T0305442

A Course in Monetary Economics

Sequential Trade, Money, and Uncertainty

To My Parents
Zahava and Shevach Eden

A COURSE IN MONETARY ECONOMICS

SEQUENTIAL TRADE, MONEY, AND UNCERTAINTY

Benjamin Eden

Blackwell
Publishing

350 Main Street, Malden, MA 02148-5020, USA
108 Cowley Road, Oxford OX4 1JF, UK
550 Swanston Street, Carlton, Victoria 3053, Australia

First published 2005 by Blackwell Publishing Ltd

Library of Congress Cataloging-in-Publication Data

Eden, Benjamin.
    A course in monetary economics : sequential trade, money, and uncertainty / Benjamin Eden.
        p. cm.
    ISBN 0-631-21565-4 (cloth : alk. paper)
    ISBN 0-631-21566-2 (pbk. : alk. paper)
1. Money–Mathematical models.
2. Uncertainty–Mathematical models.
    I. Title
        HG221.E26 2005
        332.4′01′51–dc22

                                                                                    2003020730

A catalogue record for this title is available from the British Library.

Set in $10/12\frac{1}{2}$ Dante
by Newgen Imaging Systems (P) Ltd, Chennai, India

For further information on
Blackwell Publishing, visit our website:
http://www.blackwellpublishing.com

Brief Contents

Contents

Preface

The aim of this book is to integrate the relatively new uncertain and sequential trade (UST) models with standard monetary economics. I therefore combine exposition of well-known material with that of new and sometimes yet unpublished. The exposition is at the graduate level but since mathematics is de-emphasized, it can and was used at the advanced undergraduate level.

I wrote this book while teaching monetary economics during the period 1987–2002 at the joint Master program of the Technion and the University of Haifa. I also taught earlier versions at Florida State University (First year Ph.d. level, 2001) at the University of Chicago (Second year Ph.d. level, 2002) and at Vanderbilt University (First and second year Ph.d. level, 2002–3). I have benefited from policy discussion at the Bank of Israel during the period 1992–7 where I was a consultant to the research department. This served as a reminder that monetary economics is a slow moving field not because all the problems are solved but because there are many unsolved problems that are difficult.

My interest in UST type models has started in 1979–80 while visiting Carnegie Mellon university. Initially I was motivated by the observation that the standard Walrasian model is incomplete because it uses the Walrasian tatonnement process to find the market clearing price. As a result my earlier models focused on the question of who will gather information about the market-clearing price. In these models sellers could buy information about demand but there were informational externalities arising from the fact that advertised prices can be observed by all sellers. These type of models were published in the years 1981–3 and are discussed in chapter 22. I then moved to simpler models that abstract from information acquisition. This simpler set-up proved to be rich enough and occupied most of my research efforts. The motivation has also changed. Instead of complaining about the tatonnement process I now focus on the performance of the model in explaining the monetary economy.

Since this book represents more than 20 years of effort it is difficult to remember and thank all the numerous useful comments and discussions. I have benefited mostly from comments made by students over the years. Ben Bental and Don Schlagenhauf read parts of an earlier version of the manuscript and made useful comments. I have also benefited from comments and discussions with Rick Bond, Boyan Jovanovic, Bob Lucas and Michael Woodford. Michael Bar provided excellent research assistance.

My wife Sveta contributed more than moral support and understanding. She has written a Master thesis on the subject and simulated the UST model with inventories. I hope that this book will also be of some interest to my daughter Maya and to my sons Michael and Ittai at some point in the future. Finally, I want to thank my parents Shevach and Zahava Eden for moral support and gentle push.

PART I

Introduction to Monetary Economics

In the first part of this book we use standard monetary models to talk about the joint behavior of nominal and real variables. We start with the long-run relationship focusing on the relationship between money and inflation. The focus then shifts to the short-run relationship between money and output. Special attention is devoted to the choice of fiscal and monetary policy. This introductory part sets the stage for a less standard approach in the third part of the book.

CHAPTER 1

Overview

Monetary economics is about the relationship between real and nominal variables. Its aim is to develop and test models that can help in evaluating the effects of policy on inflation, employment, nominal and real interest rates and production. We start with some evidence on the relationship between nominal and real variables and then describe some of the questions that occupy monetary economics.

1.1 MONEY, INFLATION, AND OUTPUT: SOME EMPIRICAL EVIDENCE

In his Nobel lecture Lucas (1996) summarizes the long-run effects of changes in the money supply with the aid of two figures, taken from McCandless and Weber (1995). These figures are reproduced here. Figure 1.1 plots 30-year (1960–90) average annual inflation rates against average annual growth rates of M2 (currency + demand deposits + time deposits) over the same 30-year period, for a total of 110 countries. Figure 1.2 has the growth of real output on the vertical axis. We see a high correlation between average money growth and average inflation but no correlation between average money growth and average real growth.

Consider now the point of view of a government or a central bank that wants to choose a point in the figure 1.1. Should it choose a point of low inflation and low money supply growth or should it choose a point of high inflation and high money growth? Does this matter? These questions will occupy us in the first part of the book.

As was said before figure 1.2 suggests no long-run relationship between money and output. Is there a short run relationship? Figure 1.3 is a scattered diagram of the unemployment and (CPI) inflation in the US during the years 1959:1–1999:2. Figure 1.3 uses quarterly data and each point represents unemployment and inflation in a single quarter. The first four scatter diagrams are done for each decade separately. It is evident that in the 1960s there was a negative relationship between inflation and unemployment but this relationship disappeared later. The last scatter diagram uses all observations and shows no relationship between inflation and unemployment. Stockman (1996) and Lucas (1996) obtain similar conclusions for different time periods.

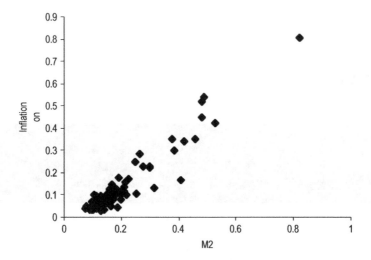

Figure 1.1   M2 growth and inflation

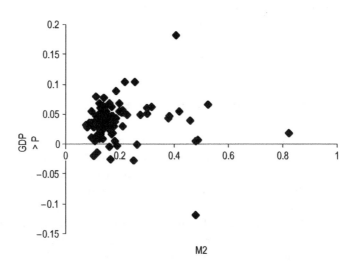

Figure 1.2   M2 and real GDP: growth rates

We may want to look at deviation of the rate of inflation from its expected value. The problem is that expected inflation cannot be directly observed. One possibility is to assume that the expected inflation is equal to the trend estimated by the Hodrick-Prescott (HP) filter (see the appendix to chapter 17). Baxter and King (1995) and Sargent (1997) use other filters and get similar results.

Figure 1.4 uses the difference of the variables from their trend value: detrended variables. As can be seen from figure 1.4, once we look at detrended variables we do get a strong and significant relationship between detrended inflation and detrended unemployment.

We now turn to some policy issues.

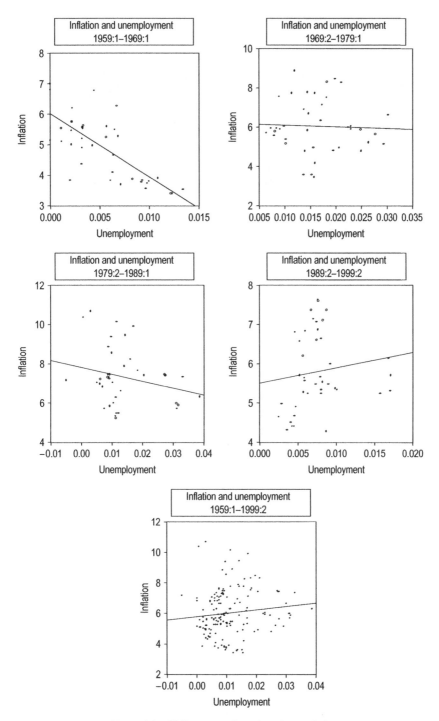

Figure 1.3 Phillips curves for various time periods

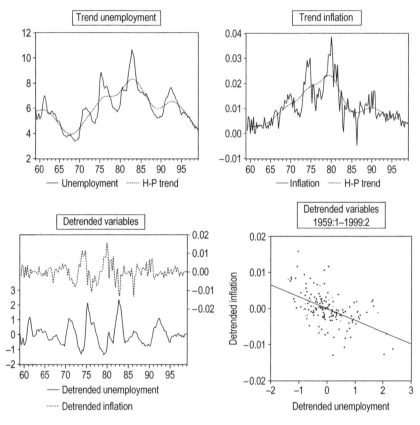

Figure 1.4   Using detrended variables

1.2   THE POLICY DEBATE

Can and should monetary policy be used to smooth output? In his essay "Of Money", David Hume observed that an increase in the money supply is "favourable to industry . . . At first, no alteration is perceived; by degrees the price rises, first of one commodity, then of another; till the whole at last reaches a just proportion with the new quantity of specie which is in the kingdom. In my opinion, it is only in this interval or intermediate situation, between the acquisition of money and rise of prices, that the encreasing quantity of gold and silver is favourable to industry" (1752, p. 38 in the 1970 edition). David Hume's conclusion with respect to the money supply is that: "The good policy of the magistrate consists only in keeping it, if possible, still encreasing; because by that means, he keeps alive a spirit of industry in the nation" (p. 39).

Figure 1.5 illustrates Hume's view by plotting the logs of money, prices and output against time. After the increase in the money supply prices rise gradually until they reach a new level proportional to the new money supply. During the period in which prices rise there is an

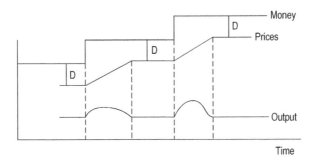

Figure 1.5 Hume's view

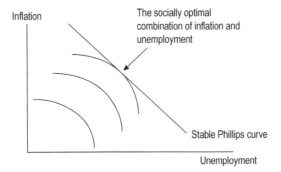

Figure 1.6 The stable Phillips curve view

increase in output but output is back to normal when prices reach the new equilibrium level. Hume suggests keeping the "spirit of industry in the nation" by increasing the money supply from time to time (or maybe increase it continuously).

In the twentieth century Phillips (1958) found a negative correlation between (wage) inflation and the rate of unemployment in British data. The Phillips curve – the relationship between inflation and unemployment – was initially accepted as a stable relationship along which policy makers could select a point. Figure 1.6 illustrates this view. The Phillips curve is drawn as a stable line. The policy-maker's indifference curves are concave to the origin and indifference curves that are closer to the origin are associated with a higher level of social welfare because both inflation and unemployment are harmful or "bads."

The stable Phillips curve view runs into difficulties when thinking about perfectly anticipated inflation. To illustrate, let us consider a hypothetical currency reform that promises to give 1.1 "new" dollars for an "old" dollar. It is expected that 1.1 "new" dollars will buy the same amount as 1 "old" dollar and therefore prices will go up by 10% immediately after the currency reform. This gimmick should have no effect on economic activity.

Friedman (1968) and Phelps (1968) make the distinction between expected and unexpected inflation. Their "natural rate hypothesis" says that in the long run, when expected inflation is the same as actual inflation, the rate of unemployment does not depend on the rate of

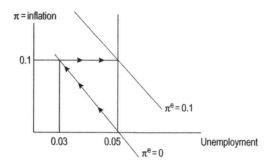

Figure 1.7   The natural rate hypothesis

inflation: The rate of unemployment when actual and expected inflation is 10% is the same as the rate of unemployment when actual and expected inflation is 20%.

The rate of unemployment which occurs when actual and expected inflation are the same is called the "natural rate of unemployment". The reasons for unemployment at the natural rate level are not in monetary policy. They are in various frictions in the process of matching workers to jobs. For example, a worker may be unemployed during the period in which he searches for a "more suitable job" because it takes time to find a new suitable job.

For the sake of concreteness let us assume that the natural rate of unemployment is 5% of the labor force, as in figure 1.7. When inflation is higher than expected workers are "excited" by the higher wages. For example, if workers expect zero inflation and the actual inflation is 10% they may be happy with their job even if they are promised a raise of less than 10% in their money wages. These workers are less likely to quit and search for a better job. Similarly firms that raise prices by 10% are less likely to fire workers who are willing to accept a less than 10% increase in their money wages. As a result, the rate of unemployment is reduced to say 3%. In terms of the graph of figure 1.7, we move on a short run Phillips curve that holds expectations fixed at $\pi^e = 0$. Eventually, however, workers learn that the rate of inflation is 10% and form correct expectations about their real wage. The rate of unemployment goes back to its normal 5% rate.

Now we are on a new short run curve that holds expectations constant at the higher level of $\pi^e = 10\%$. If we want to go back to zero inflation we must travel along this short run curve and endure unemployment which is higher than the natural rate: If when everyone expects 10% we have 5% inflation, workers who get a 5% raise will be disappointed and some will search for better jobs.

Note that the Friedman–Phelps natural rate hypothesis can be used to explain the strong negative correlation between detrended unemployment and detrended inflation (figure 1.4 in section 1.1). This explanation requires that: (1) the natural rate of unemployment is accurately measured by trend unemployment and (2) expected inflation is accurately measured by trend inflation.

Why do money surprises have real effects? This question is still not completely resolved. Friedman argued that it takes time for workers to learn about the general price level while the firm needs to know only the price of its own product. Therefore it is possible that immediately after a monetary injection the wage rate rises by less than prices but nevertheless workers

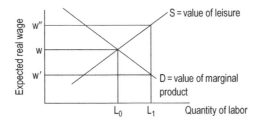

Figure 1.8   In the short run workers use the wrong deflator

think that their real wage went up. As a result workers are willing to work more and firms are willing to employ more labor.

To illustrate Friedman's argument, let us start from a long run equilibrium with $\pi^e = \pi = 0$; a nominal wage rate W, a price level P and a real wage $w = W/P$. At this real wage, workers supply L_0 units of labor as in figure 1.8. Suppose now that prices go up by 10% and the nominal wage rate goes up by 5%. At first, workers are "being fooled" and think that the real wage is $w'' = 1.05\,W/P = 1.05\,w$. As a result they are willing to supply a larger quantity of labor: L_1 in figure 1.8. The firm is perfectly informed about the price of its own product and knows that the actual real wage is $w' = 1.05\,W/1.1\,P < w$. It is therefore willing to employ a larger quantity of labor. We may even get market-clearing in the short run but this is not guaranteed. In the long run workers learn to deflate the nominal wage rate by the appropriate number and the labor market returns to the long run equilibrium in which the quantity of labor employed is L_0 and the real wage is w.

This story is not complete. Presumably the increase in money wages and prices is due to money injection. But why does the wage rate rise less than prices after an injection of money? Is it the assumption that wages are stickier than prices?

Lucas (1972) provides a complete description of the way money injections affect economic activity. A Walrasian auctioneer who knows the realizations of supply and demand announces the market-clearing price and agents use the information in this announcement. Lucas shows that even if workers know the model and form expectations by using the appropriate statistical procedures they may still respond to a purely nominal increase in their wage rate: They may attribute part of the change to real increase in the demand for their services and therefore expect that the price of the service they supply went up by more than the prices of other services that they buy (the price level).

For example, suppose that a teacher was getting 10 dollars an hour for private violin lessons. He now gets offers to teach for 20 dollars an hour. This increase may be explained as the result of doubling the money supply or as a result of an increase in the real demand for violin lessons or a combination of these factors. Optimal inference (signal extraction) will in general point to a combination of the two factors: say the price went up by 5 dollars because of monetary reasons and by 5 dollars because of real reasons. The violin teacher who makes this inference will conclude that his real wage went up by 33% and will therefore supply more lessons.

Thus, changes in the money supply may have real effects because agents in the economy are not perfectly informed about the reason for the change and attribute part of it to real changes in the demand for their product.

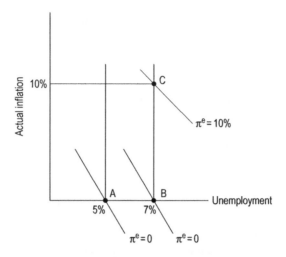

Figure 1.9 Perfectly anticipated feedback rule

An important implication is that only surprise changes in the money supply have real effects. For example, consider again the hypothetical case in which the central bank increases the money supply by 10% at the beginning of each year and as a result prices go up by 10% at the beginning of the year. In this hypothetical case, our violin teacher will know that the rise in the price of violin lessons at the beginning of the year is fully explained by the increase in the money supply. He will therefore not supply more lessons and in general economic activity will not be affected.

Similarly when the central bank increases the money supply whenever the rate of unemployment goes up, the increase in the money supply should be fully expected by agents who follow the unemployment statistics. Therefore such a transparent policy will only raise the inflation rate without affecting the probability distribution of the rate of unemployment.

To illustrate, assume that the natural rate of unemployment fluctuates randomly and may take two possible realizations: 5% and 7%. When the central bank adopts a consistent policy of zero inflation, the economy will be either at point A or at point B in figure 1.9. When it adopts a policy of creating 10% inflation whenever the rate of unemployment is 7%, agents will expect a 10% inflation whenever they observe a 7% unemployment rate. As a result we will move between points A and C in figure 1.9. Thus the central bank's attempt at reducing unemployment will lead only to inflation because the central bank's policy lacks the surprise element.

When this reasoning is generalized it leads to the conclusion that a feedback rule from unemployment to the rate of inflation will not work. Using a rather standard Keynesian type model, Sargent and Wallace (1975) show that if the central bank specifies the rate of change in the money supply as a function of the rate of unemployment, and the public understand this policy and has the same information as the central bank, then the central bank's policy will not affect the unemployment rate.

The impossibility of fighting unemployment by inflation (using a feedback rule) requires flexible prices, rational expectations and the absence of informational advantage. The debate over the effectiveness of a feedback rule is not over.

A crude summary of the main positions in the policy debate is as follows:

1   It is not possible to fight unemployment by inflation either in the short run or in the long run (Lucas, Sargent and Wallace);
2   It is possible to fight unemployment by inflation only in the short run. This is not desirable because the price of reducing the rate of inflation back to zero is too high and so is the cost of staying with high inflation rates (Friedman);
3   It is possible and desirable to fight unemployment by inflation.

1.3   MODELING ISSUES

In modeling monetary economies one often runs into the following questions: (1) why do agents hold money; (2) why do agents hold inventories and (3) how do prices adjust to various shocks?

Money

The first question arises because government bonds have the same risk characteristic as money and yield a positive nominal rate of return. Why do agents hold money when this dominating alternative is available? The answer to this question has to do with various frictions in the economy. But modeling friction is not simple. We want a model in which there are enough "frictions" so that agents choose to hold money and is still simple enough so that it can be used for analyzing the effects of alternative policies.

In the first few chapters of this book, we describe various ways of modeling money and ask whether the main policy conclusions are robust in the way in which the rate of return dominance question is solved. But we do not go into a deep discussion of the micro foundations of monetary models.

Inventories

There is wide agreement on the importance of changes in inventory investment in cyclical fluctuations. Blinder and Maccini (1991) found that the drop in inventory investment accounted for 87% of the drop in GNP during the average postwar recession in the United States (see their tables 1 and 2). There is much less agreement on how to model inventory behavior. According to the standard competitive model, inventories are held only when the expected increase in price covers storage and interest costs. This condition will not often hold but we do observe that inventories are almost always held.

The puzzle of why inventories are almost always held is similar to the money holding (rate of return dominance) puzzle. One possibility is that inventories yield convenience. This is analogous to assuming that money yields liquidity services (see chapter 2).

In the second part of the book we study the uncertain and sequential trade (UST) model. In this model sellers may fail to make a sale. When sellers fail to make a sale "undesired" inventories are carried to the next period. For this reason inventories are almost always held in the UST model and this result is obtained without having to assume convenience yield.

Prices

The short run determination of prices has strong implications for the way money affects real variables. We may distinguish between flexible prices, rigid prices and seemingly rigid prices.

Flexible prices: There is an important literature that is basically happy with the Walrasian model. This literature introduces frictions to get economic agents to hold money and to get a short run effect of money on output. Lucas's (1972) confusion model is a good example. To get money into the model Lucas assumes the overlapping generations frictions: Not all agents meet at the beginning of time. To get money non-neutrality he assumes that agents who belong to the same generation do not meet in a central Walrasian auction-place: They are distributed over disconnected islands. Another example is the limited participation model of Grossman and Weiss (1983), Lucas (1990), Fuerst (1992) and Christiano and Eichenbaum (1992). In these models money is not neutral because some agents cannot immediately adjust the amount of money balances they hold.

Rigid or sticky prices: This approach assumes that prices are set in advance. For example, Gray (1976, 1978), Fischer (1977, 1979) and Taylor (1980) develop models of the labor market in which wages are set in advance and labor unions supply the demand of the firm at the sticky wage. Phelps and Taylor (1977) and McCallum (1989, ch. 10.2) develop models in which firms set prices in advance at the level equal to the expected market-clearing price. They then supplied the quantity demanded at that price. Recently there has been a growing realization that some aspects of imperfect competition must be incorporated into a model that assumes price rigidity. Imperfect competition has become the trademark of the New Keynesian economics. See for example, Blanchard and Kiyotaki (1987), Ball and Romer (1991) and King and Watson (1996).

Seemingly rigid prices: In the uncertain and sequential trade (UST) model, prices may seem rigid but agents do not face any cost for changing prices. This approach which is developed in this book tends to yield Keynesian type behavior of inventories and prices but neoclassical policy implications.

1.4 BACKGROUND MATERIAL

In this section we introduce (review) some of the key ingredients of the monetary models used in this book: The Fisherian diagram, efficiency of the competitive outcome, the effect of distortive taxes and a non-stochastic version of the Lucas tree model (asset pricing). The last topic illustrates the working of an infinite horizon representative agent economy. The reader may choose to read this part after he or she masters the material in chapter 2.

1.4.1 The Fisherian diagram

We assume a consumer who lives for two periods ($t = 1, 2$) and consumes a single good (corn). The consumer's utility function is:

$$u(C_1, C_2) = U(C_1) + \beta U(C_2), \tag{1.1}$$

where C_t is corn consumption at time t and $0 < \beta < 1$ is a discount factor. The single period utility function $U(\ )$ is monotone and strictly concave ($U' > 0$ and $U'' < 0$).

The consumer can lend and borrow at the interest rate r. This means that if the consumer reduces his current consumption by one unit and lends it he will get $1 + r$ units of consumption in the next period. If he borrows a unit he will have to pay $1 + r$ units in the next period. The price of first period's corn in terms of second period's corn is therefore $R = 1 + r$ where R is the gross interest rate.

The consumer gets an endowment of Y_t units of corn at time t. The value of the endowment in terms of second period consumption is: $RY_1 + Y_2$. The value of the consumption bundle cannot be larger than the value of the endowment and therefore the budget constraint is:

$$RC_1 + C_2 \leq RY_1 + Y_2 = W, \tag{1.2}$$

where W is the consumer's wealth in terms of future consumption (future value). To express the budget constraint in terms of present value we divide both sides of (1.2) by R.

The consumer maximizes (1.1) subject to (1.2) and non-negativity constraints. One way of solving the problem is by substituting $C_2 = W - RC_1$ from (1.2) into (1.1). This leads to:

$$\max_{C_1} F(C_1) = U(C_1) + \beta U(W - RC_1). \tag{1.3}$$

This is a maximization problem with one variable. We now take a derivative of $F(\ )$ and equate it to zero to find the first order condition:

$$F'(C_1) = U'(C_1) - \beta RU'(W - RC_1) = 0. \tag{1.4}$$

We may write (1.4) as:

$$U'(C_1) = \beta RU'(C_2). \tag{1.5}$$

Note that a small deviation from the optimal path does not change the level of the objective function: At the optimum $\hat{C}_1$ the slope of $F(\ )$ is zero and changing C_1 a bit does not change the value of $F(\ )$. Figure 1.10 illustrates this point.

This basic principle from calculus can be used to derive the first order condition (1.5) in an alternative way. We consider a small feasible deviation from the proposed optimal path $(\hat{C}_1, \hat{C}_2)$. We cut current consumption by x units and lend it. This will result in increasing future consumption by Rx units. When x is small, the loss of current utility (the pain) is the marginal utility of current consumption times the change in current consumption: $xU'(C_1)$. Similarly the present value of the gain in future utility (the gain) is: $xR\beta U'(C_2)$. Since at the

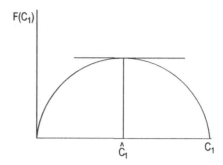

Figure 1.10 Small deviations from the optimum do not change the value of the problem

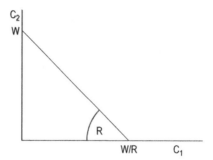

Figure 1.11 The budget line

optimum a small deviation should not change the level of the objective function the gain should equal the pain and this leads to (1.5).

The gain = pain method (sometimes refered to as calculus of variation) is more intuitive but difficult to implement. The difficulty is to think of an "easy feasible deviation" from the optimal path. Most economists proceed by deriving the first order condition in a technical way (using the substitution or the lagrangian method) and then provide an intuitive gain = pain explanation. To develop intuition we use, in this book the gain = pain method as a way of deriving first order conditions.

To solve the problem graphically we now draw the budget line: $RC_1 + C_2 = W$, in the (C_1, C_2) plane. The intersection with the horizontal axis is obtained by setting $C_2 = 0$. This leads to: $C_1 = W/R$ (as in figure 1.11). The intersection with the vertical axis is obtained by setting $C_1 = 0$. This leads to: $C_2 = W$. The slope of the budget line is obtained by taking the distance from zero to the intersection with the vertical axis and dividing it by the distance from zero to the intersection with the horizontal axis. This leads to: $W/(W/R) = R$. Thus the slope of the budget line is equal to the price of current consumption in terms of future consumption.

All points on the budget line are feasible. Points to the south west of the budget line (characterized by $RC_1 + C_2 < W$) are also feasible. Points to the north east of the budget line (characterized by $RC_1 + C_2 > W$) are not feasible.

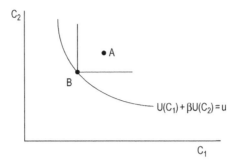

Figure 1.12 An indifference curve

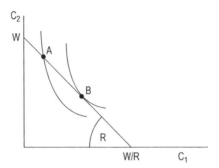

Figure 1.13 The optimal choice

We now define an indifference curve by the locus of points (C_1, C_2) that satisfy:

$$U(C_1) + \beta U(C_2) = u, \tag{1.6}$$

where here u is a given constant. All the points (C_1, C_2) that satisfy (1.6) promise the same utility level u and are illustrated by the curve that passes through point B in figure 1.12. Since the consumer is indifferent among all these points this curve is called an indifference curve. Since the utility function is strictly monotone the indifference curve is downward sloping: If we reduce C_2 we must compensate by increasing C_1 to get the same utility level. We can also verify that all points which are above the indifference curve are strictly preferred to points on the indifference curve: For each point like A, we can find a point B on the indifference curve that has less of both goods. Similarly, a point on the indifference curve is preferred to a point below the indifference curve.

At the optimal choice of consumption the indifference curve must be tangent to the budget line. Point A in figure 1.13 cannot be optimal because the consumer can get a point that is on his budget line and above the indifference curve that passes through point A. An improvement is not possible if we are at point B.

From a technical point of view, the tangency condition means that the slope of the budget line must be equal to the slope of the indifference curve that passes through the optimal point (B in figure 1.13). To find the slope of the indifference curve we take a full differential of (1.6).

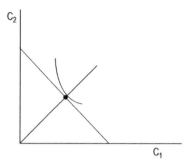

Figure 1.14 $\rho = r$

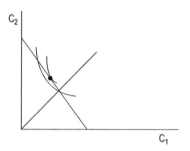

Figure 1.15 $\rho > r$

This yields:

$$U'(C_1)\,dC_1 + \beta U'(C_2)\,dC_2 = du = 0. \tag{1.7}$$

We can now solve for the slope:

$$-dC_2/dC_1 = U'(C_1)/\beta U'(C_2). \tag{1.8}$$

Equating the slope of the indifference curve (1.8) to the slope of the budget line (R) yields the first order condition (1.5).

The parameter β: To develop some intuition about the rate of discount β we define the subjective interest rate ρ by $\beta = 1/(1 + \rho)$. For a consumer whose $\rho = r$ we have $\beta R = 1$ and therefore the first order condition (1.5) implies $U'(C_1) = U'(C_2)$ and $C_1 = C_2$. Figure 1.14 illustrates this case.

For a consumer whose subjective interest rate is greater than the market interest rate ($\rho > r$) we get $\beta R < 1$. In this case (1.5) implies $U'(C_1) < U'(C_2)$ and since $U'' < 0, C_1 > C_2$. Figure 1.15 illustrates this case. Similarly when $\rho < r, C_1 < C_2$.

1.4.2 Efficiency and distortive taxes

To make policy choices we want to know if the economy works well without intervention and if not can something be done about it. As a background material we now discuss an example that demonstrates the efficiency properties of the competitive outcome (or Adam Smith's invisible hand theorem). We then use the example to talk about tax distortion. Understanding tax distortion is important for its own sake because the tax system is an important policy choice. It turns out that understanding tax distortion is also important for understanding other cases in which the invisible hand theorem does not work and there are "market failures."

We consider an economy with many identical individuals who live for one period and consume a single good (corn). Each agent owns a firm but cannot work in his own firm.

The representative firm uses labor input l to produce corn (there is no capital). Production is done according to:

$$y = f(l), \qquad (1.9)$$

where y is the quantity of corn produced, l is labor input and f( ) is a monotone and strictly concave production function (f$'$ > 0 and f$''$ < 0).

The firm's profits are given by:

$$\pi = f(l) - wl, \qquad (1.10)$$

where w is the wage rate (in units of corn per hour). The firm takes w as given and chooses l to maximize (1.10). The first order necessary condition that an interior solution (l > 0) to (1.10) must satisfy is:

$$f'(l) = w. \qquad (1.11)$$

This says that at the optimum the marginal product must equal the wage rate.

The representative individual likes corn but does not like to work. We assume the special utility function:

$$y - v(L), \qquad (1.12)$$

where y is the quantity of corn consumption, L is labor supply and v(L) is a standard cost function (v$'$ > 0 and v$''$ > 0). The representative individual takes w and π as given and maximizes (1.12) subject to the budget constraint:

$$y = wL + \pi. \qquad (1.13)$$

The first order condition for an interior solution (L > 0) to this problem is:

$$v'(L) = w. \qquad (1.14)$$

This says that at the optimum the marginal utility cost must equal the wage rate.

In equilibrium the quantity of labor demanded by the firm is equal to the quantity of labor supplied by the individual. More formally,

Equilibrium is a vector (l, L, w) that satisfies the first order conditions (1.11) and (1.14) and the market clearing condition l = L.

We substitute (1.11) and l = L in (1.14) and obtain the equilibrium condition:

$$f'(L) = v'(L). \qquad (1.15)$$

Figure 1.16 illustrates the solution $\hat{L}$ to (1.15).

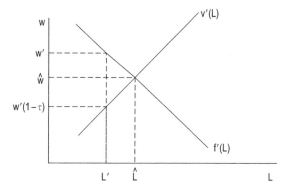

Figure 1.16 Distortive income tax

Efficiency: We now think of a hypothetical central planner who chooses L to maximize the welfare of the representative individual. The planner solves:

$$\max_{L} f(L) - v(L). \tag{1.16}$$

The first order condition for the problem (1.16) is (1.15) and therefore the equilibrium outcome $\hat{L}$ is a solution to (1.16). This means that the equilibrium outcome is efficient in the sense that a hypothetical planner cannot improve on it.

Tax distortion

We now introduce a government that collects income tax from the individuals and give it back to them as a transfer payment. The budget constraint (1.13) is now:

$$y = (1 - \tau)wL + \pi + g, \tag{1.17}$$

where $0 \leq \tau < 1$ is the income tax rate and g is the transfer payment from the government. The first order condition for the individual problem of maximizing (1.12) subject to (1.17) is:

$$v'(L) = (1 - \tau)w. \tag{1.18}$$

This says that at the optimum the marginal utility cost equals the net (after tax) wage rate.

Equilibrium with tax distortion is a vector (l, L, w) that satisfies the first order conditions (1.11) and (1.18) and the market clearing condition $l = L$.

We substitute (1.11) and $l = L$ in (1.18) and obtain the equilibrium condition:

$$v'(L) = (1 - \tau)f'(L). \tag{1.19}$$

The solution to (1.19) is $L' < \hat{L}$ in figure 1.16. It does not solve the planner's problem (1.16). The reason is in the discrepancy between the price of leisure from the individual's and the social point of view. From the individual point of view, a unit of leisure costs $w(1 - \tau) = f'(1 - \tau)$ units of corn. From the social point of view it costs $f' = w$ units of corn.

We elaborate on the choice of taxes in chapter 6. For now the reason for the inefficiency is important because it will help us understand the inefficiency caused by inflation (or more accurately by a positive nominal interest rate).

1.4.3 Asset pricing

In monetary economics we often want to abstract from distributional issues and some problem which occurs when the world ends at a finite date. We therefore often use a model in which many identical agents live for ever. In this infinite horizon representative agent economy there is no trade in equilibrium. We now demonstrate the working of such a model by considering a deterministic version of the Lucas' tree model. In chapter 13 we consider a more general version.

There are many infinitely lived identical individuals. Each individual owns a tree. All the trees are identical and promise the same path of fruits $\{d_t\}_{t=1}^{\infty}$, where d_t is the amount of fruits given by a tree at time t. At $t = 1$ the representative agent receives d_1 units of fruits as dividends. After receiving the dividends he can sell his tree for p_1 units of fruits. The total resources he has at the beginning of period 1 are thus: $p_1 + d_1$. He can use these resources for consumption (C_1) and for acquiring trees (A_1) that will give him fruits in period 2. His period 1 budget constraint is: $p_1A_1 + C_1 = p_1 + d_1$. In general the asset evolution equation is: $p_tA_t = p_tA_{t-1} + d_tA_{t-1} - C_t$. The consumer's utility function is $\sum_{t=1}^{\infty} \beta^t U(C_t)$, where $0 < \beta < 1$ and the single period utility function is strictly monotone and concave: $U' > 0$ and $U'' \leq 0$.

The representative agent takes the stream of dividends per tree $\{d_t\}_{t=1}^{\infty}$ and the path of prices $\{p_t\}_{t=1}^{\infty}$ as given and chooses the path of tree ownership $\{A_t\}_{t=1}^{\infty}$. This is done by solving the following problem:[1]

$$\max_{A_t} \sum_{t=1}^{\infty} \beta^t U(C_t)$$

$$\text{s.t.} \quad p_tA_t = p_tA_{t-1} + d_tA_{t-1} - C_t$$

$$C_t, \ A_t \geq 0 \quad \text{and} \quad A_0 = 1 \text{ is given.} \tag{1.20}$$

Suppose that $\{\hat{C}_{\tau}\}_{\tau=1}^{\infty}$ is an interior solution ($\hat{C}_{\tau} > 0$) to (1.20). To derive the first order condition we consider the following feasible deviation: Cut consumption at t by x units, use it to buy x/p_t trees and never sell the additional trees. The additional trees yield the infinite stream of dividends $\{(x/p_t)d_{\tau}\}_{\tau=t+1}^{\infty}$ which are used to augment consumption. This deviation will change the consumption path from $\{\hat{C}_{\tau}\}_{\tau=1}^{\infty}$ to $\{C_{\tau}\}_{\tau=1}^{\infty}$, where

$$C_{\tau} = \hat{C}_{\tau} \quad \text{for } \tau \leq t - 1; \qquad C_t = \hat{C}_t - x \quad \text{and} \quad C_{\tau} = \hat{C}_{\tau} + (x/p_t)d_{\tau} \quad \text{for } \tau > t.$$

For small x, the loss in utility (the pain) associated with the proposed deviation is: $\beta^t U'(\hat{C}_t)x$. The gain in utility is: $\sum_{\tau=t+1}^{\infty} \beta^{\tau} U'(\hat{C}_{\tau})(x/p_t)d_{\tau}$. At the optimum a small deviation should not make a difference in the objective function and therefore:

$$\beta^t U'(\hat{C}_t)x = \sum_{\tau=t+1}^{\infty} \beta^\tau U'(\hat{C}_\tau)(x/p_t)d_\tau. \tag{1.21}$$

Rearranging (1.21) yields:

$$p_t = \sum_{\tau=t+1}^{\infty} \beta^{\tau-t}\{U'(\hat{C}_\tau)/U'(\hat{C}_t)\}d_\tau. \tag{1.22}$$

Since there is one tree per agent, consumption per agent is $C_\tau = d_\tau$ for all τ. Substituting this in (1.22) leads to the equilibrium condition:

$$p_t = \sum_{\tau=t+1}^{\infty} \beta^{\tau-t}\{U'(d_\tau)/U'(d_t)\}d_\tau. \tag{1.23}$$

When the price satisfies (1.23) everyone wants to hold one tree and consume the stream of dividends that it promises. To appreciate the equilibrium concept it is useful to consider cases in which (1.23) does not hold. For example, when the price is less than (1.23) the right hand side of (1.21) is greater than the left hand side of (1.21). This means that the gain from cutting corn consumption and buying trees is larger than the pain. Everyone wants to sell fruits for trees but no one wants to buy fruits. This excess supply of fruits works in the direction of reducing the price of fruits and increasing the price of trees.

Note that when U is linear and U' is a constant, the price of the asset is the expected discounted sum of the future dividends that it promises: $p_t = \sum_{\tau=t+1}^{\infty} \beta^{\tau-t}d_\tau$. This will also be the case if $d_\tau = d_t$ for all τ and consumption is perfectly smooth.

Many different trees

We now assume n types of trees. A type i tree promises the stream of dividends $\{d_{ti}\}_{t=1}^{\infty}$ and its price at time t is p_{ti}. Each individual starts with a portfolio of n trees: one tree from each type. The individual's agent maximization problem is now:

$$\max_{A_{ti}} \sum_{t=1}^{\infty} \beta^t U(C_t)$$

$$\text{s.t.} \quad C_t + \sum_{i=1}^{n} p_{ti}A_{ti} = \sum_{i=1}^{n}(p_{ti}A_{t-1i} + d_{ti}A_{t-1i})$$

$$C_t, A_{ti} \geq 0 \quad \text{and} \quad A_{0i} = 1 \text{ are given.} \tag{1.24}$$

The derivation of the first order condition is similar to what we already did. We cut consumption at t by x units and invest it in x/p_{ti} trees of type i. We then use the infinite stream of dividends to augment consumption at $\tau > t$. Equating the gain to the pain yields:

$$p_{ti} = \sum_{\tau=t+1}^{\infty} \beta^{\tau-t} \{U'(\hat{C}_\tau)/U'(\hat{C}_t)\} d_{\tau i}, \tag{1.25}$$

which is similar to (1.22) except for the added index i. Since the endowment is a portfolio of n trees per agent the market clearing condition is:

$$\hat{C}_\tau = \sum_{i=1}^{n} d_{\tau i} \quad \text{for all } \tau. \tag{1.26}$$

We now substitute (1.26) into (1.25) to get the equilibrium condition:

$$p_{ti} = \sum_{\tau=t+1}^{\infty} \beta^{\tau-t} \left\{ U'\left(\sum_{i=1}^{n} d_{\tau i}\right) \Big/ U'\left(\sum_{i=1}^{n} d_{ti}\right) \right\} d_{\tau i}. \tag{1.27}$$

At the prices (1.27) each individual wants to hold his initial portfolio of n trees and consume their fruits.

Note that the dividend at time τ is multiplied by

$$S_\tau = U'\left(\sum_{i=1}^{n} d_{\tau i}\right) \Big/ U'\left(\sum_{i=1}^{n} d_{ti}\right). \tag{1.28}$$

In bad times, when $\sum_{i=1}^{n} d_{\tau i}$ is relatively small, the marginal utility of consumption is high and therefore S_τ is high. This means that fruits in bad times are weighted more heavily in the pricing formula than fruits in good times. We now turn to an example that illustrates the implication of this observation.

Example: There are n = 3 tree types. A type 1 tree yields 2 units in odd periods and 7 units in even periods. A type 2 tree yields 2 units in odd periods and no dividends in even periods. A type 3 tree yields 2 units in even periods and no dividends in odd periods. The single period utility function is: $U(C) = 2C^{0.5}$.

Here consumption is 4 units in odd periods and 9 units in even periods. The marginal utility of consumption is: $U'(C) = C^{-0.5}$. In odd periods this is: $U'(4) = 1/2$ and in even periods it is: $U'(9) = 1/3$.

Suppose we evaluate the assets in an even period t. Then $S_\tau = U'(4)/U'(9) = 1.5$ in odd periods and $S_\tau = U'(9)/U'(9) = 1$ in even periods. We now calculate the stream of dividends multiplied by the ratio of the marginal utilities:

$$\tau = t+1, t+2, t+3, t+4\ldots$$
$$d_{\tau 1} = 2.0, 7.0, 2.0, 7.0\ldots$$
$$d_{\tau 2} = 2.0, 0.0, 2.0, 0.0\ldots$$
$$d_{\tau 3} = 0.0, 2.0, 0.0, 2.0\ldots$$
$$S_\tau = 1.5, 1.0, 1.5, 1.0\ldots$$
$$S_\tau d_{\tau 1} = 3.0, 7.0, 3.0, 7.0\ldots$$
$$S_\tau d_{\tau 2} = 3.0, 0.0, 3.0, 0.0\ldots$$
$$S_\tau d_{\tau 3} = 0.0, 2.0, 0.0, 2.0\ldots$$

We can now apply the asset pricing formula $p_{ti} = \sum_{\tau=t+1}^{\infty} \beta^{\tau-t} S_\tau d_{\tau i}$ to show that the price of a type 2 tree is higher than the price of a type 3 tree.

PROBLEMS

For section 1.4.1:

1 Assume a consumer who comes to the market with an endowment of $Y_1 = Y_2$. The consumer's utility function is $U(C_1) + U(C_2)$.

(a) Show that this consumer will choose to consume his endowment if the interest rate is zero.

(b) Show that this consumer will choose to save if the interest rate is positive.

2 Consider an exchange economy in which all agents are the same and the representative agent's utility function is: $U(C_1) + U(C_2)$. Since everyone has the same endowment and the same preferences in equilibrium there is no trade. What can you say about the equilibrium real interest rate when

(a) $Y_1 = Y_2$.
(b) $Y_1 < Y_2$.
(c) $Y_1 > Y_2$.

3 How would you change your answer to 2 if storage is possible?

For section 1.4.2:

4 Solve for a competitive equilibrium vector for the special case: $f(l) = 1^{0.5}$ and $v(L) = L^{1.5}$.

5 Answer (4) for the case in which there is an income tax rate of 50% ($\tau = 1/2$).

For section 1.4.3:

6 Assume an economy with three assets (trees). Asset 1 pays a unit of consumption in all odd periods and zero in even periods. Asset 2 pays a unit of consumption in all odd periods and zero in even periods. Asset 3 pays a unit of consumption in all even periods and zero in odd periods.

(a) Compute the value of each of the three assets in (i) odd periods (ii) even periods. Assume that $\beta = 0.95$ and $U(C) = \ln(C)$.

(b) Assume that we multiply the amount of dividends paid by each of the three assets. Will this change your answer to (a)?

(c) Assume that we add a fourth asset that yields 1 unit in all periods (even and odd). Will this change your answer to (a)?

NOTE

1 Here we assume that short sales are not possible and therefore $A_t \geq 0$.

CHAPTER 2

Money in the Utility Function

Figure 1.1 establishes a connection between the average rate of change in the money supply and the average rate of inflation. There is little dispute about this long run relationship. The question is whether we want to adopt a policy of low money supply growth and low inflation or a policy of high money supply growth and high inflation. Most economists will favor the low money growth low inflation rate long run equilibrium. How low should we go?

We will examine this question using a variety of models starting from the money in the utility function approach used among others by Patinkin (1965), Sidrauski (1967) and Friedman (1969). This approach assumes that money is held because it yields some services and the way to model it is to assume a utility function in which real balances enter as an argument. It has been criticized because it does not provide an explicit description of the role of money. We will nevertheless exposit this model and derive a policy implication. In chapter 5 we will examine the robustness of the policy implication using models that are more explicit about the role of money.

The exposition here borrows from Friedman's (1969) original optimum quantity of money article and can be regarded as a diagrammatic exposition of the main ideas. We will conduct the discussion around the question of the optimum rate of change in the price level and in the money supply.

2.1 MOTIVATING THE MONEY IN THE UTILITY FUNCTION APPROACH: THE SINGLE-PERIOD, SINGLE-AGENT PROBLEM

To motivate the money in the utility function assumption, we start from the problem of an agent who comes to period t with M_{t-1} dollars and an endowment of z goods: $\bar{x}_t = (\bar{x}_{t1}, \ldots, \bar{x}_{tz})$. In addition, he gets a transfer-payment from the government of G_t dollars. The amount of money before the beginning of trade at time t is: $M_{tb} = M_{t-1} + G_t$ dollars.

We start from the case in which money is the only asset (there are no bonds and no physical capital). The agent faces the dollar prices: $p_t = (p_{t1}, \ldots, p_{tz})$, where p_{ti} denotes the dollar price of good i. Nominal spending for the period is given by: $I_t = M_{tb} - M_t + \sum_i \bar{x}_{ti} p_{ti}$, where M_t are end of period balances and $\sum_i \bar{x}_{ti} p_{ti}$ is the dollar value of the endowment. It is assumed that I_t and M_t are exogenous at this stage. (Later in the multi-period problem the agent will be able to choose these variables.) The agent's budget constraint for period t is thus:

$$\sum_i x_{ti}p_{ti} = I_t = M_{tb} - M_t + \sum_i \bar{x}_{ti}p_{ti}, \tag{2.1}$$

where $x_t = (x_{t1}, \ldots, x_{tz})$ denote quantities consumed in period t.

It takes time to exchange one vector of goods for another. The amount of time (labor) required for executing a shopping list, $x_t - \bar{x}_t = (x_{t1} - \bar{x}_{t1}, x_{t2} - \bar{x}_{t2}, \ldots, x_{tz} - \bar{x}_{tz})$, that satisfies the budget constraint (2.1) is:[1]

$$L_t = F(x_t - \bar{x}_t, p_t, M_{tb}). \tag{2.2}$$

Starting with more money reduces the amount of time required for executing a given shopping list and therefore the function $F(\ )$ is decreasing in M_{tb}. This assumption may be justified in terms of a model in which agents meet each other sequentially and bilateral trade takes place until all agents complete their desired exchange. An agent who does not have enough money will have to sell first, accumulate nominal balances and buy later. This is a constraint on the exchange process and therefore on average more time is required to complete a given exchange, when M_{tb} is low.[2]

Consider now a change in all nominal magnitudes by a factor λ: Instead of (I, p, M_{tb}) we now have $(\lambda I, \lambda p, \lambda M_{tb})$. This does not change the set of vectors x which satisfy (2.1). It is also true that the bilateral trades that a consumer can do with M_{tb} dollars at the prices p are exactly the same as the trades that he can do with λM_{tb} dollars at the prices λp. For example, suppose that a consumer wants to buy 5 units of a single good. He can do it if he has 10 dollars and the price of the good is 2. He can also do it if he has 20 dollars and the price of the good is 4. For this reason, we assume:

$$F(x - \bar{x}, p, M_b) = F(x - \bar{x}, \lambda p, \lambda M_b) \quad \text{for all } \lambda > 0, \tag{2.3}$$

where the time index is omitted.

The consumer's single period utility function is given by $u(x, L)$, where $u(\ )$ is strictly increasing in x and strictly decreasing in L. The consumer chooses x to maximize $u(x, L)$ subject to (2.1) and (2.2). Let $V(\bar{x}, I, p, M_b)$ denote the maximum single period utility the consumer can get when facing the exogenously given magnitudes $(\bar{x}, I, p, M_b)$. Thus,

$$V(\bar{x}, I, p, M_b) = \max_{x,L} u(x, L), \quad \text{s.t. (2.1) and (2.2)}. \tag{2.4}$$

The function $V(\ )$ is sometimes called an indirect utility function. The consumer does not receive utility from income or the beginning of period balances directly, but these magnitudes affect the set of feasible choices of x and L and therefore affect the maximum utility that he can achieve.

Since changing (I, p, M_{tb}) by the same proportions does not affect the set of vectors (x, L) that satisfy the constraints (2.1) and (2.2) we have:

$$V(\bar{x}, I, p, M_b) = V(\bar{x}, \lambda I, \lambda p, \lambda M_b) \quad \text{for all } \lambda > 0. \tag{2.5}$$

We now choose $\lambda = 1/p_1$ and write:

$$V(\bar{x}, Y, 1, p_2/p_1, \ldots, p_z/p_1; m_b), \tag{2.6}$$

where $Y = I/p_1$, is total expenditures in terms of good 1 and $m_b = M_b/p_1$ is the purchasing power of the nominal balances held at the beginning of trade, in terms of good 1.

For the purpose of analyzing fully anticipated changes in monetary policy, it is useful to assume that *relative* prices $(p_2/p_1, \ldots, p_z/p_1)$ and *real* endowments, $\bar{x}$, are constant and write (2.6) as:

$$V(Y, m_b), \tag{2.7}$$

where the same symbol is used to denote different functions.

2.2 THE MULTI-PERIOD, SINGLE-AGENT PROBLEM

We are now ready to discuss the choice of real balances. We assume that there exist functions $f(\ )$ and $U(\ )$ such that:

$$V(Y_t, m_{tb}) = U[Y_t + f(m_{tb})], \tag{2.8}$$

where $U(\ )$ has the standard properties of a single period utility function and $f(\ )$ has the standard properties of a production function, with $f(0) = 0$. Indeed we may think of real balances as an input in the production of consumption (liquidity services). Although money is useful only if there are many goods, we simplify the discussion by assuming that there is only one non-storable good: Corn. Under (2.8) we can define consumption as the sum of corn consumption and "liquidity services":

$$C_t = Y_t + f(m_{tb}). \tag{2.9}$$

This consumption measure is in units of corn. For example, if $m_{tb} = 4$, $Y_t = 5$ and $f(m_{tb}) = (m_{tb})^{1/2}$ then the liquidity services from 4 units of real balances are equivalent to 2 units of corn and the total consumption level is 7. This level of consumption can also be achieved with 7 units of corn and no real balances.

We start from the case in which prices are stable and there are no transfer-payments from the government. In this case, the level of real balances at the beginning of time t trade is: $m_{tb} = m_{t-1}$.

We consider the problem of an infinitely lived representative agent whose utility function is:[3]

$$\sum_{t=1}^{\infty} \beta^t U(C_t), \tag{2.10}$$

where $U(\ )$ is a single period utility function and $0 < \beta < 1$ is a discount factor. It is useful to define the subjective interest rate ρ by: $\beta = 1/(1 + \rho)$. The function $U(\ )$ is differentiable, strictly monotone and strictly concave.

The endowment of corn is constant over time and is given by $\bar{Y}$ units, per period. Since money is the only asset, the *individual* agent's real balances evolve according to:

$$m_t - m_{t-1} = \bar{Y} - Y_t. \tag{2.11}$$

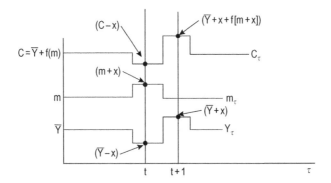

Figure 2.1 A feasible deviation from a smooth path

The representative agent's problem is to choose the levels of real balances m_t which maximize (2.10) subject to (2.9), (2.11) and

$$m_{tb} = m_{t-1} \geq 0, \quad \text{and } m_0 \text{ is given.} \tag{2.12}$$

Under what conditions will the agent want to hold his initial endowment of real balances (m_0) forever? To answer this question we define a smooth consumption path that is characterized by the level of real balances m by:

$$Y_t = \bar{Y} \quad \text{and} \quad m_t = m_0 = m \quad \text{for all t.} \tag{2.13}$$

When this smooth consumption path maximizes (2.10) subject to (2.9), (2.11) and (2.12) an agent who starts with m units of real balances will not change the amount of real balances over time.

First order condition: It must be the case that any small deviation from an optimal path does not change the value of the objective function. We now use this basic principle from calculus to derive first order conditions.

The representative agent can deviate from a smooth consumption path in the following way. He can reduce corn consumption at t by x units and accumulate x units of real balances. He can then use the additional real balances to increase corn consumption at t + 1 by x units. Thus, if a smooth consumption path which is characterized by m is feasible then the path:

$$Y_t = \bar{Y} - x; \quad Y_{t+1} = \bar{Y} + x;$$

$$Y_\tau = \bar{Y} \quad \text{for } \tau < t \text{ and } \tau > t + 1$$

$$m_t = m + x \quad \text{and} \quad m_\tau = m \quad \text{for all } \tau \neq t; \tag{2.14}$$

is also feasible. Figure 2.1 illustrates the proposed deviation (2.14).

If the agent follows the deviation (2.14), then in addition to more corn he will have $f(m + x) - f(m)$ additional units of liquidity services at time t + 1 because of the increase in the beginning of period real balances. It follows that giving up x units of corn at t yields:

$$\Delta C_{t+1} = C_{t+1} - C = x + f(m + x) - f(m), \tag{2.15}$$

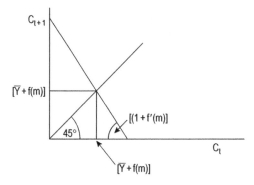

Figure 2.2 The "budget line"

units of consumption at $t + 1$, where $C = \bar{Y} + f(m)$ denotes consumption along the smooth path and ΔC is the change from the smooth path.

Dividing (2.15) by $\Delta C_t = -x$, yields the price of C_t in terms of C_{t+1}:

$$-\Delta C_{t+1}/\Delta C_t = 1 + [f(m + x) - f(m)]/x. \qquad (2.16)$$

When x is small, we may approximate:

$$[f(m + x) - f(m)]/x \approx f'(m). \qquad (2.17)$$

This approximation is used in figure 2.2, where the price of current consumption in terms of future consumption is: $1 + f'(m)$.[4]

The marginal product of real balances, $f'(m)$, plays the role of the interest rate in the standard Fisherian model. In Fisher's model if you deposit an amount of money which can buy a unit of corn in the bank you will get next period an amount that can buy $1 + r$ units of corn, where r is the real interest rate. In our model, if you add to your money holdings an amount that can buy a unit of corn, you will get the equivalent of $1 + f'(m)$ units of corn next period. Thus, here the relevant interest rate is the marginal product of money and this rate of return changes with m.

It is assumed that there exists a satiation level $\bar{m}$ such that $f'(m) > 0$ when $m < \bar{m}$; $f'(\bar{m}) = 0$; $f'(m) < 0$ when $m > \bar{m}$. The marginal product is very large for small levels of the input ($f'(0) = \infty$) and declines: $f''(m) < 0$ everywhere.[5] Figure 2.3 illustrates these properties.

Figure 2.4 illustrates the "budget lines" in the (C_{t+1}, C_t) plane. There are three "budget lines" defined for three levels of real balances: $\bar{m} > m' > m''$. Note that the slope of the budget lines goes down with m and is equal to unity when $m = \bar{m}$.

The slope of the indifference curves in the (C_{t+1}, C_t) plane can be computed by taking a full differential of (2.10) and setting $dC_\tau = 0$ for $\tau < t$ and for $\tau > t + 1$. This yields:

$$(1 + \rho)U'(C_t)/U'(C_{t+1}), \qquad (2.18)$$

and is equal to $1 + \rho$ along the 45° line, when $C_t = C_{t+1}$.

We can now use figure 2.4 to determine whether the consumer will want to stay on the 45° line. If he starts with m'' units of real balances, he will move to a point like A and accumulate

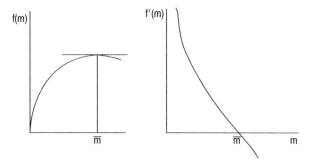

Figure 2.3 The liquidity service function

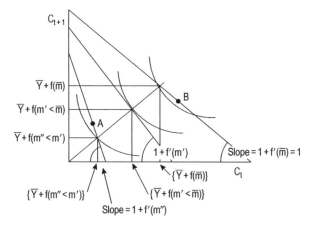

Figure 2.4 Varying m : $m'' < m' < \overline{m}$

real balances. If he starts with $\overline{m}$ units he will move to a point like B and decumulate real balances. If he starts with m' units he will not change the amount of real balances. Thus only m' characterizes an optimal smooth consumption path.

Formally if m characterizes an optimal smooth consumption path then it must satisfy the first order condition, $1 + \rho = 1 + f'(m)$, or:

$$\rho = f'(m). \tag{2.19}$$

Since $f'' < 0$ and $f'(0) = \infty$ there is a unique solution m' to (2.19), as in figure 2.5.

An alternative way of deriving (2.19): A small deviation from an optimal path should not change the level of the objective function. We now consider the following alternative deviation from a smooth path:

$$Y_t = \overline{Y} - x;$$

$$Y_\tau = \overline{Y} \quad \text{for all } \tau \neq t;$$

$$m_\tau = m + x \quad \text{for all } \tau \geq t \quad \text{and} \quad m_\tau = m \quad \text{for all } \tau < t. \tag{2.20}$$

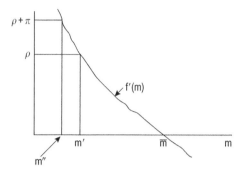

Figure 2.5 The first order condition

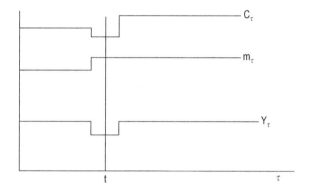

Figure 2.6 An alternative feasible deviation

In (2.20) we cut corn consumption at time t by x units ($\Delta C_t = -x$) accumulate x units of real balances and hold $m + x$ units forever. This amounts to a tradeoff between current consumption, C_t, and permanent consumption, C_p. The additional x units of real balances yield an infinite stream of $\Delta C_p = f(m+x) - f(m)$ units of consumption per period. Figure 2.6 illustrates this deviation from a smooth consumption path.

The price of current consumption in terms of permanent consumption is:

$$-\Delta C_p / \Delta C_t = \{f(m + x) - f(m)\}/x \approx f'(m). \tag{2.21}$$

The slopes of the "budget lines" in the (C_p, C_t) plane are therefore $f'(m)$ as in figure 2.7.

To find the slope of the indifference curves in the (C_p, C_t) plane, we take a full differential of (2.10) and equate it to zero: $\sum_{\tau=t}^{\infty} \beta^{\tau-t} U'(C_\tau) dC_\tau = 0$. We now substitute $dC_\tau = dC_p$ for $\tau > t$ to get:

$$-U'(C_t)\, dC_t = \sum_{\tau=t+1}^{\infty} \beta^{\tau-t} U'(C_\tau)\, dC_p. \tag{2.22}$$

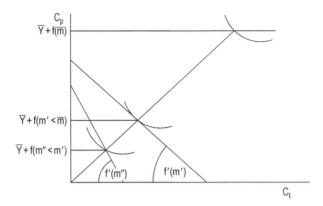

Figure 2.7   Tradeoffs between current and permanent consumption

This leads to:

$$-dC_p/dC_t = U'(C_t)\Big/ \sum_{\tau=t+1}^{\infty} \beta^{\tau-t}U'(C_\tau). \qquad (2.23)$$

Along the 45 degrees line $C_\tau = C_t$ and (2.23) implies:

$$-dC_p/dC_t = \rho. \qquad (2.24)$$

Thus the slope of the indifference curves in the (C_t, C_p) plane along the 45 degrees line is ρ.

If m characterizes an optimal smooth consumption path, then at the point: $C_t = C_p = \bar{Y} + f(m)$, an indifference curve must be tangent to a budget line. Thus, $(2.21) = (2.24)$ which is equivalent to (2.19).

2.3   EQUILIBRIUM WITH CONSTANT MONEY SUPPLY

The nominal quantity of money, M, is determined by the government. The price level P (an index of the money price of goods or the dollar price of corn in our model) is determined in equilibrium by the condition:

$$f'(M/P) = \rho. \qquad (2.25)$$

Thus the price level adjusts so that the money supply M is willingly held. To see the forces that operate to achieve (2.25), suppose that P' is a solution to (2.25) and we start with $P'' > P'$. In this case, real balances $m'' = M/P''$ are lower than the desired level: $m' = M/P'$. All agents will therefore try to exchange goods for money (move to a point like A in figure 2.4) but since the supply of money (M) is fixed, it is not possible for all agents to do it.

The attempt to exchange goods for money will drive the price of money up (and the price of corn down). This will stop when the price level reaches the equilibrium level: P'.

Note that the government determines the nominal quantity of money but the private sector determines the real quantity of money. This leads to the distinction between the social and the private cost for accumulating real balances, which is the main point of Friedman's article.

2.4   THE SOCIAL AND PRIVATE COST FOR ACCUMULATING REAL BALANCES

We start with an equilibrium in which all agents hold the equilibrium level of real balances m'. An individual agent, Mr. Loser, lost some money and as a result found himself at the beginning of period t with a quantity of real balances $m < m'$. Mr. Loser will find himself at point A in the left upper diagram of figure 2.8. He will choose to accumulate real balances by giving up x units of corn and moving to point B. At time $t + 1$ he will find himself at point D (the right upper diagram in figure 2.8) and he may choose either to continue and accumulate real balances (if $m + x < m'$) or maintain the level he has (if $m + x = m'$). In any case, to accumulate real balances Mr. Loser must give up corn consumption as in the lower diagram of figure 2.8.

Consider now the case in which all the agents in the economy lost money or paid some money as lump sum taxes to the government. In this case, they will all try to move to point B by selling corn for money. Since the money supply is constant, this leads only to a decline in the price level. A new equilibrium is achieved with the same level of real balances and the same level of corn consumption. Figure 2.9 illustrates this case: If everyone tries to accumulate real balances and move to point B they will actually move along the 45 degrees line and reach point E.

Thus, to the individual, there is a cost for accumulating real balances: he must give up corn consumption. To society, there is no such cost.

For an additional illustration, consider the trade-off between current corn consumption Y_t and permanent real balances m_p. An agent who starts from a smooth consumption path which is characterized by the level of real balances m, can cut his corn consumption and increase his

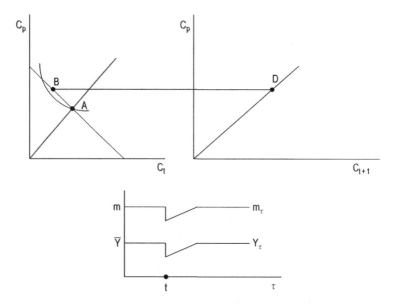

Figure 2.8   The cost of accumulating real balances from the individual's point of view

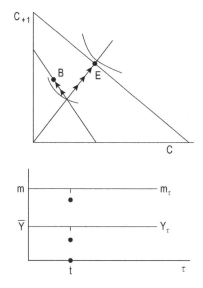

Figure 2.9   The social point of view

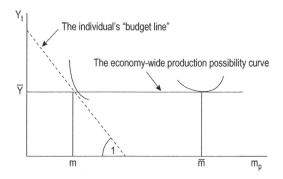

Figure 2.10   The difference between the individual and social point of view

real balances permanently as described by the deviation (2.20). From the individual point of view the trade is one for one: a unit of corn buys a unit of permanent real balances, as in the broken line of figure 2.10. From the point of view of the economy as a whole, increasing real balances is costless. The economy "production possibility curve" is the horizontal solid line in figure 2.10.

The slope of the indifference curves in the (Y_t, m_p) plane at the point of a smooth consumption path characterized by m is $f'(m)/\rho$.[6] If $m_{t-1} = m$ characterizes an equilibrium, then the indifference curve must be tangent to the budget line:

$$f'(m)/\rho = 1. \tag{2.26}$$

This is another way of deriving (2.19).

Since $f'(m)$ declines with m, the slope of the indifference curve declines with m and reaches zero at $\bar{m}$. We can therefore improve the welfare of all agents by increasing the level of real balances along the economy "production possibility curve" until we attain the maximum at the point $(\bar{Y}, \bar{m})$.

2.5 ADMINISTRATIVE WAYS OF GETTING TO THE OPTIMUM

We have shown that a competitive equilibrium with stable money supply is not Pareto efficient. This is surprising because the standard reasons for the failure of the first welfare theorem are absent: There are no external effects, no distortive taxes and no monopoly power. Nevertheless, the reason for the inefficiency is the standard reason: A divergence between the individual and the social cost.

What can we do to improve matters? It may be possible to require by law that on average agents hold $\bar{m}$ units of real balances. If this law is enforced, the price level will decline to $\bar{P}$ where $M/\bar{P} = \bar{m}$.

Alternatively, when the amount of money held by each individual is observable and lump sum taxes are possible, the government may pay interest on the holding of money. Under this subsidy scheme, an agent who increases his holding of money permanently by giving up current corn consumption, will get interest in addition to the increase in the flow of liquidity services. The slope of the budget line in the (C_t, C_p) plane is now: $f'(m) + r$, and the new equilibrium level of real balances must satisfy:

$$f'(m) + r = \rho. \tag{2.27}$$

When the policy-maker chooses $r = \rho$, $\bar{m}$ solves (2.27) and welfare is maximized.

We now turn to a solution of the efficiency problem that does not require information about the amount of money held by each individual. We start by discussing the effects of changes in the money supply.

2.6 ONCE AND FOR ALL CHANGES IN M

There are two distinct thought experiments: a once-and-for-all change in M and a change in the rate of change of M. A once-and-for-all change in M leads to an equi-proportional change in P. To see this point, let P' solve the equilibrium condition:

$$f'(M/P) = \rho. \tag{2.28}$$

Assume now that the government prints an additional M dollar per capita and transfers it to the consumers as lump sums. At the initial equilibrium position, individuals were holding the desired level of real balances. Now after they have got the transfer payment from the government, they hold more money than they want to. They will therefore try to exchange money for corn. However, since the supply of money is constant, it is not possible for all agents to do so. The attempt to exchange money for corn will only increase the price of corn. This increase in the price level will lower real balances until the quantity of real balances is equal

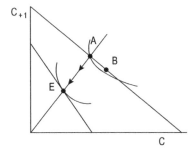

Figure 2.11   A once and for all change in the money supply

to the desired one – that is, the quantity before the transfer. The process does not necessarily require time: we may jump to the new equilibrium price level instantaneously.

In terms of our diagram, after the transfer payment all agents find themselves in a point like A in figure 2.11. They all try to move to a point like B. Since it is not possible for all agents to move to B they end up moving to the previous equilibrium: point E. The mathematics of this argument is quite simple. If P' solves the equilibrium condition $f'(M/P) = \rho$ then $2P'$ solves $f'(2M/2P) = \rho$.

What will happen if the government announces a policy of doubling the money supply each month? We will see that this thought experiment is not trivial. We start from some technical aspects of this question.

2.7   CHANGE IN THE RATE OF MONEY SUPPLY CHANGE: TECHNICAL ASPECTS

We start from the continuous time case which is a useful approximation for the discrete time case used in the theoretical analysis which follows.

The government changes the money supply at the constant rate:

$$d\ln(M)/dt = (dM/dt)/M = \mu, \qquad (2.29)$$

where M denotes the (per agent) money supply and μ is the rate of change in the money supply. The first equality in (2.29) says that the time derivative of the logarithm of a variable is equal to the rate of change in the variable.[7] For example, in figure 2.12 the government starts to increase the money supply at time t, at the rate of μ.

The rate of inflation is $\pi = d\ln P/dt$. The purchasing power of one dollar is $1/P$ and the rate of change in the purchasing power of a dollar is:

$$d\ln(1/P)/dt = -d\ln P/dt = -\pi. \qquad (2.30)$$

Thus, real balances depreciate at the rate of π. When the representative agent holds m units of real balances he loses πm per unit of time.

The government changes the money supply by printing money and transferring it to the agents in the economy. The real value of the transfer payment is:

$$(dM/dt)/P = [(dM/dt)/M][M/P] = \mu m. \qquad (2.31)$$

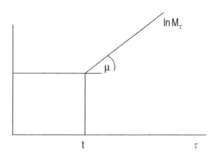

Figure 2.12 Consistent rate of growth in M

When the real value of the transfer payment is higher than the depreciation, real balances go up. The rate of change in real balances is:

$$d\ln(m)/dt = d\ln(M/P)/dt = d\ln M/dt - d\ln P/dt = \mu - \pi. \qquad (2.32)$$

Thus real balances are accumulated (decumulated) if the rate of change in M is greater (lower) than the rate of change in P.

Discrete time: We use the same symbol π to denote the discrete rate of inflation: $\pi_t = (P_t - P_{t-1})/P_{t-1}$. The discrete rate of change in the purchasing power of money (the real rate of return on money) is:

$$r_{mt} = \{(1/P_t) - (1/P_{t-1})\}/(1/P_{t-1}) = [1/(1 + \pi_t)] - 1. \qquad (2.33)$$

Since Taylor's expansion leads to: $1/(1 + \pi) = 1 - \pi + \pi^2 - \pi^3 + \cdots$, we can approximate r_m by $-\pi$ for small π.

The real value of the transfer payment is:

$$g_t = (M_t - M_{t-1})/P_t = m_t - m_{t-1}(P_{t-1}/P_t) = m_t - m_{t-1}(1 + r_{mt}). \qquad (2.34)$$

It is also true that:

$$g_t = (M_t - M_{t-1})/P_t = \mu(M_{t-1}/M_t)m_t = \mu m_t/(1 + \mu), \qquad (2.35)$$

where here $\mu = (M_t - M_{t-1})/M_{t-1}$ is the discrete rate of change in the money supply. The discrete rate of change in real balances is:

$$(m_t - m_{t-1})/m_{t-1} = (1 + \mu)/(1 + \pi) - 1 = (1 + \mu)(1 + r_m) - 1. \qquad (2.36)$$

Note that when $\mu = \pi$, the level of real balances is constant regardless of whether we use discrete or continuous time.

2.8 CHANGE IN THE RATE OF MONEY SUPPLY CHANGE: ECONOMICS

We use a discrete time analysis. At the beginning of each period, before the beginning of trade, the government transfers to the representative agent G_t dollars in a lump sum form. The agent forms expectations with respect to the sequences $\{G_t, P_t\}_{t=1}^{\infty}$ and chooses $\{M_t, Y_t\}_{t=1}^{\infty}$ to maximize:

$$\sum_{t=1}^{\infty} \beta^t U(C_t = Y_t + f[(M_{t-1} + G_t)/P_t])$$

$$\text{s.t.} \quad M_t + P_t Y_t = P_t \bar{Y} + M_{t-1} + G_t;$$

$$M_t \geq 0, \quad Y_t \geq 0, \quad \text{and } M_0 \text{ is given.} \tag{2.37}$$

The sequences $\{G_t, M_t, Y_t, P_t\}_{t=1}^{\infty}$ is an *equilibrium* if (a) given the sequence $\{G_t, P_t\}_{t=1}^{\infty}$, the sequence $\{M_t, Y_t\}_{t=1}^{\infty}$ solves the representative consumer's problem (2.37); (b) markets are always cleared: $Y_t = \bar{Y}$ and $M_t = M_0(1 + \mu)^t$, for all t and (c) the transfer payment is equal to the change in the money supply: $G_t = M_t - M_{t-1}$.[8]

The sequence $\{G_t, M_t, Y_t, P_t\}_{t=1}^{\infty}$ is a steady-state equilibrium (SSE) if it is an equilibrium with the property that M_t/P_t is the same for all t.[9] I now turn to characterize the steady state equilibrium.

Smooth consumption path: It is useful to write the problem (2.37) in real terms. We use the discrete definition of π together with (2.33) to get:

$$\max \sum_{t=1}^{\infty} \beta^t U[Y_t + f(m_{tb})]$$

$$\text{s.t.}$$

$$m_{tb} = m_{t-1}(1 + r_{mt}) + g_t$$

$$m_t = \bar{Y} - Y_t + m_{t-1}(1 + r_{mt}) + g_t$$

$$m_t, Y_t \geq 0 \quad \text{and } m_0 \text{ is given.} \tag{2.38}$$

where $g_t = G_t/P_t$ is the real value of the transfer from the government.

It is assumed that the real rate of return on money is constant over time and is given by r_m. Furthermore, the consumer starts with the level of real balances $m_0 = m$ and the real value of the transfer payment is constant and is given by:[10]

$$g_t = G_t/P_t = -m r_m, \quad \text{for all t.} \tag{2.39}$$

Under (2.39), the smooth consumption path: $Y_t = \bar{Y}$ and $m_t = m$ is feasible. To see this claim we substitute (2.39) and $m_0 = m$ in the first period budget constraint of problem (2.38) to get: $m_1 = \bar{Y} - Y_1 + m(1 + r_m) - m r_m = \bar{Y} - Y_1 + m$. We now substitute $Y_1 = \bar{Y}$ to get $m_1 = m$. This is substituted in the second period budget constraint to get: $m_2 = \bar{Y} - Y_2 + m(1 + r_m) - m r_m = \bar{Y} - Y_1 + m = m$. We keep doing it to show that $m_t = m$ for all t is feasible under (2.39).

Note that if (2.39) is not satisfied then a smooth consumption path characterized by m is not feasible. Note also that for this smooth path (2.34) implies: $m_{tb} = m(1 + r_m) + g = m$ and the liquidity services per period are given by $f(m)$.

Under what conditions will this smooth path be optimal? To answer this question, we consider the following deviation:

$$Y_t = \bar{Y} - x; \quad Y_{t+1} = \bar{Y} + x(1 + r_m);$$

$$Y_\tau = \bar{Y} \quad \text{for } \tau < t \text{ and for } \tau > t + 1;$$

$$m_t = m + x \quad \text{and} \quad m_\tau = m \quad \text{for } \tau \neq t. \tag{2.40}$$

According to the proposed deviation (2.40), we cut corn consumption at t by x units and use the accumulated real balances to increase corn consumption at $t + 1$. The change in consumption from the smooth path $C = \bar{Y} + f(m)$ is:

$$\Delta C_t = C_t - C = -x;$$

$$\Delta C_{t+1} = C_{t+1} - C = x(1 + r_m) + f[m + x(1 + r_m)] - f(m);$$

$$\Delta C_\tau = 0 \quad \text{for } \tau < t \text{ and for } \tau > t + 1. \tag{2.41}$$

And therefore:[11]

$$-\Delta C_{t+1}/\Delta C_t = (1 + r_m)[1 + f'(m)]. \tag{2.42}$$

If the smooth path is optimal, it must be the case that the slope of the indifference curve (2.18) at the point $C_t = C_{t+1}$, must equal the slope of the budget line (2.42). This leads to:

$$1 + \rho = (1 + r_m)[1 + f'(m)]. \tag{2.43}$$

When $f'(m)$ and r_m are small, (2.43) can be approximated by:

$$f'(m) \approx \rho - r_m \approx \rho + \pi. \tag{2.44}$$

To derive the first order condition (2.43) in an alternative way, consider another possible deviation from the smooth path:

$$Y_t = \bar{Y} - x;$$

$$Y_\tau = \bar{Y} + xr_m, \quad \text{for } \tau > t;$$

$$Y_\tau = \bar{Y} \quad \text{for } \tau < t \quad \text{and}$$

$$m_\tau = m + x \quad \text{for } \tau \geq t; \quad m_\tau = m \quad \text{for } \tau < t. \tag{2.45}$$

According to the proposed deviation in (2.45) the representative agent cuts his consumption of corn at time t by x units and uses it to increase the level of his real balances permanently. To maintain his real balances at the level $m + x$, he must increase his corn consumption permanently by xr_m. When r_m is negative this means that he must cut his corn consumption to cover the depreciation induced by inflation.

Under (2.45) $\Delta C_t = -x$ and the representative consumer's permanent consumption increases by:

$$\Delta C_p \approx f'(m)x + xr_m \approx f'(m)x - \pi x. \tag{2.46}$$

Therefore,

$$-\Delta C_p/\Delta C_t \approx f'(m) - \pi. \tag{2.47}$$

The slope of the indifference curve (2.23) at the point $C_p = C_t$ is ρ. If the smooth path is optimal, this must equal the slope of the budget line (2.47). Thus, $\rho \approx f'(m) - \pi$.

2.9 STEADY-STATE EQUILIBRIUM (SSE)

It is assumed that the supply of money changes at a constant rate μ. Thus,

$$G_t = (M_t - M_{t-1}) = \mu M_{t-1}. \tag{2.48}$$

The real value of the transfer payment is given by (2.34) and (2.35) which are repeated here for convenience:

$$g_t = G_t/P_t = m_t - m_{t-1}(1 + r_{mt}) = \mu m_t/(1 + \mu). \tag{2.49}$$

Substituting the steady state requirement $m_t = m$ in (2.49) leads to: $g = -r_m m = \mu m/(1+\mu)$ and $1+r_m = 1/(1+\mu)$. Since $g = -r_m m$ the transfer payment covers the depreciation (appreciation) of real balances due to inflation (deflation) and a smooth consumption path characterized by m is feasible.

Since in the steady state $1+r_m = 1/(1+\mu)$ we can write the first order condition (2.43) as:

$$(1 + \rho)(1 + \mu) = 1 + f'(m). \tag{2.50}$$

When μ and ρ are small (2.50) can be approximated by:

$$f'(m) \approx \mu + \rho. \tag{2.51}$$

Figure 2.5 can be used to show that when μ goes up the SSE level of real balances goes down and welfare goes down.

2.10 TRANSITION FROM ONE STEADY STATE TO ANOTHER

We consider an economy that before time t was in a SSE with a rate of change in the money supply $\mu = 0$. At time t the government announces a new rate of change $\mu = 0.1$. We assume that at $t' > t$ the economy will reach a new SSE with a new inflation rate $\pi = 0.1$. Can we say anything about the rate of inflation during the transition period (the period from t to t')?

For the sake of concreteness, we assume that in the initial steady state (before time t): $m = 10$, $M = 50$ and $P = 5$. In the new SSE $\mu = \pi = 0.1$ and therefore the new SSE level of real balances is lower and is given by $m = 5$.

We start with the case in which the economy reaches the new steady state equilibrium immediately at time $t (= t')$. At time t only the rate of change in the money supply has changed: the level of the money supply is still 50. Therefore to get to the lower level of real balances, the price level must jump to $P = 10$. The price level must then increase at the rate of $\pi = 0.1$ to maintain the desired level of 5 units of real balances. Figure 2.13 illustrates the instantaneous adjustment to the new steady state.

It is possible that because of long term contracts, price rigidities and imperfect information it will take time until we get to the new SSE. We now consider this case in which $t' > t$. The money supply at the end of the transition period satisfies: $\ln M_{t'} = \ln 50 + 0.1(t' - t)$. In order

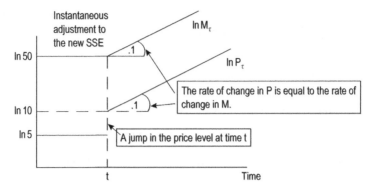

Figure 2.13   Instantaneous adjustment

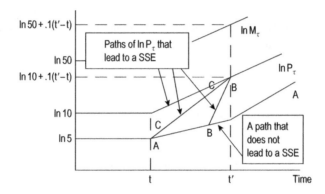

Figure 2.14   Slow adjustment

to get real balances at the desired level of 5, the price level at the end of the transition period satisfies: $\ln P_{t'} = \ln 10 + 0.1(t' - t)$. This price level at time t' can be reached if we follow a path like CC in figure 2.14. In this path, the rate of inflation during the transition period (the slope of the $\ln P_{\tau}$ line) is always greater than 0.1. We can also reach the SSE price level if we follow a path like ABB in which initially the rate of inflation is less than the steady state rate. We cannot reach the SSE price level if we follow a path like AA in which the rate of inflation is less than the SSE rate during the entire transition period.

It follows that we must have $\pi > 0.1$ at least during part of the transition period. This overshooting result can be explained as a consequence of the technical relationship (2.32). Since in the new steady state agents want to hold less real balances, they must decumulate real balances during the transition period. Since the rate of change in m is $\mu - \pi$, this can be done only if $\pi > \mu$ at least during part of the transition period.

Figure 2.15 illustrates the possible rates of inflation during the transition period. The path that is labeled "not possible" is the slope of the AA path in figure 2.15. (In this path the rate of inflation is always less than 0.1.) The two paths that are labeled "possible" are paths in which the rate of inflation is higher than 0.1 at least during part of the transition period.

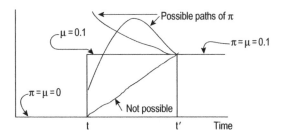

Figure 2.15   Possible inflation paths

(The instantaneous adjustment case cannot be described in this graph because it requires an infinite rate of inflation at time t.)

The "overshooting" result is relatively "model free" because it does not require a complete understanding of the transition period (the modeling of the various frictions which lead to a transition period).

2.11   REGIME CHANGES

In the previous analysis of a regime change (change in μ) the consumer was completely surprised by the announced change in policy. This is problematic because an agent with rational expectations assigns the true probability for all possible events. If the true probability of a regime change is zero (or close to zero) then regime changes are rare and do not deserve our attention.

A more satisfactory treatment would therefore assume that the agent takes into account the possibility of a regime change before it actually occurs. One way of doing it is to incorporate the probability of a regime change in the agent's maximization problem. Another approach may assume that the agent knew from the "beginning of time" that a regime change would occur at time t. Here I consider the second simpler case.

When agents expect a regime change at time t, the paths in figure 2.15, which assume zero rate of inflation until time t are no longer equilibrium paths. To see this point, note that if agents expect that the price level will go up at time t they will want to reduce their holding of real balances at time $t - 1$. Therefore the price level will go up at time $t - 1$, and by the same logic at time $t - j$, for $j = 1, 2, 3 \ldots$, as illustrated by figure 2.16.[12] Here the "transition period" starts before time t and as before, at least during part of the "transition period" π must be greater than μ.

Deflation

Deflation occurs when the government takes money from the public (by lump sum taxes) and burns it. Figures 2.17 and 2.18 describe the case in which at time t the government starts to reduce the money supply at the rate of $\mu = -0.1$. Here the level of real balances is higher in the new equilibrium and therefore $\mu - \pi$ must be positive at least during part of the transition

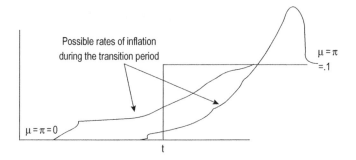

Figure 2.16 The change in policy is known in advance

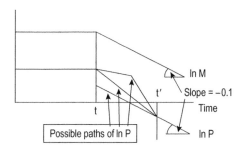

Figure 2.17 Deflation (logs of levels)

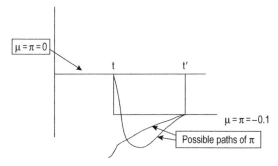

Figure 2.18 Deflation (rates of change)

period. There is also "overshooting" here in the sense that during the transition period the rate of inflation goes down below the steady-state level.

The optimum rate of inflation

The SSE condition (2.50) is: $(1 + \rho)(1 + \mu) = 1 + f'(m)$. At the social optimum f( ) is maximized and therefore: $f' = 0$. This can be achieved by setting $\mu = (1 + \rho)^{-1} - 1 \approx -\rho$. Thus, at the social optimum real balances appreciate approximately at the rate of ρ.

2.12 INTRODUCING PHYSICAL CAPITAL AND BONDS

We now add the option to sow corn and refer to corn in the soil as capital. The harvest at time $t + 1$ is given by $R(k_t)$ units of corn, where k_t denotes the amount of corn sown at time t. The marginal gross rate of return on capital is: $R'(k_t) = 1 + r(k_t)$, where $r(k_t)$ is the net rate of return. It is assumed that $r'(k) < 0$ for all $k \geq 0$ and that $r'(0) = \infty$, $r'(\infty) = 0$ as in figure 2.19.

We also add riskless private nominal bonds. We use B_t to denote the nominal quantity of bonds held by the representative consumer at time t and i_t to denote the nominal rate of return on bonds. The consumer's budget set is:

$$P_t Y_t + P_t k_t + B_t + M_t = P_t \bar{Y} + P_t R(k_{t-1}) + B_{t-1}(1 + i_t) + M_{t-1} + G_t; \qquad (2.52)$$

$$k_t, M_t \geq 0;$$

$$k_0, M_0 \text{ and } B_0 = 0 \text{ are given} \quad \text{and} \quad \lim_{t \to \infty} B_t = 0. \qquad (2.53)$$

Constraint (2.52) says that the dollar value of corn consumption and the end of period portfolio must equal the available beginning of period dollar resources (the dollar value of the endowment plus the beginning of period portfolio plus the transfer payment from the government). Constraint (2.53) specifies non-negativity constraints, initial conditions and the requirement that the consumer cannot accumulate an infinite amount of debt.

Given the sequence $\{P_t, i_t, G_t\}_{t=1}^{\infty}$, the consumer chooses $\{M_t, B_t, k_t, Y_t\}_{t=1}^{\infty}$ to maximize

$$\sum_{t=1}^{\infty} \beta^t U\{C_t = Y_t + f[(M_{t-1} + G_t)/P_t]\}$$

$$\text{subject to:} \quad (2.52) \text{ and } (2.53). \qquad (2.54)$$

The sequence $\{M_t, G_t, k_t, B_t, Y_t, i_t, P_t\}_{t=1}^{\infty}$ is an equilibrium if: (a) given $\{i_t, P_t\}$ and $G_t = M_t - M_{t-1}$, the sequence $\{M_t, k_t, B_t, Y_t\}$ solves the representative consumer's problem (2.54); and (b) markets are cleared:

$$Y_t = \bar{Y} + R(k_{t-1}) - k_t, M_t = M_0(1 + \mu)^t \quad \text{and} \quad B_t = 0 \quad \text{for all } t > 0.$$

A steady-state equilibrium sequence is an equilibrium sequence for which M_t/P_t and k_t do not change over time.

Steady-state equilibrium: As before, we express (2.52) in real terms by dividing both sides by P_t and use (2.33). This leads to:

$$Y_t + k_t + b_t + m_t = \bar{Y} + b_{t-1}(1 + r_{bt}) + m_{t-1}(1 + r_{mt}) + R(k_{t-1}) + g_t \qquad (2.55)$$

where lower case letters denote real magnitudes and $(1 + r_{bt}) = (1 + i_t)(1 + r_{mt})$ is the gross real return on bonds.[13]

The nominal interest rate and the inflation rate do not change over time and $g = -r_m m$ covers the depreciation of m units of real balances. Under these assumptions we can write (2.55) as:[14]

$$Y_t + k_t + b_t + m_t = \bar{Y} + b_{t-1}(1 + r_b) + m_{t-1}(1 + r_m) + R(k_{t-1}) - mr_m. \qquad (2.56)$$

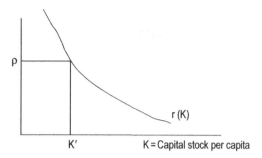

Figure 2.19   The choice of capital

The consumer starts with m units of real balances, k units of capital and no private bonds. If he does not change the amounts of assets held he will consume the smooth path:

$$Y_t = Y = \bar{Y} + R(k) - k; \quad m_t = m, \quad k_t = k, \quad b_t = 0 \quad \text{for all t.}$$

To check whether or not this smooth path is optimal, we consider three possible deviations. All of the proposed deviations assume that corn consumption is cut by x units at time t and then invested either in money (2.57) or in capital (2.58) or in bonds (2.59):

$$Y_t = Y - x; \quad Y_{t+1} = Y + x(1 + r_m);$$
$$Y_\tau = Y \quad \text{for } \tau < t \text{ and for } \tau > t + 1;$$
$$m_t = m + x \text{ and } m_\tau = m \quad \text{for } \tau \neq t; \quad k_\tau = k, \quad b_\tau = 0 \quad \text{for all } \tau. \qquad (2.57)$$

$$Y_t = Y - x; \quad Y_{t+1} = Y + x(1 + r);$$
$$Y_\tau = Y \quad \text{for } \tau < t \text{ and for } \tau > t + 1;$$
$$k_t = k + x \text{ and } k_\tau = k \quad \text{for } \tau \neq t; \quad m_\tau = m, \quad b_\tau = 0 \quad \text{for all } \tau. \qquad (2.58)$$

$$Y_t = Y - x; \quad Y_{t+1} = Y + x(1 + r_m)(1 + i);$$
$$Y_\tau = Y \quad \text{for } \tau < t \text{ and for } \tau > t + 1;$$
$$b_t = x \text{ and } b_\tau = 0 \quad \text{for } \tau \neq t; \quad m_\tau = m, \quad k_\tau = k \quad \text{for all } \tau. \qquad (2.59)$$

The slope of the budget line if savings are held as real balances is (2.42) which can be approximated by:

$$-\Delta C_{t+1}/\Delta C_t \approx 1 + f'(m) - \pi. \qquad (2.60)$$

The slope of the budget line if savings are invested in physical capital is:

$$-\Delta C_{t+1}/\Delta C_t = 1 + r. \qquad (2.61)$$

And the slope of the budget line if savings are invested in bonds is (approximately):

$$-\Delta C_{t+1}/\Delta C_t = 1 + r_b \approx 1 + i - \pi. \qquad (2.62)$$

If the smooth consumption path characterized by m is optimal, it must be the case that the slope of the indifference curve (2.18) at the point $C_t = C_{t+1}$, must equal the slope of the budget line. Using the standard approximation we get: $1 + \rho = 1 + f'(m) - \pi = 1 + r(k) = 1 + i - \pi$; or

$$\rho = f'(m) - \pi = r(k) = i - \pi. \tag{2.63}$$

Without the approximation the first order conditions are:

$$1 + \rho = (1 + r_m)[1 + f'(m)] = (1 + r_m)(1 + i) = 1 + r(k). \tag{2.64}$$

Note that the first order condition that determines real balances can be written as:

$$f'(m) = i. \tag{2.65}$$

We may therefore think of $f'(m)$ as a standard demand for money function.

In a SSE $\mu = \pi$ and we can therefore express the SSE condition by substituting $\mu = \pi$ in (2.64) and (2.63). This leads to:

$$1 + \rho = [1 + f'(m)]/(1 + \mu) = (1 + i)/(1 + \mu) = 1 + r(k)$$
$$\text{or, using the standard approximation,}$$
$$\rho = f'(m) - \mu = r(k) = i - \mu. \tag{2.66}$$

When μ goes up the SSE level of real balances goes down (see figure 2.5) but the SSE level of capital does not depend on μ. It is determined by the condition: $\rho = r(k)$.

As before we get a simple relationship between the rate of change in the money supply and welfare: When $\mu \geq -\rho$ goes up, consumption goes down and welfare goes down. At the optimum, $\mu = -\rho$ and $i = 0$.

2.13 THE GOLDEN RULE AND THE MODIFIED GOLDEN RULE

Corn consumption in the steady state is given by $Y = \bar{Y} + R(k) - k$, which is a constant plus the difference between the R(k) curve in figure 2.20 below and the 45° line. This difference is maximized at $\bar{k}$ where $R'(\bar{k}) = 1$. This is the golden rule. However the optimal steady-state level of capital is at $\hat{k}$ which satisfies the first order condition: $R'(\hat{k}) = 1 + \rho$ (see [2.64]). This is the modified golden rule.

Note that unlike real balances there is no difference between the social and the private point of view when we look at the accumulation of physical capital: To accumulate capital we must give up corn consumption. Therefore, at the social optimum we have satiation in real balances but no satiation in physical capital.

To elaborate, we consider the problem of a social planner who takes the level of real balances m as given. (As we have seen the level of real balances can be chosen optimally by an appropriate choice of μ and therefore we abstract from this choice problem here.) The

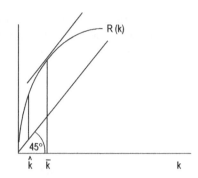

Figure 2.20 The maximum consumption level of capital and the optimum level

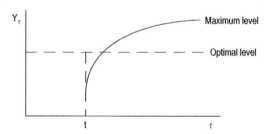

Figure 2.21 The effect of a subsidy to capital on consumption

planner's problem is:

$$\max_{k_t} \sum_{t=1}^{\infty} \beta^t U(C_t)$$

s.t.
$$C_t = Y_t + f(m)$$
$$Y_t + k_t = \bar{Y} + R(k_{t-1})$$
$$Y_{t'}, \, k_t \geq 0 \quad \text{and} \quad k_0 \text{ is given.} \tag{2.67}$$

Under what conditions will the planner choose a smooth path: $k_t = k_0 = k$? To answer this question and find the first order condition we consider the following deviation: We cut consumption at t by x units, invest it in physical capital and increase corn consumption at $t+1$ by the change in the harvest $R(k + x) - R(k)$. This deviation is the same as (2.58) and the slope of the planner's budget line is given by (2.61). Equating the slope of the budget line to the slope of the indifference curve yields the first order condition $\rho = r(k)$, which is exactly the same as the relevant part of (2.64).

This means that if a planner starts with the steady state level of capital, $\hat{k}$ he should not attempt to change it. To appreciate the implication of this result consider a subsidy scheme, financed by a lump sum tax, in which the planner pays s units per unit of capital. The first order condition for the representative private agent is now: $\rho = r(k) + s$. By choosing $s = \rho$ the central planner can induce agents to accumulate capital until they reach $\bar{k}$ and at this point $r(k) = 0$. The consumption of corn path in this case may be described by the solid line in figure 2.21.

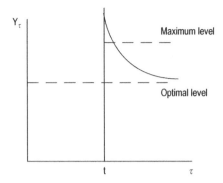

Figure 2.22   Optimal consumption when capital is above the optimal level

The above subsidy scheme reduces the welfare of the representative consumer, in spite of the fact that eventually it leads to more consumption. The reason for the reduction in welfare is that the cost of the initial reduction in consumption is too high relative to the future benefits.

Suppose now that in the past, there was a subsidy scheme of the type just described and as a result the level of capital per agent is $\bar{k}$ at time t. Should the central planner continue with the subsidy scheme? The answer is in the negative. The central planner should abolish it and as a result the private agents will choose to "eat capital" until they reach the optimal level as in the solid line of figure 2.22. This is an immediate corollary of the result that $\hat{k}$ is optimal from both the consumer's point of view and the planner's point of view.

PROBLEMS

In questions 1–5 the money supply (M) does not change over time.

1   At time t a single individual experiences a change in taste and his time preference parameter ρ goes up. What will happen to his level of corn consumption (Y_t) and total consumption (C_t)?

2   At time t a single individual experiences a change in technology: m units of real balances yield after the change $\alpha + f(m)$ units of consumption instead of the previous yield of $f(m)$ units, where $\alpha > 0$ is a constant. Does the technological change affect the individual level of current corn consumption (Y_t)?

3   The same as 2 but now the change is to $\alpha f(m)$.

4   Answer 1–3 under the assumption that all individuals in the society experience the same changes.

5   Comparing your answer 4 to 1–3 what can you say about the cost of accumulating real balances? Distinguish between the cost to an individual and the cost to society.

6 The government increases the rate of change in the money supply and as a result the economy jumps immediately (without a transition period) from one steady state to another steady state. What will happen to the price level and the rate of inflation at the jump to the new steady state?

7 Assume that the economy was in a steady state equilibrium and at time t all individuals experience a change in taste: ρ goes up. What will be the rate of inflation in the new steady state? What will happen to the rate of inflation in the transition to the new steady state?

8 Assume that liquidity services are described by the function $f(m) = m^\alpha$. What do we assume about α? What is the demand for money in a steady-state equilibrium as a function of π and ρ? (Develop a logarithmic expression).

9 In the text we wrote the budget constraint in real terms as: $m_t = \bar{Y} - Y_t + m_{t-1}(1 + r_m) + g_t$, where g_t was exogenous from the consumer's point of view (it did not depend on any of the choices he made). Assume now that the transfer payment is given in proportion to the amount of money held by each individual so that $g_t = -r_m m_{t-1}$. What is the effect of changing μ on the steady-state equilibrium level of real balances in this case?

PROBLEMS WITH ANSWERS

10 The infinite horizon problem described by (2.9)–(2.12) in the text can be written as:

$$\max_{Y_t} \sum_{t=1}^{\infty} \beta^t U[Y_t + f(m_{t-1})]$$

$$\text{s.t.} \quad Y_t + m_t = \bar{Y} + m_{t-1}$$

$$m_t \geq 0, \quad \text{and} \quad m_0 \text{ is given.}$$

Find the first order conditions for this problem using the Lagrangian method.

Answer

The Lagrangian is:

$$L = \sum_{t=1}^{\infty} \beta^t \{U[Y_t + f(m_{t-1})] + \lambda_t(\bar{Y} - Y_t + m_{t-1} - m_t)\}$$

First order conditions:

(a) $\partial L / \partial m_t = \beta^{t+1} U'(C_{t+1}) f'(m_t) + \beta^{t+1} \lambda_{t+1} - \beta^t \lambda_t = 0$

(b) $\partial L / \partial Y_t = \beta^t U'(C_t) - \beta^t \lambda_t = 0$

From (b) we get: $U'(C_t) = \lambda_t$. Substituting this in (a) yields:

(c) $1 + f'(m_t) = U'(C_t)/\beta U'(C_{t+1})$.

In the steady-state: $1 + f'(m) = 1 + \rho$. This is the first order condition (2.19) derived in the text.

11   Assume two assets: Real balances and physical capital. As in chapter 2, consumption is defined by: $C_t = Y_t + f(m_{tb})$, where Y_t is corn consumption and m_{tb} is the beginning of period real balances. But unlike the specification in chapter 2, the agent's budget constraint (asset evolution equation) is:

$$k_t + m_t = \bar{Y} - Y_t + m_{t-1}(1 + r_m) + R(k_{t-1})\theta(m_{tb}) + g_t,$$

where $R( )$ is a monotonic function with the standard properties and the function $\theta( )$ has the same properties as the function $f( )$: it is strictly concave and increasing initially. Thus we assume that in addition to yielding services to the shopper, real balances also make capital more productive.

We assume $g_t = -mr_m$ for all t.

(a) What is the consumption of corn along a smooth consumption path characterized by m?

(b) Consider the following deviation from the smooth consumption path. The consumer plans to reduce current corn consumption by x units, increase his real balances by that amount ($\Delta m_t = -\Delta Y_t = -\Delta C_t = x$) and spend it in the next period. What will be the change (ΔC_{t+1}) in t + 1 consumption relative to the smooth consumption path?

(c) Answer (b) under the assumption that instead of accumulating real balances, the agent increases the stock of capital at time t by x units.

(d) What is the slope of the budget constraint in the (C_t, C_{t+1}) plane. Give two expressions: One when you accumulate real balances as in (b) and one when you increase the stock of capital as in (c). Assume now that x is small.

(e) What are the two first order conditions?

(f) What happens to the steady-state level of capital when the steady state rate of inflation goes up? Assume that the steady-state real balances go down when inflation goes up.

(g) Derive the first order conditions using the Lagrangian method.

Answer

(a) A smooth consumption path that is characterized by m is:

$$m_t = m_0 = m; \quad k_t = k; \quad Y_t = \bar{Y} + R(k)\theta(m) - k \quad \text{for all t.}$$

(b) $\Delta C_{t+1} = x(1 + r_m) + f[m + x(1 + r_m)] - f(m)$
$\qquad + R(k)\{\theta[m + x(1 + r_m)] - \theta(m)\}$

(c) $\Delta C_{t+1} = \theta(m)[R(k + x) - R(k)]$.

(d) $-\Delta C_{t+1}/\Delta C_t = (1 + r_m) + (1 + r_m)f'(m) + (1 + r_m)R(k)\theta'(m)$
$\qquad = (1 + r_m)[1 + f'(m) + R(k)\theta'(m)]$
$-\Delta C_{t+1}/\Delta C_t = \theta(m)R'(k)$.

(e) $(1 + r_m)[1 + f'(m) + R(k)\theta'(m)] = \theta(m)R'(k) = 1 + \rho$.

(f) Since we assume that the steady state real balances goes down, the marginal product curve $R'(k)\theta(m)$ shifts to the left and the steady state level of capital is down. This is shown in figure 2.23 when comparing two steady states: The first with $i = 0.1$ and real balances $= m(0.1)$ and the second with $i = 0.2$ and real balances $= m(0.2)$.

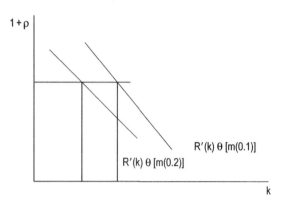

Figure 2.23   The effect of a change in the rate of inflation on the choice of capital

(g) *Solving by the lagrangian method*:

$$L = \sum_{t=1}^{\infty} \beta^t \{U(Y_t + f[m_{t-1}(1+r_m) + g_t])$$

$$+ \lambda_t(\bar{Y} - Y_t + m_{t-1}(1+r_m) + R(k_{t-1})\theta[m_{t-1}(1+r_m) + g_t]$$

$$+ g_t - k_t - m_t)\}.$$

First order conditions:

(a) $\partial L/\partial m_t = \beta^{t+1}U'(C_{t+1})(1+r_m)f'(m_{t+1b}) + \beta^{t+1}\lambda_{t+1}(1+r_m)$
$\qquad + \beta^{t+1}\lambda_{t+1}R(k_t)(1+r_m)\theta'(m_{t+1b}) - \beta^t\lambda_t = 0$

(b) $\partial L/\partial k_t = \beta^{t+1}\lambda_{t+1}R'(k_t)\theta(m_{t+1b}) - \beta^t\lambda_t = 0$

(c) $\partial L/\partial Y_t = \beta^t U'(C_t) - \beta^t\lambda_t = 0$

From (c) we get: $U'(C_t) = \lambda_t$. Substituting this in (a) and (b) yields:

(d) $(1+r_m)[1 + f'(m_{t+1b}) + R(k_t)\theta'(m_{t+1b})] = U'(C_t)/\beta U'(C_{t+1})$

(e) $R'(k_t)\theta(m_t + g_{t+1}) = U'(C_t)/\beta U'(C_{t+1})$.

In the steady state:

(f) $(1+r_m)[1 + f'(m) + R(k_t)\theta'(m)] = R'(k_t)\theta(m) = 1 + \rho$.

APPENDIX 2A   A DYNAMIC PROGRAMMING EXAMPLE

We now illustrate the use of dynamic programming by solving the infinite horizon problem (2.9)–(2.12) in section 2.2. We use two alternative ways of deriving the Bellman equation. One follows Stokey and Lucas with Prescott (1989) who starts with an infinite horizon problem. The other follows Sargent (1987) who starts from a finite horizon problem.

The infinite horizon problem (2.9)–(2.12) can be written as:

$$V_1(m_0) = \max_{Y_t} \sum_{t=1}^{\infty} \beta^{t-1} U[Y_t + f(m_{t-1})]$$

s.t.

$$Y_t + m_t = \bar{Y} + m_{t-1}$$

$$m_t \geq 0, \quad \text{and} \quad m_0 \text{ is given.} \tag{A2.1}$$

The value function $V_1(m_0)$ is the maximum utility the consumer can achieve at $t = 1$ if he starts with m_0 units of real balances. Suppose that after consuming in the first period the consumer is left with m_1 units of real balances. Then in the next period he will solve:

$$V_2(m_1) = \max_{Y_t} \sum_{t=2}^{\infty} \beta^{t-2} U[Y_t + f(m_{t-1})]$$

s.t.

$$Y_t + m_t = \bar{Y} + m_{t-1}$$

$$m_t \geq 0, \quad \text{and} \quad m_1 \text{ is given.} \tag{A2.2}$$

The value function $V_2(m_1)$ is the maximum utility that the consumer can achieve at $t = 2$ if he starts with m_1 units of real balances. Note that since the horizon is infinite, the problem at $t = 2$ looks the same as the problem at $t = 1$ and therefore $V_1(\ )$ and $V_2(\ )$ are the same. We use $V \equiv V_1 \equiv V_2$ to denote this value function.

We now write the problem (A2.1) as:

$$V(m_0) = \max_{Y_t} U[Y_1 + f(m_0)] + \beta \sum_{t=2}^{\infty} \beta^{t-2} U[Y_t + f(m_{t-1})]$$

s.t.

$$Y_t + m_t = \bar{Y} + m_{t-1}$$

$$m_t \geq 0, \quad \text{and} \quad m_0 \text{ is given.} \tag{A2.3}$$

This way of writing the problem separates the objective function into two components: The current utility component ($U[Y_1 + f(m_0)]$) and the future utility component $\left(\beta \sum_{t=2}^{\infty} \beta^{t-2} U[Y_t + f(m_{t-1})]\right)$. For any given choice Y_1 the level of the beginning of next period real balances is given by: $m_1 = \bar{Y} - Y_1 + m_0$. The maximum utility that the consumer can achieve at $t = 2$ with this predetermined level of real balances, is: $\beta V(\bar{Y} - Y_1 + m_0)$.

We can therefore write the problem (A2.3) as:

$$V(m_0) = \max_{Y_1} U[Y_1 + f(m_0)] + \beta V(\bar{Y} - Y_1 + m_0)$$

$$\text{s.t.} \quad \bar{Y} - Y_1 + m_0 \geq 0. \tag{A2.4}$$

Since the choice problem does not depend on the time it is made (again, because of the infinite horizon) we may omit the time index and write:

$$V(m) = \max_{Y} U[Y + f(m)] + \beta V(\bar{Y} - Y + m)$$

$$\text{s.t.} \quad \bar{Y} - Y + m \geq 0. \tag{A2.5}$$

This is a Bellman equation.

We now derive the first order condition for an interior solution to (A2.5) by taking a derivative with respect to Y and ignoring the non-negativity constraint. This leads to: $U'[Y + f(m)] - \beta V'(\bar{Y} - Y + m) = 0$. Using $C = Y + f(m)$ for current consumption and $m' = \bar{Y} - Y + m$ for the beginning of next period real balances we can write this first order condition as:

$$U'(C) = \beta V'(m'). \tag{A2.6}$$

To derive V' we use the envelope theorem which says that after solving the problem in (A2.5) and replacing the optimal values we can take a derivative from both sides of (A2.5) ignoring the max operator. See also Benveniste and Scheinkman (1979). This yields:

$$V'(m) = U'[Y + f(m)]f'(m) + \beta V'(\bar{Y} - Y + m) = U'(C)f'(m) + \beta V'(m'). \tag{A2.7}$$

Substituting (A2.6) in (A2.7) leads to:

$$V'(m) = U'(C)[1 + f'(m)]. \tag{A2.8}$$

The intuition is that at the optimum it does not matter what we do with an additional unit of the beginning of period real balances. In particular we may use it to increase current consumption. This yields $U'(C)$ utils. In addition the added unit increases liquidity services by f' yielding $U'(C)f'(m)$ utils.

Since (A2.8) holds for any m it also holds for the beginning of next period's real balances. We thus have: $V'(m') = U'(C')[1 + f'(m')]$ where prime is used to denote next period's magnitudes. Substituting this in (A2.6) leads to:

$$U'(C) = \beta[1 + f'(m')]U'(C'). \tag{A2.9}$$

Using time indices we can write (A2.9) as:

$$U'(C_t) = \beta[1 + f'(m_t)]U'(C_{t+1}). \tag{A2.10}$$

This first order condition (A2.10) must hold for any optimal consumption path. For a smooth path $C_t = C_{t+1}$ and we can write (A2.10) as: $\rho = f'(m)$. This is the first order condition (2.19) derived in the text.

Deriving the Bellman equation in an alternative way

We now consider a finite (T periods) horizon problem. We start with the last period problem, solve it as a function of the beginning of period real balances and use the solution to solve the two periods problem that the consumer faces at $T - 2$. The two periods problem at $T - 2$ is solved as a function of the beginning of period real balances and is used to solve the three periods problem at $T - 3$. We keep doing this (going back in time) until we reach the first period where we solve the T periods horizon problem.

The consumer enters the last period with the predetermined level of m_{T-1} units of real balances. His utility in the last period of life is:

$$V_0(m_{T-1}) \equiv U[\bar{Y} + m_{T-1} + f(m_{T-1})], \tag{A2.11}$$

where here $V_0(m)$ is the maximum utility one can achieve in a one period problem when the predetermined level of real balances is m.

Note that:

$$V_0'(m_{T-1}) = U'(C_T)(1 + f'(m_{T-1})). \tag{A2.12}$$

The intuition is that an "additional unit" of real balances will increase corn consumption by one unit and liquidity services by: $f'(m_{T-1})$ units.

Next we consider the problem in period $T - 1$. The consumer starts this period with the predetermined level of m_{T-2} units of real balances and solves:

$$V_1(m_{T-2}) = \max U[Y_{T-1} + f(m_{T-2})] + \beta V_0(m_{T-1})$$

$$\text{s.t.} \quad Y_{T-1} + m_{T-1} = \bar{Y} + m_{T-2} \quad \text{and non-negativity constraints.} \tag{A2.13}$$

Here $V_1(m)$ is the maximum utility achievable in a two periods problem when the predetermined level of real balances is m.

Using the constraint to substitute for m_{T-1} leads to:

$$\max U(Y_{T-1} + f(m_{T-2})) + \beta V_0(\bar{Y} + m_{T-2} - Y_{T-1}). \tag{A2.14}$$

Taking a derivative with respect to Y_{T-1} and equating it to zero, we obtain the first order condition:

$$U'(C_{T-1}) = \beta V_0'(m_{T-1}). \tag{A2.15}$$

Substituting (A2.12) into (A2.15) yields:

$$U'(C_{T-1}) = \beta U'(C_T)(1 + f'(m_{T-1})). \tag{A2.16}$$

This condition can be used to solve for the optimal Y_{T-1} and m_{T-1} as a function of m_{T-2}. To do that, we substitute $m_{T-1} = \bar{Y} + m_{T-2} - Y_{T-1}$ and $C_{T-1} = Y_{T-1} + f(m_{T-2})$ in (A2.16) to get:

$$U'[Y_{T-1} + f(m_{T-2})]$$
$$= \beta U'[\bar{Y} + f(\bar{Y} + m_{T-2} - Y_{T-1})][1 + f'(\bar{Y} + m_{T-2} - Y_{T-1})]. \tag{A2.17}$$

This is one equation with one unknown. We solve for $Y_{T-1}(m_{T-2})$ and then get $m_{T-1}(m_{T-2}) = \bar{Y} + m_{T-2} - Y_{T-1}(m_{T-2})$.

In general, in period t m_{t-1} is given and the consumer solves:

$$V_{T-t-1}(m_{t-1}) = \max U[Y_t + f(m_{t-1})] + \beta V_{T-t}(m_t)$$

$$\text{s.t.} \quad Y_t + m_t = \bar{Y} + m_{t-1} \quad \text{and non-negativity constraints.} \qquad (A2.18)$$

When T goes to infinity the function on both sides is the same and we get the Bellman equation (which defines the value function V):

$$V(m_{t-1}) = \max U[Y_t + f(m_{t-1})] + \beta V(m_t)$$

$$\text{s.t.} \quad Y_t + m_t = \bar{Y} + m_{t-1} \quad \text{and non-negativity constraints.} \qquad (A2.19)$$

NOTES

1 The function F( ) depends in general on what other people do and is therefore defined only in equilibrium.
2 See Kiyotaki and Wright (1993) for a formal search model.
3 Here the present value of utility is computed to date $t = 0$. For some purposes it is more convenient to discount to date $t = 1$ and write the utility function as $\sum_{t=1}^{\infty} \beta^{t-1} U(C_t)$. Since $\sum_{t=1}^{\infty} \beta^t U(C_t) = \beta \sum_{t=1}^{\infty} \beta^{t-1} U(C_t)$, they both describe the same preferences.
4 Strictly speaking, the slope of the "budget line" is $1 + f'(m)$ only in the neighborhood of the diagonal.
5 Friedman motivates the assumption that $f'(m) < 0$ for $m > \bar{m}$ by the need to employ guards for securing large quantity of real balances. This assumption is required only for the uniqueness of the social optimum.
6 This may be derived as follows. We take a full differential $\sum_{\tau=t}^{\infty} \beta^{\tau-t} U'(C) dC_\tau$, substitute $dC_t = dY_t$ and $dC_\tau = f'(m) dm_p$ for $\tau > t$ and equate to zero. This leads to: $-U'(C) dY_t = \sum_{\tau=t+1}^{\infty} \beta^{\tau-t} U'(C) f'(m) dm_p$ and to: $-dY_t/dm_p = \sum_{\tau=t+1}^{\infty} \beta^{\tau-t} f'(m) = f'(m)/\rho$.
7 The "outside" derivative $d \ln(M)/dt$ is $1/M$ and the "inside" derivative is dM/dt.
8 Thus, in equilibrium expectations about future transfer payments and prices are correct.
9 Alternatively we may define a SSE as an equilibrium with the property that the rate of inflation π does not change over time. In the present context the two definitions are equivalent.
10 For small π we can approximate (2.39) by $m\pi$.
11 This uses: $f'(m) = \lim_{x \to 0} \{f[m + x(1 + r_m)] - f(m)\}/[x(1 + r_m)]$.
12 Strictly speaking the rate of inflation should be positive from $t = -\infty$.
13 To check the interpretation of the last formula note that to invest one dollar in bonds the consumer must give up $1/P_t$ units of consumption. At the beginning of next period, the consumer will have $(1 + i)$ dollars which will buy him $(1 + i)/P_{t+1}$ units of consumption. Therefore the gross real return on bonds is: $1 + r_b = [(1 + i)/P_{t+1}]/(1/P_t) = (1 + i)(P_t/P_{t+1}) = (1 + i)(1 + r_m)$. For small π, we can use the approximation: $r_b = i - \pi$.
14 When π is small we can use the approximation:

$$Y_t + k_t + b_t + m_t = \bar{Y} + b_{t-1}(1 + i - \pi) + m_{t-1}(1 - \pi) + R(k_{t-1}) + m\pi.$$

CHAPTER 3

The Welfare Cost of Inflation in a Growing Economy

In the previous chapter we argued for the optimality of the Friedman rule. But actual economies do not follow this rule and adopt a strictly positive nominal interest rate policy. What is the welfare cost of deviation from the optimal policy? This question was addressed by Baily (1956) for the no growth case. We now use the analysis in chapter 2, to illustrate his argument.

The steady-state level of real balances is given by the solution m(i) to the first order condition: $f'(m) = i$, where i is the steady state level of the nominal interest rate. Since $i \approx \rho + \mu$, by varying μ the government can vary i. We can therefore ask what is the welfare gain from reducing i from say 0.1 to 0. In our framework, the answer is: $f[m(0)] - f[m(0.1)]$ units of corn.[1] We can estimate this welfare gain by the area under the demand for money curve: Area D in figure 3.1.

Lucas (2000) modified this approach and allowed for the case in which real income (real corn endowment in our framework) grows. He observed that over the period 1900–94, real GDP grew at an average annual rate of 3% , M1 grew at 5.6% and the GDP deflator grew at 3.2% and therefore the money-income ratio is essentially trendless. He fitted two demand for money functions: $z = Ai^{-\eta}$ and $z = Be^{-\zeta i}$, where $z = m/\bar{Y}$ is the money-income ratio, i is the nominal interest rate and A, η, B, ζ are parameters. He then computed the area D under the demand for z, which gives the welfare cost as a percentage of real income.

The first log-log specification seems to work better and yields an estimate welfare cost of about 1% or real GDP when the nominal interest rate is 4%. This welfare cost is much lower when using the semi-log specification: It is about 0.2% of real GDP.

Lucas then searched for a model that can explain the empirical findings and can be used to evaluate alternative policies. In this chapter we attempt to do the same using versions of the specification that we have already worked with in chapter 2. We start from an analysis of the steady state in a growing economy.

3.1 STEADY-STATE EQUILIBRIUM IN A GROWING ECONOMY

We require that in a SSE the rate of inflation will not change over time (and allow changes in real balances). A SSE exists if real income grows at a constant rate and the elasticity of the demand for money with respect to real income is constant.

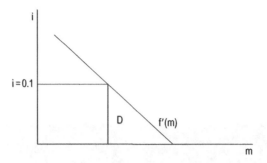

Figure 3.1   The welfare gain when there is no growth

To illustrate, we assume that real income grows at a constant rate of ϕ (thus, $\bar{Y}_t = \bar{Y}_0 e^{\phi t}$) and the money supply grows at a constant rate of μ (thus, $M_t = M_0 e^{\mu t}$). The demand for real balances is given by:

$$\ln m_t = 1.5 \ln \bar{Y}_t - 0.5 \ln \pi_t, \tag{3.1}$$

where π_t is the rate of inflation. The demand for money grows at the rate:

$$d(\ln m)/dt = 1.5 \, d(\ln \bar{Y})/dt - 0.5 \, d(\ln \pi)/dt$$
$$= 1.5\phi - 0.5 \, d(\ln \pi)/dt. \tag{3.2}$$

In the steady state the rate of inflation is constant and therefore $d(\ln \pi)/dt = 0$ and $d(\ln m)/dt = 1.5\phi$. Since the supply of real balances grow at the rate $(d \ln m)/dt = \mu - \pi$, the clearing of the money market requires:

$$\mu - \pi = 1.5\phi. \tag{3.3}$$

If, for example, $\phi = 0.1$ and the government does not print money ($\mu = 0$), the SSE rate of inflation will be -0.15 so that the supply of real balances grow at the desired rate of 0.15.

In general, when time is continuous and the demand for money grows at a constant rate of γ ($\gamma = 1.5\phi$ in our example) the steady state rate of inflation is: $\pi = \mu - \gamma$. When time is discrete and $m_t/m_{t-1} = 1 + \gamma$, we get $(M_t/M_{t-1})(P_{t-1}/P_t) = 1 + \gamma$, which leads to:

$$1 + \pi = (1 + \mu)/(1 + \gamma). \tag{3.4}$$

We will use this formula in the next section.

3.2   GENERALIZING THE MODEL IN CHAPTER 2 TO THE CASE OF GROWTH

To get a steady-state equilibrium with constant money/income ratio we must modify the specification of the liquidity services function.

We start with the indirect utility function (2.6) in section 2.1. We assume that there is only one good and that there exist functions $f(\ )$ and $U(\ )$ such that:

$$V(\bar{Y}_t, Y_t, m_{tb}) = U[C_t = \omega_1 Y_t + \omega_2 \bar{Y}_t f(m_{tb}/\bar{Y}_t) + \omega_3 Y_t f(m_{tb}/Y_t)], \tag{3.5}$$

where the $\omega_i \geq 0$ are weights. The indirect utility function $V(\bar{Y}_t, Y_t, m_{tb})$ is the maximum single period utility that the consumer can make if he starts the period with $\bar{Y}_t$ units of corn and m_{tb} units of real balances and consumes Y_t units of corn. The term $\bar{Y}_t f(m_{tb}/\bar{Y}_t)$ is designed to capture the role of money in facilitating production. The term $Y_t f(m_{tb}/Y_t)$ is designed to capture the role of money in facilitating consumption.

To motivate the production term $\bar{Y}_t f(m_{tb}/\bar{Y}_t)$ let us think of a worker who has contracted to supply 8 hours of work every day. He can get to work by bus but if he does not have enough money, he walks. In this case, the consumer will spend more time producing the same amount if he starts the period without enough money. To motivate the consumption term $Y_t f(m_{tb}/Y_t)$ think of the individual as going to shop rather than to work. Levhari and Patinkin (1968) focus on the production role of money. Karni (1973), McCallum and Goodfriend (1987) and Lucas (2000) focus on the consumption role of money.

The specification (3.5) assumes that if Y and $\bar{Y}$ grow at the rate of γ and if the agent holds a fraction z of income as real balances ($m_{tb} = z\bar{Y}_t$), then liquidity services,

$$\omega_2 \bar{Y}_t f(m_{tb}/\bar{Y}_t) + \omega_3 Y_t f(m_{tb}/Y_t), \quad \text{also grow at the rate } \gamma.$$

We follow Lucas in assuming $U(C) = C^{1-\sigma}/(1-\sigma)$, where $\sigma \neq 1$. As before we assume that income is exogenous and is given by: $\bar{Y}_t = \bar{Y}_0(1+\gamma)^t$, where γ is the constant growth rate. We start from the special case in which $\omega_1 = \omega_2 = 1$ and $\omega_3 = 0$.

A constant rate of growth path

A constant rate of growth path that is characterized by z requires: $Y_t = \bar{Y}_t$ and $m_t = z\bar{Y}_t$. We now assume that $m_0 = z\bar{Y}_0$ and the real transfer payment is given by:

$$g_t = z\bar{Y}_t - z\bar{Y}_{t-1}(1+r_m) \quad \text{for all t.} \tag{3.6}$$

Substituting (3.6) in the asset evolution equation, $m_t = \bar{Y}_t - Y_t + m_{t-1}(1+r_m) + g_t$, reveals that under the above assumptions a constant rate of growth path characterized by z is feasible. Is it optimal?

To examine this question, we consider now the following deviation from the constant rate of growth consumption path:

$$Y_t = \bar{Y}_t - x; \quad Y_{t+1} = \bar{Y}_{t+1} + x(1+r_m)$$
$$Y_\tau = \bar{Y}_\tau \quad \text{for } \tau < t \text{ and } \tau > t+1$$
$$m_t = z\bar{Y}_t + x \quad \text{and} \quad m_\tau = z\bar{Y}_\tau \quad \text{for } \tau \neq t. \tag{3.7}$$

This deviation is similar to (2.41) in section 2.8. We cut corn consumption by x units at time t and use the accumulated real balances to increase corn consumption at $t+1$.

The change of consumption from the steady state path is:

$$\Delta C_t = -x;$$
$$\Delta C_{t+1} = x(1+r_m) + \bar{Y}_{t+1}f[z + x(1+r_m)/\bar{Y}_{t+1}] - \bar{Y}_{t+1}f(z). \tag{3.8}$$

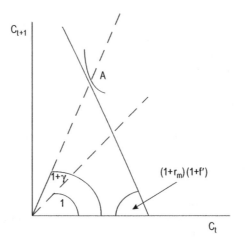

Figure 3.2 A first order condition for a constant rate of growth path

The slope of the "budget line" is given by:

$$-\Delta C_{t+1}/\Delta C_t = (1 + r_m)[1 + f'(z)], \tag{3.9}$$

because $f'(z) = \lim_{x \to 0} \bar{Y}_{t+1}\{f[z + x(1 + r_m)/\bar{Y}_{t+1}] - f(z)\}/x(1 + r_m)$.

Assuming $U(C) = C^{1-\sigma}/(1 - \sigma)$, the slope of the indifference curve at the point $C_{t+1} = C_t(1 + \gamma)$ is:

$$(1 + \rho)U'(C_t)/U'(C_{t+1}) = (1 + \rho)U'(C_t)/U'(C_t(1 + \gamma))$$

$$= (1 + \rho)(1 + \gamma)^{\sigma}. \tag{3.10}$$

The first order condition requires that the slope of the budget line equals the slope of the indifference curve:[2]

$$(1 + r_m)[1 + f'(z)] = (1 + \rho)(1 + \gamma)^{\sigma}. \tag{3.11}$$

Figure 3.2 illustrates the first order condition (3.11). A constant rate of growth path implies that consumption grows at the rate of γ. This path is optimal if the slope of the "budget line" is equal to the slope of the indifference curve at a point like A which is on a ray with a slope of $1 + \gamma$ (to the left of the 45 degrees line). For a dynamic programming formulation and a formal derivation of (3.11) see the appendix at the end of this chapter.

Steady-state equilibrium

When real balances grow at the discrete rate of γ the relationship between μ and π is given by (3.4) which implies $(1 + r_m) = (1 + \pi)^{-1} = (1 + \gamma)/(1 + \mu)$. Substituting this in (3.11) we get the steady-state equilibrium condition:

$$1 + f'(z) = (1 + \mu)/\lambda, \tag{3.12}$$

where $\lambda = (1 + \gamma)^{1-\sigma}/(1 + \rho)$. Since $f'' < 0$, an increase in μ leads to a reduction in the steady state level of z.

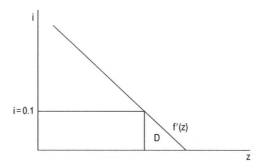

Figure 3.3 The welfare gain is a fraction D of real income

Let us now add bonds to the model. It is still true that the agent must be indifferent between investing in bonds to investing it in money. Thus,

$$(1 + r_m)[1 + f'(z)] = (1 + r_m)(1 + i), \qquad (3.13)$$

where $(1+r_m)(1+i)$ is the gross real rate of return on nominal bonds (see [2.64] in section 2.12). Combining (3.13) with (3.12) leads to:

$$1 + f'(z) = (1 + \mu)/\lambda = 1 + i. \qquad (3.14)$$

We can therefore think of $f'(z)$ as the demand for money-income ratio.

Let $z(i)$ denote the solution to (3.14). The welfare gain from reducing the steady state nominal interest rate from say 0.1 to 0 at time t is: $\bar{Y}_t\{f[z(0)] - f[z(0.1)]\}$ units of corn, or a fraction $f[z(0)] - f[z(0.1)]$ of real income. This is illustrated by the area D under the demand for z curve in figure 3.3.

Lucas' shopping specification

We now turn to the case in which consumption is defined by:

$$C_t = Y_t f(m_{tb}/Y_t). \qquad (3.15)$$

This case, considered by Lucas (2000), focuses on the role of money in facilitating shopping. Here we assume $f(0) = 0, 0 < f' < \infty$ and $f'' < 0$, everywhere.

To derive the first order condition we consider the following deviation from a steady state constant growth – constant z path. We reduce corn consumption by one unit at time t and do not change it in any other periods. The real balances accumulated at time t changes the real balances in all future periods. At $t + 1$ we have $(1 + r_m)$ additional units, at $t + 2$ we have $(1 + r_m)^2$ additional units and so on. The proposed deviation is thus:

$$Y_t = \bar{Y}_t - 1; \quad Y_\tau = \bar{Y}_\tau \quad \text{for } \tau \neq t;$$

$$m_t = z\bar{Y}_t + 1;$$

$$m_\tau = z\bar{Y}_\tau \quad \text{for } \tau < t;$$

$$m_\tau = z\bar{Y}_\tau + (1 + r_m)^{\tau-t} \quad \text{for } \tau > t. \qquad (3.16)$$

A unit cut in corn consumption at time t leads to a loss of $f(z) - zf'(z)$ units of consumption (taking the derivative of [3.15] with respect to Y_t) and to a loss of:

$$U'(C_t)[f(z) - zf'(z)], \tag{3.17}$$

time t utils.

The accumulated real balances yield an infinite stream of liquidity services. At time $t + 1$, we have $1 + r_m$ additional units of real balances (relative to the steady-state path) yielding $U'(C_{t+1})f'(z)(1 + r_m)$ utils. At time $t + 2$ we have additional $(1 + r_m)^2$ units of real balances yielding $U'(C_{t+2})f'(z)(1 + r_m)^2$ utils and so on. The total gains discounted to time t are:

$$\sum_{\tau=t+1}^{\infty} \beta^{\tau-t} U'(C_\tau) f'(z)(1 + r_m)^{\tau-t}, \tag{3.18}$$

utils. Optimality requires that the "pain" (3.17) equals the present value of the "gains" (3.18). Thus,

$$U'(C_t)[f(z) - zf'(z)] = \sum_{\tau=t+1}^{\infty} \beta^{\tau-t} U'(C_\tau) f'(z)(1 + r_m)^{\tau-t}. \tag{3.19}$$

Assuming $U(C) = C^{1-\sigma}/(1 - \sigma)$ and using the constant growth assumption, $C_\tau = C_t(1 + \gamma)^{\tau-t}$, yields:

$$U'(C_\tau)/U'(C_t) = [C_t(1 + \gamma)^{\tau-t}]^{-\sigma}/(C_t)^{-\sigma} = (1 + \gamma)^{-\sigma(\tau-t)}. \tag{3.20}$$

Substituting this in the first order condition (3.19) yields:

$$[f(z) - zf'(z)]/f'(z) = \sum_{\tau=t+1}^{\infty} \beta^{\tau-t}(1 + \gamma)^{-\sigma(\tau-t)}(1 + r_m)^{\tau-t}$$

$$= \beta(1 + \gamma)^{-\sigma}(1 + r_m)/[1 - \beta(1 + \gamma)^{-\sigma}(1 + r_m)]. \tag{3.21}$$

Rearranging and using $(1 + \pi) = (1 + \mu)/(1 + \gamma)$ leads to:

$$A(z) = 1 + f'(z)/[f(z) - zf'(z)] = (1 + \mu)/\lambda, \tag{3.22}$$

where $\lambda = (1 + \gamma)^{1-\sigma}/(1 + \rho)$. For a dynamic programming formulation of the problem and for a formal derivation of (3.22) see the appendix at the end of the chapter. We now show the following claim.

Claim: When $1 + \mu > \lambda$, there exists a unique solution $z(\mu)$ to the steady-state condition (3.22) and the function $z(\mu)$ is strictly decreasing.

Proof: Since $f'' < 0$, $A(z)$ is a decreasing function. For concave functions $f(z) - zf'(z) = z[f(z)/z - f'(z)] > 0$ and therefore $A(z) = 1 + f'(z)/[f(z) - zf'(z)]$ is greater than 1. When z goes to zero $A(z)$ goes to infinity and when z goes to infinity $A(z)$ goes to unity. It follows that there exists a solution to (3.22) if $1 + \mu > \lambda$. Figure 3.4 illustrates the solution for the case $\mu = \mu^*$. It can also be used to show that $z(\mu)$ is a decreasing function. $\square$

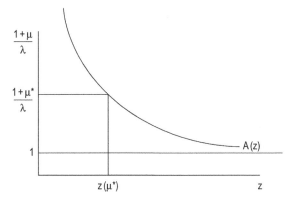

Figure 3.4   The SS level of z

The money demand relationship

We now add bonds to our model and consider the following deviation from the steady state path. We cut corn consumption by one unit. This leads to a loss of $U'(C_t)[f(z) - zf'(z)]$ time t utils. But unlike the previous case, we now invest the unit saved in bonds and use it to buy corn in the next period. The unit invested in bonds yields $(1 + r_m)(1 + i)[f(z) - zf'(z)]$ units of next period's consumption and the discounted utility from these units is: $\beta U'(C_{t+1})(1 + r_m)(1 + i)$ $[f(z) - zf'(z)]$. The "pain" equals "gain" condition for this deviation is:

$$U'(C_t)[f(z) - zf'(z)] = \beta U'(C_{t+1})[f(z) - zf'(z)](1 + r_m)(1 + i). \qquad (3.23)$$

Using the slope of the indifference curve (3.10), $1 + r_m = (1 + \gamma)/(1 + \mu)$ and $\lambda = (1 + \gamma)^{1-\sigma}/(1 + \rho)$ yields:

$$1 + i = (1 + \mu)/\lambda. \qquad (3.24)$$

Substituting this relationship in (3.22) leads to:

$$A(z) = 1 + i. \qquad (3.25)$$

We can now think of $A(z)$ as the demand schedule for z and this demand is downward sloping.

Let $z(i)$ denote the solution to (3.25). To find the welfare gain from reducing the steady state nominal interest rate to zero we should compute $f[z(0)] - f[z(i)]$. This is no longer the area under the demand for z curve. Lucas argues however that in most cases the consumer surplus formula is very close to the welfare cost.

An example: Assuming $f(z) = z^\alpha/(1 - \alpha)$. Since in this case, $f(z)$ does not have a maximum and a steady state with zero nominal interest rate does not exist, we ask what is the welfare gain from reducing the steady state nominal interest rate to 0.001 rather than zero.

In this example, $A(z) - 1 = f'(z)/[f(z) - zf'(z)] = 1/z\alpha$. Therefore $A(z) - 1 = i$, leads to: $z = 1/\alpha i$ and the welfare gain is: $(1 - \alpha)^{-1}[(1/0.001\alpha) - (1/i\alpha)]$.

Conclusions

We have extended the framework in chapter 2 to allow for growth and a measurement of the welfare cost of inflation.

There are serious debates about the measurement issue. Should we account for the resources spent on creating money substitutes? Will our calculation change if only distortive taxes are available? Does inflation introduces noise into the price system and cause agents to make "bad" choices. We will examine the money substitutes issue in the next section, the distortive tax issue in chapter 6 and the noise issue in chapter 19.

3.3 MONEY SUBSTITUTES

If the nominal quantity of money is not important why should the society spend resources on creating substitutes for money? This is not a new question. Hume (1752, p. 35 in the 1970 edition) expressed "a doubt concerning the benefit of banks and paper-credit, which are so generally esteemed advantageous to every nation". He seems to favor regulations against paper (inside) money. On page 36 he continues and says that

> it must be allowed, that no bank could be more advantageous, than such a one as locked up all the money it received, and never augmented the circulating coin, as is usual, by returning part of its treasure into commerce. A public bank, by this expedient, might cut off much of the dealings of private bankers and money-jobbers; and though the state bore the charge of salaries to the directors and tellers of this bank (for according to the preceding supposition, it would have no profits from its dealings), the national advantage, resulting from the low price of labour and the destruction of paper-credit would be a sufficient compensation. (p. 36)

Hume seems to suggest a government run bank that holds 100% reserves. In his view the private sector cannot run a bank with 100% reserve requirements because it will not generate revenues to pay for the operation. Modern discussions of 100% reserve requirements do not see that as a problem: The bank can charge fees for its services.

Alternatively the government can pay interest on reserves as in Friedman (1960, p. 66). Friedman envisaged that under 100% reserve requirement there will be two institutions. One that stores deposits and provides checking services for a fee and one that does the intermediation between lenders and borrowers.[3]

The argument for 100% reserve requirements is that it increases the stability of the financial system and does not require government intervention. On page 35 Hume says: "But there appears no reason for encreasing that inconvenience by a counterfeit money, which foreigners will not accept of in any payment, and which any great disorder to the state will reduce to nothing". Friedman who had the "benefit" of studying the collapse of the banking system in 1930–3, sees two main advantages in a 100% reserve system: (1) it does not require the federal deposit insurance and the implied government intervention in lending and investment and (2) it allows for better control of the money supply.

The question of the optimal reserve requirement is part of the larger issue of the regulation of "near monies" like credit cards. In the forties Henry Simons argued for "financial reform ... aiming at sharp differentiation between money and private obligations." He viewed his proposal for 100% reserve requirements as a first step in this direction which should be complemented by limitation with respect to "financing via the open account (book credit) and installment sales" Simons (1948, p. 171). In his discussion of Simons' legacy, Friedman objects to limiting the type of contracts between borrowers and lenders: "Why should we not have variety and diversity in the market for borrowing and lending as in other markets? Is it not desirable that borrowers tailor their obligations to the demand of lenders?" Friedman (1969, p. 83).

It seems that the issue of substitutes for money requires the distinction between the social and the individual's point of view. From the individual's point of view it makes sense to spend real resources on accumulating money. From the social point of view it does not. This distinction is made most clearly in Friedman (1969) and is exposited here in chapter 2.

The subject matter is problematic because many economists are suspicious about government regulations. But, nevertheless, many free market economists find themselves in favor of regulations aimed at restricting the private creation of money.

We now turn to extend the analysis of chapter 2 to allow for money substitutes. For a related analysis see Aiyagari, Braun and Eckstein (1998).

Generalizing the model in chapter 2 to allow for money substitutes

We assume a bank that allows agents to write checks payable at the end of the period. Using checks and buying on credit requires real resources because of the need to check collaterals and because of transaction costs associated with clearing checks. It is assumed that the consumer pays the full cost of creating credit and therefore the bank makes zero profits.

The cost of creating $cr = CR/P$ units of real credit is:

$$TC(cr), \tag{3.26}$$

where $TC(cr)$ has the properties of a standard cost function ($MC = TC' > 0$ and $MC' = TC'' > 0$, everywhere).

The amount of "effective money" available at the beginning of the period is now $M_{t-1} + G_t + CR_t$ and the representative consumer's problem ([2.37] in chapter 2) is now:

$$\max \sum_{t=1}^{\infty} \beta^t U(C_t = Y_t + f[(M_{t-1} + G_t + CR_t)/P_t]) \tag{3.27}$$

subject to:

$$M_t + P_t Y_t = P_t \bar{Y} + M_{t-1} - P_t TC(CR_t/P_t) + G_t;$$

$$M_t \geq 0, \quad Y_t \geq 0, \quad CR_t \geq 0, \quad \text{and} \quad M_0 \text{ is given.} \tag{3.28}$$

Note that the within period credit introduced here, cannot be used to change the allocation of consumption across periods. Only money can be used for this purpose. Credit here is a service that can be bought at a cost and has no "asset" characteristic.

Dividing both sides of (3.28) by P_t yields:

$$m_t = \bar{Y} - Y_t + m_{t-1}(1 + r_{mt}) - TC(cr_t) + g_t. \tag{3.29}$$

Smooth consumption path: As in chapter 2 we start from an initial level of real balances and assume a real transfer payment that can cover the depreciation of real balances: $m_0 = m$,

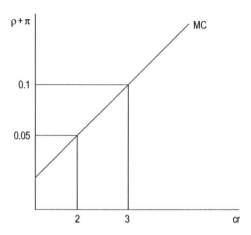

Figure 3.5 The SS level of credit

$r_{mt} = r_m$ and $g_t = -mr_m$ for all t. In this case, the smooth path:

$$m_t = m; \quad cr_t = cr; \quad Y_t = \bar{Y} - TC(cr); \qquad \text{for all t.} \tag{3.30}$$

is feasible. Is it optimal?

The first order conditions that a smooth consumption path has to satisfy are:

$$(1 + r_m)[1 + f'(m + cr)] = 1 + \rho \quad \text{or approximately,}$$
$$f'(m + cr) \approx \rho + \pi; \tag{3.31}$$

$$f'(m + cr) \leq TC'(cr) \quad \text{with equality if } cr > 0, \tag{3.32}$$

To derive (3.31) we consider the deviation (2.41)–(2.43) in chapter 2, from the proposed path: Corn consumption is reduced at time t and is used to accumulate real balances and increase corn consumption at $t + 1$.

To derive (3.32) we consider the following deviation from the proposed path. We increase credit at time t by x units and reduce corn consumption by the added cost, thus choosing: $cr_t = cr + x$ and $Y_t = \bar{Y} - TC(cr + x)$. The benefit is the additional liquidity service: $xf'(m + cr)$. The cost is the loss of corn consumption: $xTC'(cr)$. Condition (3.32) says that when $cr > 0$, the benefit is equal to the cost and when $cr = 0$, the benefit is less than the cost.

Substituting (3.31) into (3.32) and using the approximation, yields:

$$TC'(cr) \geq \rho + \pi, \quad \text{with equality if } cr > 0. \tag{3.33}$$

Condition (3.33) allows for the comparison of the level of credit across steady-state equilibria. In figure 3.5 the level of credit goes up from 2 to 3 units when inflation goes up by 5 percentage points. Since $TC'(0) > 0$, credit is not used at the Friedman rule when $\rho + \pi = 0$.

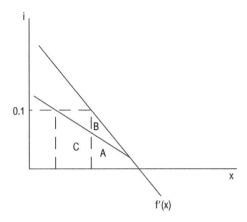

Figure 3.6 The gain in liquidity services (A + B)

The welfare cost of nominal interest rate

We now define the nominal interest rate by $1 + i = (1 + \rho)/(1 + r_m)$. Using this definition we may write the first order conditions (3.31) and (3.32) as:

$$TC'(cr) \geq f'(m + cr) = i \quad \text{with equality if } cr > 0. \tag{3.34}$$

Let $m(i)$ and $cr(i)$ denote the solution to (3.34). Let $x(i) = m(i) + cr(i)$ denote liquidity. The gains from reducing the steady-state nominal interest rate to zero are:

$$\{TC[cr(i)] - TC[cr(0)]\} + \{f[x(0)] - f[x(i)]\}, \tag{3.35}$$

units of corn. We may measure the gain in liquidity services, $f[x(0)] - f[x(i)]$, by the area under the demand for x function. This is the area A + B in figure 3.6. Most welfare estimates use the area under the demand for money function, C + A, and ignore the savings of real resources term, $TC[cr(i)] - TC[cr(0)]$.

When the initial rate of inflation is high, ignoring substitutes for money may lead to a serious underestimation of the welfare cost. In Israel the rate of inflation went up from single digit to triple digit in the 1980s and the fraction of business sector employees in the banking sector went up from 1.5% in the early 1970s to 2.8% in 1984 when the rate of inflation reached 445%. The area of bank branches per thousand people rose from 75 square meters in the early 1970s to 104 square meters in 1984. This trend stopped after the stabilization program in 1985 but significant ratchet effects remain. See Melnick (1995).

Should the government restrict the use of "near monies"?

Should we try to impose Simons type regulations and restrict the use of substitutes for money? To answer this question we consider the hypothetical case in which the government holds the steady-state nominal interest rate constant and abolishes credit. The new steady-state level of real balances m' must satisfy $f'(m') = i$. Since we start with a level x that satisfies $f'(x) = i$, it follows that $m' = x$. Thus as a result of the credit abolishing regulations real balances went up exactly by the amount of credit that was used. Welfare went up by the cost of producing the money substitute, $TC[cr(i)]$. This speaks in favor of Simons type regulations. The question is whether such regulations can be enforced.

PROBLEMS

1 The government wants a stable price level ($\pi = 0$). Compute the required rate of change in the money supply if real income, y, grows at the rate of 0.1 and the demand for money is: $\ln m^d = \ln y - \pi$.

2 Derive the steady-state level of real balances as a function of the nominal interest rate, $m(i)$, for the case: $TC(cr) = cr^2$ and $f(x) = x^{0.5}$. Show that the derivative of m with respect to i is negative and draw figure 3.6 for this special case.

PROBLEM WITH ANSWER

3 Write the Bellman equation and derive the first order conditions for the following problem:

$$\max_{Y_t\, m_t} \sum_{t=1}^{\infty} \beta^t U[Y_t + f(m_{t-1} + cr_t)]$$

$$\text{s.t.} \quad m_t = \bar{Y} + m_{t-1} - Y_t - TC(cr_t)$$

non-negativity constraints and m_0 is given.

Answer

$$V(m) = \max_{Y\, cr} U[Y + f(m + cr)] + \beta V[\bar{Y} + m - Y - TC(cr)]$$

First order conditions:

(a) $U' = \beta V'$
(b) $U'f' = \beta V'TC'$
(c) $V' = U'f' + \beta V'$
(d) $V' = U'f'/(1 - \beta)$

Substituting (d) in (a) leads to:

(e) $1 = \beta f'/(1 - \beta)$
$\quad f' = (1 - \beta)/\beta = \rho$

Substituting (d) in (b) leads to:

$$1 = \beta TC'/(1 - \beta)$$
$$TC' = \rho$$

APPENDIX 3A A DYNAMIC PROGRAMMING FORMULATION

We consider the problem of an agent who gets at time t an endowment of $\bar{Y}_t$ units of corn and a real transfer from the government of g_t units of corn. It is assumed that $\bar{Y}_t = (1 + \gamma)\bar{Y}_{t-1}$ and $g_t = \theta\bar{Y}_t$ where $\theta > 0$ is a given constant. The agent faces a constant real rate of return on money (r_m) and solves:

$$\max_{Y_t} \sum_{t=0}^{\infty} \beta^t U(C_t)$$

s.t.

$$C_t = Y_t + \bar{Y}_t f(m_{tb}/\bar{Y}_t)$$
$$m_{tb} = m_{t-1}(1 + r_{mt}) + g_t$$
$$m_t = \bar{Y}_t - Y_t + m_{t-1}(1 + r_m) + g_t$$
$$m_0 \text{ is given}, \quad Y_t, m_t \geq 0. \tag{A3.1}$$

The Bellman equation for this case is:

$$V(m_{tb}, \bar{Y}_t) = \max_{Y_t} U[Y_t + \bar{Y}_t f(m_{tb}/\bar{Y}_t)] + \beta V(m_{t+1b}, \bar{Y}_{t+1})$$

s.t.

$$m_{t+1b} = m_t(1 + r_m) + g_{t+1} = (\bar{Y}_t - Y_t + m_{tb})(1 + r_m) + g_{t+1} \tag{A3.2}$$

Omitting time indices and using m for m_b we can write (A3.2) as:

$$V(m, \bar{Y}) = \max_Y U[Y + \bar{Y}f(m/\bar{Y})] + \beta V[(\bar{Y} - Y + m)(1 + r_m)$$
$$+ \theta\bar{Y}(1 + \gamma), \bar{Y}(1 + \gamma)]. \tag{A3.3}$$

The first order condition for this problem is:

$$U'(C) = (1 + r_m)\beta V_1(m', \bar{Y}'], \tag{A3.4}$$

where V_1 denotes the derivative of V with respect to the first argument. Using the envelop theorem we get:

$$V_1(m, \bar{Y}) = U'(C)f'(z) + (1 + r_m)\beta V_1(m', \bar{Y}'), \tag{A3.5}$$

where $z = m/\bar{Y}$. We now substitute (A3.4) into (A3.5) to get:

$$V_1(m, \bar{Y}) = U'(C)[1 + f'(z)]. \tag{A3.6}$$

Since this holds for every period, $V_1(m', \bar{Y}') = U'(C')[1 + f'(z')]$. Substituting this into (A3.4) to get the first order condition:

$$U'(C) = (1 + r_m)\beta U'(C')[1 + f'(z')]. \tag{A3.7}$$

We now assume $U(C) = C^{1-\sigma}/(1 - \sigma)$ and write (A3.7) as:

$$C^{-\sigma} = (1 + r_m)\beta(C')^{-\sigma}[1 + f'(z')]. \tag{A3.8}$$

Along a constant rate of growth path $C' = C(1 + \gamma)$ and we can write (A3.8) as:

$$(1 + \rho)(1 + \gamma)^\sigma = (1 + r_m)[1 + f'(z)]. \tag{A3.9}$$

This is equation (3.11) in the text.

Lucas' shopping specification: $C_t = Y_t f(m_{tb}/Y_t)$.
In this case, the Bellmans equation is:

$$V(m, \bar{Y}) = \max_Y U[Yf(m/Y)] + \beta V[(\bar{Y} - Y + m)(1 + r_m)$$
$$+ \theta\bar{Y}(1 + \gamma), \bar{Y}(1 + \gamma)]. \tag{A3.10}$$

The first order condition for this problem is:

$$U'(C)[f(z) - f'(z)z] = (1 + r_m)\beta V_1(m', \bar{Y}'). \tag{A3.11}$$

The marginal utility of money is:

$$V_1(m, \bar{Y}) = U'(C)f'(z) + (1 + r_m)\beta V_1(m', \bar{Y}'). \tag{A3.12}$$

We now substitute (A3.11) into (A3.12) to get:

$$V_1(m, \bar{Y}) = U'(C)[f'(z) + f(z) - f'(z)z]. \tag{A3.13}$$

Since this holds for every period, $V_1(m', \bar{Y}') = U'(C')[f'(z') + f(z') - f'(z')z']$. Substituting this into (A3.11) to get the first order condition:

$$U'(C)[f(z) - f'(z)z] = (1 + r_m)\beta U'(C')[f'(z') + f(z') - f'(z')z']. \tag{A3.14}$$

We now assume $U(C) = C^{1-\sigma}/(1 - \sigma)$. Under this assumption (A3.14) is:

$$C^{-\sigma}[f(z) - f'(z)z] = (1 + r_m)\beta(C')^{-\sigma}[f'(z') + f(z') - f'(z')z']. \tag{A3.15}$$

Along a constant rate of growth path we have: $C' = C(1 + \gamma)$ and $z = z'$. We can therefore write (A3.15) as:

$$(1 + \rho)(1 + \gamma)^\sigma(1 + r_m)^{-1} = [f'(z) + f(z) - f'(z)z]/[f(z) - f'(z)z]. \tag{A3.16}$$

Substituting $(1 + r_m)^{-1} = (1 + \pi) = (1 + \mu)/(1 + \gamma)$ leads to equation (3.22) in the text.

PROBLEM

1 Solve for the first order condition using dynamic programming for the money substitutes case:

$$C_t = Y_t + \bar{Y}_t f(m_{tb}/\bar{Y}_t, X_t/\bar{Y}_t)$$

$$m_t = \bar{Y}_t - Y_t - X_t + m_{t-1}(1 + r_m) + g_t$$

and the rest is the same as (A3.1).

NOTES

1. Strictly speaking this is the welfare cost of nominal interest rate not inflation. This is because reducing the nominal interest rate to zero usually implies reducing the rate of inflation to negative levels.
2. Note that for the special case $\gamma = 0$ and $\bar{Y} = 1$, condition (3.11) is the same as (2.4.3) in section 2.8.
3. In describing "how a 100% reserves would work," Friedmans says (pp. 69–70) "The effect of this proposal would be to require our present commercial banks to divide themselves into two separate institutions. One would be a pure depository institution, a literal warehouse for money. It would accept deposits payable on demand or transferable by check . . . The other institution that would be formed would be an investment trust or brokerage firm. It would acquire capital by selling shares or debentures and would use the capital to make loans or acquire investments."

CHAPTER 4

Government

We had a rather peculiar government. It could only make lump sum transfer payments; it was interested in maximizing the welfare of the representative consumer and it could perfectly commit to its future actions. In the real world governments must finance real expenditures on military, police and other things; they typically cannot levy lump sum taxes; they may not always have the welfare of the representative consumer in mind and typically cannot perfectly commit to future policies.

Here and in chapter 6 we attempt to relax some of the assumptions made earlier about the government. In this chapter we analyze the policy of a government that is interested in maximizing revenues rather than welfare. We then talk about the appropriate definition of the inflation tax rate and the implications of the government's "budget constraint."

4.1 THE REVENUES FROM PRINTING MONEY

The government has monopoly on money creation and use it to raise revenues. How much can the government get by printing money? This question is interesting for two reasons. First, it is useful to define the feasible set. Second, there are times and places (like war for example) in which raising revenues by explicit taxation is difficult and the government may therefore choose to maximize the revenues from printing money. As we shall see it matters whether we talk about the revenues from printing money in the steady state or about the present value of revenues.

4.1.1 Steady-state revenues

The real revenues from printing money are:[1]

$$(dM/dt)/P = M[(dM/dt)/P]/M = \mu m. \tag{4.1}$$

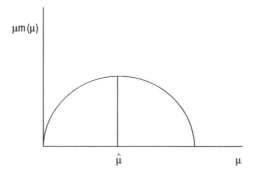

Figure 4.1 Steady-state revenues

The depreciation in the purchasing power of money is πm. In the steady state $\mu = \pi$ and therefore we may write the money demand as $m(\mu = \pi)$. We may think of π as the tax rate and m as the tax base. Since in the steady state m is a function of π, tax revenues do not always increase with π. When we increase π by say 1%, tax revenues will go up only if the base m goes down by less than 1%.

Formally, the steady-state revenues from printing money are:

$$\mu m(\mu). \tag{4.2}$$

When the money demand function is linear $(m[\mu] = a - b\mu)$ we get a "Laffer curve": revenues increase with μ up to a certain level, $\hat{\mu}$, and then start to decline as in figure 4.1.

The steady-state revenues (4.2) are maximized if they satisfy the first order condition:

$$\mu m'/m = -1. \tag{4.3}$$

This is the standard condition for maximizing revenues: Revenues are maximized when the demand elasticity is unity.

4.1.2 Out of the steady-state revenues

Empirical findings suggest that the solution to (4.3) is a relatively small μ. Can we explain high inflation rates by the desire to raise revenues?

To answer this question we now turn to out of a steady-state analysis. When $\pi \neq \mu$ the difference between tax revenues and tax payments is the change in real balances:[2]

$$\mu m - \pi m = m(\mu - \pi) = dm/dt. \tag{4.4}$$

This says that when revenues (equal here to real expenditures) are higher than tax payments, part of the money printed goes to the accumulation of real balances. When revenues are lower than payments, part of the increase in the price level is caused by the desire to decumulate real balances.

An increase in μ typically causes an initial increase in real balances. Therefore in the short run both the "tax rate" and the "tax base" go up and revenues go up. It is therefore possible that

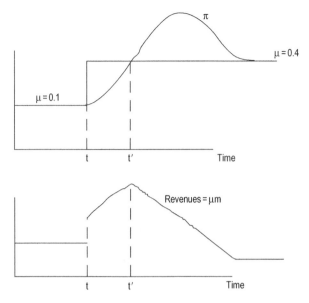

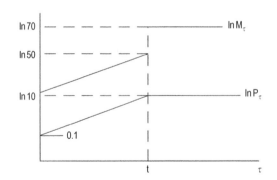

Figure 4.2   Slow adjustment

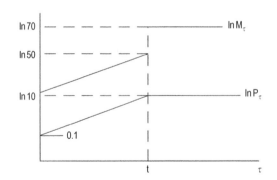

Figure 4.3   Instantaneous adjustment

a revenue maximizing government will choose to increase μ above the level that maximizes revenues in the steady state because of the short run increase in revenues.

To illustrate, we assume that at time t the economy was in a steady-state equilibrium with $\mu = \pi = 0.1$ and at this rate steady-state revenues are maximized. The government then increase the rate of growth in the money supply to $\mu = 0.4$. Figure 4.2 assumes that at first the rate of inflation is lower than 0.4 and therefore revenues increase in the short run.

A policy-maker with a relatively high discount rate may prefer the revenue path in figure 4.2 over the initial steady-state revenue path.

The argument is completely reversed if the adjustment to the new steady state is instant-aneous. In this case a policy-maker will increase short run revenues by committing to a lower rather than a higher rate of money growth. Figure 4.3 illustrates the case in which the policy-maker announces at time t a zero rate of change in the money supply. He then prints an additional amount of money (a jump in the stock occurring at time t) to satisfy the increase in the demand for money with no change in the price level. In this example the demand for money went up from 5 to 7 and as a result the policy-maker was able to collect 2 units of consumption at time t (the rate of revenue collection is infinite in this case).

We now turn to consider the problem of maximizing the present value of revenues which is the appropriate criterion for a revenue maximizing policy-maker.

4.1.3 The present value of revenues

We start with an economy that has no money and consider the problem of a revenue max-imizing government that introduces money to the economy. It is shown that maximizing the present value of revenues may lead to a choice of a relatively low rate of inflation because of the initial money creation revenues.

At $t = 0$ there is no money and no other assets. A new government is elected at $t = 0$ and is expected to stay in power indefinitely. The government can perfectly commit to its future actions and promises to give the agents at $t = 1$ an initial stock of M dollars per agent. It will then increase the money supply at the rate of μ for ever.

At $t = 1$ the economy reaches a steady state with $m(\mu) = M/P_1$ units of real balances. The real value of the transfer at $t = 1$ is: $m(\mu)$. Starting from period 2 the real value of the transfer is, approximately, $\mu m(\mu)$.[3] The present value (discounted to $t = 1$) of government expenditures financed in this way is therefore:

$$m(\mu) + \mu m(\mu) \sum_{t=2}^{\infty} (1+r)^{1-t} = m(\mu) + \mu m(\mu)/r, \qquad (4.5)$$

where r is the policy-maker's rate of discount. Maximizing (4.5) is not the same as maximizing $\mu m(\mu)$. Furthermore,

Claim 1: $\underset{\mu}{\text{Argmax}} \, [m(\mu) + \mu m(\mu)/r] < \underset{\mu}{\text{Argmax}} \, \mu m(\mu).$

This says that the rate which maximize the present value of revenues is less than the rate that maximizes the steady-state revenues.

To see claim 1, let $F(\mu) = \mu m(\mu)$ denote the steady state revenues and write (4.5) as $\max_{\mu} rm(\mu) + F(\mu)$. The first order condition for this problem is

$$rm'(\mu) + F'(\mu) = 0. \qquad (4.6)$$

Since $m' < 0$ this implies that at the solution μ^* we have $F'(\mu^*) > 0$ as in figure 4.4. Since at the rate that maximizes steady state revenues, $\hat{\mu}$, we have $F'(\hat{\mu}) = 0$, we get $\hat{\mu} \geq \mu^*$.

To build some intuition, consider the case in which we are at the rate $\hat{\mu}$, which maximizes the steady state revenues. At this point a small reduction in μ will not affect the steady state revenues, $F(\mu)$, but will increase the initial stock component $m(\mu)$ and is therefore desirable.

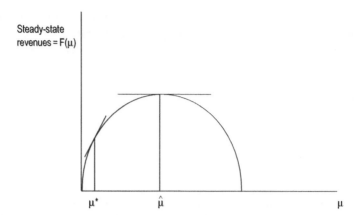

Figure 4.4   The rate that maximizes revenue in the steady state and the rate that maximizes the present value of revenues

Initial money holdings

How would our result change if at $t = 0$, the representative agent has M_0 dollars. In this case if the price level at $t = 1$ is P_1, the representative consumer will already have at $t = 1$, $m = M_0/P_1$ units of real balances and demand from the government $m(\mu) - m$ units.[4] It is therefore in the interest of the revenue maximizing government to announce a large once and for all increase in the money supply between $t = 0$ and $t = 1$ followed by the moderate rate of change μ^*. This policy will lead to a large P_1 and a small $m = M_0/P_1$ and will maximize the present value of revenues.

An initial hyper-inflation causes a massive redistribution of wealth and may not be feasible.[5] It may therefore be useful to consider the problem of a policy-maker who operates under the constraint that the value of the initial money holdings must be larger than or equal to m. In this case, the present value of revenues from the entire money printing operation is: $m(\mu) - m + \mu m(\mu)/r$. Since m is a given constant it does not change the solution. The rate that maximizes the present value of revenues remains μ^*.

APPENDIX 4A   NON-STEADY-STATE EQUILIBRIA

We consider a simple model in which money is the only asset and there are no adjustment lags (all markets are cleared). The price level and the nominal transfer payments are given by: $\{P_t, G_t\}_{t=1}^{\infty}$. Given these paths, the representative consumer solves the following problem:

$$\max \sum_{t=1}^{\infty} \beta^t U(C_t = Y_t + f[(M_{t-1} + G_t)/P_t])$$

s.t.

$$P_t Y_t + M_t = P_t \bar{Y} + M_{t-1} + G_t;$$

$$M_0 \text{ is given and } M_t \geq 0 \quad \text{for all } t > 0. \tag{A4.1}$$

We can formulate the problem (A4.1) in real terms:

$$\max \sum_{t=1}^{\infty} \beta^t U(Y_t + f[m_{t-1}(1 + r_{mt}) + g_t])$$

s.t.

$$Y_t + m_t = \bar{Y} + m_{t-1}(1 + r_{mt}) + g_t;$$

$$m_0 \text{ is given and } m_t \geq 0, \tag{A4.2}$$

where $g_t = G_t/P_t$ and
$r_{mt} = [(1/P_t) - (1/P_{t-1})]/(1/P_{t-1}) = (1 + \pi_t)^{-1} - 1 \geq -1$ is the real rate of return on holding money from $t - 1$ to t. The first order (Euler) condition for (A4.2) is:

$$U'(C_t) = \beta U'(C_{t+1})(1 + r_{mt+1})\{1 + f'[m_t(1 + r_{mt+1}) + g_{t+1}]\}. \tag{A4.3}$$

The sequence $\{m_t, g_t, r_{mt} \geq -1\}_{t=1}^{\infty}$ is an equilibrium sequence if: (a) given $\{g_t, r_{mt}\}_{t=1}^{\infty}$ the sequence $\{m_t, Y_t\}$ solves the representative consumer's problem (A4.2); and (b) markets are cleared: $Y_t = \bar{Y}$ for all $t > 0$.

In equilibrium $Y_t = \bar{Y}$ and therefore the consumer's budget constraint implies: $m_t = m_{t-1}(1 + r_{mt}) + g_t$. We can therefore substitute $C_t = \bar{Y} + f(m_t)$ in (A4.3) to get the equilibrium condition:

$$U'[\bar{Y} + f(m_t)] = \beta U'[\bar{Y} + f(m_{t+1})](1 + r_{mt+1})[1 + f'(m_{t+1})]. \tag{A4.4}$$

The solution to (A4.4) can be written as:

$$m_t = m_t(r_{mt+1}, m_{t+1}). \tag{A4.5}$$

Substituting $m_{t+1}(r_{mt+2}, m_{t+2})$ in (A4.5) leads to:

$$m_t = m_t(r_{mt+1}, m_{t+1}) = m_t[r_{mt+1}, m_{t+1}(r_{mt+2}, m_{t+2})]. \tag{A4.6}$$

We can continue and substitute $m_{t+2}(r_{mt+3}, m_{t+3})$ and so on. In this way we arrive at the following Claim.

Claim A4.1: In equilibrium m_t depends on all future rates of return on money $\{r_{m\tau}\}_{\tau=t+1}^{\infty}$ but does not depend on past rates of return.

We now look at the problem of a government that wants to maximize the present value of revenues without imposing a steady state. The government revenues at time t are given by (2.34):

$$(M_t - M_{t-1})/P_t = m_t - m_{t-1}(1 + r_{mt}). \tag{A4.7}$$

It is assumed that the government can choose the path of the rate of inflation and therefore the path of the real rate of return on money. The problem of maximizing the present value of the revenues is that of choosing $\{r_{mt} \geq -1\}_{t=1}^{\infty}$ which will solve:

$$\max \sum_{t=1}^{\infty} \beta^t [m_t - m_{t-1}(1 + r_{mt})], \tag{A4.8}$$

where β is a discount factor used by the government. Note that the revenues at $t = 1$ is:

$$m_1 - m_0(1 + r_{m1}). \tag{A4.9}$$

Since Claim A4.1 implies that m_1 does not depend on r_{m1}, this leads to the following Claim:

> *Claim A4.2:* A necessary condition for maximizing (A4.8) is: $r_{m1} = -1$.

Since $1 + r_m = 1/(1 + \pi)$, this says that the rate of inflation between $t = 0$ and $t = 1$ is infinity.

The above model says that having a hyper-inflation at the beginning of a regime is consistent with maximizing the present value of revenues from printing money.

The ability to commit

To illustrate the importance of the ability to commit, we consider now the other extreme case in which the government lasts for one period only. It is elected at time $t - 1$ and chooses $r_{mt} = -1$ to maximize the single period revenues: $m_t - m_{t-1}(1 + r_{mt})$. The public who expect this behavior will choose not to hold money. As a result revenues will be zero.

The introduction of indexed debt or more generally state contingent debt may alleviate the problem. For example, the government may eliminate the incentive to inflate by lending in nominal terms and borrowing in real terms. This type of commitment mechanism was suggested by Lucas and Stokey (1983). As was said before, such changes may be costly if, as in the Baumol–Tobin model, they require trips to the bank.

4.2 THE GOVERNMENT'S "BUDGET CONSTRAINT"

Here we follow Sargent and Wallace (1981) and derive the government's "budget constraint" in present value terms. It is shown that this budget constraint must include inflation tax revenues and the present value of the inflation tax must equal the present value of the deficit.

The analysis in chapter 2 may be a good example. There we had a government that does not levy explicit taxes. Transfer payments (positive or negative) were the only government expenditures and the real transfer payment was equal to the primary deficit. This deficit was covered by inflation tax revenues.

We start by discussing the appropriate definition of the inflation tax in an economy that has both money and bonds. We then turn to related issues. What should be the division of responsibilities between the fiscal and the monetary authorities? What will happen to the price level if the demand for money drops to zero?

The tax rate on real balances

What is the "correct" definition of the tax rate on real balances: the nominal interest rate or the rate of inflation?

This is largely an accounting question. The nominal interest rate is the more consistent measure because it takes into account the revenues received in the past from creating money. If the steady state level of real balances is m, it must be the case that the government has received for it m units of consumption in the past. The alternative to printing money was to borrow the m units of consumption. Had the government borrowed m units it would have paid an interest of rm units. The steady-state revenues from the entire money printing operation are the savings of interest payments on the steady-state level of real balances (rm) plus the revenues from the newly created money (πm), which is (r + π)m = im.

Consider now the private agents point of view. Before reaching the steady state, the representative agent sold to the government m units of consumption. Had he gotten the money for free, he would now have m units in assets earning a real interest rate of r. To maintain (cover the depreciation in) the steady-state level of real balances the agent must sell to the government πm units of consumption per period. The tax that he pays on accumulating and maintaining the steady-state level of real balances is therefore: (r + π)m.

We will now see that thinking of the nominal interest rate as the appropriate tax rate is also consistent with the government "budget constraint."

Deriving the government "budget constraint"

We consider an economy populated by N agents. All agents can produce output by using labor: One unit of labor produces one unit of output. There are two assets: bonds and money. We use r_{mt} and r_t to denote the real rate of return on money and bonds and τ_t to denote the income tax rate. The asset accumulation equation is:

$$b_t + m_t = (1 - \tau_t)L_t + m_{t-1}(1 + r_{mt}) + b_{t-1}(1 + r_t) - c_t, \tag{4.7}$$

where L = labor (= output), m = real balances, b = real bonds and c = consumption.

We start with a two period consumer who is born with no assets. His consumption at t = 1 is:

$$c_1 = (1 - \tau_1)L_1 - b_1 - m_1. \tag{4.8}$$

Consumption at t = 2 is:

$$c_2 = (1 - \tau_2)L_2 + b_1(1 + r_2) + m_1(1 + r_{m2}). \tag{4.9}$$

From (4.8) it follows that $b_1 = (1 - \tau_1)L_1 - c_1 - m_1$. Substituting this in (4.9) yields:

$$c_2 = (1 - \tau_2)L_2 + [(1 - \tau_1)L_1 - c_1 - m_1](1 + r_2) + m_1(1 + r_{m2}). \tag{4.10}$$

Dividing both sides of (4.10) by (1 + r_2) and rearranging, leads to:

$$c_1 + c_2/(1 + r_2) = (1 - \tau)L_1 + (1 - \tau)L_2/(1 + r_2) - m_1(r_2 - r_{m2})/(1 + r_2). \tag{4.11}$$

Note that the cost of holding money is the real interest rate differential ($r_t - r_{mt}$) and we can think of this cost as occurring at the beginning of the second period.

In a multi-period setting we can follow a similar procedure (see the appendix to chapter 5) and express the budget constraints (4.7) in the following present value form:

$$\sum_{t=1}^{\infty} D_t c_t^h = \sum_{t=1}^{\infty} D_t\{(1 - \tau_t)L_t^h - m_{t-1}^h(r_t - r_{mt})\}, \qquad (4.12)$$

where $D_t = (1 + r_1)^{-1} \times (1 + r_2)^{-1} \times \cdots \times (1 + r_t)^{-1}$ is the discount factor (discounting all magnitudes to $t = 0$) and the superscript h indexes the individual.

The level of government expenditures, g_t is exogenously given. The market-clearing conditions are:

$$g_t = \sum_{h=1}^{N}(L_t^h - c_t^h). \qquad (4.13)$$

Summing (4.12) over all agents and using (4.13) leads to:

$$\sum_{t=1}^{\infty} D_t \sum_{h=1}^{N} \tau_t L_t^h + m_{t-1}^h(r_t - r_{mt}) = \sum_{t=1}^{\infty} D_t \sum_{h=1}^{N} \left(L_t^h - c_t^h \right) = \sum_{t=1}^{\infty} D_t g_t. \qquad (4.14)$$

This says that the present value of income tax and inflation tax must equal the present value of government expenditures.

We can also write (4.14) as:

$$\sum_{t=1}^{\infty} D_t \sum_{h=1}^{N} m_{t-1}^h(r_t - r_{mt}) = \sum_{t=1}^{\infty} D_t \left(g_t - \sum_{h=1}^{N} \tau_t L_t^h \right) = \sum_{t=1}^{\infty} D_t d_t, \qquad (4.15)$$

where d is the primary deficit. This says that the present value of the inflation tax must equal the present value of the primary deficit.

To examine the question of the appropriate definition of the tax rate on real balances from the government's point of view, let $L_t = \sum_{h=1}^{N} L_t^h$ and $m_t = \sum_{h=1}^{N} m_t^h$. Then if the economy is in a steady state from the start we can write the expression (4.14) as:

$$\tau L + m(r - r_m) = g. \qquad (4.16)$$

Since $r_m \approx -\pi$ and $r \approx i - \pi$, the magnitude $r - r_m$ is equal approximately to the nominal interest rate. Since inflation tax is equal to the difference between g and all the explicit taxes $(g - \tau L$ in our example), it follows from (4.16) that the inflation tax is (approximately) im rather than πm.[6]

A potential pitfall: Equation (4.14) looks like a budget constraint but it is an equilibrium relationship. Therefore, the government cannot take prices as given: If it chooses to change the path of expenditures without changing the present value of expenditures ($\sum_{t=1}^{\infty} D_t g_t$) it will have to change taxes and (or) discount factors.

4.2.1 Monetary and fiscal policy: Who moves first?

We write the "government budget constraint" (4.14) as:

$$\sum_{t=1}^{\infty} D_t[\tau_t L_t(p) + (r_t - r_{mt})m_{t-1}(p)] = \sum_{t=1}^{\infty} D_t g_t, \qquad (4.17)$$

where $p = \{r_t, r_{mt}, \tau_t, g_t\}_{t=1}^{\infty}$ is policy, $L_t(p)$ is aggregate labor supply and $m_{t-1}(p)$ is aggregate real balances.

Monetary policy may be defined by the choice of the real rate of return on money: $r_m = \{r_{mt}\}_{t=1}^{\infty}$. Fiscal policy may be defined by the choice of the real interest rate, taxes and spending $(r, \tau, g) = \{r_t, \tau_t, g_t\}_{t=1}^{\infty}$. Alternatively, we may define monetary policy by $(r, r_m) = \{r_t, r_{mt}\}_{t=1}^{\infty}$ and fiscal policy by $(\tau, g) = \{\tau_t, g_t\}_{t=1}^{\infty}$.

The "budget constraint" (4.17) says that these policies cannot be chosen independently. For example, if the government moves first and credibly commits to the sequence (r, τ, g), then the central bank is constrained in its choice of monetary policy: It must choose r_m that provides enough inflation tax revenues, $\sum_{t=1}^{\infty} D_t(r_t - r_{mt})m_{t-1}(p)$, to satisfy (4.17). Sargent and Wallace (1981) analyze the implications of this constraint and show that open market operations may lead to unexpected results because of it.

A related question is about the choice of institutions: How to divide responsibilities between the government and the central bank? This has become a major issue. For example, it was suggested that the central bank should be responsible for price stability while the government should take care of the rest. This division of responsibility is not consistent with (4.17): If the government chooses a policy of long run deficit the central bank must abandon the goal of price stability.

An institutional setup and a division of responsibility which is consistent with (4.17) is in Lucas and Stokey (1983). In their model the central bank moves first and issues money by making loans to the agents in the economy. If the central bank chooses to burn the interest payments it gets (for the initial loans), not to issue any loans after the initial money creation phase and not to buy or sell any government bonds then there will be no revenues from printing money. In this case, the government will have to choose fiscal policy subject to the constraint that its budget is balanced in the present value sense: $\sum_{t=1}^{\infty} D_t \tau_t L_t(p) = \sum_{t=1}^{\infty} D_t g_t$. We will elaborate on this institutional setup shortly.

4.2.2 The fiscal approach to the price level

What will happen if the demand for money drops to zero? The standard answer to this question is an explosion of the price level. If agents want to hold zero amount of real balances and the money supply, M, is strictly positive the only way you can get $m = M/P = 0$ is with $P = \infty$.

Recently there has been a revision in this view pioneered by Sims (1994), Woodford (1995, 1998) and Cochrane (2001). This revisionist view uses the Sargent-Wallace approach to the government "budget constraint".

To illustrate, we assume that agent h has $a_0^h > 0$ units of government obligations at $t = 0$ and write his budget constraint (4.12) as:

$$\sum_{t=1}^{\infty} D_t c_t^h = a_0^h + \sum_{t=1}^{\infty} D_t \{(1 - \tau_t) L_t^h - m_{t-1}^h (r_t - r_{mt})\}. \tag{4.18}$$

Summing (4.18) over all agents and using the market-clearing condition (4.13) leads to:

$$\sum_{t=1}^{\infty} D_t [\tau_t L_t(p) + (r_t - r_{mt}) m_{t-1}(p) - g_t] = a_0, \tag{4.19}$$

where a_0 is the aggregate real value of government obligations held by agents at $t = 0$. Equilibrium condition (4.19) says that the present value of government surplus (inclusive of the inflation tax revenues) must equal the value of its obligation at $t = 0$.

We can also write:

$$a_0 = (M_0 + B_0)/P_0, \tag{4.20}$$

where M_0 is the initial money holding, B_0 is the initial bonds holdings and P_0 is the price level at $t = 0$. Note that a commitment to (fiscal and monetary) policy p, will determine the present value of the surpluses (4.19) and therefore the real value of the assets held at $t = 0$. We can then find the price level from (4.20).

We consider now the special case, $M_0 = 0$ and $a_0 = B_0/P_0$. In this case we can write (4.19) as:

$$\sum_{t=1}^{\infty} D_t [\tau_t L_t(p) - g_t] = B_0/P_0. \tag{4.21}$$

Assume further that the government "moves first" and credibly commit to fiscal policy (r, τ, g). In this case agents in this cashless economy forecast the path of government surpluses (the left hand side of [4.21]) and this determines the real value of the asset they hold. Equation (4.21) has one unknown: P_0. We can thus have a deterministic price level even in a cashless economy.

This fiscal theory of the price level is not without problems. What happens if the Walrasian auctioneer announces by "mistake" a higher price level? In this case, the right hand side of (4.21) is less than the left hand side and this means that the government will have some surplus after paying its debt. Agents may assume that the government will either lower taxes or increase spending. This speaks against the ability to commit to a policy.

4.3 POLICY IN THE ABSENCE OF PERFECT COMMITMENT: A POSITIVE THEORY OF INFLATION

We have shown that the Friedman rule is rather robust. But in reality it is not implemented. One possible explanation is that governments are interested in maximizing the present value of revenues rather than welfare. It was shown in chapter 4 that this may explain a variety of steady states inflation rates.

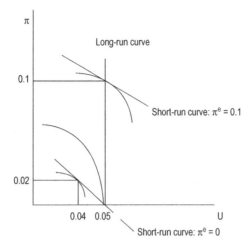

Figure 4.5 A positive theory of inflation

Another possibility was suggested by Kydland and Prescott (1977) and Barro and Gordon (1983) who assumed that the government is interested in maximizing welfare but cannot commit to its future policy. They use the Friedman and Phelps natural rate hypothesis (see section 1.2) to argue that if private agents move first and form low expectations about the rate of inflation, a policy-maker who takes these expectations as given may improve welfare by choosing a high rate of inflation. In this framework equilibrium is achieved if private agents form expectations that will be fulfilled and the policy-maker chooses actual inflation equal to the expected inflation.

To illustrate their argument, we consider a policy-maker who has preference for less unemployment (U) and less inflation (π) as in figure 4.5. The policy-maker chooses π after agents have already formed expectations π^e about his choice. The policy-maker choice of π and the expectations π^e determine the level of unemployment U on the appropriate short run curve. In figure 4.5, if agents expects $\pi^e = 0$ and the policy maker chooses $\pi = 0.02$, the unemployment level will be 0.04.

But if agents know the policy-maker preferences, the expectations $\pi^e = 0$ are not rational because the model predicts actual inflation of 0.02 (in the example used) when expected inflation is zero.

To derive a rational expectations equilibrium we now assume a specific objective function: The policy-maker's objective is to minimize: $\pi^2 + U^2$. For this specific function the slope of the policy-maker's indifference curves is: $d\pi/dU = -U/\pi$. When inflation is close to zero, the slope of the indifference curve is very large (in absolute value): An increase in inflation does not create a significant welfare loss and is therefore tempting. The slope of the policy-maker's indifference curve declines with inflation. At the equilibrium inflation rate the cost of increasing inflation is exactly equal to the benefit and the policy-maker is not tempted to use inflation for reducing unemployment.

In the example of figure 4.5, expectations of $\pi^e = 0.1$ will be fulfilled because at this rate of inflation the policy-maker's indifference curve is sufficiently flat and the trade-off between inflation and unemployment offered by the short run Philips curve is no longer attractive.

Thus in equilibrium $\pi = \pi^e = 0.1$ and $U = 0.05$. If we allow the policy-maker to commit ahead of time, say by writing the rate of inflation into the constitution, he can get the preferred outcome: $\pi = 0$, $U = 0.05$. This example provides an explanation to the observation of rates of inflation that are typically higher than the optimal rate.[7]

The proposed explanation relies on two key assumptions: (1) the policy-maker prefers unemployment which is less than the natural rate to the natural rate and (2) the slope of the indifference curves is larger in absolute value, at lower rates of inflation. The first assumption is motivated by the existence of distortive income tax and unemployment compensations which makes the level of the "natural unemployment" higher than the socially optimal level. The second assumption says that inflation is less costly when it is low: When inflation is low it is not perceived as a problem and the policy-maker is willing to pay more percentage points of inflation for a 1% reduction in unemployment.

PROBLEMS

1   The higher the rate of change in the money supply – the larger are the steady-state real revenues from the inflation tax. True or false? Explain.

2   Inflation cannot be explained by the desire to raise revenues because there are economies in which the rate of inflation is higher than the rate that maximizes the steady state real revenues from the inflation tax. True or false? Explain.

3   In 1984 Israel suffered from very high inflation rates. It was suggested that Israel would adopt the dollar as the main currency. What would have been the effect of the "dollarization" plan on both the Israeli and the US government revenues: (a) immediately after the change in currencies, (b) in the years after the implementation of the plan.

4   The observation that most countries reach a steady state with low inflation rate is not consistent with the hypothesis that governments fully exploit their monopoly power and maximize the present value of revenues from printing money. True or False? Explain.

5   Consider a small open economy that can lend and borrow at the world real interest rate of 5%. The government plans to run a primary deficit of 9 units of consumption per year.

(a) What must be the return on money (r_m) if the central bank wants to have a smooth rate of return ($r_{mt} = r_m$ for all t)? For simplicity, assume that the demand for money does not depend on the real rate of return on money and is equal to 100.

(b) Assume now that the central bank plans to have a policy of $r_m = 0.05$ for the first year. Assume that after the first year we reach a steady state. What is the steady-state level of r_m?

NOTES

1 The discrete time formula is: $(M_t - M_{t-1})/P_t = [(M_t - M_{t-1})/M_{t-1}](M_t/P_t)(M_{t-1}/M_t) = \mu m_t/(1 + \mu)$.

2 To derive it take the derivative of $\ln(M_t/P_t)$ with respect to t.

3 The real transfer for the discrete time case is: $\mu m/(1 + \mu)$.

4 The government will sell money to the public if $m(\mu) > m$. Otherwise, if $m(\mu) < m$, the public will sell the government $m - m(\mu)$ units and acquire government interest bearing debt.

5 It is also possible that the price level at $t = 1$ was already chosen by sellers at $t = 0$ and cannot be changed.

6 The budget constraint (4.14) was derived under the assumption of no financial assets at $t = 0$. Alternatively we may derive (4.14) under the assumption that at $t = 0$ the central bank lends the initial money holdings at the interest rate r (see section 4.3). In this case, an agent who takes at $t = 0$ a loan from the central bank of m units of real balances and keep it forever will pay interest to the central bank (rm) in addition to the resources which are required to cover the depreciation caused by inflation. The total real resources that the agent will pay is therefore $(r + \pi)m = im$ and in the steady state this is the amount of resources that the government gets from the entire money printing operation.

7 The diagram assumes an optimal rate of zero. It can be easily modified to the case in which the optimum is $\pi = -\rho$.

CHAPTER 5

More Explicit Models of Money

In the case of standard goods it is more or less clear that changes in monetary policy are not going to affect the utility one derives from a basket of goods. But this may not hold for money. Should the beginning of period balances enter the utility function or the end of period balances? Does inflation variability reduce the usefulness of money and should therefore enter the utility function separately?

To answer this type of questions we introduce here models that are more explicit about the role of money.

We organize the discussion around the optimal quantity of money question. Studying the efficiency properties of a model is a useful way of making oneself familiar with it. This will pay in subsequent chapters where we use the models surveyed here for analyzing various problems.

5.1 A CASH-IN-ADVANCE MODEL

The cash-in-advance (CIA) model uses the idea in Clower (1967). It assumes that goods cannot be exchanged for goods: Only money can buy goods. This assumption leads to a lag between the time of receipts and the time of expenditure: A seller/producer who sells his output this period for money will be able to use it only in the next period. Otherwise, no one will hold money in the model.

When the price level remains constant the lag between receipts and expenditures leads to a discrepancy between the social and the individual's point of view. From the social point of view output produced in the current period is consumed in the current period. From the individual's point of view the revenues from output produced in the current period are used to buy next period's consumption. When the price level is constant over time, the price of leisure from the individual's point of view is lower than the price of leisure from the social point of view and labor supply is lower than the socially efficient level.

To illustrate this point I use a simple version with elements from Lucas (1980).

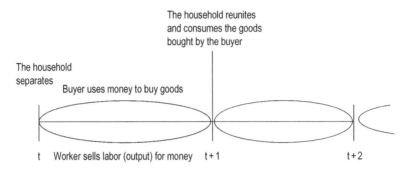

Figure 5.1   The sequence of events in a CIA model

5.1.1   A two-goods model

There is a single consumption good that can be bought only for money (there are no credit cards). Money is the only asset in the economy. The representative household is a pair of two infinitely lived agents: A worker/seller and a buyer. At the beginning of each period the buyer takes the available beginning of period balances and goes shopping. The worker goes to work and sells his output for cash. Figure 5.1 illustrates the sequence of events.

The household starts period t with M_{t-1} dollars. The shopper gets a transfer payment of G_t dollars and buys C_t units of the consumption good at the price of P_t dollars per unit. The worker produces L_t units of output (output = labor supply) and sells it for $P_t L_t$ dollars. The pre-transfer beginning of period $t + 1$ balances are:

$$M_t = P_t L_t + M_{tb} - P_t C_t, \tag{5.1}$$

dollars, where $M_{tb} = M_{t-1} + G_t$ is the post-transfer beginning of period t balances.

The shopper pays for the consumption good in cash:

$$P_t C_t \leq M_{tb}. \tag{5.2}$$

In what follows we assume that this cash-in-advance constraint is always binding.

At the end of the period the two members of the household unite and consume the good bought by the shopper. The objective function of the household is:

$$\sum_{t=1}^{\infty} \beta^t U(C_t, 1 - L_t), \tag{5.3}$$

where $0 < \beta < 1$ and $U(C_t, 1 - L_t)$ has the standard properties. The household chooses C_t and L_t to maximize (5.3) subject to (5.1), (5.2), a given initial level of nominal balances $(M_0 > 0)$ and non-negativity constraints.

As before we use: $1 + \pi_t = P_t/P_{t-1}, m_t = M_t/P_t$ and $g_t = G_t/P_t$ for the gross rate of inflation, real balances and the real transfer payment. Assuming that the cash in advance constraint is always binding $(P_t C_t = M_{tb})$ we divide (5.1) and (5.2) by P_t to get $m_t = L_t$ and $C_t = m_{t-1}(1 + \pi_t)^{-1} + g_t$. Substituting the first equation in the second leads

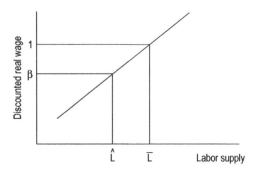

Figure 5.2 A Pareto improvement

to: $C_t = L_{t-1}(1 + \pi_t)^{-1} + g_t$. We can therefore write the consumer problem as:

$$\max_{L_t} \sum_{t=1}^{\infty} \beta^t U(C_t, 1 - L_t)$$

$$\text{s.t.} \quad C_t = L_{t-1}(1 + \pi_t)^{-1} + g_t$$

$$C_t \geq 0, \quad 0 \leq L_t \leq 1 \quad \text{and} \quad L_0 \text{ is given.} \tag{5.4}$$

To build some intuition we start from the case: $\pi_t = 0$ for all t. In this case, the agent who solves (5.4) will see an increase in one unit of next period consumption for every unit of labor supplied. Since the unit of consumption is received next period, the discounted real wage from the individual point of view is β. From the social point of view, output produced today is consumed today and therefore the real wage is unity. It follows that if labor supply is an increasing function of the discounted real wage, it will be inefficiently low: $\hat{L}$ instead of the efficient level of $\bar{L}$ in figure 5.2.

More generally, from the individual's point of view the discounted value of the real wage is $\beta/(1 + \pi)$. Efficiency requires that the discounted real wage is unity: $\beta/(1 + \pi) = 1$. This can be achieved by adopting a policy that will lead to: $(1 + \pi) = \beta$ or $\pi \approx -\rho$. This is the Friedman rule. We now develop this argument in detail.

The first order conditions for (5.4) are:

$$U_2(C_t, 1 - L_t) = \beta(1 + \pi_{t+1})^{-1} U_1(C_{t+1}, 1 - L_{t+1}) \quad \text{for all t.} \tag{5.5}$$

These say that the cost of supplying an additional unit of labor at time t (the marginal utility of leisure at time t) is equal to the discounted marginal utility of consumption (βU_1) times the real wage ($P_t/P_{t+1} = (1 + \pi_{t+1})^{-1}$).

Equilibrium in the cash-in-advance (CIA) economy is a sequence $\{C_{t+1}, L_t, \pi_{t+1}\}_{t=1}^{\infty}$ that satisfies (5.5) and the market-clearing conditions: $C_t = L_t$.

Substituting the market-clearing condition in the first order condition (5.5) and assuming a steady-state equilibrium ($L_t = L$ and $\pi_t = \pi$ for all t) leads to the equilibrium condition:

$$U_2(L, 1 - L) = \beta(1 + \pi)^{-1} U_1(L, 1 - L). \tag{5.6}$$

We now compare the equilibrium allocation to the solution of the following social planner's problem:

$$\max \sum_{t=0}^{\infty} \beta^t U(C_t, 1 - L_t)$$

$$\text{s.t.} \quad C_t = L_t. \tag{5.7}$$

The first order conditions for the problem (5.7) are:

$$U_1(C_t, 1 - L_t) = U_2(C_t, 1 - L_t) \quad \text{for all t.} \tag{5.8}$$

Conditions (5.8) say that the cost of supplying an additional unit of labor (U_2 = the marginal utility of leisure) must equal the benefit of an additional unit of consumption (U_1).

Note that the solution to the planner's problem does not change over time: $C_t = C$ and $L_t = L$ for all t. We now substitute the constraint $C = L$ in (5.8):

$$U_1(L, 1 - L) = U_2(L, 1 - L). \tag{5.9}$$

The equilibrium condition (5.6) coincides with the efficiency condition (5.9) when

$$\beta(1 + \pi_t)^{-1} = 1 \quad \text{for all t.} \tag{5.10}$$

Thus,

Claim 1: Under the Friedman rule the equilibrium allocation in the cash-in-advance economy is Pareto efficient.

5.1.2 An analogous real economy

The allocation in the CIA economy with $\pi = 0$ is not efficient. Here we examine the reason for the distortion more closely by considering a "real economy" in which workers are paid with a one period lag. This by itself does not cause inefficiency because the equilibrium real wage compensates for the payment delay. The reason for the inefficiency and for the lower real wage is in the zero real rate of return on money which occurs in the CIA economy when $\pi = 0$. When there is a delay in payment a zero real interest rate leads to a low real wage and is analogous to a tax on consumption.

To make the tax analogy we consider an economy with three goods: private consumption (c), government consumption (g) and leisure (1 − L). Government consumption is a perfect substitute for private consumption and is financed by a consumption tax at the rate T_t.

There are firms that produce output using labor input only. As before, output equals labor input. The firm pays for labor services with a one period lag (say, because the amount of output produced by the worker is observed with a one period lag).

The firm faces the wage rate w_t. Its profits (dividends) at time t are given by:

$$d_t = l_t - w_{t-1}l_{t-1}, \tag{5.11}$$

where l_t denotes the quantity of labor employed by the firm. The firm takes the wage rate as given and chooses l_t to solve:

$$\max \sum_{t=1}^{\infty} \beta^t d_t$$

s.t. (5.11), $l_t \geq 0$ and l_0 is given.   (5.12)

Claim 2: An interior solution $0 < l_t < \infty$ to (5.12) requires $w_t = 1/\beta$.

To show the claim we write the firm maximization problem (5.12) as:

$$\beta(l_1 - w_0 l_0) + \beta^2 (l_2 - w_1 l_1) + \beta^3 (l_3 - w_2 l_2) + + +$$ (5.13)

Note that l_t appears in two expressions only. Combining the terms with l_t leads to: $\beta^t(l_t - \beta w_t l_t) = A_t l_t$ where $A_t = \beta^t(1 - \beta w_t)$. The firm will choose:

$$l_t = \infty \quad \text{if } A_t > 0;$$

$$0 < l_t < \infty \quad \text{if } A_t = 0 \quad \text{and} \quad l_t = 0 \quad \text{if } A_t < 0.$$ (5.14)

Therefore $0 < l_t < 1$ is optimal only when $A_t = 0$ and $w_t = 1/\beta$. We have thus shown the claim.

The representative individual takes the wage rate, the transfer payment $\{g_t\}$ and the consumption tax rates $\{T_t\}$ as given and chooses private consumption $\{c_t\}$ and labor $\{L_t\}$ to solve:

$$\max \sum_{t=1}^{\infty} \beta^t U(c_t + g_t, 1 - L_t)$$

s.t.

$$c_{t+1}(1 + T_{t+1}) = w_t L_t + d_{t+1}$$

$$c_t \geq 0, \quad 0 \leq L_t \leq 1 \quad \text{and} \quad L_0 \text{ is given.}$$ (5.15)

Equilibrium in the analogous real economy is a sequence $\{T_t, g_t, w_t, l_t, d_t, L_t\}$ such that:

(a) given the sequence $\{w_t\}$, the sequence $\{l_t\}$ solves the firm's problem (5.12);
(b) given the sequence $\{T_t, g_t, w_t, d_t\}$, the sequence $\{L_t\}$ solves the consumer's problem (5.15);
(c) markets are cleared: $l_t = L_t$ and $c_t + g_t = L_t$.

A steady state equilibrium (SSE) in the analogous economy is an equilibrium for which $\{T_t = T, g_t = g, w_t = w, l_t = l, d_t = d, L_t = L\}$.

Claim 2 implies that the equilibrium net real wage is: $(1 + \rho)/(1 + T)$. We may refer to it also as the equilibrium gross interest rate: The worker invests a unit and gets $(1 + \rho)/(1 + T)$ with a one period delay.[1]

We now turn to examine efficiency in the analogous economy.

Efficiency

The central planner's problem for this economy is (5.7) and the first order conditions for the planner's problem are given by (5.8).

Claim 3: When $T_t = 0$, the steady-state equilibrium allocation in the analogous real economy is efficient.

To show this claim we substitute the constraint in the consumer's problem to get:

$$\beta U[(wL_0 + d_1)/(1 + T) + g_1, 1 - L_1]$$
$$+ \beta^2 U[(wL_1 + d_2)/(1 + T) + g_2, 1 - L_2]$$
$$+ \beta^3 U[(wL_2 + d_3)/(1 + T) + g_3, 1 - L_3] + + + \qquad (5.16)$$

The first order conditions for the problem of maximizing (5.16) are:

$$U_2[(wL_{t-1} + d_t)/(1 + T) + g_t, 1 - L_t]$$
$$= \beta[w/(1 + T)]U_1[(wL_t + d_{t+1})/(1 + T) + g_{t+1}, 1 - L_{t+1}]. \qquad (5.17)$$

Since in equilibrium $\beta w = 1$, if $T = 0$ we have:

$$U_2(wL_{t-1} + d_t + g_t, 1 - L_t) = U_1(wL_t + d_{t+1} + g_{t+1}, 1 - L_{t+1}). \qquad (5.18)$$

Since $wL_{t-1} + d_t + g_t = L_t$ it follows that in the steady state the equilibrium allocation must satisfy:

$$U_2(L, 1 - L) = U_1(L, 1 - L). \qquad (5.19)$$

This condition is identical to the efficiency condition (5.8) derived in the previous section. We have thus shown the Claim.

Comparison with the CIA model

Since in the analogous real model the equilibrium gross real wage is $w = 1/\beta$, the equilibrium net real wage is: $w/(1 + T) = (1 + \rho)/(1 + T)$. In the CIA model the net real wage is: $1/(1 + \pi)$. It follows that the net real wage is the same in both models if:

$$(1 + \rho)/(1 + T) = 1/(1 + \pi), \qquad (5.20)$$

or if: $(1 + T) = (1 + \rho)(1 + \pi)$. Thus,

Claim 4: Zero inflation rate in the CIA model is analogous to a consumption tax rate of $T = \rho$ in the real economy.

With a tax $T = \rho$, the net real wage and the "gross real interest rate" are: $(1+\rho)/(1+T) = 1$. We may therefore say that the source of the inefficiency in a CIA economy with $\pi = 0$ is in the "wrong" net real wage and real rate of return on money.

We have seen in this section that (a) wage payment delays by themselves are not a problem and (b) a CIA economy with a real rate of return on money that is too low is analogous to a real economy with a tax on consumption.

5.1.3 Money super-neutrality in a one-good model

Stockman (1981) and Abel (1985) consider a single good cash-in-advance economy with capital. They show that if the cash-in-advance constraint applies only to consumption then money is super-neutral: Changes in the rate of inflation will not affect real variables including the level of real balances.

This super neutrality result may be explained in terms of the tax analogy in the previous section. In the cash-in-advance model inflation is a tax on consumption and therefore in the steady state the tax rate is the same for all dated consumption goods. Since a tax on all goods at the same rate is equivalent to a lump sum tax, the inflation tax is super-neutral.

We now demonstrate the Stockman–Abel result. The utility function of the representative agent is given by:

$$\sum_{t=1}^{\infty} \beta^t U(C_t), \tag{5.21}$$

where $U' > 0$, $U'' < 0$ and $0 < \beta = 1/(1 + \rho) < 1$. The agent maximizes this utility subject to a budget constraint and a cash-in-advance constraint. The budget constraint is:

$$C_t + K_{t+1} + M_t/P_t = f(K_t) + (1 - \delta)K_t + (M_{t-1} + G_t)/P_t, \tag{5.22}$$

where K_t is the capital stock, M_t are nominal balances, C_t is consumption, P_t is the price level, G_t is the nominal money transfer received at the beginning of the period and δ is the rate of depreciation of capital. The production function $f(\ )$ has the standard properties: $f' > 0$ and $f'' < 0$.

The cash-in-advance constraint is:

$$C_t \leq (M_{t-1} + G_t)/P_t. \tag{5.23}$$

We assume that the cash-in-advance constraint is always binding and substitute $C_t = (M_{t-1} + G_t)/P_t$ in (5.21) and (5.22). The agent's problem is now:

$$\max_{M_t \, K_t} \sum_{t=1}^{\infty} \beta^t U[(M_{t-1} + G_t)/P_t]$$

s.t.

$$K_{t+1} + M_t/P_t = f(K_t) + (1 - \delta)K_t$$

$$M_0 \text{ and } K_0 \text{ are given.} \tag{5.24}$$

To solve this problem we set the following lagrangean:

$$L = \sum_{t=0}^{\infty} \beta^t \{U[(M_{t-1} + G_t)/P_t] + \lambda_t[f(K_t) + (1 - \delta)K_t - K_{t+1} - M_t/P_t]\}. \tag{5.25}$$

The first order conditions are:

$$\beta U'(C_{t+1}) - \lambda_t \Pi_{t+1} = 0 \tag{5.26}$$

$$\beta \lambda_{t+1}[f'(K_{t+1}) + (1 - \delta)] = \lambda_t, \tag{5.27}$$

where $\Pi_{t+1} = 1 + \pi_{t+1} = P_{t+1}/P_t$ is the gross rate of inflation.

In the steady state $\lambda_t = \lambda_{t+1}$ and therefore (5.27) can be written as:

$$[f'(K) + (1 - \delta)] = 1/\beta = 1 + \rho. \tag{5.28}$$

Since (5.28) implies that K does not depend on the steady state rate of inflation, the steady state level of consumption:

$$C = f(K) - \delta K, \tag{5.29}$$

and real balances do not depend on the rate of inflation. It follows that money is super-neutral in the steady state.

To make the consumption tax analogy we formulate the problem (5.24) in terms of real variables using $m_t = M_t/P_t$ and $g_t = G_t/P_t$:

$$\max_{m_t K_t} \sum_{t=1}^{\infty} \beta^t U(m_{t-1}/\Pi_t + g_t)$$

s.t.

$$K_t + m_{t-1} = f(K_{t-1}) + (1 - \delta)K_{t-1}$$

$$m_0 \text{ and } K_0 \text{ are given.} \tag{5.30}$$

We now use $c_t = m_{t-1}/\Pi_t$ to denote private consumption and write (5.30) as:

$$\max_{m_t K_t} \sum_{t=0}^{\infty} \beta^t U(c_t + g_t)$$

s.t.

$$K_t + c_t \Pi_t = f(K_{t-1}) + (1 - \delta)K_{t-1}$$

$$m_0 \text{ and } K_0 \text{ are given.} \tag{5.31}$$

Here inflation is a tax on "private consumption". In the steady state the tax rate is the same on all dated consumption good and is therefore equivalent to a lump sum tax. A lump sum tax is super-neutral.

5.2 AN OVERLAPPING GENERATIONS MODEL

The overlapping generations model was used by Samuelson (1958) and was re-examined by Cass and Yaari (1966). In the non-monetary version of this model the competitive allocation is not efficient. Money is then introduced to achieve an efficient outcome.

To illustrate, we consider an economy in which a two period lived agent is born each period. At each point in time there are thus two individuals: old and young.

Agents are endowed with x units of corn in the first period of their life. They derive utility from consumption in both periods. We start from the case in which there is no money and the only way that an agent can get consumption in the second period of his life is through storage. There is a storage cost of s units of corn per unit stored.

Let $[C_1(t), C_2(t)]$ denote quantities consumed by an agent born in period t in the first and second period of his life. The agent's choice set is given by:

$$C_2(t) = [x - C_1(t)](1 - s), \qquad (5.32)$$

or,

$$C_1(t) + C_2(t)/(1 - s) = x. \qquad (5.33)$$

The broken line in figure 5.3 illustrates the budget line (5.33). The agent chooses point A on this line.

A central planner who can take the endowment of the young and distribute it between the two existing generations faces the following constraint:

$$C_1(t) + C_2(t - 1) \leq x. \qquad (5.34)$$

In a steady state the planner's budget line is:

$$C_1 + C_2 \leq x, \qquad (5.35)$$

and is illustrated by the solid line in figure 5.3. A planner who controls the economy from $t = -\infty$ until $t = +\infty$ can improve matters by choosing point B instead of A.

The analysis is only slightly more complicated if the planner takes control at a finite point in time, say $t = 0$. In this case, the planner can improve the welfare of all current and future generations in the following way. He promises point B to all future generations and to the young agent at $t = 0$. The young agent at $t = 0$ does not eat his entire endowment. Therefore the planner can give something extra to the old agent at $t = 0$ who as a result moves from point A to point D.

Thus the free market outcome in an economy without money is not Pareto efficient. The reason for the inefficiency has to do with what Shell (1971) calls "double infinity": infinite number of agents and infinite number of goods.

Now let us introduce money. One way of doing it is to assume that the government announces at say $t = 0$, that it stands ready to exchange money for corn at the price of P dollars per unit of corn.

The old generation at $t = 0$ has no use for money and will therefore not trade with the government. If the young agent at $t = 0$ sells $x - C_1$ units of corn to the government, he will get

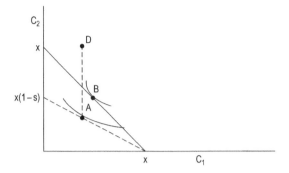

Figure 5.3   An overlapping generations model

$M = P(x - C_1)$ dollars and will be able to use it next period for buying $C_2 = M/P = (x - C_1)$ units of corn. The young agent at $t = 0$ can therefore choose out of the budget set:

$$C_1 + C_2 \leq x. \tag{5.36}$$

Let $\hat{C}_t$ denote the solution to the consumer's problem when facing the budget constraint (5.36). The amount of real balances purchased by the young is:

$$M/P = \hat{C}_2. \tag{5.37}$$

The amount of corn purchased by the government at $t = 0$ is also $\hat{C}_2$. The government transfers this amount to the old at $t = 0$.

Next period, at $t = 1$, the newly born want to purchase the same amount of real balances (5.37) and the now old generation want to sell this amount. The government can therefore stay out of the "game" and let the young trade directly with the old, and so on.

As a result of introducing money the consumption of all generations that were born after $t = 0$ moves to point B in figure 5.3 and the consumption of the old generation at $t = 0$ (born at $t = -1$) moves to point D. The introduction of money led to a Pareto improvement.

Note that here the price level, P, is exogenously determined by the government and the money supply M is determined endogenously by the agents according to (5.37): If the government doubles P agents will double M.

An alternative way of introducing money is to give the old agents at $t = 0$, M dollars. This will work if all generations expect that the price level will remain constant at the level given by (5.37). If the young agent at $t = 0$ expects that the price level will satisfy (5.37) he will choose out of the budget set (5.36) the consumption vector $[\hat{C}_1, \hat{C}_2]$ and will buy from the old $M = P\hat{C}_2$ dollars. Similarly, if the agent born at $t = 1$ expects that the price level will satisfy (5.37) he will also buy the M dollars from the old at $t = 1$ and so on.

Thus if all generations born at $t \geq 0$ expect that the price level will satisfy (5.37) they will choose out of the budget set (5.36) the consumption vector $[\hat{C}_1, \hat{C}_2]$. This choice insures that the good market is always cleared ($\hat{C}_2 + \hat{C}_1 = x$) and that the young agent always buys M dollars from the old agent (the money market is always cleared). Therefore at the price level P all agents can execute their plans and expectations about the price level are correct.

Note that the government can fix one nominal magnitude: either the price level or the money supply. The other nominal magnitude is determined by the private sector to get the desired level of real balances. If the government chooses P, the agents will determine M according to the demand for money (5.37). If the government chooses M, the agents will determine P according to (5.37).

Legal restrictions

In the above overlapping generations model the nominal asset was called "money" but we can also think of it as "bonds." To create a distinction between money and bonds and get an equilibrium in which both nominal assets are held in spite of the fact that bonds yield a positive interest rate, Sargent and Wallace (1982) consider a model in which selling bonds below a certain value is prohibited by law. As a result they get equilibrium in which agents face different rates of interest. Agents with savings below the legal minimum hold money while agents with savings above the legal minimum hold bonds. Since agents face different interest rates, the resulting allocation is not Pareto efficient.

To get an efficient allocation the government should adopt the Friedman rule (a zero nominal interest rate policy) and eliminate the difference in rates of return across assets and agents.

5.3 A BAUMOL–TOBIN TYPE MODEL

In the Baumol–Tobin model a demand for money arises because of a desire to smooth consumption: In the text book version income arrives at the beginning of the month and the consumer wants to spend it evenly during the month. Here we consider a general equilibrium version that requires heterogeneity in consumers' incomes and preferences.[2] However the analysis of the optimum policy (the Friedman rule) is simple.

The model

We consider a single good (corn) economy populated by N infinitely lived agents. Agent h receives an endowment of Y_t^h units of corn at time t. The endowment varies over time and agents in a perfectly predicted manner.

There are no private assets. The government owns a bank and uses it to create savings accounts, checking accounts and to make loans. At $t = 0$, the government announces a policy $p = \{r_t, r_{mt}, r_{Lt}\}_{t=1}^{\infty}$, where r_t is the interest rate on savings accounts, $r_{mt} \leq r_t$ is the interest rate on checking accounts and r_{Lt} is the interest rate on loans. The government then offers a loan in the form of a perpetuity: If agent h takes a loan of d_0^h units he will pay $\{r_{Lt}d_0^h\}_{t=1}^{\infty}$ interest.[3] Each agent chooses the amount of the initial loan, d_0^h, and allocates it between the savings account (b_0^h) and the checking account (m_0^h) subject to the constraint:

$$d_0^h = m_0^h + b_0^h. \tag{5.38}$$

A trip to the bank is required to change the balances in the savings account. It costs α^h units of corn per trip.

Assets (checking and savings) evolve according to:

$$b_t^h + m_t^h = Y_t^h + b_{t-1}^h(1 + r_t) + m_{t-1}^h(1 + r_{mt}) - r_{Lt}d_0^h - c_t^h - \alpha^h I_t^h; \tag{5.39}$$

$$I_t^h = \{1 \text{ if } b_t^h \neq b_{t-1}^h(1 + r_t); \ 0 \text{ otherwise}\}, \tag{5.40}$$

where c is used to denote consumption. Equation (5.40) says that a trip to the bank is required to change the amount in the savings account.

Given the announced policy, p, agent h chooses (m_0^h, b_0^h) and $\{m_t^h, b_t^h, c_t^h\}_{t=1}^{\infty}$ to solve:

$$\max \sum_{t=1}^{\infty} \beta^t u^h(c_t^h)$$

$$\text{s.t.} \quad (5.38)–(5.40) \quad \text{and}$$

$$c_t^h, m_t^h \geq 0 \text{ and } b_t^h \to 0 \quad \text{when } t \to \infty. \tag{5.41}$$

Unlike cash-in-advance models, here it is possible to consume without using money. Since $r_t \geq r_{mt}$, money will not be used if $\alpha = 0$. In this case the agent will smooth consumption by costlessly varying the amount of bonds. Money will not be used by individuals whose income is smooth ($Y_t^h = Y^h$ for all t) because those individuals will choose to consume their endowment. Money may be used however when α is sufficiently large and Y_t^h varies enough over time and agents. In this case, the yield net of transaction costs on holding money for short enough periods is greater than the yield on holding bonds for the same period length.

Equilibrium is a policy p and an allocation

$\{c_t^h, I_t^h; h = 1, \ldots, N\}_{t=1}^{\infty}$ such that:

(a) given p, $\{c_t^h, I_t^h\}_{t=1}^{\infty}$ is a solution to (5.41) for all h, and

(b) markets are cleared: $\displaystyle\sum_{h=1}^{N} c_t^h = \sum_{h=1}^{N}(Y_t^h - \alpha^h I_t^h).$

The Friedman rule in this framework is:

$$r_t = r_{mt} = r_{Lt} \quad \text{for all t.} \tag{5.42}$$

Under (5.42) the consumer will hold all his balances in the checking (money) account and will never go to the bank. Furthermore, it is shown in the appendix that under (5.42), the budget constraint (5.38)–(5.40) can be written in the present value form:

$$\sum_{t=1}^{\infty} D_t c_t = \sum_{t=1}^{\infty} D_t Y_t^h, \tag{5.43}$$

where $D_t = (1+r_1)^{-1} \times (1+r_2)^{-1} \times \cdots \times (1+r_t)^{-1}$ is the discount factor. We may therefore write (5.41) as

$$\max \sum_{t=1}^{\infty} \beta^t u^h(c_t^h) \quad \text{s.t.} \quad (5.43) \text{ and } c_t^h \geq 0. \tag{5.44}$$

An equilibrium in a Friedman rule economy is a sequence of discount factors $D = \{D_t\}_{t=1}^{\infty}$ and an allocation $\{c_t^h; h = 1, \ldots, N\}_{t=1}^{\infty}$ such that:

(a) given D, $\{c_t^h\}_{t=1}^{\infty}$ is a solution to (5.44) for all h, and
(b) markets are cleared: $\sum_{h=1}^{N} c_t^h = \sum_{h=1}^{N} Y_t^h$.

Note that a Friedman rule economy is a standard non-monetary economy. Therefore,

> *Claim:* Equilibrium in a Friedman rule economy exists under rather general conditions and the resulting allocation is Pareto efficient.

The Baumol–Tobin model is thus useful for demonstrating the optimality of the Friedman rule in a rather realistic environment. It is also useful for understanding the effects of the optimal policy because it is explicit about what happens when agents are satiated with money: They do not hold bonds and do not go to the bank.

Conclusions

In this chapter we described three models which are explicit about the role of money in the economy. In the cash-in-advance model money has value because only money can buy goods. In the overlapping generations model and the Baumol–Tobin model money is held to smooth consumption. In all three models zero nominal interest rate is optimal.

Does it matter which model we use? Wang and Yip (1992) find conditions under which various alternative approaches to modeling money yield similar qualitative results. They use continuous time analysis and consider the money in the utility function approach, the cash-in-advance approach and a transaction costs approach. In discrete time analysis it matters whether the beginning of period real balances or the end of period real balances enter the utility function. For a recent discussion on this issue and its implications see Carlstrom and Fuerst (2001).

The four models presented in chapters 2 and 5 have different implications about the possibility (and the desirability) of trade in bonds when the nominal interest rate is zero. The money in the utility function (MIU) the cash-in-advance (CIA) and the overlapping generations (OG) approaches assume that trade in bonds is costless. As we will see in the next chapter researchers using these approaches have argued for periodic changes in the composition of the government's portfolio (indexed and non-indexed debt) while keeping the nominal interest rate at zero. The Baumol–Tobin model puts a question mark on the ability of the government to trade in bonds while keeping the nominal interest rate at zero.

APPENDIX 5A

Claim: When $r_t = r_{mt} = r_{Lt}$, it is possible to write the budget constraint (5.38)–(5.40) in the present value form:

$$\sum_{t=1}^{\infty} D_t c_t^h = \sum_{t=1}^{\infty} D_t Y_t^h, \qquad (A5.1)$$

where $D_t = (1 + r_1)^{-1} \times (1 + r_2)^{-1} \times \cdots \times (1 + r_t)^{-1}$.

Proof: We start by showing that (5.38)–(5.40) imply (A5.1).

Let $a = b + m$, denote total assets. Then we can write constraint (5.39) as:

$$c_t^h + a_t^h = Y_t^h - r_t d_0^h + a_{t-1}^h(1 + r_t).\qquad\text{(A5.2)}$$

Following Barro (1984, pp. 83–8) and McCallum (1989, p. 36) We get from the $t + 1$ constraint:

$$a_t^h = \{c_{t+1}^h + a_{t+1}^h + r_{t+1}d_0^h - Y_{t+1}^h\}/(1 + r_{t+1}).\qquad\text{(A5.3)}$$

Substituting (A5.3) in (A5.2) yields:

$$c_t^h + \{c_{t+1}^h + a_{t+1}^h + r_{t+1}d_0^h - Y_{t+1}^h\}/(1 + r_{t+1}) - Y_t^h + r_t d_0^h$$
$$= a_{t-1}^h(1 + r_t).\qquad\text{(A5.4)}$$

Using a similar step to eliminate a_{t+1}^h and so on, yields:[4]

$$a_0^h = \sum_{t=1}^{\infty} D_t \left\{c_t^h + r_t d_0^h - Y_t^h\right\}.\qquad\text{(A5.5)}$$

Since $a_0^h = d_0^h = \sum_{t=1}^{\infty} D_t r_t d_0^h$ (the present value of the interest payments is equal to the value of the asset) we can write (A5.5) as (A5.1).

We have thus shown that a consumption plan that satisfies (A5.2) also satisfies (A5.1). The assumption that d_0 is a choice variable implies that for any consumption plan that satisfies (A5.1), there exists a choice d_0 such that the consumption plan satisfies (A5.2) and the non-negativity constraints. This completes the proof. □

NOTES

1   Dividends are given by: $l_t - (1/\beta)l_{t-1}$ and are negative in the steady state. However, in the first period dividends are given by: $l_1 - (1/\beta)l_0$. Without the fixed cost $(1/\beta)l_0$ dividends are positive in the first period and the present value of the operational profits is zero.

2   See Jovanovic (1982) for a general equilibrium representative consumer formulation of the Baumol–Tobin model.

3   This is similar to the way financial assets are created in Lucas and Stokey (1983).

4   Assuming here that the present value of m_t approaches zero as $t \to \infty$.

CHAPTER 6

Optimal Fiscal and Monetary Policy

How should we choose fiscal and monetary policy? This important question requires the integration of the public finance literature on optimal taxation with the macroeconomics literature on optimal monetary policy. One of the earlier writers on this topic were Lucas and Stokey (1983). Since then the literature has developed and is surveyed by Chari and Kehoe (1999) and Ljungqvist and Sargent (2000, ch. 12). Here we attempt a simple case with no capital, perfect commitment and no uncertainty.

We start by illustrating the concept of the second best in a single period framework. We then discuss the Friedman rule in the multi-period Baumol–Tobin framework of section 5.3. In this framework the Friedman rule is optimal and can be implemented. Once the Friedman rule is implemented the choice of policy can be analyzed without paying attention to the monetary aspects of the economy. This separation of the real aspects of the problem from the monetary aspects simplifies matters and allows us to solve analytically for the optimal policy when the utility function is additive.

6.1 THE SECOND-BEST ALLOCATION

We start with a representative consumer who lives for one period and can produce goods with labor input on a one to one basis. The consumer is endowed with one unit of time. His utility function is given by $U(c, 1 - L)$ where c is the quantity of consumption and L is the quantity of labor. When the income tax rate is τ, the consumption of the representative consumer is given by:

$$c = (1 - \tau)L. \tag{6.1}$$

We denote the supply of labor by $L(\tau)$ and the implied consumption by $c(\tau) = (1 - \tau)L(\tau)$. Thus, $[c(\tau), L(\tau)]$ solves the following problem:

$$\max_{L} U(c, 1 - L); \quad \text{s.t.} \quad (6.1) \text{ and } 0 \leq L \leq 1. \tag{6.2}$$

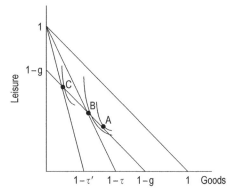

Figure 6.1   The second-best allocation

The government expenditures are exogenously given by g and the economy wide resource constraint is:

$$c(\tau) + g \le L(\tau). \tag{6.3}$$

The government chooses the tax rate τ to maximize the welfare of the representative consumer subject to the resource constraint:

$$\max_{\tau} U[c(\tau), 1 - L(\tau)]; \quad \text{s.t.} \quad (6.3). \tag{6.4}$$

The solution to (6.4) is the second best allocation. It is point B in figure 6.1. The first-best allocation (point A) can be achieved by levying a lump sum tax of g units. Note that in the second-best world the government can choose the slope of the budget line (a relative price) while in the first best world it can choose the location of the budget line.

The government's "budget constraint": Substituting (6.1) into the resource constraint (6.3) leads to

$$\tau L = g. \tag{6.5}$$

It is therefore possible to replace (6.3) by (6.5) and write the government problem as: $\max_{\tau} u[c(\tau), 1 - L(\tau)]$; s.t. $\tau L(\tau) = g$. In this formulation the government chooses the tax rate to maximize the welfare of the representative agent subject to its "budget constraint".

An additive utility function: Later we use the special additive case: $U(c, 1-L) = u(c) - v(L)$, where u is monotone and strictly concave and v is monotone and strictly convex. In this case the consumer's problem is: $\max u[(1 - \tau)L] - v(L)$. The first order condition for this problem is:

$$(1 - \tau)u'[(1 - \tau)L] = v'(L). \tag{6.6}$$

Figure 6.2 illustrates the solution $L(\tau)$ to (6.6). Note that an increase in the tax rate τ shifts the $v'(L)/(1 - \tau)$ to the left and reduces the optimal labor supply. Thus the function $L(\tau)$ is decreasing. Figure 6.2 also illustrates the first best solution $\bar{L}$ which is a solution to the problem $\max u(L - g) - v(L)$.

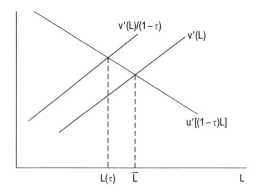

Figure 6.2 Labor as a function of the tax rate

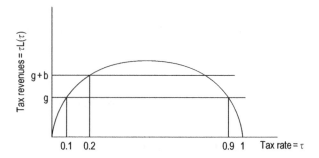

Figure 6.3 The government "budget constraint"

Having solved for the function $L(\tau)$, we now choose τ subject to the "government budget constraint" (6.5). In general the revenue function $\tau L(\tau)$ is not monotonic. This phenomenon was pointed out by Arthur Laffer and is known as the "Laffer curve". There may therefore be more than one solution to $\tau L(\tau) = g$. In figure 6.3 there are two solutions: $\tau = 0.1$ and $\tau = 0.9$. The lower tax rate maximizes welfare.

Government debt: Suppose that the government gives the private agents a claim on b units of consumption. Will this improve welfare?

Using the additive utility function the problem of the consumer is now: $\max u[(1 - \tau)L + b] - v(L)$. The first order condition for this problem is:

$$(1 - \tau)u'[(1 - \tau)L + b] = v'(L). \tag{6.7}$$

Substituting $c = (1 - \tau)L + b$ into the resource constraint (6.3) leads to:

$$\tau L = g + b. \tag{6.8}$$

Thus the government must finance the b units in addition to its expenditures. We substitute (6.8) in (6.7) to get:

$$(1 - \tau)u'(L - g) = v'(L). \tag{6.9}$$

The solution to this equation $L(\tau)$ may be illustrated by figure 6.2 after replacing $u'[(1-\tau)L]$ by $u'(L-g)$. Since the solution to (6.9) does not depend on b we have the same "Laffer curve" as before. But now we must choose a higher tax rate, 0.2 in figure 6.3.

We therefore think of an initial debt as a handicap. From the social point of view, it is better to start the period with zero government debt than with a positive government debt. A negative government debt (which means that private agents owe money to the government) is even better.

In a second-best world the government can eliminate any nominal debt it has, by creating hyperinflation. This hyperinflation may not be feasible from a political point of view because it redistributes wealth. In what follows we will call the problem of a government that has debt that cannot be eliminated, a third-best problem.

Equivalence results: In the optimal tax literature that started with Ramsey (1927), the government chooses key relative prices to maximize social welfare subject to the economy-wide resource constraints. The key relative prices are the price of leisure in terms of current consumption (the net real wage) and the price of current consumption in terms of future consumption (the real gross interest rate). There are three instruments that can be used to vary these relative prices: The income tax rate, the consumption tax rate and the nominal interest rate (treated here as a policy variable). Since there are three instruments and two relative prices there are many ways in which a particular choice of relative prices can be achieved.

To illustrate, we assume that the government chooses to reduce the net (after taxes) real wage to half of the marginal product of labor w. This may be done by choosing an income tax rate τ and a consumption tax rate T such that: $(1-\tau)w/(1+T) = (1/2)w$. The government may choose any combination of τ and T such that: $(1-\tau)/(1+T) = 1/2$.

It is also possible to use consumption tax (fiscal policy) to vary the price of current consumption. To illustrate, we assume that the producers' (before tax) prices are constant and all agents can costlessly trade in the bonds market. An agent who reduces his spending on current consumption by 1 dollar will cut current consumption by $\Delta C_t = -1/(1+T_t)$ units. This agent will get $(1+i)$ dollars in the next period and will be able to buy with it $\Delta C_{t+1} = (1+i)/(1+T_{t+1})$ units of next period's consumption. The price of a unit of current consumption in terms of next period's consumption is: $|\Delta C_{t+1}/\Delta C_t| = (1+i)(1+T_t)/(1+T_{t+1})$. And this price can be varied without varying the nominal interest rate.

There are benefits from varying the consumption tax rates rather than the interest rate. The price of current consumption is tied to the interest rate only for agents who are in the bonds market. For agents who face a cost for trading in the bonds market, the price of current consumption is often the real rate of return on money that is determined by the inflation rate of consumers' (after-tax) prices. There are also problems in choosing an interest rate that is different from the world rate because this may lead to capital inflows and outflows and may have destabilizing effects.

6.2 THE SECOND BEST AND THE FRIEDMAN RULE

Friedman (1969) argued that since real balances can be costlessly produced Pareto efficiency requires that the price of holding money – the nominal interest rate – is zero. Phelps (1973) argued that this is not the case in an economy with distorting taxes. In such an economy money should be taxed like any other good.

Recent work has shown that zero nominal interest rates may be optimal even when only distorting taxes are available. Lucas (1986) argues that "Liquidity is not 'another good' nor, indeed, a 'good' at all: It is the means to a subset of goods that an income tax has already taxed once. Tax spreading at each point in time means inflation tax fixed at zero, independent of the revenue to be raised." Kimbrough (1986) argues that money is an intermediate good and therefore should not be taxed. Woodford (1990) questions this interpretation. Chari, Christiano, and Kehoe (1996) develop a sufficient condition for the optimality of the Friedman rule (a representative agent with homothetic and separable utility function) and show that under this condition the intermediate good interpretation is correct, but there is no connection between the intermediate good result and the optimality of the Friedman rule when their sufficient conditions do not hold. See also Bewley (1983), Cooley and Hansen (1991), Eckstein and Leiderman (1992), Guidotti and Vegh (1993) and Correia and Teles (1996).

Lucas (2000) argues that in the absence of lump sum taxes the optimal nominal interest rate is small (less than 1%) but strictly positive. Lucas (2000) also points out that if the demand for real balances goes to infinity when the nominal interest rate goes to zero it may be impossible to implement the Friedman rule.

In Lucas and Stokey (1983) implementing the Friedman rule does not require taxes. The agents start with no assets. The central bank then lends to each agent as much money as he wants at the competitive real interest rate. The central bank burns the money it receives as interest payment and this leads to the desired deflation rate.

We now turn to use the Baumol–Tobin model of section 5.3 to show that by following the Lucas and Stokey (1983) scheme, we can implement the second best allocation. Since production efficiency requires no wasteful trips to the bank, there is a simple connection between Diamond and Mirrlees' (1971) case for production efficiency in an economy with distorting taxes and the case for the Friedman rule in the Baumol–Tobin model studied here.[1]

The model

In section 5.3 we allowed lump sum taxes and showed that it is possible to achieve the first best by implementing the Friedman rule. Here we allow only distorting taxes and use the same line of reasoning to argue that by implementing the Friedman rule it is possible to achieve the second best.

We consider a single good economy populated by N infinitely lived agents. As in the previous section, c is the quantity of consumption and $1 - L$ is the time spent at leisure. Consumers' h objective function is:

$$\sum_{t=1}^{\infty} \beta^t u^h(c_t^h, 1 - L_t^h). \tag{6.10}$$

Each agent allocates his non-leisure time L_t^h between productive work and going to the bank. α^h is the time cost of a trip to the bank and the time spent on this activity is $\alpha^h I_t^h$ where I_t^h is an index function that takes the value of 1 if a trip to the bank was made and zero otherwise. The amount of productive work is: $L_t^h - \alpha^h I_t^h$.

Agent h can produce according to a constant returns to scale technology that converts each unit of productive work into θ_t^h units of output. The output of agent h is thus: $\theta_t^h(L_t^h - \alpha^h I_t^h)$.

The only assets are government obligations that are held in the form of savings accounts (bonds) and checking accounts (money).

At $t = 0$ the agent gets an initial loan from the central bank, d_0^h, and allocates it between the savings account (b_0^h) and the checking account (m_0^h) subject to the constraint:

$$d_0^h = m_0^h + b_0^h. \tag{6.11}$$

The consumer's single period budget constraint is:

$$b_t^h + m_t^h = (1 - \tau_t)\theta_t^h(L_t^h - \alpha^h I_t^h) + b_{t-1}^h(1 + r_t)$$
$$+ m_{t-1}^h(1 + r_{mt}) - r_{Lt}d_0^h - c_t^h; \tag{6.12}$$

$$I_t^h = \left\{ 1 \text{ if } b_t^h \neq b_{t-1}^h(1 + r_t); \ 0 \text{ otherwise} \right\}, \tag{6.13}$$

where as before b is the real amount in the savings account, m is the real amount in the checking account, d is the initial loan taken at $t = 0$ and r, r_m, r_L are the real interest rates on savings accounts, checking accounts and the initial loan. The formulation in (6.12) and (6.13) says that it takes a trip to the bank to change the amount in the savings account but the amount in the checking account can be costlessly changed. The interest rate on savings accounts is higher than the interest rate on checking accounts: $r_t \geq r_{mt}$.

The path of government expenditures is exogenously given by: $\{g_t\}_{t=1}^{\infty}$. A policy is $p = \{\tau_t, r_t, r_{mt}, r_{Lt}\}_{t=1}^{\infty}$. The Friedman rule requires:

$$r_t = r_{mt} = r_{Lt} \quad \text{for all t.} \tag{6.14}$$

Under (6.14) the consumer will hold all his balances in the checking account and will never go to the bank. Furthermore, the budget constraint (6.12) and (6.13) can be written (see the appendix to 5.3) in the present value form:

$$\sum_{t=1}^{\infty} D_t c_t^h = \sum_{t=1}^{\infty} D_t(1 - \tau_t)\theta_t^h L_t^h, \tag{6.15}$$

where $D_t = (1 + r_1)^{-1} \times (1 + r_2)^{-1} \times \cdots \times (1 + r_t)^{-1}$ is the discount factor. Under the Friedman rule, we may therefore write the consumer's problem as:

$$\max \sum_{t=1}^{\infty} \beta^t u^h(c_t^h, 1 - L_t^h)$$

$$\text{s.t.} \quad (6.15) \quad \text{and} \quad c_t^h \geq 0, \quad 0 \leq L_t^h \leq 1. \tag{6.16}$$

Equilibrium in a Friedman rule economy is a policy choice $p = \{D_t, \tau_t\}_{t=1}^{\infty}$ and an allocation $\{L_t^h, c_t^h; h = 1, \ldots, N\}_{t=1}^{\infty}$ such that: (a) given p, $\{L_t^h, c_t^h\}_{t=1}^{\infty}$ is a solution to (6.16) for all h, and (b) markets are cleared: $g_t + \sum_{h=1}^{N} c_t^h = \sum_{h=1}^{N} \theta_t^h L_t^h$.

Second best

Let $[L_t^h(p), c_t^h(p)]$ denote the solution to (6.16) as a function of policy and let ω^h denote the weight assigned to individual h. The second-best problem is to choose p that maximizes the social welfare function:

$$\max_p \sum_{h=1}^{N} \omega^h \sum_{t=1}^{\infty} \beta^t u^h [c_t^h(p), 1 - L_t^h(p)]$$

$$\text{s.t.} \quad g_t + \sum_{h=1}^{N} c_t^h(p) \leq \sum_{h=1}^{N} \theta_t^h L_t^h(p). \tag{6.17}$$

Proposition 1: The second-best allocation can be attained as an equilibrium outcome in a Friedman rule economy.

To show proposition 1, let p^* denote the solution to (6.17). Then by construction, p^* and the second best allocation satisfy the definition of equilibrium in the Friedman rule economy. This completes the proof.

We have shown that the second-best allocation can be attained in two steps. First we commit to zero nominal interest rate (6.14). Then we choose the path of income tax and real interest rate to solve (6.17).

Third best

We now assume that at t = 0 agents hold money. An initial wealth is a handicap. See the discussion around figure 6.3. Therefore, the optimal policy is to create a large jump in the price level and make the initial holding of money worthless. But as was said before, a jump in the price level means hyperinflation that may not be feasible for political reasons. We may therefore want to consider the problem of a new regime which wants to honor some or all of the non-interest bearing obligations of the previous regime. For example, the new regime may introduce "new dollars" but agree to give x "new cents" for each old dollar.

To formulate the third best problem, let m_{nb}^h denote the amount of non-borrowed money that agent h has after the change in regime.[2] The only difference from the previous case is that now the agent has to pay interest to the central bank on $d_0^h - m_{nb}^h$ units rather than d_0^h. The budget constraint of consumer h is therefore given by (6.11), (6.13) and

$$b_t^h + m_t^h = (1 - \tau_t)\theta_t^h(L_t^h - \alpha^h l_t^h) + b_{t-1}^h(1 + r_t)$$
$$+ m_{t-1}^h(1 + r_{mt}) - c_t^h - r_{Lt}(d_0^h - m_{nb}^h). \tag{6.12'}$$

Under the Friedman rule we can write the budget constraint in the following present value form:

$$\sum_{t=1}^{\infty} D_t c_t^h = m_{nb}^h + \sum_{t=1}^{\infty} D_t (1 - \tau_t)\theta_t^h L_t^h. \tag{6.15'}$$

We can now replace (6.15) by (6.15') in problem (6.16). Let $c_t^h(p; m_{nb}^h)$ and $L_t^h(p; m_{nb}^h)$ denote the solution to:

$$\max \sum_{t=1}^{\infty} \beta^t u^h \left(c_t^h, 1 - L_t^h \right)$$

$$\text{s.t.} \quad (6.15') \quad \text{and} \quad c_t^h \geq 0, \quad 0 \leq L_t^h \leq 1. \tag{6.18}$$

The third-best problem is:

$$\max_{p} \sum_{h=1}^{N} \omega^h \sum_{t=1}^{\infty} \beta^t u^h \left[c_t^h \left(p; m_{nb}^h \right), 1 - L_t^h \left(p; m_{nb}^h \right) \right]$$

$$\text{s.t.}$$

$$g_t + \sum_{h=1}^{N} c_t^h \left(p; m_{nb}^h \right) = \sum_{h=1}^{N} \theta_t^h L_t^h \left(p; m_{nb}^h \right). \tag{6.19}$$

As in the second-best case, if p^* is a solution to (6.19) then the government can announce the policy p^* (which already assumes the Friedman rule [6.14]) and achieve the third-best allocation as an equilibrium outcome. We can restate proposition 1 for the third-best case as follows.

Proposition 1': The third-best allocation can be attained as an equilibrium outcome in a Friedman rule economy.

Using consumption tax to vary the real interest rate

The second- (and third-) best policy requires in general that both the price of leisure (the net real wage) and the price of current consumption in terms of future consumption (the gross real interest rate) vary over time. In a Friedman rule world bonds are not used and varying the real interest rate requires perfect control over the rate of deflation (the real rate of return on money). Central banks lack this level of control.

It may be possible however to maintain a constant rate of deflation in producer prices and vary the relative price of future consumption (and the rate of inflation of consumer prices) by varying the consumption tax rate.

This can be done by using the equivalence results in section 6.1. Let T_t denote the consumption tax rate. Then for the Friedman rule economy we may write the budget constraint (6.15) as follows:

$$\sum_{t=1}^{\infty} D_t(1 + T_t)c_t^h = \sum_{t=1}^{\infty} D_t(1 - \tau_t)\theta_t^h L_t^h, \tag{6.15''}$$

where as before $D_t = (1 + r_1)^{-1} \times (1 + r_2)^{-1} \times \cdots \times (1 + r_t)^{-1}$ but here $1 + r_{t+1}$ is the cost of next period's consumption in terms of current consumption before consumption taxes are paid. Thus r_{t+1} may be obtained by subtracting the rate of change in the PPI from the nominal interest rate.

Here the net real wage for $1/\theta$ units of labor is: $(1 - \tau_t)/(1 + T_t)$. The relevant price of next period consumption in terms of current period consumption is: $(1 + T_t)(1 + r_{t+1})/(1 + T_{t+1})$.

Note that we have three instruments (income tax rate, consumption tax rate and the real before tax interest rate) but we need to choose two relative prices (the price of leisure in terms of current consumption and the price of current consumption in terms of future consumption). There is therefore some redundancy and we may choose to set $r_t = r$ for all t and change the two key relative prices by manipulating T_t and τ_t.

Sticky prices and the Friedman rule

Consumption tax may also help in implementing the Friedman rule when there are menu type costs for changing nominal prices. A customer who is quoted a price of 1 dollar will add 5 cents if the consumption tax is 5% and 10 cents if it is 10%. We can thus change prices without changing the menus. Suppose, for example, that we want the CPI to go down by 4% per year. Then the government should lower the consumption tax by about 1% per quarter. When the consumption tax becomes negative the buyer gets a rebate by the amount of the negative tax.

Thus if we stabilize the producer prices (PPI) and change the consumption tax the consumer prices (CPI) will change but there will be no need to print new menus.

Summary and the implementation of the Friedman rule

In a Baumol–Tobin type model a trip to the bank is required to change balances in the savings account but no trip to the bank is required to change the balances in the checking account. Therefore when the nominal interest rate is zero agents will not use savings accounts. Agents will get a large loan from the central bank at the beginning of their adult life and will then smooth consumption by varying the amount in their checking accounts.

The adoption of the Friedman rule requires that the central bank lend large amounts of money to each person who reaches adulthood. This loan can be administered in the same way that students loans are administered and should be large enough to meet all the current and future "liquidity needs" of the person.[3] The central bank will burn the interest payments it receives and in this way reduce the money supply and create deflation.

The central bank should treat the government in the same way it treats other agents in the economy. It should lend money to the government at $t = 0$ at the same interest rate that it lends to other agents. (The central bank will then burn all the interest payments it receives including the payments from the government.)

In this institutional set-up, the government, like any other agent, will accumulate balances in its checking account when it runs a surplus and decumulate balances when it runs a deficit.

After the adoption of the Friedman rule, the problem of choosing the optimal policy is identical to the problem analyzed in the public finance literature. It will be shown in the next section that the optimal policy requires variations in the real interest rate.

Since the real interest rate in a Friedman rule economy is the rate of return on money, fluctuations in the real interest rate require fluctuations in the rate of change of the CPI. This can be achieved by changing the consumption tax rate. It is possible to follow a policy that reduces the PPI at the rate of the subjective interest rate ρ and deal with deviations of government expenditures from the steady state by changing the consumption and the income tax rates. The consumption tax rate should vary to create the desired fluctuations in the rate of change of the CPI and the income tax rate should vary to maintain a constant net real wage. If menu costs are important we can also vary the consumption tax to economize on menu changes.

6.3 SMOOTHING TAX DISTORTIONS

In the previous section we showed that we can separate the monetary aspects of the policy choice problem from the real aspects: We first apply the Friedman rule and then we get the problem of choosing relative prices subject to resource constraints.

We now attempt to solve the real aspects of the problem analytically for a special case. In our special case it is optimal to have a constant tax rate on labor. This result was obtained by Barro (1979) in a different model and is roughly true in the more general models surveyed by Chari and Kehoe (1999). We then proceed to show that high government spending is associated with high real interest rate, high labor supply and low consumption. Finally we derive similar results in the shopping time model of Bordo and Vegh (2002).

To illustrate the idea of tax smoothing we consider a two periods economy in which government expenditures are given by $g_t (t = 1, 2)$. The government cannot levy lump sum taxes and must use income tax to finance its expenditures.

The representative consumer's single period utility is: $U(c, 1 - L) = c - v(L)$, where the cost function $v( )$ is strictly monotone and strictly convex. We assume that $\beta = 1$ and therefore the consumer's objective function (two-periods utility) is:

$$c_1 + c_2 - v(L_1) - v(L_2). \tag{6.20}$$

Since the consumer's welfare depends on total consumption $(c_1 + c_2)$ and not on the way it is allocated over periods, the equilibrium real interest rate must be zero. We therefore assume that the government allows the consumer to borrow and lend at a zero real interest rate (by the mechanism described in the previous section). Productivity does not change over time and is given by $\theta = 1$. The government imposes the income tax rates τ_t and therefore the consumer's budget constraint is:

$$c_1 + c_2 = (1 - \tau_1)L_1 + (1 - \tau_2)L_2. \tag{6.21}$$

We now substitute the budget constraint (6.21) in the objective function (6.20) and write the consumer's maximization problem as follows.

$$\max_{L_t}(1 - \tau_1)L_1 + (1 - \tau_2)L_2 - v(L_1) - v(L_2). \tag{6.22}$$

The first order conditions for this problem are:

$$v'(L_t) = 1 - \tau_t. \tag{6.23}$$

We use $L(\tau_t)$ to denote the solution to (6.23) and define equilibrium as follows. Equilibrium is a vector $(\tau_1, \tau_2, L_1, L_2, c_1, c_2)$ that satisfies the market clearing conditions:

$$c_t + g_t = L(\tau_t). \tag{6.24}$$

Many equilibria exist. The government's problem is to choose an equilibrium that will maximize the welfare of the representative agent. We substitute (6.24) into the representative agent's utility function and write the government's problem as follows:

$$\max_{\tau_t} L(\tau_1) + L(\tau_2) - g_1 - g_2 - v[L(\tau_1)] - v[L(\tau_2)]. \tag{6.25}$$

We now turn to show that tax smoothing is optimal.

Claim 1: The solution to the government's problem (6.25) must satisfy the following necessary condition: $\tau_1 = \tau_2$.

To show this claim assume that $\tau_1 > \tau_2$ and $L(\tau_1) < L(\tau_2)$ as in figure 6.4. There is a tax rate τ, also illustrated by figure 6.4, such that $L(\tau) = (1/2)[L(\tau_1) + L(\tau_2)]$ is the average labor supply.

When the government imposes the tax rate τ in both periods, total output (over the two periods) remains the same. But since convexity of the cost function implies: $v\{(1/2)[L(\tau_1) + L(\tau_2)]\} \leq (1/2)v[L(\tau_1)] + (1/2)v[L(\tau_2)]$, total cost goes down. Therefore $\tau_1 > \tau_2$ cannot be optimal. The same reasoning can be used to rule out $\tau_1 < \tau_2$. This completes the proof.

We have thus shown that by smoothing the tax rate the government can achieve the same total consumption at a lower cost and therefore smoothing is optimal.[4]

Optimal real interest rate policy

In the previous example the choice of the real interest rate was trivial because only zero real interest rate was consistent with equilibrium. We now adopt the more general additive utility function and discuss the choice of the real interest rate under the assumption that smoothing the net real wage is optimal.

We assume a representative consumer with a single period utility function: $u(c) - v(L)$, where as in 6.1: $u', v' > 0, u'' < 0$ and $v'' > 0$. The economy-wide resource constraint is:

$$c_t + g_t = L_t. \tag{6.26}$$

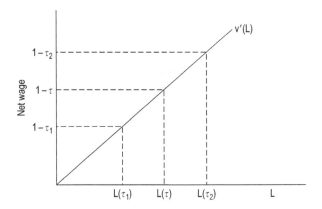

Figure 6.4   Tax smoothing and marginal cost smoothing

In a Friedman rule economy the representative consumer takes $\{D_t, w_t = 1 - \tau_t\}_{t=1}^{\infty}$ as given and solves:

$$\max_{c\,L} \sum_{t=1}^{\infty} \beta^t [u(c_t) - v(L_t)] \tag{6.27}$$

$$\text{s.t.} \quad \sum_{t=1}^{\infty} D_t c_t = \sum_{t=1}^{\infty} D_t w_t L_t, \tag{6.28}$$

where D_t is a discount factor and w_t is the real net wage. The first order conditions for this problem are given by (6.28) and:

$$u'(c_t) w_t = v'(L_t) \tag{6.29}$$

$$u'(c_t) = (D_t / D_{t+1}) \beta u'(c_{t+1}) = (1 + r_{t+1}) \beta u'(c_{t+1}). \tag{6.30}$$

Let $[c(p), L(p)]$ denotes the solution to the consumer's problem (6.27). Then we can write the government's problem as: $\max_p \sum_{t=1}^{\infty} \beta^t [u(c_t(p)) - v(L_t(p))]$ s.t. (6.26). Alternatively we may treat the first order conditions of the consumer's problem as constraints and write the government's problem as:

$$\max_{p\,L_t\,c_t} \sum_{t=1}^{\infty} \beta^t [u(c_t) - v(L_t)]$$

$$\text{s.t.} \quad (6.26) \text{ and } (6.28)–(6.30). \tag{6.31}$$

Constraint (6.26) requires that the economy wide resource constraint is satisfied. Constraints (6.28)–(6.30) require that the choice L and c is a solution to the representative agent's problem. A related approach (the primal approach) to optimal taxation is to characterize the set of allocations that can be implemented as a competitive equilibrium with distorting taxes by two conditions: a resource constraint and an implementability constraint. For this approach see Chari and Kehoe (1999).

Solving for the real interest rate policy

We now assume that the optimal policy specifies a constant net real wage w and describe an algorithm for choosing w such that constraints in the problem (6.31) are satisfied.

We choose the net real wage w arbitrarily. We then substitute the resource constraint (6.26) in the first order condition (6.29) to get:

$$u'(L - g)w = v'(L). \tag{6.32}$$

We denote the solution to this equation by $L(w, g)$. We now calculate the real interest rates that will satisfy the first order condition (6.30) when consumption is given by $c(w, g) = L(w, g) - g$. That is we find r_{t+1} that satisfies:

$$u'[L(w, g_t) - g_t] = (1 + r_{t+1})\beta u'[L(w, g_{t+1}) - g_{t+1}]. \tag{6.33}$$

We can now calculate D_t. We use these discount factors to check if the budget constraint (6.28) is satisfied. That is we check if:

$$\sum_{t=1}^{\infty} D_t[L(w, g_t) - g_t] = w \sum_{t=1}^{\infty} D_t L(w, g_t). \tag{6.34}$$

If (6.34) is satisfied we are done. Otherwise we try a different w and keep iterating with the hope of finding a solution. As in the single period case there are usually many solutions. We choose the solution that maximizes welfare.

The real interest rate must be allowed to fluctuate

We have argued that the net real wage should be smoothed. We have also argued for the Friedman rule that smooths the nominal interest rate at the level of zero. Should we also attempt to smooth the real interest rate? The answer is in the negative. Like any other relative price the real interest rate should be allowed to fluctuate in order to clear markets.

To illustrate we consider the case in which $g_t > g_{t+1}$. In figure 6.5 we solve (6.32) graphically. Using this figure we can show that $L_t = L(g_t, w) > L_{t+1} = L(g_{t+1}, w)$ and $u'(c_t) > u'(c_{t+1})$. Using (6.33) this implies $1 + r_{t+1} > 1/\beta$. The intuition is straightforward: To make people consume less you must make current consumption more expensive. This also leads to an increase in labor supply because of the increase in the marginal utility of consumption.

Similarly, we can show that when $g_{t+1} < g_{t+2}, 1 + r_{t+2} < 1/\beta$. Thus the real interest rate must be positively correlated with government expenditure as in figure 6.6. The intuition is straight forward. At time $t+1$ the consumer is "asked" to increase his consumption temporarily. To do that we must make consumption at $t + 1$ cheap both relative to consumption at t and relative to consumption at $t + 2$.

6.4 A SHOPPING TIME MODEL

In the last two sections we discussed optimal monetary and fiscal policy in a Baumol–Tobin type model. Here we follow Bordo and Vegh (2002) and discuss the choice of policy in

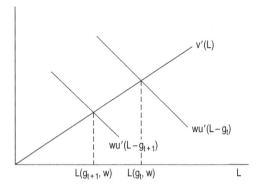

Figure 6.5   Labor and government spending: $g_t > g_{t+1}$

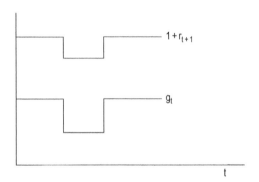

Figure 6.6   The real interest rate and government spending

a shopping time model. Bordo and Vegh assume a constant real interest rate and a logarithmic utility function. Here we extend their analysis to the case in which the interest rate varies over time and the utility function is more general (additive and separable). The results are the same as in the Baumol–Tobin type model and therefore this section can be read as a robustness check.

In the Bordo–Vegh model, the representative agent uses his time endowment to do shopping, labor and leisure. His time budget constraint is: $s_t + n_t + h_t = 1$, where s is shopping time, n is labor time and h is leisure time. Shopping time is given by:

$$s_t = \upsilon[m_t/c_t(1 + T_t)]c_t(1 + T_t) = \upsilon(x_t)c_t(1 + T_t), \tag{6.35}$$

where c is the quantity of consumption, T is the consumption tax rate, m denotes the end of period real balances and $x = m/c(1 + T)$ is the ratio of real balances to consumption expenditures. There is a satiation level $x^s > 0$. It is assumed that $\upsilon(x) \geq 0$; $\upsilon'(x) \leq 0$ when $x < x^s$ and $\upsilon(x) = \upsilon'(x) = 0$ when $x \geq x^s$. Thus shopping time is zero when $x \geq x^s$.

There are two assets: Domestic money and an internationally traded bond. The household's flow budget constraint is:

$$f_t = (1 + r_t)f_{t-1} + 1 - h_t - s_t - c_t(1 + T_t) + (1 + r_{mt})m_{t-1} - m_t \tag{6.36}$$

where f is the amount of real foreign bonds holdings, r_t $(r_{mt} = (1 + \pi_t)^{-1})$ is the real interest rate (the real rate of return on money) between time $t - 1$ and t.

The household derives utility from consumption and leisure. Its subjective discount rate is $0 < \beta < 1$ and its single period utility function, $U(c_t, h_t)$, is strictly concave and differentiable. The household takes the sequence $\{r_t, r_{mt}, T_t\}$ as given and chooses $\{c_t, h_t, m_t\}$ to solve:

$$\max_{c_t \; h_t \; m_t} \sum_{t=1}^{\infty} \beta^t U(c_t, h_t)$$

$$\text{s.t.} \quad (6.35), \; (6.36), \; f_0 = m_0 = 0. \tag{6.37}$$

We use $p = \{r_{mt}, T_t\}$ to denote policy and $c_t(p), h_t(p), m_t(p)$ to denote the solution to the representative household's problem (6.37).

Government expenditures are given by the sequence $\{g_t\}$. The government takes the international real interest rate r_t and the functions $c_t(p), h_t(p), m_t(p), x_t(p) = m_t(p)/(1+T_t)c_t(p)$ as given and chooses p to maximize the welfare of the representative consumer subject to an economy-wide resource constraint:

$$\sum_t D_t[c_t(p) + g_t] = \sum_t D_t[1 - h_t(p) - \upsilon[x_t(p)](1 + T_t)c_t(p)], \tag{6.38}$$

where $D_t = (1 + r_1)^{-1} \times (1 + r_2)^{-1} \times \cdots \times (1 + r_t)^{-1}$ is the discount factor (discounting all magnitudes to $t = 0$). The government's problem is thus:

$$\max_p \sum_{t=1}^{\infty} \beta^t U[c_t(p), h_t(p)], \quad \text{s.t.} \quad (6.38). \tag{6.39}$$

First order conditions for the household's problem (6.37)

To state the first order conditions for (6.37) we compute the price of consumption in terms of time. A unit of consumption requires $1 + T$ units of labor and some shopping time. The amount of shopping time is obtained by taking a derivative of (6.35) with respect to c. This yields:

$$ds/dc = (1 + T)[\upsilon(x) - \upsilon'(x)x]. \tag{6.40}$$

The time cost of a unit of consumption is therefore: $(1 + T_t)[1 + \upsilon(x_t) - \upsilon'(x_t)x_t]$. The first order conditions for (6.37) require that the marginal rate of substitution between consumption and leisure is equal to this relative price. That is:

$$U_1(c_t, h_t)/U_2(c_t, h_t) = (1 + T_t)[1 + \upsilon(x_t) - \upsilon'(x_t)x_t]. \tag{6.41}$$

Condition (6.41) has of course the gain equals pain interpretation. The household can deviate from the optimal plan by cutting a unit of consumption and increasing leisure by $(1+T_t)[1 + \upsilon(x_t) - \upsilon'(x_t)x_t]$ units. The pain is the marginal utility of consumption, $U_1(c_t, h_t)$. The gain is the marginal utility of leisure times the change in the amount of leisure: $(1+T_t)[1+\upsilon(x_t)-\upsilon'(x_t)x_t]U_2(c_t,h_t)$. Condition (6.41) says that the pain equals the gain and therefore at the optimum the household cannot benefit from this deviation.

The household can also deviate from the optimal plan by borrowing a unit of real balances at time t and work more to compensate for the real rate of return difference. The benefit of adding a unit of real balances is $ds_t/dm_t = -\upsilon'(x_t)$ units of (shopping) time. The difference in the gross real rate of return on the two assets is: $r_{t+1} - r_{mt+1}$. To compensate for this difference the household must work dn hours more, where $dn(1+r_{t+1}) = r_{t+1} - r_{mt+1}$. This leads to: $dn = (r_{t+1} - r_{mt+1})/(1+r_{t+1})$. Since the benefit and the cost are both in terms of time and since the household cannot benefit by this deviation from the optimal plan we get the first order condition:

$$-\upsilon'(x_t) = (r_{t+1} - r_{mt+1})/(1+r_{t+1}) = I_t, \tag{6.42}$$

where I_t is the time cost of holding a unit of real balances or the inflation tax. We denote the solution to (6.42) by $x(I_t)$.

Finally, we observe that the household can deviate from the optimal plan by taking an additional unit of leisure at time t and working $1+r_{t+1}$ units more at time $t+1$. This leads to the first order condition:

$$U_2(c_t,h_t) = \beta(1+r_{t+1})U_2(c_{t+1},h_{t+1}). \tag{6.43}$$

At the optimum the time cost of consumption can be written as $(1+T_t)[1+\upsilon[x(I_t)]+I_tx(I_t)]$. Since the present value of the time cost of consumption must equal the present value of non leisure time we have the following present value budget constraint:

$$\sum_t D_t c_t(1+T_t)\{1+\upsilon[x(I_t)]+I_tx(I_t)\} = \sum_t D_t(1-h_t). \tag{6.44}$$

Following the primal approach to optimal taxation (Lucas and Stokey [1983]) we can now state the government problem as:

$$\max_{I_t\,T_t\,c_t\,h_t} \sum_{t=1}^{\infty} \beta^t U(c_t,h_t)$$

s.t.

$$U_1(c_t,h_t)/U_2(c_t,h_t) = (1+T_t)[1+\upsilon[x(I_t)]+I_tx(I_t)]$$
$$U_2(c_t,h_t) = \beta(1+r_{t+1})U_2(c_{t+1},h_{t+1})$$
$$\sum_t D_t c_t(1+T_t)[1+\upsilon[x(I_t)]+I_tx(I_t)] = \sum_t D_t(1-h_t)$$
$$\sum_t D_t(c_t+g_t) = \sum_t D_t\{1-h_t-\upsilon[x(I_t)](1+T_t)c_t\} \tag{6.45}$$

The first three implementability constraints are obtained from the first order conditions (6.41)–(6.44). The last constraint is the economy-wide constraint (6.38) after substituting the solution to (6.42).

Proposition 1: A solution to (6.45) requires $I_t = 0$ for all t.

This says that at the optimum there is no inflation tax and $r_t = r_{mt}$. The proof is based on the observation that from the individual's point of view inflation tax is a tax on consumption and is equivalent to consumption tax. We can therefore save labor by replacing a strictly positive inflation tax with a consumption tax.

Proof: We consider the sequence $\{\hat{T}_t, \hat{I}_t, \hat{c}_t\}$ that satisfies the constraints in (6.45) and specifies $\hat{I}_t > 0$ for some t. We now consider the policy $\{T_t, I_t = 0\}$ where: $(1 + T_t) = (1 + \hat{T}_t)[1 + \upsilon[x(\hat{I}_t)] + \hat{I}_t x(\hat{I}_t)]$.

We now observe that in the first three implementability constraints of (6.45), (T_t, I_t) appears only in the expression: $q_t = (1 + T_t)[1 + \upsilon[x(I_t)] + I_t x(I_t)]$. Therefore, since the policy $\{\hat{T}_t, \hat{I}_t\}$ satisfies the implementability constraints, the policy $\{T_t, I_t = 0\}$ also satisfies these constraints.

Since $\upsilon[x(\hat{I}_t)] > 0$ when $\hat{I}_t > 0$ and the sequence $\{\hat{T}_t, \hat{I}_t, \hat{c}_t\}$ satisfies the economy-wide resource constraint, it follows that $\sum_t D_t(\hat{c}_t + g_t) < \sum_t D_t(1 - \bar{h}_t)$. Since $\upsilon[x(0)] = 0$ and since $\{T_t, I_t = 0\}$ satisfies the implementability constraints, there exists $\varepsilon_t > 0$ such that the sequence $\{T_t, I_t = 0, c_t = \hat{c}_t + \varepsilon_t\}$ satisfies all the constraints in (6.45). Therefore the sequence $\{\hat{T}_t, \hat{I}_t, \hat{c}_t\}$ cannot be a solution to (6.45). We have thus shown that a solution to (6.45) must have $I_t = 0$ for all t. □

Tax smoothing

We now turn to the question of tax smoothing under the assumption that $I_t = 0$. We start with the logarithmic utility function in Bordo and Vegh.

> *Example 1:* $U(c_t, h_t) = \log(c_t) + \log(h_t)$.

Using the log utility function and proposition 1 the first order conditions (6.41) and (6.43) are:

$$h_t/c_t = (1 + T_t) \tag{6.46}$$

$$1/h_t = \beta(1 + r_{t+1})/h_{t+1}. \tag{6.47}$$

Substituting (6.46) and $I_t = 0$ into (6.44) leads to:

$$\sum_{t=1}^{\infty} D_t h_t = \sum_{t=1}^{\infty} D_t(1 - h_t). \tag{6.48}$$

We can now solve (6.47) and (6.48) for the sequence $\{h_t\}$. This solution, denoted by $\bar{h}_t$ does not depend on the choice of policy.[5]

Taking $h_t = \bar{h}_t$ as given the government solves:

$$\max_{T_t, c_t} \sum_t \beta^t \ln c_t$$

s.t.

$$\bar{h}_t = c_t(1 + T_t);$$

$$\sum_t D_t(c_t + g_t) = \sum_t D_t(1 - \bar{h}_t). \qquad (6.49)$$

The first (implementability) constraint in (6.49) is the first order condition (6.46) and the second is the economy-wide resource constraint (6.44). We assume that $\sum_t D_t g_t < \sum_t D_t(1 - \bar{h}_t)$ and therefore some sequences of strictly positive private consumption are possible.

Claim 1: There exists a solution to (6.49) that specifies $T_t = T$ for all t.

Proof: To show this claim we first solve:

$$\max_{c_t} \sum_t \beta^t \ln c_t \quad \text{s.t.} \quad \sum_t D_t(c_t + g_t) = \sum_t D_t(1 - \bar{h}_t). \qquad (6.50)$$

This is the problem (6.49) without the implementability constraint. The first order conditions for (6.50) are:

$$c_{t+1}/c_t = \beta(1 + r_{t+1}). \qquad (6.51)$$

Since (6.47) implies $\bar{h}_{t+1}/\bar{h}_t = \beta(1 + r_{t+1})$, the first order condition (6.51) is satisfied if we choose $T_t = T$ for all t and determine c_t according to the implementability constraint in (6.49): $c_t = \bar{h}_t/(1 + T)$. We choose the constant tax rate T to satisfy the economy-wide constraint in (6.49). This leads to:

$$(2 + T)/(1 + T) = \sum_t D_t(1 - g_t)/\sum_t D_t \bar{h}_t. \qquad (6.52)$$

Let $\bar{T}$ denote the solution to (6.52). Since $\{\bar{T}, c_t = \bar{h}_t/(1+\bar{T})\}$ satisfies the constraints in (6.49) and since $c_t = \bar{h}_t/(1+\bar{T})$ is a solution to (6.50) it follows that the implementability constraint in (6.49) is not binding and $\{\bar{T}, c_t = \bar{h}_t/(1 + \bar{T})\}$ is also a solution to (6.49). Thus there exists a solution to (6.49) with perfectly smoothed tax rate.   □

Note that allowing for lump sum taxes here will not improve matters. This is because the supply of non-leisure time is inelastic in this example. We now turn to another example that shows that the perfect smoothing result occurs also when the first best is not feasible.

Example 2: $U(c_t, h_t) = 2(c_t)^{0.5} + 2(h_t)^{0.5}$.

The first order conditions (6.41) and (6.43) are now:

$$(c_t)^{-0.5} = (1 + T_t)(h_t)^{-0.5} \quad \text{or} \quad c_t = h_t(1 + T_t)^{-2}, \tag{6.53}$$

$$(h_t)^{-0.5} = \beta(1 + r_{t+1})(h_{t+1})^{-0.5} \quad \text{or} \quad h_{t+1} = h_t[\beta(1 + r_{t+1})]^2. \tag{6.54}$$

Substituting (6.53) and $I_t = 0$ into (6.44) leads to:

$$\sum_t D_t h_t/(1 + T_t) = \sum_t D_t(1 - h_t). \tag{6.55}$$

We now solve (6.54) and (6.55) explicitly. Assuming $(1 + r_1)^{-1} = \beta$ and

$D_2 = \beta(1 + r_2)^{-1}$, we use (6.54) to express h_2 in terms of h_1. This yields:
$h_2 = h_1[\beta(1 + r_2)]^2 = h_1\beta^4/(D_2)^2$. We now use
$D_3 = \beta(1 + r_2)^{-1}(1 + r_3)^{-1}$ and (6.54) to get:
$h_3 = h_2[\beta(1 + r_3)]^2 = \beta^4 h_1[(1 + r_2) \times (1 + r_3)]^2 = h_1\beta^6/(D_3)^2$. And in general,

$$h_t = h_1\beta^{2t}(D_t)^{-2} \quad \text{for } t > 1. \tag{6.56}$$

Substituting (6.56) in (6.55) yields:

$$h_1 \sum_t \beta^{2t}/D_t(1 + \theta_t) = (1/2) \sum_t D_t. \tag{6.57}$$

We assume that there exists a solution to (6.57) and denote the solution by $h_1(z)$, where $z = \sum_t \beta^{2t}/D_t(1 + T_t)$ is a weighted average of $1/(1 + T_t)$. We also use $h_t(z) = h_1(z)\beta^{2t}(D_t)^{-2}$ to write the solution for leisure at $t > 1$.

The government's problem is now:

$$\max_{T_t\ c_t} \sum_t \beta^t[2(c_t)^{0.5} + 2[h_t(z)]^{0.5}]$$

s.t.

$$z = \sum_t \beta^{2t}/D_t(1 + T_t)$$

$$h_t(z) = (1 + T_t)^2 c_t$$

$$\sum_t D_t(c_t + g_t) = \sum_t D_t[1 - h_t(z)]. \tag{6.58}$$

Similar to Claim 1 we now show the following Claim.

Claim 2: There exists a solution to (6.58) that specifies $T_t = T$ for all t.

Proof: Let $\bar{z} = \sum_t \beta^{2t}/D_t(1 + \bar{T}_t)$ denote the solution to (6.58), for the optimal policy. We start by treating $\bar{z}$ as given and solve (6.58) without the implementability constraints:

$$\max_{c_t} \sum_t \beta^t [2(c_t)^{0.5} + 2[h_t(\bar{z})]^{0.5}]$$

$$\text{s.t.} \quad \sum_t D_t(c_t + g_t) = \sum_t D_t[1 - h_t(\bar{z})]. \tag{6.59}$$

Let $\{\hat{c}_t\}$ denote the solution to (6.59). We now show that $(\bar{T}, \hat{c}_t)$ is a solution to (6.58), where $T_t = \bar{T}$ is the constant tax rate and $1 + \bar{T} = \sum_t \beta^{2t}/\bar{z}D_t$.

We first note that the choice of the constant tax rate $\bar{T}$ implies $z = \bar{z}$ and therefore the amount of leisure, $h_t(\bar{T}) = h_t(\bar{z})$, is optimal. We now observe that the first order conditions for (6.59) require: $(c_t)^{-0.5} = \beta(1 + r_{t+1})(c_{t+1})^{-0.5}$, or

$$c_{t+1} = [\beta(1 + r_{t+1})]^2 c_t. \tag{6.60}$$

Since (6.54) implies $h_{t+1}(\bar{z}) = [\beta(1 + r_{t+1})]^2 h_t(\bar{z})$, the first order condition (6.60) is satisfied if we choose $T_t = \bar{T}$ for all t and use $h_t(\bar{z}) = (1 + \bar{T})^2 c_t$ to determine c_t. Thus the implementability constraint in (6.58) is not binding and $(\bar{T}, \hat{c}_t)$ is a solution to (6.58). $\qquad\square$

We now turn to the more general case.

The general additive separable case: $U(c_t, h_t) = u(c_t) + v(h_t)$, where $u', v' > 0$ and $u'', v'' < 0$ and $u'(0) = \infty$, $v'(0) = \infty$. Note that here we use $v(\ )$ as the utility function of leisure rather than the disutility from labor function.

The first order conditions for an interior solution to (6.41) and (6.43) are now:

$$u'(c_t) = (1 + T_t)v'(h_t) \tag{6.61}$$

$$v'(h_t) = \beta(1 + r_{t+1})v'(h_{t+1}). \tag{6.62}$$

We use (6.61) to express c_t as a function of h_t and T_t: $c_t = u'^{-1}[(1 + T_t)v'(h_t)] = f(h_t, T_t)$ and substitute this and $I_t = 0$ into (6.44) to get:

$$\sum_t D_t(1 + T_t)f(h_t, T_t) = \sum_t D_t(1 - h_t). \tag{6.63}$$

We use (6.62) to write: $h_{t+1} = v'^{-1}[v'(h_t)/\beta(1 + r_{t+1})] = g(h_t, r_{t+1})$. We now substitute forward:

$$h_2 = g(h_1, r_2);$$
$$h_3 = g(h_2, r_3) = g(g(h_1, r_2), r_3);$$
$$h_4 = g(h_3, r_4) = g(g(g(h_1, r_2), r_3), r_4);$$

and in general:

$$h_t = h_t(h_1, r_2, \ldots, r_t). \tag{6.64}$$

Substituting (6.64) in (6.63) yields:

$$\sum_t D_t(1 + T_t)f[h_t(h_1, r_2, \ldots, r_t), T_t]$$

$$= \sum_t D_t[1 - h_t(h_1, r_2, \ldots, r_t)] \tag{6.65}$$

We assume that there exists a solution to (6.65) and denote it by

$$h_1 = h_1(Q), \quad \text{where } Q = \{1 + T_t\}.$$

The government's problem is now:

$$\max_{T_t\, c_t} \sum_t \beta^t u(c_t) + \beta v[h_1(Q)] + \sum_{t>1} \beta^t v\{h_t[h_1(Q), r_2, \ldots, r_t]\}$$

s.t.

$$Q = \{1 + T_t\}$$

$$c_1 = f(h_1(Q), T_1)$$

$$c_t = f\{h_t[h_1(Q), r_2, \ldots, r_t], T_t\} \quad \text{for } t > 1$$

$$\sum_t D_t(c_t + g_t) = D_1[1 - h_1(Q)] + \sum_{t>1} D_t\{1 - h_t[h_1(Q), r_2, \ldots, r_t]\}. \tag{6.66}$$

We now turn to generalize Claims 1 and 2. We assume that for a given h_1, the household's expenditure on consumption, $(1 + T)f[h_t(h_1, r_2, \ldots, r_t), T]$, is small when T is large.[6]

Proposition 2: There exists a solution to (6.66) that specifies $T_t = T$ for all t.

Proof: The proof is similar to the proofs of Claims 1 and 2. Let $\bar{Q}$ denotes the solution to (6.66) for the optimal policy. We first treat $\bar{Q}$ as given and consider (6.66) without the implementability constraint:

$$\max_{c_t} \sum_t \beta^t u(c_t) + \beta v[h_1(\bar{Q})] + \sum_{t>1} \beta^t v\{h_t[h_1(\bar{Q}), r_2, \ldots, r_t]\}$$

s.t.

$$\sum_t D_t(c_t + g_t) = D_1[1 - h_1(\bar{Q})] + \sum_{t>1} D_t\{1 - h_t[h_1(\bar{Q}), r_2 \ldots, r_t]\}. \tag{6.67}$$

Lemma: There exists a constant tax rate $\bar{T} = \{\bar{T}\}$ such that $h_1(\bar{T}) = h_1(\bar{Q})$.

Proof: When $T = 0$, the government run a permanent deficit and therefore the present value of consumption is larger than the present value of labor supply:

$$\sum_t D_t f[h_t(h_1(\bar{Q}), r_2, \ldots, r_t), 0] > \sum_t D_t[1 - h_t(h_1(\bar{Q}), r_2, \ldots, r_t)].$$

Since we assume that when T is large, $(1 + T)f[h_t(h_1(Q), r_2, \ldots, r_t), T]$ is small, continuity insures a solution, $\bar{T}$, to:

$$\sum_t D_t\{(1 + T)f[h_t(h_1(Q), r_2, \ldots, r_t), T]$$

$$= \sum_t D_t[1 - h_t(h_1(\bar{Q}), r_2, \ldots, r_t)].$$

□

We now show that the implementability constraints in (6.66) are not binding and the solution to (6.67) is also the solution to (6.66) for the optimal consumption.

For this purpose we choose $\bar{c}_t$ to satisfy the implementability constraints:

$$u'(\bar{c}_1) = (1 + \bar{T})v'[h_1(\bar{T})],$$

$$u'(\bar{c}_t) = (1 + \bar{T})v'[h_t(h_1(\bar{T}), r_2, \ldots, r_t)].$$

This leads to:

$$u'(\bar{c}_t)/u'(\bar{c}_{t+1})$$

$$= v'[h_t(h_1(\bar{T}), r_2, \ldots, r_t)]/v'[h_{t+1}(h_1(\bar{T}), r_2, \ldots, r_{t+1})]. \tag{6.68}$$

Since $h_t(h_1(\bar{T}), r_2, \ldots, r_t)$ satisfies (6.62) we have:

$$v'[h_t(h_1(\bar{T}), r_2, \ldots, r_t)]/v'[h_{t+1}(h_1(\bar{T}), r_2, \ldots, r_{t+1})] = \beta(1 + r_{t+1})$$

and therefore:

$$u'(\bar{c}_t)/u'(\bar{c}_{t+1}) = \beta(1 + r_{t+1}). \tag{6.69}$$

Condition (6.69) is the first order condition for (6.67). Therefore $\bar{c}_t$ is a solution to (6.67) and since it satisfies the implementability constraint in (6.66), $(\bar{T}, \bar{c}_t)$ is a solution to (6.66).

□

Conclusions

The Friedman rule is optimal and when the utility function is additive perfect smoothing of the net real wage is also optimal. These results were obtained here in a shopping time model for a small open economy that faces a world real interest rate that changes over time. Bordo and Vegh (2002) show that once tax collection costs are introduced the Friedman rule is no longer optimal.

PROBLEMS

1   Assume $U(c, 1 - L) = c - L^2$.

(a) Find revenues as a function of the income tax rate τ (the so called "Laffer curve").
(b) Find the tax rate that maximizes revenues.
(c) What is the maximum amount of expenditures g that can be financed in this economy?
(d) Assume that $g = 1/16$. What is the optimal tax rate?
(e) Compare the welfare of the consumer under (d) to the case in which the government expenditure is financed by a lump sum tax of $1/16$ units.

2   Consider a two periods economy in which the government spending is $g_1 = 3/16$ in the first period and $g_2 = 0$ in the second period. Assume further that the representative consumer maximizes:

$$(1 - \tau_1)L_1 + (1 - \tau_2)L_2 - (L_1)^2 - (L_2)^2.$$

Thus, here $U(c, 1 - L) = c - L^2$ and $\beta = 1$.

(a) What are the constraints on the tax choice problem? (Assume zero interest rate.)
(b) Express the tradeoff that the government faces between τ_1 and τ_2.
(c) Find the optimal tax rates.

NOTES

1   Diamond and Mirrlees (1971) show that the presence of optimal commodity taxes implies the desirability of production efficiency even when full Pareto optimum cannot be achieved. The intermediate good result is a special case of this more general claim.
2   Thus if agent h had M_0^h "old dollars" then $m_{nb}^h = xM_0^h/P_0$, where x is the rate at which the central bank is willing to exchange old dollars for new dollars and P_0 is the price level in terms of new dollars.
3   This is one possible interpretation of the "real bills" doctrine.
4   The argument for smoothing the tax rate is thus similar to the argument for equating marginal cost across plants producing the same output.
5   To solve (6.47) and (6.48) we first use (6.47) to express all h_t in terms of h_1. Assuming $D_1 = \beta$, this is:
$h_2 = \beta h_1(1 + r_2) = h_1 \beta^2/D_2$
$h_3 = \beta h_2(1 + r_3) = \beta^2 h_1(1 + r_2) \times (1 + r_3) = h_1 \beta^3/D_3$
$h_4 = \beta h_3(1 + r_4) = h_1 \beta^4/D_4$
and so on. We now substitute these in (6.48) to get:
$2h_1 \sum_t \beta^t = \sum_t D_t$. This leads to $h_1 = (1/2)(\sum_t D_t)/(\sum_t \beta^t)$. When $\sum_t \beta^t = \sum_t D_t$ we get $h_1 = 1/2$.
6   In the square root utility case $f()$ is defined by (6.53) and $(1 + T)f() = h_t(1 + T)^{-1}$. In the log utility case, $f()$ is defined by (6.46) and $(1 + T)f() = h_t$. Thus, our square root example satisfies the assumption while the log utility case does not. This implies that the assumption made is stronger than required.

CHAPTER 7

Money and the Business Cycle: Does Money Matter?

In previous chapters we studied the effects of anticipated monetary and fiscal policies and our analysis had a long run flavor. We now turn to the short run and discuss fluctuations in economic activity. We start in this chapter with some history about the "does money matter" debate and then go into a description of the empirical short run relationship between money and output.

Friedman (1964) starts his discussion of the post-war trends in monetary theory and policy with the following statement:

> The post-war period has seen a dramatic change in the views of academic students of economics about monetary theory and of governmental officials about monetary policy. At the end of the war most professional economists and most governmental officials concerned with economic policy took it for granted that money did not matter, that it was a subject of minor importance. Since then there has been something of a counter-revolution in both theory and policy.

Tobin (1970) challenged the monetarist view of Friedman. He used a Keynesian type model to argue for the possibility of "reverse causation": Income may cause money rather than money causes income.

Sims (1980) compares the interwar (1920–41) to the postwar (1948–78) period using monthly data on money (M1), industrial production and wholesale prices. He uses vector auto regression (VAR) and finds a striking difference in the variances of the innovations between the two periods. Both money and output are much more volatile in the interwar period. In addition, he finds that once a short-term interest rate is added to the VAR, money (M1) becomes unimportant in the postwar period.

More recently, there has been a change in emphasis towards "real business cycle models". This literature, pioneered by Kydland and Prescott (1982), assumes that business cycles are efficient responses to changes in technology and other real variables exogenous to the private sector, like tax rates and government purchases. King and Plosser (1984) argue that "Given the controversies surrounding the main contending hypotheses concerning money and business cycles . . . it seems worthwhile to consider alternative hypotheses."

They find that inside money (money created by the banking sector) is more highly correlated with output than outside money and interpret this finding as supporting a real business cycle model in which fluctuations in inside money are efficient and money is caused by output. More recently Coleman (1996) estimated a real business cycle model with endogenous money and notes some important discrepancies between the implied behavior of money and output in the model and the behavior of money and output in the data.

Although it seems that the academic literature has gone back to the pre-Friedman postwar era, policy-makers did not. According to Friedman (1964), "The general presumption among most economists at the end of the war was that the post-war problem was going to be depression and unemployment . . . The appropriate monetary policy in their view was very simple. The monetary authorities should keep money plentiful so as to keep the interest rates low" (Friedman, 1969, p. 71). This is very different from the current emphasis on low inflation among central bankers.

It is possible that Friedman and Lucas' success in convincing the profession at large that money surprises are harmful led to a decline in the importance of money as a major cause of the business cycle. Indeed in a hypothetical world in which all central bankers follow Friedman's k% rule and increase the money supply at a constant rate, there will be no correlation between money and output.

Even if money is becoming unimportant, it may be potentially important. We would like to know what are the effects of changes in policy even if in practice the central bank is following a relatively predictable and transparent policy. This motivated a literature, reviewed in Christiano, Eichenbaum and Evans (CEE, 1999), which studies the effects of monetary policy shocks not because these shocks are currently large but because they can help in assessing the empirical plausibility of structural economic models that can be used to think about changes in monetary policy.

The literature reviewed in CEE (1999) focuses on policy shocks and finds a surprising agreement about the effects of such shocks. There is also an agreement about the undesirability of "policy shocks": No one advocates the creation of money surprises by "policy mistakes." There is much less consensus about the effects and desirability of inside money surprises. Friedman argued for eliminating inside money by imposing 100% reserve requirements (Friedman, 1960). As was mentioned before, King and Plosser (1984) think of fluctuations in inside money as efficient responses to changes in technology. It is therefore important to study the effects of inside money surprises as well as outside money surprises on real variables.

Here we use the vector auto regression (VAR) impulse response analysis to study the rather complex relationship between output and money. We do our own VAR analysis rather than reporting the results in the literature because we are adding the stock of inventories to the list of variables.

Of course, VAR analysis is not the only way of studying the money–output relationship. For example, Friedman and Schwartz (1963) looked at specific historical episodes and more recently Romer and Romer (1989) and Boschen and Mills (1995) developed measures of the tightness of monetary policy by examining policy records directly. For an excellent review of the various approaches to the study of the money–output relationship see Walsh (1998).

7.1   VAR AND IMPULSE RESPONSE FUNCTIONS: AN EXAMPLE

A vector auto regression (VAR) is a system of ordinary least square regressions, in which each variable is regressed on lagged values of all the variables in the system (including its own lag values). The use of VAR in Macroeconomics, pioneered by Sims (1980), has been proven to be a convenient way of summarizing the dynamic relationships among variables. Here is a one lag two variables example.

Let y denote output and x a policy variable like the money supply or the federal funds rate. We start by assuming that the central bank reacts to the one period lags of y and x according to:

$$x_t = b_y y_{t-1} + b_x x_{t-1} + e_{xt}, \tag{7.1}$$

where b_y and b_x are coefficients and e_{xt} is a policy error. Output depends on the "money surprise" term e_x and the lags of y and x according to:

$$y_t = a_y y_{t-1} + a_x x_{t-1} + \theta e_{xt} + e_{yt}, \tag{7.2}$$

where a_i and θ are coefficients and e_{yt} is an error term due to supply shocks. The inclusion of the "money surprise" term in (7.2) can be justified by the discussion in chapter 1 on the natural rate hypothesis and by rational expectations models pioneered by Lucas (1972) that will be discussed later. The lags of y and x may capture technology and the quantities of fixed factors like capital and the number of employees that cannot be easily fired.

To estimate the effect of policy shocks on output, we run (7.1) and

$$y_t = c_1 y_{t-1} + c_2 x_{t-1} + c_3 x_t + s_t, \tag{7.3}$$

where c_i are coefficients and s is an error term. Substituting (7.1) into (7.3) and equating it to (7.2) yields:

$$c_1 + c_3 b_y = a_y; \quad c_2 + c_3 b_x = a_x; \quad c_3 = \theta; \quad s_t = e_{yt}. \tag{7.4}$$

Since we estimate the b coefficients by running (7.1), and the c coefficients by running (7.3), we have in (7.4), 3 equations in 3 unknowns. We can thus solve for all the coefficients. The intuition is that when lag variables are in the regression, the information added by the contemporaneous level of x_t is information about the error term e_{xt}. Therefore running (7.3) is equivalent to running (7.2).

It may be useful to think of the regression (7.3) as if it is done in two stages. In the first stage we run (7.1) and calculate the error term e_{xt}. We then use the calculated error term to run (7.2).

Calculating the impulse response functions

We keep all past and future error terms constant (say at the level of zero) but change only the realization of e_{xt} by σ units where σ is the estimated standard deviation of e_{xt}.

By construction,

$$\Delta y_t = \theta \sigma; \quad \Delta x_t = \sigma, \tag{7.5}$$

where Δ denotes the change from the initial path of current and future values of y and x. The changes (7.5) imply the following changes at $t + 1$:

$$\Delta y_{t+1} = a_y \theta \sigma + a_x \sigma; \quad \Delta x_{t+1} = b_y \theta \sigma + b_x \sigma; \tag{7.6}$$

The changes (7.6) imply the following changes at $t + 2$:

$$\Delta y_{t+2} = a_y (a_y \theta \sigma + a_x \sigma) + a_x (b_y \theta \sigma + b_x \sigma)$$
$$\Delta x_{t+2} = b_y (a_y \theta \sigma + a_x \sigma) + b_x (b_y \theta \sigma + b_x \sigma) \tag{7.7}$$

and so on.

The identification problem

Suppose that instead of (7.1) and (7.2) we have the more general model:

$$x_t = b_y y_{t-1} + b_x x_{t-1} + e_{xt} + \phi e_{yt}; \tag{7.8}$$
$$y_t = a_y y_{t-1} + a_x x_{t-1} + e_{yt} + \theta e_{xt}, \tag{7.9}$$

where ϕ is a parameter. Here everything affects everything: Shocks to policy affect output and shocks to output affect policy.

In this case, if we repeat the previous procedure (substituting [7.8] in [7.3] and equating it to [7.9]) we will get:

$$c_1 + c_3 b_y = a_y; \quad c_2 + c_3 b_x = a_x; \quad e_{yt} + \theta e_{xt} = c_3 (e_{xt} + \phi e_{yt}) + s_t. \tag{7.10}$$

This is no longer identified because (7.10) is three equations in four unknowns. Because of this identification problem we must take a stand about which variable is not affected by the contemporaneous shock. The monetarist view typically assumes that "money is exogenous" and therefore it is not affected by the shock to output. The reverse causation hypothesis assumes the opposite.

We may explain the difficulty in terms of the two-stage procedure. If we run (7.8) and compute the residuals we will now get an estimate of $e_{xt} + \phi e_{yt}$ which is no longer a pure policy shock. We cannot therefore use these residuals as a proxy for e_{xt} in the second stage.

In practice the assumption about which contemporaneous variables are allowed to have an effect on each variable in the system is reflected in the ordering of the VAR variables. For example, if we run three variables VAR with the ordering: x, y, z. Then x does not depend on any of the contemporaneous variables (it does depend however on the past realizations of the three variables), y depends on the contemporaneous realization of x but not on the contemporaneous realization of z, and z depends on the contemporaneous realizations of both x and y. Accordingly, an "x innovation" is the part of the contemporaneous realization of x which cannot be explained by the past realizations of the variables in the system, a "y innovation" is the part of the contemporaneous realization of y which cannot be explained by the past realizations of the variables in the system and by the contemporaneous realization of x and a "z innovation" is the part of the contemporaneous realization of z which cannot be explained by the past realizations of the variables in the system and by the contemporaneous realizations of both x and y.

When we choose the order x, y, z we assume the following system:

$$x_t = b_y y_{t-1} + b_x x_{t-1} + b_z z_{t-1} + e_{xt}; \tag{7.11}$$

$$y_t = a_y y_{t-1} + a_x x_{t-1} + a_z z_{t-1} + \theta e_{xt} + e_{yt}; \tag{7.12}$$

$$z_t = c_y y_{t-1} + c_x x_{t-1} + c_z z_{t-1} + \lambda e_{xt} + \alpha e_{yt} + e_{zt}. \tag{7.13}$$

Again, it may be useful to think of the estimation of (7.11)–(7.13) as if it is done in three steps. In the first step we run (7.11) and estimate the parameters b and the residuals, e_{xt}. We then use these residuals to run (7.12) and estimate the parameters a and the residuals e_{yt}. Finally, we use the residuals e_{xt} and e_{yt} to run (7.13).

Note that the specification (7.11)–(7.13) does not allow the error terms e_{yt} and e_{zt} to affect x_t. It does not allow the error term e_{zt} to have an effect on y_t. In this sense we can view these assumption as identification restrictions. Of course, if the true model does not satisfy these restrictions then we will be misled by the estimated impulse response functions. For example, the response to an x shock will no longer give us a description of the effects of unanticipated changes in monetary policy.

7.2   USING VAR IMPULSE RESPONSE ANALYSIS TO ASSESS THE MONEY–OUTPUT RELATIONSHIP

We will now use impulse response functions to examine two competing hypotheses: (a) money has a positive effect on output and (b) output has a positive effect on money. The first hypothesis may be labeled the monetarist view while the second hypothesis may be labeled the reverse causation view.

The above two hypotheses are not identical to the hypotheses (a') money cause output and (b') output cause money, where causation is in the Granger (1969) sense. The difference is that we are not looking only at the explanatory power but also at the direction of the effect. For example, output may cause money in the Granger sense but the effect of output on money may be negative, reflecting an attempt of the Fed to stabilize the economy. In this case, hypothesis (b') is not rejected but hypothesis (b) is rejected.

As was said before, Sims (1972, 1980) analyzed the Granger causality questions. The reverse causality hypothesis was suggested by, among others, Tobin (1970), King and Plosser (1984) and Coleman (1996). Coleman (1996) tests the possibility of various channels of reverse causality. For example, suppose agents choose more deposits relative to currency as interest rates rise, and high output growth is associated with rising interest rates. Then a rise in output can cause an increase in M1. Another channel of reverse causation may occur when a rise in output is associated with a high demand of firms for investment goods and a low demand by firms for cash. Coleman estimates a structural model and finds some support for the monetarist view against the reverse causation view.

Most of the recent literature has focused on M1 and even narrower definitions of money. Friedman and Schwartz (1963) use M2. Here we adopt the point of view that all assets provide some liquidity and allow for a vector of monetary aggregates to represent the theoretical concept of "money". See chapter 1 in Mishkin (2003) for a nice discussion of the alternative measures of money which takes into account the recent extensive financial innovations and

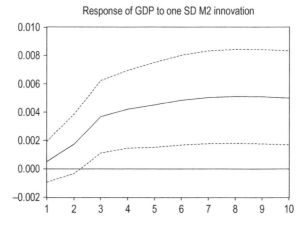

Figure 7.1   List of variables in the VAR: M2, GDP, PPIALL

Barnett, Offenbacher and Spindt (1981) for a discussion on the degree of "moneyness" in various monetary aggregates.

We use quarterly US national product and income account (NIPA) data from 1964:3–1995:2. All variables are in log form except for the rate of interest. All VARs have four lags.

We start with a three variables (four lags) VAR: A broad definition of money (M2), real gross domestic product (GDP) and a producer price index (PPIALL).[1] The ordering here is consistent with Hume's (1752) description: Money surprises affect output and prices and output surprises affect prices.

Figure 7.1 describes the response of GDP to a one standard deviation innovation in M2. The solid line is the predicted impulse response and the dashed lines describe the confidence interval (± 2 SE) of the impulse response function. The change in GDP from the base line is on the vertical axis and the time (number of quarters) is on the horizontal axis. Since GDP is in logs the units of the vertical axis are in percentage points.

As can be seen the effect of money on output is statistically significant and takes a long time: It does not die out after two years. We get a rather standard hump shape response with the maximal response of about 0.5% occurring after a year.

Figure 7.2 describes the response of M2 to a one standard deviation innovation in GDP. (Here GDP is ordered first in accordance with the hypothesis that money is caused by output). As can be seen, the response is not significantly different from zero. Figures 7.1 and 7.2 thus support the monetarist view against the reverse causation view.

We now add to the VAR a narrow definition of money (M1) and the non-borrowed reserves (NBR) held by banks. Non-borrowed reserves were used by Christiano, Eichenbaum, and Evans (1999) as one of the candidates for the instruments which are directly used by the Fed to conduct monetary policy. By running the monetary aggregates in the order NBR, M1, M2 we get the effect of each additional component. Thus an innovation to M1 is an innovation that occurred "after" the innovation to NBR. Similarly, an innovation to M2 occurs "after" the innovation to M1 and is therefore a surprise increase in the "liquid interest bearing accounts" which do not enter the M1 definition but enter the M2 definition.

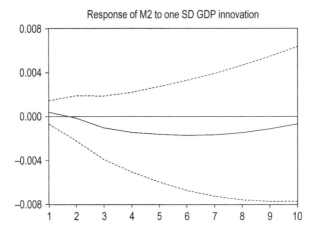

Figure 7.2 List of variables in the VAR: GDP, M2, PPIALL

Figure 7.3 is broadly consistent with the monetarist view. All three monetary aggregates have a positive effect on output except for a short period in which NBR may have a negative effect. Figure 7.4 is not consistent with the reverse causation hypothesis. Output has either an insignificant or a negative effect on the three monetary aggregates. Thus, a VAR analysis with the variables (NBR, M1, M2, GDP, PPIALL) also supports the monetarist view.

Figures 7.5 and 7.6 use the federal fund rate (FF) instead of NBR as a candidate for the policy instrument. Figure 7.5 suggests that the role of innovations to M1 that do not affect FF is negligible. The effect of M2 however, is not. The impulse response function that describes the effect of an M2 shock, looks about the same as in the previous case when NBR were used. Figure 7.6 shows a significant positive effect of FF to innovation in GDP but either negative or insignificant effect on the monetary aggregates. This picture is not consistent with the reverse causation view. It looks like the Fed is following a tight monetary policy in response to an innovation in GDP and this tight monetary policy has a negative effect on M1 but no effect on M2.

Marginal contributions

Since M_i is defined as M_{i-1} + "additional accounts" (for example: $M_2 = M_1$ + liquid time deposit type accounts) we can see if innovations in the "additional accounts" have an effect on output by running a VAR with both M_i and M_{i-1}. For this purpose, we ran the following VAR: (NBR, M0, M1, M2, M3, GDP, PPIALL), where the new variable M0 is the monetary base. Figure 7.7 reports impulse response functions without the confidence bands. In the upper graph of figure 7.7 we have the response of GDP to one standard deviation innovation in M1, M2, M3 (in that order). These impulse response functions suggest that innovations to all three monetary aggregates have an effect on output but innovations to M2 have the largest effect.

In the middle graph of figure 7.7 we compare the effect of an NBR innovation to the effect of an M2 innovation on GDP. The effect of an M2 innovation is somewhat larger. Note that

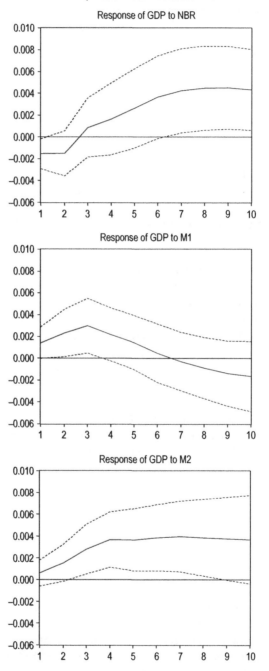

Response to one SD innovations ± 2 SE

Response of GDP to NBR

Response of GDP to M1

Response of GDP to M2

Figure 7.3   List of variables in the VAR: NBR, M1, M2, GDP, PPIALL

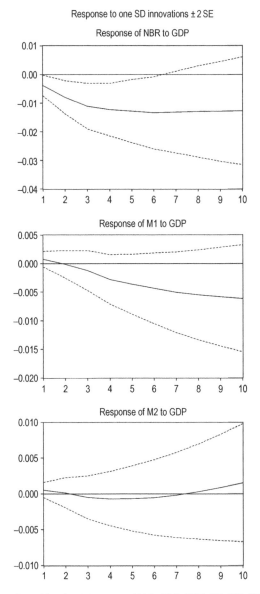

Figure 7.4 List of variables in the VAR: GDP, NBR, M1, M2, PPIALL

this is the effect of an innovation to M2 after the current innovations to (NBR, M0, M1) have already occurred. In the bottom graph of figure 7.7 we compare the effects of an NBR shock to the effect of an M1 shock. The effect of an M1 shock is larger in the first two quarters, but then becomes smaller than the effect of an NBR shock.

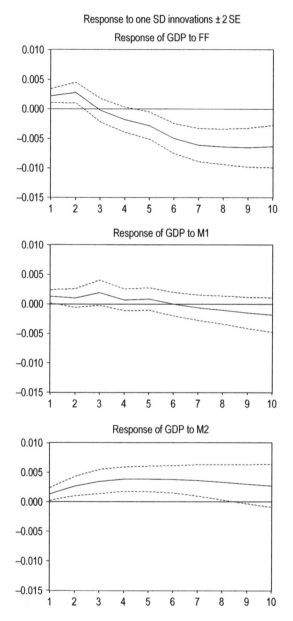

Response to one SD innovations ± 2 SE

Figure 7.5   List of variables in the VAR: FF, M1, M2, GDP, PPIALL

Conclusions

When we run a VAR with monetary variables, real output and a price index, we see that innovations to M2 have a significant and positive effect on output and this effect lasts for more than two years. But innovations to output do not affect M2. Thus M2 behaves according to

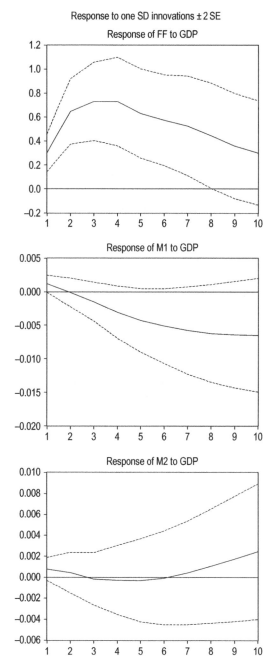

Figure 7.6   List of variables in the VAR: GDP, FF, M1, M2, PPIALL

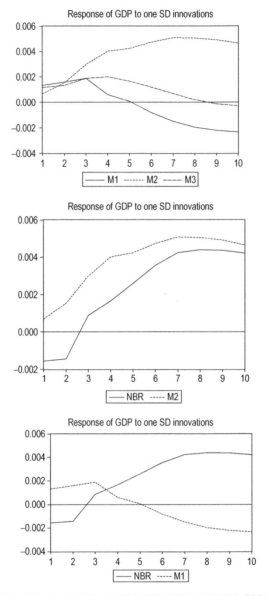

Figure 7.7   List of variables in the VAR: NBR, M0, M1, M2, M3, GDP, PPIALL

the monetarist view.[2] As was argued by Sims (1980), the behavior of M1 is not robust to the introduction of a short-term interest rate.

We did not show the effect of various innovations on prices. This is going to be our next task.

7.3 SPECIFICATION SEARCH

According to the classical view, we should come to the data with an hypothesis and test it. We should not look at the data, then formulate an hypothesis and then test it on the same data set. In practice, researchers often go to the data set with an hypothesis which is then modified as a result of looking at the data. This interaction between theory and data is useful because it is not always the case that you can find a reasonable specification that supports your hypothesis.

A good example for the interaction between theory and data is in the solution to the "price puzzle." It was observed that when FF is ordered first, an FF innovation that is interpreted as a contractory policy shock, has a positive effect on prices. This contradicted the prior of many economists and it was therefore suggested that the Fed might be reacting to contemporaneous information. For example, the Fed may be reacting to contemporaneous information about prices. When the FF variable was ordered after output and prices, the anomalous result disappeared. In their first benchmark system Christiano, Eichenbaum and Evans (1999) assumed that the Fed has information about current and four lagged values of GDP, the implicit GDP deflator (P), an index of commodity prices (PCOM) as well as four lagged values of FF, NBR, TR, and M1, where TR are total reserves. Using this specification they found that after two quarters there is a sustained decline in real GDP and the GDP deflator is flat for roughly a year and a half after which it declines.

The "price puzzle"

To illustrate the "price puzzle" and its resolution, we ran a VAR with the following variables: (FF, M1, M2, PCOM, GDP, PPIALL) in that order. The impulse response functions in figure 7.8 describe the effects of a shock to the monetary variables (FF, M1, M2) on GDP (in the upper graph) and on PPIALL (in the lower graph). As can be seen, the effects of M1 and M2 are roughly consistent with our prior. Both indicate an increase in GDP and in PPIALL. But the effects of an FF shock are not consistent with our prior. As can be expected from a contractional monetary shock an FF shock has a largely negative effect on output, but its effect on prices is positive. Figure 7.9 allows for the possibility that the Fed has information about all the contemporaneous variables by ordering FF last. The impulse response functions in figure 7.9, correspond better to our initial priors.[3]

Inventories

The impulse response functions suggest a long lasting effect of money surprises. We therefore need a propagation mechanism: Something that is affected by the current money surprise shock but unlike the surprise itself, the effect does not evaporate immediately.

One possible way of getting persistence is via inventories. A surprise increase in money increases sales and lowers inventories. Output then goes up to rebuild inventories. To see if the data lend support to this propagation mechanism we added the log of the end of period real stock of inventories (I) to the list of variables and ran a VAR with the following variables: M1,

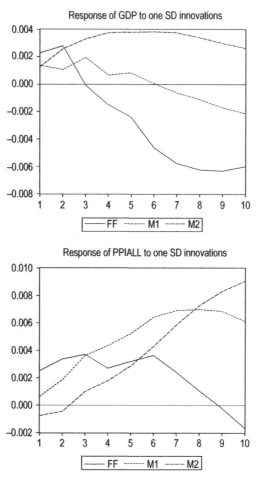

Figure 7.8   List of variables in the VAR: FF, M1, M2, PCOM, GDP, PPIALL

M2, PCOM, GDP, I, PPIALL, FF, in that order. The introduction of inventories does make a difference. The magnitude of the effect of M2 and FF shocks on output has been drastically reduced. Comparing figure 7.10 with figure 7.9 reveals that the maximal effect of these shocks is about a half of what they were without inventories. The impulse response functions in figure 7.10 suggest that inventories increase in response to an FF shock and then decline (after about 4 quarters). A similar pattern (in the opposite direction) is observed for an M1 shock. Inventories do not move in response to an M2 shock and then increase. This suggests that the inventories money output relationships are rather complex or that our specification is not correct.

The effects of shocks to (GDP, I, PPIALL) on the monetary variables are described in figure 7.11 that gives the impulse response functions when running (GDP, I, PPIALL) first. From figure 7.11 we note that: (a) M1 and M2 are not increasing in response to a GDP shock; (b) FF responds positively to a GDP shock and negatively to an inventories shock and

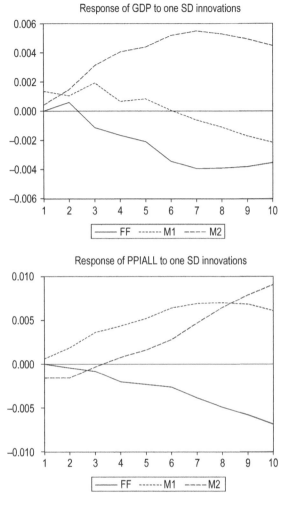

Figure 7.9   List of variables in the VAR: M1, M2, PCOM, GDP, PPIALL, FF

(c) After a short lag M2 responds positively to an inventories shock. The first observation is not consistent with our version of reverse causality. The second observation suggests that the Fed views an increase in inventories as a sign of recession and conducts a policy of "leaning against the wind". The positive effect of a I shock on M2 raises the possibility that after an inventories surprise, firms get more credit because banks use inventories as a collateral. This line of argument is related to the "credit channel" of the monetary transmission mechanism. See for example, Bernanke and Gertler (1995) and Kiyotaki and Moore (1997).

Prices

In figure 7.10 we saw that prices react to an M1 innovation but do not react much to an M2 innovation or an FF innovation. To see whether this result is robust and to examine the

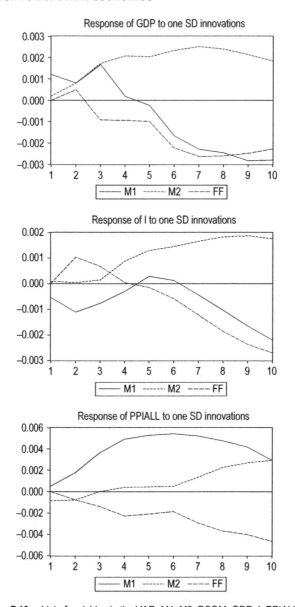

Figure 7.10   List of variables in the VAR: M1, M2, PCOM, GDP, I, PPIALL, FF

effect of inventories on prices, we add to the above VAR three price indices, the GDP deflator (P), the PPI for industrial production (PPIINDUST) and the PPI for services (PPISERV). Using the order: (M1, M2, PCOM, GDP, I, P, PPIALL, PPIINDUST, PPISERV, FF), figure 7.12 describes the responses of prices to shocks in I, M1, M2 and FF.

Note that prices respond negatively to an inventories shock. This is consistent with the view that sellers reduce prices when the level of inventories goes up. The effect of an inventories

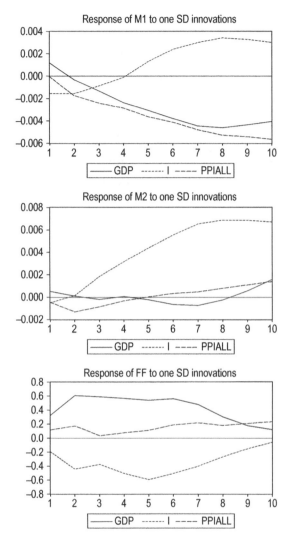

Figure 7.11   List of variables in the VAR: GDP, I, PPIALL, M1, M2, PCOM, FF

shock is relatively large. It is larger in absolute value than the effect of an FF and an M2 shock and about the same order of magnitude as the effect of an M1 shock.

Note also that an M1 shock has a larger effect on prices than an M2 shock. Since an M1 shock has a smaller effect on output, this is consistent with the view that an output effect occurs in the absence of a price effect, which goes back to Hume (1752).

The Fed reaction function

The Fed policy may neutralize the effect of a variable. To illustrate this assertion, let us assume that the Fed follows the simple rule: $M_t = \lambda M_{t-1} + \varepsilon_t$, where the shock ε_t is due to "policy

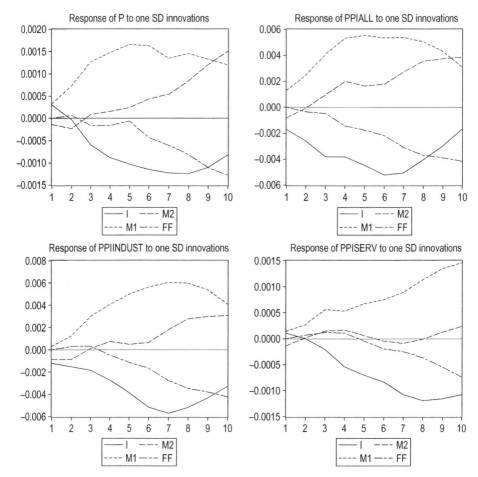

Figure 7.12   List of variables in the VAR: M1, M2, PCOM, GDP, I, P, PPIALL, PPIINDUST, PPISERV, FF

mistakes" and is assumed to be i.i.d. Let us further assume that in this case there is a strong and persistent effect of an M innovation on real output.

But what happens if the Fed can and wants to minimize output fluctuations? For example, assume that the Fed observes ε with a one period lag and the agents in the economy observe ε after a longer lag. Then after observing a large realization of ε, the Fed may want to choose a lower money supply growth. This error correction type behavior may reduce the effect of an M shock in a VAR impulse response analysis. We may reach the conclusion that money is not important in spite of the fact that it is potentially important.

It is therefore important to know the Fed reaction function. To estimate it we run the following VAR: M1, M2, PCOM, GDP, I, PPIALL, FF (in that order). The impulse response functions which describe the effects of shocks to the variables in the system on the policy variable FF are in figure 7.13. As can be seen, the Fed is reacting to innovations in M1, PCOM, GDP and I, but does not seem to react to innovations in M2 and PPIALL.

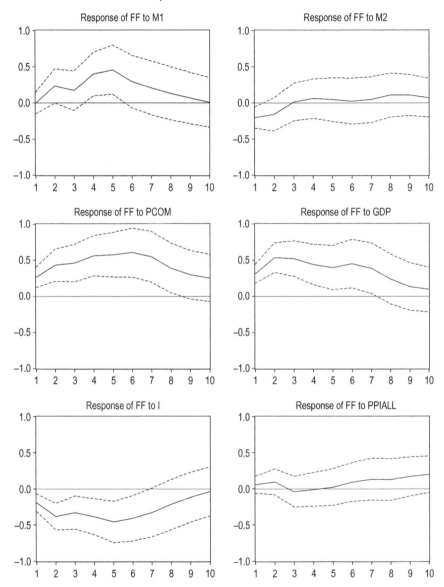

Figure 7.13   List of variables in the VAR: M1, M2, PCOM, GDP, I, PPIALL, FF

The Fed reaction may explain in part why the effect of an M2 shock on output is larger than the effect of an M1 shock on output. The reason is that the Fed successfully neutralizes the effect of an M1 shock. Similarly, a contractionary monetary shock is expected to increase inventories. But this effect is not strong in the data because the Fed is lowering the interest rate in response to an increase in inventories.

Conclusions

We used VAR impulse response analysis to get a sense of the response of real variables to a surprise change in monetary variables. Here are the main findings for the specification: M1, M2, PCOM, GDP, I, PPIALL, FF.

1 Innovations in monetary variables have an initial effect on output in the predicted direction.
2 Innovations to M2 have a relatively large effect on output.
3 The monetary aggregates M1 and M2 do not increase in response to an output shock.
4 Adding inventories to the VAR system reduces the magnitude of the effects of an FF shock and an M2 shock on output: The maximal effect is reduced by close to 50%.
5 At first, prices do not react much to an FF shock and to an M2 shock but they do react to an M1 shock and to an inventories shock.
6 M2 increases in response to an inventories shock after a lag of one to two quarters.
7 Inventories increase initially in response to an FF shock and decrease initially in response to an M1 shock but these effects are small.
8 The Fed reacts to shocks in M1, PCOM, GDP and I but does not seem to react to shocks in M2 and prices.

We should note that the Fed is trying to neutralize the effects of M1 on output and inventories. In the absence of the Fed intervention we may witness a stronger effect of M1 on output and inventories.

We should also note that prices do not appear rigid. They respond to some shocks and do not respond to other shocks.

Finally, my own prior is that a money shock should have a positive effect on both output and prices and a negative effect on inventories. M1 fits this prior. M2 does not: Innovations to M2 have a positive effect on output after a long lag and no immediate effect on prices and inventories. This may suggest that there are important elements in M2 that are not "money".

7.4 VARIANCE DECOMPOSITION

We have not answered the question in the title of this chapter. According to one possible interpretation of the question, money does not matter if you can forecast real GDP without paying attention to nominal variables (GDP may then be defined as purely exogenous). To examine this rather extreme hypothesis we may look at the variance decomposition of the system. The variance decomposition measures the percentage of the k period ahead forecast error explained by the innovation of each variable. For example, if we have two variables M and Y and innovation in M are completely unimportant for explaining innovations in Y then the variance decomposition of the Y equation will show 0% for M and 100% for Y. (This says that innovation in Y are explained by innovations in Y). If on the other hand we get 50% for M and 50% for Y, it means that innovations in M explain 50% of the variance of the innovations in Y.

In figure 7.14 we have the variance decomposition for the list of variables: M1, M2, PCOM, GDP, PPIALL, FF. If money does not matter we should observe that the GDP line is close

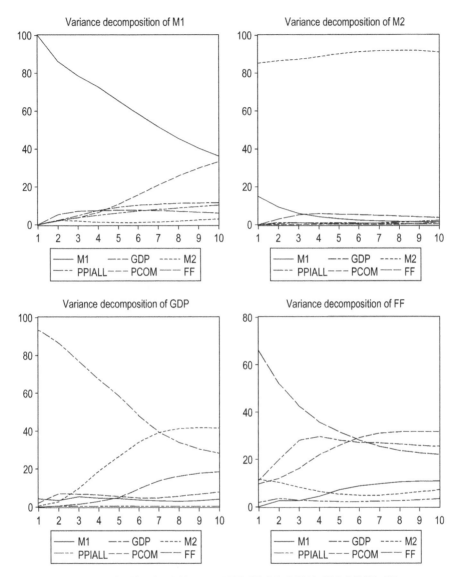

Figure 7.14   List of variables in the VAR: M1, M2, PCOM, GDP, PPIALL, FF

to the 100% level and the lines that describe the contributions of the rest of the variables are close to zero. This is not the case when looking at the variance decomposition of GDP. The variance decomposition of M2 shows that most of the innovations in M2 are not explained by innovations in other variables and therefore M2 is largely "exogenous".

In figure 7.15 we add inventories to the list of variables which is now: M1, M2, PCOM, GDP, I, PPIALL, FF. The main effect is that inventories reduce the importance of M2 innovations in forecasting GDP and reduce the percentage of the forecasting error of M2 which can be explained by its own innovation – the "exogeneity" of M2.

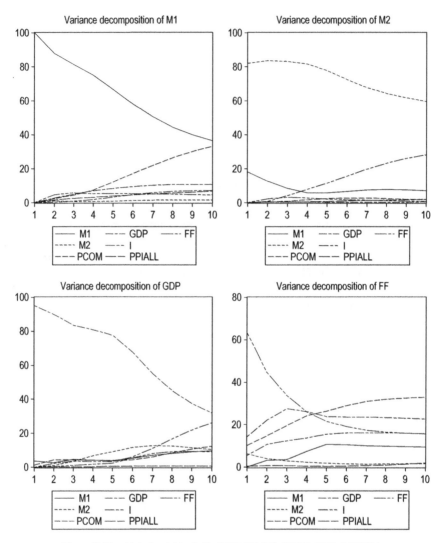

Figure 7.15 List of variables in the VAR: M1, M2, PCOM, GDP, I, PPIALL

We should note that most of the explained variance of I is due to GDP and I: Both account for more than 80% of the variance. We may therefore think of inventories as largely independent of the nominal variables in the system.

The effect of the inclusion of inventories in the system on the explanatory power of the monetary variables is described in table 7.1. As can be seen the inclusion of inventories reduces the explanatory power of both M2 and FF. The reduction in the explanatory power of M2 is most dramatic. After 8 quarters, M2 innovations account for 41% of the explained variance of GDP when inventories are not in the system. When inventories are in the system M2 innovations account for only 12%. The total explanatory power of the monetary variables is reduced by about 50% as a result of the inclusion of inventories.

Table 7.1 The contribution of the monetary variables to the explanation of GDP

	M1	M2	FF	Total
Without inventories				
After 4 quarters	4.7	18.7	2.9	26.3
After 8 quarters	2.9	41.3	16.1	60.3
With inventories				
After 4 quarters	4.1	6.5	1.6	12.2
After 8 quarters	8.0	12.4	9.1	29.1

Table 7.2 The contribution of real variables to the explanation of GDP

	GDP	I	Total
Without inventories			
After 4 quarters	67.3	0	67.3
After 8 quarters	33.9	0	33.9
With inventories			
After 4 quarters	80.7	3.1	83.8
After 8 quarters	44.9	16.5	61.4

Table 7.3 The contribution of the monetary variables to the explanation of I

	M1	M2	FF	Total
After 4 quarters	1.6	0.57	1.1	3.3
After 8 quarters	1.2	3.7	5.4	10.3

We may say that when inventories are not in the system, M2 innovations look like a dream monetarist variable: They explain a large chunk of the GDP variance and appear to be largely exogenous. When inventories are included M2 innovations explain less and appear to be less exogenous.

Which variables gained in explanatory power as a result of the inclusion of inventories? The price variable PPIALL contributes less than a percentage with and without inventories. The average contribution of PCOM (average across the forecasting horizons) does not change much with the introduction of inventories: It is about 6%. As can be seen from table 7.2, the main change occurs in the contribution of the real variables: GDP itself and inventories.

It is possible that inventories are a propagation mechanism for monetary shocks. According to this view, monetary variables have a persistent effect on output because they affect inventories. At the extreme we may attribute all of the explanatory power of inventories to monetary variables. However, this does not seem plausible in view of the low contribution of the monetary variables in explaining the inventories variance (table 7.3).

In the chapters about uncertain and sequential trade (UST) we will explore the possibility that fluctuations in inventories occur because of both demand and supply shocks and monetary shocks are only one reason for demand shocks.

Conclusions

Monetary shocks have a positive effect on output but the magnitude of the effect becomes much smaller once the stock of inventories is added to the list of variables.

We may also say that inventories play an important role in the system. We should therefore concentrate our effort in understanding the dynamic relationship between money, output and inventories.

PROBLEMS

1   Add employment and capital in the goods producing sector (EMPGOODS, KGOODS) to the list of variables and run a VAR with the following order: M1, M2, PCOM, KGOODS, EMPGOODS, GDP, I, PPIALL, FF.

(a) Does the introduction of the two additional variables change the main conclusions?
(b) Do inventories behave like the inputs (KGOODS, EMPGOODS)?

2   Find data from another country and try to answer the question in the title of this chapter.

NOTES

1   Roughly speaking, M1 = cash + demand deposits + some other checkable deposits + traveler checks; M2 = M1 + some less liquid interest bearing accounts; M_3 = M_2 + less liquid interest bearing accounts. For complete definitions see: www.stls.frb.org/fred/data/monetary.html.
2   It is possible of course that M2 reacts passively to information received by the agents that is not in the lagged variables of our system, but it is not easy to test this hypothesis.
3   In figure 7.9 M1 and M2 are still ordered first. When ordering these monetary aggregates last (after FF) we get a negative effect of an M1 innovation on output.

CHAPTER 8

Sticky Prices in a Demand-satisfying Model

The nominal quantity of money is not important: It does not matter if we carry on business in terms of dollars or cents. A monetary reform, which aims only at changing the unit of account by introducing say a "new dollar" equal to say 1,000 "old dollars," will have no effect, if all nominal magnitudes (including prices) are also divided by 1,000.

But changes in the nominal quantity of money are important. Why do changes in something that is not important become important? We discuss this question in the following chapters.

In his Nobel lecture Lucas (1996) provides an excellent survey of the answers that have been proposed starting with Hume's 1752 essays. Hume did understand that changes in the money supply do not have real effects in the long run because these are just changes in the unit of account. But Hume did not apply the same argument to the short run. Hume assumed that prices do not change immediately after an increase in the money supply. Those who got the new money face the same prices and just spend more. As a result sellers sell more and this make them produce more. In Hume's own words:

> When the quantity of money is imported into a nation, it is not at first dispersed into many hands but is confined to the coffers of a few persons ... [The artisan] carries his money to market, where he finds everything at the same price as formerly, but returns with greater quantity ... The farmer and gardner, finding that all their commodities are taken off, apply themselves with alacrity to raising more. (p. 38)

There are two difficulties in Hume's story. First, as Lucas points out, it is not clear why sellers who expect prices to rise do not increase their price immediately. Second, why are sellers selling more in response to a higher demand and why does success in selling induce more production? Under the standard formulation of a competitive environment sellers can sell as much as they want and produce more only in response to an increase in the price of their product or to changes in the cost of production.

In the spirit of Hume, Keynesian models assume that (a) prices do not adjust immediately to changes in the money supply and (b) there is a commitment on the part of the firm to supply any quantity demanded at the not fully adjusted price.

Patinkin (1965, ch. 13), Clower (1965) and Barro and Grossman (1971) question the second assumption. They argued that since trade is voluntary, the quantity transacted is the minimum between supply and demand. Subsequent literature chose to focus on the question of price determination paying little or no attention to the disequilibrium literature.

The literature pioneered by Gray (1976, 1978) and Fischer (1977, 1979) assumed that prices are set in advance at the expected market-clearing level and firms satisfy demand at this price. Phelps and Taylor (1977) and McCallum (1989, ch. 10.2) assumed that prices rather than wages are set at the expected market-clearing level.

The more recent "new Keynesian" literature has considered a monopolistically competitive environment in which the price is a choice variable. Also in this literature firms satisfy demand at their not fully adjusted prices. For some important contributions to this literature, see Akerlof and Yellen (1985), Svensson (1986), Blanchard and Kiyotaki (1987), Clarida, Gali and Gertler (1999) and Woodford (2003, ch. 3).

Here we present a simple model which is in the spirit of the "New Keynesian Economics". In this model prices are chosen optimally whenever a price choice is made. In the next chapter we will consider sticky price models in which both prices and quantities are chosen optimally.

The model

This model is based on the work of Blanchard and Kiyotaki (1987) and Woodford (2003, ch. 3). They assume that money is in the utility function. Here we use a cash-in-advance model. The model is designed to highlight the effect of money on real output and assumes self employed workers ("yeoman farmers"). For a model that distinguishes between workers and firms see chapter 16.

There is a large number of N infinitely lived households, where a household is a worker/shopper pair. The shopper takes the available cash and spends all of it. The worker produces and sells his output for cash. At the end of the period both members of the household reunite and consume whatever the shopper has bought.

Each household produces one differentiated good and consumes all goods. Normalizing $N = 1$, the single period utility function is of the Dixit-Stiglitz (1977) type:

$$\left[\sum_{j=0}^{1} (y_j)^\gamma \right]^{1/\gamma} - \upsilon(L), \tag{8.1}$$

where $0 < \gamma < 1, \upsilon(L) = (1/\delta)L^\delta$ and $\delta > 1$.

Household i starts the period with m_i normalized dollars and gets a transfer of x normalized dollars, where a normalized dollar is the beginning of the period money supply.[1] The amount of transfer x is an i.i.d. random variable with a density function $\phi(x)$. It is assumed that $\beta - 1 \le x \le g$ so the money growth rate cannot be below the Friedman rule.[2]

The buyer takes the normalized prices $(p_0, \ldots, p_1)$ as given and spends the entire available amount of $m_i + x$ normalized dollars on all goods. Buyer i solves:

$$\max_{y_j} \left[\sum_{j=0}^{1} (y_j)^\gamma \right]^{1/\gamma} \quad \text{s.t.} \quad \sum_{j=0}^{1} p_j y_j = m_i + x. \tag{8.2}$$

The first order conditions for the buyer's problem (8.2) are:

$$y_j = y_1(p_j/p_1)^\theta, \tag{8.3}$$

where $\theta = 1/(\gamma-1) < 0$. We now substitute (8.3) in the budget constraint ($\sum_j p_j y_j = m_i + x$) to get:

$$y_1 = (m_i + x)(p_1)^\theta / \sum_j (p_j)^{1+\theta}. \tag{8.4}$$

Using $z = 1/\sum_j (p_j)^{1+\theta}$ and symmetry, household's i demand for product j is $y_j = z(p_j)^\theta(m_i + x)$ and his utility from consumption is:

$$F(m_i + x, p_{-i}, p_i) = \left\{ \sum_j \left[(m_i + x)z(p_j)^\theta \right]^\gamma \right\}^{1/\gamma}, \tag{8.5}$$

where $p_{-i} = (p_0, \ldots, p_{i-1}, p_{i+1}, \ldots, p_1)$ is the prices posted by other sellers. Since there are many agents the effect of any single price on F is small and will be neglected. We therefore write $F(m + x, p_{-i})$ instead of $F(m + x, p_{-i}, p_i)$.

Our normalization implies $\sum_j m_j = 1$. Nominal spending per household is therefore $1 + x$ and the aggregate demand for product i is:

$$y_i = z(p_i)^\theta \sum_j (m_j + x) = z(p_i)^\theta(1 + x). \tag{8.6}$$

Using the aggregate demand (8.6), we compute next period's balances (in terms of next period's normalized dollars):[3]

$$m' = p_i y_i/(1 + x) = z(p_i)^{1+\theta}. \tag{8.7}$$

Note that next period's (normalized) money does not depend on x. It depends only on the relative price: $(p_i)^{1+\theta} / \sum_j (p_j)^{1+\theta}$.

The individual seller takes p_{-i} and z as given and assumes that the normalized prices charged by others will not change over time. He chooses his price p_i by solving the following Bellman's equation:

$$V(m; p_{-i}) = E_x\{F(m + x, p_{-i})\}$$
$$+ \max_{p_i} E_x\{-\upsilon[(1 + x)z(p_i)^\theta]\} + \beta V(z(p_i)^{1+\theta}; p_{-i}), \tag{8.8}$$

where E_x denotes expectations with respect to x. The first order condition for this problem is:

$$E_x\{\upsilon'[(1 + x)z(p_i)^\theta](1 + x)(p_i)^{-1}\} = \beta V'(z(p_i)^\theta)\gamma. \tag{8.9}$$

To provide an intuitive explanation of (8.9) we consider the effect of a small increase in the price p_i for a given realization of x. By increasing the price p_i the seller reduces demand and production. The change in output (obtained by taking a derivative of [8.6]) is: $\theta z(p_i)^{\theta-1}(1+x)$. The cost reduction benefit is therefore the absolute value of: $(\upsilon')\theta z(p_i)^{\theta-1}(1+x)$. The increase in the price p_i also reduces next period's balances. The change in next period balances (obtained by taking a derivative of [8.7]) is: $(1 + \theta)z(p_i)^\theta$. The loss of utility associated with that is the

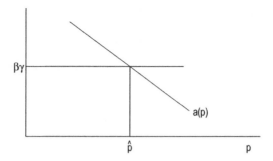

Figure 8.1   The equilibrium price level

absolute value of: $(\beta V')(1 + \theta)z(p_i)^\theta$. Since at the optimum, the cost reduction benefits must equal the loss of utility due to the loss of revenues we get (8.9).

In *equilibrium* $p_j = p$ for all j, $z = 1/\sum_j(p_j)^{1+\theta} = p^{-(1+\theta)}$ and $zp^\theta = p^{-1}$. Substituting this in (8.5) we get the utility from consumption:

$$\left[\sum_j \left(z(m + x)(p_j)^\theta\right)^\gamma\right]^{1/\gamma} = \left[\left(z(m + x)p^\theta\right)^\gamma\right]^{1/\gamma} = (m + x)/p. \qquad (8.10)$$

It follows that $V' = 1/p$. Substituting $zp^\theta = p^{-1}$ and $V' = 1/p$ in (8.9), we get the equilibrium condition:

$$E_x\{\upsilon'[(1 + x)/p](1 + x)\} = \beta\gamma. \qquad (8.11)$$

Since $\upsilon'' > 0$, the left hand side of (8.11), $a(p) = E_x\{\upsilon'[(1 + x)/p](1 + x)\}$, is decreasing in p and we get a unique solution as in figure 8.1.[4]

To interpret (8.11) we use $MC(x) = \upsilon'[(1 + x)/p]$ for the marginal cost and $MB(x) = \beta V'p/(1 + x) = \beta/(1 + x)$ for the marginal benefit and write (8.11) as:

$$E_x\{MC(x)/MB(x)\} = \gamma. \qquad (8.12)$$

Thus γ is the average ratio of marginal cost to marginal benefits (one over the markup) and low γ means high monopoly power.[5]

We can use figure 8.1 to do comparative static. An increase in γ (and a reduction of monopoly power) leads to a reduction in the equilibrium level of p and to an increase in average production. An increase in β also leads to an increase in output because of the delay in the payment for the labor effort assumed in the cash-in-advance model.

Substituting $\upsilon(L) = (1/\delta)L^\delta$ and $\upsilon'(L) = L^{\delta-1}$ in (8.11) leads to: $p = \{E_x(1+x)^\delta/\beta\gamma\}^{1/\delta-1}$. The equilibrium labor supply is therefore:

$$L(x) = (1 + x)/p = (\beta\gamma)^{1/\delta-1}(1 + x)/\{E_x(1 + x)^\delta\}^{1/\delta-1}. \qquad (8.13)$$

The elasticity of labor supply with respect to $1 + x$ is unity.

Optimal monetary policy

A social planner in this environment will solve:

$$\max_{y_j} \left[\sum_j (y_j)^\gamma \right]^{1/\gamma} - \sum_j \left[\upsilon(y_j) = (1/\delta)(y_j)^\delta \right]. \tag{8.14}$$

Imposing symmetry we can write (8.14) as $\max y - (1/\delta)y^\delta$. The solution to this problem is: $y_j = 1$ for all j.

The optimal choice of a non-random policy x solves:[6]

$$\max_x L(x) - (1/\delta)[L(x)]^\delta \quad \text{s.t.} \quad (8.13) \text{ and } x \geq \beta - 1. \tag{8.15}$$

The optimal policy is the Friedman rule: $x = \beta - 1$. To see this claim note that at the Friedman rule (8.13) implies $L = \gamma^{1/\delta - 1} < 1$. Therefore the marginal cost is less than the social benefit and increasing x is not desirable.

Are the implied quantities optimal?

After observing the realization of x and after the commitment to price was already made, the seller will want to satisfy demand if the marginal cost is less than the marginal benefit:

$$\upsilon'[(1 + x)/p] \leq \beta/(1 + x). \tag{8.16}$$

Substituting $p = \{E_x(1 + x)^\delta/\beta\gamma\}^{1/\delta - 1}$ and $\upsilon'(L) = L^{\delta - 1}$ in (8.16) leads to the following claim.

> *Claim 1:* Satisfying demand is optimal if:
>
> $$E_x(1 + x)^\delta/(1 + x)^\delta \geq \gamma \quad \text{for all } x \leq g. \tag{8.17}$$

Claim 1 says that satisfying demand is optimal when the money supply increase is largely anticipated. To advance this interpretation, we look at the expression: $\gamma(1 + x)^\delta - E_x(1 + x)^\delta$. The first term in this expression depends on the realization x while the second is an expected average term. We may therefore think of this term as a somewhat unconventional definition of money surprise and read claim 1 as saying that satisfying demand is not optimal whenever a strictly positive surprise occurs.

Note that when γ is close to unity satisfying demand when $x = g$ is not optimal. In general, we can use the condition in claim 1 to see the effect of changes in various parameters on the desire to satisfy demand. This is done in claim 2 which we bring here without the proof.

Table 8.1   Critical values of γ (demand satisfying is optimal if the true γ is less than the critical value)

g =	0.05	0.1	0.15	0.2
$x = \beta - 1$ with probability $= 0.5$ and $x = g$ otherwise.				
Expected inflation	0.005	0.030	0.055	0.08
standard deviation	0.045	0.07	0.095	0.12
Critical values of γ:				
For $\delta = 2$:	0.92	0.88	0.85	0.82
For $\delta = 3$:	0.88	0.83	0.79	0.76
For $\delta = 11$:	0.69	0.61	0.57	0.54
$x = \beta - 1$ with probability $= 0.9$ and $x = g$ otherwise.				
Expected inflation =	−0.031	−0.026	−0.021	−0.016
standard deviation	0.027	0.042	0.057	0.072
Critical values of γ:				
For $\delta = 2$:	0.85	0.79	0.73	0.68
For $\delta = 3$:	0.79	0.70	0.62	0.56
For $\delta = 11$:	0.44	0.30	0.22	0.18

Table 8.1 calculates the levels of γ for which (8.17) holds with equality. The calculations assume $\beta = 0.96$. The rate of change in the money supply is $x = \beta - 1$ or $x = g$ where $g = 0.05, 0.1, 0.15$ and 0.2. The probability that $x = \beta - 1$ is 0.5 and 0.9. The calculations are made for $\delta = 2, 3$ and 11 which correspond to labor supply elasticities of $1/(\delta - 1) = 1, 0.5$ and 0.1.

Claim 2:[7]   The following changes may cause a departure from demand-satisfying behavior: (a) an increase in γ; (b) an increase in δ; (c) replacing x by a random variable x' with a lower δth moment: $E_{x'}(1 + x')^\delta < E_x(1 + x)^\delta$ and $\beta - 1 \leq x' \leq g$; (d) replacing x by a random variable x' with a higher upper bound: $E_{x'}(1 + x')^\delta = E_x(1 + x)^\delta$ and $\beta - 1 \leq x' \leq g'$ where $g' > g$.

The intuition for claim 2 is as follows: (a) When monopoly power is low, marginal cost is larger than marginal benefits for large x; (b) When δ is high labor supply elasticity $(1/(\delta - 1))$ is low and the seller does not want to accommodate demand when the realization of x is large; (c) When a small probability event of high money supply realization occurs the surprise is large and the sellers do not want to accommodate. The same intuition applies also to (d).

A discrete example

To get a feeling for the magnitudes we now turn to a numerical example in which x may take two possible realizations: $x = \beta - 1$ and $x = g$. We use $\beta = 0.96$ and calculate the critical

Table 8.2   The demand-satisfying model

g =	0.05	0.1	0.15	0.2
Labor supply elasticity = 1 ($\delta = 2$)				
p =	1.11	1.17	1.23	1.29
L($\beta - 1$) =	0.76	0.82	0.78	0.74
L(g) =	0.95	0.94	0.93	0.93
EM =	1.11	1.14	1.23	1.21
Welfare cost =	0.005	0.009	0.015	0.022
Labor supply elasticity = 0.5 ($\delta = 3$)				
p =	1.06	1.10	1.15	1.20
L($\beta - 1$) =	0.91	0.87	0.84	0.80
L(g) =	0.99	1.00	1.00	1.00
EM =	1.12	1.16	1.21	1.27
Welfare cost =	0.004	0.008	0.015	0.022
Labor supply elasticity = 0.1 ($\delta = 11$)				
p =	1.03	1.07	1.11	1.16
L($\beta - 1$) =	0.94	0.90	0.86	0.83
L(g) =	1.02	1.03	1.03	1.03
EM =	1.36	1.81	2.53	3.68
Welfare cost =	0.010	0.023	0.040	0.059

$x = \beta - 1$ or $x = g$ with equal probabilities; $\gamma = 0.95$ and $\beta = 0.96$. The variables are normalized price (p), labor in the low money supply realization (L[$\beta - 1$]), labor in the high money supply realization (L[g]), the expected markup, (EM), the expected welfare cost of departing from the optimal policy as a percentage of labor supply (Welfare cost). Here are the details of the calculations. EM $= 0.5[L(\beta - 1)]^{1-\delta} + 0.5[L(g)]^{1-\delta}$ is the expected markup. The welfare under the optimal policy ($x = \beta - 1$ with probability 1) is:

$$W_{max} = \gamma^{1/(\delta-1)} - (1/\delta)\gamma^{\delta/(\delta-1)}.$$

The expected welfare cost as a fraction of labor supply is:

$$WC = 0.5\left\{W_{max} - \left[L(\beta - 1) - (1/\delta)[L(\beta - 1)]^{\delta}\right]\right\}/L(\beta - 1)$$
$$+ 0.5\left\{W_{max} - \left[L(g) - (1/\delta)[L(g)]^{\delta}\right]\right\}/L(g).$$

value of γ for which $E_x(1 + x)^{\delta}/(1 + g)^{\delta} = \gamma$ and (8.17) holds with equality. (Thus if the true γ is greater than the critical value then satisfying demand when $x = g$ is not optimal.) Table 8.1 makes these calculations for three alternative values of δ and alternative probability distributions for x. The example shows that when labor elasticity and the probability that $x = \beta - 1$ are low, satisfying demand is not optimal if the true γ is say 0.8.

We now use the numerical example to present the equilibrium magnitudes for the case in which $x = \beta - 1$ occurs with probability 0.5. To focus on the case in which satisfying demand is not optimal We use $\gamma = 0.95$. As can be seen from table 8.2, the expected markup as typically measured (1/marginal cost), EM is in the range 1.11–3.68.[8] The expected welfare cost of deviating from the Friedman rule ($x = \beta - 1$ with probability 1) is calculated as a percentage of the labor supply (output). It is in the range 0.4%–5.9%.

Conclusions

In the model sellers make optimal price choices whenever these choices are made and then satisfy demand. Money affects demand and since demand is always satisfied it affects production. The elasticity of output with respect to money is unity. And as in the standard cash-in-advance model, the Friedman rule is optimal.

We examined the optimality of the assumed satisfying demand behavior. In general, satisfying demand is not optimal when monopoly power and labor supply elasticity are not large and when there is a large element of surprise in the money supply increase.

NOTES

The analysis here and in chapter 9 is based on Eden (2003).

1 Thus, we divide all nominal magnitudes by the pre-transfer money supply.
2 When $x \geq \beta - 1$, the assumption that the buyer spends everything can be derived as a result. Otherwise the buyer will not spend and equilibrium does not exist.
3 Since next period's money supply increases by a factor of $1 + x$, we divide current normalized dollars by $1 + x$ to get the value in terms of next period's normalized dollars. See section 15.2 for an elaboration.
4 Existence requires $\upsilon'(0) = 0$ and $\upsilon'(\infty) = \infty$. This is the case for our assumed functional form: $\upsilon(L) = (1/\delta)L^{\delta}$.
5 The demand elasticity can be obtained by looking at the log of (8.4). It is: $|\theta = 1/(\gamma - 1)|$. Thus low γ implies low demand elasticity.
6 We cannot benefit from allowing a random choice of x because the cost function is convex.
7 Since $(1 + x)^{\delta}$ is an increasing function it is well known that (c) implies $\text{prob}(x \geq z) \geq \text{prob}(y \geq z)$ for all z (x dominates y in the first order sense).
8 The typical measure of markup assumes that the seller can use his revenues to buy goods in the same period. This is not the case in our cash-in-advance model. We use this measure here for the sake of possible comparison with estimated markups.

CHAPTER 9

Sticky Prices with Optimal Quantity Choices

In the previous chapter sellers choose prices optimally at the beginning of the period. They then satisfy all the orders they receive at their pre-announced prices. Here we relax the demand-satisfying assumption and the production to order assumption. We thus attempt to integrate the disequilibrium literature pioneered by Patinkin (1965), Clower (1965) and Barro and Grossman (1971) with the new Keynesian economics literature that began with Svensson (1986) and Blanchard and Kiyotaki (1987).

Relaxing the above assumptions is done at the cost of added complexity. But it yields new insights: (1) the correlation between money and output may be low or even negative; and (2) the welfare cost of deviating from the Friedman rule may be large even in the absence of a strong positive relationship between money and output.

The model here is different from the standard new Keynesian economics literature in three respects. We use the cash-in-advance constraint instead of the money in the utility function approach; we allow sellers/producers to choose quantities optimally and we allow for the case in which sellers receive orders only after production choices are made (the production to market case). These changes make a difference.

In a cash-in-advance model, money earned today is spent in the next period. Assuming that each unit of labor produces a unit of the consumption good, the real wage in excess demand situations is approximately P_t/P_{t+1}, where P_t is the dollar price of a unit of consumption (= labor) at time t. This real wage applies only to excess demand situations because only in these situations can the seller sell as much as he wants at his announced price and the real wage is relevant for the labor supply choice. The real wage is only approximately equal to P_t/P_{t+1} because this expression assumes that the buyer will always be able to buy in the next period at the price P_{t+1} and ignores the possibility that in the next period there may be excess demand and the buyer may not be able to make a buy.

When sellers commit to the price P_t before they know the money supply, a high money supply realization implies a high P_{t+1} and a low P_t/P_{t+1}. This inflation tax effect works in the direction of reducing labor supply in excess demand situations. In money in the utility function model this effect is missing because money earned today is typically spent today at prices that do not respond to the current money shock.

Relaxing the demand-satisfying assumption may or may not make a difference depending on the underlying parameters. It was shown in the previous chapter that the amount of monopoly power required for justifying the demand-satisfying assumption critically depends on the labor supply elasticity and the size of the monetary shock.

Relaxing the production to order assumption makes a qualitative difference regardless of the choice of parameters. When orders are received after the choice of production the seller does not sell his entire output in excess supply situations. In this case an increase in the money supply has two effects: It reduces P_t/P_{t+1} (the inflation tax effect) and it increases the fraction of output sold. These two effects cancel each other and therefore monetary shocks do not affect the equilibrium level of labor supply. In excess demand situations all the output is sold and as in the production to order case, there is a negative relationship between money and employment (labor input) because of the inflation tax effect.

In the production to order case, the welfare cost of deviating from the Friedman rule is small. In the production to market case it may be large. The intuition is as follows. When everything that is produced is sold, variations in the amount of labor supply have a small welfare cost because the change in consumption is compensated by a change in leisure: If as a result of a monetary shock the seller produces less, the household consumes less but enjoys more leisure. This compensation in terms of leisure may be absent in the production to market case: If as a result of a monetary shock the seller does not sell his entire output, the household consumes less but does not get more leisure. Therefore money shocks may be more costly in the production to market case.

Since in the production to market sector there is no positive relationship between money and employment we may get a low correlation between money and employment and a high welfare cost for departing from the Friedman rule. The analysis here thus sheds new light on the "does money matter" question. This question has two different meanings: (1) do random fluctuations in the money supply play an important role in causing the business cycle and (2) do they cause significant welfare loss. Friedman and Schwartz (1963) answer both questions in the affirmative. The real business cycle literature pioneered by Kydland and Prescott (1982) seems to answer both questions in the negative. Here we allow for a negative response to the first question and a positive response to the second.

9.1 THE PRODUCTION TO ORDER CASE

As in the previous chapter we use a cash-in-advance model. The typical household (a worker/shopper pair) derives utility from consumption and disutility from labor. We start by focusing on the choice of quantities and assume that the normalized price, p, is exogenously given and constant over time. This means that the regular dollar price $P_t = pM_t$ responds with a one period lag to changes in the money supply. Since the price is exogenous we do not need the differentiated commodities structure used in the previous chapter. We assume at this stage a single consumption good and a risk neutral utility function: $c - \upsilon(L)$, where c is the quantity consumed, L is the amount of labor supplied and $\upsilon(L)$ is the utility cost of supplying it. It is assumed that $\upsilon(L) = (1/\delta)L^\delta$, where $\delta > 1$ and $1/(\delta - 1)$ is the elasticity of labor with respect to the real wage.

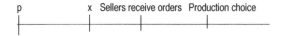

Figure 9.1   Sequence of events for the production to order case

As in chapter 8 the typical buyer receives a transfer payment of x normalized dollars, where $\beta - 1 \leq x \leq g$ is an i.i.d. random variable with a density function $\phi(x)$. The money supply transfer is realized after the price ($P_t = pM_t$) is exogenously set. Then sellers receive orders and choose production to satisfy some or all of the orders. Figure 9.1 describes the sequence of events.

In equilibrium, the typical seller receives orders to buy for the total sum of $1 + x$ normalized dollars. The revenue of the representative seller is therefore $\min(pL, 1 + x)$ if he chooses to produce L units.

Buyers arrive sequentially in an order that is determined randomly by an i.i.d lottery. Buyers who arrive late may not be able to buy. The probability that the buyer will make a buy depends on the realization x and is denoted by $\Pi(x)$. The household takes p and the probability $\Pi(x)$ as given and solves the following Bellman's equation:

$$V(m; p) = \int_{\beta-1}^{g} \Pi(x)[(m + x)/p]\phi(x)\, dx + \int_{\beta-1}^{g} \Big\{ \max_{L} -\upsilon(L)$$

$$+ \Pi(x)\beta V[\min(pL, 1 + x)/(1 + x); p]$$

$$+ [1 - \Pi(x)]\beta V[(m + x + \min(pL, 1 + x))/(1 + x); p]\Big\}\phi(x)\, dx. \qquad (9.1)$$

The first term is the expected consumption for a household that starts with m normalized dollars. Then we have the expected value of the labor choices that are made after observing the realization of x. With probability $\Pi(x)$, the buyer will make a buy and next period balances are $m' = \min(pL, 1 + x)/(1 + x)$ in terms of next period's normalized dollars. With probability $1 - \Pi(x)$, the buyer does not make a buy and next period's balances are $m' = (m + x + \min(pL, 1 + x))/(1 + x)$.

The constant marginal utility of money, V', is:

$$V' = \int_{\beta-1}^{g} \{\Pi(x)/p + [1 - \Pi(x)]\beta V'/(1 + x)\}\phi(x)\, dx = \pi/p(1 - \sigma\beta), \qquad (9.2)$$

where $\pi = \int_{\beta-1}^{g} \Pi(x)\phi(x)\, dx$ and $\sigma = \int_{\beta-1}^{g}\{[1 - \Pi(x)]/(1+x)\}\phi(x)\, dx$. To derive (9.2) note that an additional unit of money will yield $1/p$ utils if it buys in the current period. If it does not buy it will be carried to the next period yielding $\beta V'/(1 + x)$ utils. (Alternatively, you may use the envelop theorem and take a derivative of [9.1] with respect to m, using the result that under risk neutrality V' is a constant.)

Since the utility function is linear in consumption and V' is a constant we can write the labor supply choice problem (for a given x) as: $\max_L -\upsilon(L) + \beta V[\min(pL, 1 + x)/(1 + x)]$.

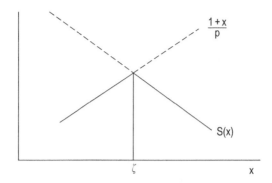

Figure 9.2   The "tent shape" solid line is the equilibrium labor supply

The first order conditions for this problem are:

$$pL \leq 1 + x; \tag{9.3}$$

$$v'(L) \leq p\beta V'/(1+x) = A/(1+x) \quad \text{with equality when } pL < 1 + x, \tag{9.4}$$

where $A = \beta\pi/(1 - \sigma\beta)$ and (9.2) is used to substitute for V'.

Condition (9.3) says that it is not optimal to produce more than the quantity demanded. Condition (9.4) says that the marginal cost must be less than the marginal benefit from selling the good and must be equal to it when there is excess demand.

Equilibrium for a given normalized price p is a pair of functions $[L(x), \Pi(x)]$ and a scalar V' such that

(a) Given $\Pi(x)$, the first order conditions (9.2)–(9.4) are satisfied;
(b) $\Pi(x) = \min\{1, pL(x)/(1+x)\}$.

The requirement (b) says that in case of excess demand, the probability of making a buy is equal to the ratio of nominal supply to nominal demand.

To solve for equilibrium we start by treating A as a constant and define $S(x; A)$ by the solution to: $v'(L) = A/(1+x)$. Using $v'(L) = L^{\delta-1}$ leads to $S(x; A) = [A/(1+x)]^{1/(\delta-1)}$.

The notional supply $S(x; A)$ is a decreasing function of x as in figure 9.2. The intuition is that when x increases, the relevant real price $P_t/P_{t+1} = pM_t/pM_t(1+x) = 1/(1+x)$, decreases. The demand is the upward sloping line $(1+x)/p$ in figure 9.2. Supply equals demand when $x = \zeta$.

The actual amount traded is the minimum between supply and demand:

$$L(x; A) = \min\{S(x; A), (1+x)/p\}. \tag{9.5}$$

Note that $L(x; A) = (1+x)/p$ when $x \leq \zeta$ and $L(x; A) = S(x; A)$ when $x > \zeta$. It therefore has a "tent like shape" as the solid lines in figure 9.2.

We now set

$$\Pi(x) = 1 \text{ if } x \leq \zeta \text{ and}$$

$$\Pi(x) = pL(x)/(1+x) = pA^{1/(\delta-1)}(1+x)^{\delta/(1-\delta)}$$

otherwise, where (9.4) is used to compute $\Pi(x)$ for $x \geq \zeta$. The cutoff point ζ is given by the solution to: $1 + \zeta = pL(\zeta)$. Using $S(x, A) = [A/(1 + x)]^{1/(\delta-1)}$ and (9.5) leads to: $\zeta(p) = p^{(\delta-1)/\delta}A^{1/\delta} - 1$. We now compute π and σ as a function of A and p:

$$\pi(A, p) = \int_{\beta-1}^{g} \Pi(x)\phi(x)\, dx$$

$$= \text{Prob}[x \leq \zeta(p)] + \int_{\zeta(p)}^{g} [pA^{1/(\delta-1)}(1 + x)^{\delta/(1-\delta)}]\phi(x)\, dx; \qquad (9.6)$$

And,

$$\sigma(A, p) = \int_{\beta-1}^{g} \{[1 - \Pi(x)]/(1 + x)\}\phi(x)\, dx$$

$$= \int_{\zeta(p)}^{g} [1 - pA^{1/(\delta-1)}(1 + x)^{\delta/(1-\delta)}](1 + x)^{-1}\phi(x)\, dx. \qquad (9.7)$$

We look for a solution (fixed point) to the following equation:

$$A = \beta\pi(A, p)/[1 - \sigma(A, p)\beta] \geq \beta^{\delta}p^{1-\delta}. \qquad (9.8)$$

The inequality is required to insure that

$$\zeta(p) = p^{(\delta-1)/\delta}A^{1/\delta} - 1 \geq \beta - 1.$$

We now turn to a discrete example and add the choice of price.

Endogenous price in a discrete example

We use the discrete example in which x can take two possible realizations: $x = \beta - 1$ and $x = g$ with equal probabilities of occurrence. We use the differentiated commodity structure of chapter 8 and formulate the price choice problem in the above discrete example under the assumption that satisfying demand is optimal when $x = \beta - 1$ but is not optimal when $x = g$.

Using equation (8.4) in chapter 8 we derive the demand for product i when $x = \beta - 1$. This is: $\beta z(p_i)^{\theta}$ where $z = 1/\sum_j (p_j)^{1+\theta}$ is an appropriate average of all prices and $\theta = 1/(\gamma - 1) < 0$. The revenues when $x = \beta - 1$ and demand is satisfied are: $p_i[\beta z(p_i)^{\theta}]/\beta = z(p_i)^{1+\theta}$. The utility derived when $x = \beta - 1$ is thus: $-\upsilon[\beta z(p_i)^{\theta}] + \beta V[z(p_i)^{1+\theta}]$.

When $x = g$ there is excess demand and the individual seller can find a buyer who could not buy any other product. This buyer will spend his money only if:

$$1/p_i \geq b, \qquad (9.9)$$

where $b = \beta V'/(1+g)$ is the value of a dollar carried to the next period. When (9.9) is satisfied and $x = g$ the worker solves the following problem:

$$G(p_i, m) = \max_L -\upsilon(L) + \Pi(g)\beta V[p_iL/(1 + g)]$$

$$+ [1 - \Pi(g)]\beta V[(m + g + p_iL)/(1 + g)], \qquad (9.10)$$

where $V(m)$ will be defined shortly. When (9.9) is not satisfied there is no demand and $L = 0$.

The household takes z and b as given and solves the following Bellman's equation:

$$V(m) = (1/2)F(m + \beta - 1) + (1/2)\Pi(g)F(m + g)$$

$$+ \max_{p_i} \left\{ (1/2)\{-\upsilon[\beta z(p_i)^\theta] + \beta V[z(p_i)^{1+\theta}]\} + (1/2)I(1/p_i \geq b)G(p_i, m) \right\},$$

(9.11)

where $I(1/p_i \geq b) = 1$ if $1/p_i \geq b$ and zero otherwise, $G(p_i, m)$ is defined by (9.10) and $F(\ )$ is the expected utility made by the buyer, defined by (8.5).

The first expression, $(1/2)F(m + \beta - 1) + (1/2)\Pi(g)F(m + g)$, is the expected current utility from consumption. When $x = \beta - 1$ demand is satisfied and the buyer spends the available cash with certainty. When $x = g$ the buyer spends his cash with probability $\Pi(g)$.

The maximization problem in (9.11) is with respect to the price p_i. When $x = \beta - 1$ the worker satisfies demand and the utility is given by $-\upsilon[\beta z(p_i)^\theta] + \beta V[z(p_i)^{1+\theta}]$. When $x = g$ demand is not satisfied and the choice of L is described by (9.10) if $1/p_i \geq b$ and $L = 0$ otherwise.

The first order condition for the labor choice problem in (9.10) is: $\upsilon'(L) = L^{\delta-1} = \beta V'p_i/(1+g)$ or $L = [\beta V'p_i/(1+g)]^{1/(\delta-1)}$. Using this and assuming (9.9) we write the price choice problem in (9.11) as:

$$\max_{p_i} -\upsilon[\beta z(p_i)^\theta] + \beta V[z(p_i)^{1+\theta}]$$

$$- \upsilon\{[\beta V'p_i/(1+g)]^{1/(\delta-1)}\} + \beta V\{p_i^{\delta/(\delta-1)}(1+g)^{\delta/(1-\delta)}(\beta V')^{1/(\delta-1)}\}.$$

(9.12)

We write the first order condition to the problem (9.12) as the sum of two terms. When the household increases its price it will typically experience a loss of utility when $x = \beta - 1$ and a gain in utility when $x = g$. The intuition is that when x is low the price is ex post "too high" and the opposite is true when x is high. Following this intuition we take the derivative of the first line in (9.12) with respect to p_i:

$$C = -\theta[\beta z(p_i)^\theta]^{\delta-1}\beta z(p_i)^{\theta-1} + (1+\theta)(\beta V')z(p_i)^\theta.$$

(9.13)

We also take the derivative of the second line in (9.12) with respect to p_i:

$$B = -(1/(\delta-1))[\beta V'p_i/(1+g)]^{2+\delta/(1-\delta)}$$

$$+ (\delta/(\delta-1))p_i^{1/(\delta-1)}[\beta V'/(1+g)]^{\delta/(\delta-1)}.$$

(9.14)

At the optimum the first order condition $C + B = 0$ is satisfied. We now turn to define equilibrium for this example.

Equilibrium for the discrete example is a vector $[\Pi(g), b, z, p, L(g), V']$ such that:

(a) Given $\Pi(g)$, b and z, the price p and the labor supply in the high demand state $L(g)$ solve the household's problem (9.10) and V' is the resulting constant marginal utility of money;

(b) $z = p^{-1-\theta}, b = \beta V'/(1+g)$ and $\Pi(g) = pL(g)/(1+g) < 1$.

Table 9.1 calculates the optimal price using the first order condition $C + B = 0$.[1] The optimal price is lower than the demand-satisfying price obtained in table 8.2. At the demand-satisfying price, $C + B < 0$. Since C is the same in both models it follows that the benefit from increasing price that occurs when $x = g$ is larger in the demand-satisfying model. This benefit is the reduction in "unwanted production" that occurs when the seller must satisfy demand.

The elasticity of output with respect to x tends to be negative and is in the range -0.61 to 0.05. The welfare cost is in the range 0.03%–1.8%.[2] This is lower than the welfare cost under the demand-satisfying model which was in the range 0.4%–5.9%. The highest welfare cost in the production to order model occurs when labor supply elasticity is high while in the demand-satisfying model it occurs when the labor supply elasticity is low.

9.2   THE PRODUCTION TO MARKET CASE

We now consider the case in which producers put their output on the market for sale, some of the output produced may not be sold and money surprises affect capacity utilization. It is shown that the change in the assumption about selling leads to a qualitatively different equilibrium labor supply function.

As in the previous section we start by assuming that the normalized price, p, is exogenously given. After observing the realization of the money supply (x) the seller chooses how much to produce and put his output on the market for sale. Buyers arrive and buy part or all of the available supply. Figure 9.3 describes the sequence of events.

As in the previous section buyers who arrive late may not make a buy and $\Pi(x)$ denotes the probability of making a buy. It is assumed that all sellers sell the same fraction, $0 \leq \Omega(x) \leq 1$, of their output. The average revenue received by the seller for a unit produced is therefore: $W(x) = p\Omega(x)$. The amount of money that the household will have at the beginning of next period is: $LW(x)/(1+x)$ if the buyer made a buy and $[LW(x) + m + x]/(1+x)$ if the buyer did not make a buy.

Figure 9.3   Sequence of events for the production to market case

Table 9.1 The production to order model

g =	0.05	0.1	0.15	0.2
Labor supply elasticity = 1 ($\delta = 2$)				
p =	1.05	1.05	1.05	1.06
π =	0.96	0.91	0.87	0.84
A =	0.956	0.948	0.937	0.925
L($\beta - 1$) =	0.91	0.91	0.91	0.91
L(g) =	0.91	0.86	0.82	0.77
EM =	1.10	1.13	1.16	1.20
Elasticity =	−0.03	−0.39	−0.54	−0.61
Welfare cost =	0.0029	0.0061	0.01	0.018
Labor supply elasticity = 0.5 ($\delta = 3$)				
p =	1.01	1.01	1.01	1.02
π =	0.96	0.93	0.90	0.87
A =	0.957	0.950	0.942	0.933
L($\beta - 1$) =	0.95	0.95	0.95	0.94
L(g) =	0.95	0.93	0.90	0.88
EM =	1.10	1.13	1.17	1.20
Elasticity =	0.05	−0.15	−0.23	−0.27
Welfare cost =	0.002	0.003	0.006	0.009
Labor supply elasticity = 0.1 ($\delta = 11$)				
p =	0.97	0.97	0.97	0.97
π =	0.96	0.93	0.91	0.89
A =	0.956	0.951	0.945	0.938
L($\beta - 1$) =	0.99	0.99	0.99	0.99
L(g) =	0.99	0.99	0.98	0.98
EM =	1.10	1.13	1.17	1.20
Elasticity =	0.01	−0.03	−0.04	−0.05
Welfare cost =	0.0003	0.0007	0.001	0.002

Table 9.1 assumes that $x = \beta - 1$ with probability 0.5 and $x = g$ otherwise; $\gamma = 0.95$ and $\beta = 0.96$. It calculates the normalized price (p) the unconditional probability of making a buy (π) the equilibrium level of $A = p\beta V'$, labor supply for the two possible realizations (L[$\beta - 1$], L[g]), the elasticity of labor supply with respect to x and the welfare cost of departing from the Friedman rule. The formulas used are:

$$p = \{E_x(1+x)^\delta/\beta\gamma\}^{1/\delta-1} = \{[0.5\beta^\delta + 0.5(1+g)^\delta]/\beta\gamma\}^{1/\delta-1};$$

$$\pi(A,p) = 0.5 + 0.5p(A)^{1/\delta-1}(1+g)^{\delta/1-\delta};$$

$$\sigma(A,p) = 0.5[1 - p(A)^{1/\delta-1}(1+g)^{\delta/1-\delta}]/(1+g)$$

$$A = \beta\pi(A,p)/[1 - \sigma(A,p)\beta]$$

$$L(\beta - 1) = \beta/p; L(g) = [A/(1+g)]^{1/\delta-1};$$

Elasticity $= [(L(g)/L(\beta - 1)) - 1]/[((1+g)/\beta) - 1]$.
Welfare cost is calculated by the formula in table 8.2.

Given p and the functions $\Pi(x)$, $W(x)$ the Bellman equation which describes the household's choice problem is:

$$V(m; p) = \int_{\beta-1}^{g} [(m + x)\Pi(x)/p]\phi(x)\, dx$$

$$+ \int_{\beta-1}^{g} \{\max_{L} -\upsilon(L) + [\Pi(x)]\beta V[LW(x)/(1 + x); p]$$

$$+ [1 - \Pi(x)]\beta V[(m + x + LW(x))/(1 + x); p]\}\phi(x)\, dx. \qquad (9.15)$$

Since the utility function is linear in consumption and V' is a constant, we can write the maximization problem in (9.15) as: $\max_L -\upsilon(L) + \beta V[LW(x)/(1 + x)]$. The first order condition for this problem is:

$$\upsilon'(L) = [W(x)/(1 + x)]\beta V' = A\Omega(x)/(1 + x), \qquad (9.16)$$

where the second equality uses $\beta V' = \beta\pi/p(1 - \sigma\beta) = A/p$ and $W(x) = p\Omega(x)$.

Equilibrium for a given normalized price p is a vector of functions $[L(x), \Pi(x), \Omega(x)]$ and a triplet $[\pi = \int_{\beta-1}^{g} \Pi(x)\phi(x)\, dx, \sigma = \int_{\beta-1}^{\infty} \{[1 - \Pi(x)]/(1 + x)\}\phi(x)\, dx, A = \beta\pi/(1 - \sigma\beta)]$ such that:

(a) $\upsilon'(L) = A\Omega(x)/(1 + x)$
(b) $\Pi(x) = \min\{1, pL(x)/(1 + x)\}$ = probability of making a buy;
(c) $\Omega(x) = \min\{1, (1 + x)/pL(x)\}$ = fraction of output sold.

Solving for equilibrium: As in the previous production to order case, the labor supply in the excess demand region $x \geq \zeta$ is given by the solution, $L(x)$, to $\upsilon'(L) = L^{\delta-1} = A/(1 + x)$. The cutoff point ζ is given by the solution to: $1 + \zeta = pL(\zeta)$ which is: $\zeta(p) = p^{(\delta-1)/\delta}A^{1/\delta} - 1$. In the excess demand range $\Omega(x) = 1$. When $x \leq \zeta$ there is excess supply, $\Omega(x) = (1 + x)/pL(x) \leq 1$ and we can write (9.16) as:

$$\upsilon'(L) = A/pL \quad \text{for } x \leq \zeta. \qquad (9.17)$$

The solution to (9.17) does not depend on x and is given by: $\hat{L} = (A/p)^{1/\delta}$. The intuition is as follows. An increase in x has two effects on the wage in terms of next period's normalized dollars: The increase in the fraction of output sold, $\Omega(x) = (1 + x)/p\hat{L}$, and the reduction in the value of a current normalized dollar. These two effects exactly offset each other and therefore the effective wage in terms of next period's normalized dollars, $W(x)/(1+x) = 1/\hat{L}$ does not depend on x. The equilibrium labor supply function $L(x)$ is therefore flat for $x \leq \zeta$ and then declines as in figure 9.4.

Endogenous price in a discrete example

We endogenize the price for the above discrete example. For a more general treatment see appendices A and B in Eden (2003).

We start by specifying the fraction of output sold by an individual seller as a function of his relative price. For this purpose we define average capacity utilization by: $CU(x) = \min\{(1 + x)/pL(x), 1\}$, where p and $L(x)$ are average (across sellers) price and labor supply.

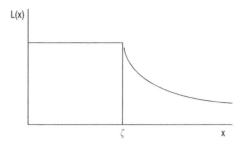

Figure 9.4   Equilibrium labor supply in the production to market case

In the low demand state there is excess supply and average capacity utilization is: $CU(\beta - 1) = \beta/p\hat{L} < 1$. It is assumed that if seller i post the price p_i he will sell a fraction:

$$\Omega(p/p_i, \beta - 1) = \min\{[\exp(\alpha p/p_i)/\exp(\alpha)]CU(\beta - 1), 1\}, \tag{9.18}$$

of his output in the low demand state, where $\alpha > 0$ is a given parameter. The specification (9.18) assumes that when $p_i = p$, seller i's capacity utilization is equal to the average, CU. In this case the parameter α is the elasticity of Ω with respect to the relative price p/p_i. We allow this elasticity to vary with CU and p and write:[3]

$$\alpha = \alpha(CU, p). \tag{9.19}$$

The household takes CU, p and the parameter $\alpha = \alpha(CU, p)$ as given and computes the effective wage in the low demand state (in terms of next period's normalized dollars):

$$W(p/p_i, \beta - 1)/\beta = p_i\Omega(p/p_i, \beta - 1)/\beta = [\exp(\alpha p/p_i)/\exp(\alpha)]p_i/p\hat{L}. \tag{9.20}$$

In the high demand state there is excess demand and average capacity utilization is: $CU(g) = 1$. In this case it does not matter whether production is made to order or to market. In both cases a seller who sets a price that satisfies (9.9) can find a buyer and make a sale. It is therefore assumed that when (9.9) is satisfied the fraction of output sold in the high demand state is: $\Omega(p/p_i, g) = 1$. The effective wage in the high demand state is therefore:

$$W(p/p_i, g)/(1 + g) = p_i\Omega(g, p/p_i)/(1 + g) = p_i/(1 + g).$$

Household i takes the average price posted by others, p, the value of a normalized dollar that is not spent in the high demand state, b, the effective wage function, $W(p/p_i, x)$ and the probability of making a buy in the high demand state, $\Pi(g)$ as given. It solves the following Bellman equation:

$$V(m) = (1/2)F(m + \beta - 1) + (1/2)\Pi(g)F(m + g)$$

$$+ \max_{p_i}(1/2)\left\{ \max_L -\upsilon(L) + \beta V[W(p/p_i, \beta - 1)L/\beta] \text{ s.t. } (20)\right\}$$

$$+ (1/2)I(1/p_i \geq b)G(p_i, m), \tag{9.21}$$

where as before I(statement) $= 1$ if the statement is true and I(statement) $= 0$ otherwise, $G(p_i, m)$ is the expected utility in the high demand state defined by (9.10) and F( ) is the expected utility that the buyer makes defined by (8.5).

Equilibrium for the discrete example is a vector $[p, \Pi(g), \Omega(p/p_i, \beta - 1), W(p/p_i, \beta - 1), b, L(\beta - 1), L(g), V']$ such that:

(a) Given $[p, \Pi(g), \Omega(p/p_i, \beta - 1), W(p/p_i, \beta - 1), b]$, the price p and the labor supplies $L(\beta - 1)$ and $L(g)$ solve the household's problem (9.21) and V' is the resulting constant marginal utility of money;

(b) $\Omega(p/p_i, \beta - 1)$ satisfies (9.18), $W(p/p_i, \beta - 1)$ satisfies (9.20), $b = \beta V'/(1 + g)$ and $\Pi(g) = pL(g)/(1 + g) < 1$.

The choice of labor in the high demand state is the same as in the production to order case. We focus here on the choice of labor in the low demand state. The first order condition that $L(\beta - 1)$ must satisfy is:

$$v'(L) = L^{\delta-1} = \beta V'[W(p/p_i, \beta - 1)/\beta] = A[\exp(\alpha p/p_i)/\exp(\alpha)]p_i/p^2\hat{L}. \qquad (9.22)$$

This leads to $L = \{A[\exp(\alpha p/p_i)/\exp(\alpha)]p_i/p^2\hat{L}\}^{1/(\delta-1)}$. The utility when demand is low can therefore be written as:

$$U(p/p_i, \beta - 1) = -v(L) + \beta V(LW(p/p_i, \beta - 1)/\beta)$$

$$= -(1/\delta)\{A[\exp(\alpha p/p_i)/\exp(\alpha)]p_i/p^2\hat{L}\}^{\delta/(\delta-1)}$$

$$+ \beta V(\{A[\exp(\alpha p/p_i)/\exp(\alpha)]p_i/p^2\hat{L}\}^{1/(\delta-1)}[\exp(\alpha p/p_i)/\exp(\alpha)]p_i/p\hat{L}). \qquad (9.23)$$

In equilibrium $p_i = p$ and, using (9.17), the derivative of (9.23) is:

$$C = (1/(\delta - 1))(1 - \alpha)p^{-1}(\hat{L})^{\delta-1}\{-\hat{L} + 1/\hat{L}\} + (1 - \alpha)(\hat{L})^{\delta/(\delta-1)}, \qquad (9.24)$$

where $C = \partial U/\partial p_i$. Note that when $\hat{L} \leq 1$, and $\alpha > 1$, $C < 0$. The first order condition that governs the choice of price is given by:

$$C + B = 0, \qquad (9.25)$$

where B is the derivative of welfare in the high demand state with respect to price. B is the same as in the production to order case and is given by (9.14).

We may solve the model by assuming a specific functional form $\alpha(CU, p)$. Rather than doing that and to facilitate the comparison with the production to order case, we treat α as an endogenous variable and compute the value of α required to get the production to order prices in table 9.1. Using (9.14) for B, (9.24) for C and (9.17) we get:

$$\alpha = 1 + B/\{(1/(\delta - 1))p^{-1}(\hat{L})^{\delta-1}\{-\hat{L} + 1/\hat{L}\} + (\hat{L})^{\delta/(\delta-1)}\}. \qquad (9.26)$$

Since $CU = \beta/p\hat{L}$ we can write (9.26) as a function of CU and p.

Table 9.2 uses (9.14) and (9.26) and the production to order prices in table 9.1 to compute α. The resulting α is a decreasing function of CU. Although prices do not react to changes in g (regime changes), capacity utilization is an increasing function of g. The reason is that an increase in g lowers the probability of making a buy (π) and the marginal utility of money V'. As a result the benefits from working go down and less excess capacity is produced.

The expected welfare cost is much larger than in the production to order case (table 9.1). It is now in the range of 0.5%–3.1% of labor supply.

Table 9.2 The production to market model

g =	0.05	0.1	0.15	0.2
Labor supply elasticity = 1 (δ = 2)				
p =	1.05	1.05	1.05	1.06
CU =	0.957	0.962	0.967	0.971
α =	1.61	1.42	1.27	1.24
EM =	1.07	1.11	1.14	1.18
Elasticity =	−0.49	−0.64	−0.69	−0.70
Welfare cost =	0.023	0.024	0.027	0.031
Labor supply elasticity = 0.5 (δ = 3)				
p =	1.01	1.01	1.01	1.02
CU =	0.968	0.969	0.971	0.972
α =	1.82	1.74	1.65	1.58
EM =	1.07	1.10	1.13	1.17
Elasticity =	−0.30	−0.35	−0.37	−0.37
Welfare cost =	0.017	0.017	0.019	0.021
Labor supply elasticity = 0.1 (δ = 11)				
p =	0.97	0.97	0.97	0.97
CU =	0.9909	0.9911	0.9913	0.9915
α =	1.93	1.88	1.83	1.79
EM =	1.06	1.09	1.12	1.16
Elasticity =	−0.09	−0.09	−0.09	−0.08
Welfare cost =	0.005	0.005	0.005	0.006

This example assumes x = β − 1 with probability 0.5 and x = g otherwise. β = 0.96. It uses the computation of A and p from table 9.1. Labor supply when x = g, L(g) is the same as in table 9.1 but labor supply when x = β − 1 is larger and is given by:

$$L(\beta - 1) = (A/p)^{1/\delta}$$

The elasticity is the percentage change in labor divided by the percentage change in x:

$$[(L(g)/L(\beta - 1)) - 1]/[(1 + g)/\beta) - 1].$$

Capacity utilization is the percentage of output sold when x = β: CU = β/pL(β − 1). Welfare cost is calculated as a percentage of labor supply according to the formula in table 8.2.

It was shown that if we relax the demand-satisfying assumption we may get a negative rather than a positive relationship between money and output. This should reduce our confidence in the sticky price model as a possible explanation for the observed positive money/output relationship.

Alternatively we may consider a model in which it is optimal to satisfy demand for some goods but not for other goods. Some goods are produced to order and some are produced to market. In such a combined model, we may get a positive relationship between money and employment but if production to market is important, we may get a low elasticity and

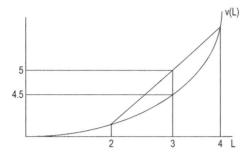

Figure 9.5   Uncertainity about L increases expected cost

a relatively high welfare cost. For a formulation of the combined model see appendix A in Eden (2003).

The welfare cost of departing from the Friedman rule

The literature on the welfare cost of inflation distinguishes between the cost of perfectly anticipated inflation and the cost of unanticipated inflation.

Perfectly anticipated inflation is costly and affects labor supply because households spend the money they earn with a lag and as a result inflation creates a distortion by affecting the real wage. This cost is the same for all the three models discussed in chapters 8 and 9.

The cost of random fluctuations in x (unanticipated inflation) varies across the three models. In the first two models (demand satisfying and production to order) it arises because random fluctuations in x cause random fluctuations in labor supply.[4] This is costly because smooth production is cheaper than non-smooth production with the same mean.

To illustrate We compare the expected cost of supplying 2 and 4 units with equal probabilities to the cost of supplying the mean of 3 units with certainty under the assumption that the cost is $v(L) = (1/2)L^2$. The expected cost of the random labor supply is $(1/2)v(2) + (1/2)v(4) = (1/4)(2^2) + (1/4)(4^2) = 5$. The cost of supplying the mean is: $(1/2)3^2 = 4.5$. Thus the cost of supplying the mean is less than the cost of supplying the distribution. Figure 9.5 illustrates this point.[5]

In the third, production to market model, the welfare cost of random fluctuations in x is large because changes in consumption may occur without changes in leisure: a drop in consumption in this model is typically not compensated by an increase in leisure. In contrast, in the production to order model a drop in consumption occurs only when there is a drop in labor supply and an increase in leisure.[6]

The cost of not making a sale in the production to market model is similar to the cost of involuntary unemployment in the old Keynesian literature which assumes that the leisure gained by unemployed workers is valueless. Here leisure is valued but output which is not sold is in a sense a waste of time.

Table 9.3 illustrates the welfare calculations for the regime (policy) in which $x = \beta - 1 = -0.04$ with probability 0.5 and $x = 0.1$ otherwise. The expected inflation in this regime is 3%.

The welfare cost of expected inflation is the cost of increasing the money supply at the rate of 3% with probability 1 relative to the Friedman rule alternative. It is in the range of

Table 9.3 The welfare cost of having $x = \beta - 1 = -0.04$ with probability 0.5 and $x = 0.1$ otherwise

$\delta =$	2	3	11
Labor supply elasticity	1	0.5	0.1
Second best L $=$	0.95	0.97	0.99
Expected inflation L $=$	0.89	0.94	0.99
Welfare cost of expected inflation $=$	0.6%	0.3%	0.1%
Demand satisfying model			
Elasticity $=$	1	1	1
Welfare cost $=$	0.9%	0.8%	2.3%
Production to order			
Elasticity $=$	−0.39	−0.15	−0.03
Welfare cost $=$	0.61%	0.3%	0.07%
Production to market with production to order prices			
Elasticity $=$	−0.64	−0.35	−0.09
Welfare cost $=$	2.4%	1.7%	0.5%
Production to market with demand-satisfying prices			
Elasticity $=$	−0.27	−0.15	−0.03
Welfare cost $=$	5.2%	4.6%	4.6%

Table 9.3 uses the elasticity and welfare cost calculations from previous tables for the case $g = 0.1$. It also adds some calculations about expected inflation. The second best L is the quantity that will be produced when the Friedman rule is implemented. Expected inflation L is the labor supply when the expected inflation of 3% occurs with probability 1.

0.1%–0.6% and its importance declines with δ. In the extreme case when labor is inelastically supplied this cost is zero.

The welfare cost in the demand-satisfying model is in the range of 0.8%–2.3%. The welfare cost in the production to order case is similar to the welfare cost of expected inflation suggesting that random fluctuations in x do not cause significant additional harm in this model. The welfare cost in the production to market case is in the range of 0.5%–2.4% if we choose α that will lead to the production to order prices and in the range of 4.6%–5.2% if the demand-satisfying prices (from table 8.2) are used.

The expected cost of deviating from the Friedman rule is probably some weighted average of the numbers in table 9.3 where the average is across models. Such an average may be obtained in a model that allows for heterogeneity in the parameters γ and δ across products. As a result some products are produced to satisfy demand and some are not. In addition because of product heterogeneity some are produced to order and some are produced to market.

The average welfare cost may potentially be a large number. If for example, the average rate of unemployment is 2% above the efficient rate and capital utilization is on average 2% less than its efficient level, then we have a loss of 2% of output. If half of this loss is due to policy "mistakes" than there is a potential gain of 1% of output which is a big number.

Conclusions

When sellers are allowed to choose quantities optimally, more money leads to a lower real wage and less output in the region of excess demand. In the region of excess supply, more money leads to more output of goods produced to order but may have no effect on the output of goods produced to market.

The welfare cost of random variations in x may be large in the production to market case because of the waste that occurs in low demand states. But there is no positive relationship between money and the output of goods produced to market.

In reality some goods are produced to order and some goods are produced to market. When production to market is relatively important, we may get a weak relationship between money and output and a large welfare cost.

NOTES

1 We substitute $z = p^{-1-\theta}$, $z(p_i)^{\theta} = p^{-1}$ and $z(p_i)^{\theta-1} = p^{-2}$ in (9.13) to get: $C = -\theta \beta^{\delta} p^{-1-\delta} + (1 + \theta)(\beta V')p^{-1}$.

2 We also made the calculations in table 9.1 using the demand satisfying prices in table 8.2. The welfare cost when using the demand satisfying prices is in the range 0.5%–5.7%. This is more than twice the welfare cost when using the optimal prices suggesting that the demand satisfying prices are poor approximations for the optimal prices.

3 When CU is relatively high, a one percent increase in the relative price p/p_i should have a relatively small effect on the percentage of output sold and therefore we expect that α should be a decreasing function of CU.

4 They may also change the mean labor supply but this effect is very small in the first two models.

5 An alternative explanation goes as follows. By cutting a unit when output is high and adding a unit when output is low we gain the difference in marginal cost.

6 It may be useful to think about the case in which the markup is close to unity. In this case small fluctuations in L in the production to order case are costless: The representative agent is willing to add (or subtract) a unit of labor in exchange for a unit of consumption.

CHAPTER 10

Flexible Prices

Is it possible to explain the money/output correlation when prices are completely flexible? The first attempt was made by Lucas (1972) and assumes a lag in the information about the money supply. The second attempt made by Grossman and Weiss (1983) and Rotemberg (1984) and more lately by Lucas (1990), Fuerst (1992) and Christiano and Eichenbaum (1992) assumes a lag in the adjustment of nominal balances. Here we illustrate the working of these models starting from Lucas (1972).

10.1 LUCAS' CONFUSION HYPOTHESIS

We consider an overlapping generations model. Agents live for two periods. They work in the first and consume in the second. The individual utility function is given by $c_{t+1} - v(L_t)$ where L_t is the quantity of labor supplied by young agents born at time t and c_{t+1} is the quantity consumed by old agents born at time t.

The representative young agent sells his output for P_t dollars per unit. He also expects to receive a transfer of $\tilde{G}_{t+1}$ dollars when old and to use his available balances $P_t L_t + \tilde{G}_{t+1}$ to buy at the next period price: $\tilde{P}_{t+1}$. The realizations of the random variables $\tilde{G}_{t+1}$ and $\tilde{P}_{t+1}$ are not known at time t. The young time t agent solves:

$$\max E\{(P_t L_t + \tilde{G}_{t+1})/\tilde{P}_{t+1}\} - v(L_t), \tag{10.1}$$

where expectations are taken with respect to the random variables $\tilde{G}_{t+1}$ and $\tilde{P}_{t+1}$. The first order condition for an interior solution to this problem is:

$$v'(L_t) = E[P_t/\tilde{P}_{t+1}] = E[1/(1 + \tilde{\pi}_{t+1})] = W_t. \tag{10.2}$$

Condition (10.2) says that the marginal cost must equal the expected real wage. Note that the expected real wage is equal to the expected real rate of return on money (one over one plus the inflation rate).

Naive expectations

Suppose that agents believe that next period's price level, $\tilde{P}_{t+1}$, does not depend on this period's price level, P_t. Then any increase in P_t implies a lower inflation and an increase in the expected real wage, W. In such an economy we will find a positive correlation between the current price level and output and, in general, also between the current money supply and output.

Expectations based on the "correct" model (rational expectations)

We now turn to specify a complete model and to derive expectations that are consistent with the model. The money supply grows at the rate $\tilde{x}_t = \ln \tilde{M}_t - \ln M_{t-1}$, where $\tilde{x}_t$ are i.i.d. The number of agents born in each period $\tilde{N}_t$ are also i.i.d. and independent of $\tilde{x}$. This implies that the rate of population growth, $\ln \tilde{N}_{t+1} - \ln N_t$, does depend on N_t: the lower N_t, the higher is on average the rate of population growth.

We use normalized dollars as the unit of account, where a normalized dollar is the pre-transfer money supply. We assume a normalized price function $p(N, x)$ such that:

$$P = p(N, x)M, \tag{10.3}$$

where N is the current realization of the number of young agents $\tilde{N}$, x is the current realization of the rate of change in the money supply, $\tilde{x}$ and M is the current pre-transfer money supply.

A normalized dollar (the pre-transfer money supply), held at the beginning of the current period buys $1/p(N, x)$ units of consumption. The expected purchasing power of next period's normalized dollar is:

$$z = E[1/p(\tilde{N}, \tilde{x})], \tag{10.4}$$

units of consumption, where expectations are taken over the next period young population $\tilde{N}$ and the next period rate of change in the money supply, $\tilde{x}$. A normalized dollar carried over to the next period will become $1/(1+x)$ next period's normalized dollars because of the increase in the money supply. It follows that the expected real wage in the current period is:

$$W(N, x) = [p(N, x)/(1 + x)]z. \tag{10.5}$$

We assume that when the current realizations N and x are observed the normalized price is proportional to the post-transfer money supply $(1 + x)$ and there exists a function $\gamma(N)$ such that:

$$p(N, x) = (1 + x)\gamma(N). \tag{10.6}$$

Substituting (10.6) in (10.5) leads to:

$$W(N, x) = z\gamma(N) \quad \text{for all x.} \tag{10.7}$$

We choose units so that $z = 1$ and use $L(\gamma)$ to denote the solution to: $v'(L) = \gamma$. Assuming that the marginal cost, v', is increasing leads to an increasing labor supply function $L(\gamma)$.

Market-clearing requires:

$$p(N, x)NL(\gamma) = 1 + x. \tag{10.8}$$

Substituting $p(N, x) = (1 + x)\gamma(N)$ in (10.8) leads to:

$$\gamma(N)L[\gamma(N)] = 1/N. \tag{10.9}$$

Since $L(\gamma)$ is an increasing function, γ must be a decreasing function.

This says that the expected real wage and real output per worker is a decreasing function of N. The intuition is in the observation that when N is large the expected population growth is low and money earned today will buy the product of a relatively small number of next generation's young agents.

Incomplete information

We now assume that the realizations (N, x) are not observed. Only the market-clearing price level is observed. But since p depends on (N, x) it provides a signal for these variables. We define the expected real wage given p by:

$$w(p) = E[W(\tilde{N}, \tilde{x}) \mid p]. \tag{10.10}$$

The market-clearing condition can now be written as:[1]

$$p(N, x)NL\{w[p(N, x)]\} = 1 + x. \tag{10.11}$$

Assume now that $L = 1$ is inelastically supplied. Then we can write (10.11) as:

$$p(N, x) = (1 + x)/N. \tag{10.12}$$

In this case there is a negative correlation between p and N. When the young agent observes high p he concludes that N is likely to be low and the expectations about the real wage, $EW(\tilde{N}, \tilde{x})$ are high. Therefore $w(p)$ is monotonically increasing.

This argument works if the equilibrium total supply, $S(N, x) = NL\{w[p(N, x)]\}$, is an increasing function of N. In this case, $p(N, x) = (1 + x)/S(N, x)$ is a decreasing function of N and a high p signals a low N and high real wage. Under this assumption young agents produce more when they see a high p. This will occur even when the reason for the high p is large x rather than low N because the agents cannot tell the difference. The equilibrium labor supply function can be written as: $L(N, x) = L\{w[p(N, x)]\}$ and is increasing in x. Therefore we will observe a positive correlation between money (x) and output (L).[2]

Rational expectations equilibrium in discrete probability space

We now consider an example with discrete random variables. We use Π_{sj} to denote the probability that $\tilde{N} = N_s$ and $\tilde{x} = x_j$. (Since the two random variables are independently distributed Π_{sj} is the probability that $\tilde{N} = N_s$ times the probability that $\tilde{x} = x_j$.) We start with a definition of rational expectations equilibrium for the discrete case and then turn to the example.

A rational expectations equilibrium is an expected real wage function, $w(p)$, a labor supply function, $L(w) = L[w(p)]$, a normalized price function, $p(N, x)$, an expected purchasing power of a normalized dollar, z, and conditional probabilities functions, $\pi_{sj}(p)$ such that:

(a) $z = E[1/p(\tilde{N}, \tilde{x})] = \sum_s \sum_j \pi_{sj}/p(N_s, x_j)$;

(b) $\pi_{sj}(p)$ are the probabilities that $\tilde{N} = N_s$ and $\tilde{x} = x_j$ given that the price is p. These probabilities are calculated as follows. We consider the set A of all possible indices (s, j) such that the realizations (N_s, x_j) solve: $p(N, x)NL\{w[p(N, x)]\} = 1+x$. We then compute the probability that we observe p by: $prob(p) = \sum_{s \text{ and } j \in A} \Pi_{sj}$. We use Bayes' law to compute the probability $\pi_{sj}(p) = \Pi_{sj}/prob(p)$ when $s, j \in A$ and $\pi_{sj}(p) = 0$ when $s, j \notin A$;

(c) $w(p) = \sum_s \sum_j \pi_{sj}(p)[p(N_s, x_j)/(1 + x_j)]z$;

(d) $v'[L(w)] = w$;

(e) $p(N, x)NL\{w[p(N, x)]\} = 1 + x$.

An example: Suppose that $\tilde{N}$ has two possible realizations with equal probability of occurrence: 1 and 2. $\tilde{x}$ has also two possible realizations: 0.1 and 0.2 with equal probability of occurrence.

For this example there is at most four possible distinct market-clearing prices:

$$p(1, 0.1)L\{w[p(1, 0.1)]\} = 1.1$$

$$p(1, 0.2)L\{w[p(1, 0.2)]\} = 1.2$$

$$p(2, 0.1)2L\{w[p(2, 0.1)]\} = 1.1$$

$$p(2, 0.2)2L\{w[p(2, 0.2)]\} = 1.2.$$

We expect that the price level will be higher when the money supply is higher:

$$p(2, 0.1) < p(2, 0.2);$$

$$p(1, 0.1) < p(1, 0.2).$$

We also expect that the price level will be higher when the number of young agents is lower:

$$p(2, 0.1) < p(1, 0.1);$$

$$p(2, 0.2) < p(1, 0.2).$$

Therefore one of the following relationships must hold:

(a) $p(2, 0.1) < p(2, 0.2) < p(1, 0.1) < p(1, 0.2)$;

(b) $p(2, 0.1) < p(1, 0.1) < p(2, 0.2) < p(1, 0.2)$;

(c) $p(2, 0.1) < p(1, 0.1) = p(2, 0.2) < p(1, 0.2)$.

Under (c) there is confusion when $p(1, 0.1) = p(2, 0.2)$ is observed and as a result we may get a positive correlation between money and output. To see this note that when $p(2, 0.1)$ is observed it must be the case that $\tilde{N} = 2$. When $p(1, 0.2)$ is observed it must be the case that $\tilde{N} = 1$. When $p(1, 0.1) = p(2, 0.2)$ is observed both realizations are possible and the young agent takes some average of the two. Because of the inverse relationship between the real wage and the perceived realization of Ñ, we get: $w[p(2, 0.1)] < w[p(1, 0.1)] = w[p(2, 0.2)] < w[p(1, 0.2)]$. It follows that:

$$(1/2)L\{w[p(2, 0.1)]\} + (1/2)L\{w[p(1, 0.1)]\}$$

$$< (1/2)L\{w[p(1, 0.2)]\} + (1/2)L\{w[p(2, 0.2)]\},$$

and therefore in case (c) we will observe a positive correlation between output and money.

Policy implications

Changes in the money supply that are based on publicly available information cannot confuse rational agents and cannot have real effects. Therefore monetary policy that tries to reduce fluctuations in output is not effective if the central bank does not have informational advantage over the public. See the discussion in section 1.2.

Discussion

Lucas (1972) changed the way macroeconomics is done. Instead of writing "reasonable" aggregate relationships it became necessary to describe the maximization problems of the agents in the model. Instead of specifying "reasonable" expectations economists started to insist that expectations will be consistent with the predictions of the model even when they are formed under incomplete information. However, over the years this model was criticized on several grounds.

1 When the random variables are discrete the equilibrium tends to be fully revealing almost always: by observing p agents will be able to tell N and x and there will be no effect of money on output. See Radner (1979).
2 It is easy to observe the current money supply and therefore the confusion hypothesis cannot explain the money/output relationship.
3 Recent studies claim that a monetary shock affects output first and prices much later (see Christiano, Eichenbaum, and Evans [1999]). This observation is not consistent with the confusion hypothesis because the change in price that follows a monetary injection plays a key role in creating the confusion and the real effects.

10.2 LIMITED PARTICIPATION

Lucas (1972) showed that information lag may cause confusion and may lead to a positive relationship between money and output. It is also possible to get the money/output relationship by assuming that some or all agents adjust their portfolios with a lag.

To provide some intuition, it is useful to review the standard neutrality argument by considering a once and for all open market operation in a frictionless Walrasian economy. We assume that the government sells bonds and reduces the money supply by x%. As a result the price level declines by x%. After the decline in prices the agents in the economy have the same amount of real balances and more bonds. But when the conditions for Ricardian equivalence hold they do not regard the acquired bonds as an addition to net wealth.[3] Therefore, an x% decline in prices brings agents to exactly the same position as they were before the open market operation and restores equilibrium.

The assumption that leads to this neutrality result is that all agents can adjust their portfolio immediately, when the open market operation occurs. To get non-neutrality, Grossman and Weiss (1983) and Rotemberg (1984) relaxed this assumption. They assumed that only half of the population is present at the bonds market (the bank) and only those who are at the bonds market can adjust their portfolio immediately. The rest adjust it with a one period lag.

To get an x% reduction in the money supply in the Grossman-Weiss-Rotemberg model, agents at the bank must reduce their nominal balances by 2x% while agents who are not at the bank cannot change their holding of money. Therefore an x% reduction in the price level implies that agents in the bank have less real balances than before. To restore equilibrium the nominal interest rate has to increase so that agents who are in the bank will be willing to hold less real balances.

In general, if not all agents participate in the bonds market, an open market operation requires a redistribution of nominal assets and therefore some changes in relative prices must occur. Lucas (1990) has taken this idea to a cash-in-advance framework. He argued "if cash is required for trading in securities, then the quantity of cash – of 'liquidity' – available for this purpose will in general influence the prices of securities traded at that time" (p. 237). In his literature review, Fuerst (1992) argues that the key to the interest effect of money is the asymmetry of the monetary injection.

Here we use a cash-in-advance model in which the limited participation effect does not work through the effect on the interest rate. For a limited participation model with an interest rate effect see chapter 16.

The model

We consider a cash-in-advance economy with a representative infinitely lived household consisting of a worker/shopper pair. The household's single period utility function is $c - v(L)$ where c denotes current period consumption and L denotes current period labor. The household's discount rate is: $0 < \beta = 1/(1 + \rho) < 1$.

The representative household starts the period with m normalized dollars (M_t regular dollars). It deposits d normalized dollars in a government run savings account that yields the gross interest rate R. After making this deposit the household gets a transfer payment of x normalized dollars, where x is an i.i.d. random variable. The price of consumption p(x) is announced after the realization of the transfer payment. The buyer then takes the available $m - d + x$ normalized dollars and buys $(m - d + x)/p(x)$ units of consumption. The worker supplies L units of labor and gets p(x)L normalized dollars for it. At the end of the period the household has $p(x)L + Rd - g$ normalized dollars, where g is a lump sum tax levied by the government. The rate of change in the money supply is $1 + x$ and therefore the balances in terms of next period's normalized dollars are: $m' = [p(x)L + Rd - g]/(1 + x)$.

Here the government run savings account is introduced to get a lag in the adjustment of the portfolio choice to change in the money supply. The key assumption is that the savings decision is made before the transfer payment is realized.

The Bellman's equation that describes the household's problem is:

$$V(m) = \max_{d} E_x\{(m - d + x)/p(x)$$

$$+ \max_{L} -v(L) + \beta V[(p(x)L + Rd - g)/(1 + x)]\}. \tag{10.13}$$

Since we have risk neutrality, V' is a constant and we can write the first order conditions for an interior solution to (10.13) as:

$$R = 1/\beta\omega \tag{10.14}$$

$$v'(L) = \beta z p(x)/(1 + x), \tag{10.15}$$

where $z = E[1/p(x)]$ is the expected purchasing power of a normalized dollar held at the beginning of the period and $\omega = E_x\{1/(1 + x)\}$ is the average of one over the gross rate of growth in the money supply. The first order condition (10.14) says that at the interest rate R the household is indifferent to the amount it puts in the savings account. The first order condition (10.15) says that the marginal cost must equal the expected real wage. Note that the wage in terms of next period's normalized dollars is: $p(x)/(1 + x)$. To get the real wage we multiply by the expected purchasing power of a normalized dollar.

Equilibrium is a vector of scalars (R, z, d) and a pair of functions $[p(x), L(x)]$ such that:

(a) $R = 1/\beta\omega$ and $z = E[1/p(x)]$;
(b) given z and the function $p(x)$, the function $L(x)$ satisfies the first order condition (10.15) for all x;
(c) the goods market is cleared: $L(x)p(x) = 1 - d + x$; for all x;
(d) $d = g/(R - 1)$.

The last requirement says that the lump sum taxes cover the interest payment on the amount deposited in the savings account: $Rd - d = g$. Therefore the rate of change in the money supply is $1 + x$.

We can now substitute the market-clearing condition, $p(x) = (1 - d + x)/L$, in (10.15) to get the equilibrium condition:

$$v'(L) = \beta z(1 - d + x)/L(1 + x) = A(x)/L, \tag{10.16}$$

where $A(x) = \beta z(1 - d + x)/(1 + x)$ is an increasing function. As can be seen from figure 10.1, the equilibrium labor supply when $x = 0.2$ is larger than the equilibrium labor supply when $x = 0.1$.

The non-neutrality here occurs because nominal spending does not increase by the percentage increase in the money supply: when the money supply increases by x%, the amount of spending increases by more than x%.[4]

The effect on current prices

Since the equilibrium price function is: $p(x) = (1 - d + x)/L(x)$, this model predicts a strong effect of money on current prices, unless labor supply is highly elastic. This is a problem

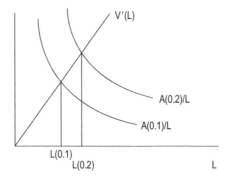

Figure 10.1 The equilibrium labor supply is increasing in x

because the work surveyed by Christiano, Eichenbaum and Evans (1999) suggests that initially prices do not move in response to a money shock.

The reasons for the non-neutrality result

The non-neutrality result is due to two key assumptions: (a) current earnings are spent next period and (b) nominal spending is not proportional to the post-transfer money supply. Therefore equilibrium prices are not proportional to the post-transfer money supply and the worker's real wage becomes a function of x.

To see the first point note that if the worker could have spent his earnings in the current period (as is the case in many models in which money is in the utility function) his real wage would have been 1 regardless of the realization of x and therefore money will be neutral.

To see the second point note that if $L(x) = L$ for all x, then $p(x) = (1 - d + x)/L$ is proportional to spending. But because earnings are spent in the next period, the real wage is proportional to the price in terms of next period's normalized dollars: $p(x)/(1 + x) = (1 - d + x)/(1 + x)L$. Because spending (the numerator in the expression) is not proportional to the post-transfer money supply (the denominator) the real wage depends on x and $L(x) = L$ for all x cannot be an equilibrium outcome.

Note that the results will not change if instead of requiring a deposit in a special account the government sells bonds that cannot be used to satisfy the cash-in-advance constraint and finance the end of period interest payments by a lump sum tax.

PROBLEM

1 Assume that instead of the above government run savings account we have government regulation that requires the household to deposit a fraction d of his

balances in a savings account that does not pay any interest. The Bellman equation for this case is:

$$V(m) = E_x\{[(1 - d)m + x]/p(x)$$
$$+ \max_{L} -v(L) + \beta V[(dm + p(x)L)/(1 + x)]\}.$$

Derive the first order conditions for this problem. What is $z = V'$ in this case?

NOTES

1   One way to think about (10.11) is to assume that the Walrasian auctioneer knows the realization (N, x).

2   Can we have an equilibrium in which the correlation between output and money is negative? To examine this possibility let us assume that $S(N, x)$ is a decreasing function of N: $S_1 = \partial S(N, x)/\partial N = L + NL'w'p_1 < 0$. Since $L' > 0$, this requires that ω' and $p_1 = \partial p/\partial N$ are of opposite signs. Since $p(N, x) = (1 + x)/S(N, x)$, if $S_1 < 0$ then $p_1 > 0$ and therefore $w' < 0$. But this contradicts (10.5) and therefore there is no equilibrium in which money and output are negatively correlated.

3   This means that agents fully discount the tax obligations implied by the new bonds. See Barro (1974).

4   The percentage increase in spending is:

$$(1 - d + x)/(1 - d) - 1 = x(1 - d) > x.$$

PART II

An Introduction to the Economics of Uncertainty

We review some of the material that is typically covered in microeconomic classes and then introduce some additional topics. We start with the expected utility hypothesis and the attitude towards risk. We then exposit the idea of trade in contingent contracts and apply it to problems of insurance, gambling and portfolio selection. Finally, we talk about efficient risk allocation and asset prices.

The analysis is relevant for monetary economics because of the debate about the importance of risk aversion for business cycle analysis. Lucas (1987) has argued quite convincingly that eliminating the business cycle is not important if risk aversion is the only reason that agents are averse to cycles.

This is related to the debate about the importance of risk aversion in general. Most economists think that there is overwhelming evidence about the importance of risk aversion. Gambling is quantitatively important but it is often discarded as primarily a game of "fun". Agents can also get "fun" by betting on stocks where the odds are in their favor. Why do agents get "fun" by gambling rather than more efficiently by investing in stocks? We will elaborate on this issue after we are done with the standard background material.

CHAPTER 11

Preliminaries

In this book we will use the expected utility hypothesis. This is a theory about the behavior of agents under uncertainty. Rather than following the axiomatic approach, we use here a version of the exposition in Friedman (1976) and Becker (1971).

It is assumed that the agent chooses among alternative lotteries, where a lottery is a probability distribution of income (or consumption). A typical lottery promises the realization I_s with probability P_s, where s is an index that runs over all possible realizations. Whenever necessary we will use the index i to distinguish among alternative lotteries and use,

$$B_i = \{I_{is} \text{ with probability } P_{is}\},$$

to denote the probability distribution of income promised by lottery i.

In general the consumer may order lotteries by the function:

$$G(B),$$

where lottery 1 is preferred to lottery 2 if $G(B_1) \geq G(B_2)$.

Special theory with some refutable implications may be obtained by assuming that there exists a utility function F( ) such that:

$$G(B_i) = \sum_s P_{is} F(I_{is}).$$

For example,

$$B = \{100 \text{ with probability (w.p.)} = 1/4, 200 \text{ w.p.} = 1/2, 300 \text{ w.p.} = 1/4\}$$

$$F(100) = 10; \quad F(200) = 20; \quad F(300) = 25$$

$$G(B) = \sum_s P_s F(I_s) = 2.5 + 10 + 5.25 = 17.75.$$

To see that the special theory has testable implications we consider the choice among the following three alternatives.

$$B_1 = \{150 \text{ w.p. } 1/2, 50 \text{ w.p. } 1/2\}$$

$$B_2 = \{200 \text{ w.p. } 1/2, 0 \text{ w.p. } 1/2\}$$

$$B_3 = \{200 \text{ w.p. } 1/4, 150 \text{ w.p. } 1/4, 50 \text{ w.p. } 1/4, 0 \text{ w.p. } 1/4\}.$$

Note that:

$$B_3 = \{B_1 \text{ w.p. } 1/2, B_2 \text{ w.p. } 1/2\}$$

Suppose now that $G(B_1) = G(B_2)$. Under the special theory $G(B_1) = G(B_2) = G(B_3)$. To see this claim note that:

$$G(B_1) = \tfrac{1}{2}[F(150) + F(50)] = G(B_2) = \tfrac{1}{2}[F(200) + F(0)]$$

implies:

$$G(B_3) = \tfrac{1}{4}[F(200) + F(150) + F(50) + F(0)] = \tfrac{1}{2}[F(200) + F(0)].$$

Therefore if the agent tells us (or shows by his behavior) that he is indifferent between lottery 1 and lottery 2, the special theory predicts that he must also be indifferent between lottery 1 and lottery 3. This is a refutable hypothesis because from the choice between 1 and 2 we predict the choice between 1 and 3.

Risk aversion

A consumer who prefers the mean of a lottery to the lottery itself is called risk averse. An agent with a concave utility function:

$$F'' < 0,$$

is risk averse. To show this claim, consider the choice between the lottery:

$$B_1 = \{I_1 \text{ w.p. } 1/2, I_2 \text{ w.p. } 1/2\}$$

and the degenerated lottery:

$$B_2 = \{\tfrac{1}{2}I_1 + \tfrac{1}{2}I_2 \text{ w.p. } 1\}.$$

We can now show with the aid of figure 11.1 that for a strictly concave utility function $F(\ )$:

$$EF(I) = \tfrac{1}{2}F(I_1) + \tfrac{1}{2}F(I_2) \leq F[\tfrac{1}{2}I_1 + \tfrac{1}{2}I_2] = F(EI)$$

Monotonic transformation of G

$G(B_1) > G(B_2)$ implies that $H[G(B_1)] > H[G(B_2)]$ if H is monotonically increasing. Thus monotonic transformation on G does not change the ordering of lotteries.

Monotonic transformation on F

$G(B_1) = \sum_s P_{1s}F(I_{1s}) > G(B_2) = \sum_s P_{2s}F(I_{2s})$ does not imply that

$$\sum_s P_{1s}H[F(I_{1s})] > \sum_s P_{2s}H[F(I_{2s})].$$

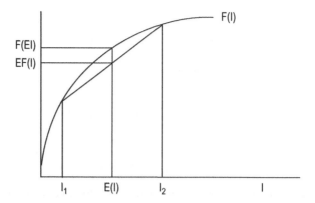

Figure 11.1   Concave utility function and risk aversion

To show this claim, suppose that $F'' < 0$ and consider a monotonic transformation: $Z(I) = H[F(I)]$, where $H' > 0$. We now take the first and second derivatives of Z:

$$Z' = H'[F(I)]F'(I) > 0$$
$$Z'' = H''[F(I)][F'(I)]^2 + F''(I)H'[F(I)]$$

Z'' may be positive if $H'' > 0$ and large and in this case the utility function Z (with $Z'' > 0$) describes the preference of a risk lover.

We started with an expected utility function F that describes the preferences of a risk averse agent. After applying a monotonic transformation to F we got a utility function that describes the preferences of a risk lover. Therefore a monotonic transformation on F may change the ranking of lotteries.

Linear transformation on F

A linear transformation on F will not change the ranking of lotteries:

$$G(B_1) = \sum_s P_{1s}F(I_{1s}) > G(B_2) = \sum_s P_{2s}F(I_{2s}) \text{ does imply that}$$

$$\sum_s P_{1s}[a + bF(I_{1s})] > G(B_2) = \sum_s P_{2s}[a + bF(I_{2s})], \quad \text{where } b > 0.$$

To show this claim note that:

$$\sum_s P_{1s}[a + bF(I_{1s})] = a + b\sum_s P_{1s}F(I_{1s})$$

$$> a + b\sum_s P_{2s}F(I_{2s}) = \sum_s P_{2s}[a + bF(I_{2s})].$$

Thus the expected utility function F is unique up to a linear transformation.

11.1 TRADE IN CONTINGENT COMMODITIES

Budget lines and indifference curves were used as early as the nineteenth century to analyze the choice between two goods with different physical characteristics: butter and cottage cheese, for example. Irving Fisher taught us how to use these tools for analyzing the choice between current and future consumption. His insight was to define goods by the time of delivery in addition to other characteristics, like physical characteristics. Thus Fisher treats cheese that will be delivered today and cheese that will be delivered tomorrow as two different goods.

Arrow and Debreu applied the same tools to analyze individual choice under uncertainty. Their insight was to define goods by the description of the events that will lead to delivery. Thus cheese that will be delivered if it rains and cheese that will be delivered if it does not rain are treated as two different goods.

To illustrate this approach We follow Hirshleifer (1966) and Becker (1971) and consider a single period economy. Trade occurs at $t = 0$. A random event takes place at $t = 1/2$: either it rains or it does not rain. Deliveries and consumption occur at $t = 1$. There are two goods with the same physical characteristics (corn). Let,

X = a claim on corn that will be delivered at $t = 1$ if it rains;

Y = a claim on corn that will be delivered at $t = 1$ if it does not rain.

X and Y are called contingent commodities because their delivery is contingent on the realizations of future events or the state of nature. We use this notation also to denote quantities of the goods.

We consider a consumer (a farmer) who comes to the market at $t = 0$ with an endowment of $(\bar{X}, \bar{Y})$. For example, he may expect to harvest 100 units if it rains and 50 units if it does not rain. In this case: $\bar{X} = 100$ and $\bar{Y} = 50$.

The price of X in terms of Y is: $P = p_x/p_y$. The consumer's budget constraint is:

$$PX + Y = P\bar{X} + \bar{Y}. \tag{11.1}$$

Let q denote the probability of rain. If $P = q/(1 - q)$ then (11.1) becomes:

$$qX + (1 - q)Y = q\bar{X} + (1 - q)\bar{Y}. \tag{11.2}$$

Under (11.2), the consumer can choose any combination of Y and X that has the same expected value as his own endowment. Therefore, we say that when $P = q/(1 - q)$ the consumer can buy actuarially fair insurance. Or alternatively we may say that the relative price P is actuarially fair.

By definition, a risk averter prefers the mean of a distribution to the distribution itself. In terms of figure 11.2 he prefers a point on the 45° line (A) to a point which is not on the 45° line

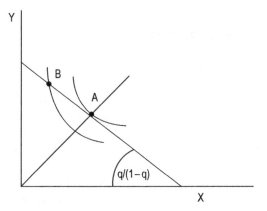

Figure 11.2   An actuarially fair price

and has the same mean (B). The indifference curves in the (X, Y) plane of a risk averter must therefore have the slope $q/(1-q)$ along the 45° line and when the relative price is actuarially fair a risk averter chooses X = Y.

We now derive this result formally for the case in which the consumer has the expected utility function:

$$qU(X) + (1-q)U(Y), \tag{11.3}$$

where U is differentiable with $U' > 0$ and $U'' < 0$. An indifference curve in the (X, Y) plane is a collection of points that satisfy:

$$qU(X) + (1-q)U(Y) = u \tag{11.4}$$

where u is the level of expected utility that characterizes the indifference curve. Taking a full differential of (11.4) leads to:

$$qU'(X)\,dX + (1-q)U'(Y)\,dY = du = 0; \tag{11.5}$$

And,

$$dY/dX = -qU'(X)/(1-q)U'(Y). \tag{11.6}$$

Note that along the 45° line, when X = Y, the slope of the indifference curves (11.6) is independent of the level of consumption and is equal to: $-q/(1-q)$.

The consumer's problem is:

$$\max \ qU(X) + (1-q)U(Y) \quad \text{s.t. (11.1).} \tag{11.7}$$

The first order condition for this problem is:

$$qU'(X)/(1-q)U'(Y) = P. \tag{11.8}$$

This says that at the optimum the slope of the indifference curve must equal the slope of the budget line. In the special case: $P = q/(1-q)$, (11.8) implies $X = Y$.

A risk neutral consumer ($U'' = 0$) has linear indifference curves with a slope $q/(1-q)$. When facing an actuarially fair price, $P = q/(1-q)$ the risk neutral consumer is indifferent among all the points on his budget line. When facing $P \neq q/(1-q)$ the risk neutral consumer specializes either in X or in Y. A risk lover ($U'' > 0$) has indifference curves which are concave to the origin. When facing the actuarially fair price he chooses to specialize either in X or in Y depending on the exact shape of his indifference curves.

Car insurance: an example

A consumer with an income of $100 may have a car accident during the period. In case of an accident he loses 50 dollars. We observe that the consumer buys an insurance contract that covers all his losses in case of an accident for a premium of 5 dollars. We now describe the trade between the insurance company and the consumer as a trade in contingent contracts. We redefine:

X = a claim on dollars that will be delivered at t = 1 if an accident does not occur;
Y = a claim on dollars that will be delivered at t = 1 if an accident does occur.

We can now think of the consumer as having at t = 0 an initial endowment of 100 units of X and 50 units of Y (100 minus the loss in case of an accident) and describe the above insurance transaction as follows. The consumer sold to the insurance company 5 units of X for 45 units of Y. As a result of trading the consumer will consume at t = 1, X = Y = 95. The price of X in terms of Y is: $P = 45/5 = 9$. This price is actuarially fair if the probability of an accident is 0.1.

Now, let us do some comparative statics under the assumption of risk aversion. Suppose that we make dollars in the good (no accident) state cheaper relative to the actuarially fair price so that $P < q/(1-q)$. Since the slope of the indifference curves is $q/(1-q)$ along the 45° line, the indifference curve that passes through the intersection of the budget line with the 45° line (point A in figure 11.3) must now intersect the budget line and the consumer will choose a point to the right of the 45° line (point B in figure 11.3). Similarly, it can be shown that if $P > q/(1-q)$ the consumer will choose a point to the left of the 45° line. Note that whenever $P \neq q/(1-q)$ the consumer chooses a point which is not on the 45° line.

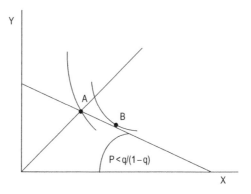

Figure 11.3   The price of X is less than fair

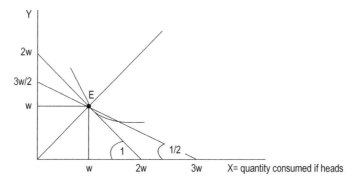

Figure 11.4   Local risk neutrality

When $P < q/(1 - q)$, the insurance offered to the consumer is less than fair from his point of view. In this case, the consumer chooses less than full coverage. For example, he may buy an insurance contract with a deductable which is the standard contract offered by insurance companies.

A consumer that starts from a position of certainty is "locally risk neutral"

Since whenever $P \neq q/(1 - q)$ a risk averter chooses a point that is not on the 45° line, a risk averter that starts from a position of certainty will take a small bet which is more than actuarially fair to him. To see this point let us redefine X as quantity consumed if the outcome of flipping a coin is "heads" and let us redefine Y as quantity consumed if the outcome of flipping a coin is "tails." The consumer starts with a non random wealth w (point E in figure 11.4). We offer him a bet in which he will gain 2 cents if the outcome of flipping the coin is "heads" and he will lose only 1 cent otherwise. The slope of the budget line proposed is now less than 1 (in absolute value) and the risk averse agent will therefore accept the bet.

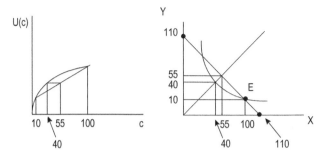

Figure 11.5   Certainty equivalence

Certainty equivalence

We consider an individual with an endowment of 100 dollars if the state is "good" and 10 dollars if the state is "bad." The minimum certain amount that the consumer is willing to receive in exchange of his random endowment, is the certainty equivalent of the endowment. In our example, the certainty equivalent, c, is a solution to:

$$U(c) = qU(100) + (1 - q)U(10). \tag{11.9}$$

Figure 11.5 uses $q = 0.5$. The certainty equivalent is 40. The maximum insurance premium that the agent will pay for full insurance is the difference between the expected value of his income and the certainty equivalent: $55 - 40 = 15$.

Application to portfolio choice

At time zero a consumer has a non-random wealth, w. He can invest it in two assets: a safe asset that promises the rate of return R and a risky asset that promises the rate r_2 if it rains and r_1 if it does not rain ($r_2 > r_1$). Let λ denote the fraction invested in the risky asset. For a given choice of λ, consumption if it rains is:

$$X = (1 - \lambda)w(1 + R) + \lambda w(1 + r_2) \tag{11.10}$$

and consumption if it does not rain is:

$$Y = (1 - \lambda)w(1 + R) + \lambda w(1 + r_1). \tag{11.11}$$

The consumer can vary his consumption between the two states by varying λ. When he chooses $\lambda = 0$, he will get a non risky point on the 45 degrees line in figure 11.6. This point is: $X = Y = w(1 + R)$. When he chooses $\lambda = 1$ the consumer will get a risky point to the right of the 45 degrees line: $X = w(1 + r_2)$ and $Y = w(1 + r_1)$. At this point he will get more if it rains.

The slope of the budget line is:

$$P = [w(1 + R) - w(1 + r_1)]/[w(1 + r_2) - w(1 + R)]$$
$$= (R - r_1)/(r_2 - R). \tag{11.12}$$

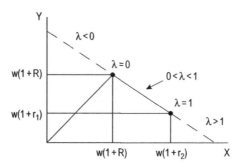

Figure 11.6   The budget line

The case in which the relative price is actuarially fair is:

$$(R - r_1)/(r_2 - R) = q/(1 - q),$$ (11.13)

where q is the probability of rain. In this case,

$$(1 - q)r_1 + qr_2 = R,$$ (11.14)

which means that the expected rate of return is the same for both assets. The risk averse consumer will choose, in this case, a point on the 45° line which in the present context implies $\lambda = 0$. When $P < q/(1 - q)$, the consumer will choose $\lambda > 0$ which implies a point to the right of the 45° line (see figure 11.3).

Note that $P < q/(1 - q)$ implies:

$$(1 - q)r_1 + qr_2 > R,$$ (11.15)

which says that the expected rate of return on the risky asset is greater than on the safe asset. Since in this case the consumer chooses $\lambda > 0$, this is an application of the claim that a risk averter who starts from a position of certainty behave locally like a risk neutral consumer.

If short sales and buying on margin are allowed, λ can be negative or greater than one. In this case we should add the broken lines in figure 11.6, to the budget line. For example, when the consumer wants to move to the right of the point $[Y = w(1 + r_1), X = w(1 + r_2)]$ he can choose $\lambda > 1$ by holding a negative amount of the safe asset (i.e., borrowing at the safe rate of return and investing it in the risky asset). This is called buying on margin. Similarly, if he wants to be to the left of the point $[Y = w(1 + R), X = w(1 + R)]$, he can choose $\lambda < 0$, by selling the risky asset short. This means that he holds a negative amount of the risky asset which is equivalent to borrowing a certain amount with an interest that is contingent on the state: r_2 if rain and r_1 if it does not rain.

11.2   EFFICIENT RISK ALLOCATION

Usually there is some aggregate risk in the economy: The total harvest when it rains is larger than the total harvest when it does not rain. Who should bear this risk? Who does bear it in a competitive environment?

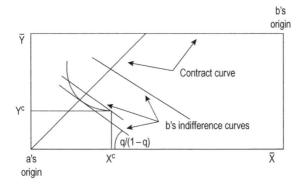

Figure 11.7 The contract curve when b is risk neutral

To analyze these questions we consider a single period economy with two agents indexed a and b. Agent a will harvest at t = 1 an amount of $\bar{X}_a$ units of corn if there is rain and $\bar{Y}_a$ units of corn if there is no rain. His endowment is: $(\bar{X}_a, \bar{Y}_a)$. Agent b's endowment is: $(\bar{X}_b, \bar{Y}_b)$. The total endowment in this economy is: $\bar{X} = \bar{X}_a + \bar{X}_b$ units of corn if there is rain and $\bar{Y} = \bar{Y}_a + \bar{Y}_b$ units of corn if there is no rain.

We now adopt the point of view of a hypothetical central planner who can take the endowments of both agents and distribute it in any way he wants. The set of all possible allocations is described by the Edgeworth box of figure 11.7. For example, the planner may choose to give X^C units of corn in the "rain" state and Y^C units of corn in the "no rain" state to agent a, and $(\bar{X} - X^C, \bar{Y} - Y^C)$ to agent b.

As a first step the planner may want to find all the points (allocations) with the property that there is no other feasible point that will make both agents better off. The set of all points with this property is called the Pareto efficient set.

To illustrate this concept, we start with the case in which agent a is risk averse and agent b is risk neutral. Assuming that the probability of rain (the good state) is q, agent b has linear indifference curves with the slope $q/(1 - q)$. Agent a, on the other hand, has indifference curves which are convex to the origin and have the slope $q/(1 - q)$ along the 45° line.

Since along the 45° line the slope of the indifference curves of both agents is $q/(1 - q)$, the set of Pareto efficient points, or the contract curve contains this line. At any other point, like point C in figure 11.7, the indifference curves intersect and a Pareto improvement is possible.

When both agents are risk averse, the contract curve must be between the two 45° lines as illustrated by figure 11.8. This claim can be shown by using $qU'(X)/(1 - q)U'(Y)$ for the slope of the indifference curves and $U'' < 0$. We then argue that the indifference curves must intersect at points like A, B, C, D in figure 11.8. For example, at point A the slope of a's indifference curve is $q/(1 - q)$. Since at point A, agent b will consume more in the good state $(X > Y)$ the slope of b's indifference curve at that point is:

$$qU'(X)/(1 - q)U'(Y) < q/(1 - q). \qquad (11.16)$$

Therefore at point A the indifference curves must intersect.

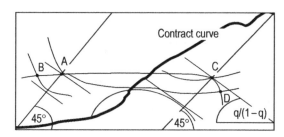

Figure 11.8   The contract curve when both are risk averse

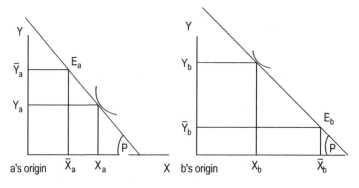

Figure 11.9   Budget lines

Thus, when the two agents are risk averse Pareto efficiency requires that X > Y for both agents: they both eat more in the good state and in that sense they both share aggregate risk.

Competitive equilibrium

To describe the Arrow-Debreu competitive equilibrium we assume an auctioneer who announces at t = 0 a relative price P. Given the endowments the relative price defines the budget lines for the two consumers as in figure 11.9.

Each consumer chooses the most preferred point on his budget line: (X_a, Y_a) for consumer a and (X_b, Y_b) for consumer b. If $X_a + X_b < \bar{X}$ there is an excess supply of X. (In this case, you can show from the consumer's budget constraints that there must be an excess demand for Y.) If $X_a + X_b > \bar{X}$ there is an excess demand for X (and excess supply of Y) and if $X_a + X_b = \bar{X}$ the market for X is cleared (and so is the market for Y). The relative price P is a market clearing price or a competitive price if $X_a + X_b = \bar{X}$, and the resulting allocation (X_a, Y_a, X_b, Y_b) is called the competitive allocation.

At the competitive allocation the slopes of the indifference curves is equal to the competitive price P and therefore the competitive allocation is Pareto efficient (i.e., it is on the contract curve). Figure 11.10 demonstrates this. (Take b's graph in figure 11.9 and flip it to create the Edgeworth box).

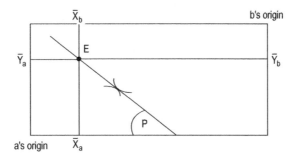

Figure 11.10   Competitive equilibrium

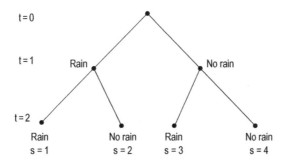

Figure 11.11   A two-periods four-states example

A generalization

We now assume a T periods horizon. At $t = 0$ the agents in the economy agree that it is possible to tell $S(<\infty)$ different stories about the evolution of the exogenous variables in the system. Each story is called a state of nature. Thus, there are S states of nature (indexed by s).

For example, suppose that $T = 2$ and at each point in time there may be two possible events: either it rains or it does not rain. In this case the following histories are possible: (a) It rains at $t = 1$ and it rains at $t = 2$; (b) it rains at $t = 1$ and it does not rain at $t = 2$; (c) it does not rain at $t = 1$ and it rains at $t = 2$; (d) it does not rain at $t = 1$ and it does not rain at $t = 2$. We have 4 states of nature as in figure 11.11.

We assume that only corn is consumed and that there are N agents in the economy. Let $\bar{C}_{ts}^h$ = the endowment of agent h in state of nature s at time t. Let C_{ts}^h = a quantity of corn which will be delivered at time t to consumer h if state of nature s occurs: ($s = 1,\ldots,S$; $t = 1,\ldots,T; h = 1,\ldots,N$).

We have ST commodities, where each commodity is defined by the time and the state of delivery. (In a more general model commodities are also defined by their physical characteristics and location). A consumption plan for agent h can be described by a choice:

$$C^h = \left(C_{11}^h,\ldots,C_{1S}^h; C_{21}^h,\ldots,C_{2S}^h,\ldots; C_{T1}^h,\ldots,C_{TS}^h\right). \tag{11.17}$$

It is assumed that each consumer can rank alternative consumption plans by:

$$V^h(C^h), \tag{11.18}$$

where V^h is a well behaved and strictly quasi concave function (from R^{ST}_+ to R).

Agents learn over time which states of nature cannot occur but they typically learn which is the true state of nature only at the end of the horizon, at time T. In the above two periods example, if there is rain at t = 1 then agents know that s cannot be strictly greater than 2, but the exact value of s will be known only at t = 2. (At t = 1, only a partition of the states of nature is observed, not the state itself.)

An agent cannot use information which he does not have: When state s is the true state and state s′ cannot be ruled out at time t he must choose:

$$C^h_{ts'} = C^h_{ts}. \tag{11.19}$$

In the two periods example of figure 11.11 the information constraint (11.19) is:

$$C^h_{11} = C^h_{12} \quad \text{and} \quad C^h_{13} = C^h_{14}. \tag{11.20}$$

The resource constraints are:

$$\sum_h C^h_{ts} \leq \sum_h \bar{C}^h_{ts}; \quad \text{for all s and t.} \tag{11.21}$$

When all agents are risk averse, an efficient allocation of risk is a choice of the magnitudes C^h_{ts} subject to (11.19) and (11.21) in a way that no other choice that satisfies the above constraints will make every individual better off.

Complete set of markets when all agents are risk averse

We now assume ST markets at t = 0. In the first market C_{11} will be traded. In the second market, C_{21}, and so on. An auctioneer announces ST prices, P_{ts}. Each consumer maximizes his utility subject to the information constraint (11.19) and the budget constraint:

$$\sum_s \sum_t P_{ts} C^h_{ts} \leq \sum_s \sum_t P_{ts} \bar{C}^h_{ts}. \tag{11.22}$$

A competitive equilibrium is attained when the prices (P_{ts}) clear all ST markets. The competitive outcome is Pareto efficient if all agents are risk averse. In the next chapter we show that this competitive outcome is not efficient when there are some risk lovers in the economy.

PROBLEMS

1   Consider an agent who consumes corn in a single period, $t = 1$. The agent's expected utility function is: $U(c) = c^{\alpha}$, where c denotes quantity of corn consumed at $t = 1$.

There may be two possible states of nature: rain and no rain, with equal probability of occurrence. Denote a quantity of corn that will be delivered if rain by x and a quantity of corn that will be delivered if no rain by y.

(a) Describe the agent's preference at $t = 0$, by indifference curves in the (x, y) plane. Distinguish among the following three cases: $\alpha > 1, \alpha = 1, 0 < \alpha < 1$. Use 3 separate graphs and indicate the slope of the indifference curve along the 45 degrees line.
(b) Assume that the opportunity cost of x in terms of y is 1. (Thus the price is actuarially fair). Assume further that the agent's endowment is 10 units of corn if it rains and zero units if it does not rain. What can you say about the agent's choice of x and y. Distinguish among three cases: $\alpha > 1, \alpha = 1, 0 < \alpha < 1$.

2   This question illustrates the Modigliani–Miller claim about the irrelevance of debt financing. Assume that at $t = 1$ there may be two states: rain and no rain. The price of a claim on a dollar that will be delivered at $t = 1$ if rain occurs is 0.5 current dollars (current dollars are dollars that will be paid at $t = 0$). The price of a claim on a dollar that will be delivered at $t = 1$ if no rain occurs is 0.25 current dollars.

There is a firm that is owned by a single individual. The firm's profits at $t = 1$ are: 1000 dollars if it rains and 500 dollars if it does not rain. The firm has a debt of 100 dollars that must be paid at $t = 1$ regardless of the state.

(a) The owner wants to sell the firm at $t = 0$, with its debt. How much he can get for it (in terms of current dollars)?
(b) Assume that the owner of the firm wants to pay the debt at $t = 0$. What is the cost of the debt in current dollars? What is the implied interest rate?
(c) The owner wants to sell the firm after paying its debt. How much can he get for it? Compare it to (a).

3   Use the state preference approach to show that if the expected rate of return on the risky asset is greater than the safe rate of return then the consumer will choose $\lambda > 0$.

4   Derive the budget line in the (X, Y) plane if instead of a safe or risky asset you have two risky assets.

5   Consider an economy in which there is cash and there are two assets which are traded in the capital market: one yielding a safe rate of return of 0.1 and the other yielding a random rate of return: 0.25 in the good state and 0.05 in the bad state. An owner of a third asset- a firm – wants to sell it for cash. The firm's profits will be 100 dollars

in the good state and 50 dollars in the bad state. For how much can the owner sell his firm?

6   Assume that b is risk neutral and a is a risk averter. Show that if $q\bar{X}_a + (1-q)\bar{Y}_a \leq \bar{Y}$ then there exists a competitive equilibrium and the competitive price must be actuarially fair $(P = q/[1-q])$.

7   Show that if both agents are risk averse then we have a competitive equilibrium in which the price of consumption in the good state is cheaper relative to the actuarially fair price $(P < q/[1-q])$.

8   Consider an economy with two agents indexed a, b. The utility function of a is: $qx^\alpha + (1-q)y^\alpha$. The utility function of b is: $qx^\beta + (1-q)y^\beta$. The aggregate endowment in the economy is: $(\bar{X}, \bar{Y})$. What can you say about the relationship between the contract curve and the diagonal of the Edgeworth box in the following three cases:

(a) $0 < \alpha = \beta < 1$ and $\bar{X} > \bar{Y}$;
(b) $0 < \alpha < \beta < 1$ and $\bar{X} > \bar{Y}$;
(c) $0 < \alpha < \beta < 1$ and $\bar{X} = \bar{Y}$.

(d) Assume that in equilibrium the price $P < q/(1-q)$ was determined. Assume that agent a's endowment is: $\bar{X}_a = \bar{Y}_a$ and he traded his endowment for the basket (X_a, Y_a). What can you say about the relationship between the expected endowment $q\bar{X}_a + (1-q)\bar{Y}_a$ and the expected consumption $qX_a + (1-q)Y_a$?

(e) How will you change your answer to d, if $\bar{X}_a > 0$ and $\bar{Y}_a = 0$?

CHAPTER 12

Does Insurance Require Risk Aversion?

We argue here that insurance-type phenomena do not require risk aversion and can be explained by the efficiency gains associated with early resolution of uncertainty. Early resolution of uncertainty can be achieved by a combination of insurance and gambling and allows for a better allocation of consumption over time regardless of the attitude towards risk. The argument is based on Eden (1977).

We consider an economy with two agents. Consumption takes place at $t = 1$ and at $t = 2$. The state of nature s is defined by the amount of rain at $t = 1.5$. The endowment of agent h at $t = 1$ is $\bar{C}_1^h$ and his endowment at $t = 2$ in state s is $\bar{C}_{2s}^h$. The aggregate endowment is non random and is given by: $\bar{C}_1 = \bar{C}_1^1 + \bar{C}_1^2$ and $\bar{C}_2 = \bar{C}_{2s}^1 + \bar{C}_{2s}^2$ for all s. Agents maximize a von Neumann Morgenstern strictly quasi-concave utility function: $U^h(C_1, C_2)$.

The endowment may be described as a probability distribution of points in the Edgeworth box of figure 12.1. Since the points $(\bar{C}_1^h, \bar{C}_{2s}^h)$ share the same first element, they must lie on the same vertical axis. For example, when there are only two states of nature $\{s = 1$ with probability q and $s = 2$ with probability $1 - q\}$ the endowment may be described as: (point A with probability q and point B with probability $1 - q$).

A feasible lottery (random allocation) can be described by a probability distribution of points in the Edgeworth box of figure 12.1. For example, the allocation point A with probability 0.2

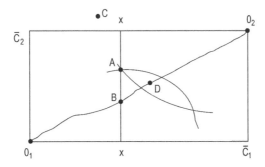

Figure 12.1 Assigning a positive probability to point A is not efficient

and point B with probability 0.8 is feasible. (The allocation [point A with probability 0.2 and point C with probability 0.8] is not feasible because point C is not in the box).

The state of nature (the amount of rain at t = 1.5) is a natural random device. We think of it as "a natural roulette wheel". Note that all allocations which are specified as a function of the state of nature are on a vertical line in the box of figure 12.1 (like points A and B). This is because the state of nature is known after the first period consumption has been allocated. It is also possible to specify the allocation as a function of the outcome of spinning an artificial roulette wheel at t = 1/2 before the irreversible choice of consumption at t = 1 is made.

Assuming that the contract curve is monotonic as in figure 12.1, leads to:

Theorem 1: Pareto efficiency requires that the allocation does not depend on the state of nature.

This Theorem is well known for the risk aversion case. It is extended here to the case in which there are risk lovers in the economy. The proof is based on the observation that an allocation that depends on the state of nature in a non-trivial way must assign a strictly positive probability to points which are not on the contract curve. We then show that by shifting the probabilities assigned to points which are not on the contract curve to points which are on it, it is possible to increase the expected utility of both agents.

Proof: We show Theorem 1 for the case in which the planner assigns a positive probability to two points only (the generalization to the case in which the number of points is greater than two is immediate).

Assume that the planner uses the "natural roulette wheel" and assigns positive probabilities to points on the same vertical line: say the probability $(1 - q)$ to point B and the probability q to point A (figure 12.1). In this case, the planner can increase the expected utility of both agents by shifting the probability q from point A to a point on the contract curve, like point D in figure 12.1.

In detail, let C_t^{Ph} denote the time t consumption of consumer h if the allocation is described by point P. Since,

$$U^h(C_1^{Ah}, C_2^{Ah}) < U^h(C_1^{Dh}, C_2^{Dh}), \tag{12.1}$$

it follows that:

$$(1 - q)U^h(C_1^{Bh}, C_2^{Bh}) + qU^h(C_1^{Ah}, C_2^{Ah})$$
$$< (1 - q)U^h(C_1^{Bh}, C_2^{Bh}) + qU^h(C_1^{Dh}, C_2^{Dh}), \tag{12.2}$$

for all h. Thus a Pareto improvement is possible when the allocation depends on the state of nature. □

To illustrate, assume that there can be only two states of nature: rain or no rain. Both agents harvest 5 units of the consumption good at t = 1. The amount harvested at t = 2, is random and depends on the amount of rain. Agent a will harvest 9 units if there is rain and 1 unit if there is no rain. Agent b will harvest 1 unit if there is rain and 9 units if there is no rain. Thus the Edgeworth box of figure 12.1, is a square in this case. Assume further that the agents have a Cobb-Douglas utility function:

$$U^h(C_1^h, C_2^h) = (C_1^h C_2^h)^2. \tag{12.3}$$

The expected utility that the representative agent can derive from his endowment in this example is:

$$\tfrac{1}{2}[(5)(9)]^2 + \tfrac{1}{2}[(5)(1)]^2 = 1012.5 + 12.5 = 1025.$$

Since both agents are risk lovers we can do better by using the natural roulette wheel and giving the entire harvest at $t = 2$ to one consumer: Agent a gets it if it rains and agent b gets it if it does not rain. This allocation which depends on the state of nature leads to the expected utility: $(1/2)[(5)(10)]^2 = 1250$.

However an efficient allocation uses an artificial roulette wheel. We flip a coin at $t = 1/2$ and give the entire resources to the winner. This yields an expected utility of: $(1/2)(100)^2 = 5000$.

The intuition is in the observation that by using an artificial roulette wheel we achieve smooth consumption. The winner gets $(10, 10)$ and the loser gets $(0, 0)$. The consumption when using the "natural roulette wheel is not smooth: It is $(5, 10)$ for the winner and $(5, 0)$ for the loser. Actually, in this example the utility of the loser is zero regardless of the amount he consumes in the first period. So why waste it on him?

In general, early resolution of uncertainty is useful for allocating consumption over time and this is achieved by a combination of insurance and gambling. Insurance type contracts are required to achieve an allocation that does not depend on the state of nature. Gambling is required to create risk (for risk lovers) in an efficient way. The combination of insurance and gambling may be viewed as a way of advancing the date at which uncertainty is resolved.

The choice of a commodity space

We know that the competitive allocation is efficient if there are markets for all the relevant commodities. What are the relevant commodities when there are risk lovers in the economy?

A commodity space is complete if: (a) any efficient outcome can be described as a point in the commodity space and (b) the initial endowment can be described as a point in that space. In our example, we should keep the "natural roulette wheel" for the purpose of describing the endowment and we should create an artificial roulette wheel that will be spun at $t = 0.5$ (before irreversible decisions are taken) to describe the efficient outcome. Let us assume that the appropriate artificial roulette wheel has Z possible outcomes, indexed z. We can then define the following $Z(S + 1)$ commodities:

C_{1z} = quantity of consumption at date 1 if the artificial roulette wheel shows z;

C_{2zs} = quantity of consumption that will be delivered at date 2 if the artificial roulette wheel shows z and the state of nature (the amount of rainfall) is s.

Trade in these commodities will lead to a Pareto efficient allocation. Trade in the standard $S + 1$ commodities (which index goods only by the state of nature and time) will suffice for the case in which all agents are risk averse.

12.1 THE INSURANCE-BUYING GAMBLER

Friedman and Savage (1948) were concerned with the puzzling phenomena of agents who simultaneously gamble and buy insurance. They propose an S shape utility of income function. Here we can use the above model to explain this phenomenon assuming a general strictly quasi-concave utility function.

We interpret insurance as aiming at reducing uncertainty that will be resolved in the future (like the amount of rain in our model) and gambling as a way of creating uncertainty that will be resolved immediately. We now provide an example, based on Eden (1979), of a strictly quasi-concave utility function that can explain the behavior of an agent who will buy any actuarially fair insurance and will participate in any actuarially fair gamble.

We assume a Cobb-Douglas utility function: $(C_1)^\gamma (C_2)^\delta$ and a zero interest rate. We define the indirect utility function from a given wealth W by:

$$V(W) = \max (C_1)^\gamma (C_2)^\delta \quad \text{s.t.} \quad C_1 + C_2 = W. \tag{12.4}$$

To solve (12.4) we set the lagrangian:

$$L = (C_1)^\gamma (C_2)^\delta + \lambda(W - C_1 - C_2). \tag{12.5}$$

We now take derivatives:

$$\partial L / \partial C_1 = \gamma(C_1)^{\gamma-1}(C_2)^\delta - \lambda = 0 \tag{12.6}$$

$$\partial L / \partial C_2 = \delta(C_1)^\gamma(C_2)^{\delta-1} - \lambda = 0. \tag{12.7}$$

Dividing (12.6) by (12.7) leads to:

$$C_2 = (\delta/\gamma)C_1. \tag{12.8}$$

Substituting (12.8) in the budget constraint and using symmetry leads to:

$$C_1 = \gamma W/(\gamma + \delta) \quad \text{and} \quad C_2 = \delta W/(\gamma + \delta). \tag{12.9}$$

Substituting the solution (12.9) in (12.4) leads to:

$$V(W) = (\gamma W/(\gamma + \delta))^\gamma (\delta W/(\gamma + \delta))^\delta = kW^{\gamma+\delta}, \tag{12.10}$$

where $k = (\gamma/(\gamma + \delta))^\gamma (\delta/(\gamma + \delta))^\delta$ is a constant.

Starting from a position of certainty, the agent will take an actuarially fair bet at $t = 1/2$ if $\gamma + \delta > 1$. To see this claim we take the following derivatives: $V'(W) = k(\gamma + \delta)W^{\gamma+\delta-1}$ and $V''(W) = k(\gamma + \delta)(\gamma + \delta - 1)W^{\gamma+\delta-1}$. Therefore, when $\gamma + \delta > 1$, $V''(W) > 0$ and the consumer will take any actuarially fair bet at $t = 1/2$.

The consumer will refuse to take a bet that will be resolved at $t = 1.5$ if $U_{22}(C_1, C_2) = \delta(\delta - 1)(C_1)^\gamma(C_2)^{\delta-2} < 0$. This requires: $\delta < 1$. Therefore the consumer will gamble and buy insurance if:

$$\gamma + \delta > 1 \quad \text{and} \quad \delta < 1. \tag{12.11}$$

This will occur for example if: $\gamma = \delta = 2/3$.

12.2 SOCIALLY HARMFUL INFORMATION

A group of consumers who distribute wealth according to the outcome of some random event will find that the sooner the outcome of the random event is known, the better the allocation of consumption will be, provided that the outcome becomes known after they had a chance to bet on it by trading in contingent contracts. In our earlier example, betting on the outcome of spinning a roulette wheel at $t = 1/2$ provides a better result than betting on the outcome of spinning the same roulette wheel at $t = 1.5$. But what about revealing information about the outcome of a random variable before there is a chance to bet on it?

Hirshleifer (1971) has shown that revealing the outcome of a relevant random variable before there is a chance to bet on it may have socially harmful results. To see his point consider the case in which all agents in our economy are risk averse and their endowment of future consumption depends on the amount of rain at $t = 1.5$. We showed that if trade in complete markets takes place at $t = 0$ agents will eliminate the effects of risk by insurance.

Consider now the case in which before trade takes place, say at $t = -1$, someone forecasts the amount of rain accurately and makes his forecast public information. This information makes insurance impossible: an insurance company that offers to exchange the random endowment for its mean will make negative profits since only agents that got less than the mean will trade with the insurance company.

Note that information in this case ruins markets. Before the forecast was announced trade in $S + 1$ contingent commodities was possible. When at $t = -1$, it was announced that state j will occur, prices of goods that will be delivered in states other than j must be zero and therefore it is possible to trade in 2 goods only. Since information that arrives too early ruins markets it may be socially harmful.

CHAPTER 13

Asset Prices and the Lucas "Tree Model"

What determines the price of a tree? This question was analyzed in the introduction (section 1.4.3) for the deterministic case. We now do it for the stochastic case. Roughly speaking the price of a tree is equal to the present value of its fruits, where the real interest rates which are used to discount future fruit dividends are determined endogenously and may vary across time and trees.

It is also true that the price of a tree is determined in a way that the available supply of trees is willingly held and no one wants to buy or sell trees. Here we merge the two answers using the Sargent (1987) and Ljungqvist and Sargent (2000) presentation of Lucas (1978).

The choice of consumption and a single asset

We start from a consumption choice problem. We consider the problem of an agent who starts with a wealth of A_0 units and expects to get labor income Y_t in each period t, $t = 1, \ldots, \infty$. The agent can invest in a single risky asset and accumulates wealth according to:

$$A_{t+1} = R_{t+1}(A_t + Y_t - C_t); \tag{13.1}$$

where C_t is consumption at time t, A_t is wealth at time t and R_{t+1} is the gross rate of return which its realization becomes known at the beginning of period $t + 1$. The consumer is not allowed to borrow an infinite amount and there exists a finite number B, such that

$$\lim_{t \to \infty} A_t \geq B, \tag{13.2}$$

where $\lim_{t \to \infty} A_t$ denotes the limit of A_t when t goes to infinity. The agent problem is to choose C_t as a function of all information available at t, to maximize:

$$\max E_0 \sum_{t=1}^{\infty} \beta^t U(C_t)$$

$$\text{s.t} \quad (13.1), (13.2) \text{ and } A_0 \text{ is given}; \tag{13.3}$$

where E_t denotes expectations taken at time t.

When A_t contains all the relevant information at time t, a solution to (13.3) is a function: $C_t = C(A_t)$. This function must satisfy the first order (Euler) conditions:

$$U'[C(A_t)] = \beta E_t\{R_{t+1}U'[C(A_{t+1})]\}, \qquad (13.4)$$

where the expectations are over the random variables R_{t+1} and A_{t+1}.

As in section 1.4.3 we may derive the first order condition (13.4) by considering a feasible deviation from the optimal path. The consumer cuts consumption at t by x units ($\Delta C_t = -x$), invests it in the risky asset and uses the proceeds to increase consumption at t + 1. Thus, $\Delta C_{t+1} = xR_{t+1}$. When x is small, the loss in utility associated with the decrease in time t consumption is: $\beta^t U'(C_t)x$. The expected gain in utility associated with the increase in time t + 1 consumption is: $\beta^{t+1}E_t R_{t+1}U'(C_{t+1})x$. At the optimum a small deviation should not change the value of the objective function and therefore:

$$\beta^t U'(C_t)x = \beta^{t+1}E_t R_{t+1}U'(C_{t+1})x, \quad \text{which is equivalent to (13.4).}$$

Bellman's equation: When A_t contains all the relevant information at time t, we may describe the problem (13.3) by a Bellman equation. The maximum utility that the consumer can achieve from time t onward depends on A_t and is denoted by $V(A_t)$. The definition of the value function V(A) is in the following Bellman's equation:

$$V(A) = \max_C U(C) + \beta EV[R(A + Y - C)]. \qquad (13.5)$$

The tradeoff in the maximization problem (13.5) is between current consumption and future wealth. Current consumption yields U(C) utils. Future wealth is given by $R(A + Y - C)$ and it yields $\beta EV[R(A + Y - C)]$ utils (discounted by β to time t).

The first order condition for the problem (13.5) is:

$$U'(C) = \beta ERV'[R(A + Y - C)]. \qquad (13.6)$$

Since by the envelope theorem $V' = U'$, it follows that

$$U'(C_t) = \beta ER_{t+1}U'(C_{t+1}). \qquad (13.7)$$

Stock prices

In the above case the distribution of the real rate of return, R, was given. We now turn to the case in which the price of the asset and the probability distribution of the stream of dividends are given. The asset evolution equation is now:

$$p_t A_t = p_t A_{t-1} + Y_t - C_t + A_{t-1}d_t, \qquad (13.8)$$

where p_t is the price of the asset at time t and d_t are the dividends per unit.

To get the first order condition in a way that relates the price to the future stream of dividends, we consider the following feasible deviation from the optimal path. The representative agent cuts consumption at t by x units, uses it to buy x/p_t shares of the asset and plans never to sell the shares and consume the infinite stream: $(x/p_t)d_\tau$, where $\tau = t + 1, \ldots, \infty$.

For small x, the loss in utility associated with the proposed deviation is: $\beta^t U'(\hat{C}_t)x$. The gain in utility is: $E_t \sum_{\tau>t} \beta^\tau U'(\hat{C}_\tau)(x/p_t)d_\tau$, where $\tau = t+1,\ldots,\infty$. At the optimum a small change should not make a difference in the objective function and therefore:

$$\beta^t U'(\hat{C}_t)x = E_t \sum_{\tau>t} \beta^\tau U'(\hat{C}_\tau)(x/p_t)d_\tau. \tag{13.9}$$

Rearranging (13.9) yields:

$$p_t = E_t \sum_{\tau>t} \beta^{\tau-t}\{U'(\hat{C}_\tau)/U'(\hat{C}_t)\}d_\tau. \tag{13.10}$$

Under risk neutrality U' is a constant and the price of the asset is the expected discounted sum of the future dividends that it promises: $p_t = E_t \sum_{\tau>t} \beta^{\tau-t}d_\tau$. This is also the case if the agent is risk averse and consumption is perfectly smooth ($\hat{C}_\tau = \hat{C}_t$ for all τ).

Asset prices in general equilibrium

It is assumed that the trees are the only asset. All trees are the same and there is one tree per agent. At the beginning of each period t, each tree yields fruit or dividends in the amount of d_t. Labor income is also exogenous and is given by Y_t. The fruit is not storable but the tree is perfectly durable. In equilibrium $\hat{C}_\tau = Y_\tau + d_\tau$ and therefore (13.10) becomes:

$$p_t = E_t \sum_{\tau>t} \beta^{\tau-t}\{U'(Y_\tau + d_\tau)/U'(Y_t + d_t)\}d_\tau. \tag{13.11}$$

To develop some intuition for this formula, suppose that the dividends d_τ are deterministic and the only random element is labor income Y_τ. Then we can think of $E_t\beta^{\tau-t}\{U'(Y_\tau + d_\tau)/U'(Y_t + d_t)\}$ as the discount factor for time τ dividends. Since $U'' < 0$, a large realization of $Y_\tau + d_\tau$ implies a low realization of $U'(Y_\tau + d_\tau)$. Therefore dividends that are expected to occur in good times, when $E_t U'(Y_\tau + d_\tau)$ is low, are discounted relatively more than dividends that are expected to occur in bad times. The implication of this can be fully appreciated when there are many assets.

Many assets: We now assume that there are n "trees" indexed i and there are n identical agents. The representative agent starts with a portfolio of assets which consists of a fraction $1/n$ of each of asset the n assets. The single period budget constraint is now:

$$\sum_{i=1}^{n} p_{ti}A_{t+1i} = \sum_{i=1}^{n} p_{ti}A_{ti} + Y_t - C_t + \sum_{i=1}^{n} d_{ti}A_{ti}, \tag{13.12}$$

where p_{ti} is the price of tree i, A_{ti} is the quantity (fraction) of tree i held at the beginning of period t and d_{ti} is the dividend from tree i.

The first order condition (13.10) can now be generalized to:

$$p_{ti} = E_t \sum_{\tau>t} \beta^{\tau-t}\{U'(\hat{C}_\tau)/U'(\hat{C}_t)\}d_{\tau i}. \tag{13.13}$$

The first order condition (13.13) can be derived in the same way that the first order condition (13.10) was derived. We consider the following deviation from the optimal path. The representative agent cuts consumption at t by x units, uses it to buy x/p_{ti} shares of asset i and plans never to sell the shares and consume the infinite stream: $(x/p_{\tau i})d_{\tau i}$, where $\tau = t + 1, \ldots, \infty$. For small x, the loss in utility associated with the proposed deviation is: $\beta^t U'(\hat{C}_t)x$. The gain in utility is: $E_t \sum_{\tau > t} \beta^\tau U'(\hat{C}_\tau)(x/p_{\tau i})d_{\tau i}$. At the optimum a small change should not make a difference in the objective function and therefore: $\beta^t U'(\hat{C}_t)x = E_t \sum_{\tau > t} \beta^\tau U'(\hat{C}_\tau)(x/p_{\tau i})d_{\tau i}$, which leads to (13.13).

In equilibrium the representative agent holds a fraction of $1/n$ of each tree and consumes: $C_\tau = Y_\tau + (1/n)\sum_{i=1}^{n} d_{\tau i}$. Substituting this in (13.13) leads to:

$$p_{ti} = E_t \sum_{\tau > t} S_t^\tau d_{\tau i}, \tag{13.14}$$

where $S_t^\tau = \beta^{\tau - t} U'[Y_\tau + (1/n)\sum_{i=1}^{n} d_{\tau i}]/U'[Y_t + (1/n)\sum_{i=1}^{n} d_{ti}]$ is the slope of the indifference curve in the (C_t, C_τ) plane.

Aggregate and "tree specific" risk

We consider now the case in which we can write the fruits of tree i as:

$$d_{\tau i} = D + b_i \theta_\tau + \varepsilon_{\tau i}; \tag{13.15}$$

where D is a constant, θ_τ is an economy-wide shock, $\varepsilon_{\tau i}$ is a firm specific shock, b_i is a parameter that measures the sensitivity of the dividends of tree i to the economy-wide shock and $\theta_\tau, \varepsilon_{\tau 1}, \ldots, \varepsilon_{\tau n}$ are serially independent and are independent of each other. We choose units such that: $E_t \theta_\tau = 0$, $E_t \varepsilon_{\tau i} = 0$ and $(1/n)\sum_i b_i = 1$.

There is no labor income and in equilibrium the representative agent consumption is:

$$C_\tau = (1/n)\sum_i d_{\tau i}. \tag{13.16}$$

Substituting (13.15) and $(1/n)\sum_i b_i = 1$, in (13.16) leads to:

$$C_\tau = D + \theta_\tau + (1/n)\sum_i \varepsilon_{\tau i}. \tag{13.17}$$

When n is large and $\mathrm{Var}(\varepsilon_{\tau i})$ are bounded, we can use the law of large numbers and the following approximation:

$$(1/n)\sum_i \varepsilon_{\tau i} = 0. \tag{13.18}$$

Substituting (13.18) in (13.17) leads to:

$$C_\tau = D + \theta_\tau. \tag{13.19}$$

We now use the definition $\mathrm{Cov}(x, y) = Exy - ExEy$ and write (13.14) as:

$$p_{ti} = E_t \sum_{\tau > t} S_t^\tau d_{\tau i}$$

$$= \sum_{\tau > t} (E_t S_t^\tau)(E_t d_{\tau i}) + \mathrm{Cov}(S_t^\tau, d_{\tau i}). \tag{13.20}$$

Since (13.19) implies that $\mathrm{Cov}(S_t^\tau, \varepsilon_{\tau i}) = 0$, we can use (13.15) to write (13.20) as:

$$p_{ti} = \sum_{\tau > t}(E_t S_t^\tau)D + b_i\, \mathrm{Cov}(\theta_\tau, S_t^\tau) \quad \text{for all } i. \tag{13.21}$$

Thus the price of two assets with the same "b" coefficient is the same: $p_{ti} = p_{tj}$ if $b_i = b_j$. The idiosyncratic risk $\varepsilon_{\tau i}$ does not require risk premium.

Quadratic utility function

For further illustration we assume now a quadratic utility function: $U(C) = \alpha C - \gamma C^2$.[1] In this case:

$$S_t^\tau = \beta^{\tau - t}\{U'(C_\tau)/U'(C_t) = [\alpha/U'(C_t)] - A_t C_\tau\}, \tag{13.22}$$

where $A_t = -U''(C_t)/U'(C_t) = 2\gamma/U'(C_t)$ is a measure of the curvature of the utility at time t. (A_t is the absolute measure of risk aversion to bets in terms of consumption. Substituting (13.19) in (13.22) to get:

$$S_t^\tau = \beta^{\tau - t}\{\alpha/U'(C_t) - A_t[D + \theta_\tau]\}. \tag{13.23}$$

Therefore,

$$\mathrm{Cov}(S_t^\tau, d_{\tau i}) = -\beta^{\tau - t}A_t b_i\, \mathrm{Var}(\theta_\tau). \tag{13.24}$$

Substituting (13.24) in (13.20) leads to:

$$p_{ti} = \sum_{\tau > t}(E_t S_t^\tau)D - A_t b_i \sum_{\tau > t}\beta^{\tau - t}\,\mathrm{Var}(\theta_\tau). \tag{13.25}$$

To get a better feel for the asset pricing formula (13.25) we now consider the special case in which $\mathrm{Var}(\theta_\tau) = \mathrm{Var}(\theta)$ for all τ and $E_t S_t^\tau = \beta^{t - \tau}$. In this case, $\sum_{\tau > t}\beta^{\tau - t}\mathrm{Var}(\theta_\tau) = \mathrm{Var}(\theta)/\rho$, where $\rho = (1/\beta) - 1$ is the subjective interest rate. We can therefore write:

$$p_{ti} = D/\rho - A_t b_i\, \mathrm{Var}(\theta)/\rho. \tag{13.26}$$

Let $p = D/\rho$ denote the price of a riskless asset. We can now define the percentage reduction in price due to the riskiness of the asset (or the risk premium) by:

$$p_{ti}/p = 1 - A_t b_i[\mathrm{Var}(\theta)/D]. \tag{13.27}$$

We see that the risk premium defined in this way is related to the importance of a measure of aggregate risk relative to the mean income, $\mathrm{Var}(\theta)/D$. It is also related to the measure of absolute risk aversion, A_t, and to the coefficient b_i.

NOTE

1. We choose a strictly positive parameters α and γ so that $U'(C) = \alpha - 2\gamma C > 0$ in the relevant range.

PART III

An Introduction to Uncertain and Sequential Trade (UST)

In the Arrow–Debreu model reviewed in chapter 11 there is uncertainty about the future but no uncertainty about current demand conditions. Trade occurs before anything happens. The number of agents who participate in trade is known and we may assume that the price of all contingent commodities is known in advance to all participants.

The situation is different if demand conditions are not known before the beginning of actual trade. In this case the standard Walrasian model assumes an auctioneer who finds the market clearing prices by the following (tatonnement) process. He calls a vector of prices and asks agents to report their demand and supply for this price vector. He then checks whether markets are cleared. If not he tries another vector of prices and keeps doing it until he finds a vector of prices that clears all markets. Actual trade is prohibited until the market clearing price vector is found.

This standard formulation is problematic for three reasons. First, the description of the Walrasian auctioneer is not complete. Why does he provide the public service of finding the market clearing prices? What is his objective function? A second problem arises from the prohibition of trade: Trade is not allowed until the market clearing price vector is found.

Finally, and maybe most importantly, prices do not behave according to the standard Walrasian model. There is ample evidence against the "law of one price" and the effect of monetary shocks on prices occurs with a significant lag.

The new Keynesian (sticky price) models reviewed in chapter 8 provide an answer to the first problem. In these models agents, rather than the Walrasian auctioneer, make price choices. But new Keynesian models typically neglect the choice of quantities and typically assume that sellers satisfy demand at their preannounced prices. An attempt to relax the demand satisfying assumption was made in chapter 9 and proved to be rather difficult.

The uncertain and sequential trade (UST) model attempts to answer the second problem by allowing trade before the resolution of uncertainty about demand (and the market clearing price). Agents know in advance the prices in all potential markets, take these prices as given and make plans accordingly. In equilibrium the plans made by all agents are mutually consistent and can be executed. But unlike the Arrow–Debreu model, in the UST model there is uncertainty about the set of markets that will open (or be active).

It is also possible to think of the UST model as an answer to the first problem. As in the Arrow–Debreu model there is no need for an auctioneer who finds the market clearing price. We may simply assume that agents know the probability distribution of demand and the prices in all potential markets before the beginning of trade. We may also think of agents in the UST model as choosing price tags (not necessarily the same tags on all units).

But the major contribution of the UST model is in explaining observations which are regarded as "puzzles" from the point of view of the standard Walrasian model. We will apply the UST approach to explain the observed deviations from the law of one price, the real effects of money and the behavior of inventories. We will then turn to some policy questions. We start from a real version of the model and then turn to monetary versions.

CHAPTER 14

Real Models

UST models use ideas in Prescott (1975) and Butters (1977). Prescott considers an environment in which sellers set prices before they know how many buyers will eventually appear. He assumes that less expensive goods will be sold before more expensive ones and obtains an equilibrium trade-off between the price and the probability of making a sale. A similar trade-off arises in Butters (1977) in a model in which sellers send price offers to potential customers. In both models sellers commit to prices before the realization of demand. Prescott thinks of his example as one "which entails monopoly power on the part of sellers" (p. 1233).

In the UST approach taken by Eden (1990), trade is sequential and equilibrium distribution of prices is obtained even though sellers have no monopoly power and are allowed to change their prices during trade.

We now turn to the comparison of the UST model with the standard Walrasian model. It turns out that the main difference is in the time in which information about the realization of demand becomes public. In the UST model information about the realization of demand is being resolved sequentially during trade while in the standard model it is resolved before the beginning of trade.

14.1 AN EXAMPLE

To illustrate the difference between the two alternative spot market models we use the example in Eden and Griliches (1993) that builds on Hall (1988).

Restaurants in a certain location produce lunches. Fixed and variable labor are the only factors of production. Preparing a meal requires λ man-hours. Serving the meal requires ϕ man-hours. The wage rate is one dollar per hour.

The number of buyers that will arrive in the marketplace is uncertain: It may be N or $N + \Delta$ with equal probabilities of occurrence. Each buyer that arrives, is willing to pay up to θ dollars for a meal, where $\theta > \phi + 2\lambda$.

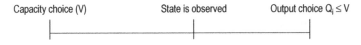

Figure 14.1 Sequence of events in the standard model

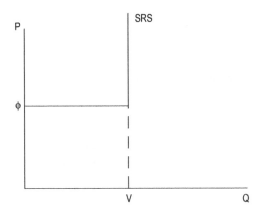

Figure 14.2 Short run supply

The standard model

There is a single price taking firm. It chooses capacity V (the number of prepared meals) on the basis of its expectations about the market-clearing price. Then buyers arrive and the market-clearing price is announced: P_1 if the demand is low (state 1) and P_2 if demand is high (state 2). The firm then chooses output (the number of served meals: $Q_i \leq V$) and sells it at the market-clearing price. Figure 14.1 describes the sequence of events.

The firm's problem is to choose capacity, V, and output in state i, Q_i, to maximize expected profits:

$$\max_{V} \left\{ \frac{1}{2} \left[\sum_{i=1}^{2} \max_{Q_i} Q_i(P_i - \phi); \text{ s.t. } Q_i \leq V \right] - \lambda V \right\}. \tag{14.1}$$

Using the logic of dynamic programming we solve (14.1) backward starting at the stage in which capacity is given. The maximum expected variable profits that can be achieved with V units of capacity is:

$$F(V) = \frac{1}{2} \left\{ \sum_{i} \max_{Q_i} Q_i(P_i - \phi); \text{ s.t. } Q_i \leq V \right\}. \tag{14.2}$$

The first order conditions for these maximization problems are:

$$Q_i = V \qquad \text{when } P_i > \phi;$$
$$0 \leq Q_i \leq V \quad \text{when } P_i = \phi;$$
$$Q_i = 0 \qquad \text{when } P_i < \phi. \tag{14.3}$$

Figure 14.2 illustrates the resulting short-run supply (SRS) curve.

Under the assumption $P_i \geq \phi$, the firm cannot do better than choosing $Q_1 = Q_2 = V$ and the expected variable profit is:

$$F(V) = \tfrac{1}{2}(P_1 - \phi)V + \tfrac{1}{2}(P_2 - \phi)V. \tag{14.4}$$

We now choose capacity by solving:

$$\max F(V) - \lambda V = \tfrac{1}{2}(P_1 - \phi)V + \tfrac{1}{2}(P_2 - \phi)V - \lambda V. \tag{14.5}$$

The first order condition for an interior solution $(0 < V < \infty)$ to (14.5) requires that the expected net revenue from an additional unit of capacity is equal to the cost of creating capacity:

$$\tfrac{1}{2}(P_1 - \phi) + \tfrac{1}{2}(P_2 - \phi) = \lambda. \tag{14.6}$$

In equilibrium, the first order conditions (14.3) and (14.6) are satisfied and the market clears. Formally, the vector (P_1, P_2, Q_1, Q_2, V) is a competitive equilibrium if: (a) given the prices (P_1, P_2), the quantities (Q_1, Q_2, V) solve (14.1) and (b) Q_i is equal to the number of buyers whose reservation price is above P_i.

Equilibrium prices are:

$$P_1 = \phi; \quad P_2 = \phi + 2\lambda, \tag{14.7}$$

and the equilibrium quantities are: $V = N + \Delta$, $Q_1 = N$ and $Q_2 = N + \Delta$.

To show this claim, we first solve (14.2) for $V = N + \Delta$. When $P_1 = \phi$, the state 1 variable profits, $Q_1(P_1 - \phi)$, are zero regardless of the choice of Q_1 and therefore the firm cannot do better than choosing $Q_1 = N < V$. Variable profits in state 2 are given by $2\lambda Q_2$ and therefore the firm will choose $Q_2 = V$. It follows that $F(V) = \lambda V$ and therefore the maximization in (14.5) yields zero profits regardless of the choice of V. Thus, the firm cannot do better than choosing: $V = N + \Delta$, $Q_1 = N$ and $Q_2 = N + \Delta$. This choice insures that the market-clearing condition (b) is satisfied.

The uncertain and sequential trade (UST) model

Buyers arrive sequentially in batches. N buyers arrive first with probability 1. After they complete trade, a second batch of Δ may arrive, with probability $1/2$. The seller is a price taker. He knows that he can sell to the first batch at the price p_1. He also knows that if the second batch arrives he can sell at the price p_2. On the basis of these expectations the seller makes a contingent plan and choose to sell x_1 units to the first batch and x_2 units to the second batch if it arrives.

It helps to talk in terms of two markets. The arrival of each batch opens a market. Since the number of batches that will arrive is random, the number of markets that will open is random. The representative firm knows that if market s opens it will be able to sell at the price p_s in this market. On the basis of these prices it chooses the amount of capacity allocated to each market (x_s). Figure 14.3 describes the sequence of events.

The representative firm is a price taker. It chooses the quantities $x_s \geq 0$, to maximize:

$$q_s(p_s - \phi)x_s - \lambda x_s; \tag{14.8}$$

Figure 14.3   Sequence of events in the UST model

where q_s is the probability of making a sale: $q_1 = 1$ and $q_2 = 1/2$.

The vector (p_1, p_2, x_1, x_2) is an equilibrium vector if: (a) given the prices p_s the quantities x_s solve (14.8) and (b) markets that open are cleared: $x_1 = N$ if $\theta \geq p_1$ and zero otherwise; $x_2 = \Delta$ if $\theta \geq p_2$ and zero otherwise.

The UST equilibrium prices are:

$$p_1 = \phi + \lambda; \quad p_2 = \phi + 2\lambda. \tag{14.9}$$

To show this claim we substitute (14.9) in (14.8). The expected profit is zero regardless of the choice of x and therefore the firm cannot do better than satisfy demand.

It is useful to define:

$$\text{ENR} = (p_1 - \phi) = \tfrac{1}{2}(p_2 - \phi) = \lambda = \text{MCC}, \tag{14.10}$$

where ENR denotes the expected net revenue per unit of capacity and MCC is the marginal capacity cost. Condition (14.10) says that ENR is the same for both goods and is equal to MCC.

Can our equilibrium unravel? Sellers who allocated capacity to market 2 may want to offer the good at an arbitrarily low price after realizing a period of low demand. But this is too late: you cannot sell another lunch to someone who has already had lunch, even at a low price.

Comparing the predictions of the two models

We now compare the time series implications of the two models under the assumption that the number of buyers each period is an identically and independently distributed (i.i.d) random variable.

Since in the UST model there are many prices for the same commodity we should distinguish between average quoted price and average transaction price. We define average quoted price by the outcome of a price survey that asks about price offers and is given by: $\bar{p} = (p_1 x_1 + p_2 x_2)/(x_1 + x_2)$. Average transaction price is the outcome of a survey that asks about prices of actual transactions. This is p_1 when demand is low and $\bar{p}$ when demand is high. The solid line in figure 14.4 illustrates a possible path for the average quoted price in the UST model. The broken line is for the average transaction price.[1]

In the standard model there is a single price that fluctuates over time between ϕ and $\phi + 2\lambda$: The solid line in figure 14.5. For comparison, the broken line is the average transaction price in the UST model.

The fluctuations of the price in the standard model are larger than the fluctuations of the average price in the UST model even if we measure transaction prices. The average transaction price fluctuates between $\bar{p}$ and $\phi + \lambda$. Since $\bar{p}$ is an average between $\phi + 2\lambda$ and $\phi + \lambda$ the

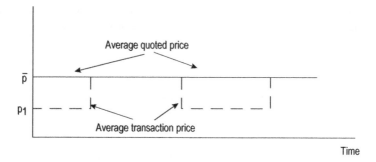

Figure 14.4   Average prices in the UST model

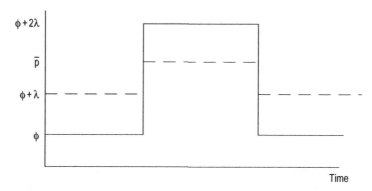

Figure 14.5   Average transaction prices in the standard model (solid line) and the UST model (broken line)

average price moves by less than λ in response to a change in demand. The price in the standard model moves by 2λ.

Therefore, if the UST is the "true" model we will reject the standard competitive model on the grounds that prices do not move much in response to changes in demand or that prices are "sticky".

Moreover, on average prices will appear to be "too high" relative to the prediction of the standard model. Average transaction price in the UST model is $(1/2)(\phi + \lambda) + (1/2)\bar{p}$ which is higher than the average price in the standard model, $\phi + \lambda$, because $\bar{p} > \phi + \lambda$. Thus if the UST is the "true" model, we may reject the standard model on the grounds that firms have market power.

A numerical example: We assume: $\lambda = 1/2$, $\phi = 1$, $N = 6$ and $\Delta = 4$. In this case the price of the 6 lunches that will be sold with probability 1 is 1.5 and the price of the 4 lunches that will be sold with probability 0.5 is 2. The data generated by the UST model is in table 14.1.

The market clearing price in the standard model is 1 if demand is low and 2 if demand is high. The data generated by the standard model is in table 14.2.

In the standard model there is one price in each period and different prices across periods. In the UST model there is a difference in prices between the two "contingent" commodities within the same period, no difference in quoted prices between periods, but no transactions in commodity 2 in the period of low demand. We get different prices for the "same" commodity

Table 14.1 Data generated by the UST model

Period	Output	Labor input	Average transaction price	Average quoted price	Wage bill	Revenue	Labor share	Profits
Low demand	6	11	1.5	1.7	11	9	1.22	−2
High demand	10	15	1.7	1.7	15	17	0.88	2

Table 14.2 Data generated by the standard model

Period	Output	Labor input	Average price	Wage bill	Revenue	Labor share	Profits
Low demand	6	11	1	11	6	1.83	−5
High demand	10	15	2	15	20	0.75	5

within the same period and smaller differences in average transaction prices across periods. Prices, labor share and profits fluctuate relatively less in the UST model.

14.1.1 Downward sloping demand

In the above example demand was inelastic and there was no difference in the predictions of both models with respect to output. We now consider the case in which all agents have the same downward sloping demand curve: $D(P)$.

Standard model: We modify the definition of equilibrium as follows.

The vector (P_1, P_2, Q_1, Q_2, V) is a competitive equilibrium if:

(a) given the prices $(P_1,\ P_2)$ the quantities (Q_1, Q_2, V) solve (14.1) and
(b) $ND(P_1) = Q_1; (N + \Delta)D(P_2) = Q_2$.

When $\lambda = 1/2$, $\phi = 1$, and $D(P) = 1/P$ the equilibrium vector (P_1, P_2, Q_1, Q_2, V) must satisfy the following 5 equations:

$$Q_1 = 0 \text{ if } P_1 < 1; \quad Q_1 = V \text{ if } P_1 > 1 \quad \text{and} \quad 0 \le Q_1 \le V \text{ if } P_1 = 1;$$
$$Q_2 = 0 \text{ if } P_2 < 1; \quad Q_2 = V \text{ if } P_2 > 1 \quad \text{and} \quad 0 \le Q_2 \le V \text{ if } P_2 = 1;$$
$$\tfrac{1}{2}(P_1 - 1) + \tfrac{1}{2}(P_2 - 1) = \tfrac{1}{2};$$
$$N/P_1 = Q_1;$$
$$(N + \Delta)/P_2 = Q_2.$$

The first equations are the first order conditions for the firm's problem (14.1) and the last two equations are the market-clearing conditions.

When $N = 6$ and $\Delta = 4$ we get an equilibrium in which capacity is always fully utilized: $P_1 = 9/8$, $P_2 = 15/8$ and $Q_1 = Q_2 = V = 16/3$. Figure 14.6 illustrates this case.

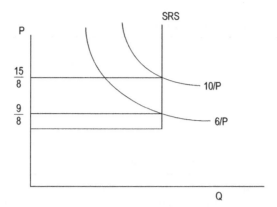

Figure 14.6   Full capacity utilization in the standard model

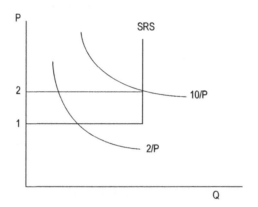

Figure 14.7   Partial utilization in the standard model

When $N = 2$ and $\Delta = 8$ we get an equilibrium in which capacity is not fully utilized in state 1: $P_1 = 1$, $P_2 = 2$, $V = 5$, $Q_1 = 2$ and $Q_2 = 5$. In this case capacity utilization in the low demand state: $Q_1/V = 2/5$. Figure 14.7 illustrates this case.

UST model: We modify the equilibrium definition as follows.

The vector (p_1, p_2, x_1, x_2) is an equilibrium vector if: (a) given the prices p_s the quantities x_s solve (14.8) and (b) $ND(p_1) = x_1$; $\Delta D(p_2) = x_2$.

When $\lambda = 1/2$, $\phi = 1$, and $D(p) = 1/p$ the equilibrium vector (p_1, p_2, x_1, x_2) must satisfy the following 4 equations:

$$p_1 - 1 = \tfrac{1}{2};$$
$$\tfrac{1}{2}(p_2 - 1) = \tfrac{1}{2};$$
$$N/p_1 = x_1;$$
$$\Delta/p_2 = x_2.$$

Table 14.3 Data generated by the UST model

Period	Output	Labor input	Av. trans. price	Capacity utilization
$N = 6$ and $\Delta = 4$				
Low demand	4	7	1.5	2/3
High demand	6	9	5/3	1
$N = 2$ and $\Delta = 8$				
Low demand	4/3	4	1.5	1/4
High demand	16/3	8	5/4	1

Table 14.4 Data generated by the standard model

Period	Output	Labor input	Price	Capacity utilization
$N = 6$ and $\Delta = 4$				
Low demand	16/3	8	9/8	1
High demand	16/3	8	15/8	1
$N = 2$ and $\Delta = 8$				
Low demand	2	9/2	1	2/5
High demand	5	15/2	2	1

The equilibrium solution for the case $N = 6$ and $\Delta = 4$ is: $p_1 = 1.5$; $p_2 = 2$, $x_1 = 4$ and $x_2 = 2$.

Capacity utilization in the low demand state: $x_1/(x_1 + x_2) = 2/3$.

When $N = 2$ and $\Delta = 8$ we get:

$$p_1 = 1.5, \quad p_2 = 2, \quad x_1 = \tfrac{4}{3} \quad \text{and} \quad x_2 = 4.$$

Capacity utilization in the low demand state: $x_1/(x_1 + x_2) = 1/4$.

Tables 14.3 and 14.4 summarize the data for the two different cases.

In the numerical examples, capacity utilization is lower in the UST model. In the first case ($N = 6$ and $\Delta = 4$) capacity is fully utilized in the standard model but is not fully utilized in the UST model. In the second case ($N = 2$ and $\Delta = 8$) capacity utilization is less than unity in both models (in the low demand case) but capacity utilization is lower in the UST model. When demand is high, the average transaction price in the UST model is lower than the standard model price. Since demand is always satisfied a lower average transaction price in the high demand state requires more capacity. When demand is low the UST first market price is higher than the standard model price and therefore output in the low demand state is lower in the UST model. Since capacity is higher and output in the low demand state is lower, capacity utilization in the low demand state is lower in the UST model. Since the above argument holds for any choice of parameters we may state the following claim.

> *Claim 1: Average capacity utilization is lower in the UST model.*

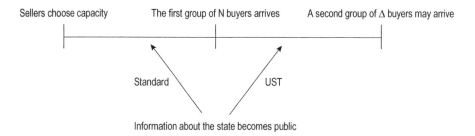

Figure 14.8 Sequence of events in the two models

Does this imply that the outcome of the standard model is better? We now turn to discuss this question.

14.1.2 Welfare analysis

To allow for welfare analysis we now provide a complete description of the economy. There are three dates (t = 0, 1, 2) and two goods (X and Y where lower case letters denote quantities of these goods). There are two states of nature (s = 1, 2) with equal probability of occurrence. There are three types of agents: one seller (S), N definite buyers (DB) and Δ possible buyers (PB).

The seller (and only the seller) can use part of his endowment of Y to produce X. It takes λ units of Y to produce a unit of capacity of X. It takes φ units of Y to convert a unit of capacity into output. Capacity choice must be made at t = 0.

The seller's utility function is: u(x, y) = y.

The definite buyers' utility function is: u(x, y) = U(x) + y, where U( ) is differentiable and strictly concave.

The possible buyers' utility function is: u(x, y) = U(x) + y if the state of nature is s = 2 and u(x, y) = y if s = 1.

Thus the seller does not like X, definite buyers like X and possible buyers like X only in state 2.

All agents are born at t = 0 with a large endowment $\bar{y}$ of the numeiraire commodity Y. Buyers (DB and PB) form a line at t = 0. At t = 1, buyers learn about their desire to consume. If s = 1 the Δ possible buyers drop out of the line and the N definite buyers arrive at the market-place. If s = 2 then all N + Δ stay in the line. The first group of N buyers go to the market at t = 1, complete their transactions and then go elsewhere. The second group of Δ buyers arrive at the market later, at t = 2.

Information about the state becomes public at time τ where the standard model assumes 0 < τ < 1 and the UST model assumes 1 < τ < 2. Figure 14.8 illustrates the sequence of events and the two alternative informational assumptions.

Let, x(i, s) = quantity of X per consumer in group i if the aggregate state is s, where i = First, Second and s = 1, 2.

Assuming x(2, 1) = 0, the total utility from X derived in state 1 is NU[x(1, 1)]. The total utility from X derived in state 2 is: NU[x(1, 2)] + ΔU[x(2, 2)]. The total utility from Y is obtained by subtracting the cost of production from the endowment. This is: $(1 + N + \Delta)\bar{y} - \lambda \max\{Nx(1,1), Nx(1,2) + \Delta x(2,2)\} - \phi Nx(1,1)$ in state 1 and $(1 + N + \Delta)\bar{y} - \lambda \max\{Nx(1,1), Nx(1,2) + \Delta x(2,2)\} - \phi[Nx(1,2) + \Delta x(2,2)]$ in state 2. The problem of maximizing the sum of expected utilities is therefore:[2]

$$\frac{1}{2}\{NU[x(1,1)] + NU[x(1,2)] + \Delta U[x(2,2)]\} + (1 + N + \Delta)\bar{y}$$
$$- \lambda \max\{Nx(1,1), Nx(1,2) + \Delta x(2,2)\}$$
$$- \frac{1}{2}\phi[Nx(1,1) + Nx(1,2) + \Delta x(2,2)]. \tag{14.11}$$

Assuming $Nx(1,1) < Nx(1,2) + \Delta x(2,2)$, a solution to (14.11) must satisfy the first order conditions:

$$U'[x(1,1)] = \phi; \quad U'[x(1,2)] = U'[x(2,2)] = 2\lambda + \phi. \tag{14.12}$$

Claim 2: The standard model's allocation maximizes (14.11).

To show this claim (the first welfare Theorem), note that when the price of X in terms of Y is P, the consumer solves: $\max U(x) + \bar{y} - Px$. The first order condition for an interior solution to this problem is:

$$U'(x) = P. \tag{14.13}$$

Substituting the equilibrium prices (14.7), $P_1 = \phi$ and $P_2 = 2\lambda + \phi$, in (14.13) leads to (14.12).

In the UST model information about the state becomes public after $t = 1$ and therefore the social planner maximizes (14.11) subject to the informational constraint:

$$x(1,1) = x(1,2) = x_1. \tag{14.14}$$

The first order conditions to this problem are:

$$U'[x(1,1)] = U'[x(1,2)] = \lambda + \phi; \quad U'[x(2,2)] = 2\lambda + \phi. \tag{14.15}$$

These first order conditions are satisfied in the UST equilibrium because the UST equilibrium prices (14.9) imply that the first group of N buyers buys at the price $\lambda + \phi$ and the second group will buy at the price $2\lambda + \phi$ if it arrives. We have thus shown,

---

Claim 3: The UST equilibrium allocation maximizes (14.11) subject to the informational constraint (14.14).

It follows that each of the two models produces an efficient outcome, where efficiency is defined relative to available information.

We may say that welfare and capacity utilization (Claim 1) are higher in the standard model because the standard model assumes more information.

Figure 14.9 illustrates the difference between the two models and the value of information to a "social planner" who maximizes (14.11). When the social planner knows the state before

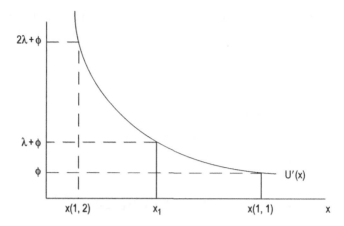

Figure 14.9   The allocation to the first group in the standard and the UST models

he chooses the allocation to the first group, he will make this choice as a function of the state: $x(1, s)$. When he does not know the state he chooses: $x(1, 2) < x_1 < x(1, 1)$. Thus information is useful for choosing the allocation to the first group.

Efficiency in the UST model and in the Prescott model

From a positive economics point of view it does not matter whether the prices in our model are flexible or rigid. But for the question of efficiency, it does matter. In the Prescott (1975) model prices are set before the arrival of buyers but actual sales occur after all buyers arrive and the realization of demand is known. At this point sellers may want to change their price but cannot. A central planner that has the same information as the sellers in the Prescott model can achieve the Walrasian allocation and will do better whenever the Walrasian allocation is different from the Prescott allocation.

Prescott assumes that each buyer demands one unit only and therefore he gets an equilibrium allocation that is the same as the Walrasian allocation. Allowing for a more general downward sloping demand curve (per buyer) will alter the efficiency result in the Prescott model because a planner that makes the actual allocation after he knows the realization of demand, will distribute the entire capacity to the first batch of buyers if he knows that the second batch will not arrive. A planner in a UST environment faces the same informational constraint as the sellers in the UST model and must therefore choose the amount given to the first batch before he knows whether the second batch will arrive or not. Therefore the allocation in the UST model is efficient even when buyers have a downward sloping demand curves.

For this reason it is useful to think of the UST model and the Prescott model as two different models, while keeping in mind that the resulting allocation is the same in both models.

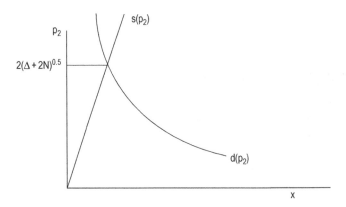

Figure 14.10   Production and prices in the UST model

14.1.3 Demand and supply analysis

Prices in the UST model are connected by an arbitrage condition. Therefore we may solve the model by standard supply and demand analysis. This will become especially useful later when we introduce storage.

To illustrate, we assume no variable costs. The cost of producing a unit of capacity is $C(x) = x^2$ and the individual demand function is $D(p) = 1/p$. The vector (x_1, x_2, p_1, p_2) is a UST equilibrium if:

$$x_1 = N/p_1; \tag{14.16}$$

$$x_2 = \Delta/p_2; \tag{14.17}$$

$$p_1 = p_2/2; \tag{14.18}$$

$$2(x_1 + x_2) = p_1. \tag{14.19}$$

The first two equations are market-clearing conditions. The third is the arbitrage condition: It says that the expected price must be the same in both markets. The fourth equation says that the marginal capacity cost is equal to the expected price (the price in the first market).

To solve for equilibrium we substitute (14.18) into (14.16) to get $x_1 = 2N/p_2$. To this quantity we add (14.17) and compute total demand as a function of p_2:

$$d(p_2) = x_1 + x_2 = (\Delta + 2N)/p_2. \tag{14.20}$$

After substituting (14.18) into (14.19) we compute supply as a function of p_2. This yields:

$$s(p_2) = x_1 + x_2 = p_2/4. \tag{14.21}$$

We can now solve for p_2 by equating supply and demand:

$$(\Delta + 2N)/p_2 = p_2/4. \tag{14.22}$$

This yields: $p_2 = 2(\Delta + 2N)^{0.5}$. Figure 14.10 illustrates this solution.

We can now do standard comparative static exercises. For example, an increase in Δ or in N will shift demand to the right and increase equilibrium prices.

PROBLEMS WITH ANSWERS[3]

1   In the UST model delivery to the first group must be made before information about the state of nature becomes public. Assume now that at $t = 1$ (before the first group arrives) sellers observe a signal about the state.

Formally the sellers observe at $t = 1$ the realization of a random variable σ. If $\sigma = 1$ the probability that the second group will arrive is $3/4$. If $\sigma = 0$ the probability that the second group will arrive is $1/4$.

A UST equilibrium for this environment is a vector of functions $[P_1(\sigma), P_2(\sigma), x_1(\sigma), x_2(\sigma)]$.

(a) Find the UST equilibrium functions for the case in which each potential buyer wants at most one unit and is willing to pay a lot for it; the fixed cost is λ per unit and the variable cost is ϕ per unit. Use the numerical example ($\lambda = 1/2$ and $\phi = 1$) to solve for the equilibrium functions numerically.

Answer

One possible solution is the following.

$P_1(1) = P_1(0) = \phi + \lambda = \frac{3}{2}$
$[P_1(1) - \phi] = \frac{3}{4}[P_2(1) - \phi] = \lambda$
$P_2(1) = \frac{4}{3}\lambda + \phi = \frac{5}{3}$
$P_2(0) = 4\lambda + \phi = 3$

(b) Compute the average quoted price as a function of σ.

Answer

$\bar{P}(\sigma) = [NP_1(\sigma) + \Delta P_2(\sigma)]/(N + \Delta)$
$\bar{P}(1) = [N(\phi + \lambda) + \Delta(\frac{4}{3}\lambda + \phi)]/(N + \Delta) = 1.56$
$\bar{P}(0) = [N(\phi + \lambda) + \Delta(4\lambda + \phi)]/(N + \Delta) = 2.1$

(c) Compare the standard deviation of the quoted price for the three informational assumptions (i) the standard model, (ii) the UST model where the signal σ is observed and (iii) the UST model where the signal σ is not observed.

Answer

(i) SD $= \lambda = 0.5$
(ii) SD $= \Delta\lambda(4 - \frac{4}{3})/2(N + \Delta) = \Delta\lambda\frac{8}{3}/2(N + \Delta) = \frac{8}{15}\lambda = 0.266$
(iii) SD $= 0$

(d) Does more information increase the standard deviation of quoted prices?

Answer

In this example, more information leads to a higher standard deviation of quoted prices. But this result does not seem to be general. We can choose parameters such that

$\Delta/(N + \Delta)$ is close to unity and therefore the SD in (ii) is close to $(4/3)\lambda$ which is greater than the standard deviation in (i).

2   Assume that the utility from X is: $U(x) = (v)[\min(x, 1)]$ and buyers who want to consume X maximize $U(x) + y$.

(a) What is the demand function, $D(p)$, in this case?

Answer

The buyer's problem is: max $v[\min(x, 1)] + y - px$. And the resulting demand function is: $D(p) = 1$ if $p \le v$ and zero otherwise.

(b) Write the (unconstraint) planner's problem (14.11) for this special case.

Answer

$\frac{1}{2}\{N(v)\min[x(1, 1), 1] + N(v)\min[x(1, 2), 1] + \Delta(v)\min[x(2, 2), 1]\} + (n + N + \Delta)\bar{y} - \lambda\max\{Nx(1, 1), Nx(1, 2) + \Delta x(2, 2)\} - \frac{1}{2}\phi[Nx(1, 1) + Nx(1, 2) + \Delta x(2, 2)].$

(c) Solve for the (unconstraint) planner's problem. Distinguish between three cases: (a) $v > 2\lambda + \phi$; (b) $\lambda + \phi < v < 2\lambda + \phi$; (c) $\lambda + \phi > v$.

Answer

If the planner chooses a unit to a member of the first group he gets v and the cost for doing that is: $\lambda + \phi$. Therefore he will supply the unit to members of the first group if $v \ge \lambda + \phi$ and will not supply otherwise.

If the planner chooses to supply a unit to a member of the second group if he arrives, he gets $(1/2)v$ and the cost for doing that is: $\lambda + (1/2)\phi$. Therefore he will supply the unit to members of the first group if $(1/2)v \ge \lambda + (1/2)\phi$ and will not supply otherwise. This considerations leads to:

(a) $x(1, 1) = x(1, 2) = x(2, 2) = 1$
(b) $x(1, 1) = x(1, 2) = 1$; $x(2, 2) = 0$. (The solution is not unique. Any solution in which the number of units distributed is N will do (this does not have to be the first group who gets it)
(c) $x(1, 1) = x(1, 2) = x(2, 2) = 0$.

(d) What is the solution to the planner's problem if we add the constraint: $x(1, 1) = x(1, 2)$.

Answer

Since the constraint is not binding the choice of the planner will be the same as in the unconstrained problem.

(e) What is the competitive UST allocation and the monopolist UST allocation in this case?

Answer

The UST allocation is the same as in (d). The monopolist will charge v. The resulting allocation is the same.

3   Let us go back to question 1 and assume that the social planner can observe the signal (the realization of σ).

(a) Assume that as in (14.11) the social planner wants to maximize the expected value of total utilities (over all agents). Write the social planner's problem for this environment.

Answer

$x(i, \sigma, s) =$ quantity delivered to group i when the observed signal is σ and the state is s.

$$\max(\tfrac{1}{4})NU[x(1, 1, 1)] + (\tfrac{3}{4})\{NU[x(1, 1, 2)] + \Delta U[x(2, 1, 2)]\} + (\tfrac{3}{4})NU[x(1, 0, 1)] +$$
$$(\tfrac{1}{4})\{NU[x(1, 0, 2)] + \Delta U[x(2, 0, 2)]\} + (n + N + \Delta)\bar{y} - \text{cost terms}$$
$$\text{s.t. } x(1, 1, 1) = x(1, 1, 2) \quad \text{and} \quad x(1, 0, 1) = x(1, 0, 2).$$

(b) Will the ability to observe the signal improve matters (increases the objective function of the social planner)? Distinguish between two cases: (a) like in question 2: $U(x) = (v)[\min(x, 1)]$ and (b) $U(x)$ is a general function with $U' > 0$, $U'' < 0$ and $U'(0) = \infty$.

Answer

Without the signal the planner will face the constraint: $x(1, 1, 1) = x(1, 1, 2) = x(1, 0, 1) = x(1, 0, 2)$. This is more restrictive than the two constraints that he faces.

14.2 MONOPOLY

We now assume that all the sellers in the sequential trade economy merge into a single monopolistic firm. There are no variable costs and the fixed cost of producing x units of capacity is given by $C(x)$, where $C(\ )$ has the standard properties of a cost function. The monopoly chooses the price to the first group (p_1) and the price to the second group (p_2).[4] Since the first group chooses the cheapest available price we require $p_1 \leq p_2$. The monopoly's problem is:

$$\max_{p_s} p_1 ND(p_1) + \tfrac{1}{2}p_2 \Delta D(p_2) - C[ND(p_1) + \Delta D(p_2)]$$

$$\text{s.t.} \quad p_1 \leq p_2. \tag{14.23}$$

Apart from the constraint, this is the problem of a monopoly that can discriminate between two markets. An alternative formulation uses the inverse demand function $p(\bullet) = D^{-1}(\bullet)$ and write the monopoly problem as:

$$\max_{x_s} p(x_1/N)x_1 + (1/2)p(x_2/\Delta)x_2 - C(x_1 + x_2)$$

$$\text{s.t.} \quad x_1/N \geq x_2/\Delta \geq 0. \tag{14.24}$$

Here x_s is the amount supplied to market s. The constraint implies $p(x_1/N) \leq p(x_2/\Delta)$.

When the constraint is not binding an interior solution to (14.24) must satisfy the following first order conditions:

$$[p'(x_1/N)x_1/N + p(x_1/N)] = \tfrac{1}{2}[p'(x_2/\Delta)x_2/\Delta + p(x_2/\Delta)] = C'(x_1 + x_2). \qquad (14.25)$$

Let $MR(z) = p'(z)z + p(z)$ denote the marginal revenue from supplying z units to an individual buyer. Then we can write (14.25) as:

$$MR(x_1/N) = \tfrac{1}{2}MR(x_2/\Delta) = C'(x_1 + x_2). \qquad (14.26)$$

Since this condition implies $MR(x_1/N) < MR(x_2/\Delta)$, the constraint in (14.24) is satisfied if the marginal revenue is a decreasing function. We therefore assume that the constraint in (14.24) is not binding.

A comparison with the UST competitive outcome

A monopoly that produces according to (14.26) produces less than the UST competitive output. The proof, based on Eden (1990, Theorem 2) uses an algorithm for computing the competitive outcome and the monopoly outcome and then comparing between the two. Here is the proof for our special case.

A competitive UST equilibrium is a vector (p_1, p_2, x_1, x_2) satisfying: (a) $p_1 = (1/2)p_2 = C'(x = x_1 + x_2)$ and (b) $x_1 = ND(p_1)$ and $x_2 = \Delta D(p_2)$. To solve for a competitive equilibrium, we choose the expected revenue per unit, π, arbitrarily and set prices as: $p_1(\pi) = \pi$ and $p_2(\pi) = 2\pi$. Given these prices the competitive output is: $x(\pi) = \operatorname{argmax}[\pi x - C(x)]$. The demand in market 1 is $ND(\pi)$ and the demand in market 2 is $\Delta D(2\pi)$. The fraction of output allocated to market 1 is

$$\mu_1(\pi) = ND(\pi)/x(\pi) \qquad (14.27)$$

and the fraction of output allocated to market 2 is:

$$\mu_2(\pi) = \Delta D(2\pi)/x(\pi). \qquad (14.28)$$

We now look at $\mu(\pi) = \mu_1(\pi) + \mu_2(\pi)$. If $\mu(\pi) = 1$ then all markets are cleared. If $\mu(\pi) > 1$ there is excess demand and if $\mu(\pi) < 1$ there is excess supply. When π goes up demand goes down and supply $x(\pi)$ goes up. Therefore, the function $\mu(\pi)$ is monotonically decreasing as in figure 14.11. The equilibrium expected profit is given by the solution $\bar\pi$ to $\mu(\pi) = 1$.

We can solve the monopoly problem in a similar way where the expected marginal revenue plays the role of the expected price. We choose the expected marginal revenue arbitrarily at the level of π and set the marginal revenues in the two markets: $MR_1(\pi) = \pi$ and $MR_2(\pi) = 2\pi$. Given this expected marginal revenue, the monopoly output is: $x(\pi) = \operatorname{argmax}[\pi x - C(x)].$[5] The demand in market 1 is $ND(\pi/[1 - (1/\varepsilon_1)])/x(\pi)$ and the demand in market 2 is $\Delta D(2\pi/[1 - (1/\varepsilon_2)])$, where ε_s is the absolute value of the price elasticity in market s. The fraction of output allocated to market 1 is $M_1(\pi) = ND(\pi/[1 - (1/\varepsilon_1)])/x(\pi)$ and the fraction of output allocated to market 2 is $M_2(\pi) = \Delta D(2\pi/[1 - (1/\varepsilon_2)])/x(\pi)$. At the optimum the monopoly satisfies demand at his announced prices and therefore the

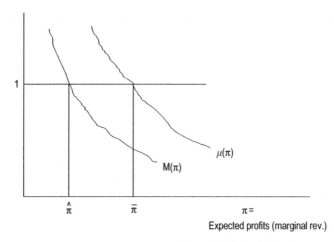

Figure 14.11 Expected marginal revenues: competition versus monopoly

expected marginal revenue for the monopoly is the solution $\hat{\pi}$ to

$$M(\pi) = M_1(\pi) + M_2(\pi) = 1.$$

We now note that the function $x(\pi) = \text{argmax}[\pi x - C(x)]$ is the same for the monopoly and the price-taker. The argument π has a different economic meaning. For the price-taker π is the expected price. For the monopoly it is the expected marginal revenue. Since for any given π, the price set by the monopoly is higher, a monopoly faces a lower demand and therefore $M(\pi) < \mu(\pi)$ for all π. It follows that the expected marginal revenue at the monopoly's optimum is less than the competitive equilibrium expected price ($\hat{\pi} < \bar{\pi}$) as illustrated by figure 14.11. Since $C'(x) = \pi$ the monopoly produces less than the price-taker. We have thus shown,

> **Claim 4:** *The UST monopoly output is less than the UST competitive output.*

This claim extends the result in the standard model to a UST environment.

14.2.1 Procyclical productivity

Rotemberg and Summers (1990) start their paper with the following statement: "Productivity, no matter how it is measured, is procyclical. Leaving aside trend growth, output rises by about 1.25 percent when man-hours employed rise by 1 percent . . . The apparent contradiction with the basic principle of diminishing returns has long troubled economists." They then offer an explanation based on price rigidity and on the Prescott (1975) model for this observation. Here we use their excellent review of the procyclical productivity issue.

Procyclical productivity is not a mystery if we allow for a two-stage production process. In our restaurant example both the standard and the UST model predict a rise in output per man-hour, the common measure of productivity, in the high demand period. Using the numerical example of tables 14.1 and 14.2, output per man-hour in the high demand period is $2/3$ and in the low demand period it is $6/11$ which is considerably less. This is because some capacity is wasted in the low demand period. This argument is related to the modeling of labor as a quasi fixed factor of production in Oi (1962).[6]

Things get more complicated when we have many goods and use prices to achieve a measure of aggregate output. If we compute PQ/L from the data generated by the standard model in table 14.2 we will get: $PQ/L = 6/11 = 0.545$ in the low demand period and $PQ/L = 20/15 = 1.333$ in the high demand period. In this case productivity should be even more procyclical because prices are procyclical.

Alternatively, total factor productivity rises from a low demand period. Alternatively, total factor productivity rises from a low demand period if $\Delta Q/Q > (WL/PQ)(\Delta L/L)$ or if $P\Delta Q > W\Delta L$. If we write the last inequality as $P > W\Delta L/\Delta Q$ we get that productivity rises if price exceed marginal cost. If $\Delta Q/Q > (WL/PQ)(\Delta L/L)$ or if $P\Delta Q > W\Delta L$. If we write the last inequality as $P > W\Delta L/\Delta Q$ we get that productivity rises if price exceeds marginal cost.

In our example, $P\Delta Q = W\Delta L = 4$ in the standard model (table 14.2) but $P\Delta Q = 6.8 > W\Delta L = 4$ if we use the data generated by the UST model (Table 1). This is because in the UST model the price in the low demand period is higher than short run marginal cost.

By measuring the extent of procyclical productivity, Hall (1988) finds that price equals more than twice marginal cost in over half of US two-digit manufacturing industries. Eden (1990) and Rotemberg and Summers (1990) argue that his findings are consistent with a competitive version of the UST model.

14.2.2 Estimating the markup

Eden and Griliches (1993) estimated the ratio of price to marginal cost – the markup – under the UST model. They assumed that capacity is determined at the beginning of the period according to:

$$V = L^{\alpha}, \tag{14.29}$$

where $0 < \alpha < 1$ is a parameter and L is the number of workers hired. Firms and workers enter into a contingent labor contract that specifies the fixed and variable inputs that will be supplied in each state of the world. Total compensation is also state contingent. It is: W_1 if only one market opens and W_2 if both markets open. The firm chooses labor input L and the supply to market s, x_s, by solving:

$$\max_{L\, x_1\, x_2} \tfrac{1}{2}[p_1x_1 - LW_1] + \tfrac{1}{2}[p_1x_1 + p_2x_2 - LW_2]$$

$$\text{s.t.} \quad x_1 + x_2 = V = L^{\alpha}. \tag{14.30}$$

An interior solution must satisfy the following first order condition:

$$R\alpha L^{\alpha-1} = W, \tag{14.31}$$

where $R = p_1 = (1/2)p_2$ is the expected revenue per unit of capacity and $W = (1/2)W_1 + (1/2)W_2$ is the expected compensation per worker. Multiplying both sides of (14.31) by L and using (14.29) leads to:

$$S \equiv WL/VR = \alpha. \tag{14.32}$$

Thus the elasticity of capacity with respect to labor, α, is approximately equal to an average of the labor share.

Output is measured according to:

$$Q = VU, \tag{14.33}$$

where Q is output and U is capacity utilization. Furthermore, we assume that capacity utilization is related to hours per worker (H) by:

$$\ln U = a + \beta \ln H, \tag{14.34}$$

where a and β are coefficients. Using $Q = VU = (L^{\alpha})U$ and $TH = (L)(H)$ for total hours leads to:

$$\ln Q = a + \alpha \ln L + \beta \ln H = a + \alpha \ln TH + (\beta - \alpha) \ln H. \tag{14.35}$$

Using Δx to denote the log difference of a variable and using $S = \alpha$ leads to:

$$\Delta Q = \gamma S \, \Delta TH + (\beta - \alpha) \, \Delta H, \tag{14.36}$$

where according to the theory $\gamma = 1$.

Following Abbot, Griliches and Hausman (1988), Eden and Griliches (1993) estimated (14.36) and could not reject the null hypothesis: $\gamma = 1$.

14.3 RELATIONSHIP TO THE ARROW–DEBREU MODEL

When buyers are ex-ante identical, we may view trade in the sequential spot markets as the execution of ex-ante contingent contracts. This interpretation of the UST model, is in the appendix of Eden (1990).

At $t = 0$, N_S ex ante identical potential buyers enter into contingent contracts with the firm. At $t = 1$, they form a line by a lottery that treats everyone symmetrically. At $t = 2$, the first Ñ buyers learn that they want to consume and execute their contracts according to their place in the line.

The random variable Ñ can take S possible realizations: $N_1 < N_2 < \cdots < N_S$ where the realization N_s occurs with probability Π_s. For notational convenience we set $N_0 = 0$. Buyers are in batch s if their place in the line is between N_s and N_{s-1}. The probability that buyers in batch s will arrive and execute their contracts is: $q_s = \sum_{i=s}^{S} \Pi_i$.

There are $N_S!$ ways of forming the line at $t = 1$ and S possible realizations of Ñ at $t = 2$. There are thus $S(N_S!)$ states of nature. There are two physical characteristics (X, Y) and therefore $2S(N_S!)$ Arrow-Debreu contingent commodities. But since buyers are ex-ante identical, we can use symmetry to simplify trade without loss of efficiency.

We define the following 2S goods: X_s (Y_s) is a good with physical characteristic X (Y) that will be delivered if the buyer is in batch s and the realization of $\tilde{N}$ is greater than N_s (which means that batch s arrives). We use P_{xs} (P_{ys}) to denote the price of X_s (Y_s). A buyer who buys a claim on X_s (Y_s) will get delivery with probability $\zeta_s q_s$ where $\zeta_s = (N_s - N_{s-1})/N_S$ is the probability that he is in batch s and q_s is the probability that batch s arrives.

The utility of the representative potential buyer is: $U(x) - y$ if he wants to consume and zero otherwise.[7] The function $U(\ )$ is differentiable and strictly concave.

The representative buyer maximizes expected utility by solving:

$$\max_{x_s\ y_s} \sum_{s=1}^{S} \zeta_s q_s [U(x_s) - y_s]$$

$$\text{s.t.} \quad \sum_{s=1}^{S} P_{xs} x_s = \sum_{s=1}^{S} P_{ys} y_s. \tag{14.37}$$

The firm produces k units of X at the cost of C(k) units of the numeraire commodity (say labor) where $C(\ )$ is strictly convex. A firm that promises k_s units of X_s to each of the N_S potential buyers will get $P_{xs} N_S k_s$ units of the numeraire commodity and will have to produce $(N_s - N_{s-1})k_s$ units to honor its promise. This is because at most $N_s - N_{s-1}$ buyers will exercise a contract to buy k_s units of X_s. The firm maximizes profits by solving:

$$\max_{k_s} \sum_{s=1}^{S} P_{xs} N_S k_s - C \left[\sum_{s=1}^{S} (N_s - N_{s-1})k_s \right]. \tag{14.38}$$

Markets are cleared if:

$$k_s = x_s. \tag{14.39}$$

Sequential delivery contracts equilibrium is a vector

$(x_1, \ldots, x_S; k_1, \ldots, k_S; P_{x1}, \ldots, P_{xS}; P_{y1}, \ldots, P_{yS})$ such that

(a) given the prices $(P_{x1}, \ldots, P_{xS}; P_{y1}, \ldots, P_{yS})$ the quantities

$(x_1, \ldots, x_S)$ maximize (14.37) and the quantities $(k_1, \ldots, k_S)$ maximize (14.38);

(b) the market-clearing condition (14.39) is satisfied.

We can also define equilibrium in sequential spot markets as follows.
UST spot markets equilibrium is a vector

$(x_1, \ldots, x_S; k_1, \ldots, k_S; p_1, \ldots, p_S)$ such that

(a) $p_s q_s = C' \left[\sum_{s=1}^{S} (N_s - N_{s-1})k_s \right]$;

(b) $U'(x_s) = p_s$;

(c) $x_s = k_s$.

The spot markets equilibrium applies to the case in which buyers and sellers meet only at $t = 2$. The condition $p_s q_s = C'$ guarantees that the UST firm produces the optimal amount and is indifferent to the way it allocates its supply across markets. The individual buyer demands in market s is determined by the first order condition $U'(x_s) = p_s$. The demand of batch s is therefore $(N_s - N_{s-1})x_s$ and in equilibrium this must be equal to the supply in market s: $(N_s - N_{s-1})k_s$. We now show the following.

Proposition 1: If $(x_1, \ldots, x_S; k_1, \ldots, k_S; p_1, \ldots, p_S)$ is a UST spot markets equilibrium, then

$$(x_1, \ldots, x_S; k_1, \ldots, k_S;$$

$$P_{x1} = p_1\zeta_1 q_1, \ldots, P_{xS} = p_S\zeta_S q_S;$$

$$P_{y1} = \zeta_1 q_1, \ldots, P_{yS} = \zeta_S q_S)$$

is a sequential delivery contracts equilibrium.

Note that at $t = 2$ goods with physical characteristics X are exchanged for goods with physical characteristics Y. In the spot markets case each buyer in market s receives x_s units of X in exchange of p_s units of Y. The proposition says that the execution of the sequential delivery contracts in market s (i.e. by buyers in batch s when batch s arrives) requires that each buyer will get x_s units of X and will deliver some Y. Because of risk neutrality the amount of Y delivered by buyers in market s is not determined but one possibility is that for each unit of X that the buyer gets he delivers to the firm $P_{xs}/P_{ys} = p_s$ units of Y. In this case, the Proposition says that an outside observer at $t = 2$ will not be able to tell whether these transactions are executions of contracts signed at $t = 0$ or spot markets transactions: The two models are observationally equivalent from the point of view of an outside observer at $t = 2$.

To show the Proposition, we start by solving for the sequential delivery contracts equilibrium. Under the proposed prices the representative buyer's problem (14.37) is:

$$\max_{x_s\, y_s} \sum_{s=1}^{S} \zeta_s q_s [U(x_s) - y_s]$$

$$\text{s.t.} \quad \sum_{s=1}^{S} p_s \zeta_s q_s x_s = \sum_{s=1}^{S} \zeta_s q_s y_s. \tag{14.37'}$$

The first order conditions for this problem are:[8]

$$U'(x_s) = p_s. \tag{14.40}$$

The firm's problem (14.38) under the proposed prices is:

$$\max_{k_s} \sum_{s=1}^{S} p_s \zeta_s q_s N_s k_s - C \left[\sum_{s=1}^{S} (N_s - N_{s-1})k_s \right]. \tag{14.38'}$$

Using $\zeta_s = (N_s - N_{s-1})/N_s$, the first order conditions for this problem are:

$$p_s q_s = C' \left[\sum_{s=1}^{S} (N_s - N_{s-1}) k_s \right]. \tag{14.41}$$

We now note that (14.39)–(14.41) define UST spot markets equilibrium. This completes the proof.

14.4 HETEROGENEITY AND SUPPLY UNCERTAINTY

Dana (1998) has generalized the Prescott (1975) model to the case of heterogeneous agents. In Dana's model buyers have a demand for one unit only but reservation prices and the probability of wanting to consume may be different across buyers. He concludes that the equilibrium allocation may not be efficient because of price rigidity. Dana compares the allocation in the Prescott model to the standard Walrasian allocation. This is the relevant comparison for the Prescott model but, as was argued in section 14.1.2; it is not the relevant comparison for the UST model.

Here we introduce heterogeneity and supply uncertainty to the UST model. We show that the UST outcome may not be efficient: Even a social planner who operates under the informational constraints faced by the UST firms can improve matters. Moreover, even a monopoly that faces the same informational constraints may improve matters. We start with some examples that illustrate the efficiency problems and then attempt at a more general treatment.

Example 1: As in section 14.1.2, there are two types of agents: Definite buyers and possible buyers. The number of agents from each type is 1. Definite buyers have a reservation price of $v_1 = 10$ dollars (units of Y) and possible buyers have a reservation price of $v_2 = 7$ dollars. There are two states of nature (indexed s) that occurs with equal probabilities. Definite buyers want to consume X in both states. Possible buyers want to consume X only if $s = 2$. The cost of production is $\lambda = 5$ per unit of capacity. Capacity can be costlessly converted into output, if there is demand for it.

At $P_1 > 10$, there is no demand. At $7 < P_1 \leq 10$ total demand is 1 and at $P_1 \leq 7$ total demand is 1 if $s = 1$ and 2 if $s = 2$. The number of buyers in the first batch is the minimum number that will arrive. It is:

$$\Delta_1(P_1) = 1 \quad \text{for } P_1 \leq 10 \quad \text{and} \quad \text{zero otherwise.} \tag{14.42}$$

Market 2 will open if there are buyers who wanted but could not buy at the first market price. This will happen if $P_1 \leq 7$ and $s = 2$. The probability that market 2 will open is:

$$q_2(P_1) = 1/2 \quad \text{for } P_1 \leq 7 \quad \text{and} \quad \text{zero otherwise.} \tag{14.43}$$

When $P_1 \leq 7$ the number of remaining buyers in state 2 is 1/2 of each type. When $P_2 \leq 7$, all the remaining buyers want to buy in market 2 and the size of the second batch is:

$$\Delta_2(P_1, P_2) = 1 \quad \text{for } P_1 < P_2 \leq 7. \tag{14.44}$$

When $7 < P_2 \leq 10$ only the definite buyers want to buy in market 2 and therefore:

$$\Delta_2(P_1, P_2) = \tfrac{1}{2} \quad \text{for } P_1 \leq 7 \text{ and } 7 < P_2 \leq 10. \tag{14.45}$$

When $P_2 > 10$ none of the remaining buyers want to buy in market 2 and therefore:

$$\Delta_2(P_1, P_2) = 0 \quad \text{for } P_1 \leq 7 \text{ and } P_2 > 10. \tag{14.46}$$

Since the second market opens in this example with probability $1/2$, equilibrium prices are: $P_1 = \lambda = 5$ and $P_2 = 2\lambda = 10$. The number of buyers in the second batch is $1/2$ according with (14.45) and production is therefore 1.5 units at the cost of 7.5. The surplus in state 1 is: $v_1 - 7.5 = 2.5$. The surplus in state 2 is: $v_1 + (1/2)v_2 - 7.5 = 6$. The average surplus over the two states is 4.25.

A monopoly will choose $P_1 = 10$ and produce one unit making a profit of 5. This profit is also the surplus in this case and is greater than the expected surplus in the competitive sequential trade.

A social planner who can set prices to maximize the expected surplus cannot do better than the monopoly: The planner will choose to produce one unit and will price it at $7 < P \leq 10$ so that only the high valuation buyers will get it. Thus the monopoly choice is efficient.

In example 1 the UST competitive firm produces more than the monopoly but this is not efficient because the additional half a unit of capacity is being used by type 2 agents whose ex-ante valuation is less than the cost of production (3.5 per unit). The reason why in example 1 the competitive firm produces too much capacity is in the failure to allocate capacity to buyers who value it the most: Low valuation buyers who arrive early are not rationed and therefore the residual demand includes high valuation buyers who arrive late. These high valuation buyers are willing to pay enough to produce goods that will be sold with probability $1/2$.

Note that the probability that a market will open and the number of buyers participating in this market are endogenous. The next market will open if there are buyers who wanted but could not buy in the last market. The probability of this event depends on the prices in previous markets. The demand in the next market is the minimum size of the residual demand. It depends on the prices in previous markets and the price in the next market.

Example 2: The same as example 1 but now $v_1 = 9$ instead of 10. In this case competitive UST prices remains the same as in the previous example: $P_1 = 5$ and $P_2 = 10$. As in the previous example, market 2 will open in state 2 but since $\Delta_2(5, 10) = 0$ it will not be active. In a UST equilibrium only one unit is produced and allocated to market 1. The surplus is: 4 in state 1 and $3(= (1/2)v_1 + (1/2)v_2 - 5)$ in state 2. The average surplus is: 3.5.

A monopoly will choose $P_1 = 9$ guaranteeing a profit (surplus) of 4.

In example 2 both the monopoly and the competitive firm produce the same amount but the monopoly does a better job in allocating the existing capacity to the buyers who value it the most.

Example 3: We now add a new type to example 1: Type 3 who wants to consume only when $s = 1$ (when type 2 does not want to consume) and is willing to pay only up to $v_3 = 4$.

Adding type 3 will not change the UST equilibrium and the monopoly choice. But it will change the planner's choice. Now the planner can do better by producing two units and pricing them at $P \leq 4$.

When $s = 1$, type 1 and type 3 will buy the good and the surplus will be $10 + 4 - 10 = 4$. When $s = 2$, type 1 and type 2 will buy the good and the surplus will be $10 + 7 - 10 = 7$. The average surplus is 5.5 which is higher than the monopoly's expected profits.

In example 3 the UST firm is producing too little relative to the sequential efficient level: 1.5 instead of 2.

The above three examples show:

Proposition 1: (a) The UST allocation is not necessarily efficient; (b) A monopoly may improve matters and (c) The UST output may be either too high or too low relative to the sequential efficient level of output.

Note that a departure from zero expected profits is required for improving on the UST competitive allocation. To improve we must either raise prices and achieve a better screening of buyers (allowing only high valuation buyers to buy) or reduce prices and allow the participation of low valuation buyers who want to consume in low demand states. This requires either positive or negative expected profits and therefore cannot occur in the UST competitive environment.

We use these examples in chapter 21 to discuss the welfare consequences of international trade. We now turn to a more general formulation and to the conditions under which efficiency can be guaranteed.

14.4.1 The model

We consider an economy with two dates ($t = 0, 1$) and two goods (X and Y with lower case letters denoting quantities). There are S possible aggregate states of nature (indexed s). There are many potential sellers and out of this group actual sellers are chosen randomly. An actual seller or just a seller for short can produce as many units as he wants at the price of λ units of Y per unit of X. In state s there are M_s actual sellers. State s occurs with probability Π_s.[9] Sellers are risk neutral and derive utility from Y only.

There are J types of buyers. The number of type j buyers is n_j. All buyers are endowed with a large quantity of Y. Ex-ante the utility of a type j agent is random and is given by: $\{u_{js}(x, y)$ with probability $\Pi_s\}$. In aggregate state s the utility function that a fraction ϕ_{js} of type j buyers realize is: $u_{js}(x, y) = U_j(x) + y$, where $U_j(x)$ is strictly monotone, strictly concave and differentiable. The remaining fraction of $1 - \phi_{js}$ who "do not want to consume X" realize the utility function: $u_{js}(x, y) = y$. The random utility of a type j buyer in aggregate state s is thus:

$$u_{js}(x, y) = \{U_j(x) + y \text{ with probability } \phi_{js} \text{ and } y \text{ otherwise}\}. \tag{14.47}$$

A type j buyer demands $d_j(p)$ units of X at the price p if he wants to consume, where the individual demand function is defined by:

$$d_j(p) = \underset{x \geq 0}{\arg\max} \, U_j(x) - px. \tag{14.48}$$

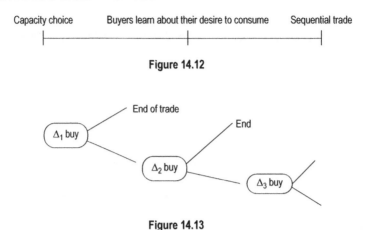

Figure 14.12

Figure 14.13

The first order condition for the problem (14.48) is:

$$U_j'(x) \leq p \quad \text{with equality if } x > 0. \tag{14.49}$$

Production occurs at $t = 0$. Then buyers realize a utility function and those who want to consume form a line. It is assumed that any batch of buyers taken from this line accurately represents the type composition of buyers who want to consume: In state s, $\sum_{j=1}^{J} \phi_{js} n_j$ buyers want to consume and the fraction of type j buyers in any batch is: $\phi_{js} n_j / \sum_{j=1}^{J} \phi_{js} n_j$. After the line is formed, buyers arrive at the market place one by one according to their place in the line and choose whether to buy at the cheapest available offer. The sequential trade does not take real time (it occurs in meta time). Figure 14.12 illustrates the sequence of events.

We start with the relatively simple case in which all types have the same demand functions (but unlike section 14.2.1 they may have different probabilities of wanting to consume).

Buyers have the same demand functions and there is no uncertainty about supply: We assume that: $U_j(x) = U(x), d_j(p) = d(p)$ for all j and $M_s = 1$ for all s. We use $N_s = \sum_{j=1}^{J} \phi_{js} n_j$ for the number of buyers and assume: $N_1 < N_2 < \cdots < N_S$.

The minimum number of buyers is: $\Delta_1 = N_1$. The first batch of Δ_1 buyers arrives with certainty. After buyers in this first batch complete trade they go away. If $s = 1$ trade ends. If $s > 1$, there are $N_s - N_1$ unsatisfied buyers. The minimum number of unsatisfied buyers is: $\Delta_2 = \min_s\{N_s - N_1\} = N_2 - N_1$. The probability that $s > 1$ is $q_2 = 1 - \Pi_1$ and this is the probability that batch 2 will arrive. After batch 2 completes trading (and disappear) there may be again two possibilities: either no additional buyers arrive or, if $s > 2$, some additional buyers do arrive. The probability that $s > 2$, is $q_3 = 1 - \Pi_1 - \Pi_2$ and this is the probability that the third batch of buyers will arrive. The minimum number of unsatisfied buyers if $s > 2$ is: $\Delta_3 = \min_s\{N_s - N_2\} = N_3 - N_2$. Proceeding in this way we define q_s and Δ_s for all $s = 1, \ldots, S$. Figure 14.13 illustrates the sequential trade process.

The seller is a price taker and behaves as if he can sell any amount at the price P_i to buyers in batch i if it arrives. He makes a contingent plan to sell x_i units to batch i if it arrives. It is convenient to think of a sequence of Walrasian markets, where batch i buys in market i and the seller supplies x_i units to market i.

Because of constant returns to scale equilibrium prices are determined by supply conditions only. The expected revenue from supplying a unit to market i is $q_i P_i$. When $q_i P_i = \lambda$ the expected profit is zero, the seller is indifferent about the quantity supplied and is willing to satisfy demand.

A UST equilibrium is a vector of prices $(P_1, \ldots, P_S)$ and a vector of supplies $(x_1, \ldots, x_S)$ such that:

(a) $P_i = \lambda/q_i = \lambda / \sum_{s=i}^{S} \Pi_s$ and
(b) $x_i = (N_i - N_{i-1})d(P_i) = \Delta_i d(P_i)$.

Thus in equilibrium markets that open are cleared. Note that prices may appear rigid because they do not respond to the realization of demand (the state). Nevertheless, sellers do not have an incentive to change prices during trade.[10]

To solve for the equilibrium quantities we substitute the equilibrium condition (a) in (b) to get:

$$x_i = \Delta_i d(\lambda/q_i). \tag{14.50}$$

We now show the following proposition which is a version of Theorem 1 in Eden (1990).

> *Proposition 2:* The equilibrium allocation (14.50) is a solution to the following social planner's problem:
>
> $$\max_{x_i} \sum_{i=1}^{S} q_i \Delta_i U(x_i/\Delta_i) - \lambda \sum_{i=1}^{S} x_i. \tag{14.51}$$
>
> Note that the objective in (14.51) is the expected utility of the sum of utilities in the economy.
>
> *Proof:* The first order condition for the problem (14.51) is:
>
> $$q_i U'(x_i/\Delta_i) \le \lambda \quad \text{with equality if } x_i > 0. \tag{14.52}$$
>
> Substituting $P_i = \lambda/q_i$ in the first order condition (14.49) leads to:
>
> $$q_i U'[d(\lambda/q_i)] \le \lambda \quad \text{with equality if } d_j(\lambda/q_i) > 0. \tag{14.53}$$
>
> In equilibrium $x_i/\Delta_i = d(\lambda/q_i)$ and therefore (14.53) implies that the UST equilibrium allocation satisfies (14.52). Since (14.52) is both sufficient and necessary condition for a solution to the problem (14.51), the UST equilibrium allocation is a solution to (14.51). □

We now turn to the general case in which buyers have different demand functions and different probabilities of wanting to consume.

The general case

As before buyers arrive in batches but here the size of each batch is endogenous. We now turn to describe an algorithm for computing the size of each batch for an arbitrarily chosen price vector $(P_1 \leq P_2 \leq \cdots \leq P_S)$. This is done under the assumption that the demand of each batch that arrives is satisfied: Batch i's demand is satisfied at the price P_i.

Roughly speaking, the size of the first batch is the minimum demand at the price P_1. Market 2 opens if there are some buyers who wanted to buy in the first market but could not. In general, an additional market opens after transactions in market $i - 1$ are complete if there is residual demand and the size of batch i is the minimum residual demand per seller. We now turn to a detailed description of this algorithm.

Demand per seller in state s at the price P_1 is: $\sum_{j=1}^{J} \phi_{js} n_j d_j(P_1)/M_s$. We choose indices such that state 1 is the state of minimum demand, $1 = \text{argmin}_s\{\sum_{j=1}^{J} \phi_{js} n_j d_j(P_1)/M_s\}$. The size of the first batch (per seller) is: $D_1(P_1) = \sum_{j=1}^{J} \phi_{j1} n_j d_j(P_1)/M_1$ units and it is assumed that each seller supplies that many units at the price P_1.

If $s = 1$ then all buyers are served in the first market and trade ends. Otherwise, if $s > 1$, a demand for $\sum_{j=1}^{J} \phi_{js} n_j d_j(P_1) - M_s D_1(P_1) \geq 0$ units was not satisfied. The fraction of demand satisfied in market 1 is: $1 - \chi_s^1(P_1) = M_s D_1(P_1)/\sum_{j=1}^{J} \phi_{js} n_j d_j(P_1)$. The residual demand per seller at the price P_2 is $\chi_s^1(P_1) \sum_{j=1}^{J} \phi_{js} n_j d_j(P_2)/M_s$. We now choose the indices $s > 1$ so that $2 = \text{argmin}_s\{\chi_s^1(P_1) \sum_{j=1}^{J} \phi_{js} n_j d_j(P_2)/M_s\}$ and the minimum residual demand per seller is in state 2. The size of batch 2 is: $D_2(P_1, P_2) = \chi_2^1(P_1) \sum_{j=1}^{J} \phi_{j2} n_j d_j(P_2)/M_2$ units.

In general, we start iteration i having already computed $\chi_s^k(P_1, \ldots, P_k)$ for $k < i - 1$ and the amount per seller supplied in market $i - 1$, $D_{i-1}(P_1, \ldots, P_{i-1})$. We then compute $\chi_s^{i-1}(P_1, \ldots, P_{i-1})$ as follows. If $s > i - 1$, the demand for $\chi \sum_{j=1}^{J} \phi_{js} n_j d_j(P_i) - M_s D_{i-1}(P_1, \ldots, P_{i-1}) \geq 0$ units was not satisfied in market $i - 1$, where $\chi = \Pi_{k=1}^{i-2} \chi_s^k(P_1, \ldots, P_k)$ is the fraction of buyers who did not buy in markets $1, \ldots, i - 2$. The fraction of demand satisfied in market $i - 1$ is:

$$1 - \chi_s^{i-1}(P_1, \ldots, P_{i-1}) = M_s D_{i-1}(P_1, \ldots, P_{i-1})/\chi \sum_{j=1}^{J} \phi_{js} n_j d_j(P_{i-1}). \qquad (14.54)$$

The residual demand per seller at the price P_i is: $\chi' \sum_{j=1}^{J} \phi_{js} n_j d_j(P_i)/M_s$, where $\chi' = \chi \chi_s^{i-1}(P_1, \ldots, P_{i-1})$. We choose indices $s > i - 1$ such that: $i = \text{argmin}_{s > i-1}\{\chi' \times \sum_{j=1}^{J} \phi_{js} n_j d_j(P_i)/M_s\}$. The size of batch i is:

$$D_i(P_1, \ldots, P_i) = \chi' \sum_{j=1}^{J} \phi_{ji} n_j d_j(P_i)/M_i, \qquad (14.55)$$

units.

Given the construction of the demand functions $D_i(P_1, \ldots, P_i)$ we can now define equilibrium as follows.

A UST equilibrium is a vector of prices $(P_1 \leq P_2 \leq \cdots \leq P_S)$ and a vector of per seller supplies $(x_1, \ldots, x_S)$ such that:

(a) $P_i = \lambda / q_i$ and
(b) $x_i = D_i(P_1, \ldots, P_i)$.

The examples at the beginning of this chapter demonstrate that efficiency cannot be guaranteed for the general case. But it is possible to show that efficiency can be guaranteed when all buyers have the same probabilities of wanting to consume.

Conclusions

The UST allocation is efficient if (1) there is no uncertainty about the number of sellers and buyers have the same downward sloping demand functions or (2) there is no uncertainty about the number of sellers and buyers have the same probabilities of "wanting to consume". Otherwise, the UST allocation may not be efficient and a monopoly may improve matters.

14.5 INVENTORIES

We have assumed that output not sold evaporates. Here we follow Bental and Eden (1993) and assume that output not sold is carried to the next period as inventories.

When demand is low the seller accumulates "undesired" inventories and next period's prices and production go down. This story has a Keynesian flavor. But here prices are completely flexible, expectations are rational and the allocation is Pareto efficient.

Our model is also different from the standard storage model in Deaton and Laroque (1992, 1996). In the standard model inventories are held only when the expected increase in price covers storage and interest costs. The UST model allows for purely speculative inventories. But in addition, inventories in the UST model are held whenever demand does not reach its highest possible realization and not all of the UST markets open.

The model

There are many identical infinitely lived risk neutral firms. Production occurs each period, before the beginning of trade. The cost of producing x units of the good is $C(x) = x^2$. The firm's discount factor is given by $0 < \beta < 1$ and for simplicity we assume that storage itself is costless.

The number of buyers (per firm) that may show up each period is an i.i.d. random variable that may take two possible realizations: N and $N + \Delta$ with equal probability of occurrence. The demand of each individual buyer that arrives is: $D(p) = 1/p$, where p is the price faced by the buyer.

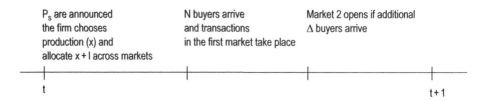

| P_s are announced
the firm chooses
production (x) and
allocate x + I across markets | N buyers arrive
and transactions
in the first market take place | Market 2 opens if additional
Δ buyers arrive |

Figure 14.14   Temporary (partial) equilibrium

14.5.1 Temporary (partial) equilibrium

The representative firm starts period t with I_t units of inventories. It takes the prices in the two UST markets (p_{1t}, p_{2t}) as given and forms expectations about next period's prices.

The expected price in next period's first market is $p_{1t+1} = \alpha(I_{t+1})$, where the function $\alpha(\ )$ is decreasing and I_{t+1} is the average beginning of next period's level of inventories per firm. Since the individual firm cannot affect the average level of inventories it cannot affect next period's prices.

The quantity supplied to market s per firm is denoted by k_s. The firm may choose to store even if all $N + \Delta$ buyers arrive and market 2 opens. The quantity that the firm chooses not to sell even if market 2 opens (purely speculative inventories) is denoted by k_3. Production at the beginning of the period is denoted by x_t.

Figure 14.14 describes the sequence of events. On the basis of the announced prices (p_{st}) and expectations about future prices (α), the firm chooses production (x_t) and allocates the available supply ($k_t = x_t + I_t$) across markets. Then the first group of N buyers arrives, trades in the first market at the price p_{1t} and goes home. If a second group of Δ buyers arrives, market 2 opens and transactions occur at the price p_{2t}.

A partial (temporary) equilibrium takes the expectation function $\alpha(\ )$ as given. It requires that markets which open are cleared and some arbitrage conditions which guarantee that in equilibrium the firm cannot increase its expected present value of profits. In the Appendix we formulate the firm's maximization problem and derive the arbitrage conditions as first order conditions.

The vector ($p_{1t}, p_{2t}, x_t, k_{1t}, k_{2t}, k_{3t}$) is a temporary equilibrium for a given expectations function, $\alpha(\ )$, and a given beginning of period inventories, I_t, if it satisfies the following conditions:

$$k_{1t} = N/p_{1t}; \tag{14.56}$$

$$k_{2t} = \Delta/p_{2t}; \tag{14.57}$$

$$p_{2t} \geq \beta\alpha(k_{3t}) \text{ with equality if } k_{3t} > 0; \tag{14.58}$$

$$p_{1t} = (1/2)p_{2t} + (1/2)\beta\alpha(k_{2t} + k_{3t}) \tag{14.59}$$

$$C'(x_t) = 2x_t = p_{1t}; \tag{14.60}$$

$$k = k_{1t} + k_{2t} + k_{3t} = x_t + I_t. \tag{14.61}$$

Conditions (14.56) and (14.57) are market-clearing conditions. The third condition governs the demand for purely speculative inventories: k_3. To develop the intuition for this condition, let us think of the seller's choice when market 2 opens. If he sells a unit he will get p_2 dollars. The alternative is to store the unit and sell it in the next period's first market. Since if both markets open this period, inventories next period are given by k_{3t}, the price in the next period's first market is: $p_{1t+1} = \alpha(k_{3t})$. The value of a unit stored in terms of current dollars is: $\beta\alpha(k_{3t})$. The market clearing condition (14.57) requires $k_2 > 0$. This can be optimal only if (14.58) holds. Otherwise, if $p_2 < \beta\alpha(k_{3t})$, it is better to carry the k_2 units to the next period as inventories. If (14.58) holds with strict inequality then we must have $k_3 = 0$, since otherwise the firm can increase its profits by selling k_3 in market 2. If (14.58) holds with equality then we may have an interior solution ($k_3 > 0$). In this case the value of inventories is the same as the revenues from selling the unit. Note that we use the assumption that market 2 opens and that the seller cannot affect average per seller magnitudes.

The fourth equation captures the main idea of the UST model. Since (14.56) and (14.57) require strictly positive k_1 and k_2, the seller must be indifferent between selling in the first market, at the price p_1, to betting that the second market will open. If the second market opens the seller will sell the unit at the higher price p_{2t}. If it does not open the unit will be stored and sold in the next period. To calculate the value of inventories note that when the second market does not open $I_{t+1} = k_{2t} + k_{3t}$ and the price in the next period's first market is: $\alpha(k_{2t} + k_{3t})$. The current value of a unit stored in this case is therefore: $\beta\alpha(k_{2t} + k_{3t})$. Condition (14.59) thus says that the seller is indifferent between selling a unit in the first market to allocating it to the second market.

The fifth equation determines current production: marginal cost = the price in the first market. To derive this condition, note that in equilibrium the firm cannot make money by increasing production and selling the additional amount in the first market. And it cannot make money by increasing production and selling the additional amount in the second market. Thus $C' = p_{1t} = (1/2)p_{2t} + (1/2)\beta\alpha(k_{2t} + k_{3t})$, as implied by conditions (14.59) and (14.60).

The last equation is a resource constraint. It says that the firm must allocate the available supply to the three markets.

The effect of storage on price dispersion: In the absence of storage, the relative price p_2/p_1 is 2. When storage is allowed the relative price p_2/p_1 is less than 2: Goods that are not sold have some value as inventories and therefore a smaller relative price is required to compensate for the risk of not making a sale. We now show this claim formally.

Claim 1: $1 \leq p_2/p_1 \leq 2$.

Proof: Since (14.59) implies that the value of inventories when only one market opens is: $\beta\alpha(k_{2t} + k_{3t}) = 2p_{1t} - p_{2t} \geq 0$, we get: $p_2/p_1 \leq 2$. To show that $p_2/p_1 \geq 1$, note that (14.58) and the fact that $\alpha(\ )$ is decreasing, implies: $p_{2t} \geq \beta\alpha(k_{3t}) > \beta\alpha(k_{2t} + k_{3t})$. Since according to (14.59) p_1 is a weighted average of p_2 and $\beta\alpha(k_{2t} + k_{3t})$ it follows that $p_1 < p_2$. □

Allowing for costly storage: Assume that (the present value of the) storage cost is ρ dollars per unit stored. When free disposal is possible the firm will store only if: $\beta\alpha(I_{t+1}) - \rho \geq 0$. The value of inventories is therefore: $\max\{\beta\alpha(I_{t+1}) - \rho, 0\}$ and conditions (14.58) and (14.59)

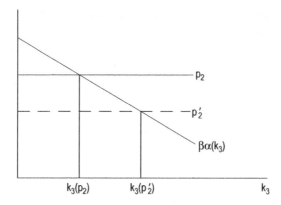

Figure 14.15   Pure speculation

are now:

$$p_{2t} \geq \beta\alpha(k_{3t}) - \rho \text{ with equality if } k_{3t} > 0; \tag{14.58'}$$

$$p_{1t} = \tfrac{1}{2}p_{2t} + \tfrac{1}{2}\max\{\beta\alpha(k_{2t} + k_{3t}) - \rho, 0\}. \tag{14.59'}$$

Storage costs do not add much because we can choose β to reflect both the interest costs and the storage costs.

14.5.2   Solving for a temporary equilibrium

We first compute the quantity demanded for a given p_2. We use (14.58) to solve for k_3 denoting the solution by $k_3(p_2)$. Figure 14.15 illustrates the solution. The demand for k_3 is strictly positive if p_2 is below the intersection of the $\beta\alpha(k_{3t})$ curve with the vertical axis. When we reduce p_2 the quantity demanded, $k_3(p_2)$, increases because the function $\alpha(\ )$ is decreasing.

We proceed by substituting the quantities $k_2 = \Delta/p_2$ and $k_3(p_2)$ in (14.59) to solve for the price in the first market p_1 (assuming $\rho = 0$):

$$p_1(p_2) = \tfrac{1}{2}p_2 + \tfrac{1}{2}\beta\alpha[\Delta/p_2 + k_3(p_2)]. \tag{14.62}$$

Since $\alpha(\ )$ is decreasing and $k_3(p_2)$ is decreasing we can show the following Claim.

> *Claim 7: The function $p_1(p_2)$ is increasing.*

The demand in the first market is:

$$k_1(p_2) = N/p_1(p_2), \tag{14.63}$$

Claim 7 implies that $k_1(p_2)$ is decreasing.

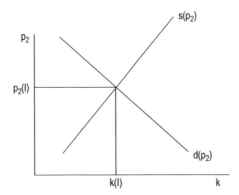

Figure 14.16 Partial equilibrium solution

We repeat this process for each price p_2 and get the demand schedule:

$$d(p_2) = k_3(p_2) + \Delta/p_2 + N/p_1(p_2). \qquad (14.64)$$

Since all $k_s(\ )$ are decreasing, the demand function $d(\ )$ is decreasing as in figure 14.16.

We now use (14.60) to calculate current production:

$$x(p_2) = \tfrac{1}{2}p_1(p_2). \qquad (14.65)$$

Supply is given by:

$$s(p_2) = x(p_2) + I_t. \qquad (14.66)$$

Since $p_1(p_2)$ is an increasing function, the supply is upward sloping as in figure 14.16.

The intersection of supply and demand yields a solution to: $d(p_2) = s(p_2)$. This solution is the temporary equilibrium level of p_2 and is denoted by $p_2(I)$. We can now solve for the other partial equilibrium magnitudes: $p_1(I) = p_1[p_2(I)], x(I) = x[p_2(I)], k_1(I) = k_1[p_2(I)]$, $k_2(I) = k_2[p_2(I)], k_3(I) = k_3[p_2(I)], k(I) = k_1(I) + k_2(I) + k_3(I)$.

We have thus solved for a partial equilibrium that assumes a given model of expectations $\alpha(\ )$ and a given level of the beginning of period inventories, I. We now vary I and get partial equilibrium functions: $[p_1(I), p_2(I), x(I), k_1(I), k_2(I), k_3(I)]$. We now turn to characterize these partial equilibrium functions.

Claim 8: The partial equilibrium functions $[p_1(I), p_2(I), x(I)]$ are monotonically decreasing and the partial equilibrium functions $[k_1(I), k_2(I), k_3(I)]$ are monotonically increasing.

We use figure 14.17 to show this claim. An increase in the beginning of period inventories shifts the supply curve to the right by the change in inventories $\Delta I = I' - I > 0$. This reduces the price in the second market from $p_2(I)$ to $p_2(I')$. By claim 7, the first market price goes down

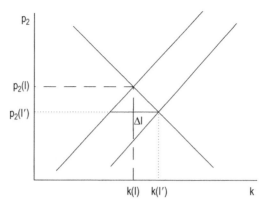

Figure 14.17   An increase in the beginning of period inventories

and since $C'(x) = p_1$, current output goes down. The supply to market s, $k_s(I) = k_s[p_2(I)]$ is decreasing in I because it is increasing in p_2.

We also have:

> *Claim 9:* A unit increase in the beginning of period inventories reduces output by less than a unit.

It is clear from figure 14.17 that $\Delta k = k(I') - k(I)$ is positive. Since $\Delta k = \Delta x + \Delta I$ it follows that: $|\Delta x| < \Delta I$.

> *Claim 10:* An increase in the beginning of period inventories increases the expected value of next period's inventories. (Thus, $E(I_{t+1}|I_t)$ is increasing in I_t.)

Since $k_s(I)$ are increasing functions, the expected next period inventories, $k_3(I) + (1/2)k_2(I)$, is an increasing function.

Claim 10 suggests that a demand shock may affect output in future periods because it changes inventories. The following claim suggests that the effect dies out gradually.

> *Claim 11:* An increase in the beginning of period inventories by one-unit increases next period expected inventories by less than a unit.

To see this claim note that an increase in I_t by one unit increases $k = k_1 + k_2 + k_3$ by less than a unit (see figure 14.17). Since claim 8 says that k_1 increases it follows that $k_2 + k_3$ increases by less than a unit and therefore: $(1/2)\Delta k_2 + \Delta k_3 < 1$.

14.5.3 Full equilibrium

We have assumed that the next period's first market price is given by the function $\alpha(I_{t+1})$. We then derived the price in the current period first market: $p_1(I_t; \alpha)$. A consistent description requires rational expectations: $\alpha(I) = p_1(I; \alpha)$. We therefore define:

The vector of functions $[p_1(I), p_2(I), x(I), k_1(I), k_2(I), k_3(I), \alpha(I)]$ is an equilibrium if it satisfies (14.56)–(14.61) and $p_1(I) = \alpha(I)$ for all I.

To solve for the equilibrium functions, we proceed as follows. We first pick $\alpha(\ )$ and I_t arbitrarily and solve for a temporary equilibrium and for $p_1(I_t; \alpha)$. We then repeat this procedure for alternative choices of I_t (keeping the same α). This yields points in the (p_1, I) space. We use these points to approximate for the partial equilibrium function $p_1(I)$. If this function is the same as $\alpha(\ )$ we are done. Otherwise, we use the approximated function $p_1(\ )$ as $\alpha(\ )$ and start the loop again.

Since a full equilibrium is also a partial equilibrium all the properties of the partial equilibrium functions hold in a full equilibrium if indeed the function $p_1(\ ) = \alpha(\ )$ is decreasing. It is shown in Bental and Eden (1993) that under certain conditions a full equilibrium with decreasing α does exist.

14.5.4 Efficiency

We consider an economy with two goods (X and Y) and $N + \Delta + 1$ infinitely lived agents. As in section 14.1.2 there are three possible types of agents: sellers (S), definite buyers (DB) and possible buyers (PB). The state is an i.i.d random variable with two possible realizations that occur with equal probabilities: $s = 1$ and $s = 2$.

All agents get income (endowment) each period in the form of a large amount, $\bar{y}$, of the numeraire commodity Y. The seller (and only the seller) can use part of their endowment of Y to produce X. It costs x^2 units of Y to produce x units of X.

The seller's single period utility function is: $u(x, y) = y$.
The definite buyers' utility function is: $u(x, y) = U(x) + y$.
The possible buyers' utility function is: $u(x, y) = \{y \text{ if } s = 1 \text{ and } U(x) + y \text{ if } s = 2\}$.

Thus the seller does not like X, definite buyers like X and possible buyers like X only in state 2.

The sum of expected utility is:[11]

$$\sum_{t=1}^{\infty} \beta^t [y_t + NU(k_{1t}/N) + (1/2)\Delta U(k_{2t}/\Delta)], \tag{14.67}$$

where k_{1t}/N is the quantity of X per DB, k_{2t}/Δ is the quantity of X per PB in state 2 and y_t is the total consumption of good Y.

The amount of inventories carried to the next period is:

$$I_{t+1}^1 = x_t + I_t - k_{t1} \text{ if } s = 1 \quad \text{and} \quad I_{t+1}^2 = x_t + I_t - k_{1t} - k_{2t} \text{ if } s = 2. \tag{14.68}$$

The total consumption of Y is:

$$y_t = \bar{y} - (x_t)^2. \tag{14.69}$$

The social planner maximizes (14.67) subject to (14.68), (14.69), an initial condition and non-negativity constraints.

Using $k_3 = x + I - k_1 - k_2$ for the aggregate purely speculative inventories we have: $I^1 = k_3 + k_2$ for next period's inventories if $s = 1$ and $I^2 = k_3$ for next period's inventories if $s = 2$. We can now describe the social planner's problem by the following Bellman equation.

$$V(I) = \max_{\{k_1\ k_2\ k_3\ x\}} NU(k_1/N) + \tfrac{1}{2}\Delta U(k_2/\Delta) + \bar{y} - x^2 + \tfrac{1}{2}\beta V(k_2 + k_3) + \tfrac{1}{2}\beta V(k_3)$$

$$\text{s.t.}\quad k_1 + k_2 + k_3 = I + x \quad k_1, k_2, k_3 \geq 0. \tag{14.70}$$

It is shown in Appendix 14B, that the first order conditions for a strictly positive solution to (14.70) are:

$$U'(k_2/\Delta) \geq \beta V'(k_3) \quad \text{with equality if } k_3 > 0; \tag{14.71}$$

$$U'(k_1/N) = \tfrac{1}{2}U'(k_2/\Delta) + \tfrac{1}{2}\beta V'(k_2 + k_3); \tag{14.72}$$

$$U'(k_1/N) = 2x. \tag{14.73}$$

We can also use the envelope Theorem to get:

$$V'(I) = 2x. \tag{14.74}$$

Proposition 5: The UST allocation maximizes the sum of expected utilities (14.67).

To show this proposition, note that a buyer who faces the price p chooses the quantity x by solving max $U(x) - px$. The first order condition for this problem is: $U'(x) = p$ and therefore in a UST equilibrium, $U'(k_1/N) = p_1$ and $U'(k_2/\Delta) = p_2$. Substituting this and $V' = \alpha$ in (14.71)–(14.73) leads to the equilibrium conditions (14.56)–(14.61).

PROBLEMS WITH ANSWERS

1   Show that an increase in the beginning of period inventories by a unit, leads to

(a) an increase in $k = k_1 + k_2 + k_3$ by less than a unit;
(b) an increase in $k_2 + k_3$ by less than a unit;
(c) an increase in k_3 by less than a unit.

Answer

(a) With the help of figure 14.17 we show that: $\Delta k < 1$.
(b) Since claim 4 says that all $k_s(I)$ are monotonically increasing, it follows that $\Delta k_1 > 0$. This and (a) imply $\Delta(k_2 + k_3) < 1$.
(c) Follows directly from claim 9.

2   In future markets people look at the difference (spread) between the current price and the price for delivery next period. Interpreting the current price as the price in the first market this is: $w_t = E(P_{1t+1}) - P_{1t}$. What can you say about the relationship between the spread (w_t) and the beginning of period inventories?

Hint: Assume full equilibrium and that the derivative $P_1'(I) = P_1'$ does not depend on I. Use your answer to question 1.

Answer

We define, $w(I) = (1/2)P_1[k_2(I) + k_3(I)] + (1/2)P_1[k_3(I)] - P_1(I)$. If I goes up by a unit, $k_2 + k_3$ goes up by less than a unit. Therefore the expected next period price $(1/2)P_1[k_2(I) + k_3(I)] + (1/2)P_1[k_3(I)]$ goes down, in absolute value, by less than the decline in the current period price $P_1(I)$ and the spread goes up.

This argument can be made by taking the derivative of $w(I)$ and using the result that $k_2' + k_3' < 1$. This yields:

$$w'(I) = (1/2)P_1'(k_2' + k_3') + (1/2)P_1'k_3' - P_1'$$
$$= P_1'\{(1/2)(k_2' + k_3') + (1/2)k_3' - 1\} > 0.$$

3   Analyze the effect of an increase in Δ on the *temporary* equilibrium levels of: $p_2(I)$ and $p_1(I)$.

Answer

The amount of speculative inventories that solves (14.58) for a given p_2, $k_3(p_2)$, is not affected by the change in Δ. Since $\alpha[\Delta/p_2 + k_3(p_2)]$ is decreasing in Δ, (14.62) implies that $p_1(p_2)$ is lower for any given p_2 . Therefore, (14.65) implies that production $x(p_2)$ will be lower for any given p_2 and as a result the supply schedule $s(p_2)$ will shift to the left as in figure 14.18.

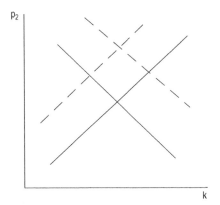

p_2

k

Figure 14.18   An increase in Δ

For any given p_2, an increase in Δ does not change the demand for purely speculative inventories $k_3(p_2)$. The demand in the second market Δ/p_2 goes up, and the demand in the first market $N/p_1(p_2)$ also goes up because $p_1(p_2)$ goes down. It follows that the demand curve (14.64) shifts to the right. The effect on the temporary equilibrium level $p_2(I)$ is unambiguous: It goes up.

Since $p_1(p_2)$ is down it is not clear what happens to the temporary equilibrium level $p_1(I)$.

4   Does your answer to the previous question imply that an increase in Δ will lead to an increase in the full equilibrium level of $p_2(I)$?

5   Consider the case: $\alpha(I) = 1/10I$, $I = 2.67$, $N = \Delta = 1$, $\beta = 0.9$ and $\rho = 0$.
Someone solved for *temporary* equilibrium and got: $p_2 = 1$. Check whether the solution is correct. In your answer solve for the temporary equilibrium magnitudes of k_3, k_2, p_1, k_1 and x. (I suggest to follow the above order). Is it a full equilibrium?

Answer

Since $p_2 = 1$, equation (14.58) implies that a strictly positive k_3 must satisfy: $1 = 0.9(1/10k_3)$. This equation yields: $k_3 = 0.09$. Substituting $p_2 = 1$ in (14.57) yields: $k_2 = 1$. The level of inventories if only one market opens is therefore: $k_2 + k_3 = 1.09$. The price in the next period's first market if only one market opens is: $\alpha(1.09) = 1/10.9 = 0.092$. Substituting this in (14.59) leads to: $p_1 = 0.54$. Substituting $p_1 = 0.54$ in (14.56) leads to: $k_1 = 1.85$. Total demand is therefore: $d(1) = 0.09 + 1 + 1.85 = 2.94$.

Substituting $p_1 = 0.54$ in (14.60) leads to: $x = 0.27$. Thus $k = x + I = 2.94$ which is equal to total demand. We have shown that $(p_1 = 0.54, p_2 = 1, k_3 = 0.09, k_2 = 1, x = 0.27)$ is a temporary equilibrium and therefore the suggested solution is correct.

This is not however a full equilibrium because $\alpha(2.67) = 0.03 \neq 0.54$.

6   Assume that α is decreasing and $k_3 = 0$.

(a) Show that an increase in storage cost (ρ) leads to an increase in the level of temporary equilibrium price in the second market (p_2).

(b) In a full equilibrium the function α changes with ρ. Assume that as a result of an increase in ρ the function $\alpha(I)$ changed to $\hat{\alpha}(I)$ where $\hat{\alpha}(I) < \alpha(I)$ for all I. What happens to the price p_2 in a full equilibrium as a result of the increase in ρ?

(c) Show that when storage cost is sufficiently high the ratio of prices (p_2/p_1) reaches a maximum level of 2.

Answer

(a) For any given p_2, the demand in the second market does not change as a result of an increase in ρ (it remains $k_2 = \Delta/p_2$). The price in the first market, $p_1(p_2) = p_2/2 + [\beta\alpha(\Delta/p_2) - \rho]/2$, is lower and therefore supply shifts to the left as in figure 14.19. Demand in the first market $N/p_1(p_2)$ goes up because $p_1(p_2)$ goes down. As a result the demand curve shifts to the right. Therefore the temporary equilibrium level of p_2 goes up as a result of the increase in storage cost.

(b) The effect of the change in α also works to increase the equilibrium level of p_2. Now, $p_1(p_2) = p_2/2 + [\beta\hat{\alpha}(\Delta/p_2) - \rho]/2$, is lower than before and this pushes the supply further to the left and the demand further to the right.

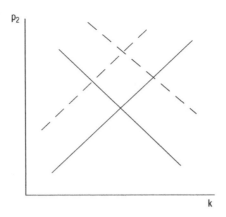

Figure 14.19 An increase in storage cost

(c) Equilibrium condition implies: $2 = p_{2t}/p_{1t} + \max[(\beta\alpha(k_{2t}+k_{3t}) - \rho), 0]/p_{1t}$. When ρ is large, storage is prohibitively expensive and $\max[(\beta\alpha(k_{2t}+k_{3t}) - \rho), 0] = 0$.

7 The result in question 6 requires $k_3 = 0$. Use the planner's problem (14.70) to discuss the effect of changes in ρ in general.

APPENDIX 14A THE FIRM'S PROBLEM

To formulate the firm's problem, let us distinguish between the level of inventories that the firm has at the beginning of the period (i) and the average per-firm level of inventories I. The price-taking firm expects that prices depend on the average per-firm level of inventories and are given by the functions: $p_s(I)$. Using this notation, the Bellman equation is:

$$V(i; I) = \max_{\{k_s, x\}} p_1(I)k_1 + \tfrac{1}{2}p_2(I)k_2 - C(x)$$
$$+ \tfrac{1}{2}\beta V(k_2 + k_3; I^1) + \tfrac{1}{2}\beta V(k_3; I^2)$$
$$\text{s.t.}\quad k_1 + k_2 + k_3 = i + x \quad \text{and non-negativity constraints.} \tag{A14.1}$$

Here V(i, I) is the expected utility of a firm that starts with i units of inventories when the average per-firm level of inventories is I and I^s denotes the expected average inventories next period given that s markets open this period.

To solve (A14.1) we set the lagrangian:

$$L = p_1(I)k_1 + \tfrac{1}{2}p_2(I)k_2 - C(x) + \tfrac{1}{2}\beta V(k_2 + k_3; I^1)$$
$$+ \tfrac{1}{2}\beta V(k_3; I^2) + \lambda(i + x - k_1 - k_2 - k_3). \tag{A14.2}$$

We now derive the following first order conditions that a solution $k_1 > 0$, $k_2 > 0$, $k_3 \geq 0$, $x > 0$ must satisfy. These are:

$$\partial L/\partial k_1 = p_1(I) - \lambda = 0; \tag{A14.3}$$

$$\partial L/\partial k_2 = \tfrac{1}{2}p_2(I) + \tfrac{1}{2}\beta V'(k_2 + k_3; I^1) - \lambda = 0; \tag{A14.4}$$

$$\partial L/\partial k_3 = \tfrac{1}{2}\beta V(k_2 + k_3; I^1) + \tfrac{1}{2}\beta V'(k_3; I^2) - \lambda \leq 0 \tag{A14.5}$$

$$\text{with equality if } k_3 > 0;$$

$$\partial L/\partial x = -C'(x) + \lambda = 0. \tag{A14.6}$$

From (A14.4) we get $(1/2)\beta V'(k_2 + k_3; I^1) - \lambda = -(1/2)p_2(I)$. Substituting this in (A14.5) leads to:

$$\beta V'(k_3; I^2) \leq p_2(I) \quad \text{with equality if } k_3 > 0. \tag{A14.7}$$

Substituting (A14.3) into (A14.4) leads to:

$$p_1(I) = \tfrac{1}{2}p_2(I) + \tfrac{1}{2}\beta V'(k_2 + k_3; I^1). \tag{A14.8}$$

Substituting (A14.3) into (A14.6) leads to:

$$C'(x) = p_1(I). \tag{A14.9}$$

The first order conditions (A14.7)–(A14.9) are the arbitrage conditions (14.48)–(14.50) in the text where V' replaces α for the value of inventories. We now observe that at the optimum it does not matter how an additional unit of inventories is used and therefore the firm cannot do better than selling it in the next period's first market.

APPENDIX 14B   THE PLANNER'S PROBLEM

To solve the maximization problem (14.60) we set the lagrangian:

$$L = NU(k_1/N) + \tfrac{1}{2}\Delta U(k_2/\Delta) + \bar{y} - x^2$$
$$+ \beta \left[\tfrac{1}{2}V(k_2 + k_3) + \tfrac{1}{2}V(k_3) \right] + \lambda(I + x - k_1 - k_2 - k_3) \tag{B14.1}$$

We now derive the first order conditions for a solution k_1, k_2, $x > 0$; $k_3 \geq 0$. These are:

$$\partial L/\partial k_1 = U'(k_1/N) - \lambda = 0; \tag{B14.2}$$

$$\partial L/\partial k_2 = \tfrac{1}{2}U'(k_2/\Delta) + \beta\tfrac{1}{2}V'(k_2 + k_3) - \lambda = 0; \tag{B14.3}$$

$$\partial L/\partial k_3 = \beta \left[\tfrac{1}{2}V'(k_2 + k_3) + \tfrac{1}{2}V'(k_3) \right] - \lambda \leq 0 \tag{B14.4}$$

$$\text{with equality if } k_3 > 0.$$

$$\partial L/\partial x = -2x + \lambda = 0. \tag{B14.5}$$

From (B14.3) we get: $-(1/2)U'(k_2/\Delta) = \beta(1/2)V'(k_2 + k_3) - \lambda$. Substituting this in (B14.4) leads to:

$$V'(k_3) \leq U'(k_2/\Delta) \quad \text{with equality if } k_3 > 0. \tag{B14.6}$$

Substituting (B14.2) in (B14.3) leads to:

$$\tfrac{1}{2}U'(k_2/\Delta) + \beta\tfrac{1}{2}V'(k_2 + k_3) = U'(k_1/N). \qquad (B14.7)$$

Substituting (B14.2) in (B14.5) leads to:

$$U'(k_1/N) = 2x. \qquad (B14.8)$$

Conditions (B14.6)–(B14.8) are the same as (14.61)–(14.63) in the text.

NOTES

1 The CPI is the outcome of a survey about quoted price.

2 Dividing (14.11) by $(1 + N + \Delta)$ yields the expected utility of the representative agent at $t = 0$.

3 Jeff Campbell suggested the first question.

4 Wilson (1988) has shown that when the individual demand function is not differentiable (a step function) a monopolist may want to charge more than one price even if there is no uncertainty about the number of buyers that will arrive. Thus a monopoly may want to charge more than one price per group (market). We assume that the individual demand function, $D(p)$ is differentiable and therefore the constraint of one price per market is not binding.

5 The first order condition for this problem is $C'(x) = \pi$ which is the same as the first order condition (14.26) for the monopoly's problem.

6 When individual demand is downward sloping, relatively more capacity is wasted in the UST model and therefore productivity should be relatively more procyclical. See Claim 1 in 14.1.1.

7 Here y is the amount paid for X. The utility could also be stated as: $U(x) - y + \bar{y}$ if he wants to consume and $\bar{y}$ otherwise, where $\bar{y}$ is the initial endowment of Y.

8 To derive these first order conditions we set the lagrangian: $L = \sum_{s=1}^{S} \zeta_s q_s[U(x_s) - y_s] + \lambda\left(\sum_{s=1}^{S} \zeta_s q_s y_s - \sum_{s=1}^{S} p_s \zeta_s q_s x_s\right)$. We then take the derivatives:

$$\partial L/\partial x_s = \zeta_s q_s U'(x_s) - \lambda p_s \zeta_s q_s = 0 \text{ and}$$

$$\partial L/\partial y_s = -\zeta_s q_s + \lambda \zeta_s q_s = 0.$$

9 The probability Π_s is the probability of state s from the actual sellers' point of view (conditional on being chosen as an actual seller). This distinction will become important later.

10 To show this claim we apply Bayes' rule and compute the probability that exactly $i > s$ markets will open given that market s opens. This is: Π_i/q_s. The probability that market i will open given that market s opens is: $\sum_{k=i}^{S} \Pi_k/q_s$. In equilibrium the unconditional expected revenue (from a unit supplied to market i) is $P_i \sum_{k=i}^{S} \Pi_k = \lambda$ and the conditional expected revenue (from a unit supplied to market i given that market s opens) is: $P_i \sum_{k=i}^{S} \Pi_k/q_s = \lambda/q_s$. Since in equilibrium $P_s = \lambda/q_s$ the opening of market s does not provide an incentive for the firm to move units from market s to market i or vice versa. Since the conditional expected revenue is λ/q_s for all $i > s$, the firm does not have an incentive to move units allocated to markets $s + 1, \ldots, S$. Thus, not surprisingly the initial plan is time consistent.

11 Note that we can divide the sum (14.79) by $(N+\Delta+1)$ to get the expected utility of the representative consumer before he knows his type.

CHAPTER 15

A Monetary Model

In chapters 15–18 we use monetary versions of the UST model to account for the money/output relationship. We start with an overlapping generations model and then use a cash-in-advance model. The overlapping generations model is simpler and does not require dynamic programming. The cash-in-advance model is useful for studying the role of inventories in propagating monetary shocks. A reader who is interested in the role of inventories may go directly to chapter 17.

In monetary UST models sellers may know the number of buyers that will arrive but do not know the amount that they will spend. This may depend on the realization of the random monetary transfer. Thus in monetary UST models uncertainty about the number of dollars that will arrive plays the role of uncertainty about the number of buyers in real UST models.

Unlike Lucas' confusion model (reviewed in chapter 10), here everyone observes the money supply process and there is no confusion. The monetary transfer process is like rain. Everyone observes the amount of monetary "rain" accumulated from the beginning of the period but no one knows when it will stop. Sellers do not sell everything they have at the beginning of the process because they speculate on the event that the monetary rain will continue and they will be able to sell at a higher price.

Changes in the money supply affect capacity utilization and output first and quoted prices later (with a one period lag). But this Keynesian feature of the model does not imply an exploitable trade-off between inflation and output.

The first generation of UST monetary models are the papers by Eden (1994) and Lucas and Woodford (1994). In the Lucas and Woodford model, trade is sequential but the transfer of money is not: Trade starts only after buyers know the total amount of money transferred. This asymmetry in information about the money supply may lead to rationing. In Eden (1994) both the money transfer and trade are perfectly synchronized processes: Each batch of dollars transferred triggers more trade. Lucas and Woodford use an infinite horizon model, a Nash equilibrium concept, and exogenous capacity. Eden uses an overlapping generations model, a competitive equilibrium concept and allows for production. Here we present the model in Eden (1994).

15.1   AN EXAMPLE

We consider an overlapping generations model. Two identical individuals are born at the beginning of each period. Each lives for two periods. In the first period of his life the representative agent produces and sells his output for money. He then uses, in the second period, the proceeds of first period sales plus a transfer that he may receives from the government to buy goods. There is a single consumption good and fiat money is the only asset.

The buyer (an old agent) shops in two locations. In the first location he spends the proceeds of period $t - 1$ sales (M_t). He then goes to the second location. If he receives a transfer at this second location he uses it to buy goods. Otherwise, he goes home. The amount of transfer is one dollar per dollar held at the beginning of the period and the probability of receiving it is $1/2$. Figure 15.1 illustrates the sequence of events from the buyer's point of view.

There is a single seller (young agent) in each location and at each round of trade a single buyer may appear in his location. (Thus buyers move but sellers do not.) From the representative seller's point of view demand arrives in batches: The first buyer spends M_t dollars with certainty and disappears. Then we have two possibilities: Either trade for the period ends or a second buyer arrives (with probability $1/2$) and spends an additional M_t dollars. Figure 15.2 illustrates the seller's point of view.

The seller is a price-taker and knows that he can sell to the first buyer at the dollar price P_{1t}. He can sell to the second buyer, if he gets the transfer payment, at the dollar price $P_{2t} > P_{1t}$. He chooses total capacity before the beginning of trade and makes a contingent plan as to how to utilize it. He may plan for example to sell 80% of his capacity to the first buyer and 20% to the second buyer if he arrives.

As in the real models, it is useful to think of Walrasian markets that open sequentially in response to the arrival of purchasing power. The first batch of M_t dollars buys in market 1 at the price P_{1t}. If the second batch of M_t dollars arrives it buys in market 2 at the price P_{2t}. Thus market 1 opens with certainty and market 2 opens with probability $1/2$.

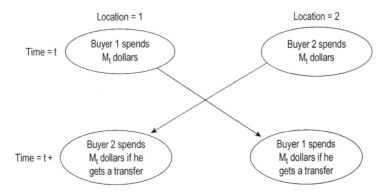

Figure 15.1   Events over time and locations

Figure 15.2   The seller's point of view

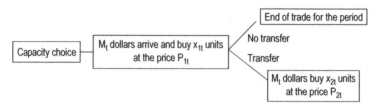

Figure 15.3   Sequence of events

It takes one unit of labor to produce one unit of capacity. The representative young agent at time t, has a utility function which is linear in consumption:

$$c_{t+1} - (x_t)^2,\tag{15.1}$$

where c_{t+1} is the expectation at time t of consumption at time $t+1$ and x_t is the total amount of work (capacity).

The representative young agent chooses total capacity, x_t, before the beginning of trade and allocates x_{1t} to market 1 and x_{2t} to market 2 ($x_{1t} + x_{2t} = x_t$). It is costless to convert capacity into output and storage is not possible. Capacity allocated to market 2 is utilized (converted to output) only if market 2 opens. Figure 15.3 describes the sequence of events from the representative seller's point of view.

Since money received today will be spent in the next period the seller must form expectations about next period's prices in order to choose capacity (effort) and to allocate it between the two markets. For this purpose it is useful to compute the expected purchasing power of a dollar earned in each market.

Let P_{it+1}^s denote the expected next period price in market i when exactly s markets open in the current period. A dollar earned this period, allows its owner to spend one dollar with certainty in the next period's first market. Since the transfer payment is proportional (a dollar per dollar held at the beginning of period) it also promises a 50% chance of spending an additional dollar in next period's market 2. The expected purchasing power of a dollar earned at time t in market 2 is therefore:

$$Z_{2t} = 1/P_{1t+1}^2 + \tfrac{1}{2}\left(1/P_{2t+1}^2\right).\tag{15.2}$$

There is no uncertainty in (15.2) about the superscript (the number of markets open in the current period) because a sale is made in market 2 only if exactly 2 markets open this period. This is not the case when the dollar is earned in market 1. The expected purchasing power of a dollar earned at time t in market 1 is:

$$Z_{1t} = \tfrac{1}{2}\left[1/P_{1t+1}^1 + \tfrac{1}{2}\left(1/P_{2t+1}^1\right)\right] + \tfrac{1}{2}\left[1/P_{1t+1}^2 + \tfrac{1}{2}\left(1/P_{2t+1}^2\right)\right].\tag{15.3}$$

The expected real revenue from a unit of capacity allocated to market 1 is $P_{1t}Z_{1t}$ and the expected revenue from a unit of capacity allocated to market 2 is: $(1/2)P_{2t}Z_{2t}$. The representative young agent's problem is to choose the capacities x_{st} that solve:

$$\max_{x_{st}} P_{1t}Z_{1t}x_{1t} + \tfrac{1}{2}P_{2t}Z_{2t}x_{2t} - (x_{1t} + x_{2t})^2. \tag{15.4}$$

The first order conditions for an interior solution to (15.4) require that the expected real revenue per unit of capacity is the same for both markets and is equal marginal cost:

$$P_{1t}Z_{1t} = \tfrac{1}{2}P_{2t}Z_{2t} = 2(x_{1t} + x_{2t}). \tag{15.5}$$

A partial equilibrium for time t is defined for given expectations (P^s_{it+1}). It is a vector $(P_{1t}, P_{2t}, x_{1t}, x_{2t})$ that satisfies (15.5) and the market-clearing conditions:

$$M_t/P_{1t} = x_{1t} \quad \text{and} \quad M_t/P_{2t} = x_{2t}. \tag{15.6}$$

A full equilibrium endogenizes expectations. To do that, we assume that agents use a quantity theory type model and expect prices proportional to the beginning of period money supply. They thus assume the existence of normalized prices p_s such that:

$$P_{st} = p_s M_t \quad \text{for all t.} \tag{15.7}$$

Using (15.7), sellers form the following rational expectations:

$$P^1_{st+1} = p_s M_t \quad \text{and} \quad P^2_{st+1} = p_s 2M_t. \tag{15.8}$$

A full equilibrium for time t is a vector $(p_1, p_2, x_{1t}, x_{2t}, P_{1t}, P_{2t}, P^1_{1t+1}, P^1_{2t+1}, P^2_{1t+1}, P^2_{2t+1}, Z_{1t}, Z_{2t})$ satisfying (15.2), (15.3) and (15.5)–(15.8).

Note that once we know normalized prices (p_1, p_2), we can easily compute (P_{1t}, P_{2t}) by using (15.7), the period t expectations $(P^1_{1t+1}, P^1_{2t+1}, P^2_{1t+1}, P^2_{2t+1})$ by using (15.8) and the expected purchasing power expression by using (15.2) and (15.3). Therefore, rather than solving for full equilibrium, we turn now to a more direct way of solving for quantities and normalized prices.

15.2 WORKING WITH THE MONEY SUPPLY AS THE UNIT OF ACCOUNT

Rather than formulating the model in terms of dollar magnitudes, we may do it directly in terms of normalized magnitudes.

To build intuition let us start with the concept of an indexed dollar. The number of cents in an indexed dollar is proportional to the money supply: If, in the current period there are 100 cents in an indexed dollar and the money supply went up by 10% then in the next period we require 110 cents per indexed dollar. A seller who posts his prices in terms of indexed dollars does not change posted prices in response to neutral changes in the money supply.

Alternatively, we may use the money supply (per household) itself as a unit of account and call it a normalized dollar. For example, if the price of a unit is one normalized dollar it means that you must pay the whole money supply (average per household) to get it. Like with an indexed dollar, a seller that posts his prices in terms of normalized dollars does not change posted prices in response to neutral money supply changes.

A normalized dollar this period is worth $\omega^s = M_t/M^s_{t+1}$ in terms of next period's normalized dollars, where M^s_{t+1} is the next period money supply if s markets open today. In our example:

$$\omega^1 = 1 \quad \text{and} \quad \omega^2 = \tfrac{1}{2}. \tag{15.9}$$

A normalized dollar earned in market 2 is thus worth ω^2 next period's normalized dollars because making a sale in market 2 implies that exactly 2 markets open this period. A normalized dollar earned in the first market is worth $\omega = (1/2)\omega^1 + (1/2)\omega^2$ in terms of next period's normalized dollars because making a sale in market 1 does not tell us anything new about the number of markets that will open.

The purchasing power of a normalized dollar held at the beginning of the period is:

$$z = (1/p_1) + \tfrac{1}{2}(1/p_2), \tag{15.10}$$

because it will be spent in the first market for sure and it promises (with probability $1/2$) a transfer of a normalized dollar that will be spent in market 2.

The young agent's problem can now be written as:

$$\max \ (p_1\omega z)x_1 + \tfrac{1}{2}(p_2\omega^2 z)x_2 - (x_1 + x_2)^2. \tag{15.11}$$

The product $p_1\omega$ is the expected number of next period's normalized dollars that a young agent can get by allocating a unit of capacity to market 1 and similarly, $(1/2)p_2\omega^2$ is the revenue from allocating a unit to market 2. Multiplying these magnitudes by the expected purchasing power of a normalized dollar (z) yields the relevant real price in each market.

The first order conditions for the problem (15.11) are:

$$p_1\omega z = \tfrac{1}{2}p_2\omega^2 z = 2(x_1 + x_2). \tag{15.12}$$

To interpret (15.12) note that a unit supplied to market 1 promises, on average, $p_1\omega z$ units of consumption. This must equal the expected amount of consumption that one can get from supplying a unit to the second market, $(1/2)p_2\omega^2 z$, and the marginal cost, $2(x_1 + x_2)$.

Since one normalized dollar will arrive in each market that is opened the market-clearing conditions can be written as:

$$1/p_1 = x_1 \quad \text{and} \quad 1/p_2 = x_2. \tag{15.13}$$

We can now define *equilibrium* as a solution (p_1, p_2, x_1, x_2) to (15.12) and (15.13). The solution is: $p_1 = 64/21; p_2 = 64/7; x_1 = 21/64; x_2 = 7/64$.

The equilibrium normalized prices and (15.7) and (15.8) can be used to compute actual and expected prices. For example, if $M_t = 1$, actual prices are equal to normalized prices and expected prices are: $P^1_{1t+1} = 64/21; P^2_{1t+1} = 128/21; P^1_{2t+1} = 64/7; P^2_{2t+1} = 128/7$.

Note that (15.12) implies:

$$p_1/p_2 = \tfrac{1}{2}\omega^2/\omega < \tfrac{1}{2}. \tag{15.14}$$

Thus unlike the real UST model, here the ratio of prices is less than the probability that market 2 will open. The intuition is that a normalized dollar earned in market 1 is worth more in terms of next period's normalized dollars and therefore $p_1 < (1/2)p_2$.

This result is analogous to the winner-curse effect in the auction literature (see for example the discussion in Milgrom and Weber [1982]). Here there is an adverse effect of a success in selling in market 2 on the value of the dollar.

15.3 ANTICIPATED AND UNANTICIPATED MONEY

We now consider a more general case that allows for a distinction between anticipated and unanticipated money. We assume $M_{t+1} = \theta \lambda M_t$, where λ is the average (anticipated) gross rate of change in the money supply and θ is the unanticipated component.

At the first location the buyer receives a transfer of $(\theta_1 \lambda - 1)$ per dollar and spends a total of $\theta_1 \lambda M_t$ dollars or $\theta_1 \lambda$ normalized dollars. With probability $1/2$ the buyer may get a transfer of $(\theta_2 - \theta_1)\lambda$ normalized dollars in the second location. We assume $E\theta = 1$. In the above numerical example: $\lambda = 3/2$, $\theta_1 = 2/3$ and $\theta_2 = 4/3$.

A normalized dollar this period will become:

$$\omega^s = M_t/M_{t+1}^s = 1/\theta_s \lambda, \tag{15.15}$$

next period's normalized dollars, if s markets open this period. The expected purchasing power of a normalized dollar held at the beginning of the period is now

$$z = (\theta_1 \lambda/p_1) + \tfrac{1}{2}(\theta_2 - \theta_1)\lambda/p_2. \tag{15.16}$$

The purchasing power of a normalized dollar earned in market 2 is: $\omega^2 z = (1/\theta_2)[\theta_1/p_1 + (1/2)(\theta_2 - \theta_1)/p_2]$. The expected consumption that a unit of output supplied to market 2 will bring is:

$$\tfrac{1}{2}p_2 \omega^2 z = \tfrac{1}{2}(1/\theta_2)\left[\theta_1 p + \tfrac{1}{2}(\theta_2 - \theta_1)\right], \tag{15.17}$$

where $p = p_2/p_1$. Similarly, $\omega z = [E(1/\theta)][(\theta_1/p_1) + \tfrac{1}{2}(\theta_2 - \theta_1)/p_2]$ and

$$p_1 \omega z = [E(1/\theta)]\left[\theta_1 + \tfrac{1}{2}(\theta_2 - \theta_1)(1/p)\right], \tag{15.18}$$

where $E(1/\theta) = (1/2)(1/\theta_1) + (1/2)(1/\theta_2)$. The first order condition (15.12) can now be written as:

$$[E(1/\theta)]\left[\theta_1 + \tfrac{1}{2}(\theta_2 - \theta_1)(1/p)\right]$$
$$= \tfrac{1}{2}(1/\theta_2)\left[\theta_1 p + \tfrac{1}{2}(\theta_2 - \theta_1)\right]$$
$$= 2(x_1 + x_2). \tag{15.19}$$

Market-clearing conditions are now:

$$\theta_1 \lambda/p_1 = x_1 \quad \text{and} \quad (\theta_2 - \theta_1)\lambda/p_2 = x_2. \tag{15.20}$$

Dividing the first equation in (15.20) by the second yields:

$$p\theta_1/(\theta_2 - \theta_1) = x_1/x_2. \tag{15.21}$$

Equilibrium is a solution (p, x_1, x_2) to (15.19) and (15.21). Note that this is a system of three equations in three unknowns: (p, x_1, x_2) which do not depend on the parameter λ.

Using the price in the first market as a numeiraire, the distribution of relative prices is: A fraction $x_1/(x_1 + x_2)$ of quoted prices is unity and a fraction $x_2/(x_1 + x_2)$ of quoted prices is $p = p_2/p_1$. This distribution of relative prices depends only on the distribution of θ and not on the expected rate of change λ. Thus,

> *Claim:* Anticipated money is neutral: It does not affect the allocation of resources and the distribution of relative prices.

15.4 LABOR CHOICE, AVERAGE CAPACITY UTILIZATION AND WELFARE

The first order condition (15.12) implies $p_1\omega z = (1/2)p_2\omega^2 z$ and $1/p = p_1/p_2 = (1/2)(\omega^2/\omega)$. Substituting this and $\omega^2/\omega = (1/\theta_2)/[E(1/\theta)]$ in (15.18) leads to:

$$w = p_1\omega z = \tfrac{3}{4} + \tfrac{1}{4}(\theta_1/\theta_2). \tag{15.22}$$

Since by construction $\theta_2 \geq \theta_1$, the real wage is maximized at the level of unity when $\theta_2 = \theta_1$ and there is no uncertainty about the money supply.

Average capacity utilization: Using the market-clearing conditions (15.20) and $1/p = (1/2)(\omega^2/\omega) = (1/2)(1/\theta_2)/[E(1/\theta)]$ leads (after substantial amount of algebra) to:

$$CU = \tfrac{1}{2}x_1/(x_1 + x_2) + \tfrac{1}{2} = \tfrac{3}{4} + \tfrac{1}{4}(\theta_1/\theta_2), \tag{15.23}$$

where CU is expected capacity utilization. When $\theta_1 = \theta_2$ there is no uncertainty about the money supply, only one market is active (the demand in the second market $(\theta_2 - \theta_1)\lambda = 0$) and average capacity utilization is maximized.

Comparing (15.23) to (15.22) reveals:

$$w = CU. \tag{15.24}$$

This is because in equilibrium a supply of one unit of labor leads to an increase in CU units of consumption on average.

Welfare: The welfare of the representative consumer can be measured by:

$$V(w) = \max_{x} wx - (x)^2. \tag{15.25}$$

Since $V(w)$ is an increasing function, welfare is maximized when monetary uncertainty is eliminated and $w = CU$ is maximized.

15.5 A GENERALIZATION TO MANY POTENTIAL MARKETS

We now generalize the transfer process. The variable θ is an i.i.d. random variable with S possible realizations: $\theta_1 < \theta_2 < \cdots < \theta_S$. The realization θ_i occurs with probability Π_i. For convenience we set $\theta_0 = 0$.

At the first location the buyer receives a transfer of $(\theta_1\lambda - 1)$ dollars per dollar, where $\lambda - 1$ denotes the anticipated rate of change in the money supply. At this stage the buyer has

$(\theta_1 - \theta_0)\lambda M_t$ dollars which he spends in the first market. If there are no additional transfers, trade for period t ends and the buyer consumes whatever was bought in the first location. But, with probability $q_2 = 1 - \Pi_1$, he gets an additional transfer of $(\theta_2 - \theta_1)\lambda M_t$ dollars. If he gets it he spends it. In general, the transfer $(\theta_s - \theta_{s-1})\lambda M_t$ will be realized with probability $q_s = \sum_{j=s}^{S} \Pi_j$ and the buyer spends it immediately after getting it. There are S different locations and each transfer is spent in a different location. The end of period money supply is: $M_{t+1} = \theta\lambda M_t$.

From the representative seller's point of view demand arrives in batches. The first batch of $(\theta_1 - \theta_0)\lambda$ normalized dollars arrives with certainty. The second batch of $(\theta_2 - \theta_1)\lambda$ normalized dollars arrives with probability q_2 and so on. Each batch of dollars that arrives opens a new market.

A normalized dollar this period is worth $\omega^s = 1/\lambda\theta_s$ normalized dollars next period if exactly s markets open this period. A normalized dollar earned in market s is worth

$$\omega_S = \sum_{j=s}^{S}(\Pi_j/q_s)\omega^j, \qquad (15.26)$$

in terms of next period's normalized dollars. To build (15.26) recall that Π_j is the unconditional probability that exactly j markets open today. When market 1 opens the seller does not learn anything and does not revise these probabilities. But when market 2 opens, the seller learns that at least 2 markets will open today. He therefore applies Bayes rule and assigns a probability of zero to the event that exactly one market will open today and Π_j/q_2 to the event that exactly $j \geq 2$ markets will open today. In general, when market s opens the revised probability that exactly j markets will open is: Π_j/q_s if $j \geq s$ and zero otherwise.[1]

There is a "winner curse" here. A seller who succeeds in selling must take into account the adverse implications of his success on the money supply. Specifically, an increase in the number of markets open today reduces the value of a normalized dollar in terms of next period's normalized dollars ($\omega^j > \omega^{j+1}$) and therefore:

$$\omega_s > \omega_{s+1}. \qquad (15.27)$$

This says that a normalized dollar earned in market s is worth on average more than a normalized dollar earned in market $s + 1$.

Since a normalized dollar held at the beginning of the period promises a transfer of $(\theta_s - \theta_{s-1})\lambda$ normalized dollars if market s opens, the expected purchasing power of a normalized dollar held at the beginning of the period is:

$$z = \sum_{s=1}^{S} q_s(\theta_s - \theta_{s-1})\lambda/p_s, \qquad (15.28)$$

where p_s is the normalized price in market s. The expected purchasing power of a normalized dollar earned in market s is $\omega_s z$ and the expected purchasing power that one can get by supplying a unit to market s is: $q_s p_s \omega_s z$. The representative young agent's problem is to choose the capacities x_s which solve:

$$\max \sum_s q_s (p_s \omega_s z) x_s - v \left(x = \sum_s x_s \right),$$ (15.29)

where $v(x)$ is the utility cost of producing x units of capacity. The first order conditions for an interior solution to (15.29) require that the expected real revenue per unit of capacity is equal to the marginal cost:

$$q_s (p_s \omega_s z) = v'(x) \quad \text{for all s.}$$ (15.30)

Since $(\theta_s - \theta_{s-1})\lambda$ normalized dollars will buy in market s if it opens, the market-clearing conditions are:

$$(\theta_s - \theta_{s-1})\lambda / p_s = x_s \quad \text{for all s.}$$ (15.31)

A solution $(p_1, p_2, \ldots, p_S, x_1, x_2, \ldots, x_S)$ to (15.30) and (15.31) is a symmetric steady-state equilibrium.

Note that from (15.27) and (15.30) it follows that

$$q_s p_s = q_{s+1} p_{s+1} (\omega_{s+1}/\omega_s) < q_{s+1} p_{s+1}.$$ (15.32)

The expected normalized price in market s is less than the expected normalized price in market s + 1 because a normalized dollar earned in market s worth more in terms of next period's normalized dollars.

Equation (15.30) implies: $p_s/p_1 = (q_1/q_s)(\omega_1/\omega_s)$. Since $\omega_1/\omega_s > 1$, the "winner curse" effect contributes to price dispersion.

15.6 ASYMMETRIC EQUILIBRIA: A PERFECTLY FLEXIBLE PRICE DISTRIBUTION IS CONSISTENT WITH INDIVIDUAL PRICES THAT APPEAR TO BE "RIGID"

In the symmetric steady-state equilibrium each seller allocates a fraction $\mu_s = x_s/x$ of his capacity to market s. Since our risk neutral sellers are indifferent about the way they allocate capacity across markets, there exists an asymmetric equilibrium in which a fraction μ_s of the sellers supply all their output to market s.[2] In this asymmetric equilibrium it is enough that only some sellers will change their posted dollar prices in response to an increase in the money supply, because most sellers are compensated for the reduction in the normalized price by the increased probability of making a sale.

To illustrate, we assume that the range of the equilibrium distribution of normalized prices $p = P/M$ is between $p = 1$ to $p = 4$. Assume that in the previous period the money supply was $M = 10$ and in the current period it doubled to $M' = 20$. A seller whose dollar price in the previous period was $P = 30$ (and his normalized price was 3) will have a normalized price of 1.5 in the current period if he does not change his dollar price. This seller will not care about the decline in his normalized price because he is compensated by the increase in the probability of making a sale. But a seller whose dollar price was $P = 15$ (and normalized price was 1.5) will have a current normalized price of 0.75 if he does not change his dollar price. Since this seller can increase his dollar price to 20 (and normalized price to 1) without affecting the probability of making a sale, he will definitely choose to increase his dollar price. Thus, the distribution of normalized prices may be always in equilibrium even when some sellers do not change their dollar prices.

15.7 SUMMARY OF THE IMPLICATIONS OF THE MODEL

The main implications of the model are as follows.

1 There is a positive correlation between capacity utilization and unanticipated money. If we measure output as capacity which is utilized (a meal prepared but not sold is not counted as output) then the model predicts a positive correlation between output and unanticipated money.
2 Money surprises affect output first and quoted prices only in the following period.
3 The distribution of relative prices (p_s/p_1) depends only on the distribution of the unanticipated rate of change in the money supply θ and not on the expected rate of change λ.
4 The expected real wage is equal to average capacity utilization. Both are maximized in the absence of monetary uncertainty (when θ is a degenerate random variable). Welfare is a monotonic function of the expected real wage and it is also maximized in the absence of monetary uncertainty.
5 Monetary uncertainty reduces the level of average output (relative to the case of no uncertainty) because it reduces average capacity utilization and the expected real wage.
6 Changes in nominal prices need not be synchronized across sellers. Sellers may let inflation erode their relative price as long as it stays in the equilibrium range. This is because the reduction in real price is compensated by the increase in the probability of making a sale. Therefore, although the distribution of dollar prices adjusts to changes in the money supply with a one period lag, the dollar price of a particular seller may appear "rigid."

PROBLEMS WITH ANSWERS

1 Consider the following variation of the example in section 15.2. We assume now that the buyer may get, with probability $1/2$, a transfer payment of two (rather than one) dollars per dollar held at the beginning of the period.

(a) Write the equilibrium conditions;
(b) What is the ratio of p_1/p_2?

Answer

(a) $\omega^1 = 1$, $\omega^2 = 1/3$, $\omega = 2/3$;

$z = 1/p_1 + 1/p_2$

First order conditions:

$p_1\omega z = (1/2)p_2\omega^2 z = 2(x_1 + x_2)$

Market-clearing conditions:

$1/p_1 = x_1$ and $2/p_2 = x_2$.

(b) $p_1/p_2 = (1/2)\omega^2/\omega = 1/4$

2   Answer 1 under the assumption that the transfer payment is in a lump sum form.

Answer

(a) $\omega^1 = 1$, $\omega^2 = 1/3$, $\omega = 2/3$;

$z = 1/p_1$

First order conditions:

$p_1 \omega z = (1/2)p_2 \omega^2 z = 2(x_1 + x_2)$

Market-clearing conditions:

$1/p_1 = x_1$ and $2/p_2 = x_2$.

(b) $p_1/p_2 = (1/2)\omega^2/\omega = 1/4$

NOTES

1   To apply Bayes rule recall that Prob $(A|B) = $ Prob$(A$ and $B)/$Prob(B). Here the event A is "exactly j markets open"; the event B is "at least s markets open"; Prob$(A$ and $B) = $ Prob$(A) = \Pi_j$ if $j \geq s$ and zero otherwise (because A implies B but not vice versa) and Prob$(B) = q_s$. Thus Prob$(A|B) = \Pi_j/q_s$ if $j \geq s$ and zero otherwise.

2   There are many other asymmetric equilibria arising from the observation that equilibrium conditions (15.36) and (15.37) determine the total capacity allocated to each market and not the number of sellers in each market.

CHAPTER 16

Limited Participation, Sticky Prices, and UST: A Comparison

Using US data, Christiano, Eichenbaum and Evans (CEE, 1997) found that in response to a contractionary monetary shock:

1 The aggregate price level initially responds very little;
2 Aggregate output falls;
3 Interest rates initially rise;
4 Real wages decline by a modest amount;
5 Profits fall.

In their article CEE compared the ability of a limited participation model and a sticky price model to account for the stylized facts. They conclude that the two alternative models cannot account for all of the above stylized facts. The limited participation model cannot explain the lack of an initial effect on prices (stylized fact [1]) while the sticky price model cannot explain the decline in profits (stylized fact [5]).

Here we provide an exposition of the two models in CEE and add a UST alternative.

16.1 LIMITED PARTICIPATION

In section 10.2 we did a version of the limited participation model that does not distinguish between workers and firms. Here we do a more standard version based on Christiano, Eichenbaum and Evans (CEE, 1997).

There is a representative infinitely lived household consisting of a worker/shopper pair. The household begins period t with M_t dollars. Both members go to the bank and deposit $D_t \leq M_t$ dollars. They then go to the firm and collect a wage payment of $W_t L_t$ dollars for a promise to deliver L_t units of labor. The two members of the household then separate. The worker stays with the firm to deliver the promised amount of labor while the shopper takes the money ($M_t - D_t + W_t L_t$ dollars) and spends it.

The representative household owns a bank and a firm. After the deposit of D_t dollars was made, the bank receives a random transfer from the government of $\widetilde{X}_t$ dollars. The amount of deposit D_t is determined prior to the realization of $\widetilde{X}_t$. All other variables are determined after the realization X_t of $\widetilde{X}_t$ is known. This includes the price level (P), the wage rate (W), the gross interest rate (R), labor supply (L) and labor demand (N).

The bank lends $D_t + X_t$ to the firm. At the end of the period it pays the household $D_t R_t$ as interest and principal and $X_t R_t$ as profits.

The firm has access to a standard production function $f(N_t)$ where N denotes labor input (no capital in this simplified version) and $f(\ )$ is strictly concave. The wage is paid at the beginning of the period. To meet this cash-in-advance constraint the firm borrows:

$$B_t = W_t N_t, \tag{16.1}$$

dollars. The firm profits are:

$$\Pi_t = P_t f(N_t) - B_t R_t. \tag{16.2}$$

The firm chooses N to maximize (16.2) subject to (16.1).

The household's single utility function is: $U(c, L) = c - v(L)$, where c denotes consumption, L denotes labor and $v(\ )$ has the standard properties of a cost function: $v' > 0$ and $v'' > 0$.

The household chooses consumption (c), the amount deposited in the bank (D), and labor (L) to solve the following problem:

$$\max E_0 \sum_{t=1}^{\infty} \beta^t [c_t - v(L_t)] \tag{16.3}$$

s.t.

$$M_{t+1} = M_t - D_t + W_t L_t - P_t c_t + R_t (X_t + D_t) + \Pi_t \tag{16.4}$$

$$0 \leq P_t c_t = M_t - D_t + W_t L_t. \tag{16.5}$$

Note that (16.1) and (16.5) assume that the cash-in-advance constraints are always binding.

We express all nominal variables in terms of the beginning of period per household money stock: $\tilde{x}_t = \tilde{X}_t / M_t$ is an i.i.d. normalized transfer; $p_t = P_t / M_t$ is the normalized price. Note that a normalized dollar this period will become $M_t / M_{t+1} = 1/(1 + x)$ normalized dollars next period.

Since prices are determined after the realization x of $\tilde{x}$ is known, we look for a steady state in which normalized prices depend on the realization of $\tilde{x}$ and use $p(\bullet)$, $w(\bullet)$ and $R(\bullet)$ to denote price functions. Figure 16.1 describes the sequence of events.

After observing the realization x and the prices $[p(x), w(x), R(x)]$ the firm chooses labor by solving:

$$\pi(x) = \max_N p(x) f(N) - R(x) w(x) N. \tag{16.6}$$

The first order condition for the firm's problem (16.6) is:

$$f'[N(x)] = R(x) w(x) / p(x). \tag{16.7}$$

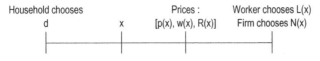

Household chooses
d   x

Prices :
[p(x), w(x), R(x)]

Worker chooses L(x)
Firm chooses N(x)

Figure 16.1   The limited participation model

This says that the marginal product must equal the real wage cost (wage plus interest on financing it).

The household chooses d before prices are known and L after prices are known. It solves the following Bellman's equation:

$$V(m) = \max_{d} E_x\{\max_{L}[c_t - v(L)] + \beta V(m')$$

s.t.

$$c = [m - d + w(x)L]/p(x)$$
$$m' = [(x + d)R(x) + \pi(x)]/(1 + x)\}. \tag{16.8}$$

To solve this Bellman's equation, we first choose the optimal L for a given realization x and a given choice d:

$$J(m, d, x) = \max_{L}[m - d + w(x)L]/p(x) - v(L)$$
$$+ \beta V\{[(x + d)R(x) + \pi(x)]/(1 + x)\}. \tag{16.9}$$

Then we choose d by solving:

$$\max_{d} E_x J(m, d, \tilde{x}). \tag{16.10}$$

The first order condition for the labor choice in the household's problem (16.9) is:

$$v'[L(x)] = w(x)/p(x). \tag{16.11}$$

This says that the marginal utility cost must equal the real wage. Note that since there is no income effect, labor supply is upward sloping.

Steady state equilibrium is a scalar d and a vector of functions $[L(\bullet), N(\bullet), p(\bullet), w(\bullet), R(\bullet), \pi(\bullet)]$ such that:

(a) $\pi(x) = p(x)f[N(x)] - R(x)w(x)N(x)$, for all realizations x of $\tilde{x}$;
(b) Given d and the prices $[p(x), w(x), R(x)]$, the labor supply $L(x)$ is a solution to (16.9) for all realizations x of $\tilde{x}$;
(c) Given the price functions $[p(\bullet), w(\bullet), R(\bullet)]$, the amount deposited in the bank d, solves (16.10);
(d) Given the prices $[p(x), w(x), R(x)]$, labor demand $N(x)$ solves the firm's problem (16.6) for all realizations x of $\tilde{x}$;

(e) markets are cleared:

$m = m' = 1$;

$L(x) = N(x)$;

$m - d + w(x)L(x) = p(x)f[N(x)]$;

$w(x)N(x) = d + x$;

for all realizations x of $\tilde{x}$.

In what follows we assume that there exists a unique steady state equilibrium and that the equilibrium functions are differentiable.

Non-neutrality

Substituting the loans market-clearing condition ($wN = d+x$) into the goods market-clearing condition ($m - d + w(x)L(x) = pc$) leads to: $pc = m + x$ and

$$wN/pc = \Gamma(x) = (d+x)/(m+x). \tag{16.12}$$

Lemma 1: In equilibrium $d < m$ and the function $\Gamma(x)$ is increasing.

This says that a change in x must affect either the real wage (w/p) or the labor to consumption ratio (N/c) or both.[1]

Proof: Since the firm makes choices after the realization x is known, equilibrium nominal profits, $pc - RwN = (m + x) - R(x)(d + x)$, must be positive. This and $R(x) \geq 1$ implies $d < m$ and $\Gamma' > 0$. □

We now turn to characterize the steady state equilibrium functions.

Lemma 2: The signs of the derivatives of the functions $N(x)$, $\alpha(x) = N(x)/f[N(x)]$ and $\gamma(x) = w(x)/p(x)$ are the same.

Thus if $N(x)$ is an increasing function then the average amount of labor per unit of output (the inverse of the average product) and the real wage are also increasing functions.

Proof: $\alpha'(x) = (N'/f)[1 - f'/(f/N)]$. Since for concave functions the marginal is less than the average, $1 - f'/(f/N) > 0$ and the sign of α' is the same as the sign of N'.

The sign of N' is the same as the sign of γ' because the first order condition (16.11) implies that labor supply is upward sloping. □

We now show that

> *Claim 1:* $N(x)$ is an increasing function.

Otherwise, lemma 2 implies that both $\gamma = w/p$ and $\alpha = N/c$ decline with x and $\Gamma(x)$ is decreasing. Lemma 1 rules this out.

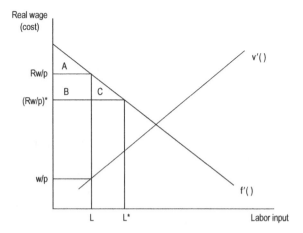

Figure 16.2   When X increases, L increases and R fails

The first order condition (16.7) and the concavity of f( ) imply that when N increases the real wage cost Rw/p must decrease. Since both N and the real wage (w/p) increase with x, it follows that:

> *Claim 2:* R(x) is a decreasing function.

Figure 16.2 illustrates Claim 2 by looking at the ratio of the labor cost to the real wage. When x is low the equilibrium level of employment is L and the ratio of the real labor cost R(w/p) to the real wage rate (w/p) is high. When x is high, employment (L*) is high and the ratio of the real labor cost to the real wage rate is low. Since the gross interest rate R is equal to the ratio of labor cost to wage, it follows that R(x) is a decreasing function.

In figure 16.2, real profits are equal to area A when the realization of $\tilde{x}$ is low (and labor supply is L). And are equal to area A + B + C when the realization of $\tilde{x}$ is high (and labor supply is L*). Thus,

> *Claim 3:* $\pi(x)$ is an increasing function.

Since $p(x) = (m + x)/f[N(x)]$, the effect of an increase in x on the price level is ambiguous. It is possible that an increase in x will lead to a sufficient increase in supply and produce no effect on prices. CEE examined this possibility and found that the required supply elasticity is too high to be empirically plausible.

16.2 STICKY PRICES

In chapter 8 we did a version of the sticky price model that does not distinguish between firms and workers. Here we introduce this distinction following CEE (1997).

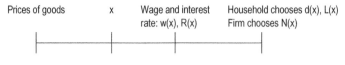

Figure 16.3 The sticky price model

Prices are set before the realization of x is known, and deposits are chosen after the realization is known. Figure 16.3 describes the sequence of events.

There are many intermediate goods that are produced by monopolistically competitive firms. A final good firm uses these goods as inputs for the production of a single final good.

The choice of prices is done in two stages. First intermediate goods firms choose prices. Then the realization of x is observed and the price of the final good, the wage rate and the interest rates are announced. It turns out that the demand of the final good firm for the products of the intermediate good firms is infinitely elastic at the price announced by the intermediate firms and therefore does not depend on x (in spite of the fact that it is announced by a Walrasian auctioneer who observes the realization of x).

We now turn to describe the model in some detail. There are G agents. Agent i owns firm i that produces intermediate good i. There is a price-taking firm that uses all intermediate goods to produce the final good according to the following CES production function:

$$Y_t = F(y_{1t}, \ldots, y_{Gt}) = \left[\sum_i (y_{it})^{1/\mu} \right]^{\mu}, \tag{16.13}$$

where y_{it} denotes the quantity of intermediate good i and $1 \le \mu < \infty$.

When the final good firm chooses the quantities of the intermediate goods, it already knows the price of the final good (p_t) and the prices of the intermediate goods (q_{it}). Being a price-taker, it chooses the quantities y_{it} to maximize profits by solving:

$$\max p_t \left[\sum_i (y_{it})^{1/\mu} \right]^{\mu} - \sum_i q_{it} y_{it}. \tag{16.14}$$

The first order condition for (16.14) is given by:

$$F_i = \left[\sum_i (y_{it})^{1/\mu} \right]^{\mu-1} (y_{it})^{(1/\mu)-1} = q_{it}/p_t \tag{16.15}$$

Raising both sides to the power of $\mu/(\mu - 1)$ yields:

$$y_{it}/Y_t = (p_t/q_{it})^{\mu/(\mu-1)}. \tag{16.16}$$

The intermediate good firm is small and ignores any effect it may have on aggregate magnitudes. It has rational expectations and uses the first order condition (16.16) to derive the following demand function: $y_{it} = Y_t(p_t/q_{it})^{\mu/(\mu-1)}$, treating Y_t and p_t as given.

Firm i produces intermediate good i according to the following Cobb–Douglas production function:

$$y_{it} = f(N_{it}) = (N_{it})^{\alpha}, \tag{16.17}$$

where N_{it} is the amount of labor input and $0 < \alpha < 1$ is the same across firms. Thus the intermediate good firms use the same production function to produce different intermediate goods.

The intermediate good firm always satisfies demand. It chooses its price (q_{it}) ex ante by solving:

$$\max_{q_{it}} E \left\{ [q_{it}Y_t(p_t/q_{it})^{\mu/(\mu-1)} - R_t w_t N_{it}]/(1+x) \right.$$

$$\left. \text{s.t.} \quad (N_{it})^{\alpha} = Y_t(p_t/q_{it})^{\mu/(\mu-1)} \right\}, \tag{16.18}$$

where expectations are taken with respect to Y_t, p_t and $R_t w_t$. Substituting the constraint in the objective function yields:

$$\max_{q_{it}} E \left\{ q_{it}Y_t(p_t/q_{it})^{\mu/(\mu-1)} - R_t w_t[Y_t(p_t/q_{it})^{\mu/(\mu-1)}]^{1/\alpha} \right\} \Big/ (1+x). \tag{16.19}$$

Symmetry: Because of symmetry all intermediate firms will choose the same price $q_{it} = q_t$ and supply the same output $y_{it} = y_t$ for all i. Substituting $y_{it} = y_t$ in (16.13) yields: $Y_t = G^{\mu}y_t$. Assuming $G = 1$ yields $Y_t = y_t$. Substituting this in the first order condition (16.16) implies: $q_t = p_t$. Thus at the price $p_t = q_t$, the demand of the final good firm is infinitely elastic: It will buy any amount of the intermediate goods.

The household behaves in a way which is similar to the one described in the previous section. The only difference is that now the household chooses its deposit (d) after the realization of $\tilde{x}$ is known. We describe the household's problem as part of the definition of steady state equilibrium.

A *symmetric steady state equilibrium* is a scalar p and a vector of functions $[d(\bullet), L(\bullet), N(\bullet), Y(\bullet), w(\bullet), R(\bullet), \pi(\bullet)]$ such that:

(a) The profits of the representative intermediate firm is:

$$\pi(x) = pY(x) - R(x)w(x)N(x);$$

(b) Given $[p, w(x), R(x), \pi(x)]$, the labor supply $L(x)$ and the amount of deposit $d(x)$ is a solution to the household's problem:

$$V(m) = E_x\{\max_{L \ d} U(c, L) + \beta V(m') \quad \text{s.t.}$$

$$pc = m - d + w(x)L$$

$$m' = [(x+d)R(x) + \pi(x)]/(1+x)\};$$

(c) Given p and the functions $[Y(\bullet), w(\bullet), R(\bullet)]$, the price $q = p$ solves the intermediate good firm's problem:

$$\max_{q} E\{[qY(x)(p/q)^{\mu/(\mu-1)} - R(x)w(x)[Y(x)(p/q)^{\mu/(\mu-1)}]^{1/\alpha}]/(1+x);$$

(d) markets are cleared:

$$m = m' = 1;$$

$$L(x) = N(x) = [pY(x)/q)^{\mu/(\mu-1)}]^{1/\alpha};$$

$$m - d(x) + w(x)N(x) = pY(x) = pf[N(x)];$$

$$w(x)N(x) = d(x) + x;$$

for all realizations x of $\tilde{x}$.

CEE argue that it is difficult to fit this type of model to the data. In particular, the interest rate may rise or fall in response to a monetary contraction. Real profits rise when the money supply contracts.

16.3   UST

In the above two models, money is non-neutral because some irreversible decisions are made before the current period money supply is known. In the limited participation model the irreversible choice is the amount deposited at the bank by households. In the sticky price model it is the prices of intermediate goods.

Money is non-neutral in the monetary UST model of chapter 15 because irreversible selling decisions are made before the resolution of uncertainty about the current period money supply. Thus the reason for the non-neutrality is fundamentally the same in all three models but as will be demonstrated the models differ in their ability to explain the stylized facts.

Here we use a cash-in-advance UST model to account for all the above-mentioned stylized facts. To get the interest (liquidity) effect of money, we make a straightforward use of the idea that "if cash is required for trading in securities, then the quantity of cash – of "liquidity" – available for this purpose will in general influence the prices of securities traded at that time" (Lucas 1990, p. 237).

The model

There are N infinitely lived households. Each household consists of two people: a seller and a buyer. At the beginning of each period they separate: The buyer takes the money and goes shopping. The seller produces and sells his output for money. After trade in the goods market is completed the seller takes his revenue in the form of cash. On the way home some sellers visit the bank (the bond market). At the end of the period the two members of the household reunite and consume the basket of goods that the buyer has bought.

Labor (L_t) is the only input and output equals labor input. The household is risk neutral and its single period utility is: $c_t - v(L_t)$, where the function $v(\ )$ has the standard properties of a cost function: $v' > 0$ and $v'' > 0$. The household's discount factor is $0 < \beta < 1$.

The amount of money available to household h at the beginning of period t is M_t^h dollars. The buyer takes the M_t^h dollars and goes shopping. Buyers arrive in the market sequentially. The order of arrival is determined by an i.i.d. Lottery.

On the way to the market the buyer may receive a transfer of G_t dollars. The number of buyers that will receive a transfer is unknown. For simplicity it is assumed that either a fraction γ or a fraction 2γ of the buyers will get a transfer with equal probability of occurrence. The identity of the buyers that will receive the transfer is determined by an i.i.d. lottery.[2]

The buyer spends all the available cash: M_t^h if he did not get a transfer and $M_t^h + G_t$ if he did get a transfer. Upon arrival, each buyer sees all the available selling offers and buys at the lowest price offer. Since cheaper goods are bought first, buyers that arrive late may face a higher price.

The average holding of money at the beginning of period t (before the beginning of the transfer process) is: $M_t = (1/N) \sum_{h=1}^{N} M_t^h$. For simplicity we assume: $G_t = M_t$. The total amount available for spending per seller is: $M_t + \gamma G_t = (1+\gamma)M_t$ if a fraction γ got a transfer and $(1 + 2\gamma)M_t$ if a fraction 2γ got a transfer.

As in previous chapters, we divide all nominal magnitudes by M_t and define a normalized dollar (ND) by the money supply per household. From the sellers' point of view purchasing power arrives in batches. The first batch of $1 + \gamma$ ND arrives with certainty and buys in the first market at the price p_1. The second batch of γ ND may arrive with probability $1/2$ and if it arrives, it buys in the second market at the price of p_2 ND per unit.

At the beginning of the period the representative seller chooses the amount of labor L and allocates the available supply across the two markets:

$$k_1 + k_2 = L, \tag{16.20}$$

where k_s is the supply to market s. This allocation may be viewed as a contingent plan that specifies how much will be sold to each batch of demand that arrives.

The seller's total revenues if s markets open are:

$$tr^s = \sum_{j=1}^{s} p_j k_j. \tag{16.21}$$

A fraction $0 < \lambda \leq 1$ of the sellers go to the bonds market after the closing of all the goods markets. The identity of the sellers who go to the bonds market is determined every period by an i.i.d. lottery.

There are only government bonds. A bond is a promise to pay one ND at the beginning of next period. The price of a bond if s markets open today is $1/R^s$ and the gross interest rate is R^s. Since nothing happens between the buying of a bond and the payment of the bond, agents who get an access to the bond market invest all their idle money in bonds at the gross interest rate: $R^s \geq 1$.

The supply of government bonds is constant over time and is given by b ND per household.[3] The interest on the government debt is paid out of lump sum taxes collected at the end of the period. The lump sum tax is: $g^s = b - b/R^s = b(1 - 1/R^s)$ ND if s markets open this period. Figure 16.4 describes the sequence of events within a typical period.

Figure 16.4 The UST model

The amount of money available to the household at the beginning of next period is:

$$m' = (R^s tr^s - g^s)/(1 + s\gamma), \quad (16.22)$$

if the seller buys bonds and $(tr^s - g^s)/(1 + s\gamma)$ if he does not buy bonds all in terms of next period's ND.[4]

A buyer who holds m normalized dollars at the beginning of the period will consume on average:

$$E_{i,s}\{(m + i)/p_s\} = \tfrac{1}{2}(m + \gamma)/p_1 + \tfrac{1}{2}[\theta(m + 2\gamma)/p_1 + (1 - \theta)(m + 2\gamma)/p_2], \quad (16.23)$$

units of consumption, where $i = 1$ if the buyer gets a transfer and zero otherwise; Expectations are taken over both i and s; $\theta = (1 + \gamma)/(1 + 2\gamma)$ is the fraction of dollars in batch 1 out of the post-transfer money supply when two markets open.[5]

The Bellman equation which describes the household's behavior is:

$$V(m) = \max_{k_s} E_{i,s}(m + i)/p_s - v(k_1 + k_2)$$

$$+ \beta\lambda E_s V \left\{ \left[R^s \left(\sum_{j=1}^{s} p_j k_j \right) - g^s \right] \Big/ (1 + s\gamma) \right\}$$

$$+ \beta(1 - \lambda)E_s V \left\{ \left[\left(\sum_{j=1}^{s} p_j k_j \right) - g^s \right] \Big/ (1 + s\gamma) \right\}, \quad (16.24)$$

where, as before, E_x denotes expectations with respect to the random variable x and the maximization is with respect to k_s. Here V(m) is the maximum expected utility that a household which starts the period with m normalized dollars can achieve. The first row is the current expected utility. The last two rows are the future expected utility: The second is for the case in which the seller buys bond (with probability λ) and the third is for the case in which he does not buy bonds.

To state the first order conditions for (16.24) it is useful to define the expected purchasing power of a normalized dollar held by the buyer at the beginning of the period. This is:

$$z = \tfrac{1}{2}(1/p_1) + \tfrac{1}{2}[\theta/p_1 + (1 - \theta)/p_2]. \quad (16.25)$$

The first term on the right hand side is the purchasing power when only one market opens times the probability of this event. The second expression applies for the case in which both markets open and the normalized dollar will buy in market 1 with probability θ.

It is also useful to introduce the coefficient:

$$\omega^s = [(1 - \lambda) + \lambda R^s]/(1 + s\gamma). \tag{16.26}$$

This coefficient converts current ND earned in the goods market to next period's ND. A current ND earned in the goods market will yield R^s if its owner buys bonds and 1 otherwise. It will therefore yield on average $(1 - \lambda) + \lambda R^s$ current ND. To convert it to next period's ND we multiply by $M_t/M_{t+1} = 1/(1 + s\gamma)$.[6]

A normalized dollar earned in the second market will therefore buy on average $\omega^2 z$ units of consumption. A normalized dollar earned in the first market will buy ωz units, where $\omega = (1/2)\omega^1 + (1/2)\omega^2$.

The first order conditions that must be satisfied for an interior solution ($k_s > 0$) to (16.24) are:

$$v'(k_1 + k_2) = \beta p_1 \omega z = \tfrac{1}{2}\beta p_2 \omega^2 z. \tag{16.27}$$

To interpret (16.27) note that from selling a unit in market 2 the seller will get p_2 ND which, on average, will become $p_2 \omega^2$ next period's ND and buy $p_2 \omega^2 z$ units of consumption. The expression $(1/2)\beta p_2 \omega^2 z$ is therefore the real price in market 2, where the real price is defined by the expected discounted consumption. Similarly, the expression $\beta p_1 \omega z$ is the real price in market 1. Thus, (16.27) says that at the optimum the marginal cost (v') must equal the real price.

Steady state equilibrium is a vector $(k_1, k_2, p_1, p_2, R^1, R^2, \omega^1, \omega^2, z)$ such that:

(a) $R^s \geq 1; z = (16.25); \omega^s = (16.26)$;
(b) given $(p_1, p_2, R^1, R^2, \omega^1, \omega^2, z)$, the quantities (k_1, k_2) satisfy the first order condition (16.27);
(c) goods markets which open are cleared: $p_1 k_1 = 1 + \gamma; p_2 k_2 = \gamma$;
(d) the bond market is cleared: $\lambda \left(\sum_{j=1}^{s} p_j k_j \right) = b/R^s$ for $s = 1, 2$.

A numerical example: To solve for the nine equilibrium magnitudes: $(k_1, k_2, p_1, p_2, R^1, R^2, \omega^1, \omega^2, z)$, we use the five equations in (16.25)–(16.27) and the four market-clearing conditions. Assuming for example $(\gamma = 0.1, b = 1, \lambda = 3/4, v(L) = L^2, \beta = 1)$, yields the following solution: $(k_1 = 0.458, k_2 = 0.019, p_1 = 2.397, p_2 = 5.195, R^1 = 1.21, R^2 = 1.11, \omega^1 = 1.054, \omega^2 = 0.902, z = 0.408)$.

Note that it is possible to solve the bond markets variables $(R^1, R^2, \omega^1, \omega^2)$ before solving for the other variables.

The nominal interest rate

The goods markets clearing conditions imply: $\sum_{j=1}^{s} p_j k_j = 1 + s\gamma$. Therefore, the clearing of the bonds market implies:

$$R^s = b/\lambda \left(\sum_{j=1}^{s} p_j k_j \right) = b/\lambda(1 + s\gamma). \tag{16.28}$$

The bond market is active, if $b > \lambda(1 + s\gamma)$ and the gross nominal rate is greater than one.

The equilibrium relationship (16.28) implies a negative relationship between R and the end of period money supply. Limited participation ($\lambda < 1$) and trading uncertainty are not necessary for this result. The negative relationship arises as a special case of Lucas' argument cited in the introduction: The cash in advance in the bonds market implies that the amount of liquidity affects the interest rate.[7]

Substituting (16.28) in (16.26) yields:

$$\omega^s = [(1 - \lambda) + b/(1 + s\gamma)]/(1 + s\gamma), \qquad (16.29)$$

and implies $\omega^1 > \omega^2$. Therefore, a normalized dollar earned in the first market is worth more than a normalized dollar earned in the second market: $\omega = (1/2)(\omega^1 + \omega^2) > \omega^2$. This result will be used later.

Adding variable costs

We now assume that it costs one unit of fixed labor to create a unit of capacity and it costs one unit of variable labor to convert a unit of capacity into output at the time of sale. As in chapter 14, we may think of a restaurant as an example. It takes a unit of fixed labor to prepare a meal (create capacity) and a unit of variable labor to serve it and wash the dishes (convert capacity into output).

Unlike the previous section, here each household owns a firm that hires (fixed and variable) labor, but cannot supply labor to his own firm. The wage rate for the fixed factor is denoted by w_f. The wage rate for the variable factor supplied if market s opens is denoted by w_{vs}, all in normalized dollars.

The firm's profits if s markets open are:

$$\psi^s = \sum_{j=1}^{s}(p_j - w_{vj})k_j - w_f(k_1 + k_2). \qquad (16.30)$$

The firm maximizes the expected purchasing power of profits. It chooses $k_s \geq 0$ to solve:

$$\max \tfrac{1}{2}\psi^1\omega^1 z + \tfrac{1}{2}\psi^2\omega^2 z \quad \text{s.t.} \quad (16.30). \qquad (16.31)$$

An interior solution to (16.31) requires a strictly positive net price $(p_j - w_{vj})$ and

$$(p_1 - w_{v1})\omega = \tfrac{1}{2}(p_2 - w_{v2})\omega^2 = w_f\omega. \qquad (16.32)$$

This says that the expected net revenue (in terms of next period's ND) from supplying an additional unit to market 1 is the same as the expected net revenue from supplying an additional unit to market 2 and is equal to marginal cost.

The household's utility function is: $U(c, L, l) = c - v(L) - \eta l$, where L is the quantity of fixed labor, l is the quantity of variable labor and η is a strictly positive parameter. We use l_s to denote the quantity of variable labor supplied to market s if it opens and describe the household's problem by the following Bellman's equation:

$$V(m) = \max E_{i,s}(m+i)/p_s - v(L) - \eta l_1 - \tfrac{1}{2}\eta l_2$$

$$+ \beta\lambda E_s V\left\{\left[R^s(w_f L + \sum_{j=1}^{s} w_{vj}l_j + \psi^s) - g^s\right]\middle/(1+s\gamma)\right\}$$

$$+ \beta(1-\lambda)E_s V\left\{\left[(w_f L + \sum_{j=1}^{s} w_{vj}l_j + \psi^s) - g^s\right]\middle/(1+s\gamma)\right\},\qquad(16.33)$$

where the maximization is with respect to L and l_s. The first order conditions for an interior solution to this problem are:

$$v'(L) = \beta w_f \omega z,\qquad(16.34)$$

and

$$\eta = \beta w_{v1}\omega z = \beta w_{v2}\omega^2 z.\qquad(16.35)$$

These first order conditions require that marginal cost equals the appropriate real price. Since $\omega > \omega^2$,

$$w_{v1} < w_{v2}.\qquad(16.36)$$

This is because a normalized dollar earned in market 1 is worth more in terms of next period's normalized dollars and therefore the wage rate for the variable factor in market 1 is lower, in spite of the fact that we assume constant marginal variable labor cost. Assuming increasing marginal variable labor cost will only strengthen this result.

Substituting (16.34) in (16.32) leads to:

$$v'(L) = \beta(p_1 - w_{v1})\omega z = \tfrac{1}{2}\beta(p_2 - w_{v2})\omega^2 z\qquad(16.37)$$

which is the same as (16.27) when $w_{v1} = w_{v2} = 0$.

Steady-state equilibrium is a vector $(k_1, k_2, L, l_1, l_2, p_1, p_2, w_f, w_{v1}, w_{v2}, \psi^1, \psi^2, R^1, R^2, \omega^1, \omega^2, z)$ such that:

(a) $R^s \geq 1$; $p_j - w_{vj} \geq 0$; $L = k_1 + k_2$; $l_s = k_s$;
(b) $z = (16.25)$; $\omega^s = (16.26)$; $\psi^s = (16.30)$;
(c) Given $(p_1, p_2, w_f, w_{v1}, w_{v2}, \omega^1, \omega^2, z)$ the quantities (k_1, k_2) solve (16.31);
(d) Given $(p_1, p_2, R^1, R^2, w_f, w_{v1}, w_{v2}, \psi^1, \psi^2)$, the labor supplies (L, l_1, l_2) solve (16.33);
(g) Markets that open are cleared:

$$p_1 k_1 = 1 + \gamma;\ p_2 k_2 = \gamma;\quad \text{and}\quad \lambda\left(\sum_{j=1}^{s} p_j k_j\right) = b/R^s;\ \text{for } s = 1, 2.$$

Back to the stylized facts

The UST model can account for all the effects documented in CEE (1997).

The lack of price level response (stylized fact [a]) occurs because quoted prices do not change in response to current changes in the money supply.[8]

The fall in aggregate output (stylized fact [b]) occurs because when money is low, fewer markets open and capacity utilization is low. Measured output is therefore low for two reasons. First, unused capacity is often not measured as output: A meal that was prepared in a restaurant but was not sold is not measured as output even when fixed costs were used in the preparation of the meal. Second, low capacity utilization implies the use of less variable factors of production.

When the money supply is low, the sellers' revenue is low and less idle money arrives at the bonds market. Since the supply of bonds does not depend on the end of period money supply, low money leads to a low price of bonds and high rate of return. This accounts for stylized fact (c).

Since a dollar earned in a higher index market is worth less than a dollar earned in a lower index market, $w_{v1} < w_{v2}$ and the average real wage of the variable factor is lower when the money supply is low: $w_{v1} < (w_{v1}l_1 + w_{v2}l_2)/(l_1 + l_2)$. This is in accordance with stylized fact (d).

An interior solution to the firm's problem (16.31) requires a strictly positive net price $(p_j - w_{vj})$. Using the definition of profits in (16.30) this implies: $\psi^2 - \psi^1 = (p_2 - w_{v2})k_2 > 0$. Thus in accordance to the stylized fact (e) profits are low when the money supply is low.

16.4 A REAL BUSINESS CYCLE MODEL WITH WEDGES: SOME EQUIVALENCE RESULTS

Chari, Kehoe and McGrattan (2002) suggest that the allocations obtained in models with frictions can also be obtained in a prototype growth model with time varying wedges. Their approach is useful as an organizing tool.

To illustrate, we consider the following neo-classical model without capital. The representative consumer solves:

$$\max E \sum_t \beta^t U(c_t, L_t)$$

s.t.

$$c_t + b_t = (1 - \tau_{Lt})w_t L_t + b_{t-1}[1 + r_t(1 - \tau_{rt})] + g_t + \pi_t$$

where, c_t is the quantity consumed, b_t are real bonds, w_t is the real wage rate, L_t is labor input, g_t is a lump sum transfer or tax from the government, π_t are profits, r_t is the real interest rate from time $t - 1$ to time t and τ_{Lt}, τ_{rt} are taxes (wedges) on labor and interest income.

Firms maximize $A_t f(L_t) - w_t L_t$. The equilibrium is summarized by:

$$c_t = A_t f(L_t) \tag{16.38}$$

$$-U_{2t}/U_{1t} = (1 - \tau_{Lt})A_t f'(L_t) \tag{16.39}$$

$$U_{1t} = \beta[1 + r_t(1 - \tau_{rt})]E_t U_{1t+1} \tag{16.40}$$

The first equation is the resource constraint. Conditions (16.39) and (16.40) are the consumer's first order condition after substituting $w = A_t f'(L_t)$ from the firm's problem.

Suppose now that the data is generated by the UST model in section 16.3 but we try to fit a neo-classical model which is summarized by (16.38)–(16.40). What will we find? We start by making some general remarks and then go to a numerical example.

(1) We may assume constant technology, $A_t = 1$, and a Cobb–Douglas production function, $f(L) = L^{\alpha}$. In this case we may find increasing returns to scale ($\alpha > 1$) because of fixed labor costs. This short run increasing returns to labor is a well known observation and is discussed in section 14.2.

Alternatively, we may use the observed labor share (say $\alpha = 0.64$) in a calibration exercise. In this case we will observe procyclical fluctuations in technology (A_t).

(2) Will we observe fluctuations in the labor wedge (τ_{Lt})?

The average wage (across both fixed and variable labor) is:

$$W^1 = (w_f L + w_{v1} l_1)/(L + l_1) \text{ in low demand periods and}$$

$$W^2 = (w_f L + w_{v1} l_1 + w_{v2} l_2)/(L + l_1 + l_2) \text{ in high demand periods.}$$

If $W^1 > w_{v2}$ we may get that the average wage in the low demand state is higher making fluctuations in the labor wedge necessary for explaining the data.[9]

(3) Will we observe fluctuations in the capital market wedge (τ_{rt})?

In our model when the money supply is low, consumption is low and the real interest rate is high. We may therefore account for (16.40) without a time varying wedge.

Numerical example

We use the numerical example in section 16.3 to generate data from the UST model and then fit the prototype growth model. As before, we assume: $\gamma = 0.1$, $b = 1$, $\lambda = 3/4$, $v(L) = L^2$, $\beta = 1$. To simplify, we assume $\eta = 0$. Thus the firm can get variable labor for free.

The equilibrium solution is: $k_1 = 0.458$, $k_2 = 0.019$, $p_1 = 2.397$, $p_2 = 5.195$, $R^1 = 1.21$, $R^2 = 1.11$, $\omega^1 = 1.054$, $\omega^2 = 0.902$, $z = 0.408$, $w_f = 2.391$, $w_{v1} = w_{v2} = 0$, $L = 0.477$, $l_1 = 0.458$, $l_2 = 0.019$.

From this we can compute:

$$L^1 = L + l_1 = 0.935 = \text{total labor input in state 1}$$

$$L^2 = L + l_1 + l_2 = 0.954 = \text{total labor input in state 2}$$

$$Y^1 = k_1 = 0.458 = \text{measured output and consumption in state 1}$$

$$Y^2 = k_1 + k_2 = 0.477 = \text{measured output and consumption in state 2}$$

$$r^1 = (R^1/1.1) - 1 = 0.1 = \text{real interest rate in state 1}$$

$$r^2 = (R^2/1.2) - 1 = -0.075 = \text{real interest rate in state 2}$$

The prototype growth model

We assume $f(L) = (L)^{0.64}$ and $U(c, L) = \log c + \log(3 - L)$. We now use (16.38)–(16.40) to solve for the distortion parameters in the low demand period (period 1) and the high demand period (period 2). That is we solve for the technology shocks (A_1, A_2), the labor tax rates (τ_{L1}, τ_{L2}) and the tax rates on real interest (τ_{r1}, τ_{r2}).

We start from the technology shocks:

$$A_1 = Y^1/f(L^1) = 0.458/(0.935^{0.64}) = 0.478$$

$$A_2 = Y^2/f(L^2) = 0.491.$$

Thus as expected the estimated prototype model shows an increase in productivity in the high demand state.[10]

We now use the equilibrium condition: $-U_{2t}/U_{1t} = Y^s/(3 - L^s) = (1 - \tau_{Ls})A_s f'(L^s)$ to solve for the labor distortion parameter $(1 - \tau_{Ls})$. This yields:

$$1 - \tau_{L1} = [Y^1/(3 - L^1)]/A_1 f'(L^1) = 0.708$$

$$1 - \tau_{L2} = [Y^2/(3 - L^2)]/A_2 f'(L^2) = 0.729$$

Thus the labor tax rate is higher in the low demand state.

Finally, we use the equilibrium condition $U_{1s} = \beta[1 + r^s(1 - \tau_{rs})]EU_{1t+1}$ to solve for the implied interest rate tax. Using $U_{1s} = 1/Y^s$ and $EU_{1t+1} = (1/2)(1/Y^1 + 1/Y^2)$, this yields:

$$(1 - \tau_{r1}) = 0.203$$

$$(1 - \tau_{r2}) = 0.271.$$

Thus we need a substantial tax on interest to explain the fluctuations in consumption.[11]

16.5   ADDITIONAL TESTS BASED ON UNIT LABOR COST AND LABOR SHARE

Sbordone (1998, 2002) proposed a new test of price stickiness that is useful to distinguish among the alternatives in this chapter. She used the standard Walrasian model to show that the rate of inflation is equal to the rate of change in unit labor cost (ULC). But in the data the unit labor cost varies much more than the rate of inflation.

The average labor cost per unit produced (unit labor cost) is:

$$ULC_t = W_t N_t/Y_t, \tag{16.41}$$

where N is the quantity of labor, W is the wage rate and Y is output. We assume a Cobb–Douglas production function:

$$Y_t = A(N_t)^\alpha, \tag{16.42}$$

where $0 < \alpha < 1$. In the standard Walrasian model the price (P) is equal to the marginal cost:

$$P_t = W_t/MPL_t = W_t/\alpha A(N_t)^{\alpha-1} = W_t N_t/\alpha A(N_t)^\alpha = (1/\alpha)ULC_t. \tag{16.43}$$

Taking log differences from both sides of (16.43) yields:

$$dP = \ln P_t - \ln P_{t-1} = dULC = \ln ULC_t - \ln ULC_{t-1}. \tag{16.44}$$

Thus, according to the standard model, the rate of inflation is equal to the rate of change in ULC.

Sbordone (1998, 2002) found that the rate of inflation in the US is smooth relative to the rate of change in ULC and on the basis of this observation rejected (16.44).

The *limited participation model* deviates from the standard Walrasian model in the requirement that wages should be paid in advance. Under the Cobb–Douglas production function (16.42), $MPL = \alpha A[N(x)]^{\alpha-1}$ and the first order condition for the firm's problem ([16.2] in section 16.1) is:

$$P = RW/\alpha AN^{\alpha-1} = (1/\alpha)R(ULC), \tag{16.45}$$

where as before, R is the gross interest rate. Thus, as in the standard Walrasian model, price equals marginal cost but here marginal cost includes also an interest rate component.

To see if this improve matters, we took the T bills interest rate and computed the variable $RULC = R(ULC)$. The results did not improve.[12]

In the *sticky price model* and the *UST* model prices do not depend on the realization of the money supply and unit labor cost does depend on it. Therefore, these models are consistent with Sbordone's observation.

Countercyclical labor share

Rotemberg and Woodford (1998) found a small negative correlation between labor share and detrended GDP. They also cite Boldrin and Horvath (1996) and Gomme and Greenwood (1995) for similar findings. This observation can also be used to distinguish among our competing models.

Labor share is the fraction of the wage bill in total revenues:

$$LS = WN/PY = ULC/P. \tag{16.46}$$

In the *limited participation model* (16.45) and (16.46) imply:

$$LS = ULC/P = \alpha/R. \tag{16.47}$$

Since R is countercyclical it follows that LS is procyclical. This is not consistent with the small negative correlation found by Rotemberg and Woodford (1998).

In the *sticky price model* normalized prices do not change over time. We may write $LS_t = w_t N_t/p(N_t)^{\alpha}$, where p is the normalized price, $w_t = w(x_t)$ is the normalized wage and $N_t = N(x)$ is labor input. Taking log differences yields:

$$\text{Ln}(LS_t) - \text{Ln}(LS_{t-1}) = (\ln w_t - \ln w_{t-1}) + (1 - \alpha)(\ln N_t - \ln N_{t-1}). \tag{16.48}$$

Since prices are constant and workers choose their labor supply on the basis of the real wage rate, the nominal wage must be high when labor supply is high. Therefore, (16.48) also implies a positive correlation between labor share and output.

In *the UST model* the relationship between labor share and output is ambiguous. To see this point, note that $LS = (W/P)/(Y/N) = w/APL$, where here w is the real wage and APL is the average product of labor. When demand is high both w and APL go up. The real wage goes up because of the "winner-curse" effect and because of fatigue. Productivity (APL) goes up because of the increase in capacity utilization.

Conclusions

The CEE stylized facts about the effect of a contractionary monetary policy shock are:

(a) The aggregate price level initially responds very little;
(b) Aggregate output falls;
(c) Interest rates initially rise;
(d) Real wages decline by a modest amount;
(e) Profits fall.

To these we added:

(f) The rate of inflation is smooth relative to the rate of change in unit labor cost (Sbordone 1998);
(g) labor share is weakly countercyclical (Rotemberg and Woodford 1998).

The limited participation model does not do well on explaining (a), (f) and (g). The sticky price model does not do well on explaining (e) and (g). The UST model can explain all of the above stylized facts. We now turn to study additional empirical observations about inventories behavior.

PROBLEM

1 Assume that the shopper cannot use the wage payments and therefore $pc = m - d$.

(a) Write the Bellman equation (16.8) for this case. How does the new cash-in-advance constraint affect the first order condition (16.11)?
(b) What can you say about the relationship between the price level and x in this case?

NOTES

1 It can be shown that money is neutral if d is chosen after the realization of $\tilde{x}$ is known. This implies that anticipated money is neutral and only money surprises matter.
2 We may think in terms of a welfare program that pays G_t dollars to households that qualifies. The criteria for qualification is not well understood by the public and therefore ex ante all households assign the same probability to winning the welfare lottery. This probability itself is a random variable that may take the realizations γ and 2γ depending on the bureaucrat that implement the policy.

3 The supply in terms of regular dollars does change and is given by $B_t = bM_t$.

4 Note that since the money supply increases at the rate of γs the number of regular dollars in the current period normalized dollar is a fraction $1/(1 + s\gamma)$ of the amount of regular dollars in next period's normalized dollars. Therefore, to convert current into next period normalized dollars we divide by $1 + s\gamma$.

5 To compute (16.23), note that if only one market opens, the buyer will buy at the price p_1 with probability one. If he gets a transfer (with probability γ) he will buy $(m+1)/p_1$ units of consumption. Otherwise, he will buy m/p_1 units. The expected consumption if only the first market opens is therefore: $[\gamma(m + 1) + (1 - \gamma)m]/p_1 = (m + \gamma)/p_1$. If two markets open in the current period, then the buyer will participate in the first market with probability $\theta = (1 + \gamma)/(1 + 2\gamma)$ and receive a transfer with probability 2γ. The expected consumption given that two markets open is therefore: $\theta(m + 2\gamma)/p_1 + (1 - \theta)(m + 2\gamma)/p_2$. And the unconditional expected consumption is (16.23).

6 Here we assume bonds that reach maturity immediately. The analysis can be extended to more conventional bonds that reach maturity after T periods by using an appropriate conversion coefficient. Specifically, let $d = \beta E_s[1/(1 + s\gamma)]$ denote the value of a normalized dollar that will be paid next period in terms of todays normalized dollar. Then if the government issues a T periods bonds the conversion coefficient (16.26) becomes: $\omega^s = (1 - \lambda)/(1 + s\gamma) + \lambda d^T R^s/(1 + s\gamma)$.

7 The role of the limited participation assumption is to allow for the possibility that both cash and bonds are held while bonds have a higher rate of return. In this model all sellers invest their idle cash in bonds if they have a chance to do so. Only sellers who did not make it to the bank, hold idle cash.

8 Average transactions prices do change but the data is about quoted prices, not transaction prices.

9 $W^1 > w_{v2}$ implies: $w_f > w_{v2}$. To see that note that $W^1 > w_{v2}$ implies: $L(w_f - w_{v2}) + l_1(w_{v1} - w_{v2}) > 0$. Since $w_{v1} - w_{v2} < 0$, this inequality implies $w_f - w_{v2} > 0$.

10 Alternatively we may assume constant technology and estimate $f(L^s) = L^\lambda$ rather than assuming $\lambda = 0.64$. Under this alternative, we will get the following two equations: $0.458 = 0.935^\lambda$ and $0.477 = 0.954^\lambda$. The percentage difference in output between a high and low demand period is: $\ln 0.477 - \ln 0.458 = 0.04$. The percentage difference in labor is: $\ln 0.954 - \ln 0.935 = 0.02$. Therefore $\lambda = 0.04/0.02 = 2$. Thus if we assume constant technology we will get increasing returns to scale.

11 This may change if we make the fraction of sellers who get to the bonds market endogenous and depend on the interest rate.

12 In the nonfarm private business sector (Sbordone's data) the estimated standard deviation is: $SD(dRULC) = 0.0112$ which is slightly higher than $SD(dULC) = 0.0108$.

CHAPTER 17

Inventories and the Business Cycle

Changes in inventories are volatile and small. Christiano (1988) reports that quarterly changes in inventory investment are on average 0.6% of GDP but about half the size of changes in GDP. Blinder (1981, p. 500) concludes that "to a great extent, business cycle are inventory fluctuations."

Figures 17.1 and 17.2 use NIPA quarterly data to illustrate the size and volatility of inventories. Figure 17.1 plots the change in business inventories (CBI) and fixed private investment (FPI) as a fraction of GDP. Relative to fixed private investment, changes in business inventories are indeed small and volatile. Figure 17.2 plots changes in the beginning of period inventories and GDP.

The extreme volatility of inventory investment has made it a prime candidate as an explanatory variable of the business cycle. Metzler's (1941) pure inventory cycle is exposited in many text-books (see for example, Sachs and Larrain [1993, ch. 17]) and Abramovitz (1950) is often cited for early empirical work.

The earlier work on inventories tended to treat the accumulation of inventories as an external shock. In the UST model the accumulation of inventories occurs mainly because of a demand shock. Inventories do not cause the business cycle but play an important role in propagating the underline shocks.

Here we explore the implications of the UST model with storage. The models discussed here are monetary versions of the real model in section 14.5 and are based on the work of Bental and Eden (1996) and Eden (2001a). As in the real model, a negative demand shock leads to the accumulation of "undesired" inventories and as a result next period's prices and production go down. But here normalized prices (which are nominal magnitudes) play the role of relative prices in the real model. What we hope to accomplish is a model that can explain the joint behavior of real variables (output, employment and inventories) and nominal variables (the money supply and the price level).

We start, with the analysis of i.i.d demand shocks. We then add serially correlated supply shocks and discuss the correlations between the beginning of period stock of inventories and output. Finally we introduce credit and use vector auto regression analysis to study the effects of outside and inside money. We focus on the computational aspect of the problem with the hope that the material in these chapters will be useful for calibration exercises.

Fixed private investment (FPI) and change in business inventories (CBI) as a fraction of GDP

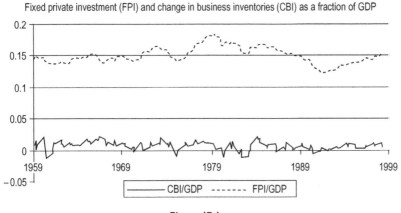

Figure 17.1

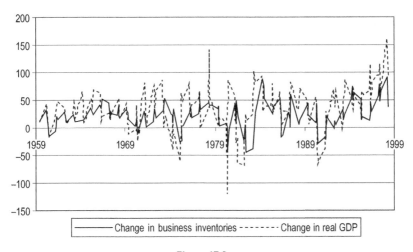

Figure 17.2

The "undesired inventories" hypothesis

In section 14.5 we showed that the equilibrium level of real output is a decreasing function of the beginning of period level of inventories. Figure 17.3 illustrates the main idea. The price in the second market (p_2) is on the vertical axis while total supply (k = inventories + output) is on the horizontal axis. Equilibrium prices move together and therefore we can think of p_2 as representing the average price. An increase in the beginning of period inventories (which occurs say as a result of a negative demand shock in the previous period) shifts the supply curve to the right without affecting the demand curve. As a result, normalized prices go down. From the diagram we can see that a unit increase in inventories is associated with less than a unit increase in k. Therefore, output goes down in response to the increase in inventories.

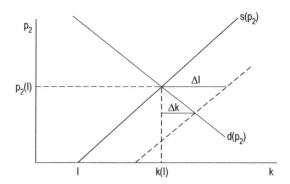

Figure 17.3   An increase in the beginning of period inventories

This is different from the real business cycle model in Kydland and Prescott (1982) and Cooley and Prescott (1995) who treat inventories as part of capital. This input view of inventories suggests a positive correlation between the beginning of period level of inventories (input) and output.

Blinder and Fischer (1981) build on Lucas' confusion hypothesis and write down a modified Lucas-type supply curve where production depends not only on the price level and trend output but also on the difference between desired and final goods inventories. This should lead to a negative relationship between the beginning of period inventories and output.[1] Ramey and West (1997) consider a linear-quadratic model in which inventories are held to smooth production and to meet a desired ratio of inventories to sales. They use the model to explain the positive correlation between output and change in inventories. Kahn and Bils (2000) find that the ratio of sales to the "stock available for sale" (k in our notation) is strongly procyclical or that inventories are highly countercyclical relative to sale. There is thus a difference between the behavior of the stock of inventories and the behavior of the change in inventories. Here we focus on the behavior of the stock.

17.1   INTRODUCING COSTLESS STORAGE

We now introduce storage to the model in 16.3. As in that model, the representative household consists of two people: a seller and a buyer. They start the period with inventories and money. They then separate: The buyer takes the money and goes shopping. The seller takes the inventories and produces some additional output. He then sells the available supply (inventories + the newly produced output) for money. The two members of the family reunite at the end of the period and consume whatever the buyer has bought.

Money is the only financial asset (there are no bonds). Labor (L_t) is the only input and output equals labor input. The household is risk neutral and its single period utility is: $c_t - v(L_t)$, where the function $v(\ )$ has the standard properties of a cost function: $v' > 0$ and $v'' > 0$. The household's discount factor is $0 < \beta < 1$.

Buyers arrive in the market sequentially in an order that is exogenously determined by an i.i.d. lottery. On the way to the market the buyer may receive a transfer of G_t dollars.

The fraction of buyers that will receive a transfer is unknown. It may be γ or 2γ with equal probability of occurrence. The identity of the buyers that will receive the transfer is determined by an i.i.d. lottery.

The buyer spends all the available cash: M_t^h if he did not get a transfer and $M_t^h + G_t$ if he did get a transfer. Upon arrival, each buyer sees all the selling offers and buys at the lowest available offer. Since cheaper goods are bought first, buyers that arrive late face a higher price.

The average holding of money at the beginning of period t (before the transfer) is M_t. To economize on notations we assume: $G_t = M_t$. The total amount available for spending per seller is: $M_t + \gamma G_t = (1 + \gamma)M_t$ dollars or $1 + \gamma$ normalized dollars (ND) if a fraction γ got a transfer and $1 + 2\gamma$ ND if a fraction 2γ got a transfer.

From the sellers' point of view purchasing power arrives in batches. The first batch of $\Delta_{1t} = 1 + \gamma$ ND arrives with certainty. The second batch of $\Delta_{2t} = \gamma$ ND may arrive with probability $1/2$. The first batch of dollars buys in the first market at the price p_{1t} (ND per unit). The second batch of dollars buys, if it arrives, in the second market at the price p_{2t}.

The household's current consumption depends on the initial stock of money (m), on whether it gets a transfer payment and on the market at which the buyer buys. The probability that a dollar is in batch j, given that two markets open is θ_j: $\theta_1 = (1 + \gamma)/(1 + 2\gamma)$, $\theta_2 = \gamma/(1 + 2\gamma)$. The expected current consumption is denoted by $E_{i,j}\{(m + i)/p_j\}$, where $i = 1$ if the buyer gets a transfer and zero otherwise. Expectations are taken over both $i = 0, 1$ and $j = 1, 2$ and are equal to:

$$E_{i,j}\{(m + i)/p_j\} = \tfrac{1}{2}[\gamma(m + 1)/p_1 + (1 - \gamma)m/p_1]$$
$$+ \tfrac{1}{2}\theta_1[2\gamma(m + 1)/p_1 + (1 - 2\gamma)m/p_1]$$
$$+ \tfrac{1}{2}\theta_2[2\gamma(m + 1)/p_2 + (1 - 2\gamma)m/p_2]. \qquad (17.1)$$

The first term in (17.1) is the expected consumption given that only one market opens (times the probability of this event). The second term is the expected consumption given that two markets open and the buyer buys in market 1 (times the probability). The third term is the expected consumption given that two markets open and the buyer buys in market 2 (times the probability).

At the beginning of the period seller h chooses the amount of labor (output) L^h and allocates the available supply across the two markets:

$$k_1^h + k_2^h \leq k^h = L^h + I^h, \qquad (17.2)$$

where k_j^h is the supply to market j and I^h is the beginning of period level of inventories. Pure speculation occurs when $k_1 + k_2 < k$. In this case, the amount $k - (k_1 + k_2)$ will not be sold even if both markets open. In general, the amount of inventories carried to the next period when s markets open today is: $k - \sum_{j=1}^{s} k_j$.

In equilibrium prices depend on the average per household level of inventories I. We denote the level of next period's inventories when exactly s markets open today by I^s and describe the behavior of the household by the following Bellman's equation.

$$V(m^h, I^h; I) = \max \left[E_{i,j} \left(m^h + i \right) \Big/ p_j(I) \right] - v(L^h)$$

$$+ \beta \frac{1}{2} \sum_{s=1}^{2} V \left\{ \left(\sum_{j=1}^{s} p_j k_j^h \right) \Big/ (1 + s\gamma), k^h - \sum_{j=1}^{s} k_j^h; I^s \right\}$$

s.t.   (17.1), $k_1^h + k_2^h \le k^h = L^h + I^h$ and non negativity constraints.   (17.3)

Here $V(m^h, I^h; I)$ is the maximum expected utility possible when starting the period with m^h normalized dollars and I^h units of inventories given that the per household level of inventories is I and normalized prices are $[p_1(I), p_2(I)]$.

We now derive the first order conditions for (17.3) under the assumption that in equilibrium all magnitudes depends on I. The expected purchasing power of a normalized dollar is:

$$z(I) = \tfrac{1}{2}[1/p_1(I)] + \tfrac{1}{2}[\theta_1/p_1(I) + \theta_2/p_2(I)],   (17.4)$$

where θ_s is the probability that a dollar is in batch s given that two markets open.

The average per household level of next period inventories if exactly s markets open today is $I^s(I) = k(I) - \sum_{j=1}^{s} k_j(I)$ and expected prices when exactly s markets open today are $p_j(I^s)$. The expected purchasing power of a normalized dollar next period is: $z(I^s) = (1/2)[1/p_1(I^s)] + (1/2)[\theta_1/p_1(I^s) + \theta_2/p_2(I^s)]$. The first order condition that governs the choice of labor is:

$$v'(L^h) = \beta p_1(I)E_s[\omega^s z(I^s)],   (17.5)$$

where, $\omega^s = 1/(1 + s\gamma)$ is the value of a normalized dollar in terms of next period's normalized dollars.

The right hand side of (17.5) is the real wage – the expected discounted consumption from a unit supplied to the first market. When s markets open this period $p_1 \omega^s$ is the price in terms of next period's normalized dollars. We multiply it by the expected purchasing power of a normalized dollar to get the price in terms of expected next period consumption $(p_1 \omega^s z[I^s])$ and take expectations over the number of markets open. The first order condition (17.5) therefore requires that the marginal cost equals the real wage.

In equilibrium the seller must be indifferent between supplying to the first and the second market:

$$p_1(I)E_s[\omega^s z(I^s)] = \tfrac{1}{2}p_2(I)[\omega^2 z(I^2)] + \tfrac{1}{2}v'[L(I^1)],   (17.6)$$

where $L(I^s)$ is the next period labor supply when the beginning of next period's inventories are I^s. The left hand side of (17.6) is the expected purchasing power that the seller can get by supplying a unit to the first market. The right hand side is the expected utility that can be derived from a unit supplied to the second market. It has two elements. The first is the expected purchasing power given that market 2 opens. The second is the value of inventories when market 2 does not open: In this case, the unit of inventories can be used to substitute for a unit of next period's production and save the marginal cost v'.

The last first order conditions governs the pure speculation choice: A choice to hold inventories even if the second market opens. Pure speculation occurs only if the purchasing power that the seller will get from selling a unit in the second market is equal to next period's marginal cost:

$$p_2(I)[\omega^2 z(I^2)] \geq v'[L(I^2)] \quad \text{with strict equality if } k > k_1 + k_2. \tag{17.7}$$

Steady state equilibrium is a vector of functions $[p_1(I), p_2(I), L(I), k(I), k_1(I), k_2(I), z(I), I^1(I), I^2(I)]$ such that:

(a) $k(I) = L(I) + I \geq k_1(I) + k_2(I); I^s(I) = k(I) - \sum_{j=1}^{s} k_j(I) \geq 0; z(I) = (1/2)[1/p_1(I)] + (1/2)[\theta_1/p_1(I) + \theta_2/p_2(I)];$
(b)   Given the prices $[p_1(I), p_2(I)]$ and next period's inventories $[I^1(I), I^2(I)]$ the quantities $[L(I), k_1(I), k_2(I)]$ satisfy (17.5), (17.7) and (17.8);
(c)   Markets that open are cleared: $1 + \gamma = p_1(I)k_1(I); \gamma = p_2(I)k_2(I);$ for all $I \geq 0$ and $s = 1, 2$.

Solving for a temporary (partial) equilibrium

Expectations about future marginal cost are given by a decreasing function $MC(I^s) = v'[L(I^s)]$ and expectations about future purchasing power of a normalized dollar are given by an increasing function: $z(I^s)$. We further assume that there exists a number I_{max} such that: $0 \leq I \leq I_{max}$. We solve the current period magnitudes $k_s(I)$ and $p_s(I)$ under the above assumptions starting with the case in which pure speculation does not occur.

> Case 1: $k(I) = k_1(I) + k_2(I)$ for all $0 \leq I \leq I_{max}$.

To solve for a partial equilibrium for this case we choose the price in the last market (p_2) and the level of beginning of period inventories (I) arbitrarily. The price in the first market must satisfy (17.6) which can now be written as:

$$p_1 E_s[\omega^s z(I^s)] = \tfrac{1}{2}p_2[\omega^2 z(I^2)] + \tfrac{1}{2}MC(I^1). \tag{17.8}$$

When both markets open, the beginning of next period inventories is: $I^2 = 0$. When only one market opens, the beginning of next period inventories to the supply to market 2. Assuming that the supply to market 2 is equal to the demand in this market yields: $I^1 = \gamma/p_2$. Substituting $I^2 = 0$ and $I^1 = \gamma/p_2$ in (17.8) leads to:

$$p_1[\tfrac{1}{2}\omega^1 z(\gamma/p_2) + \tfrac{1}{2}\omega^2 z(0)] = \tfrac{1}{2}p_2[\omega^2 z(0)] + \tfrac{1}{2}MC(\gamma/p_2). \tag{17.9}$$

Denote the solution to (17.9) by $p_1(p_2)$. Since $z(\ )$ is an increasing function and $MC(\ )$ is a decreasing function $p_1(p_2)$ is an increasing function.

The demand in market 2 at the price p_2 is: γ/p_2. The demand in market 1 at this price is: $(1 + \gamma)/p_1(p_2)$. Total demand at the price p_2 is therefore:

$$d(p_2) = \gamma/p_2 + (1 + \gamma)/p_1(p_2), \tag{17.10}$$

which is a decreasing function of p_2 as in Figure 17.3.

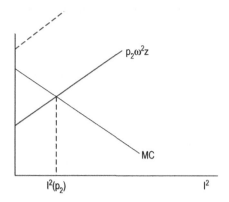

Figure 17.4   Speculative inventories

To find labor supply we substitute (17.9) in (17.5) to get:

$$v'(L) = \beta \left\{ \tfrac{1}{2} p_2 [\omega^2 z(0)] + \tfrac{1}{2} MC(\gamma/p_2) \right\}. \tag{17.11}$$

Since MC( ) is a decreasing function and $v'' > 0$, the solution $L(p_2)$ to (17.11) is an increasing function. Total supply

$$s(p_2) = L(p_2) + I, \tag{17.12}$$

is also an increasing function.

The partial equilibrium level of p_2 is obtained by equating supply and demand, $s(p_2) = d(p_2)$, as in figure 17.3. We use $p_2(I)$ to denote this solution.

> ### Case 2: Allowing for pure speculation.

As before we choose p_2 arbitrarily. We now start by solving for the amount of purely speculative inventories. This is done by finding a solution to (17.7) which can now be written as:

$$p_2 \omega^2 z(I^2) \geq MC(I^2), \quad \text{with strict equality if } I^2 > 0. \tag{17.13}$$

Figure 17.4 illustrates the solution $I^2(p_2)$ to (17.13). The function $I^2(p_2)$ is decreasing because an increase in p_2 shifts the $p_2 \omega^2 z(I^2)$ curve to the left as in the broken line of figure 17.4.

When $I^2(p_2) = 0$ we proceed according to case 1. We now focus on the case $I^2(p_2) > 0$. In this case (17.13) holds with equality and we can write the first order condition (17.6) as:

$$p_1 E_s[\omega^s z(I^s)] = \tfrac{1}{2} MC(I^2) + \tfrac{1}{2} MC(I^1), \tag{17.14}$$

Substituting $I^2 = I^2(p_2)$ and $I^1 = I^2(p_2) + \gamma/p_2$ in (17.14) leads to:

$$p_1 \left\{ \tfrac{1}{2} \omega^1 z[I^2(p_2)] + \tfrac{1}{2} \omega^2 z[I^2(p_2) + \gamma/p_2] \right\}$$
$$= \tfrac{1}{2} MC[I^2(p_2)] + \tfrac{1}{2} MC[I^2(p_2) + \gamma/p_2]. \tag{17.15}$$

Since $I^2(\ )$ and $MC(\ )$ are decreasing functions and $z(\ )$ is an increasing function, the solution to (17.15), $p_1(p_2)$, is an increasing function. It follows that total demand, $d(p_2) = I^2(p_2) + \gamma/p_2 + (1+\gamma)/p_1(p_2)$, is a decreasing function.

To find labor supply we substitute (17.13) with equality into (17.11) to get:

$$v'(L) = \beta \left\{ \tfrac{1}{2}MC[I^2(p_2)] + \tfrac{1}{2}MC[I^2(p_2) + \gamma/p_2] \right\}. \tag{17.16}$$

The solution $L(p_2)$ to (17.16) is an increasing function because $MC(\ )$ and $I^2(\ )$ are decreasing functions. The supply $s(p_2) = L(p_2) + I$ is therefore increasing and we can therefore use figure 17.3 to solve for $k(I)$ and $p_2(I)$ as in case 1.

Properties of the temporary equilibrium functions

We have solved for $k(I)$ and $p_2(I)$. We think of these partial equilibrium magnitudes as functions of the beginning of period inventories. As can be seen from figure 17.3, an increase in the beginning of period level of inventories by ΔI increases the partial equilibrium level of total supply by Δk and reduces the partial equilibrium level of p_2. Since $L(I) = k(I) - I$ and $\Delta k \leq \Delta I$, it follows that:

> *Claim 1:* $L(I)$ is a decreasing function.

This implies that $v'[L(I)]$ is a decreasing function of I in accordance with our assumption about $MC(I)$. Figure 17.3 also implies that $p_2(I)$ is a decreasing function. Since $p_1(p_2)$ is an increasing function, it follows that $p_1(I) = p_1[p_2(I)]$ is a decreasing function. Thus,

> *Claim 2:* The partial equilibrium functions $p_1(I)$, $p_2(I)$, are decreasing.

Claim 2 implies that the expected purchasing power of a normalized dollar, $(1/2)(1/p_1(I)) + (1/2)[\theta_1/p_1(I) + \theta_2/p_2(I)]$, is increasing in I. This is in accordance with our assumption about $z(I)$.

Thus we have assumed an increasing function $z(I)$ and a decreasing function $MC(I)$ and solved for temporary equilibrium functions with the same properties.

Solving for a steady state (full) equilibrium

We now check if the temporary equilibrium functions are consistent with our assumptions about expectations. That is, we check if:

$$v'[L(I)] = MC(I) \quad \text{and}$$

$$\tfrac{1}{2}(1/p_1(I)) + \tfrac{1}{2}[\theta_1/p_1(I) + \theta_2/p_2(I)] = z(I) \quad \text{for all } 0 \leq I \leq I_{max}. \tag{17.17}$$

If (17.17) is satisfied we further check whether our assumption about I_{max} is consistent with the levels of inventories that the model can generate. That is, we compute $k_1(I) = (1 + \gamma)/p_1(I)$ and check whether:

$$k(I) - k_1(I) \le I_{max} \quad \text{for all } 0 \le I \le I_{max}. \tag{17.18}$$

If both (17.17) and (17.18) are satisfied, then we have solved for a full equilibrium. If (17.18) is not satisfied we choose a larger I_{max}. If (17.17) is not satisfied, we start again using the solution of the temporary equilibrium functions to construct our next guess about future magnitudes. That is, we use the partial equilibrium function $v'[L(I)]$ as our new guess of $MC(I)$ and the function $(1/2)(1/p_1(I)) + (1/2)[\theta_1/p_1(I) + \theta_2/p_2(I)]$ as our new guess of $z(I)$. We keep doing it until the current magnitudes are consistent with what we have assumed about future magnitudes. There is no guarantee that this process will converge but some examples do work.

Properties of the steady state equilibrium functions

Claim 3: The steady state equilibrium functions $p_1(I)$, $p_2(I)$, $L(I)$ are decreasing and the steady state equilibrium functions $k(I)$, $k_1(I)$, $k_2(I)$, $z(I)$, $I^1(I)$, $I^2(I)$ are increasing.

Since a full equilibrium is also a partial equilibrium it follows that claim 1 and claim 2 hold and $p_1(I)$, $p_2(I)$, $L(I)$ are decreasing. Figure 17.3 can be used to show that $k(I)$ is increasing.

$$k_1(I) = (1 + \gamma)/p_1(I), \quad k_2(I) = \gamma/p_2(I) \quad \text{and}$$
$$z(I) = (1/2)(1/p_1(I)) + (1/2)[\theta_1/p_1(I) + \theta_2/p_2(I)]$$

are increasing because $p_s(I)$ are decreasing. It was shown that in a partial equilibrium $I^2(p_2)$ is a decreasing function (see figure 17.4). Since $p_2(I)$ is decreasing $I^2(I) = I^2[p_2(I)]$ is increasing. This implies that $I^1(I) = I^2(I) + \gamma/p_2(I)$ is also increasing.

17.2 ADDING SUPPLY SHOCKS

In the previous section equilibrium output could be fully explained by the beginning of period inventories. To run a regression of output on inventories we must add a random disturbance to this relationship. We do it here by adding a supply shock. In addition, we change our story a bit to talk about changes in employment, hours per employee and productivity over the cycle.

There are n households. Each household consists of many people: a seller (manager) a buyer and a large number of workers. The manager chooses the number of workers that will be employed (N^h), the number of hours per employee (H^h) and effort per hour (F^h). Total productive hours (labor input) is given by:

$$L^h = (N^h)(H^h)(F^h). \tag{17.19}$$

The household is risk neutral and dislikes all three components of labor. Its single period utility is:

$$c^h - \upsilon(N^h, H^h, F^h), \tag{17.20}$$

where c is consumption and the function $\upsilon()$ is the disutility from the labor supply components. Labor is the only input and the production function takes the Cobb–Douglas form:

$$y^h = \varepsilon_t(L^h)^\alpha, \tag{17.21}$$

where ε_t is an i.i.d. supply shock. Total supply is:

$$k^h = y^h + I^h_{-1}, \tag{17.22}$$

where I^h_{-1} is the beginning of period inventories.[2]

Demand

As in the previous section the buyer takes the beginning of period balances (M^h dollars) and goes shopping. On the way to the market some buyers get a transfer of one normalized dollar. The fraction of buyers who get this transfer is γ or 2γ with equal probability of occurrence.

The average per household beginning of period inventories is: $I_{-1} = (1/n) \sum_{h=1}^{n} I^h_{-1}$. We use $x = (I_{-1}, \varepsilon)$ to denote the current aggregate state and assume an equilibrium in which all magnitudes are functions of x. We use:

$$k(x) = \varepsilon[L(x)]^\alpha + I_{-1}, \tag{17.23}$$

to denote total supply per household and

$$I^s(x) = k(x) - \sum_{j=1}^{s} k_j(x), \tag{17.24}$$

to denote the per household level of next period inventories if exactly s markets open today.

To simplify, we assume that purely speculative inventories are not held. In equilibrium household h chooses $(N^h, H^h, F^h, k_1^h, k_2^h)$ to solve the following Bellman equation:

$$V(m^h, I^h_{-1}; x) = \max_{N^h\ H^h\ F^h\ k_1^h\ k_2^h} E\{(m^h + \tilde{i})/p_{\tilde{j}}(x)\} - \upsilon(N^h, H^h, F^h)$$

$$+ \beta(1/2) \sum_{s=1}^{2} EV\left\{ \left(\sum_{j=1}^{s} p_j k_j^h \right) \middle/ (1 + s\gamma),\ k^h - \sum_{j=1}^{s} k_j^h;\ [I^s(x), \tilde{\varepsilon}] \right\}$$

s.t.

$$L^h = (N^h)(H^h)(F^h),$$

$$(1), \quad k_1^h + k_2^h = k^h = \varepsilon(L^h)^\alpha + I^h_{-1} \quad \text{and non negativity constraints.} \tag{17.25}$$

Here $V(m^h, I^h_{-1}; x)$ is the maximum expected utility when the aggregate state is x and the household starts the period with the predetermined variables (m^h, I^h_{-1}). The expected current consumption is $E\{(m^h + \tilde{i})/p_{\tilde{j}}(x)\}$, where expectations are taken with respect to getting a transfer payment ($\tilde{i} = 1$ if the buyer got a transfer and zero otherwise) and with respect to the price $p_{\tilde{j}}$. The expected consumption term is more fully described in equation (17.1).

Equilibrium conditions

To state the first order conditions for an interior solution to (17.25), we compute the expected purchasing power of a normalized dollar held by the buyer at the beginning of the period. This is done by replacing x for I in equation (17.22) of the previous section. This yields:

$$z(x) = \tfrac{1}{2}[1/p_1(x)] + \tfrac{1}{2}[\theta_1/p_1(x) + \theta_2/p_2(x)]. \tag{17.26}$$

The expected purchasing power of a normalized dollar next period given that s markets open this period is:

$$Z[I^s(x)] = E\{z[I^s(x), \tilde{\varepsilon}]\}. \tag{17.27}$$

The minimum cost of supplying L units of labor is given by:

$$v(L) = \min \upsilon(N, H, F) \quad \text{s.t.} \quad (N)(H)(F) = L. \tag{17.28}$$

To simplify, we assume that υ is symmetric and there exists a unique solution to (17.28): $N = H = F = L^{1/3}$. It is further assumed that $v(L)$ has the standard properties of a cost function: $v'(0) = 0, v' > 0$ and $v'' > 0$.

At the optimum producing an additional unit and supplying it to the first market will not change the expected utility. The marginal cost must therefore equal the expected discounted real price in the first market:

$$mc(x) = v'[L(x)]/\varepsilon\alpha[L(x)]^{\alpha-1} = \beta p_1(x)E\{\omega^{\tilde{s}}Z[I^{\tilde{s}}(x)]\}. \tag{17.29}$$

where $\omega^{\tilde{s}} = 1/(1 + \tilde{s}\gamma)$. The right hand side of (17.29) is the expected discounted real price: p_1 is the price in terms of current normalized dollar, $p_1\omega^s$ is the price in terms of next period normalized dollars and $p_1\omega^sZ$ is the price in terms of next period expected consumption.

The expected marginal cost next period given that s markets open today is:

$$MC[I^s(x)] = E\{mc[I^s(x), \tilde{\varepsilon}]\}. \tag{17.30}$$

Since at an interior optimum the seller must be indifferent between supplying to the first and to the second market we have:

$$p_1(x)E\{\omega^{\tilde{s}}Z(I^{\tilde{s}})\} = \tfrac{1}{2}p_2(x)\omega^2Z(I^2) + \tfrac{1}{2}MC(I^1). \tag{17.31}$$

The left hand side of (17.31) is the expected consumption from supplying a unit to the first market. The right hand side is the expected utility from supplying a unit to the second market. The right hand side has two elements. The first is the expected consumption given that market 2 opens and the unit is sold. The second is the value of the unit if market 2 does not open and it is carried as inventories to the next period. Since in this case, the unit may be used to substitute for next period production, the value of inventories is equal to next period's expected marginal cost.

Full (steady state) equilibrium is a vector of functions $[p_1(x), p_2(x), L(x), N(x), H(x), F(x),$ $k(x), k_1(x), k_2(x), z(x), mc(x), I^1(x), I^2(x), Z[I^s(x)], MC[I^s(x)], V(m,I; x)]$ such that: (17.23)–(17.31) are satisfied and markets which open are cleared:

$$1 + \gamma = p_1(x)k_1(x); \quad \gamma = p_2(x)k_2(x). \tag{17.32}$$

Solving for a partial equilibrium: A partial equilibrium is defined for a given current state x and given expectation functions: $A = \{Z(\bullet), MC(\bullet)\}$.

We now solve for the current period magnitudes $k_s(x; A)$ and $p_s(x; A)$ under the assumption that $Z(\bullet)$ is an increasing function and $MC(\bullet)$ is a decreasing function. As in the previous section we start by choosing p_2 arbitrarily. The price in the first market must satisfy (17.31) which can now be written as:

$$p_1 E[\omega^s Z(I^s)] = \tfrac{1}{2}p_2[\omega^2 Z(I^2)] + \tfrac{1}{2}MC(I^1). \tag{17.33}$$

Substituting $I^2 = 0$ and $I^1 = \gamma/p_2$ leads to:

$$p_1 \left[\tfrac{1}{2}\omega^1 Z(\gamma/p_2) + \tfrac{1}{2}\omega^2 Z(0) \right] = \tfrac{1}{2}p_2[\omega^2 Z(0)] + \tfrac{1}{2}MC(\gamma/p_2). \tag{17.34}$$

Denote the solution to (17.34) by: $p_1(p_2)$. Since $Z(\ )$ is an increasing function and $MC(\ )$ is a decreasing function, $p_1(p_2)$ is an increasing function.

Total demand at the prices p_2 and $p_1(p_2)$ is:

$$d(p_2) = \gamma/p_2 + (1 + \gamma)/p_1(p_2), \tag{17.35}$$

which is a decreasing function of p_2 as in figure 17.3.

To find labor supply we substitute (17.34) in (17.29) to get:

$$mc = v'(L)L^{1-\alpha}/\varepsilon\alpha = \beta \left\{ \tfrac{1}{2}p_2[\omega^2 Z(0)] + \tfrac{1}{2}MC(\gamma/p_2) \right\}. \tag{17.36}$$

Let $mc(p_2)$ and $L(p_2)$ denote the solution to this equation. Since $MC(\ )$ is a decreasing function, $mc(\ )$ is an increasing function of p_2. Since $v'' > 0, L(p_2)$ is also an increasing function. Total supply is given by:

$$s(p_2) = \varepsilon[L(p_2)]^\alpha + I_{-1}, \tag{17.37}$$

which is an increasing function. A solution can be obtained by equating supply and demand: $s(p_2) = d(p_2)$, as in figure 17.3.

Solving for a full equilibrium: The above partial equilibrium solution was computed for a given x. We now vary x to get the partial equilibrium functions and compute the functions $\{Z(\bullet, A), MC(\bullet, A)\}$. We then check whether the assumed functions $A = \{Z(\bullet), MC(\bullet)\}$ are the same as the partial equilibrium functions: $A' = \{Z(\bullet; A), MC(\bullet; A)\}$. If they are the same, we are done. If not we use A' to compute a new partial equilibrium. We keep doing that with the hope that this iteration procedure will converge.

Properties of the equilibrium functions

Since a full equilibrium is also a partial equilibrium, we can derive the properties of the equilibrium functions by using the algorithm for computing partial equilibrium. Changes in I_{-1} and ε affect the supply schedule $s(p_2)$ but not the demand schedule $d(p_2)$. An increase in I_{-1} will shift the supply curve to the right, reduce prices and increase total supply by less than the increase in inventories: $\Delta k < \Delta I$. It follows that an increase in the beginning of period inventories reduces output and labor supply. An increase in ε will not change the right hand side of (17.36) and will therefore increase $L(p_2)$. It follows that the supply curve (17.37) will shift to the right. As a result p_2 will go down and k will go up. Since k is up and I_{-1} did not change it follows that output is up. This type of diagrammatic analysis leads to:

Claim 4: The equilibrium functions $L(x)$, $N(x)$, $H(x)$, $F(x)$ are decreasing in I and increasing in ε. The equilibrium functions $k(x)$, $k_1(x)$, $k_2(x)$, $z(x)$, $I^1(x)$, $I^2(x)$ are increasing in I and in ε. The equilibrium functions $p_1(x)$, $p_2(x)$ are decreasing in I and in ε.

Serially correlated supply shocks

We now assume that the supply shock follows an AR(1) process:[3]

$$\varepsilon_t = \rho \varepsilon_{t-1} + u_t, \tag{17.38}$$

where here ε is in a log form and u_t are i.i.d error terms. This case can be analyzed by redefining the expected purchasing power and the expected marginal cost as follows:

$$Z[I^s(x), \varepsilon] = E\{z[I^s(x), \tilde{\varepsilon}_{+1} = \rho \varepsilon + \tilde{u}]\}, \tag{17.39}$$

$$MC[I^s(x), \varepsilon] = E\{mc[I^s(x), \tilde{\varepsilon}_{+1} = \rho \varepsilon + \tilde{u}]\}, \tag{17.40}$$

where expectations are taken with respect to $\tilde{u}$.

It can be shown that as in the i.i.d. case, changes in I_{-1} shifts the supply curve only and therefore:

Claim 5: When the supply shocks are AR(1), the equilibrium functions $L(x)$, $N(x)$, $H(x)$, $F(x)$, $p_1(x)$, $p_2(x)$ are decreasing in I_{-1} and the equilibrium functions $k(x)$, $k_1(x)$, $k_2(x)$, $z(x)$, $I^1(x)$, $I^2(x)$ are increasing in I_{-1}.

Unlike the i.i.d. case changes in ε will in general affect both supply and demand and therefore the sign of the partial derivatives with respect to ε cannot be determined without some additional assumptions.

17.3 TESTING THE MODEL WITH DETRENDED VARIABLES

We do not have capital in our model and there are no technological changes. These factors contribute to the upward trend of time series we are interested in. We therefore interpret the model as talking about deviations from the trend assuming that the trend itself is explained by the omitted factors (capital and technology). We use the Hodrick–Prescott filter, described in the appendix, to estimate the trend.[4]

In equilibrium all magnitudes are functions of the state $x = (I_{-1}, \varepsilon)$. Here We assume the following log linear specification:

$$Y_t = \alpha L_t + \varepsilon_t \tag{17.41}$$

$$TH_t = N_t + H_t \tag{17.42}$$

$$L_t = TH_t + F_t \tag{17.43}$$

$$TH_t = -\beta_1 I_{t-1} + \beta_2 \varepsilon_t \tag{17.44}$$

$$F_t = -\gamma_1 I_{t-1} + \gamma_2 \varepsilon_t \tag{17.45}$$

$$I_t = \delta_1 I_{t-1} + \delta_2 \varepsilon_t - \delta_3 s_t, \tag{17.46}$$

where here the same symbols are used to denote the detrended log of the variables; $TH = N + H$ denotes total hours, F denotes effort and $L = F + TH$ is labor input. To save notation the intercept term was omitted from all equations (but is present in all regressions).

Equation (17.41) is a Cobb–Douglas production function. Equation (17.42) defines total hours (TH) as the sum of employment and average hours per employee. Equation (17.43) defines labor supply as the sum of total hours and effort. Equations (17.44)–(17.45) specify total hours and effort as a function of the beginning of period inventories and the supply shock. Equation (17.46) specifies end of period inventories as a function of the beginning of period inventories, the supply shock ε and the number of markets open (s).

Under the assumption that supply shocks are i.i.d claim 4 implies: $\alpha, \beta_i, \gamma_i, \delta_i > 0$ for all i. Under the assumption that supply shocks are serially correlated claim 5 implies: $\alpha, \beta_1, \gamma_1, \delta_1, \delta_3 > 0$.

Substituting (17.43)–(17.45) in (17.41) leads to:

$$Y_t = -\alpha(\beta_1 + \gamma_1)I_{t-1} + \alpha(\beta_2 + \gamma_2 + 1)\varepsilon_t = -\phi_1 I_{t-1} + \phi_2 \varepsilon_t, \tag{17.47}$$

where $\phi_1 = \alpha(\beta_1 + \gamma_1)$ and $\phi_2 = \alpha(\beta_2 + \gamma_2 + 1)$. In the serially correlated supply shocks case we get:[5]

$$\begin{aligned} Y_t &= -\phi_1 I_{t-1} + \phi_2 \varepsilon_t = -\phi_1 I_{t-1} + \phi_2(\rho\varepsilon_{t-1} + u_t) \\ &= -\phi_1 I_{t-1} + \rho(Y_{t-1} + \phi_1 I_{t-2}) + \phi_2 u_t \\ &= \rho Y_{t-1} - \phi_1 I_{t-1} + (\rho\phi_1)I_{t-2} + \phi_2 u_t. \end{aligned} \tag{17.48}$$

The specification (17.48) says that lag variables matter. In a similar way we can show that in the serially correlated case lag variables should appear in all the equations in which ε_t appears because lag variables serve as a proxy for ε_{t-1}. The number of lag depends of course on the number of lags in the AR process.[6] We therefore experiment with various lags starting from VAR with one lag only. The main hypothesis is in claim 5. It says that the beginning of period inventories have a negative effect on all components of labor supply (employment, hours per employee and effort) and therefore on output and a positive effect on the end of period inventories.

Table 17.1 The correlation matrix for the detrended (ln) variables

	G	I_{-1}	TH	D	I_{-1}	TH	ND	I_{-1}	TH
G	1								
I_{-1}	*0.2*	1							
TH	0.9	0.39	1						
D	0.94	0.19	0.89	1					
I_{-1}	0.29	0.9	0.39	*0.2*	1				
TH	0.91	0.39	0.98	0.92	0.4	1			
ND	0.64	0.17	0.47	0.35	0.26	0.43	1		
I_{-1}	−0.05	0.59	0.16	0	0.19	0.14	*−0.1*	1	
TH	0.82	0.1	0.89	0.8	0.07	0.85	0.46	0.1	1

All variables were logged before the H–P filter was applied. We have three concepts of outputs: goods (G), durable goods (D) and non-durable goods (ND). For each output concept we have the beginning of period stock of inventories (I_{-1}) and hours (TH). The correlations between output and inventories are in italic.

Disaggregation by stage-of-fabrication

The model at this stage of development does not point to the appropriate definition of inventories: There is no distinction among inventories at different stages of the production process (work in progress and final goods) and no special category for materials and supplies.[7] Blinder (1986) has argued that given the accounting procedures which are used, only the aggregate concept of inventories (finished goods + work in progress) satisfies the equation: output = sales + change in inventories. Since this equation is used in the model, we follow Blinder in using the aggregate concept of inventories.

Data: We use NIPA data from 1959:1 to 1997:4. We use data on the stock of inventories rather than the change in inventories.[8] The data have three concepts of outputs: output in the goods sector, output in the durable goods sector and output in the non-durable goods sector. In 1997:4 the goods producing sector was about 40% of GDP and was equally divided between durables (20%) and non-durables (20%).

The standard deviation of the detrended (cyclical) variables in the goods sector are 0.026 for output, 0.011 for sales, 0.014 for inventories and 0.035 for total hours.

The correlation matrix for the detrended variables is in table 17.1. The correlation between the beginning of period inventories and output (levels of detrended variables) is positive for the durable sector (0.2) and negative for the non-durable sector (−0.1). The correlation for the goods sector as a whole is positive (0.2). The correlation between hours and lag inventories are all positive and somewhat higher: 0.4 for the goods and durable sectors and 0.1 for the non-durable sector.

The vector auto regressions are in table 17.2. The sign of the inventories coefficients are as predicted by theory: An increase in the beginning of period inventories has a depressing effect on output and total hours and a positive effect on the beginning of period inventories. All the coefficients of the inventories variable are significantly different from zero. The lags of output and total hours are also statistically significant. This suggests the rejection of the i.i.d. supply shocks hypothesis in favor of the serially correlated supply shocks.

Table 17.2   VAR using H-P detrended log variables

	Y_{-1}	TH_{-1}	I_{-1}	Adj.R^2
Goods measures				
Dependent var: Y	0.59	0.33	−0.69	0.72
	(6.0)	(4.2)	(−6.8)	
Dependent var: TH	0.22	0.92	−0.70	0.84
	(2.2)	(11.2)	(−6.6)	
Dependent var: I	0.09	0.09	0.68	0.90
	(2.6)	(3.3)	(20.0)	
Durables measures				
Dependent var: Y	0.49	0.61	−0.90	0.68
	(4.2)	(4.2)	(−6.8)	
Dependent var: TH	0.14	0.96	−0.64	0.85
	(1.9)	(10.5)	(−7.7)	
Dependent var: I	0.05	0.15	0.65	0.90
	(1.6)	(3.9)	(18.8)	
Non-durables measures				
Dependent var: Y	0.37	0.21	−0.38	0.33
	(5.0)	(4.2)	(−4.3)	
Dependent var: TH	0.03	0.84	−0.16	0.69
	(0.4)	(16.6)	(−1.8)	
Dependent var: I	0.06	0.05	0.81	0.73
	(1.7)	(2.0)	(18.4)	

t statistics in parentheses. There are three regressions per output concept. In the first regression the left hand side variable is output. In the second regression it is total hour and in the third it is the end of period stock of inventories. The right hand side variables are lag output, lag total hours and beginning of period inventories. The adjusted R^2 for each regression is reported in the last column.

We can examine the joint hypothesis about the effect of inventories on effort by running two stage least squares regression of output on total hours and lag inventories, using lag variables as instruments. The results in table 17.3 show that an increase in I_{-1} reduces output, holding TH constant. This can happen in our model only if effort goes down in response to an increase in I_{-1}.

In tables 17.4 and 17.5 we test the hypothesis about the effect of the beginning of period inventories on employment and hours per employee. The results are consistent with the prediction of a negative effect of inventories on these variables.

Conclusions

The negative relationship between the beginning of period inventories and output is a key prediction of the UST model. The raw correlation between these variables is positive (and small) when using H-P detrended variables.

Table 17.3 Dependent variable = Y; 2SLS using H-P detrended log variables

	Y_{-1}	I_{-1}	TH	Adj.R^2
Goods measures		−0.27	0.69	0.83
		(−4.1)	(23.3)	
	0.51	−0.44	0.36	0.83
	(5.6)	(−6.1)	(5.4)	
Durables measures		−0.31	1.04	0.87
		(−4.4)	(26.3)	
	0.40	−0.49	0.64	0.84
	(4.1)	(−5.6)	(5.9)	
Non-durables measures		−0.25	0.38	0.23
		(−2.7)	(6.5)	
	0.37	−0.34	0.26	0.35
	(4.9)	(−3.9)	(4.2)	

t statistics are in parentheses. In this table we use lag variables as instruments for the TH variable. The first line reports the regression of output on (the estimated level of) total hours and the beginning of period inventories. In the second line we add lag output to the list of explanatory variables. This is done for the three output measures: goods, durables and non-durables.

Table 17.4 Dependent variable = number of employees (N); using H-P detrended log variables

	Y_{-1}	I_{-1}	N_{-1}	Adj.R^2
Goods measures	0.25	−0.43	0.88	0.89
	(4.9)	(−5.5)	(12.7)	
Durables measures	0.15	−0.41	0.95	0.89
	(4.6)	(−5.9)	(12.6)	
Non-durables measures	0.09	−0.09	0.86	0.78
	(2.2)	(−1.9)	(19.7)	

t statistics are in parentheses.

Table 17.5 Dependent variable = hours per employee (H); using H-P detrended log variables

	Y_{-1}	I_{-1}	H_{-1}	Adj.R^2
Goods measures	0.04	−0.26	0.82	0.72
	(0.9)	(−5.4)	(10.4)	
Durables measures	0.06	−0.27	0.78	0.79
	(1.6)	(−6.8)	(8.8)	
Non-durables measures	−0.05	−0.07	0.79	0.58
	(−1.2)	(−1.4)	(14.1)	

t statistics are in parentheses.

But when lag variables are held constant, the effect of inventories on output is negative and highly significant. In this case, inventories have a negative effect on all three components of labor supply: employment, hours per employee and effort.

The following estimates were obtained for the goods sector, when controlling for lag total hours and lag output. A 1% increase in the beginning of period inventories leads to 0.7% reduction in total hours (table 17.2). This reduction can be decomposed into: 0.4% reduction in the number of employees (table 17.4) and 0.3% reduction in hours per employee (table 17.5). The reduction in effort that is associated with a 1% increase in inventories is 1.2% (table 17.3, see Eden [2001a] for the details of the calculation).

Thus controlling for lag variables drastically changes the conclusion about the effects of the beginning of period inventories.

In our model we should control for lag variables if the supply shocks are serially correlated. Since lag variables appear to be highly significant in most of the regressions, we reject the i.i.d. hypothesis in favor of the serially correlated supply shock hypothesis.

17.4 USING AN IMPULSE RESPONSE ANALYSIS WITH NON-DETRENDED VARIABLES TO TEST FOR PERSISTENCE

According to our model, a negative demand shock leads to the accumulation of inventories and, since output is negatively related to the beginning of period level of inventories, to a decline in output. The effect of demand shock on output is persistent because the effect on inventories dies out slowly: An increase in the beginning of period inventories by one unit leads on average to less than a unit increase in the beginning of next period inventories and this leads to even smaller effect on the beginning of two periods ahead inventories and so on until the effect dies out.

Vector-auto-regression-impulse-response analysis is a good way of testing for persistence. This type of analysis was introduced to the Macro literature by Sims (1980) and was reviewed in chapter 7. According to this approach there is no need to use detrended variables because the trend is embodied in the past variables of the system.

We use (17.47) to substitute $\varepsilon_t = (Y_t + \phi_1 I_{t-1})/\phi_2$ in (17.46). Taking the lag of the resulting equation leads to:

$$I_{t-1} = cY_{t-1} + dI_{t-2} - \delta_3 s_{t-1}. \tag{17.49}$$

where $c = \delta_2/\phi_2$, $d = \delta_2\phi_1/\phi_2$. Equation (17.49) says that when the lag variables are in the system a shock to inventories is a negative demand shock. We also use (17.48) which is reproduced here as:

$$Y_t = \rho Y_{t-1} - \phi_1 I_{t-1} + \rho\phi_1 I_{t-2} + \phi_2 u_t. \tag{17.50}$$

The system (17.49) and (17.50) can be estimated by running two variables VAR system with the ordering: I_{-1}, Y. Since a shock to the beginning of period inventories is caused by a negative demand shock in the previous period we can learn about the effect of a demand shock by estimating the response of output to an inventories shock. We expect that the maximal effect will occur immediately after the demand shock and then the effect should die out gradually. We should thus observe impulse response functions that qualitatively look as in figure 17.5.

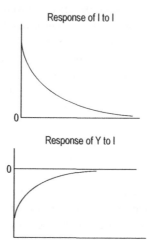

Figure 17.5   The predicted effects of an inventories shock in a two variables VAR: I, Y

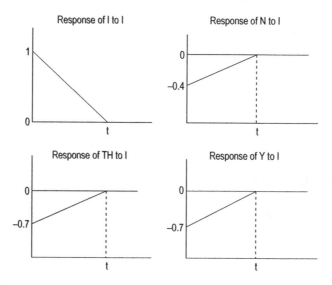

Figure 17.6   The predicted effect of an inventories shock in a four variables VAR: I, N, TH, Y

Figure 17.6 describes the qualitative response to an inventories shock when running the four variables VAR of inventories, employment, total hours and output (I_{-1}, N, TH, Y). We should expect that a 1% increase in the beginning of period inventories will lead to a decline in employment (say by -0.4%) and to a larger decline in total hours (say of -0.7%) reflecting the hypothesis that hours per employee decline in response to an inventories shock. The effect on labor input should be even higher because of the negative effect on effort. Since a percentage decline in labor input causes α% decline in output, the effect on Y may be larger or smaller

Response to one SD. Innovations ±2 SE

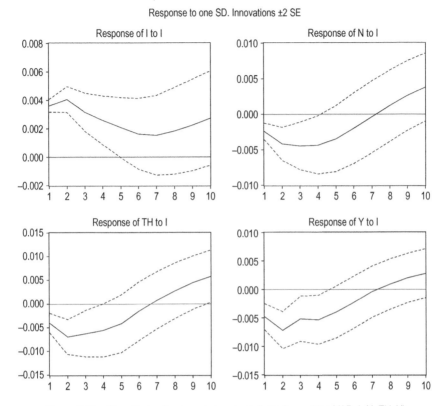

Figure 17.7   The effects of an inventories shock (based on a 4-lag VAR: I, N, TH, Y)

than the effect on TH. Finally the effect should die out when inventories are back to the baseline.

We use the NIPA data described in the previous section on the goods producing sector in the period 1965:2 to 1997:4 and allow for 4 lags to estimate the four variables VAR: I_{-1}, N, TH, Y. The results in figure 17.7 are not very different from the prediction in figure 17.6. The effect of a shock to inventories on inventories is significantly positive for about 5 quarters. The effect of an inventories shock on employment total hours and output is significantly negative for about 4 quarters. The maximal effect occurs in period 2 instead of period 1 as predicted by the theory. The effect on total hours is larger than the effect on employment (in absolute value).

The estimates are somewhat different from what we got in the previous section when we allowed for 1 lag only. A 1% increase in inventories leads to about 0.7% decline in employment and 1.1% decline in total hours in the first period. These are larger than our previous estimates of 0.4% and 0.7%.

Figure 17.8 describes the responses to an inventories shock when there are 10 lags in the VAR. These are similar to the responses in figure 17.7 when allowing for 4 lags. The initial response to the shock is almost identical to the previous VAR: a 1% increase in the beginning of period inventories leads to 0.7% decline in employment and to a 1.1% decline in total hours in the first period.

Response to one SD. Innovations ±2 SE

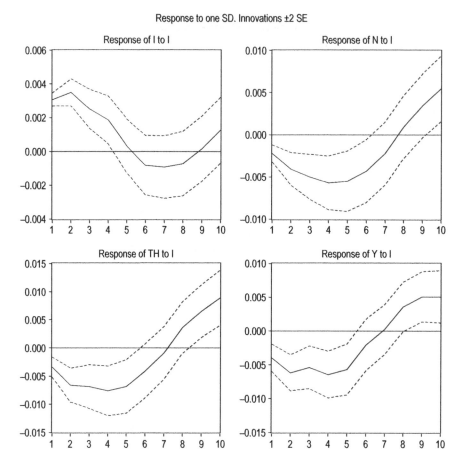

Figure 17.8   The effects of an inventories shock (based on a 10-lag VAR: I, N, TH, Y)

Conclusions

According to our model a negative demand shock leads to the accumulation of inventories and to a persistent negative effect on employment, hours per employee, effort and real output. The maximal effect should occur immediately after the shock and then die out gradually. The estimated impulse response functions are not very different from the theoretical prediction. The maximal effect occurs after some lag but the difference between the initial impact and the maximal effect is not large.

APPENDIX 17A   THE HODRICK–PRESCOTT (H–P) FILTER

Let y_t be a time series which can be decomposed into a cyclical component, y_t^c, and a growth component, y_t^g, such that $y_t = y_t^c + y_t^g$. We observe y_t and we want to separate the relatively smooth growth component from the cyclical component. One way of doing that is to run a regression of y on time: $y_t = a + bt + e_t$. We then use the predicted value, $y_t^g = a + bt$, as the growth component and the estimated error term, $y_t^c = e_t$, as the cyclical component. When y_t is in log form the coefficient b is the predicted rate of growth of y. Hodrick and Prescott (1997) have observed that for many time series the regression parameter b is not stable over time. They allow the rate of growth coefficient to change in a smooth way and choose the two components by minimizing:

$$\sum_{t=1}^{T} \left(y_t^c\right)^2 + \lambda \sum_{t=1}^{T} \left[\left(y_{t+1}^g - y_t^g\right) - \left(y_t^g - y_{t-1}^g\right)\right]^2, \qquad (A17.1)$$

where λ is a parameter. The first term is the variance of the cyclical component. The second term is the variance of the rate of growth (in case that y_t is in log form) of the growth component. The minimization problem treats both variances as undesired. When $\lambda = 0$, the growth component is equal to y_t and the cyclical component is zero. When $\lambda \to \infty$ the growth component approaches a linear trend. For quarterly data it is customary to choose $\lambda = 1600$.

NOTES

1 The major difference between the implications of the Blinder–Fischer model and the implications of the UST model is about the effect of the initial monetary shock. As in the Lucas' model the initial effect of the monetary shock in the Blinder–Fischer model is on the price level. This shock creates confusion and inventories are used as a propagation mechanism. In the UST model current prices do not move in response to a monetary shock.
2 Here we denote the beginning of period inventories by sub $t - 1$ rather than sub t. This is because in the NIPA data end of period inventories are reported.
3 The log form is required because otherwise the supply shock (and output) may be negative.
4 We used the Hodrick–Prescott (H–P) filter with $\lambda = 1600$ to detrend the logs of the variables.
5 We used the lag of (17.28) to substitute for ε_{t-1} in the second row.
6 When the supply shock follows an AR(p) process we should modify the theoretical section and define the aggregate state by: $x = (\varepsilon, \varepsilon_{-1}, \dots, \varepsilon_p, I_{-1})$. This should not change the result in claim 2.
7 See for example, Abramovitz (1950) for an early study and Reagan and Sheehan (1985) for a more recent study that distinguishes among these types of inventories.
8 The data is on the internet at: www.stat-usa.gov

CHAPTER 18

Money and Credit in the Business Cycle

In chapter 7 we discussed the importance of money in the business cycle. Taking an eclectic view we found that: (1) When inventories are added to a VAR system with money and output, the importance of money (in explaining output) is drastically reduced; (2) When M1 and M2 are both in the system, M2 innovations are more important than M1 innovations. Should we evaluate the importance of money by a system that has inventories in it? Do inside and outside money have different effects?

Here we examine these questions from the point of view of a UST model that assigns a similar role to inside and outside money.

18.1 A UST MODEL WITH CREDIT

As in the previous chapters, the typical household is a worker–buyer pair. It starts the period with some inventories and money. The buyer takes the money and goes to shop. The worker takes the inventories and goes to produce. He then tries to sell the available supply (inventories plus currently produced output) for money.

The buyer may get a transfer from the government and an interest-free single period credit from banks. The transfer payment from the government is μ dollars per dollar held at the beginning of the period and the credit from the bank is θ dollars per dollar held at the beginning of the period.

It may be useful to think in terms of an environment in which the money in advance constraint can be satisfied by checks and cash. The buyer first goes to the bank and opens a checking account. For each dollar deposited in the checking account the bank allows the buyer to spend $1 + \theta$ dollars by writing checks. He then gets a cash transfer from the government which is spent as cash. At the end of the period the household returns the loan from the revenues received by the seller. It is assumed that θ is not too large and that bankruptcy does not occur.

The sum $\mu + \theta$ is an i.i.d. random variable that can take S possible realizations. We choose indices in a way that: $\mu_1 + \theta_1 \leq \mu_2 + \theta_2 \leq \cdots \leq \mu_S + \theta_S$. We use Π_s to denote the probability that the realization of $\mu + \theta$ is $\mu_s + \theta_s$.

The amount spent during the period is $M_t(1 + \mu_s + \theta_s)$ with probability Π_s, where M_t denotes the average per household beginning of period money supply. As in previous chapters, we use M_t as the unit of account and call it a normalized dollar (ND). The amount spent in terms of normalized dollars is thus: $1 + \mu_s + \theta_s$ with probability Π_s. Since $M_{t+1} = M_t(1 + \mu_s)$, a normalized dollar this period will become $\omega^s = 1/(1 + \mu_s)$ normalized dollars in the next period if the transfer is μ_s dollars per dollar.

From the sellers' point of view money arrives sequentially. The minimal amount that will arrive is $\Delta_1 = 1 + \mu_1 + \theta_1$ normalized dollars and this amount buys in the first market at the price of p_1 ND per unit. If no more money arrives then trade ends for the period. But with probability $q_2 = 1 - \Pi_1$, an additional amount of $\Delta_2 = \mu_2 + \theta_2 - (\mu_1 + \theta_1)$ ND will arrive. If it arrives it opens the second market and buys at the price p_2. Similarly, if no more money arrives after the end of transactions in market 2, then trade ends for the period. But with probability $q_3 = 1 - \Pi_1 - \Pi_2$ an additional amount of $\Delta_3 = \mu_3 + \theta_3 - (\mu_2 + \theta_2)$ normalized dollars will arrive and so on.

A buyer who holds m^h normalized dollars at the beginning of the period will buy on average:

$$\sum_{s=1}^{S} \Pi_s \sum_{j=1}^{s} v_j^s m^h (1 + \mu_s + \theta_s)/p_j, \tag{18.1}$$

units of consumption, where $v_j^s = \Delta_j/(1 + \mu_s + \theta_s)$ is the probability that a dollar will buy in market j given that s markets open.

Prior to trade the worker takes the beginning of period inventories (I_{t-1}^h) and goes to work. He produces output (y_t^h) using labor input (L_t^h) according to a linear production function:

$$y_t^h = \varepsilon_t L_t^h, \tag{18.2}$$

where ε_t is a supply shock. He then takes the total supply:

$$k_t^h = y_t^h + I_{t-1}^h, \tag{18.3}$$

and allocates it across the S potential markets:

$$\sum_{s=1}^{S} k_{st}^h \leq k_t^h, \tag{18.4}$$

where k_{st}^h is the supply to market s.

The household is risk neutral and its single period utility function is given by:

$$c_t^h - v(L_t^h), \tag{18.5}$$

where $v(\ )$ is a standard cost function ($v' > 0$ and $v'' > 0$).

We drop the superscript to denote average per household magnitudes and use $x = (I_{-1}, \varepsilon)$ to denote the current aggregate state. In equilibrium all magnitudes are functions of x. We use,

$$k(x) = \varepsilon[L(x)] + I_{-1}, \tag{18.6}$$

to denote average supply per household and

$$I^s(x) = k(x) - \sum_{j=1}^{s} k_j(x) \geq 0, \tag{18.7}$$

to denote the average per household level of next period inventories if exactly s markets open today.

The household takes the price functions, $p_s(x)$, and the next period average inventories functions, $I^s(x)$, as given. Given these functions it chooses L^h and k_j^h to solve the following Bellman's equation:

$$V(m^h, I_{-1}^h; x)$$

$$= \max_{L^h k_j^h} \sum_{s=1}^{S} \Pi_s \sum_{j=1}^{s} v_j^s m^h (1 + \mu_s + \theta_s)/p_j(x) - v(L^h)$$

$$+ \beta \sum_{s=1}^{S} \Pi_s EV \left\{ \left[\sum_{j=1}^{s} p_j(x) k_j^h - \theta_s m^h \right] \middle/ (1 + \mu_s), k^h - \sum_{j=1}^{s} k_j^h, [I^s(x), \tilde{\varepsilon}] \right\}$$

s.t.

$$\sum_{s=1}^{S} k_s^h \leq k^h = \varepsilon L^h + I_{-1}^h, \quad \text{and non-negativity constraints.} \tag{18.8}$$

Here $V(m^h, I_{-1}^h; x)$ is the maximum expected utility possible in aggregate state x for a household that starts this period with m^h normalized dollars and I_{-1}^h units of inventories. The first row is the expected utility in the current period. The second row is the expected future utility. The expectations operator E is taken with respect to the next period supply shock $\tilde{\varepsilon}$.

Equilibrium is a vector of functions $[p_1(x), \ldots, p_S(x), L(x), k(x), k_1(x), \ldots, k_S(x), I^1(x), \ldots, I^S(x)]$ which satisfy (18.6)–(18.7) and
(a) given the functions $[p_s(x), I^s(x)]$, $[L^h = L(x), k_s^h = k_s(x)]$ solve the household's problem (18.8) for all x;
(b) markets which open are cleared:

$$p_s(x) k_s(x) = \Delta_s, \quad \text{for all s.} \tag{18.9}$$

Claims 4 and 5 of the previous chapter hold also in this more general model and are repeated here for convenience, without proof (the proof is not a trivial extension of the discussion in the previous chapter).

Claim 1: When the supply shocks are iid, the equilibrium labor supply function, $L(x)$, is decreasing in I and increasing in ε. The equilibrium supply functions $k_s(x)$ and end of period inventories functions, $I^s(x)$ are increasing in I and in ε. The equilibrium price functions $p_s(x)$ are decreasing in I and in ε.

Claim 2: When the supply shocks are AR(1), the equilibrium functions $L(x)$, $p_s(x)$ are decreasing in I_{-1} and the equilibrium functions $k(x)$, $k_s(x)$, $I^s(x)$ are increasing in I_{-1}.

Endogenous money

The results in claim 2 are robust to allowing for the possibility that changes in the supply of money (outside and inside) depend on the state of the economy (x). To show this claim, we assume that changes in the money supply occur in two stages: A perfectly anticipated stage and a random process that was described above. In the first stage, the government gives a transfer of $\lambda(x)$ dollars per dollar and the banks extend credit of $\psi(x)$ dollars per dollar. We then start the random process in which the government gives a transfer of μ dollars per dollar and the banks give credit of θ dollars per dollar. Thus total spending is given by:

$$[1 + \lambda(x) + \psi(x)][1 + \mu + \theta]M_t, \tag{18.10}$$

and the money supply evolves according to: $M_{t+1} = [1 + \lambda(x)][1 + \mu]M_t$. We now normalize all magnitudes by the anticipated purchasing power $[1 + \lambda(x) + \psi(x)]M_t$ instead of by M_t and the rest of the model is the same.

18.2 INVENTORIES ARE A SUFFICIENT STATISTIC FOR PAST DEMAND SHOCKS

The theory tells us that inside and outside money surprises have similar effects. They both lead to more spending and the decumulation of inventories. This leads in the next period to a decline in prices and output. The simplest VAR system that can capture the main equilibrium relationship specifies real output and the beginning of period inventories as a function of the underline supply and demand shocks. We therefore start with the VAR system (17.46) and (17.47) from the previous chapter and reproduce it here for convenience:

$$Y_t = -\phi_1 I_{t-1} + \phi_2 \varepsilon_t \tag{18.11}$$

$$I_t = \delta_1 I_{t-1} + \delta_2 \varepsilon_t - \delta_3 s_t, \tag{18.12}$$

where Y_t is the log of real output, I_t is the log of the end of period inventories, ε_t is the supply shock and s_t is the demand shock. This specification is a log linearization of the equilibrium functions. Output $(L[x])$ is a function of the state $x = (I_{-1}, \varepsilon)$. Since the end of period inventories $(I^s[x])$ depends also on the number of markets open during the period, inventories depends in addition to x on the demand shock s.

When the supply shock is i.i.d., the beginning of period inventories is a sufficient statistic for all past variables. Under this assumption, lag output should not appear as an explanatory variable in the output equation. As was shown in the previous chapter, this hypothesis is strongly rejected by the data.

When the supply shock is serially correlated, inventories are a sufficient statistic for past demand shocks (but not for past supply shocks). To show this claim we substitute

$\varepsilon_t = \rho\varepsilon_{t-1} + u_t$ in (18.11) and use the lag, $(Y_{t-1} + \phi_1 I_{t-2})/\phi_2 = \varepsilon_{t-1}$, to get:

$$Y_t = -\phi_1 I_{t-1} + \rho Y_{t-1} + (\rho\phi_1)I_{t-2} + \phi_2 u_t. \tag{18.13}$$

We now use the lag of (18.12) to substitute out I_{t-1}:

$$\begin{aligned} Y_t &= -\phi_1 I_{t-1} + \rho Y_{t-1} + (\rho\phi_1)I_{t-2} + \phi_2 u_t \\ &= -\phi_1(\delta_1 I_{t-2} + \delta_2 \varepsilon_{t-1} - \delta_3 s_{t-1}) + \rho Y_{t-1} + (\rho\phi_1)I_{t-2} + \phi_2 u_t \\ &= a I_{t-2} + b Y_{t-1} + c s_{t-1} + \phi_2 u_t, \end{aligned} \tag{18.14}$$

where $a = -\phi_1\delta_1 + \rho\phi_1$; $b = \rho$ and $c = \phi_1\delta_3$.

We see that in (18.13) when lag inventories are in the regression, demand shocks do not appear in the regression. In (18.14) when the first lag of inventories is not in the regression, the demand shock s_{t-1} does appear in the regression. We can now repeat this procedure and use the lag of (18.12) to substitute I_{t-2} in (18.14). This will lead to an equation in both s_{t-1} and s_{t-2}. We keep doing it to get in the equation all the lag values of s. Thus, by comparing (18.14) to (18.13) we can show that:

Claim 3: Lag inventories are sufficient statistics for the demand shocks.

It follows that when both inventories and the demand shocks are in the system we run into a multicollinearity problem. This may explain why monetary variables appear to be relatively unimportant when we add inventories to the list of variables in the VAR system (see the discussion in chapter 7).

18.3 ESTIMATING THE RESPONSES TO A MONEY SHOCK

Claim 3 implies that the effect of the monetary variables on output should be estimated from a VAR system without inventories. This is because demand shocks affect inventories that then become a sufficient statistic and take some or all of the credit for the explanation of output. According to our model, a demand shock leads to the decumulation of inventories and to an increase in output in the following period. Since a reduction of one unit of inventories leads on average to less than a unit reduction in the end of period inventories, the effect on output is persistent and diminishing over time.

The effect of money on output

Since our theory assigns a symmetric role to inside and outside money, we should use a wide (as opposed to narrow) definition of money. But as is well known, the definition of money is problematic. We therefore use here both M1 and M2 as a proxy for M.

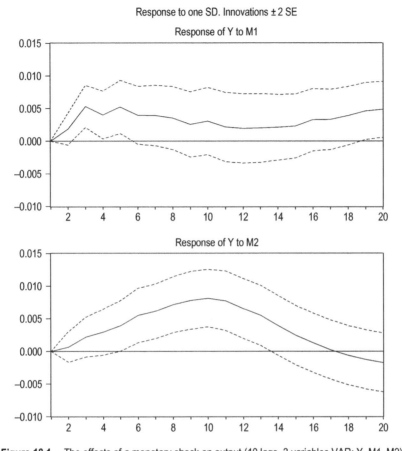

Figure 18.1   The effects of a monetary shock on output (10 lags, 3 variables VAR: Y, M1, M2)

Figure 18.1 uses 10 lags VAR with the variables (Y, M1, M2). As can be seen the effect of monetary shocks is quite large. M1 reaches a peak of about 0.5% after 2 quarters while M2 reaches a peak of 0.8% after 9 quarters. The effect of M1 is roughly consistent with the theoretical impulse response function: The peak occurs early and then the effect diminishes over time. This is not the case for the effect of a credit (M2) shock that peaks much later.

The effect of money on inventories, prices and sales

According to the model a money shock should increase sales in the first period. This will reduce the beginning of next period inventories and prices. Since inventories are low in the following period, prices should be high and sales should be low. Since the effect on inventories dies out gradually the effect on prices and sales should also die out gradually. We should thus expect impulse response functions that look like the responses in figure 18.2.

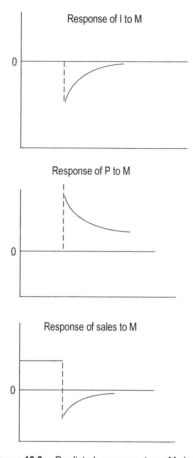

Figure 18.2   Predicted responses to an M shock

Figure 18.3 is based on 10 lags five variables VAR of I, P, M1, M2, S where S is the log of real final sales in the goods producing sector. An M1 shock reduces inventories in the period following the shock and increase sales in the period of the shock. But there is no effect on prices in the period following the shock. An M2 shock does not affect inventories and prices in the period that follows the shock and does not affect sales in the period of the shock. Thus, the initial response to an M2 shock is not consistent with the theory.

One possible story is as follows. Buyers allocate their liquid portfolio between checking and saving type accounts. The funds allocated to checking accounts are spent immediately. They typically spend the funds allocated to saving accounts after some time, say two years. Therefore when the balances in saving type accounts go up, everyone knows that spending will go up in the future and producers build up inventories to face the increase in demand.

Response to one SD. Innovations ± 2 SE

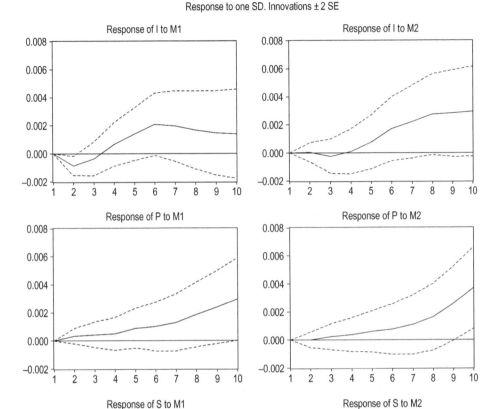

Figure 18.3   The effects of money shock on inventories, prices, and sales (based on a 10-lag VAR: 1, P, M1, M2, S)

The effect of an M shock on prices is generally positive but unlike the prediction of the theory, the maximal effect does not occur in the following period but occurs with a considerable lag. The maximal effect on prices of an M2 shock is after 18 quarters while the maximal effect of this shock on sales is after 8 quarters. One possible story is that measured prices are biased

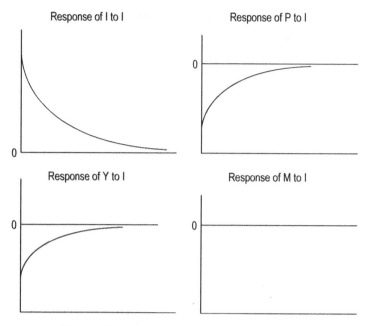

Figure 18.4   Predicted responses to an inventories shock

toward the list prices. Stigler and Kindahl (1970) argued that list prices change slowly while actual prices that include various discounts change more frequently.

18.4   ESTIMATING THE RESPONSES TO AN INVENTORIES SHOCK

According to our model, a negative demand shock leads to the accumulation of inventories and to a decline in output and prices. Since on average a one-unit increase in I_{-1} leads to less than a unit increase in I, the effect on inventories declines over time and so does the effect on output and prices. Qualitatively we should get impulse response functions as in figure 18.4.

To test these predictions we ran a 10 lag VAR with the following list of variables: I, P, Y, M1, M2 where P is the log of PPI for finished goods and I ($= I_{-1}$) is the beginning of period stock of inventories. The impulse response functions in figure 18.5 show a persistent positive effect of an inventories shock on inventories and a persistent negative effect of an inventories shock on output and prices. Inventories behave as expected, reaching a peak immediately after the shock and going back to normal after about 6 quarters. Output declines and then returns to normal after about 6 quarters. Prices decline but reach a trough after 8 quarters. Money increases after an inventories shock, which suggests that the effect on prices would have been stronger in the absence of central bank intervention.

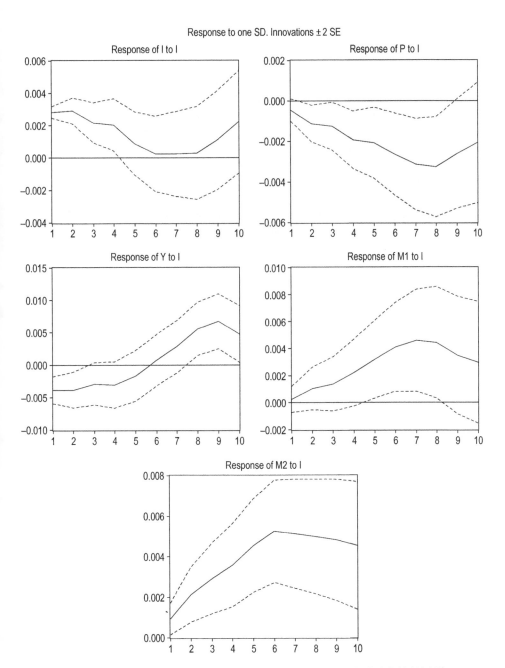

Figure 18.5 The effects of an inventories shock (based on a 10-lag VAR: I, P, Y, M1, M2)

18.5   CONCLUDING REMARKS

We have studied a model in which inside and outside money have similar effects on sales and the end of period inventories. When supply shocks are serially correlated inventories are a sufficient statistic for all past demand shocks (because demand shocks are i.i.d.). This may explain why the importance of the monetary variables in the explanation of output is drastically reduced once inventories are added to the system (see chapter 7).

The observation that inventories are a sufficient statistic for all past demand shock may also explain why the estimated effects of an inventories shock are more in line with the theory than the estimated effects of a money shock. Since the theory says that all demand shocks have a similar effect and they all work by affecting inventories, looking at an inventories shock is appropriate. Another possibility is that money shock (especially M2 shocks) affect demand with a lag.

CHAPTER 19

Evidence from Micro Data

In the previous two chapters we tested the implication of the UST model using aggregate data. Here we use disaggregate data to test the implications of some sticky price models against the UST alternative. The analysis is based on Eden (2001b) and Baharad and Eden (2003). The exposition here omits some indices and definitions but transmit, we hope, the flavor of the results. For the exact definitions see Eden (2001b).

Nominal price changes occurs discretely, in jumps (see, for example, Carlton [1986], Cecchetti [1986] and Lach and Tsiddon [1992]). This observation is consistent with fixed menu-type costs for changing nominal prices. It is also consistent with the UST model.

In a UST equilibrium there is price dispersion and sellers are indifferent among prices in the equilibrium range because a lower real price promises a higher probability of making a sale. When inflation erodes the real price many sellers are fully compensated by the increase in the probability of making a sale and therefore may choose not to change their nominal price even in the absence of menu type costs. The observation that nominal price changes occur in jumps cannot therefore distinguish between the two types of models. We need more observations.

To derive additional predictions of menu costs models, we start by describing the key relationship between the time since the last nominal price change and the nominal price jump.

19.1 A MENU COST MODEL

A seller who does not change his nominal price (P) will experience a change in his real price $P/\bar{P}$, if the relevant deflator (the index of prices $\bar{P}$) changes. His real price will appreciate by $d\ln(P/\bar{P})/dt = -d\ln(\bar{P})/dt = -\pi$, where π is the inflation rate of the relevant price index $\bar{P}$. Price erosion – the depreciation in the real price since the last nominal price change – can therefore be measured by the multiplication of the time since the last nominal price change (Δt) and the rate of inflation (π). For example, when the monthly inflation rate is 5%, the real value of a nominal price that was not changed for 3 months declines by about 15%.

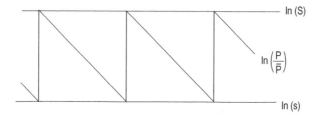

Figure 19.1   (S, s) policy in the real price

One hypothesis is that whenever stores change their nominal price they achieve the same real price target:

$$\Delta p = \pi \Delta t, \tag{19.1}$$

where Δp is the rate of change in the nominal price at the time of the "jump" and $\pi \Delta t$ is the price erosion variable. A good example for a theory that leads to (19.1) is the (S, s) model of nominal price changes.

Simple (S, s) models assume that stores have some monopoly power and face a fixed cost for changing their nominal price. The tradeoff is between the frequency of nominal price changes and the average deviation from the optimal monopoly price. Barro (1972) and Sheshinski and Weiss (1977) show that the optimal strategy in a stationary environment is to increase the nominal price whenever the real price hits a certain threshold level s to the target level S. Figure 19.1 illustrates this strategy by plotting the log of the real price, ln $(P/\bar{P})$, under the assumption that $\pi = d\ln(\bar{P})/dt$ does not change over time.

The UST alternative says that stores do not care about their real price as long as it stays in the equilibrium range. The target in the UST model is a range rather than a point. Under the UST alternative we may run the following regression:

$$\Delta p = a + b\Delta t + e, \tag{19.2}$$

where a and b are coefficients and e is an error term. The error term in (19.2) may be large and there are no strong restrictions on the coefficients. Under (19.1), $a = 0$, $b = \pi$ and $e = 0$ implying perfect correlation between Δp and Δt.

We ran (19.2) using monthly Israeli data about prices of specific products (for example 500 gram Hala bread) in a sample of stores that sold this product. The data are from three periods: 1978–1979, 1981–1982 and 1991–1992. The monthly inflation rate was 4.3% in 78–79, 6.3% in 81–82 and 0.7% in 91–92. There were 26 products in the first two samples and 390 products in the 91–92 sample. 23 of the 26 products in the earlier samples are also in the 91–92 sample. Here we report only the results of this "comparable" sample.[1]

Table 19.1 reports the OLS regression results when running (19.2). As can be seen the simple (S, s) model does not do well. The adjusted R^2 is very small. The intercept is significantly different from zero in all cases. The coefficient of Δt is significant and positive in two out of the three samples but it is much lower than the rate of inflation during the corresponding periods.

In (19.1) we assumed that all sellers use the same price index to compute the real price and this price index changes at a constant rate. In their 1983 article, Sheshinski and Weiss extended

Table 19.1 Running non-zero nominal price changes on the time interval
$(\Delta P = a + b\Delta t)$

	Observations	Intercept*	Coefficient of Δt*	Adjusted R^2
78–9	2503	0.051	0.022	0.08
		(13.9)	(14.6)	
81–2	3586	0.085	0.013	0.02
		(25.6)	(7.6)	
91–2	1767	0.016	0.000	−0.0005
		(4.0)	(0.3)	

Based on table 7 in Eden (2001b); t statistics in parentheses.

the analysis to the case in which inflation is a stochastic process. The rate of change of the price level can be positive or zero and the time spent in each state is of random duration. They show that the optimal policy in this stochastic environment is (S, s) in the real price.

To allow for a stochastic product specific inflation rate we computed the jump in nominal price per month $(\Delta p_{ijn}/\Delta t_{ijn})$ for each store j that changed the nominal price of product i in month n and then used the average across sellers π_{in} as an estimate of the realized product specific inflation rate in the time interval Δt_{ijn}. The correlations between Δp_{ijn} and the depreciation variable $d_{ijn} = \pi_{in}\Delta t_{ijn}$ are 0.4, 0.2 and 0.5 for the 78–79, 81–82 and 91–92 samples. These correlations are somewhat less than the correlations between Δp_{ijn} and the average jump across stores that changed the price of product i in month n, Δp_{in}. Thus for prediction purposes one would do better with the naive hypothesis that nominal price changes are equal to the average nominal price change (across stores who changed the nominal price of the same product). The time since the last nominal price change (Δt_{ijn}) is not useful for predicting the size of the jump.

19.2 THE SERIAL CORRELATION IN THE NOMINAL PRICE CHANGE

The simple (S, s) model has a prediction about non-zero nominal price changes even when the realized inflation rate is both product and store specific. That is even if each store uses a store and product specific price index $\bar{P}_{ij}$ to compute its real price $P/\bar{P}_{ij}$ and the price index $\bar{P}_{ij}$ changes at a stochastic rate.

In this case, we may write (19.1) as:

$$\Delta p_{ijn} = \pi_{ijn}\Delta t_{ijn} = S_{ij} - s_{ij}, \tag{19.3}$$

where Δp_{ijn} is the jump in the nominal price of product i in store j at month n, π_{ijn} is the rate of product and store specific inflation rate realized during the time interval Δt_{ijn} and $S_{ij} - s_{ij}$ is the product and store specific size of the band. The critical assumption here is that the size of the band is stable over time. This assumption gives the model in (19.3) its predictive power.

The model in (19.3) implies that the current nominal price change is equal to the last nominal price change. This is not the case in the data. The correlations between the current and the last nominal price change are negative. They are: −0.10, −0.18 and −0.28 for the 78–9, 81–2 and the 91–2 samples.

316 UNCERTAIN AND SEQUENTIAL TRADE

Table 19.2 OLS estimates of (19.5)

	Coefficient of z_{-1}
78–9	−0.194
	(−9.3)
81–2	−0.264
	(−15.9)
91–2	−0.352
	(−15.1)

Based on table 9 in Eden (2001b). The table reports the regression of the relative nominal price change, z, on its lagged value; t statistics are in parentheses.

To allow for changes in the size of the band, we examined the model:

$$\Delta p_{ij} = S_{ij} - s_{ij} = z_{ij} + \Delta p_i, \qquad (19.4)$$

where i is an index for the product, j is an index for the store and z_{ij} is the difference between the average and the store specific size of the band. The assumption that gives the model in (19.4) its predictive power is that the difference between the store specific band size and the average band size, $z_{ij} = \Delta p_{ij} - \Delta p_i$, does not change over time. To test (19.4), we ran:

$$z = bz_{-1} + \varepsilon, \qquad (19.5)$$

where z_{-1} is the value of z at the previous nominal price change episode and the error term ε arises from sampling and measurement errors. The model (19.4) predicts: $b = 1$. As can be seen from table 19.2, the actual coefficients are negative and highly significant.

Thus, it seems that the simple (S, s) model does not work even if we allow a product and store specific rate of realized inflation which changes over time. We now turn to examine the implication of a two sided (S, s) model.

19.3 A TWO-SIDED POLICY

Vial (1972) and Tsiddon (1993) consider a two sided (S, s) policy which allows for nominal price reductions. The policy is characterized by three parameters: (b, u, I). The store changes its nominal price whenever the real price hits the lower bound (b) or the upper bound (u) to reach the target level (I). Figure 19.2 illustrates this policy.

According to two sided (S, s) policy, the level of the real price (I) after a nominal price change should not depend on the sign of the nominal price change. To test this hypothesis, we define the relative price (r) by the price divided by the average price across all stores that changed the price of the same product. We then calculate the mean of the relative price for the group that increased its nominal price ($\Delta p > 0$) and for the group that reduced it ($\Delta p < 0$). As can be seen from table 19.3, the relative price of stores that reduced their nominal price is lower by about 8 to 4 percent relative to stores that increased their nominal price. To test whether the difference in the mean between the two groups is significant, we ran r on

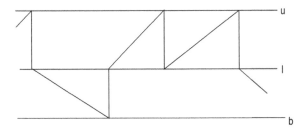

Figure 19.2   Two-sided (S, s) policy in the real price

Table 19.3   Relative price conditional on the sign of the nominal price change

	Observations	r	SD(r)	t statistic for dummy
1978–79; $\Delta p > 0$	2382	1.005	0.125	−5.8
$\Delta p < 0$	306	0.960	0.140	
1981–82; $\Delta p > 0$	3536	1.006	0.157	−8.2
$\Delta p < 0$	278	0.925	0.157	
1991–92; $\Delta p > 0$	1197	1.017	0.149	−6.3
$\Delta p < 0$	736	0.973	0.142	

Based on table 10 in Eden (2001b). The first column reports the number of observations of nominal price increases and nominal price reductions in each sample. The second column (r) reports the means of the relative price for the stores that increased the nominal price and for the stores that decreased it. The third column reports the standard deviation of the relative price in each group and the fourth is the t statistic for the dummy variable in a regression of the relative price on a constant and a dummy that gets unity in the case of a nominal price reduction and zero otherwise.

a constant and a dummy variable that gets unity if $\Delta p < 0$ and zero otherwise. The t statistics for this dummy variable are reported in the last column. They suggest that the differences in the means are highly significant.

We can therefore reject the hypothesis that the relative price immediately after the change does not depend on the sign of the change.[2]

19.4   RELATIVE PRICE VARIABILITY AND INFLATION

There is a large literature that studies the effect of inflation on some measure of the dispersion of prices. As a result of this literature many researchers believe that there is a positive relationship between inflation and price dispersion.

Reinsdorf (1994) challenges this view. He distinguishes between price change variability (PCV) and relative price variability (RPV). The first is measured by the standard deviation of the rate of change in nominal prices across sellers of the same product. The second is measured by the standard deviation of the levels of relative prices. Most researchers have assumed that PCV is a good proxy for RPV. Using US data Reinsdorf (1994) claims that this is not the case.

Table 19.4 Price-change variability (PCV)

	Observations	Monthly inflation (average of ΔP)	SD(ΔP)
1978–9	5934	0.043	0.089
1981–2	6394	0.063	0.099
1991–2; comparable	5842	0.007	0.069

Based on table 1 in Eden (2001b). The first column reports the number of observations in each sample. The second column reports the mean of the nominal price change (across all products stores and months). The third reports the standard deviation of the nominal price change.

Table 19.5 Relative price variability (RPV)

	Observations	SD(R)	SD(lnR)
78–9	6192	0.141	0.144
81–2	6672	0.169	0.175
91–2	6096	0.184	0.210

Based on table 2 in Eden (2001b). SD(R) is the standard deviation of the relative prices and SD(lnR) is the standard deviation of the natural log of relative prices.

Also in our data PCV is not a good proxy for RPV. Table 19.4 reports the standard deviations of price changes (PCV). It suggests the standard positive relationship between inflation and PCV: The highest standard deviation occurs in the highest inflation period and the lowest standard deviation occurs in the lowest inflation period.

Table 19.5 reports the standard deviation of relative prices $R = P/\bar{P}_i$, where $\bar{P}_i$ is the average price across all sellers who sell product i.[3] Here the highest standard deviation occurs in the lowest inflation period.

In what follows we use the standard deviation of the log of nominal prices in each product (i) month (t) cell as a measure of relative price variability (RPV). That is, we compute for each product (i) month (t) cell:

$$
SD(\ln P_{it}) = \left\{ \sum_j \left[\ln P_{ijt} - \left(\sum_j \ln P_{ijt}/N_{it} \right) \right]^2 \middle/ N_{it} \right\}^{0.5}, \qquad (19.6)
$$

where $\ln P_{ijt}$ is the natural log of the price of product i quoted by store j and SD($\ln P_{it}$) is the standard deviation across all the N_{it} stores which quoted a price for product i in month t. Note that if the deflator $\bar{P}_{it}$ is the same for all stores in the (i, t) cell, the variance of $\ln(P_{ijt}/\bar{P}_{it})$ is the same as the variance of $\ln P_{ijt}$.

We obtained measures of SD($\ln P_{it}$) and $\Delta P_{it} = \sum_j \Delta P_{ijt}/N_{it}$ for each (i = product, t = month) cell and ran a simple OLS regression of SD($\ln P_{it}$) on ΔP_{it}. As can be seen from table 19.6 the coefficient of ΔP_{it} is not significantly different from zero. When running a regression of a measure of PCV on ΔP_{it} one obtains the standard highly significant positive relationship.

Table 19.6 OLS of relative price variability on inflation: dependent variable $= SD(\ln P_{it})$

	Observations	Coefficient of ΔP_{it}	Adjusted t^a
78–9	575	0.067	1.0
81–2	552	−0.160	−1.1
91–2; all	8740	−0.138	−1.6

Based on table 11 in Eden (2001b). We calculated a measure of relative price variability and the mean rate of nominal price change for each (month, product) cell. The table reports the results of OLS regression of the relative price variability on the mean.
[a] Adjusted t $=$ t statistic adjusted for asymptotic variance.

Which measure is more meaningful: PCV or RPV? When changes in nominal prices are not synchronized across stores, the measurement of PCV depends on the length of the period in the data. To demonstrate this claim, consider the case in which $1/3$ of the stores changes their nominal price in the first month of each quarter, $1/3$ changes it in the second month of the quarter and $1/3$ in the last month of the quarter. They all change it by k%. In this case, we will find no variation in the rate of nominal price change in quarterly data but we will find positive variation ($\text{Var}(\Delta P) = 2k^2/9$) in monthly data because of the difference between the mean of those who changed their nominal price (k) and the mean of those who did not change their nominal price (0). Furthermore, the correlation between inflation and PCV can arise spuriously as a result of sampling errors.

To demonstrate this claim, let γ_{it} denote the fraction of stores in the sample, which changed the nominal price of good i at month t. Because of sampling errors γ_{it} may be different from $1/3$. The estimated mean of the rate of nominal price change in cell (i,t) is: $\Delta P_{it} = \gamma_{it}k$. The estimated variance is: $\text{Var}(\Delta P_{it}) \equiv \gamma_{it}(1 - \gamma_{it})k^2$. When $\gamma_{it} \leq 1/2$, the derivative of both the estimated mean and the estimated variance with respect to γ_{it} is positive. In this case, cells in which the fraction of stores which did change their nominal price is high will have both a high mean and a high variance, leading to a positive correlation between the estimated mean and the estimated variance.

This suggests that for the purpose of distinguishing among abstract competing theories that are not specific about the definition of the "period", we should focus on the behavior of RPV rather than PCV.

19.5 A STAGGERED PRICE SETTING MODEL[4]

In a staggered price-setting model of the type suggested by Taylor (1980) and more recently studied by Chari, Kehoe and McGrattan (CKM, 2000), a fraction $1/N$ of the sellers may change their nominal price in any given period and individual sellers change their nominal price every N periods.

What happens to relative price variability (RPV) as a result of a shock in this model? To build some intuition it may be useful to consider the effect of a once and for all change in the money supply. We start from an equilibrium in which the money supply has been constant

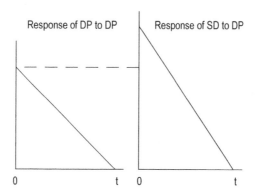

Figure 19.3 Possible responses to a DP shock

for a long time and all sellers post the same price. We then increase the money supply. Since only a fraction $1/N$ of the sellers can change their price immediately after the change in the money supply, this shock will create a price difference between sellers who could change their nominal prices to sellers who could not. RPV will gradually go back to zero as all sellers adjust their prices and the economy reaches the new equilibrium. Thus a money supply shock is expected to have a persistent positive effect on RPV.

For the sake of concreteness, we assume that at the initial steady state all sellers post the price of 1 and immediately after the change a fraction $1/N$ of the sellers change their price by Δ percent. The rate of inflation immediately after the change is the weighted average:

$$DP_t = \Delta(1/N) + 0[(N-1)/N] = \Delta/N.$$

The variance of the log of prices is:[5]

$$VAR_t = (DP)^2 + \Delta^2[1 - (2/N)](1/N).$$

It follows that when $N \geq 2$,

Claim 1: A shock that affects the rate of inflation (DP_t) also affect the standard deviation of the log of prices (SD_t). The effect on the standard deviation is larger: $SD_t > DP_t$.

This claim derives the impact effect of any shock. We expect that after the initial impact effect both DP and SD will gradually go back to the baseline (steady state). Figure 19.3 illustrates this possibility by plotting a theoretical impulse response functions to a shock of DP in a vector auto regression (VAR) with two variables: DP and SD.

In the UST model of chapter 15 with iid money supply shocks the distribution of quoted relative prices does not change in response to the realization of the money supply. In this model equilibrium prices are proportional to the beginning of period money supply:

$$P_{st} = p_s M_t, \tag{19.7}$$

where P_{st} is the dollar price in market s and p_s is the normalized price in market s. The rate of inflation is the same for all markets and is given by:

$$DP_t = \ln P_{st} - \ln P_{st-1} = \ln M_t - \ln M_{t-1} \quad \text{for all s.} \tag{19.8}$$

Thus prices adjust with a one period lag to changes in the money supply.

The average quoted price is given by:

$$P_t = \sum_s \psi_s P_{st}, \tag{19.9}$$

where ψ_s is the fraction of output allocated to market s. The variance of the log of prices is:

$$\text{VAR}(\ln P_t) = \sum_s \psi_s (\ln P_{ts} - \ln P_t)^2. \tag{19.10}$$

We define the stationary mean and variance of normalized prices by: $\ln p = \sum_s \psi_s \ln p_s$ and $\text{VAR}(\ln p) = \sum_s \psi_s (\ln p_s - \ln p)^2$. Since M_t is common across all markets we may use (19.7) to write:

$$\text{VAR}(\ln P_t) = \text{VAR}(\ln p) + \text{VAR}(\ln M_t) = \text{VAR}(\ln p). \tag{19.11}$$

This says that a shock to the money supply does not affect the variance of the log of dollar prices. (In general, the variance of the log of a variable does not depend on the unit at which this variable is measured.)

It follows that in response to a money supply shock we should observe an increase in the inflation rate (19.8) but no effect on the variance of the log of prices (19.11).

> *Claim 2:* In the UST model a monetary shock affects the current rate of inflation but does not affect the (current and future) variance of relative prices and future inflation rates.

Figure 19.4 illustrates the prediction of the UST model about the responses to a DP shock in a two variables VAR.

It was shown that the staggered price-setting model and the UST model have different predictions about the response of DP and SD to a monetary shock. Estimating these responses may therefore be useful for distinguishing between the two competing hypotheses.

Vector auto regression analysis

The staggered price-setting model suggests the following 2 variables vector auto regression relationships:

$$DP_t = a + b_1 DP_{t-1} + \cdots + b_q DP_{t-q}$$
$$+ c_1 SD_{t-1} + \cdots + c_q SD_{t-q} + \theta_t \tag{19.12}$$

$$SD_t = A + B_0 DP_t + B_1 DP_{t-1} + \cdots + B_q DP_{t-q}$$
$$+ C_1 SD_{t-1} + \cdots + C_q SD_{t-q} + \varepsilon_t. \tag{19.13}$$

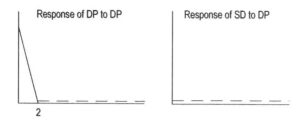

Figure 19.4   Theoretical impulse response functions in the UST model

The error term θ in the DP equation may arise as a result of serially independent money supply shocks. It may also arise as a result of sampling errors: It makes a difference if we sample sellers who changed their nominal price or sellers who did not change their nominal price. Since the contemporaneous level of DP is an explanatory variable in the SD equation (and serves as a proxy for the money supply shock), the error term ε in the SD equation is due to sampling errors. Since current DP affects the standard deviation we place DP first when estimating the vector auto regression (VAR). The coefficients in (19.12) and (19.13) may be product specific if we allow for product specific length of the contract (N).

Under the UST model with a random walk money supply, all the coefficients in (19.12) and (19.13) are zero, except the intercept. We therefore estimate the impulse response functions twice. We first allow for product specific coefficients and then impose the same coefficients on all products.

Allowing for product specific coefficients

We start by running vector auto regressions for each product separately, allowing for four lags. The typical VAR had 23 observations (months) and two variables: DP, SD (in this order). We then compute the average impulse response (AV) across all the products in the sample (about 25 products per sample). To obtain this average we computed the impulse response function in a table form for each product and took the average (AV) across products. We also calculated the standard deviation (STD) across the 25 products.

Figures 19.5–19.7 describe the average response (AV) and two bounds: AV + STD is the average plus the standard deviation and AV − STD is the average minus the standard deviation. In all the samples the average DP returns to the baseline in the month following the shock. The average effect of a shock to DP on SD is close to zero. These findings are consistent with the theoretical impulse response functions from the UST model but not with the staggered price setting model.

Imposing the same coefficients on all products

We now impose the same VAR coefficients across products. We think of a hypothetical world that lives for GT periods, where G is the number of products in the sample (about 25 goods

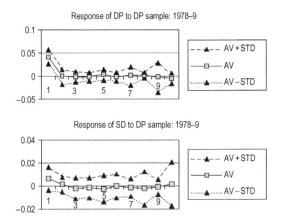

Figure 19.5   Average (across products) impulse response functions for the 1978–1979 sample

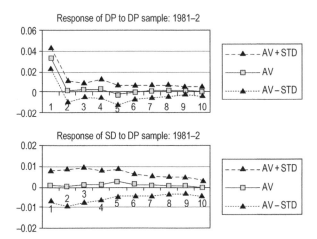

Figure 19.6   Average (across products) impulse response functions for the 1981–1982 sample

per sample) and T is the number of months (23). In this hypothetical world agents produce one product only and each 23 months the identity of the product changes.

We create an artificial time series of about $(23)(25) = 575$ periods.[6] The results of this exercise are in figures 19.8–19.10. These impulse response functions look very much like the average computed in figures 19.5–19.7 and may serve as a test for robustness.

Conclusions

We used datasets on prices by products and stores from three inflationary periods in Israel to estimate two variables VAR: DP (average inflation across sellers who sell the same product) and SD (the standard deviation of prices in log forms across sellers who sell the

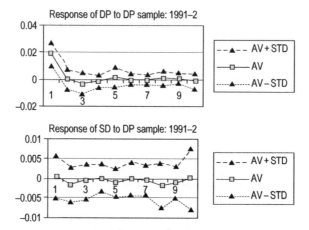

Figure 19.7   Average (across products) impulse response functions for the 1991–1992 sample

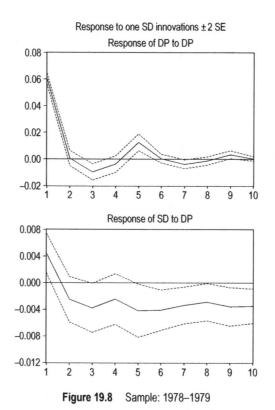

Figure 19.8   Sample: 1978–1979

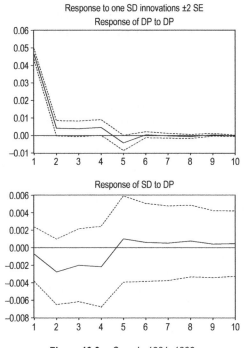

Figure 19.9   Sample 1981–1982

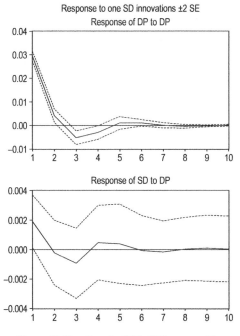

Figure 19.10   Sample 1991–1992 comparable

same product). We found that a shock to DP has no effect on SD and no persistent effect on DP. These findings are not consistent with a staggered price setting model of the type considered by Taylor (1980) and CKM (2000) but are consistent with a UST model.

NOTES

1   These data were collected by Israel's Central Bureau of Statistics as inputs for computing the CPI and are described in Eden (2001b). The first two samples were used by Lach and Tsiddon (1992).

2   There are models that assume a cost for changing nominal prices which depend on the size of the change. For example, Rotemberg (1982) assumes that the cost depends on the square of the price change. These type of models leads to a four parameters policy (u, b, I, i). A store that hit the upper bound u will change its real price to I while a store that hits the lower bound b will change its real price to i. Since large nominal price changes are costly, i < I. This means that the real price of stores with $\Delta p > 0$ should be less than the real price of stores with $\Delta p < 0$. The findings in table 19.3 do not support this prediction.

3   Here we use the entire sample to compute R. In table 19.3 we used the subsample of stores that actually changed their nominal price.

4   The following sections are based on Baharad and Eden (2001).

5   The derivation is as follows. A fraction $1/N$ post P. A fraction $(N - 1)/N$ post 1. $\Delta = \ln P$. The average of the log of prices is: $(1/N) \ln P = \Delta/N$. The variance of the log of prices is:

$$
\begin{aligned}
\text{VAR}_t &= (\Delta/N)^2[(N - 1)/N] + (\Delta - \Delta/N)^2(1/N) \\
&= (DP)^2[(N - 1)/N] + (\Delta - DP)^2(1/N) \\
&= (DP)^2[(N - 1)/N] + [\Delta^2 - 2\Delta DP + (DP)^2](1/N) \\
&= (DP)^2 + (\Delta^2 - 2\Delta DP)(1/N) \\
&= (DP)^2 + \Delta^2(1 - 2/N)(1/N).
\end{aligned}
$$

6   We separate each good by an appropriate number of blanks so that the lags of product i will not be taken as observations from product i − 1.

CHAPTER 20

The Friedman Rule in a UST Model

The Friedman rule was discussed in the first part of this book and was found to be rather robust. But in practice this policy recommendation is not implemented. One possible explanation is in the cost of collecting explicit taxes (Bordo and Vegh, 2002). Here we explore the possibility that an operative bonds market may play a useful role and therefore a small deviation from the Frieman rule may be desirable.

The argument is based on Eden (1986) and Williamson (1996). In the absence of an operative market for bonds taste shocks may cause uncertainty about nominal demand because agents who experience negative taste shocks do not spend their money. In a UST model this uncertainty about demand leads to waste (less than full capacity utilization).

Adding an operative bonds market may elevate the problem because agents who experience negative taste shocks lend their money to agents who want to spend it. As a result all the money supply is spent regardless of the aggregate taste shock, there is no uncertainty about nominal demand and capacity is fully utilized.

When trading in the bonds market is costly, an operative bonds market requires a positive nominal interest rate. In this case the policy-maker faces a trade-off between capacity utilization and intertemporal distortion.

20.1 A SINGLE-ASSET ECONOMY

We use a cash-in-advance model in which the uncertainty about demand arises as a result of taste shocks rather than shocks to the money supply. There are N infinitely lived households. Each household consists of two people: a seller (worker) and a buyer. At the beginning of the period the worker goes to work. The buyer learns about his demand (the realization of the taste shock) and if he wants to consume he takes the available money and goes shopping. After trade in the goods market is completed the seller takes his revenue in the form of cash. At the end of the period the two members of the household reunite and consume whatever the shopper has bought.

The amount of money available to household h at the beginning of period t is M_t^h dollars. In addition, all households get the same perfectly anticipated lump sum transfer of G_t dollars.

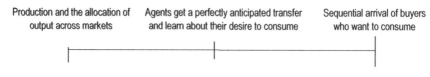

| Production and the allocation of output across markets | Agents get a perfectly anticipated transfer and learn about their desire to consume | Sequential arrival of buyers who want to consume |

Figure 20.1   A single asset economy

The average pre-transfer amount of money is: $M_t = (1/N) \sum_{h=1}^{N} M_t^h$. The rate of change in the money supply is constant over time and is given by: $M_{t+1}/M_t = 1 + \mu \geq \beta$, where $0 < \beta < 1$ is the household's discount factor.

The representative household is risk neutral and its single period utility is: $\tilde{\theta} c_t - v(L_t)$, where c is the quantity consumed, L is the quantity produced and $\tilde{\theta}$ is a random variable that takes two possible realizations: $\tilde{\theta} = 0$ if the household does not want to consume and $\tilde{\theta} = 1$ if it does. The cost function v( ) has the standard properties of a cost function ($v' > 0$ and $v'' > 0$ everywhere).

A fraction $\tilde{\phi}$ of the buyers experience $\tilde{\theta} = 1$ and want to consume. The variable $\tilde{\phi}$ is an i.i.d. random variable with S possible realizations: $\phi_1 < \phi_2 < \ldots < \phi_S$. For notational convenience we set $\phi_0 = 0$. The probability that $\tilde{\phi} = \phi_s$ is Π_s and the probability that $\tilde{\phi} \geq \phi_s$ is q_s. The probability that $\tilde{\theta} = 1$ is the same for all agents and is equal to ϕ_s if the aggregate state is s.

Buyers who want to consume spend all the money they have. From the seller's point of view nominal demand in aggregate state s is $\phi_s M_t(1 + \mu)$ dollars or ϕ_s normalized dollars, where here normalized magnitudes are nominal magnitudes divided by the post-transfer money supply, $M_t(1 + \mu)$.

As in previous UST models buyers arrive sequentially at the market place. The first ϕ_1 normalized dollars arrive with certainty and buy in the first market at the price p_1 (normalized dollars per unit). After transactions in the first market have been completed there can be two possible events: either trade ends or an additional batch of $\phi_2 - \phi_1$ normalized dollars arrive (with probability q_2). If the second batch arrives it buys in the second market at the price p_2. In general, after the completion of trade in market s there can be two possibilities: either trade ends or an additional batch of $\phi_{s+1} - \phi_s$ arrives and open market $s + 1$.

Figure 20.1 illustrates the sequence of events within the period. The worker produces at the beginning of the period and allocates his output across the potential markets: k_s to market s. Buyers then receive a transfer payment and learn about their desire to consume. They then arrive sequentially at the marketplace.

Given that s markets open this period, a normalized dollar that is spent this period will buy on average:

$$z_s = \sum_{j=1}^{s} (\upsilon_j^s / p_j), \tag{20.1}$$

units, where $\upsilon_j^s = (\phi_j - \phi_{j-1})/\phi_s$, is the probability that the dollar will buy in market j when s markets open. A household that starts with m normalized dollars will get a transfer payment of g normalized dollars and will consume on average $\sum_{s=1}^{S} \Pi_s \phi_s (m + g) z_s$ units in the current period.

The Bellman equation that describes the household's choice problem is:

$$V(m) = \max_{k_s} \sum_{s=1}^{S} \Pi_s \phi_s (m + g) z_s - v \left(\sum_{s=1}^{S} k_s \right)$$

$$+ \beta \sum_{s=1}^{S} \Pi_s \left\{ \phi_s V \left[\left(\sum_{j=1}^{S} p_j k_j \right) \omega \right] + (1 - \phi_s) V \left[\left(m + g + \sum_{j=1}^{S} p_j k_j \right) \omega \right] \right\},$$

$$(20.2)$$

where lower case letters denote nominal magnitudes in terms of normalized dollars, $\omega = (1 + \mu)^{-1}$ is used to convert current normalized dollars into next period's normalized dollars and the maximization is with respect to k_s. Here $V(m)$ is the maximum expected utility that the household can achieve if he starts with a pre-transfer balances of m normalized dollars; $\sum_{s=1}^{S} \Pi_s \phi_s (m + g) z_s$ is the expected current consumption and $v(\sum_{s=1}^{S} k_s)$ is the utility cost of producing $L = \sum_{s=1}^{S} k_s$ units. To understand the future utility terms note that the worker's revenue is $\sum_{j=1}^{S} p_j k_j$ if s markets open this period. When $\tilde{\theta} = 1$ the buyer spends everything he has and the household will have at the end of the period $\sum_{j=1}^{S} p_j k_j$ normalized dollars. This is multiplied by ω to convert it to next period's normalized dollars. When $\tilde{\theta} = 0$ the buyer does not spend and the household will start next period with $(m + g + \sum_{j=1}^{S} p_j k_j)\omega$ normalized dollars.

To state the first order conditions for an interior solution to (20.2), let

$$\zeta = \sum_{s=1}^{S} \Pi_s (1 - \phi_s), \qquad (20.3)$$

denote the probability that $\tilde{\theta} = 0$. The expected utility from a normalized dollar held at the beginning of the period (before the realization of the taste shock) is:

$$V' = z = \sum_{s=1}^{S} \Pi_s \phi_s z_s + \zeta \beta \omega z \quad \text{or} \quad z = (1 - \zeta \beta \omega)^{-1} \sum_{s=1}^{S} \Pi_s \phi_s z_s. \qquad (20.4)$$

The first order conditions can be written in the familiar way:

$$q_s \beta p_s \omega z = \beta p_1 \omega z = v' \left(\sum_{s=1}^{S} k_s \right). \qquad (20.5)$$

The expected utility from supplying a unit to market s is $q_s p_s \omega z$: If the market opens (with probability q_s) the seller gets p_s normalized dollars which are worth $p_s \omega$ next period's normalized dollars and bring on average $p_s \omega z$ utils. Condition (20.5) says that the discounted expected utils from supplying a unit is the same across markets and is equal to the marginal cost.

Equilibrium requires (20.5) and the market-clearing conditions:

$$p_s k_s = \phi_s - \phi_{s-1}; \quad \text{for all s}. \qquad (20.6)$$

We now show the following claim.

Claim 1: In equilibrium $\beta p_1 \omega z < \beta \omega$.

The claim implies that the equilibrium (expected discounted) real wage is less than $\beta \omega$ and therefore even if we adopt the Friedman rule and set $\beta \omega = 1$, the real wage will be less than unity. The reason is in the uncertainty about demand which leads on average to less than full capacity utilization.

Proof: The equilibrium condition (20.5) implies $p_1 < p_s$ for all $s > 1$. Therefore, $z_s = \sum_{j=1}^{s}(\upsilon_j^s/p_j) < 1/p_1$ and $z = (1 - \zeta\beta\omega)^{-1}\sum_{s=1}^{S}\Pi_s\phi_s z_s < (1/p_1)(1 - \zeta)(1 - \zeta\beta\omega)^{-1} \le (1/p_1)$. It follows that $\beta p_1 \omega z < \beta \omega$. □

20.2   ADDING A COSTLESS BONDS MARKET

We now add a costless bonds market. The sequence of events within each period is as follows. First the worker chooses capacity k and buyers get a perfectly anticipated transfer payment of g normalized dollars. They then go to a bond market. Buyers who experience $\theta = 0$ and do not want to consume lend to buyers who experience $\theta = 1$ and do want to consume. After buyers complete trade in the bonds market they go to the goods markets. Buyers who want to consume arrive sequentially at the market place and spend all the cash that they have, including the borrowed cash. Since all the money is spent there is no uncertainty about nominal spending and only one market opens.

We use p to denote the price, $R = 1+i \ge 0$, to denote the gross nominal interest rate and b_s to denote the amount borrowed in state s by buyers who want to consume. It is assumed that buyers who do not want to consume lend all their money at any positive nominal interest rate.

The Bellman equation that describes the household's problem is now:

$$V(m) = \max_{k\,b_s} \sum_{s=1}^{S}\Pi_s\phi_s(m + g + b_s)/p - v(k)$$

$$+ \beta\sum_{s=1}^{S}\Pi_s\{\phi_s V[pk\omega - b_s R\omega] + (1 - \phi_s)V[\omega R(m + g) + pk\omega]\}. \qquad (20.7)$$

The expected utility from a normalized dollar held at the beginning of the period (before the realization of the taste shock) is now:

$$z = (1 - \zeta)(1/p) + \zeta\beta\omega Rz \quad \text{or} \quad z = (1 - \zeta\beta\omega R)^{-1}(1 - \zeta)/p. \qquad (20.8)$$

Note that when $R = 1/\omega\beta$, $z = 1/p$. This leads to the following claim.

Claim 2: The demand for borrowing is infinitely elastic at the interest rate $R = 1/\omega\beta$.

To see this claim note that a buyer who realizes a taste shock $\theta = 1$ and borrows a normalized dollar will get 1/p units of additional consumption in the current period at the cost of $\beta\omega Rz$ utils. When $R = 1/\omega\beta$, $z = 1/p$ and the benefit is equal to the cost.

Therefore in equilibrium the interest rate is R $= 1/\omega\beta$. At the equilibrium interest rate, $z = 1/p$ and the expected discounted real wage is $\beta\omega pz = \beta\omega$. The first order condition that governs the labor choice is:

$$v'(k) = \beta\omega. \tag{20.9}$$

We can now compare (20.9) and claim 1 and conclude that,

Claim 3: The introduction of the bonds market increased the expected discounted real wage, labor supply and capacity utilization.

This is because trading in bonds eliminates the uncertainty about demand.

As in section 15.4, welfare here can be measured by the expected discounted real wage, w. The single period welfare of the representative household is: $A(w) = \max_k wk - v(k)$ and the household ex-ante life-time utility is: $A(w) \sum_{t=1}^{\infty} \beta^t = A(w)/\rho$. Since the introduction of the bonds market increases w, it improves welfare. Since $\omega \leq 1/\beta$ welfare is maximized when $\omega = 1/\beta$ and $w = 1$.

To derive the optimal ω in an alternative way we may consider the problem of a social planner. Since the utility function is linear the distribution of consumption across households does not matter and we may state the social welfare function as $k - v(k)$, where k is output per household. Maximizing the social welfare function leads to:

$$v'(k) = 1. \tag{20.10}$$

The first order condition (20.9) implies that the equilibrium outcome is efficient only if the Friedman rule is adopted and $\omega = 1/\beta$.

20.3 COSTLY TRANSACTIONS IN BONDS

We now introduce a cost for lending: It costs δ units of consumption per normalized dollar lent. Borrowing is costless.

We know from the previous section that when the bonds market operates only one goods market opens, $z = 1/p$ and $R = 1/\beta\omega$. Potential lenders will choose to lend only if:

$$\beta\omega Rz - \delta > \beta\omega z \quad \text{or} \quad 1 - \beta\omega > \delta/z = \delta p. \tag{20.11}$$

Therefore,

Claim 4: Under the Friedman rule, $\beta\omega = 1$, and the bonds market does not operate.

This and claim 3 suggests that:

Claim 5: When δ is small and strictly positive, the Friedman rule is not optimal.

To elaborate, note that when $\beta\omega = 1$, the bonds market does not operate, there is uncertainty about nominal spending and the equilibrium real wage is less than unity (claim 1). The policy-maker can choose $\beta\omega = 1 - \delta p$. In this case the bonds market does operate and the real wage is given by $1 - \delta p$. When δ is small the second alternative dominates.

Conclusions

At the Friedman rule the nominal interest rate is zero and no one pays the cost for trading in the bonds market. As a result there is uncertainty about demand arising from aggregate taste shocks. When the nominal interest rate is sufficiently high, agents who do not want to spend lend their money to agents who do want to spend and the entire money supply is spent regardless of the realization of the aggregate taste shock. The adoption of the Friedman rule may therefore increase uncertainty about nominal demand and reduce average capacity utilization.

Williamson (1996) reaches a similar conclusion in a model that distinguishes between credit and cash goods (as in Lucas and Stokey [1987]). In his model, cash goods are sold on sequential markets while credit goods are sold on a Walrasian market. Supply choices are made first. Then agents experience a taste shock and go to the bonds market. Entering the bonds market is costless and all households experience the same taste shock. At the bonds market the monetary authorities may transfer money to the agents. It turns out that smoothing the nominal interest at the level of zero requires random changes in the money supply. These money surprises reduce average capacity utilization because cash goods are sold on sequential markets. In a calibration exercise Williamson finds that the Friedman rule is not optimal because it requires too much unanticipated variations in the money supply that cause a substantial reduction in average capacity utilization.

CHAPTER 21

Sequential International Trade[1]

The following observations have provoked a lot of discussion in the international trade literature: (1) countries trade in similar goods; (2) there are government made barriers to trade; and (3) there is a strong correlation between changes in the real and the nominal exchange rates.

These observations are sometimes regarded as puzzles because they are at odds with the implications of the standard Walrasian model. On the basis of the standard model we expect that only the benefits from trade in goods that are not close substitutes will cover transaction and transportation costs. In the classic Heckscher-Ohlin model countries with a relatively large endowment of labor export labor intensive goods and import capital intensive goods. We also expect that in the absence of transactions costs governments will reach efficient agreements among themselves and promote free trade. Finally, the law of one price suggests no correlation between changes in the real and the nominal exchange rate but Obstfeld and Rogoff (1996) argue that for countries with floating currencies and open capital markets the exchange rates are an order of magnitude more volatile than the ratio of the CPIs which hardly moves at all (p. 606, see their figure 9.2). An immediate corollary is "that the short-run volatility of real exchange rates is very similar to that of nominal exchange rates." Earlier Mussa (1986) has observed that an increase in the volatility of the nominal exchange rate leads to an increase in the volatility of the real exchange rate.

Models with increasing returns to scale and monopolistic competition are often used to account for the trade in similar goods puzzle. See for example, Helpman and Krugman (1985). In Newbery and Stiglitz (1984) there is trade in the same good to smooth consumption over time but in a given period each country is either exporting the good or importing it. It does not do both. Newbery and Stiglitz show that when agents are risk averse and insurance markets are incomplete trade may be Pareto inferior to autarky. This may provide a partial explanation for the barriers to trade question. A different approach is taken in the political economy literature. Schattschneider (1935) and Olson (1971) argue that the benefits from a tariff is concentrated in a relatively small group while the cost is spread over a large group that cannot form an effective lobby.

Rogoff survey the extensive literature on the purchasing power parity puzzle. He concludes that

> International goods markets, though becoming more integrated all the time, remain quite segmented, with large trading frictions across a broad range of goods. These frictions may be due to transportation costs, threatened or actual tariffs, nontariff barriers, information costs, or lack of labor mobility. As a consequence of various adjustment costs, there is a large buffer within which nominal exchange rates can move without producing an immediate proportional response in relative domestic prices. (Rogoff 1996, p. 665)

Here we analyze these questions in an uncertain and sequential trade (UST) model that assumes a competitive environment, a single good, constant or diminishing returns to scale and risk neutrality. Residents of the same country are ex-ante identical. There are no "natural barriers to trade" like transportation costs. The only so called friction is the UST friction: buyers arrive sequentially and some irreversible trade must be made before the complete resolution of uncertainty about demand and supply.

We discuss the incentives for trade from the individual agent's point of view, from the individual country's point of view and from the world's point of view. We also discuss the effect of trade on output. This is done in two models: A real model that assumes a constant per unit cost of production and a single unit demand function and a monetary cash-in-advance model that assumes increasing marginal cost of production.

21.1 A REAL MODEL

We now apply the analysis in 14.4 to international trade problems. For convenience we repeat the description of the model.

We consider an economy with two dates ($t = 0, 1$) and two goods (X and Y with lower case letters denoting quantities).

There are S possible aggregate states of nature (indexed s) where state s occurs with probability Π_s. There are J types of sellers. The ability to produce depends on the aggregate state. If a seller is able to produce he can produce as many units as he wants at the price of λ units of Y per unit of X. The number of type j sellers is m_j and a fraction μ_{js} of them can produce in state of nature s. The total number of sellers who can produce in state of nature s is:

$$M_s = \sum_j \mu_{js} m_j. \tag{21.1}$$

There are J types of buyers. A type j buyer demands one unit of X at any price less than v_j if he wants to consume and zero otherwise. There are n_j type j buyers and in state s a fraction ϕ_{js} of them want to consume. Aggregate demand per seller over all type j buyers in state s at the price p is thus:

$$N_{js}(p) = \phi_{js} n_j / M_s \quad \text{if } v_j \geq p \text{ and zero otherwise.} \tag{21.2}$$

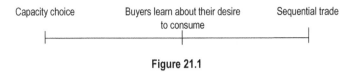

Figure 21.1

Aggregate demand per seller over all types in state s is:

$$N_s(p) = \sum_j N_{js}(p). \tag{21.3}$$

Production occurs at $t = 0$. The state becomes public information only after the completion of trade at $t = 1$.

The $\sum_{j=1}^{J} \phi_{js} n_j$ buyers who want to consume form a line by a lottery that treats everyone symmetrically. After the line is formed, buyers arrive at the market place one by one according to their place in the line and choose whether to buy at the cheapest available offer. Figure 21.1 illustrates the sequence of events.

From the individual seller's point of view demand arrives in batches. The first batch with Δ_1 buyers per seller arrives with certainty. After the buyers in the first batch complete trade a second batch of Δ_2 buyers (per seller) may arrive. In general, there can be two possible events after buyers in batch i complete trade: Either trade ends or an additional batch of Δ_{i+1} buyers arrives.

Sellers are price-takers. They behave as if they can sell any amount at the price P_i to buyers in batch i if it arrives. Each seller makes a contingent plan to sell x_i units to batch i if it arrives.

It helps to think in terms of markets that open sequentially. The first batch of buyers opens the first market. If the second batch of buyers arrives, it opens the second market and so on. The price in market i is P_i, the quantity supplied to market i is x_i per seller and the quantity demanded in market i is Δ_i per seller. In equilibrium markets that open are cleared:

$$\Delta_i = x_i \quad \text{for all i.} \tag{21.4}$$

Trade occurs sequentially but does not take real time. The only information that the sellers receive during the trading process is about the number of batches that arrive: at stage i of the trading process sellers know that i batches already arrived.

The probability that market i will open, q_i, the price in market i, P_i, and the size of the batch that will trade in this market if it opens (Δ_i) are all determined endogenously. An algorithm for computing these equilibrium magnitudes is as follows. The first market opens when some buyers want to consume (regardless of their reservation price). The probability that the first market will open is the probability that a state with strictly positive demand occurs. This probability is denoted by q_1. The price in the first market is: $P_1 = \lambda/q_1$. At this price suppliers to the first market make zero expected profits ($q_1 P_1 = \lambda$). Market 2 opens if there are some buyers who wanted to buy in the first market but could not. In general, an additional market opens after transactions in market $i - 1$ are complete if there is residual demand: There are buyers who wanted to buy in market $i - 1$ at the price P_{i-1} but could not make a buy. We compute the probability that there is residual demand after trade in market $i - 1$ is complete and denote it by q_i. We use this probability to compute the zero expected profit price in market i: $P_i = \lambda/q_i$. To determine Δ_i we compute the minimum (strictly positive) number of unsatisfied customers who are willing to pay the price P_i.

A more general treatment is in 14.4.1. We now turn to examples in which the allocation is not necessarily efficient. Some of the examples here are taken from 14.4 and are repeated here for convenience.

Example 1: There are n buyers in each country. Type 1 buyers reside in country 1 and each demands one unit if the price is less than 7 and zero otherwise ($v_1 = 7, \phi_{11} = \phi_{12} = 1$). Type 2 buyers reside in country 2 and each demands one unit if the price is less than 7 and s = 2 and demands zero otherwise ($v_2 = 7, \phi_{21} = 0$ and $\phi_{22} = 1$). There is one seller in each country who can produce in both states at the unit cost of $\lambda = 5$.

Under *autarky* there will be only one market (a standard Walrasian market) in country 1 that opens with certainty at the price of $\lambda = 5$. The quantity produced in country 1 is n and the generated surplus is $(v_1 - \lambda)n = 2n$. There is a market in country 2 that opens with probability $1/2$ at the price of 10 but there is no demand in country 2 at this price. The quantity produced in country 2 is zero and the generated surplus is zero.

We now allow *free trade*. The demand at the price 5 is n in state 1 and 2n in state 2. The minimum demand per seller at the price of $\lambda = 5$ and hence the number of buyers in the first market is: $\Delta_1 = n$.

Market 2 will open if there are buyers who wanted to buy at the first market but could not. This will occur in state 2 with probability $q_2 = 1/2$ and the price in the second market is therefore: $P_2 = 2\lambda = 10$. At this price there is no demand in market 2. Total production is therefore n and total surplus is 2n.

In state 2 $(1/2)n$ buyers from each country make a buy in market 1. The surplus is therefore divided between the two countries: The buyers in country 1 get on average a surplus of 1.5n while the buyers in country 2 get on average a surplus of 0.5n. Autarky is better for the residents in country 1 and free trade is better for the residents of country 2.

Trading in ex-ante contracts: Suppose that we allow ex-ante trade (at t = 0) in non-contingent promises to deliver X. The equilibrium price of a promise to deliver a unit of X is 5. Only type 1 buyers will choose to buy this contract and the resulting surplus is 2n.

Thus, here allowing for trade in ex-ante contracts is equivalent to autarky.

Example 2: The same as example 1 but now $v_1 = 10$.

Under *autarky* there will be only one market in country 1 that opens with certainty at the price of $\lambda = 5$. There is a market in country 2 that opens with probability $1/2$ at the price of 10 but there is no demand in country 2 at this price. The quantity produced in country 1 is n and the generated surplus is 5n.

To define the market structure under *free trade* we specify the demand at the price of 5 per seller as a function of the state: n in state 1 and 2n in state 2. The minimum demand at the price of 5 is therefore n and this is the number of buyers served in the first market. Market 2 opens with probability $1/2$ at the price of 10. When s = 2, $(1/2)n$ buyers from each type make a buy in market 1 and the number of unsatisfied customers is $(1/2)n$ of each type. But at the price of 10 only type 1 buyers are willing to buy. Therefore, $\Delta_2 = (1/2)n$. Production is the total amount supplied to both markets: $(1.5)n$ units at the cost of $(7.5)n$. The surplus in state 1 is: $(v_1 - 7.5)n = (2.5)n$. The surplus in state 2 is: $(v_1 + (1/2)v_2 - 7.5)n = 6n$. The average surplus is $(4.25)n$.

The world surplus is less than under autarky.

Table 21.1 Autarky, free trade, and monopoly

	World surplus	Surplus to buyers in country 1	Surplus to buyers in country 2	Output
Type 1 wants to consume in both states, type 2 wants to consume in state 2 only				
$v_1 = v_2 = 7$ (example 1):				
Autarky	2	2	0	1
Free trade	2	1.5	0.5	1
monopoly	2	0	0	1
$v_1 = 10, v_2 = 7$ (example 2):				
Autarky	5	5	0	1
Free trade	4.25	3.75	0.5	1.5
monopoly	5	0	0	1
Type 1 wants to consume in state 1 and type 2 in state 2				
$v_1 = v_2 = 7$ (example 3):				
Autarky	0	0	0	0
Free trade	2	1	1	1
monopoly	2	0	0	1

Table 21.1 gives the results in examples 1–3 when $n = 1$. The first column is world surplus calculated as the expected value of the output sold minus the cost of production. Then we have the surplus of the buyers in each country and the world output. There is one type of buyer (seller) per country. v_j is the reservation price of type j buyer. In examples 1–2 type 1 buyers have stable demand. In example 3 demand is negatively correlated.

A *monopoly* (that faces the same informational constraints as the sellers in our model) will choose $P_1 = 10$ and produce n units making a profit of 5n. This is one way of showing that in the general case the UST allocation may not be efficient in the relevant sense.

Example 3: Type 1 wants to consume in state 1 only while type 2 wants to consume only in state 2. They are both willing to pay up to 7 units for the good in the state that they want to consume.

Under *autarky* there will be no trade.

Under *free trade* n units are supplied to a single market that opens with certainty at the price of 5. In state 1 type 1 buyers buy n units and in state 2 type 2 buyers buy n units. Surplus is 2n.

In this example trade improve welfare in both countries.

Table 21.1 summarizes the results of the above three examples. It shows that when agents differ both in their demand function and the probability that they want to consume free trade may either increase or decrease the world's surplus. The country with the stable demand tends to lose from trade while the country with the unstable demand tends to gain from trade. These conclusions are very different from what one will get from a standard Walrasian model of trade. The reason is in the UST friction: Irreversible choices are made before the state is known. On a less abstract level there are two reasons why free trade may change the world surplus relative to autarky. It may reduce average capacity utilization and it may allow buyers with low valuation to get the good before buyers with high valuation who end up getting rationed.

Note that the adverse effect of trade on welfare occurs here under risk neutrality and is therefore different from the result in Newbery and Stiglitz (1984). In their model the strongest case against trade is in the case of perfectly negative correlation between the supply and demand conditions in the two countries. As shown by example 3, in our model this is the strongest case for (rather than against) trade.

Intra-industry trade

In the present model the marginal cost is constant and the location of production is not determined. Furthermore, sellers are indifferent about the allocation of supplies to the sequential trade markets. To determine the trade patterns we need to break these ties. We therefore introduce the following assumptions: (1) the quantity produced is the same across all sellers who can produce and (2) sellers allocate their output across markets to minimize expected trade.

The first assumption can be justified in terms of a model in which sellers face increasing marginal cost schedules (strictly convex cost functions). The second assumption may be justified in terms of transportation costs but other considerations (like risk aversion) may lead to a different conclusion. We therefore regard the second assumption as ad-hoc.

In *example 1* each seller produces $(1/2)n$ units. When $s = 1$ country 2 exports $(1/2)n$ units of the good. When $s = 2$ each seller sells to buyers in his own country and there is no trade.

In *example 2* each seller produces $(3/4)n$ units. It can be shown that the minimal trade allocation is symmetric: Each seller supplies $1/2$ a unit to the first market and $1/4$ units to the second market. When $s = 1$, country 2 exports $1/2$ a unit and when $s = 2$ country 2 exports $1/4$ units.

To see whether we can generate an example in which country 2 simultaneously exports and imports the good We consider the more general case in which π is the probability of state 2 and $v_1 = 5/\pi$ is the reservation price of the buyers in country 1. All the other features of the example remain unchanged. We now show:

Claim: If $\pi \leq 1/3$, expected trade is minimized when seller 1 allocates his entire output to market 1 (and seller 2 allocates $(1/4)n$ units to market 1 and $(1/2)n$ units to market 2).

Proof: Let X (Y) denote the supply of seller 1 to the first (second) market and let lower case letters denote the supply of seller 2. These magnitudes should be positive and satisfy the following conditions: $X + x = 1$; $Y + y = 1/2$; $X + Y = x + y = 3/4$. When $s = 1$, world trade is x. When $s = 2$, world trade is: $y + \max\{X, x\} - 1/2$. The expected trade is:

$$(1 - \pi)x + \pi(y + \max(X, x) - 1/2]$$

$$= (1 - \pi)x + \pi(3/4 - x) + \pi[\max(1 - x, x) - 1/2]. \qquad (21.5)$$

We now look at the problem minimizing (21.5) subject to: $x \geq 1/4$. When $x = 1/4$ and $\pi \leq 1/3$ the derivative of (21.5) with respect to x is positive and therefore $x = 1/4$ minimizes the expected trade expression (21.5). Note also that $x > X$ cannot be a solution because the derivative of (21.5) is strictly positive in this case. We have thus shown that $x = 1/4$ is the minimal trade allocation. $\qquad \square$

Note that under the condition of the claim, in state 2, country 2 both exports and imports the same good: It imports $(1/4)n$ units at the price of 5 and exports $(1/2)n$ units at the price of 10. We have thus shown that the UST model can be used to generate examples in which intra-industry trade occurs and in which a country can both imports the good and exports it at the same period.

Supply shocks

Uncertainty about supply seems to be the more important source of departure from efficiency. We now turn to discuss this case and show by example that barriers to trade may be beneficial.

Example 4: In country 1 there is a seller who can produce in both states. In country 2 there is a seller who can produce only in state 1. Type 1 must choose production before he knows the state.

Buyers in country 1 want to consume in both states and are willing to pay up to 10 for a unit. Buyers in country 2 do not want to consume good X (in any state).

Under *autarky* there is one market that opens with certainty in country 1 and the price in this market is 5. Production in country 1 is n and buyers in country 1 get a surplus of 5n. There is no production in country 2.

Under *free trade*, total demand per seller at the price of 5 is: $(1/2)n$ in state 1 and n in state 2. The minimum demand per seller and hence the number of buyers in the first market is: $\Delta_1 = (1/2)n$.

In state 2 there will be some unsatisfied buyers. The probability that market 2 will open is $1/2$ and the price in this market is 10. The demand in the second market if it opens is $(1/2)n$.

Type 1 seller supplies $(1/2)n$ at the price 5 and $(1/2)n$ at the price of 10. Type 2 supplies in state 1 $(1/2)n$ units at the price of 5. When s = 2, n units are produced and the surplus is $(10 - 5)n = 5n$. When s = 1, 1.5n units are produced and the surplus is: $(10 - 7.5)n = 2.5n$. The average surplus is: 3.75n.

Thus here free trade is Pareto inferior to autarky.

Dumping

According to the World Trade Organization definition, dumping occurs "if a company exports a product at a price lower than the price it normally charges on its own home market."[2] In our model the average price in country 2 may be higher than the average price in country 1 if there is more demand uncertainty in country 2. In this case a seller located in country 2 may be accused of dumping. But anti-dumping laws tend to reduce welfare in this case.

Example 5: Buyers in country 1 want to consume in both states and are willing to pay up to 7. Buyers in country 2 want to consume only in state 2 and are willing to pay up to 10. There is one seller who is located in country 2 and can produce in both states.

Under *autarky* there will be no supply to country 1. In country 2 there is one market that opens with probability $1/2$ at the price of 10. Production is n and this amount is sold only in state 2. Surplus in state 1 is: $-5n$. Surplus in state 2 is: 5n. Average surplus is zero.

Under *free trade* demand at the price of 5 in state 1 is: $\Delta_1 = n$. Demand in state 2 at the price of 10 is n and since $(1/2)$n type 2 buyers already bought in the first market the size of the second batch is: $\Delta_2 = (1/2)$n. Total production is 1.5n. In state 1 n units are sold to type 1 buyers and the surplus is -0.5n. In state 2 $(1/2)$n units are sold to type 1 buyers and n units are sold to type 2 buyers. The surplus in state 2 is 6n. Average world's surplus is: (2.75)n.

The seller may be accused of dumping. If anti-dumping laws are enforced we may revert to autarky.

In the absence of data about prices in the country that exports the good, dumping may be defined as "export sales at a price below the cost of production" (Ethier, 1982, page 489). The following example illustrates that dumping in this sense is also possible in our model provided that sellers can discriminate.

Example 6: As in example 3 type 1 buyers want to buy in state 1 only and type 2 buyers want to buy in state 2 only. Type 2 buyers are willing to pay up to 7 in state 2. But unlike example 3 type 1 buyers are willing to pay only up to 4. There is one seller in country 2 who can produce in both states.

Under free trade, the total demand at the price of 5 is zero in state 1 and n in state 2. Therefore only one market will open with probability $1/2$ at the price of 10. Since at this price there is no demand there is no production.

We now allow the seller to discriminate between the two types. We may think of the case in which delivery occurs after actual trade and the seller observes the address of the buyer. In this case, a seller may produce n units and offer them for sale at the price of 3 to buyers in country 1 and at the price of 7 to buyers in country 2 (or 4 to buyers in country 1 and 6 to buyers in country 2). This seller who is making zero expected profits, may be accused of dumping. If anti-dumping laws are imposed in country 1 there will be no production and country 1 buyers will lose $(1/2)$n units of consumer surplus.

Note that a discriminatory monopoly will produce n units and charge the price of 7 in country 2 and 4 in country 1 making an expected profits of 0.5n. If the discriminating monopoly is shut down by anti-dumping measures the welfare of buyers will not be affected but the monopoly loses profits. Table 21.2 summarizes examples 4–6.

The analysis of dumping here has elements in common with both the traditional analysis of dumping as price discrimination between nations (Viner [1923]) and the modern theory of cyclical dumping in Ethier (1982). Unlike the traditional view, discrimination here is explained by the difference in capacity utilization and not by monopoly power. Ethier demonstrates that firms with high fixed cost due to labor contracts that promise secure employment may sell below average cost in downturns. In his model there is a single price that clears the international market (for steel in his example) and therefore at any given point in time the firm charges the same price at home and at the foreign country. Ethier's analysis is somewhat similar to the analysis of peak load pricing in Williamson (1966) where the competitive price is equal to the short run marginal cost when demand is low and capacity is not fully utilized.

Conclusions

Trade may reduce welfare because of two reasons. First, it may increase the uncertainty about the demand per seller and lead to a reduction in average capacity utilization. Second, it may

Table 21.2 Supply shocks and dumping

	World surplus	Surplus to buyers in country 1	Surplus to buyers in country 2	Output
Buyers in country 1 want to buy in both states. Buyers in country 2 only in state 2.				
One seller in country 1 who can produce in both states. One seller in country 2 who can produce only in state 1;				
$v_1 = 10; v_2 = 0$ (example 4):				
Autarky	5	5	0	1
Free trade	3.75	3.75	0	1.5
One seller in country 2 who can produce in both states				
$v_1 = 7; v_2 = 10$ (example 5):				
Autarky	0	0	0	1
Free trade	2.75	1.5	1.25	1.5
Type 1 buyers want to buy in state 1 only and type 2 buyers want to buy in state 2 only. There is one seller per country who can produce in both states.				
$v_1 = 4; v_2 = 7$ (example 6):				
Autarky	0	0	0	0
Free trade	0	0	0	0
Discr. free trade	0.5	0.5	0	1
Discr. monopoly	0.5	0	0	1

Table 21.2 gives the results in examples 4–6. The first column is world surplus calculated as the expected value of the output sold minus the cost of production. Then we have the surplus of the buyers in each country and the world output. In examples 4–5 type 1 buyers want to consume in both states and type 2 buyers want to consume in state 2 only. In example 6 demand is negatively correlated.

allow buyers with low valuation to get in "line" before buyers with high valuation and this may lead to the rationing of high valuation buyers.

The model may be used to explain the purchasing power parity puzzle, the trade in similar goods puzzle, some barriers to trade and dumping.

Sellers whose home country has a relatively unstable demand may be viewed as "dumping" goods on the country with the more stable demand. This is because average capacity utilization is lower and average price is higher in the country with the unstable demand.

21.2 A MONETARY MODEL

We now turn to explore the connection between average capacity utilization, output and welfare. This is done in a cash-in-advance economy with a downward sloping demand and increasing marginal cost. We start with the taste shock model of chapter 20.

There are N infinitely lived households each consisting of a seller (worker) and a buyer pair. At the beginning of the period the worker goes to work. The buyer learns about his demand (taste shock) and if he wants to consume he takes the available money and goes shopping. After trade in the goods market is complete the seller takes his revenue in the form of cash, reunites with the shopper and consumes whatever the shopper has bought.

The household is risk neutral and its single period utility is: $\theta c_t - v(L_t)$, where c is the quantity consumed, L is the quantity produced and θ is a random variable that takes two possible realizations: 0 if the household does not want to consume and 1 if it does. The cost function v( ) has the standard properties ($v' > 0$ and $v'' > 0$ everywhere) and the household's discount factor is $0 < \beta < 1$.

Aggregate demand is an i.i.d. random variable. In each period there are S possible states of aggregate demand. In state s a fraction ϕ_s of the agents experience $\theta = 1$ and want to consume. It is assumed that: $0 < \phi_1 \leq \phi_2 \leq \cdots \leq \phi_S$. State s occurs with probability Π_s. The probability that the state is greater than or equal to s is $q_s = \sum_{i=s}^{S} \Pi_i$. The probability that $\theta = 1$ is the same for all agents and is equal to ϕ_s in state s. For notational convenience we set $\phi_0 = 0$.

We start by assuming a single world currency – the dollar. Household h starts the period with M_t^h dollars and gets in addition, a perfectly anticipated lump sum transfer of G_t dollars. The average per-household post transfer amount of money is: $M_t = G_t + (1/N)\sum_{h=1}^{N} M_t^h$ dollars. The deterministic rate of change in the world money supply is: $M_{t+1}/M_t = 1 + \mu$.

Buyers who want to consume spend all the money they have. As in the previous section buyers who want to consume arrive sequentially at the marketplace, buy at the cheapest available price and disappear. Buyers who arrive early buy at low prices. Buyers who arrive late do not find cheap merchandise and buy at relatively high prices.

From the seller's point of view nominal demand in aggregate state s is $\phi_s M_t(1 + \mu)$ dollars or ϕ_s normalized dollars, where normalized magnitudes are nominal magnitudes divided by the post transfer money supply, $M_t(1 + \mu)$.

Dollars arrive in batches. The size of the first batch is the minimum amount that will be spent: ϕ_1 normalized dollars. The size of the second batch is the minimum additional amount that will be spent if $s \geq 2$: $\min_{s \geq 2}\{\phi_s - \phi_1\} = \phi_2 - \phi_1$ normalized dollars. In general, the size of batch i is the minimum additional amount that will be spent if $s \geq i$ and $i - 1$ batches completed trade: $\min_{s \geq i}\{\phi_s - \phi_{i-1}\} = \phi_i - \phi_{i-1}$ normalized dollars. Batch i buys in market i at the price of p_i normalized dollars per unit if it arrives.

Workers/sellers choose how much to produce and make a contingent plan which specifies the amount that they will sell to each batch if it arrives. This contingent plan is described as an allocation of output across the potential markets: k_i to market i.

The sequence of events within the period is as follows. Prices are announced for each of the S markets and the workers choose production and the allocation of output across the potential markets.[3] Buyers then learn about their desire to consume and those who want to consume arrive sequentially at the market-place. Figure 21.2 illustrates the sequence of events.

The expected purchasing power of a dollar when exactly s markets open is:

$$z_s = \sum_{i=1}^{s}(v_i^s/p_i),$$

(21.6)

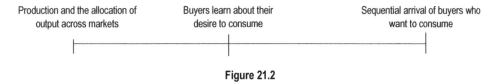

Figure 21.2

where v_i^s is the probability that the dollar will buy in market i: $v_i^s = (\phi_i - \phi_{i-1})/\phi_s$.

The household starts with m normalized dollars and receives a transfer worth g normalized dollars.[4] It solves the following Bellman's equation:

$$V(m) = \sum_{s=1}^{S} \Pi_s \phi_s (m + g) z_s + \max_{k_s} -v \left(\sum_{s=1}^{S} k_s \right)$$

$$+ \beta \sum_{s=1}^{S} \Pi_s \left\{ \phi_s V \left[\left(\sum_{i=1}^{s} p_i k_i \right) \omega \right] + (1 - \phi_s) V \left[\left(m + g + \sum_{i=1}^{s} p_i k_i \right) \omega \right] \right\},$$

(21.7)

where $\omega = (1 + \mu)^{-1}$ is used to convert current normalized dollars into next period's normalized dollars. Here V(m) is the maximum expected utility that the household can achieve; $\sum_{s=1}^{S} \Pi_s \phi_s (m + g) z_s$ is the expected current consumption; $v(\sum_{s=1}^{S} k_s)$ is the utility cost of producing $L = \sum_{s=1}^{S} k_s$ units. To understand the future utility terms note that the worker's revenue is $\sum_{i=1}^{s} p_i k_i$ if exactly s markets open this period. When $\theta = 1$ the buyer spends everything he has and the household will have at the end of the period $\sum_{i=1}^{s} p_i k_i$ normalized dollars which will be worth, in the next period, $(\sum_{i=1}^{s} p_i k_i) \omega$ normalized dollars. When $\theta = 0$ the buyer saves everything and the household will start next period with $(m + g + \sum_{i=1}^{s} p_i k_i) \omega$ normalized dollars.

In aggregate state s, a normalized dollar will buy on average z_s units if the buyer want to consume (with probability ϕ_s) and will be saved and become ω normalized dollars in the next period if the buyer does not want to consume. The expected utility from a normalized dollar is thus:

$$z = \sum_{s=1}^{S} \Pi_s [\phi_s z_s + (1 - \phi_s) \beta \omega z].$$

(21.8)

Using $\zeta = \sum_{s=1}^{S} \Pi_s \phi_s$ to denote the unconditional probability of wanting to consume, we can solve (21.8) and get:

$$z = (1 - \beta \omega + \zeta \beta \omega)^{-1} \sum_{s=1}^{S} \Pi_s \phi_s z_s.$$

(21.9)

The expected benefits from supplying a unit to market s is $q_s p_s \omega z$ utils: If the market opens (with probability q_s) the seller gets p_s current normalized dollars which will become $p_s \omega$ next period's normalized dollars and bring on average $p_s \omega z$ utils. The first order conditions for an interior solution to (21.7) can therefore be written as:

$$q_s \beta p_s \omega z = \beta p_1 \omega z = v' \left(\sum_{s=1}^{S} k_s \right).$$

(21.10)

This says that the discounted expected benefit from supplying a unit is the same for all markets and is equal to the marginal cost. We will refer to $\beta p_1 \omega z$ as the expected discounted real wage or the real wage for short.

Equilibrium requires that the first order conditions (21.10) are satisfied and markets which open are cleared:

$$p_s k_s = \phi_s - \phi_{s-1} \quad \text{for all s.} \tag{21.11}$$

Welfare in equilibrium is an increasing function of the real wage, $w = \beta p_1 \omega z$, and can be measured by:

$$A(w) = \max_L \quad wL - v(L), \tag{21.12}$$

where $wL - v(L)$ is the expected utility that the worker gets for a given choice of L (as a function of L and w) and $A(w)$ is the maximum expected utility as a function of w. It is therefore useful to characterize the equilibrium real wage as a function of the probability distribution of ϕ.

In equilibrium average capacity utilization must equal average consumption per unit of labor supplied and is therefore related to the real wage. The capacity utilization when exactly s markets open is: $CU_s = \sum_{i=1}^{s} k_i / \sum_{s=1}^{S} k_s$. The expected capacity utilization is:

$$CU = \sum_{s=1}^{S} \Pi_s CU_s. \tag{21.13}$$

We now show the following claim.

Claim 1: The equilibrium expected capacity utilization is:

$$CU = 1 - \left[\sum_{s=1}^{S} \Pi_s \sum_{i=s+1}^{S} \Pi_i (\phi_i - \phi_s)/\zeta \right].$$

The proof of this and all other claims is in appendix 21.A. We now turn to show that the real wage is related to average capacity utilization.

Claim 2: The equilibrium real wage is:

$$w = \beta \omega p_1 z = CU\{\beta \omega \zeta /(1 - \beta \omega + \zeta \beta \omega)\}.$$

Note that when $\beta \omega = 1$, $w = CU$. This is because when $\beta \omega = 1$ (a policy known as the Friedman rule) workers are fully compensated for the delay in spending their money income. In general the real wage is increasing in $\beta \omega$, average capacity utilization (CU) and the unconditional probability that a buyer will want to consume (ζ). The probability of wanting to consume plays a role only when $\beta \omega < 1$ because a higher probability of wanting to consume means, on average, less delay in spending the money.

To study the effect of changes in the distribution of ϕ on capacity utilization and the real wage, we now show the following Claim.

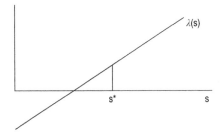

Figure 21.3   An increase in ϕ_s increases CU if $s \leq s^*$ and reduces CU otherwise

Claim 3: $CU = 1 - \sum_{s=1}^{S} \phi_s \Pi_s \lambda(s)/\zeta$, where $\lambda(s) = \sum_{i=1}^{s-1} \Pi_i - \sum_{i=s+1}^{S} \Pi_i = 1 - q_s - q_{s+1}$.

Note that $\lambda(s)$ is an increasing function, $\lambda(1) < 0$ and $\lambda(S) > 0$. Since $0 < \sum_{i=1}^{S} \phi_i \Pi_i \lambda(i)/\sum_{i=1}^{S} \Pi_i \phi_i < 1$, there exists a cut-off point s^* such that

$$\lambda(s) \leq \sum_{i=1}^{S} \phi_i \Pi_i \lambda(i)/\sum_{i=1}^{S} \Pi_i \phi_i \quad \text{for } s \leq s^* \quad \text{and}$$

$$\lambda(s) > \sum_{i=1}^{S} \phi_i \Pi_i \lambda(i)/\sum_{i=1}^{S} \Pi_i \phi_i \quad \text{otherwise.}$$

Figure 21.3 illustrates the cut-off point.
  An immediate corollary is as follows.

Corollary: A small increase in ϕ_s (holding other ϕ_i constant) increases CU if $s \leq s^*$ and reduces CU otherwise.

The intuition is as follows. Increasing the fraction of buyers who want to consume in states that this fraction is low or reducing it in states that it is high reduce the uncertainty about demand and therefore increase average capacity utilization.

Incentives to trade from the individual and the social point of view

When the probability distribution of ϕ is country specific there are incentives to trade in the same good, at least from the individual's point of view. This is because equilibrium prices (the solution to [21.10] and [21.11]) depend on the probability distribution of ϕ and are country specific under autarky. When prices are country specific, a seller in country j will have, for example, an incentive to sell in country j' if there is a market s for which: $p_{j's} > p_{js}$.

An individual that takes prices as given can only benefit from trade. But a country as a whole that recognize the effect of trade on prices and capacity utilization may actually suffer from trade.

We now turn to characterize the condition under which free trade can improve the welfare for an individual country j. For this purpose let ϕ_{js} denote the fraction of buyers who want to consume in country j in state s and for simplicity let us assume: $0 = \phi_{j0} \leq \phi_{j1} \leq \phi_{j2} \leq \cdots \leq \phi_{js}$ for all j. The real wage under autarky can be derived by adding the country index j to the expression in Claim 2. It is:

$$\beta\omega p_{j1}z_j = CU_j[\beta\omega\zeta_j/(1 - \beta\omega + \zeta_j\beta\omega)], \qquad (21.14)$$

where $CU_j = 1 - [\sum_{s=1}^{S} \Pi_s \sum_{i=s+1}^{S} \Pi_i(\phi_{ji} - \phi_{js})/\zeta_j]$ and $\zeta_j = \Sigma_{s=1}^{S} \Pi_s \phi_{js}$.

Free trade equilibrium We now assume n countries of equal size and calculate the real wage under free trade. Although prices are the same for all buyers, the real wage is country specific because the probability of wanting to consume is country specific.

We use:

$$\phi_s = (1/n) \sum_{j=1}^{n} \phi_{js}, \qquad (21.15)$$

to denote the worldwide fraction of buyers who want to consume. The probability that a dollar will buy in market i when s markets open is not type specific and is given by $v_i^s = (\phi_i - \phi_{i-1})/\phi_s$. Since prices are also common to all buyers the expected purchasing power of a dollar when s markets open is: $z_s = \sum_{i=1}^{s}(v_i^s/p_i)$ and is not type specific. We can now modify (21.7) to formulate type j's Bellman's equation:

$$V_j(m) = \sum_{s=1}^{S} \Pi_s \phi_{js}(m + g)z_s + \max_{k_{js}} - v\left(\sum_{s=1}^{S} k_{js}\right)$$

$$+ \beta \sum_{s=1}^{S} \Pi_s \left\{ \phi_{js} V_j\left[\left(\sum_{i=1}^{s} p_i k_{ji}\right)\omega\right] + (1 - \phi_{js})V_j\left[\left(m + g + \sum_{i=1}^{s} p_i k_{ji}\right)\omega\right]\right\}.$$

$$(21.16)$$

To state the first order conditions for this problem we modify (21.9) and define the expected utility from a normalized dollar by:

$$z_j = \sum_{s=1}^{S} \Pi_s[\phi_{js}z_s + (1 - \phi_{js})\beta\omega z_j] = (1 - \beta\omega + \zeta_j\beta\omega)^{-1} \sum_{s=1}^{S} \Pi_s \phi_{js}z_s, \qquad (21.17)$$

where $\zeta_j = \sum_{s=1}^{S} \Pi_s \phi_{js}$ is the probability that type j will want to consume. We can now state the first order condition to (21.16) by:

$$\beta\omega q_s p_s z_j = \beta\omega p_1 z_j = v'\left(\sum_{s=1}^{S} k_{js}\right). \qquad (21.18)$$

The average per country supply to market s is:

$$k_s = (1/n) \sum_{j=1}^{n} k_{js}. \qquad (21.19)$$

The market clearing conditions can now be stated as:

$$p_s k_s = \phi_s - \phi_{s-1}. \tag{21.20}$$

Claim 4: Under free trade, $CU = 1 - \sum_{s=1}^{S} \Pi_s \sum_{i=s+1}^{S} \Pi_i (\phi_i - \phi_s)/\zeta$ and the real wage for type j sellers is:

$$\beta \omega p_1 z_j = CU\{\beta \omega E(\phi_j/\phi)\zeta/(1 - \beta \omega + \zeta_j \beta \omega)\},$$

where

$$E(\phi_j/\phi) = \sum_{s=1}^{S} \Pi_s(\phi_{js}/\phi_s) \text{ and } \zeta = \sum_{s=1}^{S} \Pi_s \phi_s.$$

We can now compare the expected wage under free trade and autarky. $CU\{\beta \omega E(\phi_j/\phi)\zeta/(1 - \beta \omega + \zeta_j \beta \omega) > CU_j\{\beta \omega \zeta_j/(1 - \beta \omega + \zeta_j \beta \omega)\}$ implies: $CU > CU_j/\delta_j$ and vise versa, where $\delta_j = \zeta_j/\zeta E(\phi_j/\phi) = E(\phi_j)/E(\phi)E(\phi_j/\phi)$. Thus,

---

Claim 5: Free trade increases welfare in country j if: $CU > CU_j/\delta_j$.

The magnitude $\delta_j = E(\phi_j)/E(\phi)E(\phi_j/\phi)$ may be either larger or smaller than unity.[5] Therefore the condition $CU > CU_j$ is neither sufficient nor necessary.

Example 7: There are two countries with the same population. The residents of country 1 always want to consume. In country 2 either half of the residents want to consume or all of the residents want to consume; with equal probabilities of occurrence.

Thus we assume: $\phi_{11} = \phi_{12} = 1, \phi_{21} = 1/2; \phi_{22} = 1$. We compute: $CU_1 = 1, CU_2 = 2/3$, $CU = 6/7, \delta_1 = 48/49$ and $\delta_2 = 36/35$. Since $CU_2/\delta_2 = 70/108 = 0.648 < CU = 6/7 = 0.857$ country 2 gains from trade. Since $CU_1/\delta_1 = 49/48 = 1.02 > CU = 0.857$ country 1 loses from trade.

The detailed equilibrium solutions for this example is in appendix 21.B.

Example 8: There are two countries with the same population and the same independent distribution of demand: Either half of the residents want to consume or all of the residents want to consume; with equal probabilities of occurrence.

There are four states of the world which occur with equal probabilities. In state 1 demand is low in both countries; in state 2 and 3 it is low in one country and high in the other and in state 4 it is high in both countries. In this symmetric example: $\phi_{11} = \phi_{21} = 1/2; \phi_{12} = 1$ and $\phi_{22} = 1/2; \phi_{13} = 1/2$ and $\phi_{23} = 1; \phi_{14} = \phi_{24} = 1$.

We compute average capacity utilization under autarky: $CU_1 = CU_2 = 2/3$.

To compute average capacity utilization under free trade, note that the average fraction of buyers who want to consume is: $\phi_1 = 1/2; \phi_2 = 3/4; \phi_3 = 3/4$ and $\phi_4 = 1$. Average capacity utilization under free trade is: $CU = 1 - 7/48 = 41/48 = 0.854$. In this symmetric example, $\delta_j = 1$. Since $CU > CU_j$ both countries benefit from trade.

21.3 EXCHANGE RATES

We now assume J currencies (indexed j). Let M_{jt}^h denotes the amount of currency j held by household h at time t and let E_{jt} denotes the value of currency j in terms of dollars. The dollar value of the portfolio of currencies held by household h is:

$$M_t^h = \sum_{j=1}^{J} E_{jt} M_{jt}^h. \tag{21.21}$$

In addition, all households get a perfectly anticipated lump sum transfer. The dollar value of the transfer payment is the same for all households and is equal to G_t. The average per-household post-transfer world money supply is: $M_t = G_t + (1/N) \sum_{h=1}^{N} M_t^h$ dollars. As in the single currency case the rate of change in the world money supply is non-random and is given by: $M_{t+1}/M_t = 1 + \mu$.

Exchange rates are determined at the beginning of the period in a random manner but, as in Karaken and Wallace (1981), on average they are expected to remain constant:

$$E(E_{jt+1} \mid E_{jt}) = E_{jt}, \tag{21.22}$$

where E denotes the expectations operator.

Since the world money supply in terms of dollars grow at a constant rate, equilibrium prices in terms of dollars grow at a constant rate. In our formulation we divide all dollar magnitudes by the post transfer money supply ($M_t[1 + \mu]$) and assume that prices in terms of normalized dollars do not change over time. This allow us to use the amount of normalized dollar held at the beginning of the period as the only state variable in our dynamic programming formulation and write the Bellman equation (21.7), where m is now interpreted as the value of the beginning of period portfolio in terms of normalized dollars.

Sellers may be viewed as maximizing revenues in terms of next period's normalized dollars and because of (21.22) they are willing to accept any currency. If the seller sells a unit at a price of 1 dollar he will get $1/(1 + \mu)$ in terms of next period's normalized dollars. If instead he sells the unit for $1/E_{jt}$ units of currency j he will have next period E_{jt+1}/E_{jt} dollars, which under (21.22) will equal on average to 1 dollar or $1/(1 + \mu)$ normalized dollars. Thus under (21.22) a seller who maximizes the expected value of revenues in terms of next period's normalized dollars will accept payment in any currency.

Since dollar prices increases at a constant rate sellers also behave as if they maximize revenues in terms of dollars (rather than next period's normalized dollars). Is this true also for, say, marks? A seller who maximizes revenues in terms of next period's expected marks will prefer 1 dollar (which is worth on average $E[1/E_{jt+1}]$ marks in the next period) to $1/E_{jt}$ marks. This is because Jensen's inequality and (21.22) imply: $E(1/E_{jt+1}) \geq 1/E(E_{jt+1}) = 1/E_{jt}$. But our sellers are indifferent between marks and dollars.

To resolve this apparant paradox (sometimes called the Siegel's paradox) we formulated the dynamic programming problem in terms of normalized marks, where a normalized mark is the per household mark money supply. This revealed that the beginning of period normalized marks can be used as the only state variable and our seller may be viewed as maximizing the expected value of revenues in terms of next period *normalized* marks. But this is different from maximizing the expected revenues in terms of next period's regular marks. To see this point, let $DM_t = M_t/E_{jt}$ denote the money supply in terms of marks. Since the dollar money supply grows at the rate of μ, $E_{jt+1}DM_{t+1}/E_{jt}DM_t = 1 + \mu$ and therefore $DM_{t+1}/DM_t = E_{jt}(1 + \mu)/E_{jt+1}$. Since E_{jt+1} is a random variable the rate of growth of the world money supply in terms of marks is a random variable. It follows that a normalized mark will become $\omega_j = E_{jt+1}/E_{jt}(1 + \mu)$ next period's normalized marks, where now ω_j is a random variable. Now 1 dollar will become on average $E(1/E_{jt+1})\omega_j = 1/E_{jt}(1 + \mu)$ next period's normalized marks. And $1/E_{jt}$ marks will also become on average $1/E_{jt}(1 + \mu)$ next period's normalized marks. Therefore a seller who maximize revenues in terms of next period's normalized marks will be indifferent between accepting 1 dollar to accepting $1/E_{jt}$ marks.

Asymmetric equilibria and the correlation between the nominal and the real exchange rate

The above symmetric formulation assumes that the representative household allocates capacity to all S markets. We may think of this allocation as a price-setting choice: The seller posts many prices and puts the price tag p_s on k_s units.

We now assume that each seller quotes one price only and a fraction k_s/L of the sellers choose to participate in market s and offer to sell at the price p_s. The expected utility of the seller does not depend on his choice of market.

We also assume that sellers in country j (type j) quote their price in terms of currency j (but nevertheless are willing to accept payment in any other currency). We assume that a seller changes his price in terms of the local currency only if there are strictly positive benefits from doing it. This assumption may be motivated by the existence of small menu type costs for changing nominal price quotations.

To get the observed correlation between the nominal exchange rate and the real exchange rate We assume a continuum of countries and two potential markets. Equilibrium prices are 1 dollar worth in market 1 and 2 dollars worth in market 2.

Suppose now that at time t the exchange rate of currency j was 1 and sellers in country j supplied to market 2. Currency j depreciated at $t + 1$ and is now worth 0.5 dollars. Sellers in country j do not change their nominal price quotations (in terms of their currency) and as a result the dollar value of their price goes down by the percentage of the devaluation. After the devaluation, country j supplies to market 1 instead of market 2 but because the country is small all the equilibrium conditions are satisfied and country j sellers have no incentive to change their price quotation.

Conclusions

The sequential trade model abandons the law of one price in favor of an equilibrium price distribution. Therefore we may get deviations from the purchasing power parity (PPP) and a high correlation between the real and the nominal exchange rates.

350 UNCERTAIN AND SEQUENTIAL TRADE

Under autarky the distribution of equilibrium prices are in general country specific and therefore individual agents have an incentive to trade, in the same good, with agents in other countries. However, the country (or the world) as a whole may be better off under autarky. This occurs when trade increases the uncertainty about supply and demand conditions.

An individual country benefits from trade if as a result of trade average capacity utilization increases by a sufficient amount. The exact condition is: $CU > CU_j/\delta_j$, where CU is average capacity utilization under free trade, CU_j is average capacity utilization under autarky and δ_j is a country specific constant. This constant is close to unity in the examples we have worked out.

A possible application is to historical episodes in which the uncertainty about supply and demand conditions was substantial. Recently Cole and Ohanian (2001) describe the new deal policies which were designed to limit competition. They think of these policies as a huge "mistake" that contributed to the persistent of the depression. But it is possible that in 1933 there was a lot of uncertainty about supply and demand conditions and limiting competition may have worked in the direction of reducing this uncertainty.

APPENDIX 21A PROOFS OF THE CLAIMS IN THE MONETARY MODEL

Proof of claim 1: Using the market clearing condition (21.11) we get:

$$k_i = k_1(\phi_i - \phi_{i-1})p_1/p_i\phi_1 = k_1(\phi_i - \phi_{i-1})q_i/\phi_1. \qquad (A21.1)$$

Average waste if exactly s markets open is:

$$\sum_{i=s+1}^{S} k_i / \sum_{i=1}^{S} k_i = \sum_{i=s+1}^{S} (\phi_i - \phi_{i-1})q_i / \sum_{i=1}^{S}(\phi_i - \phi_{i-1})q_i \qquad (A21.2)$$

We now use the definition $q_s = \sum_{i=s}^{S} \Pi_i$ to get:

$$\sum_{i=s+1}^{S} (\phi_i - \phi_{i-1})q_i = (\phi_{s+1} - \phi_s)q_{s+1} + (\phi_{s+2} - \phi_{s+1})q_{s+2} + \cdots + q_S(\phi_S - \phi_{S-1})$$

$$= -\phi_s q_{s+1} + \phi_{s+1}(q_{s+1} - q_{s+2}) + \cdots + q_S\phi_S$$

$$= -\phi_s q_{s+1} + \phi_{s+1}\Pi_{s+1} + \cdots + \Pi_S\phi_S$$

$$= \sum_{i=s+1}^{S}\Pi_i\phi_i - \phi_s \sum_{i=s+1}^{S} \Pi_i = \sum_{i=s+1}^{S} \Pi_i(\phi_i - \phi_s). \qquad (A21.3)$$

We can now get the expected waste by substituting (A21.3) in (A21.2) and computing the expected value of this expression. This leads to: $\sum_{s=1}^{S} \Pi_s \sum_{i=s+1}^{S} \Pi_i(\phi_i - \phi_s)/ \sum_{s=1}^{S} \Pi_s\phi_s$. Since expected capacity utilization is one minus the expected waste we get:

$$CU = 1 - \sum_{s=1}^{S}\Pi_s \sum_{i=s+1}^{S} \Pi_i(\phi_i - \phi_s)/ \sum_{s=1}^{S}\Pi_s\phi_s. \qquad \square$$

Proof of claim 2: Substituting (21.9) in the real wage (21.10) leads to:

$$\beta\omega p_1 z = \beta\omega p_1 (1 - \beta\omega + \zeta\beta\omega)^{-1} \sum_{s=1}^{S} \Pi_s \phi_s z_s. \tag{A21.4}$$

Substituting (21.6), $q_i p_i = p_1$, $v_i^s = (\phi_i - \phi_{i-1})/\phi_s$ and $\zeta = \sum_{s=1}^{S} \Pi_s \phi_s$ in (A21.4) leads to:

$$\beta\omega p_1 z = \beta\omega p_1 (1 - \beta\omega + \zeta\beta\omega)^{-1} \sum_{s=1}^{S} \Pi_s \phi_s \sum_{i=1}^{s} (v_i^s / p_i)$$

$$= \beta\omega(1 - \beta\omega + \zeta\beta\omega)^{-1} \sum_{s=1}^{S} \Pi_s \phi_s \sum_{i=1}^{s} q_i v_i^s$$

$$= \beta\omega(1 - \beta\omega + \zeta\beta\omega)^{-1} \sum_{s=1}^{S} \Pi_s \sum_{i=1}^{s} q_i (\phi_i - \phi_{i-1})$$

$$= \beta\omega \sum_{s=1}^{S} \Pi_s \sum_{i=1}^{s} q_i (\phi_i - \phi_{i-1}) \bigg/ \left[1 - \beta\omega + \beta\omega \sum_{s=1}^{S} \Pi_s \phi_s \right]. \tag{A21.5}$$

We now use $q_s = \sum_{i=s}^{S} \Pi_i$ to get:

$$\sum_{i=1}^{s} q_i (\phi_i - \phi_{i-1}) = \phi_1 + q_2(\phi_2 - \phi_1) + q_3(\phi_3 - \phi_2) + \cdots + q_s(\phi_s - \phi_{s-1})$$

$$= (1 - q_2)\phi_1 + (q_2 - q_3)\phi_2 + q_s\phi_s$$

$$= \Pi_1\phi_1 + \Pi_2\phi_2 + \Pi_3\phi_3 + q_s\phi_s$$

$$= \sum_{i=1}^{s-1} \Pi_i\phi_i + q_s\phi_s = \sum_{i=1}^{s-1} \Pi_i\phi_i + \phi_s \sum_{i=s}^{S} \Pi_i$$

$$= \sum_{s=1}^{S} \Pi_s\phi_s - \sum_{i=s}^{S} \Pi_i(\phi_i - \phi_s). \tag{A21.6}$$

Substituting (A21.6) in (A21.5) and using claim 1 leads to:

$$\beta\omega p_1 z = \beta\omega \left[\sum_{s=1}^{S} \Pi_s\phi_s - \sum_{s=1}^{S} \Pi_s \sum_{i=s}^{S} \Pi_i(\phi_i - \phi_s) \right] \bigg/ \left[1 - \beta\omega + \beta\omega \sum_{s=1}^{S} \Pi_s\phi_s \right].$$

$$= \beta\omega CU \sum_{s=1}^{S} \Pi_s\phi_s \bigg/ \left[1 - \beta\omega + \beta\omega \sum_{s=1}^{S} \Pi_s\phi_s \right]. \qquad \square$$

Proof of claim 3:

$$\sum_{s=1}^{S} \Pi_s \sum_{i=s+1}^{S} \Pi_i (\phi_i - \phi_s)$$

$$= \Pi_1 \Pi_2 (\phi_2 - \phi_1) + \Pi_1 \Pi_3 (\phi_3 - \phi_1) + \Pi_1 \Pi_4 (\phi_4 - \phi_1)$$

$$+ \cdots + \Pi_1 \Pi_S (\phi_S - \phi_1) + \Pi_2 \Pi_3 (\phi_3 - \phi_2) + \Pi_2 \Pi_4 (\phi_4 - \phi_2)$$

$$+ \cdots + \Pi_2 \Pi_S (\phi_S - \phi_2) + \Pi_3 \Pi_4 (\phi_4 - \phi_3) + \Pi_3 \Pi_5 (\phi_5 - \phi_3)$$

$$+ \cdots + \Pi_3 \Pi_S (\phi_S - \phi_3) + \cdots + \phi_S \Pi_S \left(\sum_{i=1}^{S-1} \Pi_i \right)$$

$$= \phi_1 \Pi_1 (-\Pi_2 - \Pi_3 - \Pi_4 - \cdots - \Pi_S)$$

$$+ \phi_2 \Pi_2 (\Pi_1 - \Pi_3 - \Pi_4 - \cdots - \Pi_S)$$

$$+ \phi_3 \Pi_3 (\Pi_1 + \Pi_2 - \Pi_4 - \cdots - \Pi_S) + \cdots + \phi_S \Pi_S \left(\sum_{i=1}^{S-1} \Pi_i \right)$$

$$= \sum_{s=1}^{S} \phi_s \Pi_s \left\{ \sum_{i=1}^{s-1} \Pi_i - \sum_{i=s+1}^{S} \Pi_i \right\} = \sum_{s=1}^{S} \phi_s \Pi_s \{ (1 - q_s) - q_{s+1} \}.$$

Substituting this in claim 1 leads to the claim. $\qquad\qquad\square$

Proof of claim 4: Substituting (21.17) in the real wage (21.18) leads to:

$$\beta \omega p_1 z_j = \beta \omega p_1 (1 - \beta \omega + \zeta_j \beta \omega)^{-1} \sum_{s=1}^{S} \Pi_s \phi_{js} z_s. \qquad (A21.7)$$

Substituting (21.6), $q_i p_i = p_1$, $v_i^s = (\phi_i - \phi_{i-1})/\phi_s$ and $\zeta_j = \sum_{s=1}^{S} \Pi_s \phi_{js}$ in (A21.7) leads to:

$$\beta \omega p_1 z_j = \beta \omega p_1 (1 - \beta \omega - \zeta_j \beta \omega)^{-1} \sum_{s=1}^{S} \Pi_s \phi_{js} \sum_{i=1}^{S} (v_i^s / p_i)$$

$$= \beta \omega (1 - \beta \omega + \zeta_j \beta \omega)^{-1} \sum_{s=1}^{S} \Pi_s \phi_{js} \sum_{i=1}^{S} q_i v_i^s$$

$$= \beta \omega (1 - \beta \omega + \zeta_j \beta \omega)^{-1} \sum_{s=1}^{S} \Pi_s (\phi_{js}/\phi_s) \sum_{i=1}^{S} q_i (\phi_i - \phi_{i-1})$$

$$= \beta \omega \sum_{s=1}^{S} \Pi_s (\phi_{js}/\phi_s) \sum_{i=1}^{S} q_i (\phi_i - \phi_{i-1}) \Big/ \left[1 - \beta \omega + \beta \omega \sum_{s=1}^{S} \Pi_s \phi_{js} \right].$$

$$(A21.8)$$

Substituting (A21.6) in (A21.5) and using claim 1 leads to:

$$\beta\omega p_1 z_j = \beta\omega \sum_{s=1}^{S} \Pi_s(\phi_{js}/\phi_s) \left[\sum_{s=1}^{S} \Pi_s \phi_s - \sum_{i=s}^{S} \Pi_i(\phi_i - \phi_s) \right] \bigg/ \left[1 - \beta\omega + \beta\omega \sum_{s=1}^{S} \Pi_s \phi_{js} \right]$$

$$= \beta\omega CU \sum_{s=1}^{S} \Pi_s(\phi_{js}/\phi_s) \sum_{s=1}^{S} \Pi_s \phi_s \bigg/ \left[1 - \beta\omega + \beta\omega \sum_{s=1}^{S} \Pi_s \phi_{js} \right].$$

□

APPENDIX 21B EXAMPLE 7 IN DETAIL

Example 7: There are two countries with the same population. The residents of country 1 always want to consume. In country 2 either half of the residents want to consume or all of the residents want to consume; with equal probabilities of occurrence.

We start by calculating the equilibria under *autarky*. In country 2 there are two potential markets: Market 1 opens with certainty and face the demand of 1/2 normalized dollar per seller. Market 2 opens with probability 1/2 and if it opens it will face the demand of 1/2 normalized dollar per seller. The expected utility from a normalized dollar (Using equations [21.6] and [21.8] in the text) is:

$$z_1 = 1/p_1;$$
$$z_2 = \tfrac{1}{2}(1/p_1) + \tfrac{1}{2}(1/p_2);$$
$$z = \tfrac{1}{2}\left[\tfrac{1}{2}z_1 + \tfrac{1}{2}\beta\omega z\right] + \tfrac{1}{2}z_2. \tag{B21.1}$$

To allow for numerical solutions, We assume $v(L) = L^2$. Under this assumption, the first order condition for the household's problem (21.10) are:

$$2L = \beta\omega p_1 z = \tfrac{1}{2}\beta\omega p_2 z; \quad L = k_1 + k_2. \tag{B21.2}$$

And market clearing conditions are:

$$p_1 k_1 = \tfrac{1}{2}; \quad p_2 k_2 = \tfrac{1}{2}. \tag{B21.3}$$

Equilibrium under autarky in country 2 is a solution $(p_1, p_2, z_1, z_2, z, k_1, k_2, L)$ to (B21.1)–(B21.3). The analytical solution is:

$$p_1 = 2.4/\beta\omega - 0.6; \quad p_2 = 4.8/\beta\omega - 1.2;$$
$$z_1 = 1.666\beta\omega/(4 - \beta\omega); \quad z_2 = 1.25\beta\omega/(4 - \beta\omega); \quad z = 4.16\beta\omega/(4 - \beta\omega)^2;$$
$$k_2 = 0.416\beta\omega/(4 - \beta\omega); \quad k_1 = 0.833\beta\omega/(4 - \beta\omega); \quad L = 1.25\beta\omega/(4 - \beta\omega). \tag{B21.4}$$

Table 21.B1 computes the numerical solution for various levels of $\beta\omega$.

The expected real wage in country 2 under autarky is:

$$w = \beta\omega p_1 z = 9.984\beta\omega/(4 - \beta\omega)^2 - 2.5(\beta\omega)^2/(4 - \beta\omega)^2. \tag{B21.5}$$

Under autarky there is only one market in country 1. Using x to denote the purchasing power of a normalized dollar in country 1 we can define equilibrium as a vector (p, x, L)

Table 21B.1 Equilibria in country 2 under autarky

	p_1	p_2	z	k_1	k_2	L
$\beta\omega = 1$	1.8	3.6	0.463	0.278	0.139	0.417
$\beta\omega = 0.95$	1.926	3.853	0.426	0.260	0.130	0.39
$\beta\omega = 0.90$	2.066	4.133	0.390	0.242	0.121	0.362
$\beta\omega = 0.5$	4.2	8.4	0.170	0.120	0.060	0.18

Table 21B.2 Equilibria under autarky for country 1

	$p = 2/\beta\omega$	$x = \beta\omega/2$	$L = \beta\omega/2$
$\beta\omega = 1$	2	0.5	0.5
$\beta\omega = 0.95$	2.105	0.475	0.475
$\beta\omega = 0.90$	2.222	0.450	0.450
$\beta\omega = 0.5$	4	0.25	0.25

such that:

$$x = 1/p \tag{B21.6}$$

$$v'(L) = 2L = \beta\omega px = \beta\omega \tag{B21.7}$$

$$pL = 1. \tag{B21.8}$$

The analytical solution for (B21.6)–(B21.8) is: $p = 2/\beta\omega$, $x = L = \beta\omega/2$. Table 21B.2 illustrates the solutions for different values of $\beta\omega$.

Allowing for international trade

Assume now that these two asymmetric countries open to trade.

The fraction of households who want to consume out of the entire world population is: $3/4$ or 1 with equal probabilities of occurrence. There will therefore be two markets. Market 1 will open with certainty and will face the demand of $3/4$ normalized dollars per seller. Market 2 will open with probability $1/2$ and will face the demand of $1/4$ normalized dollars per seller.

The expected purchasing power of a normalized dollar if exactly s markets open is now given by:

$$z_1 = 1/p_1 \tag{B21.9}$$

$$z_2 = \tfrac{3}{4}(1/p_1) + \tfrac{1}{4}(1/p_2). \tag{B21.10}$$

The expected utility from a normalized dollar is not the same for the residence of both countries because of the difference in the desire to consume. We use x (y) to denote the expected utility from a normalized dollar held by a resident in country 1 (country 2). These are defined by:

$$x = \tfrac{1}{2}z_1 + \tfrac{1}{2}z_2 \tag{B21.11}$$

$$y = \tfrac{1}{2}\left[\tfrac{1}{2}z_1 + \tfrac{1}{2}\beta\omega y\right] + \tfrac{1}{2}z_2. \tag{B21.12}$$

Table 21B.3   Equilibria for the integrated world economy

	p_1	p_2	x	y	L_1	L_2	k_1	k_2
$\beta\omega = 1$	1.888	3.775	0.499	0.486	0.469	0.458	0.397	0.066
$\beta\omega = 0.95$	2.003	4.006	0.468	0.450	0.445	0.428	0.374	0.062
$\beta\omega = 0.90$	2.131	4.263	0.440	0.416	0.422	0.399	0.352	0.059
$\beta\omega = 0.5$	4.062	8.124	0.231	0.193	0.234	0.196	0.185	0.031

Since the expected utility from a normalized dollar varies across countries the real wage and labor supply varies across countries. Using L_j to denote the labor supply in country j and using $v'(L) = 2L$, leads to the following first order conditions (assuming an interior solution):

$$2L_1 = \beta\omega p_1 x, \tag{B21.13}$$

$$2L_2 = \beta\omega p_1 y, \tag{B21.14}$$

$$p_1 = \tfrac{1}{2}p_2. \tag{B21.15}$$

In equilibrium, markets which open must clear:

$$p_1 k_1 = \tfrac{3}{4}, \tag{B21.16}$$

$$p_2 k_2 = \tfrac{1}{4}, \tag{B21.17}$$

$$k_1 + k_2 = \tfrac{1}{2}(L_1 + L_2), \tag{B21.18}$$

where the last equation requires that the total supply is equal to the average per seller labor supply.

Equilibrium for this world is a vector

$$(p_1, p_2, z_1, z_2, x, y, L_1, L_2, k_1, k_2) \text{ that satisfies (B21.9)–(B21.18).}$$

The full analytical solution for all the variables is rather complicated. But the analytical solution for L_1 is simple. It is: $L_1 = 0.469\beta\omega$. This is less than the supply in country 1 under autarky $(0.5\beta\omega)$. Since labor supply is increasing in the expected real wage and welfare, we conclude that welfare in country 1 went down as a result of trade.

The analytical solution for the labor supply in country 2 is: $1.375\beta\omega/(4 - \beta\omega)$. This is larger than the labor supply in country 2 under autarky $(1.25\beta\omega/(4 - \beta\omega))$, indicating an improvement in welfare as a result of trade. For the sake of comparison, the solutions for alternative values of $\beta\omega$ are in table 21B.3.

NOTES

This chapter is based on Eden (2003). It benefited from many useful discussions with Rick Bond.

1   See the WTO website for details: www.wto.org/english/tratop_e/adp_e.htm
2   It is possible to show that during trade there are no incentive to change the allocation of goods across markets or to change prices.
3   Since we normalize by the post transfer money supply: $g = \mu/(1 + \mu)$.
4   $E(\phi_j/\phi) = E(\phi_j)E(1/\phi) + \text{Cov}(\phi_j, 1/\phi) \leq E(\phi_j)E(1/\phi) \geq E(\phi_j)/E(\phi)$. The first inequality is because $\text{Cov}(\phi_j, 1/\phi) < 0$. The second is because of Jensen's inequality.

CHAPTER 22

Endogenous Information and Externalities

In this chapter we extend the basic UST model by allowing sellers to buy information about demand. Sellers can also free ride by deducing the information about demand from prices posted by others. It turns out that this extension leads to an equilibrium in which sellers adjust prices in random intervals as in the Calvo (1983) model. But unlike the Calvo model here the time intervals are endogenously determined and sellers produce the optimal amount rather than satisfying demand. Another important difference is that here and in other UST models sellers do not have an incentive to change prices during trade. The model is particularly close to the version of the Calvo model studied by Mankiw and Reis (2001). In their sticky information framework sellers may change their prices at any time but only a fraction of the sellers choose prices on the basis of current information.

Endogenizing information and using a maximization framework to get a Calvo type model comes at the cost of added complexity. There are two benefits. In terms of positive economics we achieve a better understanding of the economy once we endogenize more variables (like information in this case) and describe behavior by maximization problems. In terms of normative economics we get a model that is more immune to the Lucas' (1976) critique and may be more suitable for evaluating alternative policies.

The analysis in this chapter is based on Eden (1981, 1982, 1983). Since we assume that information becomes public, we have a public good problem of the type studied by Grossman and Stiglitz (1980). In their article the public good problem leads to an existence of equilibrium problems. Here sellers adopt a mixed strategy and in equilibrium only a fraction of the sellers are informed about the current realization of the money supply. For related papers on the effects of informational externalities see Chamley and Gale (1994) and Caplin and Leahy (1998).

22.1 A REAL MODEL

To illustrate the main idea it may be useful to start with an extension of a simple real UST model of the type studied in chapter 14. The number of buyers is a random variable, $\tilde{N}$, that can take two possible realizations: N and N $+$ Δ with equal probability of occurrence.

Each potential buyer has a downward sloping demand curve D(P). There are n sellers each supplying one unit of a non-storable good inelastically.

Buyers arrive sequentially. A first batch of N buyers arrives with certainty and trades in the first market. A second batch of Δ buyers arrives with probability $1/2$ and if it arrives it buys in the second market. The representative seller allocates x_i units to market i.

A UST equilibrium is a positive vector (P_1, P_2, x_1, x_2) satisfying: $x_1 + x_2 = 1$;

$$P_1 = \tfrac{1}{2}P_2; \tag{22.1}$$

and

$$ND(P_1) = nx_1; \quad \Delta D(P_2) = nx_2. \tag{22.2}$$

Condition (22.1) says that sellers are indifferent about the way they allocate their unit across markets. Condition (22.2) says that markets which open must clear.

The value of information

We now allow sellers to buy information about the realization of demand before the beginning of trade. We start by computing the maximum amount that a seller will pay for this information under the assumption that other sellers do not buy information and do not change their equilibrium strategies.

In the above UST equilibrium the expected payoff is P_1 dollars per seller. A seller who has the information about the realization of demand will supply to market 1 if demand is low and to market 2 if it is high. The expected payoff for an informed seller is thus: $\bar{P} = (1/2)P_1 + (1/2)P_2$. The maximum amount that a seller will pay for the information, or the value of information is:

$$VI = \bar{P} - P_1 = \tfrac{1}{2}P_1. \tag{22.3}$$

The private value of information when information may leak

We now assume that other sellers may buy the information and allow the individual seller to get the information for free if someone else in his neighborhood buys it. For example, if he knows that an individual seller buys the information he may observe the quantity that this individual supplies to market 1.

We thus distinguish between two ways of getting the information: (a) directly and (b) by free riding and deducing the information from the behavior of others. For simplicity we assume at this stage that the prices in the two potential markets are not affected by the acquisition of information.

Let ζ denotes the probability that the seller will not be able to free ride. The maximum amount that the seller will pay for direct information – or the private value of infromation – is:

$$\zeta VI. \tag{22.4}$$

To show (22.4) note that a seller who does not buy the information directly will get P_1 if he cannot free ride and $\bar{P}$ if he can free ride. The payoff in this case is thus: $\zeta P_1 + (1 - \zeta)\bar{P}$. A seller who buys the information directly will get: $\bar{P}$. The private value of information is therefore: $\bar{P} - [\zeta P_1 + (1 - \zeta)\bar{P}]$ which is equal to (22.4).

A mixed strategy partial equilibrium

We now consider a game in which each seller must choose whether or not to buy information. The cost of information is α units of the numeraire commodity. It is assumed that all sellers can costlessly observe the supply choices made by other sellers and therefore if someone buys information all others can free ride.

If $\alpha \geq$ VI, information is prohibitively expensive and no one buys the information. But if $\alpha <$ VI we cannot get a symmetric equilibrium in pure strategies. If everyone buy the information than the individual seller should free ride, but if no one buys it than he should buy it. There exists however a symmetric equilibrium in mixed strategies.

Let each seller buy the information with probability:

$$q = 1 - (\alpha/\text{VI})^{1/n-1}. \tag{22.5}$$

Then the probability that no other seller will buy the information and an individual seller will not be able to free ride is: $\zeta = (1 - q)^{n-1} = \alpha/\text{VI}$. It follows that the cost of information is equal to the private value of information $(\alpha = \zeta \text{VI})$ and therefore sellers cannot do better than choosing a mixed strategy.

General equilibrium analysis

The above discussion assumed that the acquisition of information does not affect prices. Here we consider a complete model in which information is a local public good: It is shared by all sellers in the neighborhood. In equilibrium prices and the fraction of informed sellers are determined simultaneously.

There are many neighborhoods. The number of buyers per neighborhood is N or $N + \Delta$ and the individual demand function is given by D(P). Buyers see all prices in all neighborhoods and can freely move across neighborhoods.

There are two potential markets. The price in market 1 is P_1 and the price in market 2 is P_2. Before the beginning of trade sellers may buy information about the realization of $\tilde{N}$. As in other UST models, it is assumed that a market opens if there is a demand to trade in it.

There are n sellers per neighborhood. Information is shared among the sellers in the neighborhood but not among sellers who belong to different neighborhoods.[1] A neighborhood is informed if at least one of its members bought the information. We assume that n is large and use $\zeta = (1 - q)^{n-1} \approx (1 - q)^n$ to denote the probability that the neighborhood is not informed.

Sellers in an informed neighborhood supply to market 1 if the realization of $\tilde{N}$ is N and to market 2 if the realization of $\tilde{N}$ is $N + \Delta$.

Sellers in uninformed neighborhoods supply to market 1 if $P_1 \geq (1/2)P_2$ and to market 2 otherwise.

Equilibrium is a vector (P_1, P_2, ζ, VI) such that

$$VI = \tfrac{1}{2}P_1 + \tfrac{1}{2}P_2 - \max\left\{P_1, \tfrac{1}{2}P_2\right\};$$ (22.6)

$$\zeta VI = \alpha;$$ (22.7)

$$ND(P_1) = n \quad \text{if } P_1 \geq \tfrac{1}{2}P_2 \quad \text{and}$$

$$[N/(1 - \zeta)]D(P_1) = n \quad \text{otherwise;}$$ (22.8)

$$[N + \Delta/(1 - \zeta)]D(P_2) = n \quad \text{if } P_1 \geq \tfrac{1}{2}P_2 \quad \text{and}$$

$$(N + \Delta)D(P_2) = n \quad \text{otherwise.}$$ (22.9)

Condition (22.6) defines the value of information. The expected private benefit from buying information is ζVI and condition (22.7) says that in equilibrium sellers are indifferent between buying to not buying the information.

Conditions (22.8) and (22.9) require that markets which open will clear. To understand these conditions, let us focus on the case in which $P_1 \geq (1/2)P_2$. In this case, (22.8) and (22.9) can be written as:

$$ND(P_1) = n \quad \text{and} \quad [N + \Delta/(1 - \zeta)]D(P_2) = n.$$ (22.10)

When the number of buyers is N per neighborhood all sellers supply to market 1 and the requirement $ND(P_1) = n$ insures that this market is cleared. When the number of buyers is $N + \Delta$ per neighborhood sellers in informed neighborhoods supply to market 2 and sellers in uninformed neighborhoods supply to market 1. At the price P_1 uninformed neighborhoods will satisfy the demand of N buyers per uninformed neighborhood. Since ζ is the fraction of uninformed neighborhoods, the number of buyers who could not buy at the cheaper price P_1 is $\Delta + (1 - \zeta)N$ per neighborhood and $[\Delta/(1 - \zeta)] + N$ per informed neighborhood. The clearing of the second market therefore requires: $[N + \Delta/(1 - \zeta)]D(P_2) = n$.

When $P_1 < (1/2)P_2$, uninformed neighborhoods supply to the second market. In this case, we may write (22.8) and (22.9) as:

$$[N/(1 - \zeta)]D(P_1) = n \quad \text{and} \quad (N + \Delta)D(P_2) = n.$$ (22.11)

When the number of buyers is $N + \Delta$ per neighborhood, everyone supplies to the second market and the first market does not open. Equilibrium condition $(N + \Delta)D(P_2) = n$ ensures that market 2 clears in this case. If the number of buyers is N per neighborhood, informed neighborhoods supply to market 1 and satisfy the demand of all buyers and market 2 does not open. The number of buyers per informed neighborhood is $N/(1 - \zeta)$ and the clearing of the first market condition is: $[N/(1 - \zeta)]D(P_1) = n$. Thus when $P_1 < (1/2)P_2$, only one market opens but uninformed sellers do not know which one.

To discuss the existence of equilibrium, let θ_1 (θ_2) denote the Walrasian price when the number of buyers are N $(N + \Delta)$ per neighborhood. Thus, $ND(\theta_1) = n$ and $(N + \Delta)D(\theta_2) = n$. We assume that α is small; the individual demand curve $D(P)$ intersects the price axis at P_{max}

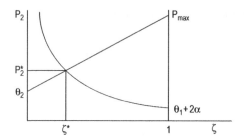

Figure 22.1 Uninformed supply to the first market

and $\theta_1 + 2\alpha < P_{max} < 2\theta_1$. Under these assumptions,

Proposition 1: There exists a unique equilibrium in which $P_1 = \theta_1 \geq (1/2)P_2$.

In this equilibrium market 1 always opens and market 2 opens only when the number of buyers is $N + \Delta$ per neighborhood.

Proof: When $P_1 = \theta_1 \geq (1/2)P_2$, the value of information is: $VI = (1/2)(P_2 - \theta_1)$ and equation (22.7) is:

$$P_2 = \theta_1 + 2\alpha/\zeta. \tag{22.12}$$

For this case equation (22.9) is:

$$[N + \Delta/(1-\zeta)]D(P_2) = n. \tag{22.13}$$

These are two equations in two unknowns (ζ, P_2). The locus of points that satisfy (22.12) is downward sloping as in figure 22.1. When $\zeta = 1$, $P_2 = \theta_1 + 2\alpha$ and when ζ goes to zero P_2 goes to infinity. The locus of points that satisfy (22.13) is upward sloping. When $\zeta = 0$, $P_2 = \theta_2$. When $\zeta = 1$, $P_2 = P_{max}$. Since $P_{max} > \theta_1 + 2\alpha$, there is a unique solution to our two equations: ζ^*, P_2^* in figure 22.1.

Since $P_2^* < P_{max} < 2\theta_1$, it follows that $(1/2)P_2^* < \theta_1$. Thus, there exists an equilibrium in which $P_1 = \theta_1 \geq (1/2)P_2$. $\qquad\square$

We have shown that if the intersection point P_{max} is not too high, there exists an equilibrium in which uninformed sellers supply their entire endowment to the first market. The other type of equilibrium exists when the intersection point is high.

Proposition 2: When $P_{max} > 2\alpha$ and Δ is large there exists a unique equilibrium in which $P_2 = \theta_2 \geq 2P_1$.

In this equilibrium only one market opens. If the number of buyers is large, only market 2 opens. Otherwise, only market 1 opens.

Proof: When $P_1 < (1/2)P_2$, $P_2 = \theta_2$ and the value of information is: $VI = (1/2)P_1$. Equation (22.7) is:

$$\zeta P_1 = 2\alpha; \tag{22.14}$$

And equation (22.8) is:

$$[N/(1-\zeta)]D(P_1) = n. \tag{22.15}$$

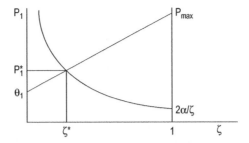

Figure 22.2   Uninformed supply to the second market

This is a system of two equations in two unknowns (ζ, P_1). With the help of figure 22.2 we can show that there exists a solution to these two equations.

When Δ is large, θ_2 is large and $P_1^* < (1/2)\theta_2$. Thus under the above conditions there exists a unique equilibrium in which uninformed sellers choose to supply to market 2.   □

Note that Proposition 1 requires that θ_2 is not large and Proposition 2 requires that θ_2 is large. We can vary θ_2 without affecting θ_1 by varying Δ.

Conclusions

We considered the case in which sellers can buy information about the realization of demand before the beginning of trade. As in the standard UST model, there are two potential markets and sometimes only one opens. But here sellers typically allocate their entire supply to one market. Informed sellers allocate their entire supply to the highest price market that opens while uninformed sellers allocate their entire supply to the market that promises the highest expected revenues.

22.2   A MONETARY MODEL

We now modify the overlapping generations model in chapter 15 to the case in which information about the end of period money supply can be obtained at a cost.

At the beginning of each period many ex ante identical individuals are born: n agents per neighborhood. Individuals live for two periods. They produce and sell their output for money in the first period. They then use, in the second period, the proceeds of first period sales plus a transfer that they may receive from the government to buy goods.

The utility function of an agent born at t is:

$$c_{t+1} - (x_t)^2, \tag{22.16}$$

where c_{t+1} is the amount of consumption when old and x_t is the amount of production when young. The expected utility for a young agent who faces the expected real wage w is:

$$V(w) = \max wx - x^2. \tag{22.17}$$

And the supply at the real wage w is denoted by:

$$S(w) = \text{argmax} \, wx - x^2. \tag{22.18}$$

Later we use the explicit solutions to (22.18) and (22.17):

$$S(w) = \tfrac{1}{2}w \quad \text{and} \quad V(w) = \tfrac{1}{4}w^2.$$

The buyer (an old agent) spends the proceeds of last period sales. Then, if he receives a transfer payment he goes to a second location and buys goods with the transfer payment money. Otherwise, he goes home. The amount of transfer is γ dollars per dollar held at the beginning of the period and the probability of receiving it is $1/2$.

We use M to denote the money supply in the current period and M^s to denote the next period money supply in state s: $M^1 = M$ and $M^2 = \Gamma M = (1 + \gamma)M$. We use normalized dollars (ND) as the unit of account, where a normalized dollar is the pre-transfer money supply per agent. In terms of current normalized dollars the post-transfer money supply is $m' = 1$ if there is no transfer payment and $m' = \Gamma$ if there is a transfer payment.

A normalized dollar this period is worth $\omega^s = M/M^s$ in terms of next period's normalized dollars:

$$\omega^1 = 1 \quad \text{and} \quad \omega^2 = 1/(1 + \gamma) = 1/\Gamma. \tag{22.19}$$

In steady-state equilibrium, the buyer will spend his initial holdings of money in market 1 at the price p_1 (ND per unit). Then, if he receives a transfer payment he will spend it in market 2 at the price p_2. Since a normalized dollar promises a transfer of γ ND with probability $1/2$, the expected purchasing power of a normalized dollar held at the beginning of the period is:

$$z = (1/p_1) + \tfrac{1}{2}(\gamma/p_2). \tag{22.20}$$

From the seller's (young agent) point of view there are two potential markets. Market 1 will open with certainty at the price p_1 and market 2 will open if there is a transfer payment (with probability $1/2$) at the price p_2.

Before the choice of production the seller (young agent) can buy information about the end of period money supply for α units of next period's consumption and learn about the number of markets that will open. Information is a local public good: It is shared with all the sellers in the neighborhood. As before, a neighborhood is informed if at least one seller in the neighborhood has bought the information.

In equilibrium $p_2 > p_1$ and an informed seller supplies $S(w^1)$ units to market 1 (and zero to market 2) if the post transfer money supply is $m' = 1$ and $S(w^2)$ units to market 2 (and zero to market 1) if $m' = \Gamma$, where $w^1 = p_1\omega^1 z$ and $w^2 = p_2\omega^2 z$ are the relevant real wages.

Sellers in uninformed neighborhoods face the expected real wage $w = \max[p_1\omega z, (1/2)p_2\omega^2 z]$, where as in previous chapters:

$$\omega = \tfrac{1}{2}\omega^1 + \tfrac{1}{2}\omega^2, \tag{22.21}$$

is the unconditional expected value of a ND in terms of next period's NDs. We start by assuming that $p_1\omega \geq (1/2)p_2\omega^2$ and sellers in uninformed neighborhoods choose to supply to market 1.

Uninformed neighborhoods supply to market 1

Sellers in uninformed neighborhoods make the expected utility $V(w = p_1 \omega z)$. The expected utility of a seller in an informed neighborhood is: $(1/2)V(p_1 \omega^1 z) + (1/2)V(p_2 \omega^2 z)$. The value of information is therefore:

$$\text{VI} = \tfrac{1}{2}V(p_1 \omega^1 z) + \tfrac{1}{2}V(p_2 \omega^2 z) - V(p_1 \omega z). \tag{22.22}$$

Sellers buy the information with probability q. We assume that n is large and use $\zeta = (1 - q)^{n-1} \approx (1 - q)^n$ to denote the probability that no other seller in the neighborhood buys the information.

A seller who buys information will increase his expected utility by VI if no one else in the neighborhood has bought the information and by zero otherwise. The expected private benefit from buying information is therefore ζVI, where ζ is the probability that he cannot free ride. To justify a mixed strategy we require that the private value of information is equal the cost of information:

$$\zeta \text{VI} = \alpha. \tag{22.23}$$

The number of neighborhoods is large and in equilibrium a fraction ζ of the neighborhoods are uninformed. Unlike the standard UST model, here the supply to each market depends on the state of nature. When $m' = 1$ all neighborhoods supply to market 1. When $m' = \Gamma$, only uninformed neighborhoods supply to market 1. The supply per neighborhood to market 1 is therefore:

$$\zeta S(p_1 \omega z) + (1 - \zeta) S(p_1 \omega^1 z) \quad \text{if } m' = 1$$
$$\zeta S(p_1 \omega z) \quad \text{if } m' = \Gamma. \tag{22.24}$$

The supply per neighborhood to market 2 is:

$$0 \quad \text{if } m' = 1;$$
$$(1 - \zeta) S(p_2 \omega^2 z) \quad \text{if } m' = \Gamma. \tag{22.25}$$

Market clearing requires:

$$1 = p_1 [\zeta S(p_1 \omega z) + (1 - \zeta) S(p_1 \omega^1 z)]; \tag{22.26}$$
$$\Gamma = p_2 (1 - \zeta) S(p_2 \omega^2 z) + p_1 \zeta S(p_1 \omega z). \tag{22.27}$$

Note that these conditions say that buyers can always find goods at some price. When $m' = 1$ all the money is spent in market 1 and condition (22.26) guarantee that all buyers spend their money. When $m' = \Gamma$, $p_1 \zeta S(p_1 \omega z)$ normalized dollars buy in market 1 and the rest in market 2.

Equilibrium for the case $p_1 \omega \geq (1/2) p_2 \omega^2$ requires (22.22), (22.23) and (22.26)–(22.27). We also require $p_1 \leq p_2$ so that an informed seller who observed $m' = \Gamma$ will advertise p_2 rather than p_1.

Uninformed neighborhoods supply to market 2

We now turn to the case $p_1\omega < (1/2)p_2\omega^2$. In this case, uninformed neighborhoods supply to market 2 making an expected utility of $V[(1/2)p_2\omega^2 z]$ and, as before, informed neighborhoods make the expected utility $(1/2)V(p_1\omega^1 z) + (1/2)V(p_2\omega^2 z)$, by supplying their entire output to market 1 if $m' = 1$ and market 2 if $m' = \Gamma$. The value of information in this case is:

$$VI = \tfrac{1}{2}V(p_1\omega^1 z) + \tfrac{1}{2}V(p_2\omega^2 z) - V[\tfrac{1}{2}p_2\omega^2 z]. \tag{22.28}$$

The supply per neighborhood to market 1 is:

$$(1 - \zeta)S(p_1\omega^1 z) \quad \text{if } m' = 1$$
$$0 \quad \text{if } m' = \Gamma. \tag{22.29}$$

The supply per neighborhood to market 2 is:

$$\zeta S[(1/2)p_2\omega^2 z] \quad \text{if } m' = 1;$$
$$\zeta S[(1/2)p_2\omega^2 z] + (1 - \zeta)S(p_2\omega^2 z) \quad \text{if } m' = \Gamma. \tag{22.30}$$

Note that when $m' = 1$ only market 1 opens and when $m' = \Gamma$ only market 2 opens. The market-clearing conditions are:

$$1 = p_1(1 - \zeta)S(p_1\omega^1 z); \tag{22.31}$$
$$\Gamma = p_2\zeta S[(1/2)p_2\omega^2 z] + p_2(1 - \zeta)S(p_2\omega^2 z). \tag{22.32}$$

Equilibrium for this case requires (22.28), (22.23) and (22.31)–(22.32) as well as $p_1 \le p_2$.

We can now summarize the discussion and define equilibrium that allows for the two cases. Equilibrium is a vector (p_1, p_2, z, VI, ζ) such that $p_1 \le p_2$ and

$$z = (1/p_1) + \tfrac{1}{2}(\gamma/p_2); \tag{22.33}$$

$$VI = \tfrac{1}{2}V(p_1\omega^1 z) + \tfrac{1}{2}V(p_2\omega^2 z) - \max\{V(p_1\omega z), V[\tfrac{1}{2}p_2\omega^2 z]\}; \tag{22.34}$$

$$\zeta VI = \alpha; \tag{22.35}$$

$$1 = p_1[\zeta S(p_1\omega z) + (1 - \zeta)S(p_1\omega^1 z)] \quad \text{if } p_1\omega \ge \tfrac{1}{2}p_2\omega^2 \quad \text{and}$$
$$1 = p_1(1 - \zeta)S(p_1\omega^1 z) \quad \text{otherwise}; \tag{22.36}$$

$$\Gamma = p_1\zeta S(p_1\omega z) + p_2(1 - \zeta)S(p_2\omega^2 z) \quad \text{if } p_1\omega \ge (1/2)p_2\omega^2 \quad \text{and}$$
$$\Gamma = p_2\{\zeta S[(1/2)p_2\omega^2 z] + (1 - \zeta)S(p_2\omega^2 z)\} \quad \text{otherwise}. \tag{22.37}$$

We now turn to the relationship between money and output.

Proposition: When uninformed sellers supply to market 1, equilibrium output is positively related to the end of period money supply:

$$(1 - \zeta)S(p_2\omega^2 z) + \zeta S(p_1\omega z) > (1 - \zeta)S(p_1\omega^1 z) + \zeta S(p_1\omega z). \tag{22.38}$$

Proof: Since uninformed sellers supply does not depend on the end of period money supply, we need to show that the expected real wage of the informed sellers is higher when $m' = \Gamma$. That is: $p_2\omega^2 > p_1\omega^1$. For this purpose, note that the revenue per uninformed seller in terms of next period's normalized dollars is:

$$\mu_1 = p_1\zeta S(p_1\omega z) \quad \text{when } m' = 1 \quad \text{and} \quad \mu_2 = p_1\zeta S(p_1\omega z)/\Gamma \quad \text{when } m' = \Gamma. \tag{22.39}$$

The revenue (in terms of next period's normalized dollars) per informed seller is $1 - \mu_s$. The expected consumption per informed seller in state s is $c_s = (1 - \mu_s)z$. Since $\mu_1 > \mu_2$, it follows that:

$$c_1 = (1 - \mu_1)z < c_2 = (1 - \mu_2)z. \tag{22.40}$$

It is also true that consumption is equal to the expected real wage times the quantity supplied: $c_s = w_s S(w_s)$. Since the supply function $S(w_s)$ is increasing, (22.40) implies: $w_2 > w_1$. Thus the real wage of informed young agents is higher when $m' = \Gamma$ and therefore their output is higher. Since the output of the uninformed sector is the same in both states, aggregate output is positively related to the end of period money supply. □

We have thus shown that when the uninformed supply to market 1, the informed will work harder when $m' = \Gamma$ because in this case their market share is higher and therefore their real wage is higher.

When Γ is large we may get the other type of equilibrium in which the uninformed supply to market 2. In this case, there is no clear relationship between the end of period money and output because the informed agents will work harder when $m' = 1$ and their market share is 1. The uninformed do not sell in this case and therefore their measured output may be zero.

Welfare

A planner in this economy will command each young agent to produce: $x = 1/2 = $ argmax $x - x^2$. This allocation can be achieved as an equilibrium outcome if there are no money surprises ($\gamma = 0$). Otherwise there will be distortions arising from the following equilibrium features: (a) Sellers produce different amounts depending on their information (b) When uninformed supply to market 2 and the money supply is low, some output is wasted and (c) Some resources are being spent on buying information. (This last item is negligible when n is large.)

A numerical example

We assume that $p_1\omega \geq (1/2)p_2\omega^2$. In this case uninformed supply to market 1 and solve the system of equations (22.22), (22.23), (22.26), (22.27), $S(w) = (1/2)w$ and $V(w) = (1/4)w^2$.

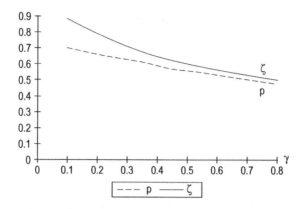

Figure 22.3   The fraction of uninformed and the relative price as a function of the potential shock

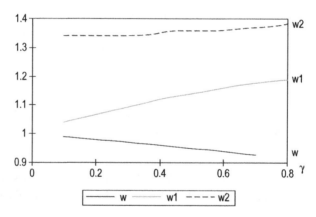

Figure 22.4   Real wages

We use $\alpha = 0.1$ and vary γ in the range 0.1 to 0.8. Figure 22.3 graphs the solutions to the relative price $p = p_1/p_2$ and the fraction of uninformed ζ. The monetary policy parameter γ is on the horizontal axis. In this example, the fraction of uninformed neighborhoods (ζ) and the relative price ($p = p_1/p_2$) are both decreasing functions of γ. Finally we check whether: $p_1\omega \geq (1/2)p_2\omega^2$ and $p_1 \leq p_2$. These conditions hold for all the points in figure 22.3.

Figure 22.4 describes the behavior of the real wages, where $w = p_1\omega z$ is the real wage of the uninformed, $w1 = p_1\omega^1 z$ is the real wage of the informed when $m' = 1$ and $w2 = p_2\omega^2 z$ is the real wage of the informed when $m' = \Gamma$. In this example, the real wages of the informed go up with γ while the real wage of the uninformed goes down. Therefore the equilibrium value of information (VI) increases with γ but since the fraction of uninformed (ζ) goes down, the private value of information (ζVI) remains constant at the level of α.

Conclusions

When the cost of information is not prohibitive, we get an equilibrium in which some but not all sellers are informed about the end of period money supply. When uninformed sellers supply to market 1, we get a positive relationship between money and output. This relationship is due to the behavior of the informed sellers: When the end of period money supply is high, informed sellers see a high real wage and work harder.

22.3 RELATIONSHIP TO THE NEW KEYNESIAN ECONOMICS

There are some similar elements with the new Keynesian economics literature that builds on the work of Taylor (1980), Rotemberg (1982) and Calvo (1983) and surveyed in Clarida, Gali and Gertler (1999).

Small costs can cause large welfare losses

Akerlof and Yellen (1985) and Mankiw (1985) advanced the idea that small costs can create large welfare losses. Figure 22.5 here is based on figure 3 in Mankiw (1985): p_m is the optimal monopoly price and MC is the constant marginal cost. Suppose now that because of menu costs the monopoly failed to adjust his price and post a price $p > p_m$. In this case, the monopoly's profits are reduced by B − A but the sum of consumer and producer surplus is reduced by B + C. Therefore the social loss is greater than the private loss. Furthermore, since small deviations from the optimum do not affect the objective function, for small deviations $(p - p_m)$, B − A is zero while the social loss of B + C is strictly positive.

In our model small information costs can also lead to large welfare losses. When $\alpha > VI$ information is prohibitively expensive and no one buys information. In this case we get the standard UST model that implies substantial waste: When realized demand is low some goods are produced but not sold. This occurs even when the cost per agent α/n is negligible. Even when $\alpha < VI$, we get a relatively large welfare loss because of informational externalities. In this case only a fraction of the neighborhoods are informed and a difference between the labor supply across sellers will emerge.

Calvo (1983)

It was mentioned in the introduction that this is a Calvo type model. In Calvo's model sellers can change their prices at random intervals that are exogenously determined. In a recent article Mankiw and Reis (2001) have assumed that sellers can change their prices at any point in time but only a fraction of the sellers get information about the current state of the economy.

To make the connection with our overlapping generations model we may think of father and son as belonging to the same firm. Firms do not make profits but we can think of the time series of prices posted by firms. Using this interpretation, the prices of all firms changes in response to last period change in the money supply but only the informed sector responds

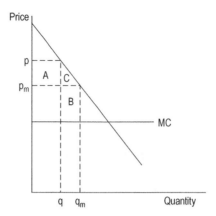

Figure 22.5   Mankiw's model

to the current change in the money supply. The model thus predicts frequent nominal price changes but only a fraction of these price changes are based on updated information.

There are two differences. In our model the time interval is endogenous and as we saw in the numerical example, when the uncertainty about the money supply goes up (measured by γ in our model) more agents are informed. Another difference is about labor supply. In Mankiw and Reis (2001) firms satisfy demand and therefore uninformed sellers who post a relatively low price work more than informed sellers. The opposite is true in our model.

Effective monetary policy?

Sargent and Wallace (1975) point out that under rational expectations monetary policy can be effective only if the government has better information than the public. In the presence of informational externalities a government that attempt to maximize welfare may have information advantage over the agents. In our model, the government may buy information even if $\alpha > VI$, while private agent will buy information with a strictly positive probability only if $\alpha < VI$ and even in this case there will be uninformed neighborhoods because of the local public good problem.

It thus seems that informational externalities, like externalities in general, can be used to justify some government intervention.

NOTE

1   Since there are many neighborhoods sellers cannot benefit by keeping the information private.

CHAPTER 23

Search and Contracts

Up to now we have abstracted from search and assumed that upon arrival the buyer saw all prices and spent all his money on the cheapest available alternative. This level of abstraction may be suitable for analyzing aggregate data but it is not likely to be suitable for analyzing micro level data.

We start by completing the model in section 17.1 and allow buyers to search over time. This extension allows us to talk about delivery lags which is an aspect of sales stressed by Carlton (1989). We then turn to the case in which buyers may make "mistakes" and may not succeed in buying at the cheapest available price. This add realism to our model because it leads to an equilibrium in which some expensive goods are sold even when the realization of demand is low.

23.1 SEARCH OVER TIME

We now extend the model with storage in section 17.1 and allow buyers the choice of the amount of money that they will spend. This can be interpreted as search over time. To advance this interpretation note that in section 17.1 buyers who arrive early find low price offers (in market 1) and buyers who arrive late find only high price offers. Here a buyer who arrives when market 2 opens may choose not to buy with the hope of arriving early next period and participating in next period's market 1.

To formulate this search choice, let $r_s(I)$ denote the value of a normalized dollar held by the buyer in market s as a function of the beginning of period inventories. The value of a normalized dollar held at the beginning of the period is:

$$\zeta(I) = \tfrac{1}{2}r_1(I) + \tfrac{1}{2}[\theta_1 r_1(I) + \theta_2 r_2(I)], \qquad (23.1)$$

where θ_s is the probability that a dollar is in batch s given that two markets open. Note that in the special case $r_s(I) = 1/p_s(I)$, the function $\zeta(I)$ is identical to the function $z(I)$ in equation (17.4) of 17.1.

We can now define the functions $r_s(I)$ recursively for given expectations (I^1, I^2) about future inventories:

$$r_2(I) = \max\{1/p_2(I), \beta\omega^2\zeta(I^2)\};\qquad(23.2)$$

$$r_1(I) = \max\left\{1/p_1(I), \beta\left[\tfrac{1}{2}\omega^1\zeta(I^1) + \tfrac{1}{2}\omega^2\zeta(I^2)\right]\right\}.\qquad(23.3)$$

The definition (23.2) says that the value of a normalized dollar held by the buyer in market 2 is the maximum between the purchasing power in market 2 and the expected purchasing power in case the normalized dollar is carried over to the next period. The definition (23.3) is the value of a normalized dollar held by the buyer in market 1 when he does not know how many markets will open this period.

Since the utility is linear in consumption the buyer will spend everything he has in market 1 if $1/p_1(I) \geq \beta E\omega^s\zeta(I^s)$. The demand in market 1 is therefore:

$$d_1(I) = 1+\gamma \quad \text{if } 1/p_1(I) \geq \beta\left[\tfrac{1}{2}\omega^1\zeta(I^1) + \tfrac{1}{2}\omega^2\zeta(I^2)\right], \quad \text{and} \quad \text{zero otherwise.}\qquad(23.4)$$

Similarly, the demand in market 2 (if it opens) is:

$$d_2(I) = \gamma \quad \text{if } 1/p_2(I) \geq \beta\omega^2\zeta(I^2) \quad \text{and} \quad \text{zero otherwise.}\qquad(23.5)$$

The first order conditions which governs the supply decisions can now be stated by substituting the function ζ for z in (17.5), (17.6) and (17.7) in section 17.4. This yields:

$$v'[L(I)] = \beta p_1(I)E_s\{\omega^s\zeta(I^s)\},\qquad(23.6)$$

$$p_1(I)E_s\{\omega^s\zeta(I^s)\} = \tfrac{1}{2}p_2(I)[\omega^2\zeta(I^2)] + \tfrac{1}{2}v'[L(I^1)],\qquad(23.7)$$

$$p_2(I)[\omega^2\zeta(I^2)] \geq v'[L(I^2)] \quad \text{with strict equality if } k > k_1 + k_2.\qquad(23.8)$$

We can now define a steady state equilibrium as follows.

Steady state equilibrium is a vector of functions

$$[L(I), d_1(I), d_2(I), k(I), k_1(I), k_2(I), p_1(I), p_2(I), \zeta(I), r_1(I), r_2(I), I^1(I), I^2(I)]$$

such that (23.1)−(23.8) are satisfied and:

(a) $k(I) = L(I) + I \geq k_1(I) + k_2(I); I^s(I) = k(I) - \sum_{j=1}^{s} k_s(I) \geq 0;$

(b) markets that open are cleared: $d_s(I) = p_s(I)k_s(I);$ for all $I \geq 0$ and $s = 1, 2.$

The solution method is the same as in section 17.1 where the function ζ plays the role of z. We first guess the functions $\zeta(I^s)$ and $MC(I^s) = v'[L(I^s)]$ and use these functions to specify expectations. We then solve for current magnitudes and then check whether the assumed expectations are correct. If not we try another guess. Once we have solved for the function $\zeta(I)$ and for equilibrium prices we use (23.2) and (23.3) to solve for $r_s(I)$.

23.2   RANDOM CHOICE OF MARKETS

Rotemberg and Summers (1990, p. 865–6) argue quite convincingly that the rationing of buyers in a UST type model is realistic. When an item is on sale, some individuals are often unable to obtain it on demand at the sale price. Moreover, buyers who arrive first often get a better quality than buyers who arrive late, which is equivalent to paying a low price. For example, buyers who make early plane reservation get better seats.

The rationing of sellers in the UST model is however, not realistic. Sellers in the model either sell their entire supply at a given price or do not sell anything at that price. In the real world sellers usually sell a fraction of the goods offered at a given price and the fraction sold varies over time.

To gain some realism we outline here a model that allows for the possibility that cheaper goods may not sell first. The additional complexity may be required for explaining micro level data about prices and sales that are becoming available as scanner data.

The model

We extend the model in section 14.1 assuming a real (non-monetary) economy with no storage technology. There are N potential buyers and S possible states of nature. In state of nature s, N_s buyers want to consume, where $N_1 < N_2 < \cdots < N_S$. The probability that state of nature s will occur is Π_s and $q_s = \sum_{j=s}^{S} \Pi_j$ is the probability that $N \geq N_s$.

Buyers who want to consume arrive sequentially at the market place, demand one unit and are willing to pay a high price for it. The demand for $\Delta_1 = N_1$ units arrives with certainty. This batch of buyers completes trade and disappears. Then there are two possibilities. Either trade ends for the period or, if the realization of N is greater than N_1, an additional demand for $\Delta_2 = N_2 - N_1$ units arrives. This process continues until all the buyers who want to consume arrive and trade.

As in other UST models there are S markets. But unlike other UST models, here buyers do not always buy at the cheapest available price. Instead each buyer draws a market randomly. The probability that the buyer will buy in market s depends on the price in this market relative to the prices in other markets with available supplies. We may think of the lottery that allocates buyers across markets as standing for a more complex choice problem in which the buyer chooses the location of his shopping on the basis of where he happens to be at the time he makes the choice and relative prices. For this type of discrete choice models see McFadden (2000).

The description of the lottery uses the concept of markets. As in other UST models, the seller chooses capacity before the beginning of trade and allocates it among the S potential markets. Here it is useful to think of this choice as a choice of price tags: A seller who chooses the price tag p_s for a given unit supplies it to market s. Like in previous UST models it is assumed that if the first s batches arrive then all the quantity supplied to market s is sold. Unlike previous models it is assumed here that a fraction of the quantity supplied to market s is sold if only $j < s$ batches arrive. Figure 23.1 illustrates the sequential trade process.

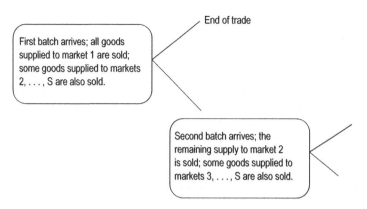

Figure 23.1

After the completion of trade in market $j - 1$ the available price offers are $(p_j, \ldots, p_S)$ and the average price offer is:

$$\bar{p}_j = [1/(S + 1 - j)] \sum_{i=j}^{S} p_i. \tag{23.9}$$

If batch j arrives then the lottery that allocates buyers to markets will send a fraction $w_s / \sum_{i=j}^{S} w_i$ of the buyers in this batch to market s $(s \geq j)$, where $w_i = \exp[\alpha(\bar{p}_j/p_i)]$. Here the fraction of buyers in batch j that will buy in market s is not random, but there is uncertainty from the individual buyer's point of view. The probability that a buyer in batch j will buy in market s, $w_s / \sum_{i=j}^{S} w_i$, depends on the price in this market relative to the prices in other markets with available supplies.

A seller who quotes the price p_s will get a fraction:

$$F_j(\bar{p}_j, p_s) = \exp[\alpha(\bar{p}_j/p_s)] / \sum_{i=j}^{S} \exp[\alpha(\bar{p}_j/p_i)], \tag{23.10}$$

of the buyers in batch $j \leq s$ if this batch arrives.[1] The expected revenue for a seller who quotes the price p_s and satisfies demand until transactions in market s are completed is therefore:

$$p_s \sum_{j=1}^{s} q_j \Delta_j F_j(\bar{p}_j, p_s), \tag{23.11}$$

where $q_j = \sum_{s=j}^{S} \Pi_s$ is the probability that batch j will arrive and $\Delta_j = N_j - N_{j-1}$ is the number of buyers in batch j.

The quantity required for satisfying the demand at the price p_s until transactions in market s are completed is:

$$k_s = \sum_{j=1}^{s} \Delta_j F_j(\bar{p}_j, p_s). \tag{23.12}$$

The expected revenue per unit supplied at the price p_s is denoted by Γ_s and is obtained by dividing (23.11) by (23.12). Thus,

$$\Gamma_s = p_s \sum_{j=1}^{S} q_j \Delta_j F_j(\bar{p}_j, p_s) \Big/ \sum_{j=1}^{S} \Delta_j F_j(\bar{p}_j, p_s). \tag{23.13}$$

The term $\sum_{j=1}^{s} q_j \Delta_j F_j(\bar{p}_j, p_s) / \sum_{j=1}^{s} \Delta_j F_j(\bar{p}_j, p_s)$ is the selling probability of a unit supplied to market s. It is obtained by a weighted average of the probabilities that batches $1, \ldots, s$ will arrive where the weights are equal to the fraction of the supply to market s which is sold in each market $j \leq s$.

Production occurs before the beginning of trade at the cost of $C(k)$ units of the numeraire commodity, where $C'(0) = 0$ and $C'' > 0$. The seller takes the expected revenues per unit $(\Gamma_1, \ldots, \Gamma_S)$ as given and solves:

$$\max_{\{k_s\}} \sum_{s=1}^{S} \Gamma_s k_s - C\left(\sum_{s=1}^{S} k_s\right), \tag{23.14}$$

where k_s is the amount allocated to market s.

The first order conditions for this problem are:

$$\Gamma_s = C'\left(\sum_{s=1}^{S} k_s\right) \quad \text{for all s.} \tag{23.15}$$

Equilibrium is a vector $(p_1, \ldots, p_S; \Gamma_1, \ldots, \Gamma_S; k_1, \ldots, k_S)$ that satisfies (23.12), (23.13) and (23.15).

Note that the equilibrium concept is competitive in the sense that sellers take the relevant price (the expected revenue per unit, Γ_s) in each market as given and equate marginal cost to the price.

Solving for equilibrium

We say that market s opens when batch s arrives. This language is useful in spite of the fact that some of the supply to market s is sold before it opens. We use $\pi_s = \sum_{j=s}^{S} \Pi_j / q_{s-1}$ to denote the probability that market s will open given that market $s - 1$ opens. We now solve for equilibrium under the assumption that π_s is close to unity. This will be the case when the probability distribution of x can be approximated by a continuous distribution with a mass point at $x = x_S$.

We choose p_S arbitrarily and start by looking for a price p_{S-1} that will make the seller indifferent between selling a unit in market $S - 1$ when it opens to allocating it to market S. For this purpose we first compute the expected revenue per unit allocated to market S, given that market $S - 1$ opens.

The expected revenue of the entire supply to market S, given that market $S - 1$ opens is:

$$p_S[\Delta_{S-1} F_{S-1}(\bar{p}_{S-1}, p_S) + \pi_S \Delta_S], \tag{23.16}$$

where $\bar{p}_{S-1} = (1/2)(p_S + p_{S-1})$ is the average price when market $S-1$ opens; $\pi_S = \Pi_S / q_{S-1}$ is the probability that market S will open given that market $S - 1$ opens.

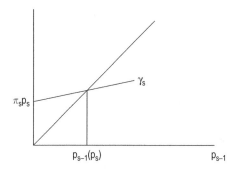

Figure 23.2   Solving p_{S-1} as a function of p_S

The quantity required to satisfy demand at the price p_S is:

$$[\Delta_{S-1}F_{S-1}(\bar{p}_{S-1}, p_S) + \Delta_S]. \tag{23.17}$$

The revenue per unit allocated to market S, conditional on market $S-1$ being open is obtained by dividing (23.16) by (23.17). This yields:

$$\gamma_S = p_S[\Delta_{S-1}F_{S-1}(\bar{p}_{S-1}, p_S) + \pi_S \Delta_S]/[\Delta_{S-1}F_{S-1}(\bar{p}_{S-1}, p_S) + \Delta_S]. \tag{23.18}$$

When market $S-1$ opens, the seller can sell the entire unit at the price p_{S-1}. He can also put the price tag p_S on it and get the expected revenue γ_S. We require that the expected per unit revenue will be the same for both price tags:

$$p_{S-1} = \gamma_S. \tag{23.19}$$

Note that (23.18) implies $p_S > \gamma_S$ and therefore $p_S > p_{S-1}$.

We now use (23.18) and (23.19) to solve for the price p_{S-1} as a function of the price p_S. When $p_{S-1} = 0, F_{S-1} = 0$ and $\gamma_S = \pi_S p_S$. Since we assume that π_S is close to unity, the derivative of γ_S with respect to p_{S-1} is small. Under this condition there is a solution, $p_{S-1}(p_S)$, to (23.18) and (23.19). Figure 23.2 illustrates this solution.

We can now use $p_{S-1}(p_S)$ to find the price p_{S-2} that will make the seller indifferent to changing the price tag on a given unit from p_{S-2} to $p_{S-1}(p_S)$, when market $S-2$ opens. We keep doing that until we find all prices: $p_1(p_S), \ldots, p_{S-1}(p_S)$.

We now use (23.12) to compute the total amount required to satisfy the demand in market s:

$$k_s(p_S) = \sum_{j=1}^{s} \Delta_j F_j[\bar{p}_j(p_S), p_s(p_S)]. \tag{23.20}$$

Supply, $s(p_S)$, is the solution to (23.15) which can be written as:

$$C'(k) = p_1(p_S). \tag{23.21}$$

We now equate supply and demand:

$$s(p_S) = d(p_S) = \sum_{s=1}^{S} k_s(p_S). \tag{23.22}$$

We denote the solution to (23.22) by $\hat{p}_S$ and compute all equilibrium prices and quantities: $p_s(\hat{p}_S), k_s(\hat{p}_S)$.

Conclusions

In previous UST models the probability distribution of sales at a given price could take only two possible realizations: Either you sell everything or nothing. The reason for this unrealistic sale distribution was in the assumption that cheaper goods are sold first. Here buyers may buy at prices which are higher than the cheapest alternative and therefore we get a more realistic sale distribution.

We also get realistic contingent demand-satisfying behavior. Rotemberg and Summers (1990) provide some direct evidence against unconditional demand-satisfying behavior. For example, they cite studies which report that, on average, 12.2 percent of major brand items carried by supermarkets are out of stock at any point in time and 30 percent of the customers at the typical store are unable to purchase all the items on their shopping lists. If we are after realism we should therefore look for a milder form of demand-satisfying behavior.

When there are many prices and capacity limits, a commitment to satisfy demand may take two forms. A store may plan to sell at the announced price up to the capacity limit. A store may also plan to sell a certain quantity at a lower "sale" price and then, if demand is high, to sell at a higher "list price" to late arrivals. Our model allows for both types of demand-satisfying behavior. In general sellers can make contingent demand-satisfying commitments of the type: "I will satisfy the demand at the price p_s if demand is less than N_s." In equilibrium these contingent demand satisfying commitments are not binding and the seller has no incentive to renege on them.

23.3 CAPACITY UTILIZATION CONTRACTS AND CARLTON'S OBSERVATIONS

The sun rises in the east and falls in the west. For a long time this was taken as direct evidence that the sun moves around earth. But we do not think so anymore.

It was argued in chapters 14 and 15 that in the UST model prices that appear rigid may not be rigid at all. This is not the only example of seemingly rigid prices. The labor contract literature pioneered by Azariadis (1975), Baily (1974), and Gordon (1975), focus on the insurance explanation of wage rigidity and Barro (1977) shows that rigid real wages do not necessarily imply labor misallocation.

Here we apply the contracting argument to observations made by Carlton (1986, 1989). Using the Stigler and Kindahl (1970) data about prices of transactions between large firms and their suppliers, Carlton found that it is not unusual in some industries for prices to individual buyers to remain unchanged for several years. But more surprisingly, the correlation of price changes across buyers is low even for what appears to be homogeneous commodities. He argues that the low correlation of price changes across buyers "emphasizes how erroneous it is to focus attention on price as the exclusive mechanism to allocate resources. Non-price rationing is not a fiction, it is a reality of business and may be the efficient response to economic uncertainty and the cost of using the price system" (Carlton 1986, p. 638).

Here we assume that using the price system is costless and use a variant of the Walrasian–Arrow–Debreu model to account for Carlton's observations. Sellers choose capacity before the realization of demand is known and sell state contingent capacity utilization contracts. Since we do not observe the entire basket of contingent commodities bought by the buyer, the price actually paid by the buyer, when executing the contract, may appear rigid and the correlation between price changes across buyers may be low.

The argument is different from the labor contracting argument because here all agents are risk neutral. Like in the UST model the problem here is to choose capacity in the face of uncertain demand. But unlike the UST model here trade is not sequential and the standard Walrasian outcome is achieved.

The model

We consider an economy with two dates ($t = 0, 1$) and two goods (X and Y with lower case letters denoting quantities). There is a price-taking firm with a constant returns to scale technology: It can produce X at the cost of λ units of Y per unit of X. Production occurs at $t = 0$.

There are S possible aggregate states of nature (indexed s) where state s occurs with probability Π_s. There are J types of buyers. A type j buyer demands one unit of X at any price less than v_j if he wants to consume and zero otherwise. At $t = 1$ the state becomes public information and the buyer learns about his desire to consume.

There are n_j type j buyers and in state s a fraction ϕ_{js} of them want to consume. Aggregate demand over all type j buyers in state s at the price p is thus:

$$N_{js}(p) = \phi_{js}n_j \quad \text{if } v_j \geq p \quad \text{and} \quad \text{zero otherwise.} \tag{23.23}$$

Aggregate demand over all types in state s is:

$$N_s(p) = \sum_j N_{js}(p). \tag{23.24}$$

In the standard Walrasian auction model the realization of demand is observed before announcing the market clearing price: p_s. Formally, standard Walrasian auction equilibrium is a non-negative vector of prices $(p_1, \ldots, p_S)$ and total production (capacity) x such that:

(a) $\sum_{s=1}^{S} \Pi_s p_s = \lambda$;
(b) $N_s(p_s) \leq x$ for all s and $p_s = 0$ when the inequality is strict.

Condition (a) ensures that the firm makes zero expected profits; (b) is a market clearing condition.

To define efficiency we consider the problem of a central planner who can observe the state of nature and the reservation price of each buyer. Let I(statement) $= 1$ when the statement is true and zero otherwise. The central planner's problem may be stated as that of choosing shadow prices p_s and capacity x which solve:

$$\max \sum_s \Pi_s \sum_j \phi_{js} n_j v_j I(v_j \geq p_s) - \lambda x$$

$$\text{s.t.} \quad \sum_j \phi_{js} n_j I(v_j \geq p_s) \leq x \quad \text{for all s.} \tag{23.25}$$

An allocation is Walrasian efficient if it solves (23.25). The first welfare Theorem says that the standard Walrasian auction prices and the equilibrium choice of x solve (23.25) and therefore the equilibrium allocation is Walrasian efficient.

We now turn to discuss the possibility of using ex-ante contracts. Here agents are risk neutral and there is no insurance motive for trading in contracts. But it may be cheaper to implement the Walrasian auction allocation in two stages. In the first stage buyers delegate their preferences to a relatively small number of firms and then after the state is revealed, these firms participate in a spot market auction. We use the term delegated auction for this two stages procedure and use the airline industry as an example.

Delegated auctions

The airline industry must choose and allocate capacity in the face of uncertainty about demand. One possibility is to run an auction at the gate. Alternatively, trade may be done in two stages. In the first stage the airlines sell tickets. Then, close to the time of departure, there is an auction in which airlines participate but individual passengers do not. The two stages alternative may save time if it is easier to run an auction with a smaller number of participants. It may also be a way of transmitting information about prices and allow buyers to make an informed decision about whether or not to take a cab to the airport. We now describe the second alternative in detail.

We start from the case in which the type of the buyer is observed. At $t = 0$, the airlines sell contracts to buyers. A contract (a ticket) is a triplet (μ, α, β): If at $t = 1$ the buyer reports that he wants to fly and the airline chooses to deliver the buyer pays the price μ. If the buyer reports that he does not want to fly he pays α (get a refund of $\mu - \alpha$). If he reports that he wants to fly but there is "overbooking" and the airline does not deliver the buyer gets β (pays $-\beta$).[2] To insure that a buyer who does not want to fly will truthfully report to the airline, we require: $\mu \geq \alpha \geq 0$.

At $t = 1$ all the refund options are exercised and the state of nature is revealed. At this stage airlines trade in a spot market auction at the price p_s.

The airline problem is to choose capacity and choose whether to sell it on the spot market or in advance. In equilibrium the airline is indifferent about the capacity it produces and the way it sells it.

The airline expected profits from producing a unit of capacity at $t = 0$ and selling it on the $t = 1$ spot market are zero:

$$\sum_s \Pi_s p_s = \lambda. \tag{23.26}$$

Since the type is observed the expected revenue from producing a unit and selling a ticket (μ, α, β) at $t = 0$ to a type j buyer is:

$$\sum_s \Pi_s \{\phi_{js}[\max(\mu, p_s - \beta)] + (1 - \phi_{js})(p_s + \alpha)\}. \tag{23.27}$$

The term $\max(\mu, p_s - \beta)$ reflects the choice of the firm: Only if $\mu > p_s - \beta$ will it choose to deliver. The term $(p_s + \alpha)$ is the payoff to the firm when the buyer chooses not to fly: The airline gets α from the buyer and p_s from selling the seat on the spot market.

The expected profits from producing a unit and selling a ticket in advance is zero and therefore airlines let customers choose their tickets subject to the constraint that the expected revenue (23.27) is equal to λ. The problem of type j buyer is thus to choose $T = (\mu, \alpha, \beta)$ which solves the following problem:

$$\max_T \sum_s \Pi_s \phi_{js}\{(v_j - \mu)I(\mu > p_s - \beta) + \beta I(\mu \le p_s - \beta)\} - \sum_s \Pi_s (1 - \phi_{js})\alpha$$

s.t.

$$\sum_s \Pi_s \{\phi_{js}[\max(\mu, p_s - \beta)] + (1 - \phi_{js})(p_s + \alpha)\} = \lambda; \quad \mu \ge \alpha \ge 0. \tag{23.28}$$

The objective in (23.28) is the expected consumer surplus. Delivery occurs if $\mu > p_s - \beta$ and the buyer wants to fly. Therefore the term $(v_j - \mu)I(\mu > p_s - \beta) + \beta I(\mu \le p_s - \beta)$ is the consumer surplus when the buyer wants to fly: He gets $v_j - \mu$ if the airline delivers and β otherwise. The last term is the loss which occurs when the buyer does not want to fly and pays α.

We now turn to solve this problem.

Proposition 1: The following is a solution to (23.28):

$$\beta = v_j - \mu$$

$$\mu = \sum_s \Pi_s \phi_{js} \min(p_s, v_j) / \sum_s \Pi_s \phi_{js}$$

$$\alpha = 0.$$

Under the proposed solution $\max(\mu, p_s - \beta) = \max(\mu, \mu + p_s - v_j)$ and the ticket will not be delivered if $p_s - v_j > 0$.

Given the choice of β, a buyer who wants to fly pays μ and receives v_j. To elaborate on this interpretation of the contract note that the buyer who wants to fly gets delivery which is valued at v_j if $p_s \le v_j$ and pays $-\beta = \mu - v_j$ otherwise. The payment of $\mu - v_j$ is equivalent to paying μ and getting v_j. Thus, regardless of the realization of p_s he pays μ and gets v_j. The cost to the airline of guaranteeing v_j to the buyer if he wants to fly is: $\min(p_s, v_j)$. At the proposed solution the expected revenue $\mu \sum_s \Pi_s \phi_{js}$ is equal to the expected cost $\sum_s \Pi_s \phi_{js} \min(p_s, v_j)$.

We now turn to prove the Proposition.

Proof: We show that the proposed solution maximizes the joint surplus (buyer + firm) and the firm gets only the expected revenue of λ.

The joint surplus (buyer + firm) is:

$$\sum_s \Pi_s \phi_{js}\{v_j I(\mu > p_s - \beta) + p_s I(\mu \le p_s - \beta)\} + \sum_s \Pi_s(1 - \phi_{js})p_s - \lambda. \quad (23.29)$$

The choice $\beta = v_j - \mu$ maximizes (23.29) because it implies delivery if and only if $v_j > p_s$.

To show that the firm's expected profits are exactly λ, we substitute (23.26), $\beta = v_j - \mu$ and $\alpha = 0$ in the expected profits constraint in the problem (23.28) to get:

$$\sum_s \Pi_s\{\phi_{js}[\mu + \max(0, p_s - v_j)] + (1 - \phi_{js})p_s\} = \sum_s \Pi_s p_s. \quad (23.30)$$

After some algebra we get $\mu = \sum_s \Pi_s \phi_{js} \min(p_s, v_j) / \sum_s \Pi_s \phi_{js}$ as the solution to (23.30). Thus we have shown that the proposed solution maximizes total surplus and the expected revenue of the firm is exactly λ. It must therefore maximize the expected consumer surplus subject to the constraints in (23.28). $\qquad \square$

Corollary: The solution to (23.28) is not unique. Any μ and α that imply the expected payment:

$$\mu \sum_s \Pi_s \phi_{js} I(v_j > p_s) + \alpha \sum_s \Pi_s(1 - \phi_{js}) = \sum_s \Pi_s \phi_{js} I(v_j > p_s)p_s,$$

and satisfy the constraint $\mu \ge \alpha \ge 0$ is a solution.

We now define equilibrium as follows. Delegated auction equilibrium is a vector of spot prices $(p_1, \ldots, p_S)$, a vector of contracts $(T_1, \ldots, T_J)$ and total capacity x such that:

(a) $\sum_s \Pi_s p_s = \lambda$;
(b) Given the prices $(p_1, \ldots, p_S)$ type j's choice $T_j = (\mu_j, \alpha_j, \beta_j)$ solves (23.28) for all j;
(c) $x = \max_s\{\sum_j \phi_{js}n_j I(\mu_j > p_s - \beta_j)\}$.

To find a delegated auction equilibrium we pick a standard Walrasian auction equilibrium vector: $(p_1, \ldots, p_S; x)$. We then let agents choose contracts by solving (23.28). Under the solution proposed in Proposition 1, a buyer will get the seat only if he wants to fly and $v_j > p_s$. This is precisely the allocation rule used in the standard spot market model. Therefore the market clearing condition (c) is satisfied. We have thus shown that for this equilibrium solution.

Proposition 2: The delegated auction allocation is the same as the standard Walrasian auction allocation.

As was said before, we may view the advance purchase of tickets as a practical way of running a spot market auction. We now argue that this delegated auction generates observations that have been interpreted as evidence of price rigidity. We start from the airline example and then discuss the application to the Stigler–Kindahl data.

We observe the price actually paid by a given passenger over many periods. When buyers do not change preferences (types) often we will observe that the price actually paid by each individual buyer (μ_j) when executing the contract remains constant for a long time. When there is a change in preferences we will observe a change in the actual price paid. But this change need not be correlated with the change experienced by other buyers. We may thus get Carlton's observations in spite of the fact that there are no costs for using the price system.

It may be useful to describe the delegated auction in terms of trade in contingent commodities. Typically each buyer buys a basket of contingent commodities but if we misspecify the commodity space and assume that the airlines sell one good only, we may erroneously conclude that the law of one price is violated. We now illustrate this point by an example.

Example 1: There are three types and two states of nature. A type 1 buyer wants to consume in both states and his reservation price is $v_1 = 10$. A type 2 buyer wants to consume only when $s = 2$ and his reservation price is $v_2 = 7$. A type 3 buyer wants to consume only when $s = 1$ and his reservation price is $v_3 = 4$. There are the same numbers of agents from each type. The cost of production is $\lambda = 5$ per unit of capacity.

A standard Walrasian equilibrium vector for this case is:

$$p_1 = 3, \quad p_2 = 7, \quad x = 2.$$

A delegated auction equilibrium specifies, in addition, the tickets sold to each type. We can have an equilibrium with $\alpha_j = \beta_j = 0$,

$$\mu_1 = 5, \mu_2 = 7 \text{ and } \mu_3 = 3.$$

In this example, the type 2 buyer has bought flight in state 2 for 7 units of the numeiraire commodity. The type 3 buyer has bought flight in state 1 for 3 units. The type 1 buyer has bought a basket of two commodities for a total of 10 units. His actual payment may be 3 in state 1 and 7 in state 2. But because of risk neutrality this is equivalent to paying 5 in both states.[3] If we misspecify the commodity space and assume that the airlines sell one good instead of two, we may erroneously conclude that the law of one price is violated.

Carlton's data are about long-term relationship between large firms (typically in the fortune 500) and their suppliers. In a long term relationship the type is revealed and therefore our underline assumption may be quite realistic. We now use the Corollary to show that the above analysis may apply even if the type is not revealed because the free parameter (α) can be used to get a separating equilibrium without loss of efficiency.

The type is not observed

We now consider the case in which the buyer's type cannot be observed at $t = 0$. We follow the adverse selection literature and assume that the firm offers a choice of contracts and asks each buyer to choose out of the proposed menu. The buyer thus chooses a contract out of a menu $(T_1, \ldots, T_J)$ where the menu satisfies the "truth telling constraint":

$$\sum_s \Pi_s \phi_{js}\{(v_j - \mu_j)I(\mu_j > p_s - \beta_j) + \beta_j I(\mu \leq p_s - \beta_j)\} - \sum_s \Pi_s(1 - \phi_{js})\alpha_j$$

$$\geq \sum_s \Pi_s \phi_{js}\{(v_j - \mu_{j'})I(\mu_{j'} > p_s - \beta_{j'}) + \beta_{j'}I(\mu \leq p_s - \beta_{j'})\}$$

$$- \sum_s \Pi_s(1 - \phi_{js})\alpha_{j'} \quad \text{for all } j \text{ and } j'. \tag{23.31}$$

The "truth telling" or incentive compatibility constraint says that type j will prefer ticket T_j out of all the tickets offered. In equilibrium there are no incentives to change the menu and a firm cannot offer a contract that promises the same expected surplus to type j consumers and promise the firm an expected payment higher than λ.

Since the Corollary to Proposition 1 implies that we have a "free parameter" the incentive compatability constraint (23.31) may not bind. The airline may issue tickets with high μ and low α and tickets with relatively low μ and high α. Buyers with low probability of "wanting to fly" will buy tickets with high μ and low α.

To illustrate the importance of partial refunds as a selection device, we add the following example.

Example 2: There are two types, one consumer per type and two states of nature. As before $\lambda = 5$.

      Type 1: $v_1 = 6$ and he always want to consume;

      Type 2: $v_2 = 7$ and he wants to consume in state 2 only.

In this example the efficient level of production is unity and it should be allocated to type 1 in state 1 and type 2 in state 2.

The standard Walrasian prices for this example are: $p_1 = 4$; $p_2 = 6$. An efficient allocation (first best) can be achieved with the following menu:

$$T_1 = (\mu_1 = 5; \beta_1 = 1; \alpha_1 = 5);$$

$$T_2 = (\mu_2 = 6; \beta_2 = 1; \alpha_2 = 0).$$

Given this menu, type 1 will prefer contract 1 because he always want delivery and the price when the good is delivered is less than the alternative $(\mu_1 < \mu_2)$. Type 2 prefers contract 2 because the payment when not flying is much less than the payment under the alternative $(\alpha_2 \ll \alpha_1)$.

Concluding remarks

Prices that do not behave according to the standard Walrasian model can arise even in the absence of costs for changing prices and do not always imply market failure.

In our airline example, delivery occurs simultaneously to all buyers. The airline can conduct an auction at the gate just before departure but it may be better to conduct a delegated auction in which the airlines collect information through travel agents that sell tickets to potential passengers. This delegated auction may achieve the same outcome as an auction at the gate but leads to observations about prices (paid at the execution stage of the contract) that have been interpreted as evidence for price rigidity.

PROBLEM WITH ANSWERS

Using 23.1 to model delivery lags

1   Consider the case in which the money supply can take only two realizations and therefore at most two markets open. Assume that buyers have the option to pay now and get their order in the next period at the first market price. For example, if a buyer arrives in market 2 with 1 normalized dollar he can choose between buying and getting $1/p_2(I)$ units to having $1/p_1(I^2)$ units that will be delivered next period. Assume further that buyers who choose not to spend in the current period utilize this option.

(a) What is the expected value of a normalized dollar held by the buyer in market s $(r_s(I), s = 1, 2)$?

Answer

$$r_2(I) = \max\{1/p_2(I),\ \beta\omega^2/p_1(I^2)\};$$
$$r_1(I) = \max\{1/p_1(I),\ \tfrac{1}{2}\beta\omega^1/p_1(I^1) + \tfrac{1}{2}\beta\omega^2/p_1(I^2)\}$$

(b) What is the equilibrium nominal demand in market s $(s = 1, 2)$?

Answer

$d_2(I) = \gamma$ if $1/p_2(I) \geq \beta\omega^2/p_1(I^2)$ and   zero otherwise.
$d_1(I) = 1 + \gamma$ if $1/p_1(I) \geq \tfrac{1}{2}\beta\omega^1/p_1(I^1) + \tfrac{1}{2}\beta\omega^2/p_1(I^2)$ and zero otherwise.

(c) Let $b_j^s(I)$ denotes the amount sold in advance in market j if exactly s markets open. Define $b_2^1(I) = 0$ and find $b_2^2(I), b_1^1(I), b_1^2(I)$.

Answer

$b_2^2(I) = \gamma/p_1(I^2)$ if $1/p_2(I) < \beta\omega^2/p_1(I^2)$ and   zero otherwise.
$b_1^s(I) = (1 + \gamma)/p_1(I^s)$ if $1/p_1(I) < \tfrac{1}{2}\beta\omega^1/p_1(I^1) + \tfrac{1}{2}\beta\omega^2/p_1(I^2)$
and   zero otherwise.

(d) What is the appropriate definition of the beginning of period inventories for this case?

Answer

Inventories should be defined as the quantity carried from the previous period minus the quantity sold in advance.

(e) What is the amount of the beginning of next period's inventories if exactly s markets open this period?

Answer

$$I^s(I) = k(I) - \sum_{j=1}^{s}[k_j(I) + b_j^s(I)]$$

Inventories may be negative.

(f) Define steady state equilibrium.

Answer

Steady state equilibrium is a vector of functions

$[L(I), d_1(I), d_2(I), k(I), k_1(I), k_2(I), p_1(I), p_2(I), \zeta(I), r_1(I), r_2(I), b_1^1(I), b_1^2(I), b_2^2(I),$

$I^1(I), I^2(I)]$ such that:

$r_2(I) = \max\{1/p_2(I), \beta\omega^2/p_1(I^2)\};$

$r_1(I) = \max\{1/p_1(I), \frac{1}{2}\beta\omega^1/p_1(I^1) + \frac{1}{2}\beta\omega^2/p_1(I^2)\};$

$\zeta(I) = \frac{1}{2}r_1(I) + \frac{1}{2}[\theta_1 r_1(I) + \theta_2 r_2(I)];$

$d_2(I) = \gamma$ if $1/p_2(I) \geq \beta\omega^2/p_1(I^2)$ and zero otherwise;

$d_1(I) = 1 + \gamma$ if $1/p_1(I) \geq \frac{1}{2}\beta\omega^1/p_1(I^1) + \frac{1}{2}\beta\omega^2/p_1(I^2)$ and zero otherwise;

$b_2^2(I) = \gamma/p_1(I^2)$ if $1/p_2(I) < \beta\omega^2/p_1(I^2)$ and zero otherwise;

$b_1^s(I) = (1+\gamma)/p_1(I^s)$ if $1/p_1(I) < \frac{1}{2}\beta\omega^1/p_1(I^1) + \frac{1}{2}\beta\omega^2/p_1(I^2)$

and zero otherwise;

The first order conditions are satisfied:

$$v'[L(I)] = \beta p_1(I)E_s\{\omega^s\zeta(I^s)\},$$

$$p_1(I)E_s\{\omega^s\zeta(I^s)\} = \frac{1}{2}p_2(I)[\omega^2\zeta(I^2)] + \frac{1}{2}v'[L(I^1)],$$

$$p_2(I)[\omega^2\zeta(I^2)] \geq v'[L(I^2)] \quad \text{with strict equality if } k > k_1 + k_2.$$

Feasibility:

$$k(I) = L(I) + I \geq k_1(I) + k_2(I);$$

$$I^s(I) = k(I) - \sum_{j=1}^{s}[k_j(I) + b_j^s(I)];$$

Market clearing: $d_s(I) = p_s(I)k_s(I)$.

NOTES

1 Note that when α is large, $F_j(p_j, q_s) = \exp[\alpha(p_j/q_s)]/\sum_{i=j}^{s} \exp[\alpha(p_j/q_i)]$ approaches unity for $s = j$ and zero otherwise. In this case, buyers always buy at the cheapest available price as in previous uncertain and sequential trading (UST) models.

2   In the "real world" tickets often have two parameters only (μ, α). In the case of overbooking there is an auction: The airline buys back the number of seats which were "overbooked." This will lead to the same qualitative results as the contracts we assume.

3   In general our environment requires many commodities. There are S aggregate state and there are many individual histories which are possible for any given aggregate state. In an Arrow–Debreu world there will therefore be many commodities and a typical basket of these commodities will be described as a ticket with many parameters. Here we used risk neutrality and symmetry to reduce the number of parameters to three.

References

Abbott, Thomas A. III, Zvi Griliches, and Jerry A. Hausman, 1988: "Short Run Movements in Productivity: Market Power versus Capacity Utilization," presented at the NBER Summer Institute, August.

Abel, Andrew B., 1985: "Dynamic Behavior of Capital Accumulation in a Cash-in-advance Model," *Journal of Monetary Economics*, 16, 55–71.

Abramovitz, M., 1950: *Inventories and Business Cycles, with Special Reference to Manufacturers' Inventories.* New York: NBER.

Aguirregabiria, Victor, 1999: "The Dynamics of Markups and Inventories in Retailing Firms," *Review of Economic Studies*, 66, 275–308.

Aiyagari, S. Rao, Anton Braun, and Zvi Eckstein, 1998: "Transaction Services Inflation and Welfare," *Journal of Political Economy*, 106 (6), 1247–1301.

Akerlof, George and Janet Yellen, 1985: "Can Small Deviations from Rationality Make Significant Differences to Economic Equilibria?," *American Economic Review*, 75, 708–21.

Arrow, Kenneth J., 1964: "The Role of Securities in the Optimal Allocation of Risk-Bearing," *Review of Economic Studies*, 31 (April), 91–6.

——, 1971: *Essays in the Theory of Risk Bearing*, Chicago: Markham.

Auernheimer, L., 1974: "The Honest Government's Guide to the Revenue from the Creation of Money," *Journal of Political Economy*, May, 598–606.

Azariadis, Costas, 1975: "Implicit Contracts and Underemployment Equilibria," *Journal of Political Economy*, 83 (6), 1183–1202.

Baharad, E. and B. Eden, 2001: "Price Rigidity and Price Dispersion: Evidence from Micro Data," mimeo. On Eden's web page: http://econ.haifa.ac.il/~b.eden/. Accepted for publication in the *Review of Economic Dynamics*.

Bailey, M., 1956: "The Welfare Cost of Inflationary Finance," *Journal of Monetary Economics*, April, 93–110.

Baily, Martin Neil, 1974: "Wages and Employment under Uncertain Demand," *Review of Economic Studies*, 41 (1), 37–50.

Ball, Laurence and David Romer, 1991: "Sticky Prices as Coordination Failure," *American Economic Review*, 81 (3), 539–52.

Barnett, William, Edward Offenbacher, and Paul Spindt, 1981: "New Concepts of Aggregate Money," *Journal of Finance*, 36 (May), 487–505.

Barro, R.J., 1972: "A Theory of Monopolistic Price Adjustment," *Review of Economic Studies*, 34, 205–72.

——, 1974: "Are Government Bonds Net Wealth?," *Journal of Political Economy*, 82 (6), 1095–1117.

——, 1977: "Long-Term Contracting, Sticky Prices, and Monetary Policy," *Journal of Monetary-Economics*, 3 (3), 305–16.

——, 1979: "On the Determination of the Public Debt," *Journal of Political Economy*, 87 (5), part 1, 940–71.

——, 1993: *Macroeconomics*, 4th edn. New York: Wiley.

Barro, R.J. and Herschel I. Grossman, 1971: "A General Disequilibrium Model of Income and Employment," *American Economic Review*, 61 (1), 82–93.

Barro, R.J. and D.B., Gordon, 1983: "A Positive Theory of Monetary Policy in a Natural-Rate Model," *Journal of Political Economy*, 91 (4), 589–610.

Baumol, W.J., 1952: "The Transaction Demand for Cash: An Inventory Theoretic Approach," *Quarterly Journal of Economics*, 66, 545–56.

Baxter, Marianne and Robert G. King, 1995: "Measuring Business Cycles: Approximate Band-Pass Filters for Economic Time Series," NBER working paper 5022.

Becker, Gary S., 1971: *Economic Theory*, Knopf.

Bental, Benjamin and Benjamin Eden, 1993: "Inventories in a Competitive Environment," *Journal of Political Economy*, 101 (5), 863–86.

——, 1996: "Money and Inventories in an Economy with Uncertain and Sequential Trade," *Journal of Monetary Economics*, 37, 445–59.

——, 2002: "Reserve Requirements and Output Fluctuations," *Journal of Monetary Economics*, 49 (8), 1597–1620. Also on Eden's webpage: http://econ.haifa.ac.il/~b.eden/.

Benveniste, Lawrence and Jose Scheinkman, 1979: "On the Differentiability of the Value Function in Dynamic Models of Economics," *Econometrica*, 43 (3), 727–32.

Bernanke, S.B. and M. Gertler, 1995: "Inside the Black Box: The Credit Channel of Monetary Policy Transmission," *Journal of Economic Perspectives*, 9 (4), 27–48.

Bewley, Truman, 1983: "A Difficulty with the Optimum Quantity of Money," *Econometrica*, 51, 1485–1504.

Blanchard Olivier, Jean and Kiyotaki Nobuhiro, 1987: "Monopolistic Competition and the Effects of Aggregate Demand," *American Economic Review*, 77 (4), 647–66.

Bils, Mark and James Kahn, 2000: "What Inventory Behavior Tells Us about Business Cycles," *American Economic Review*, June.

Bils, Mark and Peter Klenow, 2002: "Some Evidence on the Importance of Sticky Prices," mimeo, January.

Blinder, A.S., 1981: "Retail Inventory Behavior and Business Fluctuations," *Brooking Papers on Economic Activity*, 2, 443–505.

——, 1986: "Can the Production Smoothing Model of Inventories Behavior be Saved?," *Quarterly Journal of Economics*, 101 (3), 431–53.

Blinder, A.S. and Stanley Fischer, 1981: Inventories, Rational Expectations, and the Business Cycle," *Journal of Monetary Economics*, 8, 277–304.

Blinder, A.S. and Louis J. Maccini, 1991: "Taking Stock: A Critical Assessment of Recent Research on Inventories," *Journal of Economic Perspective*, 5 (1), 73–96.

Boldrin, Michele and Michael Horvath, 1996: "Labor Contracts and Business Cycles," *Journal of Political Economy*, 103, 972–1004.

Bordo, Michael D. and Carlos A. Vegh, 2002: "What if Alexander Hamilton had been Argentinean? A Comparison of the Early Monetary Experiences of Argentina and the United States," *Journal of Monetary Economics*, 49, 459–94.

Boschen, J.F. and L.O. Mills, 1995: "The Relation between Narrative and Money Market Indicators of Monetary Policy," *Economic Inquiry*, 33 (1), 24–44.

Brock, W., 1975: "A Simple Perfect Foresight Monetary Model," *Journal of Monetary Economics*, April, 131–50.

Butters, G., 1977: "Equilibrium Distribution of Sales and Advertising Prices," *Review of Economic Studies*, 44, 467–491.

Calvo, G.A., 1978: "Optimal Seigniorage from Money Creation," *Journal of Political Economy*, August.

——, 1983: "Staggered Prices in a Utility-Maximizing Framework," *Journal of Monetary Economics*, 12, 383–98.

Caplin, Andrew and John V. Leahy, 1998: "Miracle on Sixth Avenue: Informational Externalities and Search," *Economic Journal*, 108 (January), 60–74.

Carlton, D.W., 1986: "The Rigidity of Prices," *American Economic Review*, 76, 637–58.

——, 1989: "The Theory and the Facts of How Markets Clear: Is Industrial Organization Valuable for Understanding Macroeconomics?" In R. Schmalensee and R.D. Willig, eds, *Handbook of Industrial Organization*, vol. I. Elsevier Science Publishers B.V.

Carlstrom, Charles T. and Timothy S. Fuerst, 2001: "Timing and Real Indeterminacy in Monetary Models," *Journal of Monetary Economics*, 47 (2), 285–98.

Cass, David and Yaari Menaham E., 1966: "A Re-examination of the Pure Consumption Loans Model," *Journal of Political Economy*, 74 (4), 353–67.

Cecchetti, S.G., 1986: "The Frequency of Price Adjustment: A Study of the Newsstand Prices of Magazines," *Journal of Econometrics*, 31, 255–74.

Chamberlin, Edward H., 1933: *The Theory of Monopolistic Competition*. Cambridge, Mass.: Harvard University Press.

Chamley, Christophe and Douglas Gale, 1994: "Information Revelation and Strategic Delay in a Model of Investment," *Econometrica*, 62, 1065–85.

Chari, V.V., Larry E. Jones, and Rodolfo E. Manuelli, 1995: "The Growth Effects of Monetary Policy," Federal Reserve Bank of Minneapolis, *Quarterly Review*, fall, 18–32.

Chari, V.V., Lawrence J. Christiano, and Patrick J. Kehoe, 1996: "Optimality of the Friedman Rule in Economies With Distorting Taxes," *Journal of Monetary Economics*, 37 (2), 203–23.

——, 1999: "Optimal Fiscal and Monetary Policy." In J.B. Taylor and M. Woodford, eds, *Handbook of Macroeconomics*, vol.1. Elsevier Science B.V.

Chari, V.V., Patrick J. Kehoe, and Ellen McGrattan, 2001: "Sticky Price Models of the Business Cycle: Can the Contract Multiplier Solve the Persistence Problem?," *Econometrica*, 68 (5), 1151–79.

——, 2002: "Business Cycle Accounting," Federal Reserve Bank of Minneapolis, Research Department Staff Report 350.

Christiano, Lawrence J., 1988: "Why Does Inventory Investment Fluctuate So Much?," *Journal of Monetary Economics*, 21, 247–80.

Christiano, Lawrence J., and Martin Eichenbaum, 1992: "Liquidity Effects and the Monetary Transmission Mechanism," *American Economic Review*, 82 (2), Papers and Proceedings, 346–53.

Christiano, Lawrence J., M. Eichenbaum and C. Evans, 1997: "Sticky Price and Limited Participation Models: A Comparison," *European Economic Review*, 41 (6), 1201–49.

——, 1999: "Monetary Policy Shocks: What Have We Learned and to What End?," In Michael Woodford and John Taylor, eds, *Handbook of Macroeconomics*. North Holland.

Clarida, Richard, Gertler Mark, and Gali Jordi, 1999: "The Science of Monetary Policy: A New Keynesian Perspective," *Journal of Economic Literature*, 37 (4), 1661–1707.

Clower, R.W., 1965: "The Keynesian Counter-Revolution: A Theoretical Appraisal." In F.H. Hahn and F.P.R. Brechling, eds, *The Theory of Interest Rate*. London.

——, 1967: "A Reconsideration of the Microfoundations of Monetary Theory," *Western Economic Journal*, 6 (1), 1–9.

Cochrane, John H., 2001: "Long Term Debt and the Optimal Policy in the Fiscal Theory of the Price Level," *Econometrica*, 69, 69–116.

Cole, Harold L. and Lee E. Ohanian, 2001: "New Deal Policies and the Persistence of the Great Depression: A General Equilibrium Analysis," Minneapolis Fed. WP 597, revised May.

Coleman, Wilbur John II, 1996: "Money and Output: A Test of Reverse Causation," *American Economic Review*, 86 (1), 90–111.

Cooley, Thomas, F. and Prescott Edward C., 1995: "Economic Growth and Business Cycles." In *Frontiers of Business Cycle Research*, Princeton: Princeton University Press.

Cooley, Thomas F. and Gary D. Hansen, 1991: "The Welfare Cost of Moderate Inflations," *Journal of Money, Credit, and Banking*, 23, 485–503.

Correia, Isabel and Teles Pedro, 1996: "Is the Friedman Rule Optimal When Money Is an Intermediate Good?," *Journal of Monetary Economics*, 38, 223–44.

Cukierman, Alex, 1983: "Relative Price Variability and Inflation: A Survey and Further Results," *Carnegie Rochester Series on Public Policy*, autumn, 103–158.

Dana, James D. Jr., 1998: "Advance-Purchase Discounts and Price Discrimination in Competitive Markets," *Journal of Political Economy*, 106 (2), 395–422.

Deaton, Angus, 1981: "Optimal Taxes and the Structure of Preferences," *Econometrica*, 49 (5), 1245–60.

Deaton, Angus and Laroque Guy, 1992: "On the Behavior of Commodity Prices," *Review of Economic Studies*, 59 (1), 1–23.

——, 1996: "Competitive Storage and Commodity Price Dynamics," *Journal of Political Economy*, 104 (5), 896–923.

Diamond, P.A. and J.A. Mirrlees, 1971: "Optimal Taxation and Public Production I: Production Efficiency and II: Tax Rules," *American Economic Review*, 61 (1) (March) 8–27; 3 (June), 261–78.

Dixit, Avinash and Joseph Stiglitz, 1977: "Monopolistic Competition and Optimum Product Diversity," *American Economic Review*, 67 (June), 297–308.

Dotsey, M., R.G. King, and A.L. Wolman, 1999: "State-Dependent Pricing and the General Equilibrium Dynamics of Money and Output," *Quarterly Journal of Economics*, May, 655–90.

Eckstein, Zvi and Leonard Leiderman, 1992: "Seigniorage and the Welfare Cost of Inflation," *Journal of Monetary Economics*, 29, 389–410.

Eden, Benjamin, 1977: "The Role of Insurance Gambling in Allocating Risk Over Time," *Journal of Economic Theory*, 16 (2), 228–46.

——, 1979: "An Expected Utility for the Insurance Buying Gambler," *Review of Economic Studies*, October, 741–2.

——, 1981: "Toward a Theory of Competitive Price Adjustment," *Review of Economic Studies*, April, 199–216.

——, 1982: "Competitive Price Adjustment to Changes in the Money Supply," *Quarterly Journal of Economics*, August, 499–517.

——, 1983: "Competitive Price Setting, Price Flexibility and Linkage to the Money Supply." In K. Brunner and A.H. Meltzer, eds, *Carnegie–Rochester Conference Series on Public Policy*, vol. 19. Amsterdam: North Holland, pp. 253–300.

——, 1986: "Trading Uncertainty and the Cash-in-advance Constraint," *Journal of Monetary Economics*, 18, 285–93.

——, 1990: "Marginal Cost Pricing When Spot Markets are Complete," *Journal of Political Economy*, 98 (6), 1293–1306.

——, 1994: "The Adjustment of Prices to Monetary Shocks When Trade is Uncertain and Sequential," *Journal of Political Economy*, 102 (3), 493–509.

——, 2001a: "Inventories and the Business Cycle: Testing a Sequential Trading Model," *Review of Economic Dynamics*, 4, 562–74.

——, 2001b: "Inflation and Price Adjustment: An Analysis of Microdata," *Review of Economic Dynamics*, 4, 607–36.

——, 2002: "Seemingly Rigid Prices," mimeo, April. On Eden's webpage: http://econ.haifa.ac.il/~b.eden/.

——, 2003: "Sequential International Trade," mimeo. On Eden's webpage: http://econ.haifa.ac.il/~ b.eden/.

——, 2003: "Sticky Prices in a Cash-in-advance Model: Does Money Matter?," mimeo, January. On Eden's webpage: http://econ.haifa.ac.il/~b.eden/.

Eden, Benjamin and Zvi Griliches, 1993: "Productivity, Market Power and Capacity Utilization When Spot Markets are Complete," *American Economic Review*, Papers and Proceedings, May.

Engel, Charles M., 1993: "Real Exchange Rates and Relative Prices: An Empirical Investigation," *Journal of Monetary Economics*, 32 (August), 35–50.

——, 1999: "Accounting for U.S. Real Exchange Rate Changes," *Journal of Political Economy*, 107 (June), 507–38.

Ethier, Wilfred J., 1982: "Dumping," *Journal of Political Economy*, 90 (3), 487–506.

Fischer, S., 1977: "Long-term Contracts, Rational Expectations, and the Optimal Money Supply Rule," *Journal of Political Economy*, 85, 191–205.

——, 1979: "Anticipations and the Nonneutrality of Money," *Journal of Political Economy*, 87 (2), 225–52.

Flood, R. and P. Garber, 1980: "An Economic Theory of Monetary Reform," *Journal of Political Economy*, 88 (1), 48–58.

Friedman Milton, 1960: *A Program for Monetary Stability*. New York: Fordham University.

——, 1967: "The Monetary Theory and Policy of Henry Simons," *Journal of Law and Economics*, 1967, 10. Reprinted in *The Optimum Quantity of Money and Other Essays*. Chicago: Aldine, pp. 1–50.

——, 1968: "The Role of Monetary Policy," *American Economic Review*, 58 (March), 1–17.

——, 1969a: "The Optimum Quantity of Money." In *The Optimum Quantity of Money and Other Essays*. Chicago: Aldine, pp. 1–50.

——, 1969b: "Post-War Trends in Monetary Theory and Policy," *National Banking Review*, 1964, 2 (1). Reprinted in The *Optimum Quantity of Money and Other Essays*. Chicago: Aldine.

——, 1976: *Price Theory*. Chicago: Aldine.

Friedman, Milton and Anna J. Schwartz, 1963: *A Monetary History of the United States*. Princeton, NJ: Princeton University Press.

Friedman, Milton and L.J. Savage, 1948: "The Utility Analysis of Choices Involving Risk," *Journal of Political Economy*, 56 (4), 279–304.

Fuesrt, T.S., 1992: "Liquidity, Loanable Funds, and Real Activity," *Journal of Monetary Economics*, 16 (3), 309–27.

Gertler, M. and S. Gilchrist, 1994: "Monetary Policy, Business Cycles, and the Behavior of Small Manufacturing Firms," *Quarterly Journal of Economics*, 109 (2), 309–40.

Gomme, Paul and Jeremy Greenwood, 1995: "On the Cyclical Allocation of Risk," *Journal of Economic Dynamics and Control*, 19, 91–124.

Gordon, Donald F., 1975: "A Neo-Classical Theory of Keynesian Unemployment." In Karl Brunner and Allan Meltzer, eds, *The Phillips Curve and Labor Markets*, Vol. 1, *Carnegie-Rochester Conference Series on Public Policy, Journal of Monetary Economics*, Suppl., 65–97.

Granger, C.W.J., 1969: "Investigating Causal Relations by Econometric Models and Cross-Spectral Methods," *Econometrica*, 37 (July), 424–38.

Gray, J.A., 1976: "Wage Indexation: A Macroeconomic Approach," *Journal of Monetary Economics*, 2, 221–35.

——, 1978: "On Indexation and Contract Length," *Journal of Political Economy*, 86 (1), 1–18.

Grossman, Sanford and Laurence Weiss, 1983: "A Transactions-Based Model of the Monetary Transmission Mechanism," *American Economic Review*, 73 (5), 871–80.

Guidotti, Pablo E. and Carlos A. Vegh, 1993: "The Optimal Inflation Tax When Money Reduces Transaction Costs: A Reconsideration," *Journal of Monetary Economics*, 31, 189–206.

Hall, Robert E., 1988: "The Relation between Price and Marginal Cost in U.S. Industry," *Journal of Political Economy*, 96 (October), 921–47.

Helpman, Elhanan and Paul R. Krugman, 1985: *Market Structure and Foreign Trade: Increasing Returns, Imperfect Competition and the International Economy*, Cambridge, Mass.: MIT Press.

Hicks, John R., 1946: *Value and Capital*, 2nd edition. Oxford: Clarendon Press.

Hirshleifer, J., 1966: "Investment Decision under Uncertainty: Application of the State-Preference Approach," *Quarterly Journal of Economics*, 80 (2), 252–7.

——, 1971: "The Private and Social Value of Information and the Reward to Inventive Activity," *American Economic Review*, 61 (September), 561–74.

Hirshleifer, J. and John G. Riley, 1979: "The Analytics of Uncertainty and Information: An Expository Survey," *Journal of Economic Literature*, 17 (4), 1375–1421.

Hodrick, R.J. and Edward C. Prescott, 1997: "Postwar U.S. Business Cycles: An Empirical Investigation," *Journal of Money, Credit and Banking*, 29 (1), 1–16.

Hume, David, 1970: *Writing on Economics*, ed. Eugene Rotwein. Madison: University of Wisconsin Press.

Jovanovic, Boyan, 1982: "Inflation and Welfare in the Steady State," *Journal of Political Economy*, 90, 561–77.

Karaken, John and Neil Wallace, 1981: "The Indeterminacy of Equilibrium Exchange Rates," *Quarterly Journal of Economics*, 96 (May), 207–22.

Karni, Edi, 1973: "The Transaction Demand for Cash: Incorporating the Value of Time into the Inventory Approach," *Journal of Political Economy*, 81, 1216–25.

Kimbrough Kent, P., 1986: "The Optimum Quantity of Money Rule in the Theory of Public Finance," *Journal of Monetary Economics*, 18, 277– 84.

King, Robert G. and Plosser, Charles I., 1984: "Money, Credit, and Prices in a Real Business Cycle Model," *American Economic Review*, 74 (3), 363–80.

King, Robert G. and Mark W. Watson, 1996: "Money, Prices, Interest Rates and the Business Cycle" (in Symposium on Development in Business Cycle Research), *Review of Economics and Statistics*, 78 (1), 35–53.

Kiyotaki, Nobuhiro and John Moore, 1997: "Credit Cycles," *Journal of Political Economy*, 105 (2), 211–48.

Kiyotaki, Nobuhiro and Randall Wright, 1993: "A Search-Theoretic Approach to Monetary Economics," *American Economic Review*, 83 (1), 63–77.

Kreps, D.M. and E.L. Porteus, 1978: "Temporal Resolution of Uncertainty and Dynamic Choice Theory," *Econometrica*, 46, 185–200.

Kydland, F.E. and E.C. Prescott, 1977: "Rules Rather than Discretion: The Inconsistency of Optimal Plans," *Journal of Political Economy*, 85 (3), 473–92.

——, 1982: "Time to Build and Aggregate Fluctuations," *Econometrica*, 50 (6), 1345–70.

Lach, S. and D. Tsiddon, 1992: "The Behavior of Prices and Inflation: An Empirical Analysis of Disaggregated Price Data," *Journal of Political Economy*, 100 (2), 349–89.

Laffont, Jean-Jacques, 1989: *The Economics of Uncertainty and Information*. Cambridge, Mass.; London: MIT Press.

Levhari, David and Don Patinkin, 1968: "The Role of Money in a Simple Growth Model," *American Economic Review*, 58 (4), 713–53.

Ljungqvist, Lars and Thomas J. Sargent, 2000: *Recursive Macroeconomic Theory*. Cambridge, Mass.: MIT Press.

Lucas, Robert E., Jr. 1972: "Expectations and the Neutrality of Money," *Journal of Economic Theory*, 4 (April), 103–24.

——, 1976: "Econometric Policy Evaluation: A Critique," *Carnegie-Rochester Conference Series on Public Policy*, 1, 19–46.

——, 1978: "Asset Prices in an Exchange Economy," *Econometrica*, 46 (6), 1426–45.

——, 1980: "Equilibrium in a Pure Currency Economy." In John H. Karaken and Neil Wallace, eds, *Models of Monetary Economies*. Minneapolis: Federal Reserve Bank of Minneapolis.

——, 1986: "Principles of Fiscal and Monetary Policy," *Journal of Monetary Economics*, 17, 117–34.

——, 1990a: "Liquidity and Interest Rates," *Journal of Economic Theory*, 50 (2), 237–64.

——, 1990b: *Models of Business Cycles*. Oxford: Basil Blackwell.

——, 1996: "Nobel Lecture: Monetary Neutrality," *Journal of Political Economy*, 4 (4), 661–82.

——, 2000: "Inflation and Welfare," *Econometrica*, 68 (2), 247–74.

Lucas, Robert E., Jr. and Nancy L. Stokey, 1983: "Optimal Fiscal and Monetary Policy in an Economy Without Capital," *Journal of Monetary Economics*, 12, 55–93.

——, 1987: "Money and Interest in a Cash-in-advance Economy," *Econometrica*, 55, 491–513.

Lucas, Robert E., Jr. and Michael Woodford, 1994: "Real Effects of Monetary Shocks in an Economy With Sequential Purchases," preliminary draft, University of Chicago, April.

Luce, R.D., 1959: *Individual Choice Behavior*, New York: Wiley.

Mankiw, N. Gregory, 1985: "Small Menu Costs and Large Business Cycles: A Macroeconomic Model of Monopoly," *Quarterly Journal of Economics*, 100 (May), 529–37.

Mankiw, N. Gregory and Ricardo A.M.R. Reis, 2001: "Sticky Information Versus Sticky Prices: A Proposal to Replace the New Keynesian Phillips Curve" mimeo, revised September.

Manski, Charles F., 2000: "Daniel McFadden and the Econometric Analysis of Discrete Choice," November. Taken from Charles Manski's webpage, Department of Economics, Northwestern University: www.faculty.econ.northwestern.edu/faculty/mauski./

Marquez, Jaime and D. Vining, 1984: "Inflation and Relative Price Behavior: A Survey of the Literature." In M. Ballobon, ed., *Economic Perspectives: An Annual Survey of Economics*, vol. 3. New York: Harwood Academic Publishers, pp. 1–52.

Mas-Colell, Andreau, Michael D. Whinston, and Jerry R. Green, 1995: *Microeconomic Theory*, Oxford: Oxford University Press.

McCallum, B.T., 1989: *Monetary Economics*, London: Macmillan.

McCallum, B.T. and Marvin S. Goodfriend, 1987: "Demand for Money: Theoretical Studies." In *The New Palgrave: A Dictionary of Economics*, ed. John Eatwell, Murray Milgate, and Peter Newman. London: Macmillan; New York: Stockton Press, pp. 775–81.

McFadden, Daniel, 2000: "Disaggregate Behavioral Travel Demand's RUM Side: A 30-Year Retrospective," mimeo, March. Taken from McFadden's webpage: www.ethlab.berkeley.edu/users/mcfadden/.

McGrattan, Ellen, R. and Edward C.Prescott, 2000: "Is the Stock Market Overvalued?," *Federal Reserve Bank of Minneapolis Quarterly Review*, 24 (4), 20–40.

Mehra, R. and E.C. Prescott., 1985: "The Equity Premium: A Puzzle," *Journal of Monetary Economics*, 15, 145–61.

Melnick, Rafi, 1985: "Financial Services, Cointegration, and the Demand for Money in Israel," *Journal of Money, Credit and Banking*, 27 (1), 140–53.

Metzler, Lloyd, 1941: "The Nature and Stability of Inventory Cycles," *Review of Economics and Statistics*, 23 (3), 113–29.

Milgrom, Paul R. and Robert J. Weber, 1982: "A Theory of Auctions and Competitive Bidding," *Econometrica*, 50 (5), 1089–122.

Mussa, Michael, 1986: "Nominal Exchange Rate Regimes and the Behavior of the Real Exchange Rates: Evidence and Implications," *Carnegie-Rochester Series on Public Policy*, 25, (autumn), 117–214.

Newbery, David, M.G. and Joseph E. Stiglitz, 1984: "Pareto Inferior Trade," *Review of Economic Studies*, 51 (1), 1–12.

Obstfeld Maurice and Kenneth Rogoff, 1996: *Foundations of International Macroeconomics*. Cambridge, Mass.: MIT Press.

Oi, Walter Y., 1962: "Labor as a Quasi-Fixed Factor," *Journal of Political Economy*, 70, 538–55.

Olson, Mancur, 1971: *The Logic of Collective Action: Public Goods and the Theory of Groups*. Cambridge, Mass.: Harvard University Press.

Patinkin, Don, 1965: *Money, Interest, and Prices: An Integration of Monetary and Value Theory*, 2nd edn. New York: Harper and Row.

Phelps, Edmund S., 1968: "Money-Wage Dynamics and Labor-Market Equilibrium," *Journal of Political Economy*, 76 (4), part 2, 678–711.

——, 1973: "Inflation in the Theory of Public Finance," *Swedish Journal of Economics*, 75, 67–82.

Phelps, Edmund S. and J.B. Taylor, 1975: "Stabilizing Powers of Monetary Policy under Rational Expectations," *Journal of Political Economy*, 85, 163–190.

Philips, A.W., 1958: "The Relationship between Unemployment and the Rate of Change of Money Wage Rates in the United Kingdom, 1861–1957," *Economica*, 25 (November), 283–99.

Pratt, J., 1964: "Risk Aversion in the Small and in the Large," *Econometrica*, 32, 122–36.

Prescott, Edward C., 1975: "Efficiency of the Natural Rate," *Journal of Political Economy*, 83 (December), 1229–36.

Radner, Roy, 1979: "Rational Expectations Equilibrium: Generic Existence and the Information Revealed by Prices," *Econometrica*, 47 (3), 655–78.

Ramey, Valerie A. and Kenneth D. West, 1997: "Inventories," NBER working paper 6315, December.

Ramsey, F.P., 1927: "A Contribution to the Theory of Taxation," *Economic Journal*, 37 (145), 47–61.

Reagan, Patricia and Sheehan Dennis P., 1985: "The Stylized Facts about the Behavior of Manufacturers' Inventories and Backorders Over the Business Cycle: 1959–1980," *Journal of Monetary Economics*, 15, 217–46.

Reinsdorf, M., 1994: "New Evidence on the Relation Between Inflation and Price Dispersion," *American Economic Review*, June, 720–31.

Rogoff, Kenneth, 1996: "The Purchasing Power Parity Puzzle," *Journal of Economic Literature*, 34 (June), 647–68.

Romer, C.D., and D.H. Romer, 1989: "Does Monetary Policy Matter? A New Test in the Spirit of Friedman and Schwartz." In O.J. Blanchard and S. Fischer, eds, NBER Macroeconomics Annual, Cambridge, Mass.: MIT Press, pp. 121–70.

Rotemberg, Julio, J., 1982: "Monopolistic Price Adjustment and Aggregate Output," *Review of Economic Studies*, 44, 517–31.

——, 1984: "A Monetary Equilibrium Model with Transactions Costs," *Journal of Political Economy*, 92 (1), 40–58.

——, 1998: "The Cyclical Behavior of Prices and Costs" mimeo (July). Prepared for John B. Taylor and Michael Woodford, eds, *Handbook of Macroeconomics*. Amsterdam: North-Holland.

—— and Larry H. Summers, 1990: "Inflexible Prices and Procyclical Productivity," *Quarterly Journal of Economics*, 105 (November), 851–74.

Sachs, Jeffrey, D. and Felipe Larrain B., 1993: *Macroeconomics in the Global Economy*. New York: Prentice-Hall.

Samuelson, Paul A., 1985: "An Exact Consumption-Loan Model of Interest with or without the Social Contrivance of Money," *Journal of Political Economy*, 66 (6), 467–82.

Sargent, Thomas, J., 1986: "The End of Four Big Inflations." In his *Rational Expectations and Inflation*. New York: Harper and Row, pp. 40–109.

——, 1987: *Dynamic Macroeconomic Theory*, Cambridge, Mass.: Harvard University Press.

——, 1997: "The Conquest of American Inflation" Mimeo, November 4. Text of a "Marshall lecture" given at the University of Cambridge in October 1996.

Sargent, Thomas J. and Wallace, Neil, 1975: "Rational Expectations: The Optimal Monetary Instrument, and the Optimal Money Supply Rule," *Journal of Political Economy*, 83 (2), 241–54.

——, 1981: "Some Unpleasant Monetarist Arithmetic," *Federal Reserve Bank of Minneapolis Quarterly Review*, fall, 1–17.

——, 1982: "The Real-Bills Doctrine versus the Quantity Theory: A Reconsideration," *Journal of Political Economy*, 90 (6), 1212–36.

Sbordone Argia M., 1998: "Prices and Unit Costs: Testing Models of Pricing Behavior," mimeo (July).

——, 2002: "Prices and Unit Labor Costs: A New Test of Price Stickiness," *Journal of Monetary Economics*, 49, 265–92.

Schattschneider, E.E., 1935: *Politics, Pressures and the Tariff*, New York: Prentice-Hall.

Selden, Larry, 1978: "A New Representation of Preferences over 'Certain × Uncertain' Consumption Pairs: The 'Ordinal Certainty Equivalent' Hypothesis," *Econometrica*, 46, 1045–60.

Shell, Karl, 1971: "Notes on the Economics of Infinity," *Journal of Political Economy*, 79 (5), 1002–11.

Sheshinski, Eytan and Weiss, Yoram, 1977: "Inflation and Costs of Price Adjustment," *Review of Economic Studies*, 44, 287–303.

——, 1983: "Optimum Pricing Policy Under Stochastic Inflation," *Review of Economic Studies*, 50, 513–29.

Sidrauski, Miguel, 1967: "Inflation and Economic Growth," *Journal of Political Economy*, 75, 798–810.

Simons, Henry, 1948: *Economic Policy for a Free Society*. Chicago, Ill.: University of Chicago Press.

Sims, Christopher A., 1972: "Money, Income, and Causality," *American Economic Review*, 62 (3), 540–52.

——, 1980: "Comparison on Interwar and Post-war Business Cycles: Monetarism Reconsidered," *American Economic Review*, 70 (1), 250–7.

——, 1994: "A Simple Model for the Determination of the Price Level and the Interaction of Monetary and Fiscal Policy," *Economic Theory*, 4, 381–99.

Stigler, George J. and James K. Kindahl, 1970: *The Behavior of Industrial Prices*. New York: NBER General Series, Columbia University Press.

Stockman, Alan C., 1981: "Anticipated Inflation and the Capital Stock in a Cash-in-advance Economy," *Journal of Monetary Economics*, 8, 387–93.

——, 1996: *Introduction to Economics*. Fort Worth, Tex.: Dryden.

Svensson, Lars E.O., 1986: "Sticky Goods Prices, Flexible Asset Prices, Monopolistic Competition, and Monetary Policy," *Review of Economic Studies*, 53 (3), 385–405.

Taylor, John B., 1980: "Aggregate Dynamics and Staggered Contracts," *Journal of Political Economy*, 88, 1–23.

——, 1999: "Staggered Price and Wage Setting in Macroeconomics." In John B. Taylor and Michael Woodford, eds, *Handbook of Macroeconomics*, vol. 1B. New York: Elsevier, ch. 15.

Tsiddon, Daniel, 1993: "The (Mis)Behaviour of the Aggregate Price Level," *Review of Economic Studies*, 60, 889–902.

Tobin, James, 1956: "The Interest Elasticity of the Transactions Demand for Cash," *Review of Economics and Statistics*, 38 (3), 241–7.

——, 1970: "Money and Income: Post Hoc Ergo Propter Hoc?," *Quarterly Journal of Economics*, 84 (2), 301–17.

Vial, J.P., 1972: "A Continuous Time Model for the Cash Balance Problem." In G.P. Szëgo and K. Shell, eds, *Mathematical Methods in Investment and Finance*. Amsterdam: North Holland, pp. 244–91.

Wallace Neil, 1992: "Lucas's Signal Extraction Model: A Finite State Exposition with Aggregate Real Shocks," *Journal of Monetary Economics*, 30, 433–47.

Wang, Ping and Yip Chong K., 1992: "Alternative Approaches to Money and Growth," *Journal of Money, Credit and Banking*, 24 (4), 553–62.

Weiss, Yoram, 1993: "Inflation and Price Adjustment: A Survey of Findings from Micro Data." In E. Sheshinski and Y. Weiss, eds, *Individual and Aggregate Price Dynamics*. Cambridge, Mass.: MIT Press.

Walsh, Carl E., 1998: *Monetary Theory and Policy*. Cambridge, Mass.: MIT Press.

Williamson, Stephen D., 1996: "Sequential Markets and the Suboptimality of the Friedman rule," *Journal of Monetary Economics*, 37 (3), 549–72.

Wilson, Charles A., 1988: "On the Optimal Pricing Policy of a Monopolist," *Journal of Political Economy*, 96, 164–76.

Woodford, Michael, 1990: "The Optimum Quantity of Money." In Benjamin M. Friedman and Frank H. Hahn, eds, *Handbook of Monetary Economics*, vol. 2. Elsevier Science Publishers B.V., pp. 1068–1152.

———, 1995: "Price Level Determinacy without Control of a Monetary Aggregate," *Carnegie-Rochester Conference Series on Public Policy*, 43, 1–46.

———, 1996: "Loan Commitments and Optimal Monetary Policy," *Journal of Monetary Economics*, 37 (3), 573–605.

———, 1998: "Doing Without Money: Controlling Inflation in a Post Monetary World," *Review of Economic Dynamics*, 1, 173–219.

———, 2002: "Optimizing Models with Nominal Rigidities," mimeo. Revised, December 2002: www.princeton.edu/~woodford/.

Index

Printed and bound by CPI Group (UK) Ltd, Croydon, CR0 4YY

23/04/2025

14660945-0004